HOUGHTON MIFFLIN HARCOURT

Literacy and Language Guide

Consultants
Irene C. Fountas
Shane Templeton

Grade 1

Printed in the U.S.A.

ISBN   978-0-547-86646-8

22   0877   21 20 19 18

4500707224   E F G

Houghton Mifflin Harcourt.

Literacy and Language Guide
Table of Contents

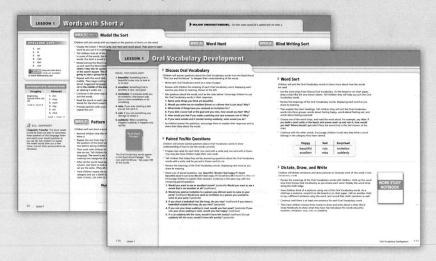

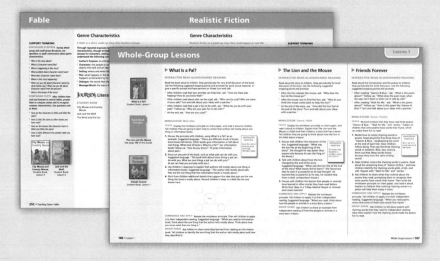

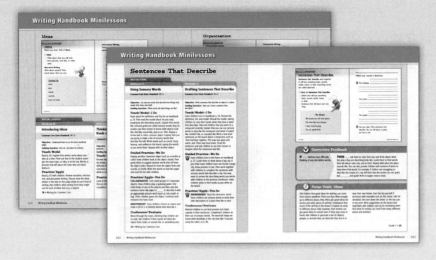

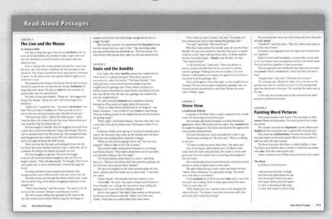

- Linguistic Transfer Support
- Qualitative Spelling Inventory
- Comprehensive Word List
- Leveled Readers Database
- Literature Discussion
- Bibliography

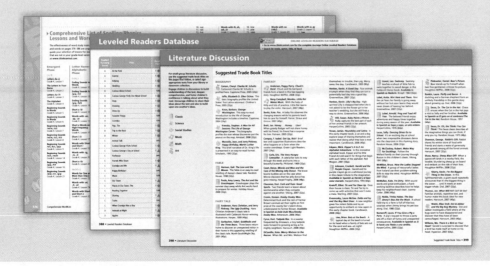

Literacy and Language Guide
Overview

In this Guide, you will find weekly lesson plans for Word Study, Reading, and Writing. A Planning page for each lesson provides a clear pathway through each week of instruction, connecting the parts of the plan cohesively and seamlessly.

INSTRUCTIONAL FOCUS
Each week's instructional focus at a glance— literature selections, comprehension skills, word work, and writing

READ ALOUD PASSAGES
Read Aloud Passages are reproduced in this Guide for ease of use

READING SELECTIONS
Reading selections for the week from the *Journeys* Student Book and Teacher's Edition

WORD STUDY
Spelling/Phonics and Oral Vocabulary Development lessons for the week

WRITING
Writing minilessons connect to *Journeys* instruction and provide students with additional handbook resources for writing practice during the week

GUIDED READING
Options for small-group teaching also appear in the complete Leveled Readers Database in the Resources section of this Guide

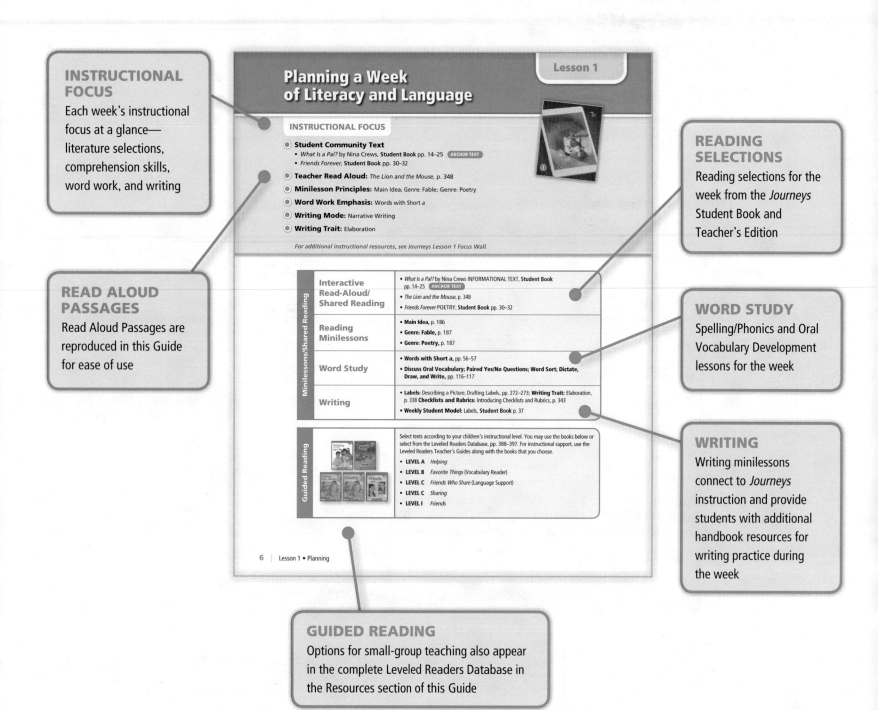

Planning a Week of Literacy and Language — Lesson 1

INSTRUCTIONAL FOCUS
- **Student Community Text**
  - *What Is a Pal?* by Nina Crews, **Student Book** pp. 14–25 ANCHOR TEXT
  - *Friends Forever,* **Student Book** pp. 30–32
- **Teacher Read Aloud:** *The Lion and the Mouse,* p. 348
- **Minilesson Principles:** Main Idea; Genre: Fable; Genre: Poetry
- **Word Work Emphasis:** Words with Short *a*
- **Writing Mode:** Narrative Writing
- **Writing Trait:** Elaboration

For additional instructional resources, see Journeys Lesson 1 Focus Wall.

Minilessons/Shared Reading		
Interactive Read-Aloud/ Shared Reading	• *What Is a Pal?* by Nina Crews INFORMATIONAL TEXT, **Student Book** pp. 14–25 ANCHOR TEXT • *The Lion and the Mouse,* p. 348 • *Friends Forever* POETRY, **Student Book** pp. 30–32	
Reading Minilessons	• **Main Idea,** p. 186 • **Genre: Fable,** p. 187 • **Genre: Poetry,** p. 187	
Word Study	• **Words with Short *a*,** pp. 56–57 • **Discuss Oral Vocabulary; Paired Yes/No Questions; Word Sort; Dictate, Draw, and Write,** pp. 116–117	
Writing	• **Labels:** Describing a Picture, Drafting Labels, pp. 272–273; **Writing Trait:** Elaboration, p. 338 **Checklists and Rubrics:** Introducing Checklists and Rubrics, p. 343 • **Weekly Student Model:** Labels, **Student Book** p. 37	

Guided Reading	
	Select texts according to your children's instructional level. You may use the books below or select from the Leveled Readers Database, pp. 388–397. For instructional support, use the Leveled Readers Teacher's Guides along with the books that you choose. • **LEVEL A** *Helping* • **LEVEL B** *Favorite Things* (Vocabulary Reader) • **LEVEL C** *Friends Who Share* (Language Support) • **LEVEL C** *Sharing* • **LEVEL I** *Friends*

6 | Lesson 1 • Planning

Planning for Literacy and Language

Table of Contents

Instructional Focus and Planning

Planning a Week of Literacy and Language

INSTRUCTIONAL FOCUS

- **Student Community Text**
  - *What Is a Pal?* by Nina Crews, **Student Book** pp. 14–25   ANCHOR TEXT
  - *Friends Forever*, **Student Book** pp. 30–32
- **Teacher Read Aloud:** *The Lion and the Mouse*, p. 348
- **Minilesson Principles:** Main Idea; Genre: Fable; Genre: Poetry
- **Word Work Emphasis:** Words with Short *a*
- **Writing Mode:** Narrative Writing
- **Writing Trait:** Elaboration

For additional instructional resources, see Journeys Lesson 1 Focus Wall.

Minilessons/Shared Reading		
Interactive Read-Aloud/ Shared Reading	• *What Is a Pal?* by Nina Crews INFORMATIONAL TEXT, **Student Book** pp. 14–25 ANCHOR TEXT • *The Lion and the Mouse*, p. 348 • *Friends Forever* POETRY, **Student Book** pp. 30–32	
Reading Minilessons	• **Main Idea,** p. 186 • **Genre: Fable,** p. 187 • **Genre: Poetry,** p. 187	
Word Study	• **Words with Short *a*,** pp. 56–57 • **Discuss Oral Vocabulary; Paired Yes/No Questions; Word Sort; Dictate, Draw, and Write,** pp. 116–117	
Writing	• **Labels:** Describing a Picture, Drafting Labels, pp. 272–273; **Writing Trait:** Elaboration, p. 338 **Checklists and Rubrics:** Introducing Checklists and Rubrics, p. 343 • **Weekly Student Model:** Labels, **Student Book** p. 37	

Guided Reading

Select texts according to your children's instructional level. You may use the books below or select from the Leveled Readers Database, pp. 388–397. For instructional support, use the Leveled Readers Teacher's Guides along with the books that you choose.

- **LEVEL A**   *Helping*
- **LEVEL B**   *Favorite Things* (Vocabulary Reader)
- **LEVEL C**   *Friends Who Share* (Language Support)
- **LEVEL C**   *Sharing*
- **LEVEL I**   *Friends*

Planning a Week of Literacy and Language

INSTRUCTIONAL FOCUS

- **Student Community Text**
  - *The Storm* by Raúl Colón, **Student Book** pp. 42–53   ANCHOR TEXT
  - *Storms!,* **Student Book** pp. 58–60
- **Teacher Read Aloud:** *Susie and the Bandits,* p. 348
- **Minilesson Principles:** Understanding Characters; Understanding Characters; Genre: Informational Text
- **Word Work Emphasis:** Words with Short *i*
- **Writing Mode:** Narrative Writing
- **Writing Trait:** Elaboration

For additional instructional resources, see Journeys *Lesson 2 Focus Wall.*

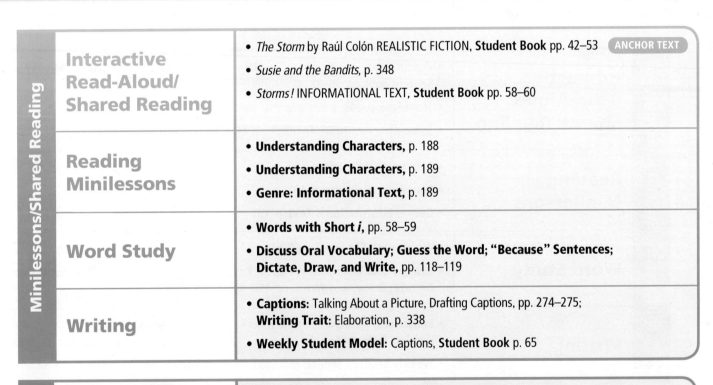

Minilessons/Shared Reading		
Interactive Read-Aloud/ Shared Reading	• *The Storm* by Raúl Colón REALISTIC FICTION, **Student Book** pp. 42–53 ANCHOR TEXT • *Susie and the Bandits,* p. 348 • *Storms!* INFORMATIONAL TEXT, **Student Book** pp. 58–60	
Reading Minilessons	• **Understanding Characters,** p. 188 • **Understanding Characters,** p. 189 • **Genre: Informational Text,** p. 189	
Word Study	• **Words with Short *i*,** pp. 58–59 • **Discuss Oral Vocabulary; Guess the Word; "Because" Sentences; Dictate, Draw, and Write,** pp. 118–119	
Writing	• **Captions:** Talking About a Picture, Drafting Captions, pp. 274–275; **Writing Trait:** Elaboration, p. 338 • **Weekly Student Model:** Captions, **Student Book** p. 65	

Guided Reading

Select texts according to your children's instructional level. You may use the books below or select from the Leveled Readers Database, pp. 388–397. For instructional support, use the Leveled Readers Teacher's Guides along with the books that you choose.

- **LEVEL A**   *Granny*
- **LEVEL B**   *Grandpa* (Vocabulary Reader)
- **LEVEL C**   *Grandpa and Me*
- **LEVEL C**   *When Grandpa Was a Boy* (Language Support)
- **LEVEL J**   *A Mexican Festival*

Planning a Week of Literacy and Language

INSTRUCTIONAL FOCUS

◉ **Student Community Text**
- *Curious George at School* based on Margret and H.A. Rey's Curious George, **Student Book** pp. 70–81 `ANCHOR TEXT`
- *School Long Ago*, **Student Book** pp. 86–88

◉ **Teacher Read Aloud:** *Stone Stew*, p. 349

◉ **Minilesson Principles:** Sequence of Events; Sequence of Events; Genre: Informational Text

◉ **Word Work Emphasis:** Words with Short *o*

◉ **Writing Mode:** Narrative Writing

◉ **Writing Trait:** Purpose

For additional instructional resources, see Journeys Lesson 3 Focus Wall.

Minilessons/Shared Reading		
Interactive Read-Aloud/ Shared Reading	• *Curious George at School* based on Margret and H.A. Rey's Curious George FANTASY, **Student Book** pp. 70–81 `ANCHOR TEXT` • *Stone Stew*, p. 349 • *School Long Ago* INFORMATIONAL TEXT, **Student Book** pp. 86–88	
Reading Minilessons	• **Sequence of Events,** p. 190 • **Sequence of Events:** p. 191 • **Genre: Informational Text,** p. 191	
Word Study	• **Words with Short *o*,** pp. 60–61 • **Discuss Oral Vocabulary; Paired Yes/No Questions; Describe It or Act It Out; Dictate, Draw, and Write,** pp. 120–121	
Writing	• **Sentences:** Writing a Complete Thought, Drafting Sentences, pp. 276–277; **Writing Trait:** Purpose, p. 338 • **Weekly Student Model:** Sentences, **Student Book** p. 93	

Guided Reading

Select texts according to your children's instructional level. You may use the books below or select from the Leveled Readers Database, pp. 388–397. For instructional support, use the Leveled Readers Teacher's Guides along with the books that you choose.

- **LEVEL B**   *Curious About School* (Vocabulary Reader)
- **LEVEL B**   *Curious George Finds Out About School*
- **LEVEL C**   *Curious George Visits School* (Language Support)
- **LEVEL C**   *Curious George's Day at School*
- **LEVEL I**   *Curious George at the Library*

Planning a Week of Literacy and Language

INSTRUCTIONAL FOCUS

- **Student Community Text**
  - *Lucia's Neighborhood* by George Ancona, **Student Book** pp. 98–109 ANCHOR TEXT
  - *City Mouse and Country Mouse* retold by Debbie O'Brien, **Student Book** pp. 114–116
- **Teacher Read Aloud:** *Painting Word Pictures,* p. 349
- **Minilesson Principles:** Text and Graphic Features; Genre: Poetry; Genre: Fable
- **Word Work Emphasis:** Words with Short e
- **Writing Mode:** Narrative Writing
- **Writing Trait:** Elaboration

For additional instructional resources, see Journeys *Lesson 4 Focus Wall.*

Minilessons/Shared Reading		
Interactive Read-Aloud/ Shared Reading	• *Lucia's Neighborhood* by George Ancona INFORMATIONAL TEXT, **Student Book** pp. 98–109 ANCHOR TEXT • *Painting Word Pictures,* p. 349 • *City Mouse and Country Mouse* retold by Debbie O'Brien FABLE, **Student Book** pp. 114–116	
Reading Minilessons	• **Text and Graphic Features,** p. 192 • **Genre: Poetry** p. 193 • **Genre: Fable,** p. 193	
Word Study	• **Words with Short e,** pp. 62–63 • **Discuss Oral Vocabulary; Word Associations; True or Not True; Dictate, Draw, and Write,** pp. 122–123	
Writing	• **Class Story:** Thinking of Events, Drafting a Class Story, pp. 278–279; **The Writing Process:** Prewriting, p. 332; **Writing Trait:** Elaboration, p. 338 • **Weekly Student Model:** Class Story, **Student Book** p. 121	

Guided Reading

Select texts according to your children's instructional level. You may use the books below or select from the Leveled Readers Database, pp. 388–397. For instructional support, use the Leveled Readers Teacher's Guides along with the books that you choose.

- **LEVEL A**   *At the Park*
- **LEVEL C**   *Firehouse* (Vocabulary Reader)
- **LEVEL C**   *Our Town*
- **LEVEL C**   *The Places in Our Town* (Language Support)
- **LEVEL I**   *Neighbors*

Planning a Week of Literacy and Language

INSTRUCTIONAL FOCUS

- ◉ **Student Community Text**
  - *Gus Takes the Train* by Russell Benfanti, **Student Book** pp. 126–137   ANCHOR TEXT
  - *City Zoo*, **Student Book** pp. 142–144

- ◉ **Teacher Read Aloud:** *Training Around the Town*, p. 350

- ◉ **Minilesson Principles:** Story Structure; Genre: Informational Text; Genre: Informational Text

- ◉ **Word Work Emphasis:** Words with Short *u*

- ◉ **Writing Mode:** Narrative Writing

- ◉ **Writing Trait:** Elaboration

For additional instructional resources, see Journeys Lesson 5 Focus Wall.

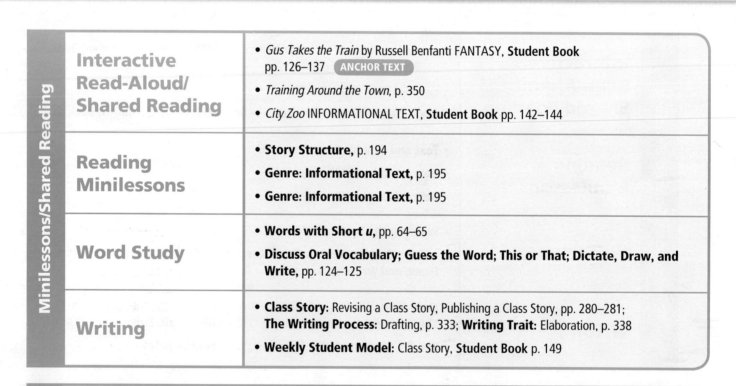

Minilessons/Shared Reading		
Interactive Read-Aloud/ Shared Reading	• *Gus Takes the Train* by Russell Benfanti FANTASY, **Student Book** pp. 126–137 ANCHOR TEXT • *Training Around the Town*, p. 350 • *City Zoo* INFORMATIONAL TEXT, **Student Book** pp. 142–144	
Reading Minilessons	• **Story Structure**, p. 194 • **Genre: Informational Text**, p. 195 • **Genre: Informational Text**, p. 195	
Word Study	• **Words with Short *u***, pp. 64–65 • **Discuss Oral Vocabulary; Guess the Word; This or That; Dictate, Draw, and Write**, pp. 124–125	
Writing	• **Class Story:** Revising a Class Story, Publishing a Class Story, pp. 280–281; **The Writing Process:** Drafting, p. 333; **Writing Trait:** Elaboration, p. 338 • **Weekly Student Model:** Class Story, **Student Book** p. 149	

Guided Reading

Select texts according to your children's instructional level. You may use the books below or select from the Leveled Readers Database, pp. 388–397. For instructional support, use the Leveled Readers Teacher's Guides along with the books that you choose.

- **LEVEL A**   *Sledding*
- **LEVEL C**   *Trains* (Vocabulary Reader)
- **LEVEL D**   *Ben the Cat*
- **LEVEL D**   *A Cat Named Ben* (Language Support)
- **LEVEL J**   *A Job for Jojo*

Planning a Week of Literacy and Language

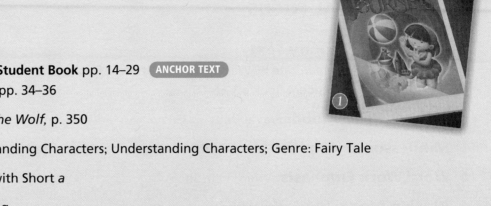

INSTRUCTIONAL FOCUS

○ **Student Community Text**
- *Jack and the Wolf* by Chris Sheban, **Student Book** pp. 14–29 ANCHOR TEXT
- *The Three Little Pigs,* **Student Book** pp. 34–36

○ **Teacher Read Aloud:** *Night of the Wolf,* p. 350

○ **Minilesson Principles:** Understanding Characters; Understanding Characters; Genre: Fairy Tale

○ **Word Work Emphasis:** Words with Short *a*

○ **Writing Mode:** Informative Writing

○ **Writing Trait:** Elaboration

For additional instructional resources, see Journeys Lesson 6 Focus Wall.

Minilessons/Shared Reading		
Interactive Read-Aloud/ Shared Reading	• *Jack and the Wolf* by Chris Sheban FABLE, **Student Book** pp. 14–29 ANCHOR TEXT • *Night of the Wolf,* p. 350 • *The Three Little Pigs* FAIRY TALE, **Student Book** pp. 34–36	
Reading Minilessons	• **Understanding Characters,** p. 196 • **Understanding Characters,** p. 197 • **Genre: Fairy Tale,** p. 197	
Word Study	• **Words with Short *a*,** pp. 66–67 • **Discuss Oral Vocabulary; Riddles; Complete Sentences; Dictate, Draw, and Write,** pp. 126–127	
Writing	• **Sentences That Describe:** Using Sensory Words, Drafting Sentences That Describe, pp. 282–283; **Writing Trait:** Elaboration, p. 338; **Checklists and Rubrics:** Introducing Checklists and Rubrics, p. 343 • **Weekly Student Model:** Sentences That Describe, **Student Book** p. 41	

Guided Reading

Select texts according to your children's instructional level. You may use the books below or select from the Leveled Readers Database, pp. 388–397. For instructional support, use the Leveled Readers Teacher's Guides along with the books that you choose.

- **LEVEL B** *The Pigs*
- **LEVEL D** *Go Turtle! Go Hare!* (Language Support)
- **LEVEL D** *Reading* (Vocabulary Reader)
- **LEVEL D** *Turtle and Hare*
- **LEVEL I** *Fox and Crow*

Planning a Week of Literacy and Language

INSTRUCTIONAL FOCUS

- **Student Community Text**
  - *How Animals Communicate* by William Muñoz, **Student Book** pp. 46–61 `ANCHOR TEXT`
  - *Insect Messages*, **Student Book** pp. 66–68
- **Teacher Read Aloud:** *Prairie Dogs*, p. 351
- **Minilesson Principles:** Details; Details; Genre: Informational Text
- **Word Work Emphasis:** Words with Short *i*
- **Writing Mode:** Informative Writing
- **Writing Trait:** Elaboration

For additional instructional resources, see Journeys *Lesson 7 Focus Wall.*

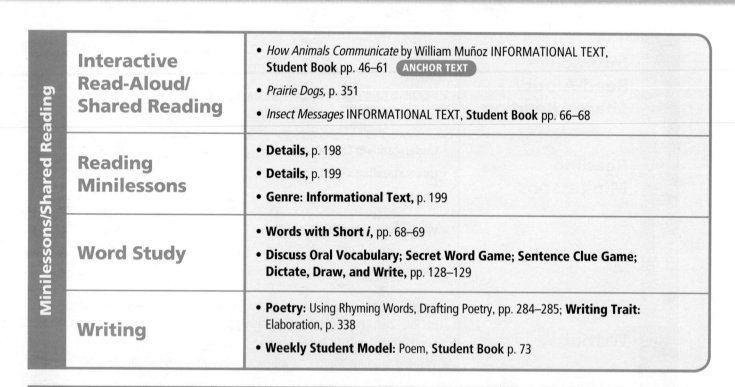

Minilessons/Shared Reading		
Interactive Read-Aloud/ Shared Reading	• *How Animals Communicate* by William Muñoz INFORMATIONAL TEXT, **Student Book** pp. 46–61 `ANCHOR TEXT` • *Prairie Dogs*, p. 351 • *Insect Messages* INFORMATIONAL TEXT, **Student Book** pp. 66–68	
Reading Minilessons	• **Details**, p. 198 • **Details**, p. 199 • **Genre: Informational Text**, p. 199	
Word Study	• **Words with Short *i*,** pp. 68–69 • **Discuss Oral Vocabulary; Secret Word Game; Sentence Clue Game; Dictate, Draw, and Write,** pp. 128–129	
Writing	• **Poetry:** Using Rhyming Words, Drafting Poetry, pp. 284–285; **Writing Trait:** Elaboration, p. 338 • **Weekly Student Model:** Poem, **Student Book** p. 73	

Guided Reading

Select texts according to your children's instructional level. You may use the books below or select from the Leveled Readers Database, pp. 388–397. For instructional support, use the Leveled Readers Teacher's Guides along with the books that you choose.

- **LEVEL B** *Dogs*
- **LEVEL C** *Animal Talk* (Vocabulary Reader)
- **LEVEL D** *Animals at Night*
- **LEVEL D** *Busy Animals at Night* (Language Support)
- **LEVEL J** *Dog Talk*

Planning a Week of Literacy and Language

INSTRUCTIONAL FOCUS

◉ **Student Community Text**
- *A Musical Day* by Jerdine Nolen, **Student Book** pp. 78–93 ANCHOR TEXT
- *Drums* by Tim Pano, **Student Book** pp. 98–100

◉ **Teacher Read Aloud:** *The Neighbors*, p. 352

◉ **Minilesson Principles:** Sequence of Events; Sequence of Events; Diagram

◉ **Word Work Emphasis:** Words with Short *o*

◉ **Writing Mode:** Informative Writing

◉ **Writing Trait:** Purpose

For additional instructional resources, see **Journeys** *Lesson 8 Focus Wall.*

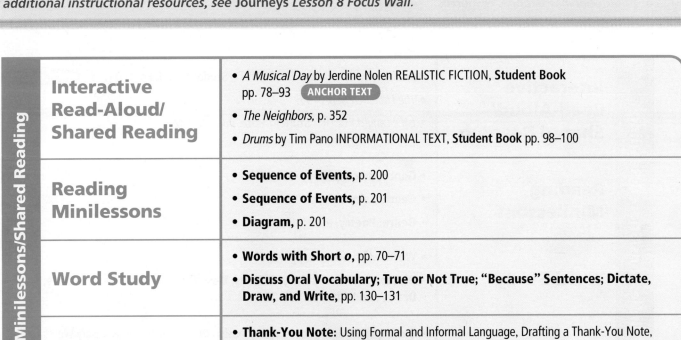

Minilessons/Shared Reading		
Interactive Read-Aloud/ Shared Reading	• *A Musical Day* by Jerdine Nolen REALISTIC FICTION, **Student Book** pp. 78–93 ANCHOR TEXT • *The Neighbors*, p. 352 • *Drums* by Tim Pano INFORMATIONAL TEXT, **Student Book** pp. 98–100	
Reading Minilessons	• **Sequence of Events,** p. 200 • **Sequence of Events,** p. 201 • **Diagram,** p. 201	
Word Study	• **Words with Short *o*,** pp. 70–71 • **Discuss Oral Vocabulary; True or Not True; "Because" Sentences; Dictate, Draw, and Write,** pp. 130–131	
Writing	• **Thank-You Note:** Using Formal and Informal Language, Drafting a Thank-You Note, pp. 286–287; **Writing Trait:** Purpose, p. 338 • **Weekly Student Model:** Thank-You Note, **Student Book** p. 105	

Guided Reading

Select texts according to your children's instructional level. You may use the books below or select from the Leveled Readers Database, pp. 388–397. For instructional support, use the Leveled Readers Teacher's Guides along with the books that you choose.

- **LEVEL B** *Dress Up*
- **LEVEL C** *Music* (Vocabulary Reader)
- **LEVEL D** *Nana's House*
- **LEVEL D** *Our Day at Nana's House* (Language Support)
- **LEVEL J** *The Beach*

Planning a Week of Literacy and Language

INSTRUCTIONAL FOCUS

- **Student Community Text**
  - *Dr. Seuss* by Helen Lester, **Student Book** pp. 110–125 `ANCHOR TEXT`
  - *Let's Laugh!*, **Student Book** pp. 130–132
- **Teacher Read Aloud:** *The Little Red Hen*, p. 352
- **Minilesson Principles:** Genre: Biography; Genre: Fairy Tale; Genre: Poetry
- **Word Work Emphasis:** Words with Short *e*
- **Writing Mode:** Informative Writing
- **Writing Trait:** Evidence

For additional instructional resources, see Journeys Lesson 9 Focus Wall.

Minilessons/Shared Reading		
Interactive Read-Aloud/ Shared Reading	• *Dr. Seuss* by Helen Lester BIOGRAPHY, **Student Book** pp. 110–125 `ANCHOR TEXT` • *The Little Red Hen*, p. 352 • *Let's Laugh!* POETRY, **Student Book** pp. 130–132	
Reading Minilessons	• **Genre: Biography,** p. 202 • **Genre: Fairy Tale,** p. 203 • **Genre: Poetry,** p. 203	
Word Study	• **Words with Short *e*,** pp. 72–73 • **Discuss Oral Vocabulary; Riddles; Describe It or Act It Out; Dictate, Draw, and Write,** pp. 132–133	
Writing	• **Description:** Listing Topics and Choosing One, Brainstorming Sensory Words, pp. 288–289; **The Writing Process:** Prewriting, p. 332; **Writing Trait:** Evidence, p. 336 • **Weekly Student Model:** Web, **Student Book** p. 137	

Guided Reading

Select texts according to your children's instructional level. You may use the books below or select from the Leveled Readers Database, pp. 388–397. For instructional support, use the Leveled Readers Teacher's Guides along with the books that you choose.

- **LEVEL B** *Drawing*
- **LEVEL C** *Reading Together* (Vocabulary Reader)
- **LEVEL E** *Jim Henson, the Puppet Man*
- **LEVEL E** *The Man Who Made Puppets* (Language Support)
- **LEVEL J** *Margret and Hans Rey*

Planning a Week of Literacy and Language

INSTRUCTIONAL FOCUS

- **Student Community Text**
  - *A Cupcake Party* by David McPhail, **Student Book** pp. 142–157 ANCHOR TEXT
  - *Happy Times,* **Student Book** pp. 162–164
- **Teacher Read Aloud:** *Chipper Chips In,* p. 353
- **Minilesson Principles:** Story Structure; Story Structure; Genre: Poetry
- **Word Work Emphasis:** Words with Short *u*
- **Writing Mode:** Informative Writing
- **Writing Trait:** Organization

For additional instructional resources, see Journeys Lesson 10 Focus Wall.

Minilessons/Shared Reading		
Interactive Read-Aloud/ Shared Reading	• *A Cupcake Party* by David McPhail FANTASY, **Student Book** pp. 142–157 ANCHOR TEXT • *Chipper Chips In,* p. 353 • *Happy Times* POETRY, **Student Book** pp. 162–164	
Reading Minilessons	• **Story Structure,** p. 204 • **Story Structure,** p. 205 • **Genre: Poetry,** p. 205	
Word Study	• **Words with Short *u*,** pp. 74–75 • **Discuss Oral Vocabulary; Paired Yes/No Questions; Word Sort; Dictate, Draw, and Write,** pp. 134–135	
Writing	• **Description:** Writing a Clear Topic Sentence, Drafting a Description, 290–291; **The Writing Process:** Revising, p. 334; **Writing Trait:** Organization, p. 337 • **Weekly Student Model:** Description, **Student Book** p. 169	

Guided Reading

Select texts according to your children's instructional level. You may use the books below or select from the Leveled Readers Database, pp. 388–397. For instructional support, use the Leveled Readers Teacher's Guides along with the books that you choose.

- **LEVEL B** *Trip to the Rock*
- **LEVEL C** *Happy Birthday!* (Vocabulary Reader)
- **LEVEL E** *Happy Birthday, Toad* (Language Support)
- **LEVEL E** *Toad's Birthday*
- **LEVEL I** *Chipmunk's New Home*

Planning a Week of Literacy and Language

INSTRUCTIONAL FOCUS

- **Student Community Text**
  - *At Home in the Ocean* by Rozanne Lanczak Williams, **Student Book** pp. 14–29 ANCHOR TEXT
  - *Water,* **Student Book** pp. 34–36
- **Teacher Read Aloud:** *The Piano Lessons,* p. 353
- **Minilesson Principles:** Author's Purpose; Author's Purpose; Genre: Informational Text
- **Word Work Emphasis:** Words with *th*
- **Writing Mode:** Informative Writing
- **Writing Trait:** Evidence

For additional instructional resources, see Journeys Lesson 11 Focus Wall.

Minilessons/Shared Reading

Interactive Read-Aloud/ Shared Reading	• *At Home in the Ocean* by Rozanne Lanczak Williams INFORMATIONAL TEXT, **Student Book** pp. 14–29 ANCHOR TEXT • *The Piano Lessons,* p. 353 • *Water* INFORMATIONAL TEXT, **Student Book** pp. 34–36
Reading Minilessons	• **Author's Purpose,** p. 206 • **Author's Purpose,** p. 207 • **Genre: Informational Text,** p. 207
Word Study	• **Words with *th*,** pp. 76–77 • **Discuss Oral Vocabulary; Paired Yes/No Questions; Synonyms; Dictate, Draw, and Write,** pp. 136–137
Writing	• **Sentences That Inform:** Using Words That Tell *How, When,* and *Where*; Drafting Sentences That Inform, pp. 292–293; **Writing Trait:** Evidence, p. 336; **Using the Computer:** Using the Computer to Find Information, p. 341 • **Weekly Student Model:** Sentences That Inform, **Student Book** p. 41

Guided Reading

Select texts according to your children's instructional level. You may use the books below or select from the Leveled Readers Database, pp. 388–397. For instructional support, use the Leveled Readers Teacher's Guides along with the books that you choose.

- **LEVEL D** *In the Sea*
- **LEVEL D** *Shark* (Vocabulary Reader)
- **LEVEL G** *Life in the Coral Reefs* (Language Support)
- **LEVEL H** *Coral Reefs*
- **LEVEL L** *The Amazing Octopus*

Planning a Week of Literacy and Language

INSTRUCTIONAL FOCUS

◉ **Student Community Text**
  - *How Leopard Got His Spots* by Gerald McDermott, **Student Book** pp. 46–63 ANCHOR TEXT
  - *The Rain Forest*, **Student Book** pp. 68–70

◉ **Teacher Read Aloud:** *Turtle, Frog, and Rat*, p. 354

◉ **Minilesson Principles:** Sequence of Events; Genre: Folktale; Genre: Informational Text

◉ **Word Work Emphasis:** Words with *ch*

◉ **Writing Mode:** Informative Writing

◉ **Writing Trait:** Organization

For additional instructional resources, see Journeys Lesson 12 Focus Wall.

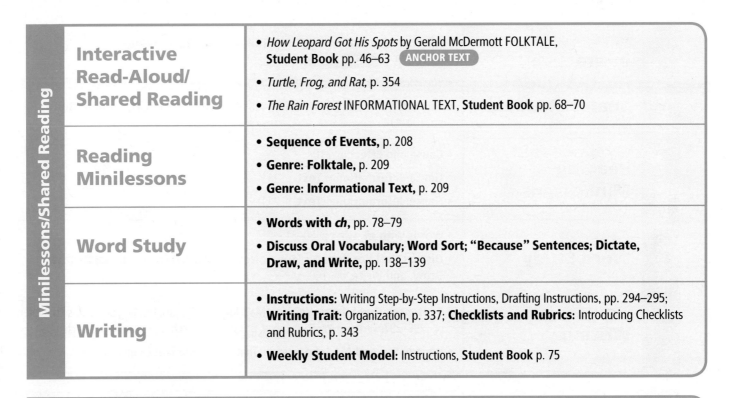

Minilessons/Shared Reading		
Interactive Read-Aloud/ Shared Reading	• *How Leopard Got His Spots* by Gerald McDermott FOLKTALE, **Student Book** pp. 46–63 ANCHOR TEXT • *Turtle, Frog, and Rat*, p. 354 • *The Rain Forest* INFORMATIONAL TEXT, **Student Book** pp. 68–70	
Reading Minilessons	• **Sequence of Events,** p. 208 • **Genre: Folktale,** p. 209 • **Genre: Informational Text,** p. 209	
Word Study	• **Words with *ch*,** pp. 78–79 • **Discuss Oral Vocabulary; Word Sort; "Because" Sentences; Dictate, Draw, and Write,** pp. 138–139	
Writing	• **Instructions:** Writing Step-by-Step Instructions, Drafting Instructions, pp. 294–295; **Writing Trait:** Organization, p. 337; **Checklists and Rubrics:** Introducing Checklists and Rubrics, p. 343 • **Weekly Student Model:** Instructions, **Student Book** p. 75	

Guided Reading

Select texts according to your children's instructional level. You may use the books below or select from the Leveled Readers Database, pp. 388–397. For instructional support, use the Leveled Readers Teacher's Guides along with the books that you choose.

- **LEVEL D** *Spots* (Vocabulary Reader)
- **LEVEL E** *Giraffe's Neck*
- **LEVEL H** *Bear's Long, Brown Tail* (Language Support)
- **LEVEL H** *Bear's Tail*
- **LEVEL L** *Peacock's Tail*

Planning a Week of Literacy and Language

INSTRUCTIONAL FOCUS

- **Student Community Text**
  - *Seasons* by Pat Cummings, **Student Book** pp. 80–99 [ANCHOR TEXT]
  - *Four Seasons for Animals* by Ashley Wolff, **Student Book** pp. 104–114
- **Teacher Read Aloud:** *The Prickly Pride of Texas*, p. 355
- **Minilesson Principles:** Cause and Effect; Genre: Informational Text; Genre: Informational Text
- **Word Work Emphasis:** Words with *sh, wh*
- **Writing Mode:** Informative Writing
- **Writing Trait:** Purpose

For additional instructional resources, see Journeys *Lesson 13 Focus Wall.*

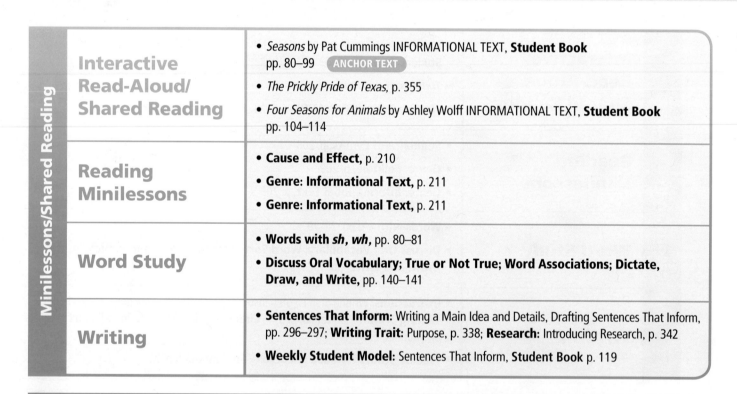

Minilessons/Shared Reading		
Interactive Read-Aloud/ Shared Reading	• *Seasons* by Pat Cummings INFORMATIONAL TEXT, **Student Book** pp. 80–99 [ANCHOR TEXT] • *The Prickly Pride of Texas*, p. 355 • *Four Seasons for Animals* by Ashley Wolff INFORMATIONAL TEXT, **Student Book** pp. 104–114	
Reading Minilessons	• **Cause and Effect**, p. 210 • **Genre: Informational Text**, p. 211 • **Genre: Informational Text**, p. 211	
Word Study	• **Words with *sh, wh*,** pp. 80–81 • **Discuss Oral Vocabulary; True or Not True; Word Associations; Dictate, Draw, and Write,** pp. 140–141	
Writing	• **Sentences That Inform:** Writing a Main Idea and Details, Drafting Sentences That Inform, pp. 296–297; **Writing Trait:** Purpose, p. 338; **Research:** Introducing Research, p. 342 • **Weekly Student Model:** Sentences That Inform, **Student Book** p. 119	

Guided Reading

Select texts according to your children's instructional level. You may use the books below or select from the Leveled Readers Database, pp. 388–397. For instructional support, use the Leveled Readers Teacher's Guides along with the books that you choose.

- **LEVEL B** *Winter*
- **LEVEL D** *Ducks* (Vocabulary Reader)
- **LEVEL H** *In the Fall* (Language Support)
- **LEVEL I** *Fall Changes*
- **LEVEL K** *Seasons Around the World*

Planning a Week of Literacy and Language

INSTRUCTIONAL FOCUS

- **Student Community Text**
  - *The Big Race* by Pam Muñoz Ryan, **Student Book** pp. 124–143 **ANCHOR TEXT**
  - *Rules and Laws* by J.C. Cunningham, **Student Book** pp. 148–154

- **Teacher Read Aloud:** *The Tortoise and the Hare,* p. 355

- **Minilesson Principles:** Conclusions; Conclusions; Genre: Informational Text

- **Word Work Emphasis:** Words with Long *a*

- **Writing Mode:** Informative Writing

- **Writing Trait:** Evidence

For additional instructional resources, see Journeys *Lesson 14 Focus Wall.*

Minilessons/Shared Reading	**Interactive Read-Aloud/ Shared Reading**	• *The Big Race* by Pam Muñoz Ryan FANTASY, **Student Book** pp. 124–143 **ANCHOR TEXT** • *The Tortoise and the Hare,* p. 355 • *Rules and Laws* by J.C. Cunningham INFORMATIONAL TEXT, **Student Book** pp. 148–154
	Reading Minilessons	• **Conclusions,** p. 212 • **Conclusions,** p. 213 • **Genre: Informational Text,** p. 213
	Word Study	• **Words with Long *a*,** pp. 82–83 • **Discuss Oral Vocabulary; Describe It; Complete Sentences; Dictate, Draw, and Write,** pp. 142–143
	Writing	• **Report:** Selecting a Topic, Planning a Report, pp. 298–299; **The Writing Process:** Prewriting, p. 332; **Writing Trait:** Evidence, p. 336 • **Weekly Student Model:** Chart, **Student Book** p. 159

Guided Reading		Select texts according to your children's instructional level. You may use the books below or select from the Leveled Readers Database, pp. 388–397. For instructional support, use the Leveled Readers Teacher's Guides along with the books that you choose. • **LEVEL D** *Izzy's Move* • **LEVEL E** *Desert Animals* (Vocabulary Reader) • **LEVEL I** *The Map and the Treasure* (Language Support) • **LEVEL I** *The Treasure Map* • **LEVEL K** *Cam the Camel*

Planning a Week of Literacy and Language

INSTRUCTIONAL FOCUS

◉ **Student Community Text**
  - *Animal Groups* by James Bruchac, **Student Book** pp. 164–183 `ANCHOR TEXT`
  - *Animal Picnic* by Debbie O'Brien, **Student Book** pp. 188–190

◉ **Teacher Read Aloud:** *The Dancing Wolves*, p. 355

◉ **Minilesson Principles:** Compare and Contrast; Story Structure; Compare and Contrast

◉ **Word Work Emphasis:** Words with Long *i*

◉ **Writing Mode:** Informative Writing

◉ **Writing Trait:** Elaboration

For additional instructional resources, see Journeys *Lesson 15 Focus Wall.*

Minilessons/Shared Reading		
Interactive Read-Aloud/ Shared Reading	• *Animal Groups* by James Bruchac INFORMATIONAL TEXT, **Student Book** pp. 164–183 `ANCHOR TEXT` • *The Dancing Wolves*, p. 355 • *Animal Picnic* by Debbie O'Brien PLAY, **Student Book** pp. 188–190	
Reading Minilessons	• **Compare and Contrast,** p. 214 • **Story Structure,** p. 215 • **Compare and Contrast,** p. 215	
Word Study	• **Words with Long *i*,** pp. 84–85 • **Discuss Oral Vocabulary; True or Not True; Sentence Clue Game; Dictate, Draw, and Write,** pp. 144–145	
Writing	• **Report:** Writing a Strong Closing, Drafting a Report, pp. 300–301; **The Writing Process:** Revising, p. 334; **Writing Trait:** Elaboration, p. 338 • **Weekly Student Model:** Report, **Student Book** p. 195	

Guided Reading

Select texts according to your children's instructional level. You may use the books below or select from the Leveled Readers Database, pp. 388–397. For instructional support, use the Leveled Readers Teacher's Guides along with the books that you choose.

- **LEVEL D** *Making a Home*
- **LEVEL E** *Animals* (Vocabulary Reader)
- **LEVEL J** *All About Bats*
- **LEVEL J** *Many Kinds of Bats* (Language Support)
- **LEVEL L** *Bald Eagles*

Planning a Week of Literacy and Language

INSTRUCTIONAL FOCUS

◉ **Student Community Text**
  - *Let's Go to the Moon!* by Stephen R. Swinburne, **Student Book** pp. 14–35 `ANCHOR TEXT`
  - *Mae Jemison* by Debbie O'Brien, **Student Book** pp. 40–42

◉ **Teacher Read Aloud:** *One Giant Leap,* p. 356

◉ **Minilesson Principles:** Main Idea and Details; Main Idea and Details; Genre: Biography

◉ **Word Work Emphasis:** Words with Long *o*

◉ **Writing Mode:** Narrative Writing

◉ **Writing Trait:** Purpose

For additional instructional resources, see Journeys *Lesson 16 Focus Wall.*

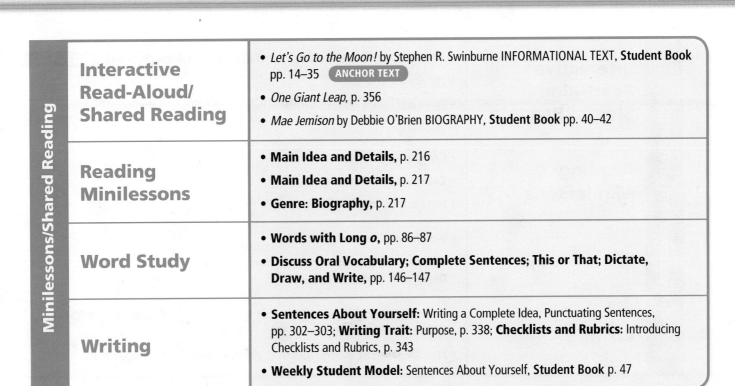

Minilessons/Shared Reading		
Interactive Read-Aloud/ Shared Reading	• *Let's Go to the Moon!* by Stephen R. Swinburne INFORMATIONAL TEXT, **Student Book** pp. 14–35 `ANCHOR TEXT` • *One Giant Leap,* p. 356 • *Mae Jemison* by Debbie O'Brien BIOGRAPHY, **Student Book** pp. 40–42	
Reading Minilessons	• **Main Idea and Details,** p. 216 • **Main Idea and Details,** p. 217 • **Genre: Biography,** p. 217	
Word Study	• **Words with Long *o*,** pp. 86–87 • **Discuss Oral Vocabulary; Complete Sentences; This or That; Dictate, Draw, and Write,** pp. 146–147	
Writing	• **Sentences About Yourself:** Writing a Complete Idea, Punctuating Sentences, pp. 302–303; **Writing Trait:** Purpose, p. 338; **Checklists and Rubrics:** Introducing Checklists and Rubrics, p. 343 • **Weekly Student Model:** Sentences About Yourself, **Student Book** p. 47	

Guided Reading

Select texts according to your children's instructional level. You may use the books below or select from the Leveled Readers Database, pp. 388–397. For instructional support, use the Leveled Readers Teacher's Guides along with the books that you choose.

- **LEVEL D** *In the Sky* (Vocabulary Reader)
- **LEVEL D** *The Sun*
- **LEVEL I** *Seasons*
- **LEVEL I** *The Seasons of the Year* (Language Support)
- **LEVEL J** *Living and Working in Space*

Planning a Week of Literacy and Language

INSTRUCTIONAL FOCUS

- **Student Community Text**
  - *The Big Trip* by Valerie Gorbachev, **Student Book** pp. 52–73 `ANCHOR TEXT`
  - *Lewis and Clark's Big Trip*, **Student Book** pp. 78–80
- **Teacher Read Aloud:** *The Rainy Trip*, p. 357
- **Minilesson Principles:** Compare and Contrast; Compare and Contrast; Genre: Informational Text
- **Word Work Emphasis:** Words with Long *e*
- **Writing Mode:** Narrative Writing
- **Writing Trait:** Development

For additional instructional resources, see Journeys Lesson 17 Focus Wall.

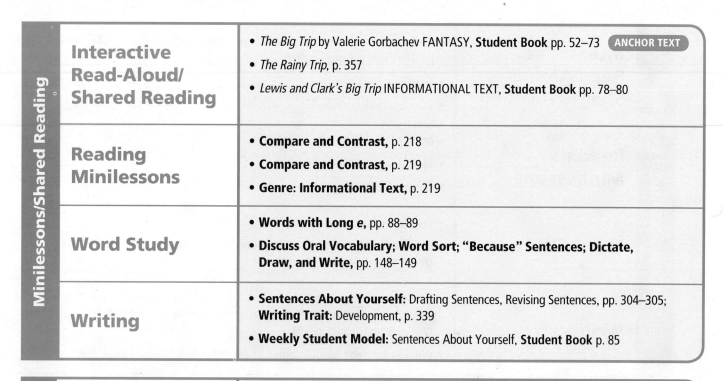

Minilessons/Shared Reading		
Interactive Read-Aloud/ Shared Reading	• *The Big Trip* by Valerie Gorbachev FANTASY, **Student Book** pp. 52–73 `ANCHOR TEXT` • *The Rainy Trip*, p. 357 • *Lewis and Clark's Big Trip* INFORMATIONAL TEXT, **Student Book** pp. 78–80	
Reading Minilessons	• **Compare and Contrast,** p. 218 • **Compare and Contrast,** p. 219 • **Genre: Informational Text,** p. 219	
Word Study	• **Words with Long *e*,** pp. 88–89 • **Discuss Oral Vocabulary; Word Sort; "Because" Sentences; Dictate, Draw, and Write,** pp. 148–149	
Writing	• **Sentences About Yourself:** Drafting Sentences, Revising Sentences, pp. 304–305; **Writing Trait:** Development, p. 339 • **Weekly Student Model:** Sentences About Yourself, **Student Book** p. 85	

Guided Reading

Select texts according to your children's instructional level. You may use the books below or select from the Leveled Readers Database, pp. 388–397. For instructional support, use the Leveled Readers Teacher's Guides along with the books that you choose.

- **LEVEL E** *Bear Swims*
- **LEVEL E** *Going to School* (Vocabulary Reader)
- **LEVEL H** *Flying*
- **LEVEL H** *Flying in an Airplane* (Language Support)
- **LEVEL J** *The Mountain*

Planning a Week of Literacy and Language

INSTRUCTIONAL FOCUS

- **Student Community Text**
  - *Where Does Food Come From?* by Shelley Rotner and Gary Goss, **Student Book** pp. 90–111 **ANCHOR TEXT**
  - *Jack and the Beanstalk,* **Student Book** pp. 116–118
- **Teacher Read Aloud:** *The Three Wishes,* p. 357
- **Minilesson Principles:** Author's Purpose; Genre: Fairy Tale; Genre: Fairy Tale
- **Word Work Emphasis:** Words with Long *a*
- **Writing Mode:** Narrative Writing
- **Writing Trait:** Conventions

For additional instructional resources, see Journeys *Lesson 18 Focus Wall.*

Minilessons/Shared Reading		
Interactive Read-Aloud/ Shared Reading	• *Where Does Food Come From?* by Shelley Rotner and Gary Goss INFORMATIONAL TEXT, **Student Book** pp. 90–111 **ANCHOR TEXT** • *The Three Wishes,* p. 357 • *Jack and the Beanstalk* FAIRY TALE, **Student Book** pp. 116–118	
Reading Minilessons	• **Author's Purpose,** p. 220 • **Genre: Fairy Tale,** p. 221 • **Genre: Fairy Tale,** p. 221	
Word Study	• **Words with Long *a*,** pp. 90–91 • **Discuss Oral Vocabulary; Describe It or Act It Out; Multiple-Meaning Words; Dictate, Draw, and Write,** pp. 150–151	
Writing	• **Friendly Letter:** Using Letter Format, Drafting a Friendly Letter, pp. 306–307; **Writing Trait:** Conventions, p. 340 • **Weekly Student Model:** Friendly Letter, **Student Book** p. 123	

Guided Reading	
	Select texts according to your children's instructional level. You may use the books below or select from the Leveled Readers Database, pp. 388–397. For instructional support, use the Leveled Readers Teacher's Guides along with the books that you choose. • **LEVEL D** *Apples* • **LEVEL D** *My Favorite Foods* (Vocabulary Reader) • **LEVEL G** *How We Get Food* (Language Support) • **LEVEL H** *Food for You* • **LEVEL K** *A World of Food*

Planning a Week of Literacy and Language

INSTRUCTIONAL FOCUS

- **Student Community Text**
  - *Tomás Rivera* by Jane Medina, **Student Book** pp. 128–143 **ANCHOR TEXT**
  - *Life Then and Now*, **Student Book** pp. 148–150
- **Teacher Read Aloud:** *Christina's Work*, p. 358
- **Minilesson Principles:** Sequence of Events; Conclusions; Compare and Contrast
- **Word Work Emphasis:** Words with Long *o*
- **Writing Mode:** Narrative Writing
- **Writing Trait:** Organization

For additional instructional resources, see Journeys Lesson 19 Focus Wall.

Minilessons/Shared Reading	**Interactive Read-Aloud/ Shared Reading**	• *Tomás Rivera* by Jane Medina BIOGRAPHY, **Student Book** pp. 128–143 **ANCHOR TEXT** • *Christina's Work*, p. 358 • *Life Then and Now* INFORMATIONAL TEXT, **Student Book** pp. 148–150
	Reading Minilessons	• **Sequence of Events,** p. 222 • **Conclusions,** p. 223 • **Compare and Contrast,** p. 223
	Word Study	• **Words with Long *o*,** pp. 92–93 • **Discuss Oral Vocabulary; Paired Yes/No Questions; "Because" Sentences; Dictate, Draw, and Write,** pp. 152–153
	Writing	• **Personal Narrative:** Using Time Order, Planning a Personal Narrative, pp. 308–309; **The Writing Process:** Prewriting, p. 332; **Writing Trait:** Organization, p. 337 • **Weekly Student Model:** Flow Chart, **Student Book** p. 155

Guided Reading		Select texts according to your children's instructional level. You may use the books below or select from the Leveled Readers Database, pp. 388–397. For instructional support, use the Leveled Readers Teacher's Guides along with the books that you choose. • **LEVEL D** *People in the Town* (Vocabulary Reader) • **LEVEL E** *Working in the Park* • **LEVEL H** *Our Bakery* • **LEVEL H** *Our Day at the Bakery* (Language Support) • **LEVEL J** *What I Want to Be*

Planning a Week of Literacy and Language

INSTRUCTIONAL FOCUS

Student Community Text
- *Little Rabbit's Tale* by Wong Herbert Yee, **Student Book** pp. 160–179 ANCHOR TEXT
- *Silly Poems*, **Student Book** pp. 184–186

Teacher Read Aloud: *Chicken Little*, p. 358

Minilesson Principles: Cause and Effect; Genre: Folktale; Genre: Poetry

Word Work Emphasis: Compound Words

Writing Mode: Narrative Writing

Writing Trait: Development

For additional instructional resources, see Journeys Lesson 20 Focus Wall.

Minilessons/Shared Reading		
Interactive Read-Aloud/ Shared Reading	• *Little Rabbit's Tale* by Wong Herbert Yee FOLKTALE, **Student Book** pp. 160–179 ANCHOR TEXT • *Chicken Little*, p. 358 • *Silly Poems* POETRY, **Student Book** pp. 184–186	
Reading Minilessons	• **Cause and Effect,** p. 224 • **Genre: Folktale,** p. 225 • **Genre: Poetry,** p. 225	
Word Study	• **Compound Words,** pp. 94–95 • **Discuss Oral Vocabulary; Word Sort; Word Associations; Dictate, Draw, and Write,** pp. 154–155	
Writing	• **Personal Narrative:** Adding Details, Drafting a Personal Narrative, pp. 310–311; **The Writing Process:** Editing and Publishing, p. 335; **Writing Trait:** Development, p. 339 • **Weekly Student Model:** Personal Narrative, **Student Book** p. 191	

Guided Reading

Select texts according to your children's instructional level. You may use the books below or select from the Leveled Readers Database, pp. 388–397. For instructional support, use the Leveled Readers Teacher's Guides along with the books that you choose.

- **LEVEL D**   *Putting Frosting on the Cake*
- **LEVEL E**   *The Weather* (Vocabulary Reader)
- **LEVEL G**   *Polly's Pet Polar Bear* (Language Support)
- **LEVEL H**   *Polar Bear Pete*
- **LEVEL J**   *Bobcat Tells a Tale*

Planning a Week of Literacy and Language

INSTRUCTIONAL FOCUS

- **Student Community Text**
  - *The Garden* by Arnold Lobel, **Student Book** pp. 14–29 `ANCHOR TEXT`
  - *Garden Good Guys* by Timothy Thomas, **Student Book** pp. 34–36

- **Teacher Read Aloud:** *Grandpa's Tree*, p. 359

- **Minilesson Principles:** Story Structure; Story Structure; Genre: Informational Text

- **Word Work Emphasis:** Words with *ar*

- **Writing Mode:** Narrative Writing

- **Writing Trait:** Development

For additional instructional resources, see Journeys Lesson 21 Focus Wall.

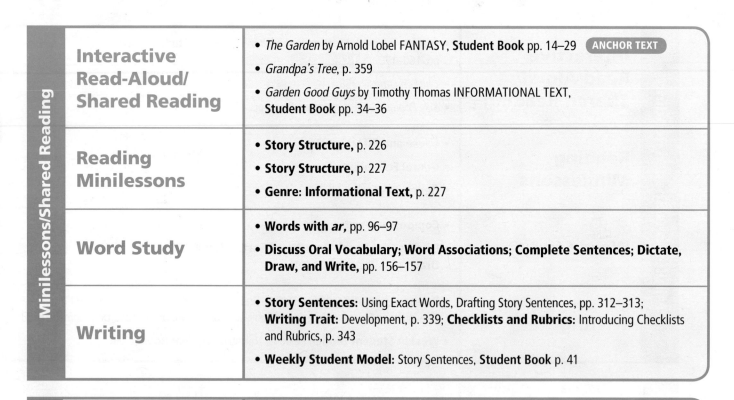

Minilessons/Shared Reading		
Interactive Read-Aloud/ Shared Reading	• *The Garden* by Arnold Lobel FANTASY, **Student Book** pp. 14–29 `ANCHOR TEXT` • *Grandpa's Tree*, p. 359 • *Garden Good Guys* by Timothy Thomas INFORMATIONAL TEXT, **Student Book** pp. 34–36	
Reading Minilessons	• **Story Structure,** p. 226 • **Story Structure,** p. 227 • **Genre: Informational Text,** p. 227	
Word Study	• **Words with *ar*,** pp. 96–97 • **Discuss Oral Vocabulary; Word Associations; Complete Sentences; Dictate, Draw, and Write,** pp. 156–157	
Writing	• **Story Sentences:** Using Exact Words, Drafting Story Sentences, pp. 312–313; **Writing Trait:** Development, p. 339; **Checklists and Rubrics:** Introducing Checklists and Rubrics, p. 343 • **Weekly Student Model:** Story Sentences, **Student Book** p. 41	

Guided Reading

Select texts according to your children's instructional level. You may use the books below or select from the Leveled Readers Database, pp. 388–397. For instructional support, use the Leveled Readers Teacher's Guides along with the books that you choose.

- **LEVEL E**   *A Seed for Sid*
- **LEVEL G**   *Trees* (Vocabulary Reader)
- **LEVEL H**   *Forest Stew*
- **LEVEL H**   *Skunk Cooks Soup* (Language Support)
- **LEVEL J**   *Lena's Garden*

Planning a Week of Literacy and Language

INSTRUCTIONAL FOCUS

- **Student Community Text**
  - *Amazing Animals* by Gwendolyn Hooks, **Student Book** pp. 46–65 ANCHOR TEXT
  - *The Ugly Duckling*, **Student Book** pp. 70–72

- **Teacher Read Aloud:** *How Bat Learned to Fly*, p. 359

- **Minilesson Principles:** Conclusions; Conclusions; Genre: Folktale

- **Word Work Emphasis:** Words with *er, ir, ur*

- **Writing Mode:** Narrative Writing

- **Writing Trait:** Development

For additional instructional resources, see Journeys Lesson 22 Focus Wall.

Minilessons/Shared Reading		
Interactive Read-Aloud/ Shared Reading	• *Amazing Animals* by Gwendolyn Hooks INFORMATIONAL TEXT, **Student Book** pp. 46–65 ANCHOR TEXT • *How Bat Learned to Fly*, p. 359 • *The Ugly Duckling* FOLKTALE, **Student Book** pp. 70–72	
Reading Minilessons	• **Conclusions,** p. 228 • **Conclusions,** p. 229 • **Genre: Folktale,** p. 229	
Word Study	• **Words with *er, ir, ur*,** pp. 98–99 • **Discuss Oral Vocabulary; Paired Yes/No Questions; Word Sort; Dictate, Draw, and Write,** pp. 158–159	
Writing	• **Story Sentences:** Using Vivid Verbs, Publishing Story Sentences, pp. 314–315; **Writing Trait:** Development, p. 339; **Using the Computer:** Introducing Using the Computer, p. 341 • **Weekly Student Model:** Story Sentences, **Student Book** p. 77	

Guided Reading

Select texts according to your children's instructional level. You may use the books below or select from the Leveled Readers Database, pp. 388–397. For instructional support, use the Leveled Readers Teacher's Guides along with the books that you choose.

- **LEVEL E** *Animal Homes*
- **LEVEL E** *Baby Birds* (Vocabulary Reader)
- **LEVEL I** *Baby Kangaroos*
- **LEVEL I** *Tiny Baby Kangaroos* (Language Support)
- **LEVEL J** *How Animals Move*

Planning a Week of Literacy and Language

INSTRUCTIONAL FOCUS

- **Student Community Text**
  - *Whistle for Willie* by Ezra Jack Keats, **Student Book** pp. 82–103 ANCHOR TEXT
  - *Pet Poems*, **Student Book** pp. 108–110
- **Teacher Read Aloud:** *Around the World in a Day,* p. 360
- **Minilesson Principles:** Cause and Effect; Genre: Realistic Fiction; Genre: Poetry
- **Word Work Emphasis:** Words with *oo* (/o͞o/)
- **Writing Mode:** Narrative Writing
- **Writing Trait:** Organization

For additional instructional resources, see Journeys Lesson 23 Focus Wall.

Minilessons/Shared Reading		
Interactive Read-Aloud/ Shared Reading	• *Whistle for Willie* by Ezra Jack Keats REALISTIC FICTION, **Student Book** pp. 82–103 ANCHOR TEXT • *Around the World in a Day,* p. 360 • *Pet Poems* POETRY, **Student Book** pp. 108–110	
Reading Minilessons	• **Cause and Effect,** p. 230 • **Genre: Realistic Fiction,** p. 231 • **Genre: Poetry,** p. 231	
Word Study	• **Words with *oo* (/o͞o/),** pp. 100–101 • **Discuss Oral Vocabulary; True or Not True; Word Associations; Dictate, Draw, and Write,** pp. 160–161	
Writing	• **Story Summary:** Using Your Own Words, Drafting a Story Summary, pp. 316–317; **Writing Trait:** Organization, p. 337 • **Weekly Student Model:** Story Summary, **Student Book** p. 115	

Guided Reading

Select texts according to your children's instructional level. You may use the books below or select from the Leveled Readers Database, pp. 388–397. For instructional support, use the Leveled Readers Teacher's Guides along with the books that you choose.

- **LEVEL E** *Amy's Airplane*
- **LEVEL F** *So Many Sounds* (Vocabulary Reader)
- **LEVEL I** *Len's Tomato Plant* (Language Support)
- **LEVEL I** *Len's Tomatoes*
- **LEVEL L** *The Lemonade Stand*

Planning a Week of Literacy and Language

INSTRUCTIONAL FOCUS

- **Student Community Text**
  - *A Tree Is a Plant* by Clyde Robert Bulla, **Student Book** pp. 120–147 ANCHOR TEXT
  - *Grow, Apples, Grow!*, **Student Book** pp. 152–154
- **Teacher Read Aloud:** *Visiting Butterflies*, p. 361
- **Minilesson Principles:** Sequence of Events; Sequence of Events; Genre: Informational Text
- **Word Work Emphasis:** Words with *oo, ou, ew*
- **Writing Mode:** Narrative Writing
- **Writing Trait:** Development

For additional instructional resources, see Journeys Lesson 24 Focus Wall.

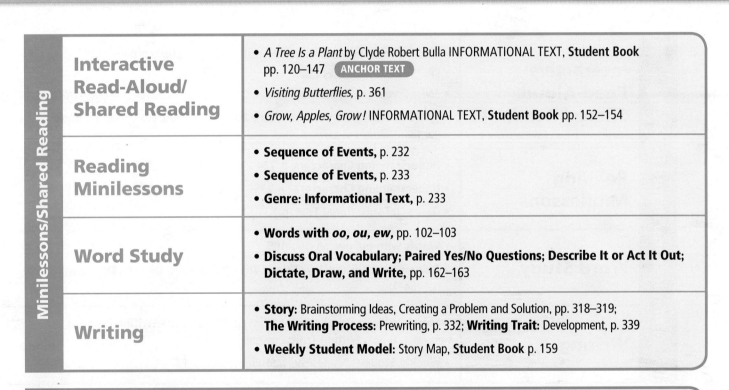

Minilessons/Shared Reading		
Interactive Read-Aloud/ Shared Reading	• *A Tree Is a Plant* by Clyde Robert Bulla INFORMATIONAL TEXT, **Student Book** pp. 120–147 ANCHOR TEXT • *Visiting Butterflies*, p. 361 • *Grow, Apples, Grow!* INFORMATIONAL TEXT, **Student Book** pp. 152–154
Reading Minilessons	• **Sequence of Events,** p. 232 • **Sequence of Events,** p. 233 • **Genre: Informational Text,** p. 233
Word Study	• **Words with *oo, ou, ew*,** pp. 102–103 • **Discuss Oral Vocabulary; Paired Yes/No Questions; Describe It or Act It Out; Dictate, Draw, and Write,** pp. 162–163
Writing	• **Story:** Brainstorming Ideas, Creating a Problem and Solution, pp. 318–319; **The Writing Process:** Prewriting, p. 332; **Writing Trait:** Development, p. 339 • **Weekly Student Model:** Story Map, **Student Book** p. 159

Guided Reading

Select texts according to your children's instructional level. You may use the books below or select from the Leveled Readers Database, pp. 388–397. For instructional support, use the Leveled Readers Teacher's Guides along with the books that you choose.

- **LEVEL H** *An Acorn Grows*
- **LEVEL J** *From Pit to Plum*
- **LEVEL J** *A Plum Grows* (Language Support)
- **LEVEL J** *Worms* (Vocabulary Reader)
- **LEVEL M** *The Story of a Rose*

Planning a Week of Literacy and Language

INSTRUCTIONAL FOCUS

- **Student Community Text**
  - *The New Friend* by María Puncel, **Student Book** pp. 164–181 `ANCHOR TEXT`
  - *Symbols of Our Country* by Agatha Jane, **Student Book** pp. 186–192

- **Teacher Read Aloud:** *Señor Coyote, the Judge,* p. 361

- **Minilesson Principles:** Understanding Characters; Understanding Characters; Genre: Informational Text

- **Word Work Emphasis:** Words with *ou, ow*

- **Writing Mode:** Narrative Writing

- **Writing Trait:** Conventions

For additional instructional resources, see Journeys *Lesson 25 Focus Wall.*

Minilessons/Shared Reading

Interactive Read-Aloud/ Shared Reading	• *The New Friend* by María Puncel REALISTIC FICTION, **Student Book** pp. 164–181 `ANCHOR TEXT` • *Señor Coyote, the Judge,* p. 361 • *Symbols of Our Country* by Agatha Jane INFORMATIONAL TEXT, **Student Book** pp. 186–192
Reading Minilessons	• **Understanding Characters,** p. 234 • **Understanding Characters ,** p. 235 • **Genre: Informational Text,** p. 235
Word Study	• **Words with *ou, ow,*** pp. 104–105 • **Discuss Oral Vocabulary; This or That; Antonyms; Dictate, Draw, and Write,** pp. 164–165
Writing	• **Story:** Drafting a Story, Revising a Story, pp. 320–321; **The Writing Process:** Revising, p. 334; **Writing Trait:** Conventions, p. 340 • **Weekly Student Model:** Story, **Student Book** p. 197

Guided Reading

Select texts according to your children's instructional level. You may use the books below or select from the Leveled Readers Database, pp. 388–397. For instructional support, use the Leveled Readers Teacher's Guides along with the books that you choose.

- **LEVEL F** *Molly's New Team*
- **LEVEL G** *Moving* (Vocabulary Reader)
- **LEVEL H** *First Day of Second Grade* (Language Support)
- **LEVEL I** *Ready for Second Grade*
- **LEVEL J** *Tag-Along Tim*

Planning a Week of Literacy and Language

INSTRUCTIONAL FOCUS

- ○ **Student Community Text**
  - *The Dot* by Peter H. Reynolds, **Student Book** pp. 14–33 `ANCHOR TEXT`
  - *Artists Create Art!* by Anne Rogers, **Student Book** pp. 38–40

- ○ **Teacher Read Aloud:** *The Art Contest,* p. 362

- ○ **Minilesson Principles:** Compare and Contrast; Compare and Contrast; Genre: Biography

- ○ **Word Work Emphasis:** Base Words with *-ed, -ing*

- ○ **Writing Mode:** Opinion Writing

- ○ **Writing Trait:** Conventions

For additional instructional resources, see Journeys *Lesson 26 Focus Wall.*

Minilessons/Shared Reading		
Interactive Read-Aloud/ Shared Reading	• *The Dot* by Peter H. Reynolds REALISTIC FICTION, **Student Book** pp. 14–33 `ANCHOR TEXT` • *The Art Contest,* p. 362 • *Artists Create Art!* by Anne Rogers BIOGRAPHY, **Student Book** pp. 38–40	
Reading Minilessons	• **Compare and Contrast,** p. 236 • **Compare and Contrast,** p. 237 • **Genre: Biography,** p. 237	
Word Study	• **Base Words with *-ed, -ing,*** pp. 106–107 • **Discuss Oral Vocabulary; True or Not True; Complete Sentences; Dictate, Draw, and Write,** pp. 166–167	
Writing	• **Opinion Sentences:** Thinking About Fact vs. Opinion, Drafting Opinion Sentences, pp. 322–323; **Writing Trait:** Conventions, p. 340; **Checklists and Rubrics:** Introducing Checklists and Rubrics, p. 343 • **Weekly Student Model:** Opinion Sentences, **Student Book** p. 45	

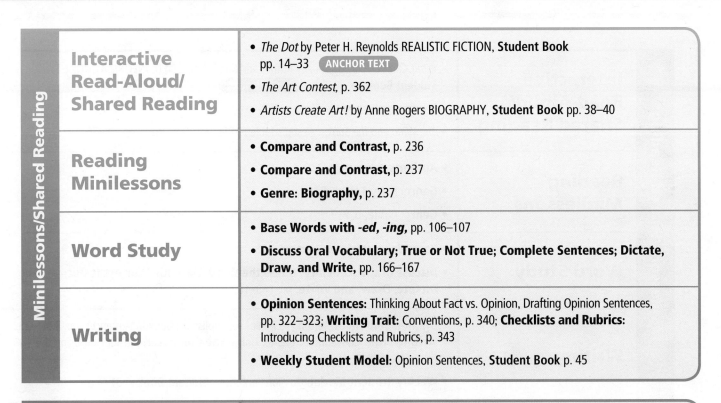

Guided Reading

Select texts according to your children's instructional level. You may use the books below or select from the Leveled Readers Database, pp. 388–397. For instructional support, use the Leveled Readers Teacher's Guides along with the books that you choose.

- **LEVEL F**   *Our School*
- **LEVEL H**   *The Bumpy Snowman* (Language Support)
- **LEVEL H**   *Kamala's Art* (Vocabulary Reader)
- **LEVEL I**   *Paco's Snowman*
- **LEVEL J**   *A Surprise for Ms. Green*

Planning a Week of Literacy and Language

INSTRUCTIONAL FOCUS

- **Student Community Text**
  - *What Can You Do?* by Shelley Rotner and Sheila Kelly, Ed.D., **Student Book** pp. 50–69 **ANCHOR TEXT**
  - *The Wind and the Sun* an Aesop's fable, **Student Book** pp. 74–76
- **Teacher Read Aloud:** *The Shoemaker and the Elves,* p. 362
- **Minilesson Principles:** Author's Purpose; Genre: Fairy Tale; Genre: Fable
- **Word Work Emphasis:** Base Words with *-er, -est*
- **Writing Mode:** Opinion Writing
- **Writing Trait:** Conventions

For additional instructional resources, see Journeys Lesson 27 Focus Wall.

Minilessons/Shared Reading		
Interactive Read-Aloud/ Shared Reading	• *What Can You Do?* by Shelley Rotner and Sheila Kelly, Ed.D. INFORMATIONAL TEXT, **Student Book** pp. 50–69 **ANCHOR TEXT** • *The Shoemaker and the Elves,* p. 362 • *The Wind and the Sun* an Aesop's fable FABLE, **Student Book** pp. 74–76	
Reading Minilessons	• **Author's Purpose,** p. 238 • **Genre: Fairy Tale,** p. 239 • **Genre: Fable,** p. 239	
Word Study	• **Base Words with *-er, -est*,** pp. 108–109 • **Discuss Oral Vocabulary; Guess the Word; Describe It or Act It Out; Dictate, Draw, and Write,** pp. 168–169	
Writing	• **Opinion Sentences:** Writing to Persuade, Publishing Opinion Sentences, pp. 324–325; **Writing Trait:** Conventions, p. 340; **Using the Computer:** Introducing Using the Computer, p. 341 • **Weekly Student Model:** Opinion Sentences, **Student Book** p. 81	

Guided Reading

Select texts according to your children's instructional level. You may use the books below or select from the Leveled Readers Database, pp. 388–397. For instructional support, use the Leveled Readers Teacher's Guides along with the books that you choose.

- **LEVEL E**   *Helping at Home* (Vocabulary Reader)
- **LEVEL E**   *Our Class*
- **LEVEL H**   *A Fun Baseball Game* (*Language Support*)
- **LEVEL I**   *The Baseball Game*
- **LEVEL K**   *Always Learning*

Planning a Week of Literacy and Language

INSTRUCTIONAL FOCUS

- **Student Community Text**
  - *The Kite* by Arnold Lobel, **Student Book** pp. 86–101   ANCHOR TEXT
  - *Measuring Weather,* **Student Book** pp. 106–108

- **Teacher Read Aloud:** *A Hopeful Song,* p. 363

- **Minilesson Principles:** Story Structure; Genre: Informational Text; Genre: Informational Text

- **Word Work Emphasis:** Words with Long *i*

- **Writing Mode:** Opinion Writing

- **Writing Trait:** Elaboration

For additional instructional resources, see Journeys Lesson 28 Focus Wall.

Minilessons/Shared Reading		
Interactive Read-Aloud/ Shared Reading	• *The Kite* by Arnold Lobel FANTASY, **Student Book** pp. 86–101 ANCHOR TEXT • *A Hopeful Song,* p. 363 • *Measuring Weather* INFORMATIONAL TEXT, **Student Book** pp. 106–108	
Reading Minilessons	• **Story Structure,** p. 240 • **Genre: Informational Text,** p. 241 • **Genre: Informational Text,** p. 241	
Word Study	• **Words with Long *i*,** pp. 110–111 • **Discuss Oral Vocabulary; Paired Yes/No Questions; Word Sort; Dictate, Draw, and Write,** pp. 170–171	
Writing	• **Opinion Sentences:** Stating a Strong Opinion, Revising Opinion Sentences, pp. 326–327; **Writing Trait:** Elaboration, p. 338 • **Weekly Student Model:** Opinion Sentences, **Student Book** p. 113	

Guided Reading

Select texts according to your children's instructional level. You may use the books below or select from the Leveled Readers Database, pp. 388–397. For instructional support, use the Leveled Readers Teacher's Guides along with the books that you choose.

- **LEVEL F**   *A Chunk of Cheese*
- **LEVEL F**   *Kite Flying* (Vocabulary Reader)
- **LEVEL J**   *The Boat Race* (Language Support)
- **LEVEL J**   *The Sailboat Race*
- **LEVEL K**   *The Sand Castle*

Planning a Week of Literacy and Language

INSTRUCTIONAL FOCUS

- **Student Community Text**
  - *Hi! Fly Guy* by Tedd Arnold, **Student Book** pp. 118–141 `ANCHOR TEXT`
  - *Busy Bugs,* **Student Book** pp. 146–148
- **Teacher Read Aloud:** *A Stone Goes to Court,* p. 364
- **Minilesson Principles:** Understanding Characters; Cause and Effect; Genre: Poetry
- **Word Work Emphasis:** Words with Suffixes *-ly, -y, -ful*
- **Writing Mode:** Opinion Writing
- **Writing Trait:** Evidence

For additional instructional resources, see **Journeys Lesson 29 Focus Wall.**

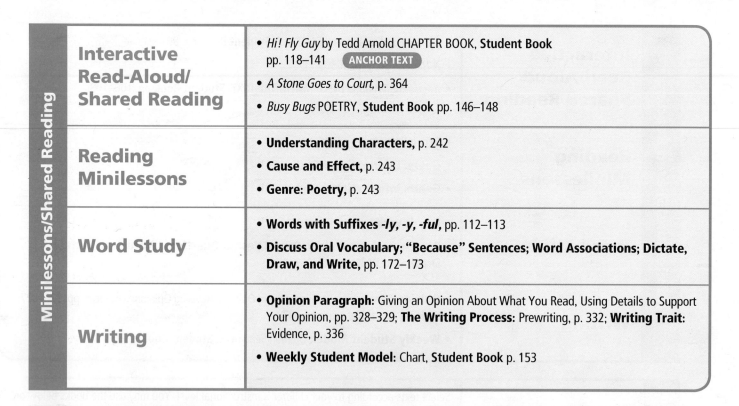

Minilessons/Shared Reading		
Interactive Read-Aloud/ Shared Reading	• *Hi! Fly Guy* by Tedd Arnold CHAPTER BOOK, **Student Book** pp. 118–141 `ANCHOR TEXT` • *A Stone Goes to Court,* p. 364 • *Busy Bugs* POETRY, **Student Book** pp. 146–148	
Reading Minilessons	• **Understanding Characters,** p. 242 • **Cause and Effect,** p. 243 • **Genre: Poetry,** p. 243	
Word Study	• **Words with Suffixes *-ly, -y, -ful,*** pp. 112–113 • **Discuss Oral Vocabulary; "Because" Sentences; Word Associations; Dictate, Draw, and Write,** pp. 172–173	
Writing	• **Opinion Paragraph:** Giving an Opinion About What You Read, Using Details to Support Your Opinion, pp. 328–329; **The Writing Process:** Prewriting, p. 332; **Writing Trait:** Evidence, p. 336 • **Weekly Student Model:** Chart, **Student Book** p. 153	

Guided Reading

Select texts according to your children's instructional level. You may use the books below or select from the Leveled Readers Database, pp. 388–397. For instructional support, use the Leveled Readers Teacher's Guides along with the books that you choose.

- **LEVEL F** *Let's Play Ball*
- **LEVEL H** *Butterflies* (Vocabulary Reader)
- **LEVEL I** *Birds* (Language Support)
- **LEVEL I** *More Than One Bird*
- **LEVEL K** *A Cat Trick*

Planning a Week of Literacy and Language

INSTRUCTIONAL FOCUS

- **Student Community Text**
  - *Winners Never Quit!* by Mia Hamm, **Student Book** pp. 158–177 ANCHOR TEXT
  - *Be a Team Player*, **Student Book** pp. 182–184

- **Teacher Read Aloud:** *The Parts of the House Have a Fight*, p. 364

- **Minilesson Principles:** Main Idea and Details; Genre: Folktale; Genre: Informational Text

- **Word Work Emphasis:** Words with Syllable Pattern CV

- **Writing Mode:** Opinion Writing

- **Writing Trait:** Organization

For additional instructional resources, see Journeys Lesson 30 Focus Wall.

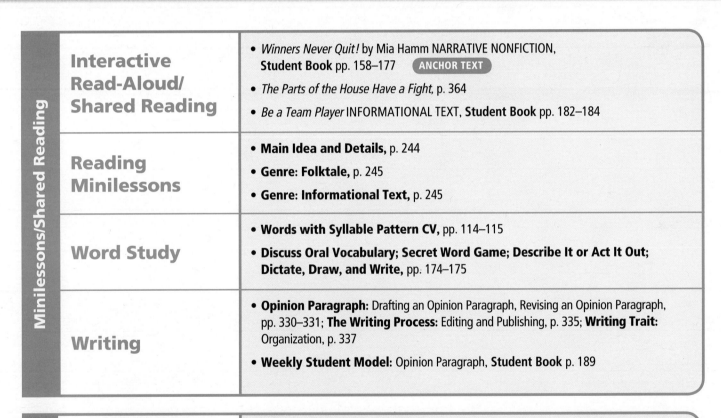

Minilessons/Shared Reading		
Interactive Read-Aloud/ Shared Reading	• *Winners Never Quit!* by Mia Hamm NARRATIVE NONFICTION, **Student Book** pp. 158–177 ANCHOR TEXT • *The Parts of the House Have a Fight*, p. 364 • *Be a Team Player* INFORMATIONAL TEXT, **Student Book** pp. 182–184	
Reading Minilessons	• **Main Idea and Details**, p. 244 • **Genre: Folktale**, p. 245 • **Genre: Informational Text**, p. 245	
Word Study	• **Words with Syllable Pattern CV**, pp. 114–115 • **Discuss Oral Vocabulary; Secret Word Game; Describe It or Act It Out; Dictate, Draw, and Write**, pp. 174–175	
Writing	• **Opinion Paragraph:** Drafting an Opinion Paragraph, Revising an Opinion Paragraph, pp. 330–331; **The Writing Process:** Editing and Publishing, p. 335; **Writing Trait:** Organization, p. 337 • **Weekly Student Model:** Opinion Paragraph, **Student Book** p. 189	

Guided Reading	
	Select texts according to your children's instructional level. You may use the books below or select from the Leveled Readers Database, pp. 388–397. For instructional support, use the Leveled Readers Teacher's Guides along with the books that you choose. • **LEVEL F** *Michelle Wie* • **LEVEL G** *Soccer* (Vocabulary Reader) • **LEVEL J** *Two Sisters Play Tennis* (Language Support) • **LEVEL J** *The Williams Sisters* • **LEVEL L** *Lance Armstrong*

Teacher's Notes

Word Study

Table of Contents

(continued)

Word Study

Table of Contents

Vocabulary

Why Is Word Study Important?

Word study is a developmentally based approach to phonics, spelling, and vocabulary instruction. Because of the critical role that word knowledge plays in reading and in writing, it is essential that our instruction be matched to students' developmental levels. The word study approach is grounded in research that has identified how learners develop an understanding of the structure of written words and how this structure reflects the alphabetic, pattern, and meaning layers of the language (Templeton, 2011).

Effective word study develops students' underlying *orthographic knowledge*—the understanding of how letters and letter patterns represent sound and meaning in language. As the diagram shown below illustrates, over time students move from an understanding of (1) alphabetic/sound relationships to (2) pattern/sound relationships to (3) *morphology*, or meaning, relationships. Orthographic knowledge forms the foundation of students' development in fluency, reading comprehension, and writing.

By understanding how we can best assess what our students know about word structure, we can then target our instruction most effectively at those aspects of word study that each of our students needs and is ready to learn (Bear, Invernizzi, Templeton, & Johnston, 2012).

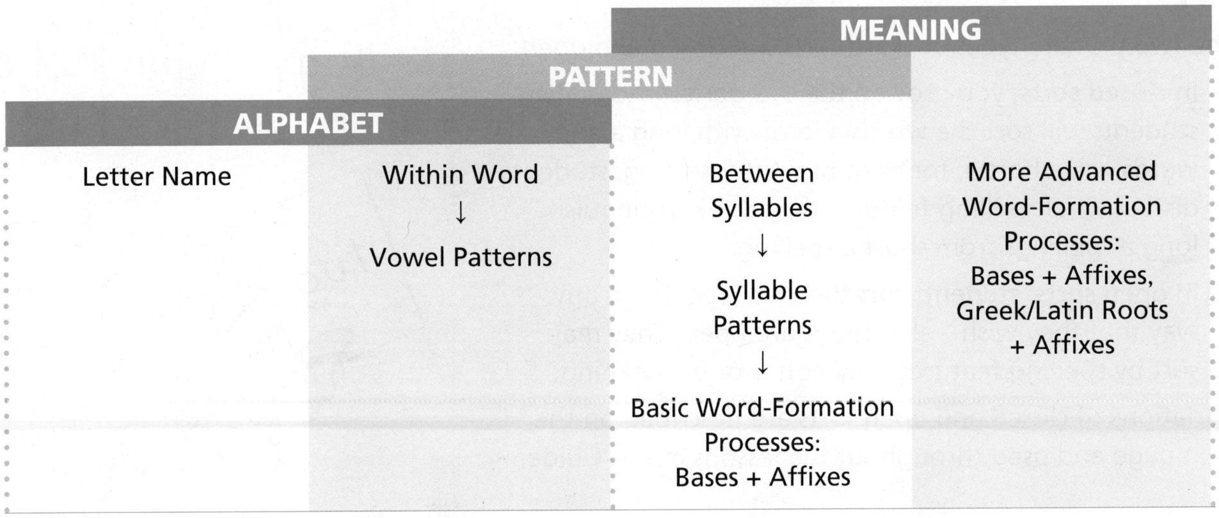

ALPHABET		PATTERN	MEANING
Letter Name	Within Word ↓ Vowel Patterns	Between Syllables ↓ Syllable Patterns ↓ Basic Word-Formation Processes: Bases + Affixes	More Advanced Word-Formation Processes: Bases + Affixes, Greek/Latin Roots + Affixes

▸ Engaging and Effective Word Study

For word study to be effective, we need to make sure that our students are experiencing, examining, and talking about words from a variety of perspectives—taking them apart and putting them together (Ehri, 2005; Templeton & Bear, 2011). Through this type of analysis and synthesis, students will best internalize the features of words and apply this understanding efficiently in their reading and writing.

The most effective framework in which students may productively explore words and their patterns is through the process of comparing, contrasting, and analyzing in interactive word sort activities. Word sorts actively engage and motivate students, and the discussions allow students to share insights and discover generalizations about words. Word sorting combines student-exploratory and teacher-directed learning.

In *Journeys* and in this Guide, you are provided with words that will support students' discoveries and generalizations about the spelling of words at the alphabet, pattern, and meaning layers. First, you will guide students' explorations with appropriate modeling and questioning. As students follow up in their seatwork, they internalize these questions and develop ways to think critically about words.

Because word sorts are hands-on, they are motivating to students. Students work with *known* words because they cannot search for and discover patterns if they cannot identify some or most of the words they are examining. This involvement is in sharp contrast to many phonics and spelling approaches in which the "rule" is stated at the beginning of the lesson. Sorting words leads students towards generating the rule themselves. This framework supports the kind of processing that is the foundation of efficient, fluent reading and spelling.

Types of Word Sorts

The two primary types of word sorts are *closed* and *open*.

- In **closed sorts**, you provide the categories into which students will sort the words: words with long *a* and words with short *a*, for example. After sorting, students discuss what spelling features they think distinguish long *a* spellings from short *a* spellings.

- In **open sorts**, students sort the words provided any way that they wish—all options are open. They may sort by spelling features they notice or by meaning.

Variations of closed and open sorts are described on the next page and used throughout the lessons in this Guide.

Word Sort Variations

Repeated Sorting   It is important that students have multiple opportunities to sort and write the words for the week. Repeated sorting may be done after the initial group sort on Day 1. You may also send words home to be sorted with family members.

Blind Sorts   A blind sort focuses on strengthening the bond between sound and spelling. In blind sorts, students do not see the words to be sorted; they sort them based on the targeted sound/feature that the words represent. Words are shuffled and read aloud by you or a buddy without showing them to the writer. A key word is used to represent each of the sort categories. Students write the word that is called out under the appropriate key word.

Word Hunts   This activity helps students establish the connection between spelling words and reading words. After exploring the targeted features/patterns through sorting, students look back through familiar reading selections, hunting for words that are examples of these features/patterns. They record their discoveries in their Word Study Notebooks (see below).

Picture Sorts   Children in the early phases of spelling development sort both words and pictures. Pictures are particularly effective when children are focusing on sound because they must attend to particular sound patterns or phonemes within the pronounced word. Then they are able to focus more precisely on the sounds as they are represented either alphabetically or by spelling pattern.

Draw and Label, Cut-and-Paste   As children are learning the names and sounds of particular letters, they will draw pictures of things that begin with or contain these sounds. They label the pictures with the appropriate letter or try to spell as much of the label as they are able. Later, when words are sorted, they may be pasted into categories.

Guess My Category   This activity involves students in trying to guess categories after words have been sorted by you or by other students. The categories may be based on spelling patterns or on concepts. Students grow more creative in their categorization and guessing as they are exposed to more words and their features.

Speed Sorts   As students sort the words later in the week, they enjoy timing their sorts to see how rapidly they are able to complete the sort while maintaining accuracy. Many students keep track of their progress in their Word Study Notebooks.

Meaning/Concept Sorts   Pictures and words may be sorted according to meaning categories. When known words are grouped in different ways, new conceptual relationships are established. For example, younger children may sort a group of pictures according to things that may be found *indoors* and those that may be found *outdoors*; older students may sort a group of words according to concepts such as *mammal*, *amphibian*, or *bird*.

Word Study Notebooks

The Word Study Notebook is the home for word sorts, writing sorts, word hunts, interesting new words encountered in reading, and important new vocabulary. For younger children, the notebook may be a few pages of construction paper stapled or tied together. For older students, a loose-leaf binder works especially well because as more words and patterns are explored it is easy to add pages. Students may record and work with new spelling and vocabulary words—doing concept sorts, creating graphic organizers, or drafting sentences for the vocabulary.

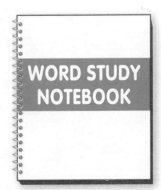

▶ Spelling/Phonics

The spelling/phonics lessons in this Guide may be used apart from or to complement the lessons in *Journeys*, providing additional exposure to and exploration of targeted word features. The five-day format of each lesson begins with an introduction and walk-through of the features and patterns in the spelling words. On subsequent days, the spelling words are compared and contrasted through the variety of sorts and activities described on page 41.

Throughout each lesson, there are several opportunities for students to share and discuss what they are observing and thinking with partners and with the group. The fifth day of each lesson is an assessment. Dictation sentences that include the spelling words are provided in Grades 1–6.

It is important that students interact with the spelling words every day. At all levels, you will introduce important phonics and spelling features at the beginning of the lesson. Depending on the students' developmental level, you may meet with some students on subsequent days. Every day, however, activities are provided that may be completed by the students at their seats, either in small groups or independently.

Components of a Typical Grade 1 Spelling/Phonics Lesson

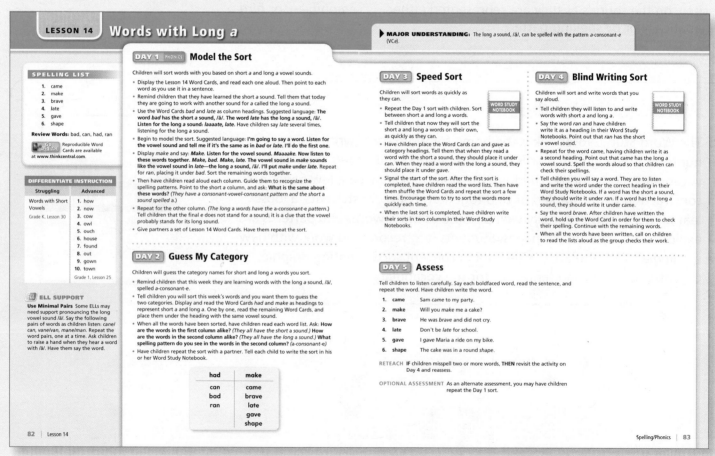

Characteristics of Most Grade 1 Spellers

- In the early part of the year, most children will need to continue to explore short vowel spellings introduced in Kindergarten: the basic consonant-vowel-consonant (CVC) pattern. They will use a single vowel letter to stand for a long vowel sound: LAT for *late*, SKI for *sky*.

- They learn consonant digraphs such as *ch* and *th* in the context of the CVC pattern: *chip, bath*.

- As children grow their sight vocabularies in reading, they will become aware of the vowel-consonant-e pattern (VCe) and explore different vowel sounds that are represented by this pattern.

- Common errors at this phase are MAEK (*make*) and RIED, RAIDE (*ride*). Such spellings indicate that children are moving from the letter name–alphabetic spelling phase to the within word pattern phase.

- In this phase, as children learn about the common -*ay* spelling for long *a*, it is common for them to overgeneralize this pattern to spellings for long *a* learned previously, even occasionally including the silent *e*: MAYK *(make)* and RAYK, RAYKE *(rake)*.

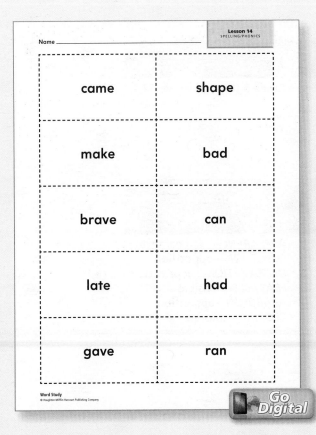

Word Study Spelling/Phonics Lessons

- **Day 1:** Words are sorted by vowel sound. Then the patterns that represent those sounds are examined. The basic long vowel pattern (VCe) is contrasted with the basic short vowel pattern (CVC).

- **Day 2:** Children apply understanding of the short *a* and long *a* spelling patterns through an engaging category guessing game.

- **Day 3:** Children develop fluency in recognizing and categorizing the words by vowel sounds and spelling patterns.

- **Day 4:** Children write words from memory and sort them under key words that have the same target vowel sounds and spelling patterns.

- **Day 5:** Assesses children's understanding.

Reproducible Word Cards

- Available at **www.thinkcentral.com**
- The lesson's Word Cards are used in a variety of ways throughout the week.

▶ Spelling/Phonics Development

What the Research Says

Word study instruction must match the needs of each student. A student's **instructional level** is a powerful determinant of what may be learned. Simply put, we must teach within each child's zone of understanding. The word features that are examined at each grade in *Journeys* should match the developmental level of most students. Students for whom the word study curriculum is not the appropriate developmental "fit," however, will have appropriate patterns and words provided.

The lower chart below presents the developmental nature of orthographic knowledge as students learn the relationships between letters in the printed word and the types of information the letters represent. The spellings reflect the types of orthographic information to which developing learners pay attention, from alphabetic through a deeper understanding of the structure of single-syllable words, two-syllable and multisyllabic words, and morphological relationships.

A developmental perspective on phonics and spelling instruction reveals that knowledge does not occur simply through repetition and memorization. For most students throughout the primary, intermediate, and middle grades, memory for words and patterns is supported by an awareness of underlying interrelationships among sound, spelling, meaning, and morphology.

Levels of Literacy Development

Emergent Literacy	Beginning Literacy	Transitional Literacy	Intermediate Literacy	Skilled/ Advanced Literacy
Pre-K to middle of Grade 1	Kindergarten to middle of Grade 2	Grade 1 to middle of Grade 4	Grade 3 through Grade 8	Grade 5 through Grade 12

Levels of Spelling Development

Emergent Phase	Letter Name-Alphabetic Phase	Within Word Pattern Phase	Syllables and Affixes Phase	Derivational Relations Phase
B—bed *CUS*—see you soon	*DT*—dot *BAD*—bed *SEP*—ship *LUP*—lump *JRIV*—drive	*TRANE*—train *FLOWT*—float *CATOL*—cattle *THOUT*—throat	*HABBIT*—habit *CAPCHURE*—capture *MIDDEL*—middle	*APPEARENCE*—appearance *OPPISITION*—opposition *DEPRAVATION*—deprivation *FEASABLE*—feasible *APARITION*—apparition *CLORINE*—chlorine

Phases of Spelling Development

Emergent Most preschoolers and kindergartners, as well as some first graders at the beginning of the school year, are emergent spellers. Emergent spelling may range from random marks to recognizable letters that correspond in some way to sound. Notably, children at the emergent phase are not yet phonemically aware—that is, they are not able consciously to attend to consonant and vowel sounds within syllables.

Letter Name-Alphabetic Becoming letter name-alphabetic spellers depends upon learning the *alphabetic principle*—the understanding that letters represent sounds in a systematic way and that words can be segmented into phonemes from left to right. Early on, children use the names of the letters to represent sounds. Beginning and ending sounds in syllables are represented, and medial vowels come in a bit later: BD spells *bed*; *we* may be spelled YE because the name of letter *y* contains the /w/ sound.

Typically, short vowel sounds may be spelled with the letter whose name is *closest* to the sound the child wants to spell: *bed* is spelled BAD because the name of the letter *a* is pronounced with a mouth position that is very similar to the mouth position that is used to pronounce the short *e* sound—more similar than any other vowel sound. As children learn about the conventional spellings for short vowel sounds, they learn about consonant digraphs and blends, or how to separate the sound that each letter represents.

Within Word Pattern Within word pattern spellers are able to spell correctly most single-syllable short-vowel words, consonant blends, consonant digraphs, and the sounds that *m* and *n* represent when they occur before consonants, as in *bump* and *stand*. They are able to think in more than one dimension about word structure—how letters may be grouped into patterns that correspond predictably to sound—and they examine words by sound and pattern simultaneously. Because of this, within word pattern spellers come to understand that how sounds are spelled often depends on the following: where the sounds occur within words (long *a* at the end of words is spelled *ay*; in the middle, usually *a*-consonant-*e* or *ai*); other sounds that are around them (if a long vowel comes before a /j/ sound, /j/ is spelled *ge*; otherwise, /j/ is spelled *dge*); letters provide clues about the pronunciation of other letters within the word (the final *e* in *slide*).

During the within word pattern phase, students will first explore the common long vowel patterns (long *o* can be spelled *o*-consonant-*e* as in *broke*, *oa* as in *boat*, and *ow* as in *grow*), then less common patterns (VCC pattern in *told* and *host*), and later more challenging patterns (*au* in *taught*, *ough* in *through* and *though*).

Students begin to explore the role of *meaning* in the spelling system when they examine *homophones* such as *sail/sale* and *pail/pale*. The different spellings for the same sound are often explained by the fact that they occur in homophones, and we support children as they keep the word's meaning in mind while examining its spelling.

Syllables and Affixes Students' understanding about spelling patterns in single-syllable words is the foundation that supports their growth into the syllables and affixes phase. This understanding helps them to explore two-syllable words and the syllable patterns that determine what goes on at the juncture of syllables and morphemes. The juncture conventions all depend on an awareness of the relationship between sound and spelling. Morphological analysis—the exploration of word-formation processes involved in combining prefixes, suffixes, bases, and roots—may be facilitated by exploring how these units are represented in spelling.

The syllables and affixes phase is typically achieved in the intermediate grades. The first major convention to be explored at this phase is the addition of inflectional endings to base words. The vowel pattern in the base word determines what happens at the juncture of the base word and the ending: *make* + *ing* = *making* (drop *e*); *hit* + *ing* = *hitting* (double the final consonant to keep the short vowel sound in the base word); *wait* + *ing* = *waiting* (vowel pair in the base word, so no change when adding the ending).

Students' understanding of the relationship between short and long vowel sounds/patterns in base words and how they determine spelling when inflectional endings are added provides a solid foundation for their exploration of syllable patterns—what happens *within* words at the juncture of syllables. The vowel-consonant-consonant-vowel (VC/CV) pattern in *hitting* occurs in *hammer*. In both cases, the doubled consonant keeps the vowel in the first syllable short. The vowel-consonant-vowel (V/CV) pattern in *making* occurs in *diner*. In both cases, the single consonant signals a long vowel in the first syllable.

Derivational Relations   Some students may move into the derivational relations phase in Grade 4 or 5, but most students in this phase are in middle school and above. It is important to note that students will be *reading* many of the words to be studied at this phase when they are still syllables and affixes spellers.

In this phase, students explore the full range in which words are *derived* from a common base or Greek/Latin root to form spelling-meaning families. Word study at this level has the potential to expand students' vocabularies exponentially because most words students will encounter in specific domains of study will be understood and learned by examining their morphological structure. Students' spelling errors at this level are fairly sophisticated: schwas in unaccented syllables within multisyllabic words (DEPRAVATION/*deprivation*, DOMINENT/*dominant*) and consonant doubling in assimilated or "absorbed" prefixes (APARITION/*apparition*). Assimilated prefixes reflect the convention of changing the last consonant in a prefix to the first consonant of the base word or root (*in* + *mediate* = *immediate*; *ad* + *point* = *appoint*).

Where Do the Spelling/Phonics Words Come From?

The resources we have drawn upon to guide the selection of words in *Journeys* and in this Guide include extensive word frequency counts of English (Zeno et al., 1996). This informs us about the most frequently occurring words at each grade level in oral language as well as in print. To determine which words are likely to be known by students at different grade levels, we have used Biemiller's (2005) adaptation of Dale et al.'s (1981) extensive study. We have also drawn upon the developmental research that, as described above, has determined the scope and sequence of word features (Henderson & Templeton, 1986; Templeton & Bear,

1992). Consolidating this information allows us to select words representing the features that need to be addressed at each developmental level.

At the beginning of each grade, several lessons address important patterns that were also addressed in the previous grade. The words that represent the patterns, however, are appropriate for the new grade level. This is done in order to revisit and consolidate knowledge that may not have been exercised over the preceding break. If you teach in a year-round or multi-track system, you may decide whether or which students need to work through these lessons.

▶ Vocabulary

The vocabulary lessons in this Guide build on and extend the lessons and activities in *Journeys*. Each lesson addresses the research-based criteria for effective instruction using a grade-appropriate approach:

- Develop **word consciousness**—the appreciation of and interest in words, their meanings, and how they are used.

- Through discussion, **activate background knowledge** to determine what students already know about the words and the concepts they represent. Usually there is a range of understandings among students, so getting them involved in discussion is very important.

- Use a **variety of activities** that involve students in using words and thinking about their meanings. These include **sorting/categorizing** words, thinking of **words that are related** morphologically and semantically, **discussing** the words with examples and non-examples, and using **graphic organizers**.

- Reinforce how the structure or **morphology** of the words—affixes, base words, and roots—provides clues to their meanings.

- Teach and model the development of independent word-learning strategies that integrate the use of **contextual and morphological clues**.

- When necessary, **explain the meaning and give examples** of how the words are used. Make a point of using the words often.

Components of a Typical Grade 1 Oral Vocabulary Development Lesson

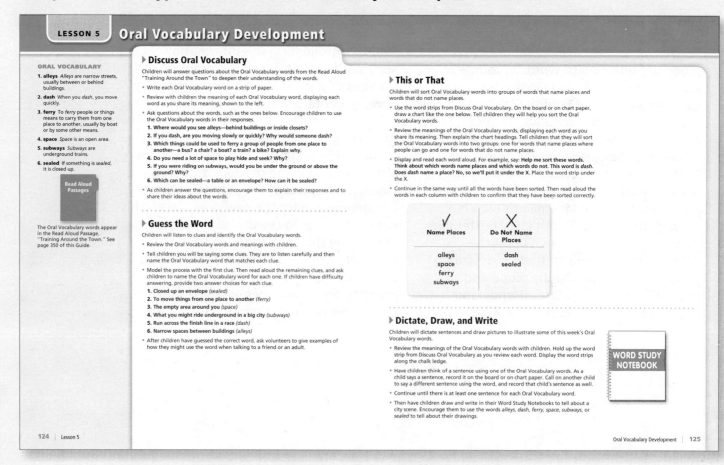

Word Study Oral Vocabulary Development Lessons

- Oral Vocabulary words that appear in a *Journeys* Read Aloud are introduced using student-friendly definitions. Oral questioning focuses on applying the words to various contexts to support an understanding of their meanings.

- Meaning is reinforced through wordplay and game-like activities in which children apply their knowledge of the Oral Vocabulary words.

- A word sort activity with teacher prompting has children categorize Oral Vocabulary words by how they are used.

- Children apply their understanding by dictating sentences and drawing pictures about a given topic that is based on the Oral Vocabulary words. Children then write about their drawings using the lesson's Oral Vocabulary words.

▸ Vocabulary Development

What the Research Says

We know that vocabulary knowledge is the single most powerful predictor of reading comprehension and academic learning. In Kindergarten and Grade 1, developing *oral* vocabulary is critical and absolutely necessary as a foundation for later vocabulary growth and learning.

For younger children who are not yet reading widely, there is a substantial, convincing body of research that supports the role of teacher read-alouds in developing language and vocabulary (Santoro, Chard, Howard, & Baker, 2008; Pilkulski & Templeton, 2010). However, significant vocabulary growth will occur only when teachers spend time with *explicit* attention to vocabulary in the contexts of both narrative and informational texts.

In Grades 2–6, we need to address the two major areas of vocabulary development: general academic vocabulary and content-area, or domain-specific, vocabulary (*Common Core State Standards*, 2010).

- **General academic vocabulary** includes those words that do not often occur in everyday spoken language—for example *transmit*, *paradox*, and *product*—but which students may encounter frequently in their reading across all content areas. These words also occur in more formal spoken language, such as a lecture format. Students may often have the underlying concept that such a word represents, but they lack the label that stands for that concept.

- **Content-area or domain-specific vocabulary** refers to words that occur primarily in specific content or subject matter areas such as science, history and social science, mathematics, and the arts. In contrast to general academic vocabulary, much content-specific academic vocabulary—for example *equilateral*, *condensation*, and *feudalism*—represents new concepts, and can therefore be more challenging to learn.

Journeys and this Guide offer a research-based, rich, and robust approach to vocabulary instruction using the important words that students need to learn. The lessons also teach them *about* words—for example, how prefixes, suffixes, base words, and roots combine to result in the meaning of words. When learners understand how this process works, they possess one of the most powerful understandings for vocabulary growth.

Where Does the Target Vocabulary Come From?

As with the selection of words for the spelling/phonics lessons, at Grades 2–6 we used Biemiller's (2005) adaptation of Dale et al.'s (1981) study to guide the selection of words for a particular grade level. We then used Zeno et al.'s frequency corpus (1996) as well as Hiebert's corpus (2005) to identify morphologically related words and cross-checked with Harris-Jacobsen (1982), Dale-Chall, and the Academic Word List.

This process ensured that words would be sufficiently challenging to be academic rather than conversational vocabulary, yet not so challenging that students will find them too difficult to learn and remember, even with good instruction and careful repetition. In Kindergarten and Grade 1, we used Zeno as well as cross-checking with traditional word frequency lists that still correlate highly with recent analyses.

Teacher's Notes

Teacher's Notes

▶ Differentiated Instruction

Teachers differentiate for appropriate reading levels in their classrooms. It is important that children and older students be placed at their appropriate levels for word study as well. This will ensure that they have the experience with words and patterns that they are ready to explore.

Specific guidelines for determining your students' appropriate developmental levels for word study are provided on the next page and on pages 373–386 in the Resources section of this Guide. The Qualitative Spelling Inventory will help you determine your students' developmental spelling levels at the beginning of the school year. It may be administered again at the middle of the school year, and then toward the end of the year.

The relationship between word knowledge and reading level is very close. You will likely find that your below-level, on-level, and above-level students in word study are almost always your below-, on-, and above-level readers. This allows you to differentiate your instruction more effectively. For example, when meeting with your below-level reading group at the beginning of the week, you may introduce and sort the leveled spelling words after students have read an appropriately leveled selection.

For most students, the grade-level words and features that are presented in *Journeys* and in this Guide will be appropriate. For your students who are not on grade level, the Struggling and Advanced words and features offered in each lesson will address the needs of most. For those students who are significantly below- or above-level, use the word lists on pages 376–386 and access the appropriate lessons in another grade level of this Guide on **www.thinkcentral.com**.

Occasionally, it may be necessary to adjust the level for particular students, just as you adjust reading levels. The weekly assessments on Day 5 of each spelling/phonics lesson provide effective progress monitoring so that you will be able to know how students are progressing. This insight is also very helpful as you evaluate students' writing since that is where the depth of your students' learning is observed.

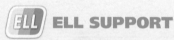 **ELL SUPPORT**

In addition to the point-of-use notes located in the spelling/phonics lessons in this Guide, the information on the next page and on pages 368–372 of the Resources section will help you address the unique transfer support needs of your students who are English language learners (ELLs).

▶ Assessment to Inform Instruction

Assessing a student's spelling developmental phase is a powerful and precise method for planning instruction. By following the steps below and using the tools on the pages that follow, you can determine the phase of spelling development for each of your students and use the results to select appropriate lessons for students at varying phases.

1 ASSESS

Administer the Qualitative Spelling Inventory (QSI) on pages 373–375 in the Resources section of this Guide. Also collect a selection of each student's first-draft writing for comparison. The QSI results combined with examples from daily writing will offer a strong sampling for analysis. Emphasize to students that the assessment is not a test for a grade and it is okay if they don't know all the answers. Explain that their work will help you understand what they already know and what you need to help them learn.

2 ANALYZE

Determine a spelling developmental phase for each student. Use the Qualitative Spelling Inventory Checklist (pages 374–375) to guide your decisions.

3 PLAN AND MONITOR

Organize small groups based on your diverse classroom needs. Monitor students' progress, and reorganize groups as needed throughout the year. For on-level students, use the lessons in your grade-level of this Guide. Select lessons for Struggling and Advanced students:

- Suggested lessons for Differentiated Instruction are provided in each lesson in Grades 1–6.

- If your students' needs do not align with the suggested lessons, select an appropriate lesson using the word lists organized by spelling phase on pages 376–386.

Words with Short *a*

DIFFERENTIATE INSTRUCTION

Struggling	Advanced
Beginning Sounds /m/m, /s/s, /t/t	1. chin
	2. chop
	3. much
Grade K, Lesson 8	4. chip
	5. rich
	6. chick
	Grade 1, Lesson 12

 ELL SUPPORT

Linguistic Transfer The short vowel sound /ă/ does not exist in Cantonese. Have speakers of this language listen and watch your mouth position as you say /ă/. Ask children to repeat the vowel sound after you a few times. Correct their pronunciation as necessary.

DAY 1 PHONICS **Model the Sort**

Children will sort words with you based on the position of short *a* in the word.

- Display the Lesson 1 Word Cards, and read each word aloud. Then point to each word as you use it in a sentence.
- Tell children that all of this week's words have the short *a* sound, /ă/. Explain that in some of the words, the short *a* sound is at the beginning of the word. In other words, the short *a* sound is in the middle of the word.
- Model sorting the Word Cards according to the position of the short *a* sound. Hold up and read the Word Card *am*. Suggested language: *Am.* I'll listen for the place where I hear the /ă/ sound—is it at the beginning of the word or in the middle of the word? *Aaaam.* The short *a* sound, /ă/, is at the beginning of the word. I'm going to start a group for words that begin with short *a*.
- Repeat with the word *dad,* and start a group for words that have short *a* in the middle. Then begin sorting the other words. Display the Word Card *sat*, and read it aloud. Suggested language: *Sat.* I listen for the sound /ă/. *Saaaat.* I hear the sound /ă/ in the middle of the word *sat*. So I'll put *sat* under *dad*. Repeat the process for *at*, placing it under *am*.
- Continue in the same way with the remaining Word Cards, having children help you sort the words.
- Read the words in each column with children. Guide them to notice that the letter *a* stands for the short vowel sound /ă/.
- Provide partners with a set of Lesson 1 Word Cards. Have them work together to repeat the sort.

DAY 2 **Pattern Sort**

Children will sort short *a* words according to spelling patterns.

- Remind children that this week's words have the short *a* sound, /ă/, spelled with the letter *a*.
- Repeat the sort from Day 1, working with children to sort the Word Cards based on the position of the short vowel *a* (beginning or middle). Model sorting a word or two before asking children to name the correct category for the remaining words.
- Then work with children to identify the words that rhyme with *cat* and the words that do not. Tell children to listen as you read each Word Card aloud. Suggested language: **The word is *am*. Does *am* rhyme with *cat*?** Repeat for each word, creating two categories of words on the board.
- After all the words have been sorted, have children read aloud the words in each column. Ask them to look at the words and explain how the words that rhyme with *cat* are the same. *(They all end with the letters* at *and the sounds /ăt/.)*
- Have children repeat the sort with a partner. They may draw a cat to represent one category and use a blank word card to represent the other category. When children have finished, tell them to write their sorts in their Word Study Notebooks.

Rhymes with *cat*	Other
at	am
sat	man
mat	dad

DAY 3 Word Hunt

Children will write short *a* words that they find in their reading.

- Remind children that they have been learning about short *a*. Tell them that they will go on a word hunt to find short *a* words in a story they have read.

- Use a copy of the Decodable Reader story "Dan and Nan" to demonstrate how to scan text for words. Suggested language: **When I go on a word hunt, I don't need to read every word. If I am hunting for short *a* words, I run my eyes quickly over each page to find the words with short *a*. I read the words aloud to make sure the words have the /ă/ sound.**

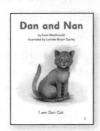

- Have partners read "Dan and Nan" together. Then have them go through the selection a second time, looking for words with short *a*. As children find words, have them write each one in their Word Study Notebooks.

- Have children read their finished word list aloud. Tell them to compare their list with another pair's list.

(Possible responses: am, Dan, Cat, sat, Nan, and, can)

DAY 4 Blind Writing Sort

Children will sort and write words that you say aloud.

- Tell children they will listen to and write words with short *a*.

- Say the word *at*. Have children write *at* as a heading in their Word Study Notebooks. Display the corresponding Word Card for children to check their spelling. Point out that *at* has the short *a* sound at the beginning.

- Repeat for *mat*, having children write it as a second heading. Point out that *mat* has short *a* in the middle.

- Explain that you will say one word at a time. Tell children to write the word under the correct column heading: under *at* if the word begins with short *a* and under *mat* if the word has short *a* in the middle.

- Say the word *dad*. After children finish writing, display the Word Card *dad* so they can confirm or correct their spelling. Continue with the remaining spelling words.

- When all the spelling words have been written, call on children to read the lists aloud as the group checks category placement.

DAY 5 Assess

Tell children to listen carefully. Say each boldfaced word, read the sentence, and repeat the word. Have children write the word.

1. **am**   I *am* in first grade.

2. **at**   The boy is *at* the store.

3. **sat**   The girl *sat* in a chair.

4. **man**   The *man* sang a song.

5. **dad**   My *dad* is a good cook.

6. **mat**   Come and sit on the *mat*.

RETEACH IF children misspell two or more words, **THEN** revisit the activity on Day 2 and reassess.

OPTIONAL ASSESSMENT As an alternate assessment, you may have children repeat the Day 1 sort.

Words with Short *i*

DIFFERENTIATE INSTRUCTION

Struggling	Advanced
Beginning Sounds /t/t, /k/c, /p/p Grade K, Lesson 9	1. ship 2. shop 3. which 4. when 5. whip 6. fish Grade 1, Lesson 13

 **ELL SUPPORT**

Use Minimal Pairs The short vowel sound /ĭ/ may present a challenge to ELLs. Have children listen carefully to the following pairs of words: *pin/pan*, *fin/fan*, *tin/tan*. Say each pair of words again, and have children repeat them.

DAY 1 PHONICS **Model the Sort**

Children will sort words with you based on their short vowel sounds.

*   Display the Lesson 2 Word Cards. Read each word with children.
*   Tell children you are going to sort words with short vowel sounds.
*   Display the Word Cards *sat* and *him* as column headings, and read each word. Suggested language: *Sat* **is at the top of the first column.** *Him* **is at the top of the second column. I am going to read a word. You will tell me if the word has the same vowel sound as** *sat* **or** *him*. **Listen while I do the first one.**
*   Hold up the Word Card *man*, and read it aloud. Suggested language: *Man*. **Listen for the vowel sound.** *Maaaan*. **Now I will compare the words.** *Man, sat. Man, him.* **The vowel sound in** *man* **sounds like the vowel sound in** *sat*, **the short** *a* **sound, /ă/. So I'll put** *man* **under** *sat*. **Repeat for** *if*, **placing it under** *him*.
*   Sort the words *pin* and *at* so that children see the pattern. Then sort the remaining words by reading one at a time and asking children where to place each word. Read the word lists with children. Then shuffle the cards and have children sort the words with you again.
*   Read the words in the short *i* column with children. Ask them what is similar about each of the words. Elicit that the letter *i* stands for the short vowel sound /ĭ/.
*   Give each child a set of Lesson 2 Word Cards, and have them repeat the sort independently.

DAY 2 **Guess My Category**

Children will guess the category names for words you sort according to the number of letters.

*   Remind children that this week's spelling words have the short *i* sound, /ĭ/.
*   Work with children to repeat the sort from Day 1, grouping the words by short vowel sound. Then tell children that you are going to sort the words in a different way, and they will try to guess how the words are the same.
*   Place the Word Cards *if* and *rip* as category headings. Read each word. Then read *am* and place the Word Card under *if*. Read *man* and place the Word Card under *rip*. Continue to read and sort the remaining words, placing two-letter words in the first column and three-letter words in the second column.
*   Read the words in the first column with children and ask them to look closely at the words and tell how the words are alike. *(They each have two letters.)* Guide children to recognize that each of the two-letter words begins with a vowel letter and a short vowel sound.
*   Read the words in the second column with children. Ask how these words are alike. *(They each have three letters with a consonant-short vowel-consonant pattern.)*
*   Have partners repeat the sort and then write it in their Word Study Notebooks. Direct children to circle the words with the letter *i* and the short *i* sound.

if	rip
am	man
is	him
at	fit
	pin
	sat

DAY 3 Speed Sort

Children will sort words as quickly as they can.

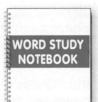

- Repeat the Day 1 sound sort with children.
- Tell children that now they will sort the short *i* and short *a* words on their own.
- Have children place the Word Cards *pin* and *at* side by side. Explain that these are the sorting categories. Point out that *pin* has short *i* and *at* has short *a*. Words with short *i* go under *pin* and words with short *a* go under *at*.
- Model how to sort by reading each word quietly and placing it in the correct category. Then tell children that everyone, including you, is going to sort the Word Cards as quickly as possible.
- When children are ready, signal the start of the sort. Repeat the sort a few times, encouraging children to improve their speed.
- After the last sort, call on individuals to read aloud the words in each category. Emphasize this week's spelling words by having everyone read aloud the short *i* words. Then have children write the short *i* spelling words in their Word Study Notebooks.

DAY 4 Word Hunt

Children will write short *i* words that they find in their reading.

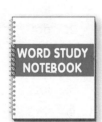

- Remind children that they have been reading and writing short *i* words. Tell them they will hunt for short *i* words in a story they have read.
- Have partners read the Decodable Reader story "Can It Fit?" together. Then have them go through the selection a second time, looking for words with the short *i* sound.

- As children find each word, have them read it aloud to make sure it has the /ĭ/ sound. Then have children write each of the short *i* words in their Word Study Notebooks.
- When children have finished, tell partners to take turns reading their word lists aloud. Have them check that each word has the short *i* sound, /ĭ/.

(Possible responses: it, is, fit, in, tin, sit, his)

DAY 5 Assess

Tell children to listen carefully. Say each boldfaced word, read the sentence, and repeat the word. Have children write the word.

1. **if**   I will nap *if* I can.
2. **is**   Who *is* that?
3. **him**   Give the pen to *him*.
4. **rip**   Try not to *rip* the paper.
5. **fit**   Does the shoe *fit*?
6. **pin**   Put the *pin* on your hat.

RETEACH   **IF** children misspell two or more words, **THEN** revisit the activity on Day 3 and reassess.

OPTIONAL ASSESSMENT   As an alternate assessment, you may have children repeat the Day 1 sort.

Words with Short *o*

Model the Sort

Children will sort words with you based on their short vowel sounds.

- Display the Lesson 3 Word Cards. Read each word with children. Then point to each word as you use it in a sentence.

- Remind children that they have been learning about words with short vowel sounds. Tell them that today they will look at some more words that have short vowels.

- Place the Word Cards *fit* and *log* side by side. Point to and read each word. Suggested language: **I'm going to read a word. Listen for the vowel sound and tell me if it's the same as in *fit* or *log*. I'll do the first one to show you how.**

- Display the Word Card *top,* and read the word aloud. Suggested language: *Top.* **Listen for the vowel sound.** *Tooop.* **Now listen to these words together.** *Top, fit. Top, log.* **The vowel sound in *top* sounds like the vowel sound in *log*. *Top* and *log* both have the short o sound, /ŏ/, so I'll put *top* under *log*. Repeat the process for *is*, placing it under *fit*.**

- Use the same procedure with the remaining words. Allow children to name the column for each word. Read the lists together to confirm that the words are sorted correctly. Then shuffle the cards and have children help you sort the words again.

- Read the words in the short o column with children. Guide them to notice that the letter o stands for the short o sound, /ŏ/, and can appear at the beginning or in the middle of a word.

- Distribute the Lesson 3 Word Cards. Have children repeat the sort independently.

Guess My Category

Children will guess the category names for short o words you sort.

- Remind children that this week they are learning about words that have the short o sound, /ŏ/, spelled with the letter o.

- Repeat the sort from Day 1, having children help you sort the words by short vowel sounds. Then remove the short i words.

- Display the Word Cards *hot* and *top* as category headings to represent words that end with the letters *ot* and words that do not. Read each word. Then read *dot* and place the Word Card under *hot*. Read *log* and place the Word Card under *top*. Do the same for the Word Cards *lot* (under *hot*) and *ox* (under *top*).

- After all the words have been sorted, read the words in the first column together. Help children identify the category by asking: **How are the words alike?** (*They all end with the letters* ot *and the sounds* /ŏt/.) Guide children to understand that the words *hot*, *dot*, and *lot* are rhyming words.

- Read the words in the second column together. Have children guess the category. (*The words all have the letter* o *and the short* o *sound. They do not rhyme.*)

- Have partners repeat the sort. Tell children to write their sorts in their Word Study Notebooks.

hot	top
dot	log
lot	ox

SPELLING LIST

1. log
2. dot
3. top
4. hot
5. lot
6. ox

Review Words: is, him, rip, fit

 Go Digital Reproducible Word Cards are available at **www.thinkcentral.com**.

DIFFERENTIATE INSTRUCTION

Struggling	Advanced
Short *a* /ă/	1. came
Grade K, Lesson 12	2. make
	3. brave
	4. late
	5. gave
	6. shape
	Grade 1, Lesson 14

ELL SUPPORT

Linguistic Transfer Spanish speakers may pronounce the short vowel sound /ŏ/ as /ō/. Read the list of spelling words, elongating the short o sound in each word (*looog*). Then read the words normally. Have children repeat the words after you.

DAY 3 Open Sort

Children will sort words according to categories of their choice.

WORD STUDY NOTEBOOK

- Tell children that they will sort their Word Cards using their own categories.
- Model how to choose categories. Suggested language: **I look at the words carefully. I see that some words begin with the letter *l* and some do not. Those could be my categories:** *begin with* l *and do not begin with* l.
- Have children work in small groups. Provide examples of other categories, such as *rhyme, do not rhyme; two letters, three letters; end with* t*, other*. Help children write their headings in their Word Study Notebooks.
- Then have the groups sort the words. Have them read each word and write it under the appropriate heading in their Word Study Notebooks.
- Have groups share their work by reading aloud their headings and the words they sorted under each one.

DAY 4 Blind Writing Sort

Children will sort and write words you say.

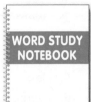
WORD STUDY NOTEBOOK

- Tell children they will listen to and write words with short *o*.
- Have children divide a page in their Word Study Notebooks into two columns. Say the word *dot*. Have children write it as the first column heading. Help them write *Other* as the second column heading.
- Tell children you will read a spelling word and they are to decide if the word belongs under the heading *dot* or *Other*. If the word ends with the letters *ot*, children should write it under *dot*. If the word does not end with *ot*, children should write it under *Other*.
- Say the word *ox*. When children finish writing, display the corresponding Word Card so children can check their spelling and the category. Have them correct any errors before you move on to the next word.
- When the sort is complete, have children read aloud and spell the words in each column.

DAY 5 Assess

Tell children to listen carefully. Say each boldfaced word, read the sentence, and repeat the word. Have children write the word.

1. **log**   We sit on a *log*.
2. **dot**   Look at the *dot*.
3. **top**   He plays with a *top*.
4. **hot**   The pan is *hot*.
5. **ox**   Did you see the *ox*?
6. **lot**   They play in the *lot*.

RETEACH   **IF** children misspell two or more words, **THEN** revisit the activity on Day 4 and reassess.

OPTIONAL ASSESSMENT   As an alternate assessment, you may have children repeat the Day 1 sort.

Words with Short *e*

Model the Sort

Children will sort words with you based on their short vowel sounds.

- Display the Lesson 4 Word Cards, and read each one aloud. Then point to each word as you use it in a sentence.
- Remind children that they have been learning about words with short vowel sounds. Tell them that today they will look at more words with short vowels.
- Display the Word Cards *dot* and *web*. Read the words. Suggested language: **I'll put *dot* and *web* at the top of two columns. I'll read a word, and I want you to tell me if the vowel sound is the same as in *dot* or *web*. Listen as I do the first one.**
- Display the Word Card *pen*, and read the word. Suggested language: ***Pen*. Listen for the vowel sound. *Peeeen*. I ask myself: *Does* pen *have the same vowel sound as in* dot *or does it have the same vowel sound as in* web? *Pen, dot. Pen, web. Pen *and* web *have the same vowel sound. So I'll put* pen *under* web.** Use the same procedure for *log*, placing it under *dot*.
- Continue in the same way with each Word Card, asking children to indicate in which column each word belongs. Read the word lists together. Then shuffle the Word Cards. Work with children to sort the words again.
- Call attention to the words in the short *e* column. Read the words with children. Help them recognize that the short vowel sound, /ĕ/, is spelled with the letter *e*.
- Give each child a set of Lesson 4 Word Cards. Have them repeat the sort independently.

SPELLING LIST

1. yet
2. web
3. pen
4. wet
5. leg
6. hen

Review Words: ox, log, dot, top

 Reproducible Word Cards are available at www.thinkcentral.com.

DIFFERENTIATE INSTRUCTION

Struggling	Advanced
Words with -*an*, -*ap*, -*at*	1. time
	2. like
Grade K, Lesson 13	3. kite
	4. bike
	5. white
	6. drive
	Grade 1, Lesson 15

 **ELL SUPPORT**

Use Minimal Pairs Some ELLs may need support pronouncing the short vowel sound /ĕ/. Say the following pairs of words as children listen: *pen/pan, men/man, ten/tan*. Repeat the word pairs, one at a time. Ask children to raise a hand when they hear a word with /ĕ/. Have them say the word.

DAY 2 **Pattern Sort**

Children will sort short *e* words according to spelling patterns.

- Remind children that this week's words have the short *e* sound, /ĕ/, spelled with the letter *e*.
- Work with children to repeat the Day 1 sort. Then set aside the short *o* words.
- Display the Word Cards *yet* and *pen* as column headings. Write *Other* as a third column heading. Read the words. Then display the Word Card *hen* and sort it according to ending sounds. Suggested language: ***Hen*. Hen *ends with the letters* en*, so I'll put* hen *under* pen. **Both words end with the sounds /ĕn/.** Have children help you sort the remaining words.
- Have children read aloud the words in the first column. Ask them to tell how *yet* and *wet* are alike. *(They both end with the letters* et *and the sounds* /ĕt/.) Elicit that *yet* and *wet* rhyme. Repeat with the second column words, *pen* and *hen*. Have children read the words in the third column and tell why they do not fit under *yet* or *pen*. Provide help as necessary.
- Have children copy their sorts into their Word Study Notebooks. When children have finished, call on individuals to read aloud their word lists.

yet	pen	Other
wet	hen	web
		leg

DAY 3 Blind Writing Sort

Children will sort and write spelling words.

WORD STUDY NOTEBOOK

- Tell children that they will listen to and write words with short *e*.
- Have children make three columns in their Word Study Notebooks. Lead them to write the following words as column headings: *wet, hen,* and *Other*.
- Explain that you will read a spelling word. Children are to listen carefully and then write it under the correct heading in their Word Study Notebooks.
- If a word ends with the letters *et*, children should write it under *wet*. If a word ends with the letters *en*, they should write it under *hen*. If a word does not end with *et* or *en*, they should write it under *Other*.
- Say the word *leg*. Allow time for children to write the word. Then display the Word Card *leg* so children can check the spelling and category. Have children make corrections as necessary. Repeat the procedure for the remaining spelling words.
- When the sort is complete, have children read their lists aloud to confirm that they sorted the words correctly.

DAY 4 Speed Sort

Children will sort words as quickly as they can.

WORD STUDY NOTEBOOK

- Repeat the sort from Day 1 with children, grouping words by short vowel sound *e* and short vowel sound *o*.
- Explain that children will work to sort short *e* and short *o* words as quickly as they can. Read aloud the words together.
- Have children set out the Word Cards *yet* and *log* as category headings. Tell them that when they read a word with short *e*, they should place it under *yet*. When they read a word with short *o*, they should place it under *log*. Tell children to sort as quickly as they can.
- Give the signal to begin sorting. When children finish, lead them to check their work. Then have them shuffle the Word Cards and sort again. Repeat a few times so that children can work to improve their speed.
- After the last sort, have children remove the short *o* cards. Then have partners take turns reading and writing the short *e* words. As one partner reads a word, the other partner writes it in his or her Word Study Notebook. Then partners switch roles.

DAY 5 Assess

Tell children to listen carefully. Say each boldfaced word, read the sentence, and repeat the word. Have children write the word.

1. **yet**   Are you done with your homework *yet*?
2. **web**   The spider made a tiny *web*.
3. **pen**   I like to write with a red *pen*.
4. **wet**   We are all *wet* from the rain.
5. **leg**   My *leg* is tired from the walk.
6. **hen**   The *hen* laid a green egg!

RETEACH **IF** children misspell two or more words, **THEN** revisit the activity on Day 4 and reassess.

OPTIONAL ASSESSMENT   As an alternate assessment, you may have children repeat the Day 1 sort.

Words with Short *u*

DIFFERENTIATE INSTRUCTION

Struggling	Advanced
Short *a* Words and High-Frequency Words	1. so
	2. go
Grade K, Lesson 15	3. home
	4. hole
	5. no
	6. rope
	7. joke
	8. bone
	9. stove
	10. poke
	Grade 1, Lesson 16

 **ELL SUPPORT**

Linguistic Transfer Speakers of Spanish, Cantonese, Tagalog, and Korean may pronounce the short vowel sound /ŭ/ as /ŏ/. Say the spelling word *up* several times, elongating the short *u* sound: *uuuup.* Then say the word normally. Have children repeat the word. Continue with other spelling words.

DAY 1 PHONICS **Model the Sort**

Children will sort words with you based on their short vowel sounds.

- Display the Lesson 5 Word Cards, and read each one aloud. Then point to each word as you use it in a sentence.
- Remind children that they have been learning about words with short vowel sounds. Tell them that today they will learn about more words with short vowels.
- Display the Word Cards *yet* and *mud* as column headings. Read each word. Suggested language: **Yet is at the top of the first column. *Mud* is at the top of the second column. I'm going to read a word. Tell me if the word has the same vowel sound as *yet* or *mud*. Listen while I do the first one as an example.**
- Hold up the Word Card *hen*, and read it aloud. Suggested language: **Hen. Listen for the vowel sound. *Heeeen.* Now I will compare the words. *Hen, yet. Hen, mud.* The vowel sound in *hen* sounds like the vowel sound in *yet*, the short e sound, /ĕ/. So I'll put *hen* under *yet*.** Repeat for *tub*, placing it under *mud*.
- Sort the remaining Word Cards by reading them one at a time and asking children where to place each word. Read the word lists with children. Then shuffle the cards and have children sort the words with you a second time.
- Read aloud the words under *mud* with children. Ask them what is similar about the words. Elicit that the words have the letter *u* and the short *u* vowel sound, /ŭ/.
- Distribute the Lesson 5 Word Cards. Have children repeat the sort independently.

DAY 2 **Guess My Category**

Children will guess the category names for short *u* words you sort.

- Repeat the sort from Day 1, allowing children to guide you to place each word in the correct category, short e or short u. Then set aside the short e words.
- Display the Word Cards *hug* and *tub* as category headings. Read each word. Then read *bug* and place the Word Card under *hug*. Read *up* and place the Word Card under *tub*. Repeat for the Word Cards *mud* and *nut* (under *tub*).
- Once the words are sorted, have children read aloud the first column. Ask them to tell how the two words are alike. (They both end with the letters ug *and the sounds* /ŭg/.) Have children read aloud the second column and tell how these words are alike. (They all have the letter u *and the short* u *sound.*)
- Have children read both word lists again. Ask them to tell which column has rhyming words and to read the words. (the first column; hug, bug)
- Have children repeat the sort independently and write their sorts in their Word Study Notebooks.

hug	tub
bug	up
	mud
	nut

DAY 3 Word Hunt

Children will write short *u* words that they find in their reading.

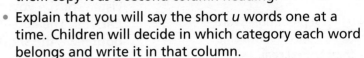

- Tell children that today they will go on a word hunt for short *u* words in a story they have read.
- Have children read aloud the Decodable Reader story "Fun in the Sun" together in small groups. Then ask group members to take turns looking at one page at a time and reading aloud any short *u* words they find.

- Once a short *u* word is identified, have all group members write the word in their Word Study Notebooks. Have children read their word list aloud to make sure each of the words contains short *u*.
- When children complete their word hunt, call on group members to read aloud the words for everyone to hear.

(Possible responses: fun, tug, up, sun)

DAY 4 Blind Writing Sort

Children will sort and write words you say.

- Tell children they will listen to and write short *u* words.
- Say the word *bug*. Have children write *bug* as a column heading in their Word Study Notebooks. Write *Other* on the board. Have them copy it as a second column heading.
- Explain that you will say the short *u* words one at a time. Children will decide in which category each word belongs and write it in that column.
- If a word ends with the letters *ug*, children should write it under *bug*. If a word does not end with the letters *ug*, children should write it under *Other*.
- Begin with the word *nut*. After children write the word, hold up the corresponding Word Card in order for them to confirm or correct the spelling or category. Continue with the remaining spelling words.
- When the sort is finished, ask children to read aloud the words in each column and double-check their work.

DAY 5 Assess

Tell children to listen carefully. Say each boldfaced word, read the sentence, and repeat the word. Have children write the word.

1. **up**   Look *up* in the tree!
2. **bug**   I saw a funny *bug*.
3. **mud**   The pigs splash in the *mud*.
4. **nut**   The squirrel hid a *nut*.
5. **hug**   Peg gives Gus a *hug*.
6. **tub**   Elephants get a bath in the *tub*.

RETEACH **IF** children misspell two or more words, **THEN** revisit the activity on Day 4 and reassess.

OPTIONAL ASSESSMENT As an alternate assessment, you may have children repeat the Day 1 sort.

Words with Short *a*

Model the Sort

Children will sort words with you based on their short vowel sounds.

- Display the Lesson 6 Word Cards. Read the words with children. Then point to each word as you use it in a sentence.

- Remind children that they have learned about short *a* words. Tell them that today they will look at more words with short *a*.

- Place the Word Cards *nut* and *ran* side by side. Point to and read each word. Suggested language: **I'm going to read a word. Listen for the vowel sound and tell me if it's the same as in *nut* or *ran*. I'll do the first one.**

- Display the Word Card *cat*, and read the word aloud. Suggested language: *Cat.* **Listen for the vowel sound.** *Caaaat.* **Now listen to these words together.** *Cat, nut. Cat, ran.* **The vowel sound in *cat* sounds like the vowel sound in *ran*. *Cat* and *ran* both have the short *a* sound, /ă/. So I'll put *cat* under *ran*.** Repeat for *bug*, placing it under *nut*.

- Continue in the same way with each Word Card, asking children to tell where each word belongs. Read the word lists with children. Then shuffle the Word Cards, and work with children to sort the words again.

- Read the words in the short *a* column with children. Ask them what is similar about each of the words. Elicit that the letter *a* stands for the short vowel sound /ă/.

- Provide partners with a set of Lesson 6 Word Cards. Have them repeat the sort.

Pattern Sort

Children will sort short *a* words according to spelling patterns.

- Remind children that this week they are learning about words that have the short vowel sound, /ă/, spelled with the letter *a*.

- Repeat the sort from Day 1, having children help you sort the words by short vowel sound. Then remove the short *u* words.

- Display the Word Cards *can* and *had* as column headings. Write *Other* as a third column heading. Then show the Word Card *ran*. Read the word. Suggested language: *Ran. Ran* **ends with the letters *an* and the sounds /ăn/. I'll put *ran* under *can*.** Work with children to sort the remaining words. Then ask them to read aloud the words in each column.

- Point out the rhyming words in the first column: *can, ran, an*. Ask children to name other words that could be added to the list. *(Possible responses: fan, man, tan)* Repeat for the second column. *(Possible responses: mad, dad, sad)*

- Have small groups repeat the sort. Then tell children to write their sorts in their Word Study Notebooks.

can	had	Other
ran	bad	cat
an		

SPELLING LIST

1. an
2. bad
3. can
4. had
5. cat
6. ran

Review Words: up, bug, nut, tub

 Reproducible Word Cards are available at **www.thinkcentral.com**.

DIFFERENTIATE INSTRUCTION

Struggling	Advanced
Short *i* /ĭ/	1. me
Grade K, Lesson 17	2. be
	3. read
	4. feet
	5. tree
	6. keep
	7. eat
	8. mean
	9. sea
	10. these
	Grade 1, Lesson 17

ELL SUPPORT

Linguistic Transfer If ELLs pronounce the short vowel sound /ă/ as /ŏ/, help them practice correct pronunciation. Read the list of spelling words, elongating the short *a* sound in each word (*baaaad*). Then read the words normally. Have children repeat the words after you.

DAY 3 Speed Sort

Children will sort words as quickly as they can.

- Repeat the Day 1 sort with children, working to sort the short *a* and short *u* words.

- Tell children that today they will sort the short *a* and short *u* words as quickly as they can.

- Have children place these Word Cards as column headings: *cat, bug*. Explain that when they read a word with short *a*, they should place it under *cat*. When they read a word with short *u*, they should place it under *bug*.

- Give the signal to begin. After the sort is completed, have children shuffle the cards and repeat the sort. Have them do this several times, trying to sort faster each time.

- After the last sort, have partners take turns reading and writing the words in their Word Study Notebooks.

DAY 4 Blind Writing Sort

Children will sort and write words you say.

- Tell children they will listen to and write words with short *a*.

- Have children make three columns in their Word Study Notebooks.

- Write these words on the board: *ran, bad, Other*. Ask children to read *ran* and *bad*. Identify the word *Other*. Have children write the words as column headings in their Word Study Notebooks.

- Explain that you will say one word at a time. Children are to write the word under the correct column heading: under *ran* if the word ends with the letters *an*, under *bad* if the word ends with the letters *ad*, and under *Other* if the word does not end with *an* or *ad*.

- Say the word *can*. After children finish writing, display the Word Card *can* so they can confirm or correct their spelling. Continue with the remaining spelling words.

- When finished, call on volunteers to read aloud the lists. Ask children to identify rhyming words. Then have them check that their words are in the correct columns.

DAY 5 Assess

Tell children to listen carefully. Say each boldfaced word, read the sentence, and repeat the word. Have children write the word.

1.	**an**	Rosa saw *an* elephant.
2.	**bad**	Please don't be *bad*.
3.	**can**	I *can* ride my bike.
4.	**had**	She *had* her hat in her hands.
5.	**cat**	The *cat* cleaned his face.
6.	**ran**	I *ran* home from school.

RETEACH **IF** children misspell two or more words, **THEN** revisit the activity on Day 2 and reassess.

OPTIONAL ASSESSMENT As an alternate assessment, you may have children repeat the Day 1 sort.

Words with Short *i*

SPELLING LIST

1. in
2. will
3. did
4. sit
5. six
6. big

Review Words: an, had, cat, ran

 Reproducible Word Cards are available at **www.thinkcentral.com**.

DIFFERENTIATE INSTRUCTION

Struggling	Advanced
Words with Short *a* and Short *i*	1. play
	2. grain
Grade K, Lesson 19	3. sail
	4. mail
	5. may
	6. rain
	7. way
	8. day
	9. stay
	10. pain
	Grade 1, Lesson 18

 **ELL SUPPORT**

Use Minimal Pairs Some ELLs may need support pronouncing the short vowel sound /ĭ/. Say the following pairs of words as children listen: *will/well, bill/bell, fill/fell.* Repeat the word pairs, one at a time. Ask children to raise a hand when they hear a word with /ĭ/. Have them say the word.

DAY 1 PHONICS Model the Sort

Children will sort words with you based on their short vowel sounds.

- Display the Lesson 7 Word Cards. Read the words with children. Then point to each word as you use it in a sentence.
- Remind children that they have learned about short *i* words. Tell them that today they will look at more words with short *i*.
- Display the Word Cards *ran* and *big* as column headings. Suggested language: **We are going to sort words into two groups—one group with the same vowel sound as *ran* and another group with the same vowel sound as *big*. I'll do the first one. The first word is *did*. I listen for the vowel sound in *did*. diiid. *Did* has the same vowel sound as *big*. I'll put *did* under *big*. Repeat for *had*, placing it under *ran*.**
- Use a similar procedure with the remaining words, having children name the correct column for each word. Read each list together to confirm that the words are sorted correctly. Then shuffle the cards and have children help you sort the words again.
- Read the words in the short *i* column with children. Guide them to notice that the short vowel sound, /ĭ/, is spelled with the letter *i*.
- Distribute the Lesson 7 Word Cards. Have children repeat the sort independently.

DAY 2 Open Sort

Children will sort words according to categories of their choice.

- Remind children that this week's words have the short *i* sound, /ĭ/, spelled with the letter *i*.
- Work with children to repeat the short vowel sort from Day 1, grouping words by short *a* and short *i*. Then set aside the short *a* words.
- Tell children they will choose their own categories for sorting the spelling words. Read the short *i* words with children. Make a few suggestions for categories: *same beginning letter; same beginning and ending letter, different beginning and ending letters; two letters, three letters, four letters.*
- Have children work in pairs. Tell them to talk about ways the short *i* words are alike and different.
- Once children have decided on their categories, help them write column headings in their Word Study Notebooks.
- Then have partners sort the words according to their categories. Have children complete their sorts in their Word Study Notebooks. Ask partners to explain their categories to the group and read the words in each column.

DAY 3 Blind Writing Sort

Children will sort and write words you say.

- Tell children that they will listen to and write words with short *a* and short *i*.
- Have children make two columns in their Word Study Notebooks. Say the word *cat* and have children write it as the first column heading. Say the word *six* and have them write it as the second column heading.
- Tell children you will say a word. They are to listen and then write the word under the correct heading. If the word has short *a*, they should write it under *cat*. If the word has short *i*, they should write it under *six*.
- Say *in*. After children finish writing, display the Word Card *in* so they can confirm or correct their spelling. Repeat the procedure for the remaining words.
- When the sort is complete, have children read their lists aloud to check that the words are sorted correctly.

DAY 4 Word Hunt

Children will write short *i* words that they find in their reading.

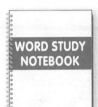

- Remind children that they have been reading and writing short *i* words. Tell them that today they will go on a short *i* word hunt in a story they have read.
- Have partners take turns reading pages in the Decodable Reader story "Brad and Cris." Then have them page through the selection, looking for words with the short *i* sound.

- Tell children to write each short *i* word they find in their Word Study Notebooks.
- When the word hunt is complete, ask children to read their word list aloud to confirm that each word has the short *i* sound, /ĭ/.

(Possible responses: is, his, Cris, will, trip, it, did)

DAY 5 Assess

Tell children to listen carefully. Say each boldfaced word, read the sentence, and repeat the word. Have children write the word.

1. **in**   The dog is *in* the house.
2. **will**   I *will* play in the sand.
3. **did**   She *did* her homework.
4. **sit**   Please *sit* next to me.
5. **six**   Daniel has *six* books.
6. **big**   My school is *big*.

RETEACH **IF** children misspell two or more words, **THEN** revisit the activity on Day 1 and reassess.

OPTIONAL ASSESSMENT As an alternate assessment, you may have children repeat the Day 1 sort.

Words with Short *o*

1. on
2. got
3. fox
4. pop
5. not
6. hop

Review Words: in, six, sit, big

 Reproducible Word Cards are available at **www.thinkcentral.com**.

DIFFERENTIATE INSTRUCTION

Struggling	Advanced
Short *o* /ŏ/	1. show
Grade K, Lesson 22	2. row
	3. grow
	4. low
	5. blow
	6. snow
	7. boat
	8. coat
	9. road
	10. toad
	Grade 1, Lesson 19

 **ELL SUPPORT**

Use Minimal Pairs In Korean, there are no short/long vowel distinctions. Help children hear the short vowel sound /ŏ/ by saying these word pairs: *not/note, got/goat, cot/coat*. Have children practice saying the words with you, gradually allowing them to say the words on their own.

DAY 1 PHONICS Model the Sort

Children will sort words with you based on their short vowel sounds.

- Display the Lesson 8 Word Cards, and read them aloud. Then point to each word as you use it in a sentence.
- Remind children that they have learned about short *o* words. Tell them that today they will look at some more words with short *o*.
- Explain that you will sort words by their vowel sounds. Display the Word Cards *sit* and *hop* as column headings and establish the categories. Suggested language: *Sit.* **The word** *sit* **has the short** *i* **sound. The word** *hop* **has the short** *o* **sound.**
- Display the Word Card *fox*. Suggested language: **Now here's another word. Does** *fox* **belong with** *sit* **or with** *hop*? **Listen for the vowel sound in** *fox*: *fooox. Fox* **and** *hop* **both have the short** *o* **sound, /ŏ/. I'll put** *fox* **under** *hop*. Repeat for *big*, placing it under *sit*.
- Continue in the same way with each Word Card, asking children to tell where each word belongs. After the Word Cards have been sorted, shuffle them and work with children to sort them again.
- Read the words in each column with children. Then focus on the column of short *o* words. Guide children to notice that the short vowel sound, /ŏ/, is spelled with the letter *o*.
- Distribute the Lesson 8 Word Cards. Have children repeat the sort independently.

DAY 2 Guess My Category

Children will guess the category names for short *o* words you sort.

- Remind children that this week's words have the short *o* sound, /ŏ/, spelled with the letter *o*.
- Repeat the sort from Day 1, allowing children to place each word in the correct category: short *o* or short *i*. Then remove the short *i* words.
- Display the Word Cards *not, pop,* and *on* as category headings. Read each word. Then display and read the Word Card *got*. Place it under *not*. Repeat for the Word Card *hop*, placing it under *pop*. Read the Word Card *fox* and place it under *on*.
- After the words are sorted, have children read aloud the words in each column. Have them guess each category. Guide children by asking: **How are the words** *not* **and** *got* **alike?** (*They both end with the letters* ot *and the sounds* /ŏt/.)
- Repeat for the second column. (*Both words end with the letters* op *and the sounds* /ŏp/.) Ask children to tell how the words in the third column are alike. (*Both words have the letter* o.)
- Guide children to recognize the rhyming words *not/got* and *pop/hop*.
- Have partners repeat the sort. Then tell them to write their sorts in their Word Study Notebooks.

not	pop	on
got	hop	fox

DAY 3   Speed Sort

Children will sort words quickly.

WORD STUDY NOTEBOOK

- Repeat the Day 1 sort with children. Together, sort words by short vowel sounds, short *o* and short *i*.
- Tell children they will work on a speed sort and try to sort the words as quickly as they can.
- Have children place these Word Cards as column headings: *fox, big*. Tell them that when they read a word with short *o*, they should place it under *fox*. When they read a word with short *i*, they should place it under *big*.
- Begin the sort, monitoring children's work. Then have children shuffle the cards and repeat the sort several times to improve their speed.
- When the last sort is completed, have partners take turns reading and writing the words in their Word Study Notebooks.

DAY 4   Blind Writing Sort

Children will sort and write words you say.

WORD STUDY NOTEBOOK

- Tell children that they will listen to and write words with the short *o* sound.
- Have children set up three columns in their Word Study Notebooks. Guide them to write these words as column headings: *got, hop, Other*.
- Explain that you will say the short *o* words one at a time. Children will decide in which category each word belongs and write it in that column.
- If a word ends with the letters *ot*, children should write it under *got*. If a word ends with the letters *op*, they should write it under *hop*. If the word does not end with *ot* or *op*, they should write it under *Other*.
- Say the word *pop*. After children write it, hold up the corresponding Word Card so they can confirm or correct their spelling. Continue with the remaining words.
- When the sort is complete, have children read aloud each list to check that the words are sorted correctly.

DAY 5   Assess

Tell children to listen carefully. Say each boldfaced word, read the sentence, and repeat the word. Have children write the word.

1. **on**   The book is *on* my desk.
2. **got**   She *got* a lot of presents.
3. **fox**   The *fox* ran into the woods.
4. **pop**   *Pop* went the wheel.
5. **not**   I will *not* eat that.
6. **hop**   The bunnies *hop* around.

RETEACH   **IF** children misspell two or more words, **THEN** revisit the activity on Day 4 and reassess.

OPTIONAL ASSESSMENT   As an alternate assessment, you may have children repeat the Day 1 sort.

Words with Short e

SPELLING LIST

1. yes
2. let
3. red
4. ten
5. bed
6. get

Review Words: got, not, on, hop

 Reproducible Word Cards are available at **www.thinkcentral.com**.

DIFFERENTIATE INSTRUCTION

Struggling	Advanced
Words with -at, -it, -ot	1. bedtime
	2. sunset
Grade K, Lesson 24	3. bathtub
	4. sailboat
	5. flagpole
	6. backpack
	7. playpen
	8. raincoat
	9. inside
	10. himself
	Grade 1, Lesson 20

 **ELL SUPPORT**

Linguistic Transfer In Cantonese, vowel sounds may change based on the surrounding consonants. Read the spelling list to help children hear the consistency of the short vowel sound /ĕ/.

DAY 1 PHONICS Model the Sort

Children will sort words with you based on their short vowel sounds.

- Display the Lesson 9 Word Cards, and read them aloud. Then point to each word as you use it in a sentence.
- Remind children that they have been learning about words with short vowel sounds. Tell them that today they will read and sort words with the short e sound.
- Use the Word Cards *got* and *ten* as column headings. Read each word. Suggested language: ***Got. Ten. I'm going to say another word. You will tell me if the word has the same vowel sound as*** *got* **or** *ten*. **Listen while I do the first one.**
- Say *yes* as you hold up the Word Card. Suggested language: ***Yes. Listen for the vowel sound. Yeees. Now I will compare the words. Yes, got. Yes, ten. The vowel sound in*** *yes* **sounds like the vowel sound in** *ten*—**the short e sound, /ĕ/. I'll put** *yes* **under** *ten*. **Use the same procedure for** *hop*, **placing it under** *got*.
- Sort the remaining words by reading them one at a time and asking children where to place the Word Card. Shuffle the cards and have children sort the words with you a second time. Then read the word lists with children.
- Read the words in the short e column with children. Guide them to notice that the letter e stands for the short vowel sound /ĕ/.
- Distribute the Lesson 9 Word Cards. Have children repeat the sort independently.

DAY 2 Pattern Sort

Children will sort short e words according to spelling patterns.

- Remind children that this week's spelling words have the short e sound, /ĕ/.
- Repeat the sort from Day 1, working with children to sort the words by short vowel sounds. Then set aside the short o words.
- Place the Word Cards *let* and *bed* as two column headings. Make a card for *Other* as the heading for a third column. Read the headings. Then show the Word Card *red*. Suggested language: ***Red ends with the letters*** *ed* **and the sounds /ĕd/. So does** *bed*. **I'll put** *red* **under** *bed*.
- Continue to sort the remaining words, asking children to tell you in which category they belong. Then read the words in each column with children.
- Point out the rhyming words in the first column: *let, get*. Ask children to name other *et* words that could be added to the list. *(Possible responses: wet, set, net)* Repeat for the second column with *ed* words. *(Possible responses: led, fed)*
- For the third column, ask children why they think *yes* and *ten* are in a column with the heading *Other*. *(The words do not rhyme with each other or with* let *or* bed.)
- Tell partners to repeat the sort of short e words. Have children write their sorts in their Word Study Notebooks.

let	bed	Other
get	red	yes
		ten

DAY 3 Word Hunt

Children will write short *e* words that they find in their reading.

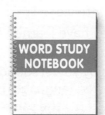

- Tell children that they will go on a word hunt to find words with short *e* in a story they have read.
- Have small groups take turns reading aloud the Decodable Reader selection "Step Up!"

- Then direct the groups to study one page at a time to look for and read aloud short *e* words. If everyone in the group agrees on the short *e* words, they should write each one in their Word Study Notebooks.
- When children have finished, call on a member from each group to read aloud the group's word list. Have children check that each word has the short *e* sound, /ĕ/.

(*Possible responses: step, Jess, yes, spell, Peg, Bess, Jen*)

DAY 4 Speed Sort

Children will sort words as quickly as they can.

- Work with children to repeat the Day 1 sort of short *e* and short *o* words.
- Tell children that now they will sort those words as quickly as they can.
- Have children place the Word Cards *get* and *not* as column headings. Children will read the other words and place short *e* words under *get* and short *o* words under *not*.
- Signal the start of the sort. After the first sort is completed, have children read the word lists. Then have them shuffle the Word Cards and repeat the sort a few times. Encourage them to try to sort the words faster each time.
- After the last sort, have partners take turns reading and writing the words. One partner reads the words while the other partner writes them in his or her Word Study Notebook. Then partners switch roles.

DAY 5 Assess

Tell children to listen carefully. Say each boldfaced word, read the sentence, and repeat the word. Have children write the word.

1. **yes**   *Yes*, I will go with you.

2. **let**   My mother will *let* me go to your house.

3. **red**   The apple is *red*.

4. **ten**   We have *ten* fingers.

5. **bed**   I like to sleep in my *bed*.

6. **get**   Can you *get* me a book?

RETEACH **IF** children misspell two or more words, **THEN** revisit the activity on Day 1 and reassess.

OPTIONAL ASSESSMENT As an alternate assessment, you may have children repeat the Day 1 sort.

Words with Short *u*

SPELLING LIST

1. us
2. sun
3. but
4. fun
5. bus
6. run

Review Words: ten, bed, red, get

 Reproducible Word Cards are available at **www.thinkcentral.com**.

DIFFERENTIATE INSTRUCTION

Struggling	Advanced
Words with Short *o* and Short *e*	1. far
	2. arm
Grade K, Lesson 25	3. yard
	4. art
	5. jar
	6. bar
	7. barn
	8. bark
	9. card
	10. yarn
	Grade 1, Lesson 21

 **ELL SUPPORT**

Use Minimal Pairs The short vowel sound /ŭ/ may be a challenge for ELLs. To help children hear the correct pronunciation, say the following pairs of words: *but/bat, cut/cat, hut/hat.* Say each pair of words again, and have children repeat them.

DAY 1 PHONICS Model the Sort

Children will sort words with you based on their short vowel sounds.

- Display the Lesson 10 Word Cards. Read the words with children. Then point to each word as you use it in a sentence.
- Remind children that they have learned about short *u* words. Tell them that now they will look at more words with short *u*.
- Model sorting the words by vowel sound. Use the Word Cards *get* and *fun* as column headings. Suggested language: **I'm going to read a word. Listen for the vowel sound and tell me if it's the same as in *get* or *fun*. I'll do the first one.**
- Display the Word Card *bus.* Suggested language: **Bus. Listen for the vowel sound. Buuus. Now listen to these words together. *Bus, get. Bus, fun.* The vowel sound in *bus* sounds like the vowel sound in *fun*—the short *u* sound, /ŭ/. I'll put *bus* under *fun*.** Repeat the process for *ten*, placing it under *get*.
- Continue to sort the remaining words, asking children to guide you as you place the Word Card in the correct column. When all the words have been sorted, shuffle the Word Cards and sort the words with children again.
- Read aloud the words in each column. Then reread the short *u* words. Ask children what is similar about each of the words. Elicit that the letter *u* stands for the short vowel sound /ŭ/.
- Provide partners with a set of Lesson 10 Word Cards. Have them work together to repeat the sort.

DAY 2 Guess My Category

Children will guess the category names for short *u* words you sort.

- Remind children that this week's spelling words have the short *u* sound, /ŭ/, spelled with the letter *u*.
- Repeat the Day 1 sort with short *u* and short *e* words. Then set aside the short *e* words.
- Tell children you will sort the short *u* words and you want them to guess the two categories. Read these Word Cards and place them as column headings: *run, us.*
- Explain that you will read and sort one word at a time. When children recognize the pattern in each category, they should raise a hand.
- Display and read *bus.* Place the Word Card under *us.* Continue with *sun* and *fun*, placing them under *run.* Read the lists with children. Guide them to recognize that the words in each column rhyme, and they end with the same letters and sounds. Have them reread each group of words, paying attention to the ending letters and sounds.
- Then ask children if a Word Card is missing. Elicit that the word *but* does not fit in either category. Add a third column with the heading *Other.* Place *but* in the new category.
- Have children repeat the sort independently and write their sorts in their Word Study Notebooks.

run	us	Other
sun	bus	but
fun		

DAY 3 Blind Writing Sort

Children will sort and write words you say.

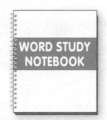

- Tell children they will listen to and write words with the short *u* sound.
- Have children fold a page in their Word Study Notebooks into two columns. Guide them to label the columns *sun* and *Other*.
- Tell children you will say a word. They should decide whether the word rhymes with *sun*. If the word rhymes with *sun*, children should write it under *sun*. If it does not rhyme, they should write it under *Other*.
- Say the word *run*. After children write the word, display its Word Card. Have children check the spelling and category. Continue with the remaining spelling words.
- After the sort, have children read the lists aloud. Review that the words in the first column rhyme. Ask if any words in the second column rhyme. Elicit that *us* and *bus* rhyme. Have children circle those words.

DAY 4 Open Sort

Children will sort words according to categories of their choice.

- Have partners work together to choose their own categories for sorting the short *u* spelling words and the short *e* words.
- Read the words with children. Provide some examples of categories, such as these: *words that begin with* b *and words that do not begin with* b; *two-letter words, three-letter words; words that rhyme.*
- Have partners discuss the words and choose categories. Help them write the column headings in their Word Study Notebooks.
- Have partners work together to sort the Word Cards. Tell them to write each word under the correct heading in their Word Study Notebooks.
- When all pairs have finished, encourage children to explain how they sorted the words. Ask them to read aloud the words in their lists.

DAY 5 Assess

Tell children to listen carefully. Say each boldfaced word, read the sentence, and repeat the word. Have children write the word.

1.	**us**	Will you come with *us*?
2.	**sun**	The *sun* is in the sky.
3.	**but**	I like rice *but* not cheese.
4.	**fun**	It is *fun* to ride a bike.
5.	**bus**	The *bus* takes me to school.
6.	**run**	Lisa can *run* fast.

RETEACH   **IF** children misspell two or more words, **THEN** revisit the activity on Day 3 and reassess.

OPTIONAL ASSESSMENT   As an alternate assessment, you may have children repeat the Day 1 sort.

Words with *th*

SPELLING LIST

1. that
2. then
3. this
4. them
5. with
6. bath

Review Words: ten, tub, wet, sat

 Reproducible Word Cards are available at **www.thinkcentral.com**.

DIFFERENTIATE INSTRUCTION

Struggling	Advanced
Words with -*et* and -*en*	1. her
	2. fern
Grade K, Lesson 26	3. girl
	4. sir
	5. stir
	6. bird
	7. fur
	8. hurt
	9. turn
	10. third
	Grade 1, Lesson 22

ELL SUPPORT

Modified Instruction During the Day 3 Word Hunt, pair ELLs with more proficient English speakers. The ELL partner may point to the *th* words in the Decodable Reader story, while the English speaker reads the words. Both partners record the words.

DAY 1 PHONICS **Model the Sort**

Children will sort words with you based on their consonant sounds.

- Display the Lesson 11 Word Cards, and read each word aloud. Then point to each word as you use it in a sentence.
- Point out that some of this week's words have the /t/ sound and some have the /th/ sound. Explain that some words have /t/ or /th/ at the beginning. Some words have /t/ or /th/ at the end. Tell children they will help you sort the words by the sounds /t/ and /th/.
- Display the Word Cards *tub* and *then*. Suggested language: **Listen as I say** *tub.* **Tub has the /t/ sound. I'll make a group for words with the /t/ sound.** Repeat for *then*, starting a group of words with the /th/ sound.
- Sort the words *sat* (under *tub*) and *with* (under *then*) to help children see that *t* and *th* may also come at the end of words. Then work with children to sort the other words. Point out that the word *that* fits in both categories because it has the sounds /th/ and /t/. Read the word lists with children. Then shuffle the cards and have them sort the words with you again.
- Read the words in the *th* column with children. Lead them to understand that sometimes two letters stand for one sound and that the letters *th* together stand for the /th/ sound.
- Draw attention to the *th* words. Remind children that sometimes the /th/ sound is at the beginning of words and sometimes it is at the end of words. Have children help you group the Word Cards by initial and final *th*.
- Distribute the Lesson 11 Word Cards to children. Have them repeat the sort independently.

DAY 2 **Pattern Sort**

Children will sort words based on the position of the letters *th*.

- Remind children that this week's spelling words have two letters, *th*, that stand for one sound, /th/.
- Repeat the Day 1 sort, asking children to tell whether each word has the sound /t/ or /th/. Then set aside the words with *t*.
- Display the Word Cards *them* and *bath* as column headings. Read the words. Begin to sort by whether *th* is in the initial or final position. Read the Word Card *that* and sort according to the initial position of *th*. Suggested language: *That.* **Do you hear the /th/ sound at the beginning or at the end?** After children respond, place *that* under *them*. Continue in the same way with the remaining words.
- When all the words are sorted, have children read aloud the words in each column. Ask them to explain how the words in each column are alike. (*The words in the first column begin with the letters* th *and the sound /th/. The words in the second column end with the letters* th *and the sound /th/.*)
- Have children work in pairs to repeat the sort. Tell them to write their sorts in their Word Study Notebooks.

them	bath
that	with
then	
this	

▶ **MAJOR UNDERSTANDING:** Sometimes one sound is spelled with two letters. The sound /th/ is spelled with the letters *th*.

DAY 3 Word Hunt

Children will sort *th* words they find in their reading.

- Remind children that they have been reading and writing words with *th*. Tell them that today they will look for *th* words in a story they have read.

- Have children write these two column headings in their Word Study Notebooks: *this, with*. Point out that the first column is for words that begin with *th*. The second column is for words that end with *th*.

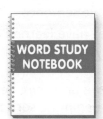

- Then have partners read the Decodable Reader story "Seth and Beth."

- Tell children to go through the story again, this time looking for words with the letters *th*. Children should write words that begin with *th* under *this* and words that end with *th* under *with*.

- When children have finished, tell partners to take turns reading their word lists aloud. Have them check that each word is in the correct column.

  (Possible responses: Seth, Beth, path, with, they, this, them, then, their)

DAY 4 Blind Writing Sort

Children will sort and write words that you say aloud.

- Tell children they will listen to and write words with *th*.

- Have children divide a page in their Word Study Notebooks into two columns.

- Say the word *then* and have children write it as the first column heading. Say the word *bath* and have them write it as the second heading. Display the Word Cards *then* and *bath* for children to check their spelling.

- Tell children you will say one spelling word at a time. They are to listen and write the word under the correct heading: under *then* if the word begins with *th* and under *bath* if the word ends with *th*.

- Say the word *this*. After children have written the word, display the corresponding Word Card. Have children confirm or correct the spelling and category. Provide time for children to make corrections as necessary. Continue with the remaining spelling words.

- When the sort is complete, have children read their lists aloud.

DAY 5 Assess

Tell children to listen carefully. Say each boldfaced word, read the sentence, and repeat the word. Have children write the word.

1. **that**   *That* is my hat.

2. **then**   Come to my house and *then* we will bake cookies.

3. **this**   *This* is my bed.

4. **them**   Please tell *them* to go slow.

5. **with**   Alex will go *with* you to the store.

6. **bath**   I take a *bath* every night.

RETEACH **IF** children misspell two or more words, **THEN** revisit the activity on Day 2 and reassess.

OPTIONAL ASSESSMENT As an alternate assessment, you may have children repeat the Day 1 sort.

Words with *ch*

SPELLING LIST

1. chin
2. chop
3. much
4. chip
5. rich
6. chick

Review Words: that, this, with, bath

 Reproducible Word Cards are available at www.thinkcentral.com.

DIFFERENTIATE INSTRUCTION

Struggling	Advanced
Short *u* /ŭ/	1. look
Grade K, Lesson 27	2. book
	3. good
	4. hook
	5. brook
	6. took
	7. foot
	8. shook
	9. wood
	10. hood
	Grade 1, Lesson 23

ELL SUPPORT

Linguistic Transfer Speakers of Hmong and Vietnamese may find the /ch/ sound challenging to pronounce. Read the list of spelling words, repeating the *ch* sound in each word (ch-ch-ch-op). Have children watch your mouth and tongue position as you pronounce the /ch/ sound. Then read the words again. Have children repeat the words after you.

DAY 1 PHONICS Model the Sort

Children will sort words with you based on their consonant digraph sounds.

- Display the Lesson 12 Word Cards. Read each word with children. Then point to each word as you use it in a sentence.
- Remind children that they have learned about two letters that stand for one sound. Tell them that today they will work with words with the sound for *th*, /th/, and the sound for *ch*, /ch/.
- Display the Word Cards *this* and *chip*. Read them with children. Then arrange them as column headings and begin the sort. Suggested language: **I will say a word. You tell me if the word has the sound /th/ or /ch/. I'll do the first one.** Display the Word Card *chin*, and say: **Chin. Chin has the /ch/ sound, just like *chip*. I'll put *chin* under *chip*.** Repeat for *that*, placing it under *this*.
- Sort the words *with* (under *this*) and *much* (under *chip*) to help children see that *th* and *ch* may also come at the end of words. Then work together to sort the other words. Read the word lists together. Then shuffle the cards and have children help you sort the words again.
- Focus on the *ch* words. Point out that the /ch/ sound can be at the beginning of words or at the end of words. Guide children to recognize how the /ch/ sound is spelled. Then work with children to group the words by initial and final *ch*.
- Give each child a set of Lesson 12 Word Cards, and have them repeat the sort independently.

DAY 2 Pattern Sort

Children will sort words based on the position of the digraph *ch*.

- Remind children that this week's words have the /ch/ sound spelled *ch*.
- Work with children to repeat the sort from Day 1, grouping the words by *th* and *ch*. Then set aside the words with *th*.
- Display the Word Cards *chop* and *much* as column headings. Read the words with children and have them tell where they see *ch* in each word. Then sort words by initial and final *ch*. Display the Word Card *rich*. Suggested language: ***Rich.* Do you hear the /ch/ sound at the beginning or at the end?** After children respond, place *rich* under *much*. Sort the remaining words in the same way.
- Have children read the words in the first column. Ask: **How are the words alike?** *(They all begin with the letters* ch *and the sound /ch/.)*
- Have children read the words in the second column. Ask how these words are alike. *(They both end with the letters* ch *and the sound /ch/.)*
- Tell children to repeat the sort independently and write their sorts in their Word Study Notebooks.

chop	much
chin	rich
chip	
chick	

DAY 3 Open Sort

Children will sort words according to their own categories.

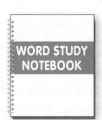

- Lead children in a sort of the *ch* words, grouping the words by initial and final position of *ch*. Then tell children that they can choose their own categories to sort the words again.
- Read the words with children. Make a few suggestions for categories: *end with* p, *do not end with* p; *words with* i, *words with* o, *and words with* u; *things, actions, and describing words.*
- Have children work in pairs. Tell them to talk about the words and choose their categories. Help them write the column headings in their Word Study Notebooks.
- Then have partners sort the Word Cards into their categories. Ask partners to name each category and read the words in each column.
- Guide children to understand and correct any errors and then write their sorts in their Word Study Notebooks.

DAY 4 Speed Sort

Children will sort words as quickly as they can.

- Repeat the initial and final *ch* sort with children.
- Tell them that today they will work to sort the words as quickly as possible.
- Have children place these Word Cards as column headings: *chick, rich.* Explain that when they read a word that begins with *ch*, they should place it under *chick*. When they read a word that ends with *ch,* they should place it under *rich*.
- Begin the sort and check children's work when it is finished. Then tell children to shuffle the Word Cards. Repeat the sort a few more times to give children the chance to improve their speed.
- After the last sort, have children write their sorts in their Word Study Notebooks.

DAY 5 Assess

Tell children to listen carefully. Say each boldfaced word, read the sentence, and repeat the word. Have children write the word.

1. **chin**   A fly was on his *chin.*
2. **chop**   *Chop* the apples into small pieces.
3. **much**   How *much* does that toy cost?
4. **chip**   The cup has a *chip* in it.
5. **rich**   He is *rich* and has many things.
6. **chick**   The baby *chick* was yellow.

RETEACH **IF** children misspell two or more words, **THEN** revisit the activity on Day 2 and reassess.

OPTIONAL ASSESSMENT As an alternate assessment, you may have children repeat the Day 1 sort.

Words with *sh, wh*

SPELLING LIST

1. ship
2. shop
3. which
4. when
5. whip
6. fish

Review Words: chin, chop, chip, chick

 Reproducible Word Cards are available at **www.thinkcentral.com**.

DIFFERENTIATE INSTRUCTION

Struggling	Advanced
Words with Short *e* and Short *u*	1. soon
	2. new
Grade K, Lesson 28	3. noon
	4. zoo
	5. boot
	6. too
	7. moon
	8. blew
	9. soup
	10. you
	Grade 1, Lesson 24

ELL **ELL SUPPORT**

Modified Questioning During the Day 2 Guess My Category sort, phrase questions so ELLs may answer *yes* or *no*. For example, point to the first column of words and ask: **Do all these words have the letters *sh*? Do all these words begin with *sh*? Does the word *fish* begin with *sh*? Does *fish* end with *sh*?** Use a similar approach for the words in the second column.

DAY 1 PHONICS **Model the Sort**

Children will sort words with you based on their consonant digraph sounds.

- Display the Lesson 13 Word Cards. Read each word aloud. Then point to each word as you use it in a sentence.
- Remind children that they have learned about words with the sound /ch/. Tell them that today they will work with words with the sounds /ch/, /sh/, and /hw/.
- Explain the sorting categories as you display these Word Cards as column headings: *chop, ship, when.* Suggested language: **I'm going to make three groups. The first is for words with the /ch/ sound. The second is for words with /sh/. The third is for words with /hw/.**
- Display the Word Card *whip.* Suggested language: **Whip. I hear /hw/ in *whip.* I'll put *whip* under *when.*** Repeat for *chip*, placing it under *chop*, and for *shop*, placing it under *ship*.
- Continue the sort, having children guide you in placing each word in the correct column. Point out that the word *which* has both /ch/ and /hw/. Read the word lists together. Then shuffle the cards and ask children to help you sort them again.
- Call attention to the words under *ship* and *when.* Have children read each column aloud. Guide them to notice that the letters *sh* stand for the sound /sh/ and the letters *wh* stand for the sound /hw/.
- Give partners a set of Lesson 13 Word Cards. Have them work together to repeat the sort.

DAY 2 **Guess My Category**

Children will guess the category names for *sh* and *wh* words you sort.

- Remind children that this week they are learning words with the sounds /sh/ and /hw/. Review the sound/spellings *sh* and *wh.* Set aside the words with /ch/.
- Display the Word Cards *shop* and *whip* as category headings. Read each word. Then sort the remaining words by *sh* and *wh.* Read *ship* and place the Word Card under *shop.* Read *which* and place the Word Card under *whip.* Repeat for *fish* (under *shop*) and *when* (under *whip*).
- Once the words are sorted, guide children to identify the categories. Have them read aloud the first column. Ask them to tell how the words are alike. *(They all have the letters* sh *and the sound /sh/.)* Have children read aloud the second column and tell how these words are alike. *(They all have the letters* wh *and the sound /hw/.)*
- Call attention to the first column. Ask: **Why is the word *fish* different from *shop* and *ship*?** *(It has the letters* sh *and the sound /sh/ at the end.)* Name a few other words that end with *sh*, such as *wish, dish,* and *hush.*
- Have children repeat the sort independently. Have them write the sorted words in two columns in their Word Study Notebooks.

shop	whip
ship	which
fish	when

DAY 3 Speed Sort

Children will sort words as quickly as they can.

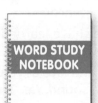

WORD STUDY NOTEBOOK

- Repeat the Day 2 *sh-wh* sort with children. Then tell children that today they will work on a speed sort, sorting the words as quickly as possible.
- Have children set out the Word Cards *fish* and *which* as category headings. Tell them that when they read a word with *sh*, they should place it under *fish*. When they read a word with *wh*, they should place it under *which*.
- After you help children check their work, ask them to shuffle the Word Cards and sort again. Repeat a few times so that children can practice improving their speed. Monitor children to make sure they maintain accuracy.
- After the last sort, call on individuals to read aloud the words as everyone copies their sorts into their Word Study Notebooks.

DAY 4 Blind Writing Sort

Children will sort and write words you say aloud.

WORD STUDY NOTEBOOK

- Tell children they will listen to and write words with *sh* and *wh*.
- In their Word Study Notebooks, have children write *ship* and *when* as column headings. Ask them to underline *sh* and *wh* in the headings, and display the corresponding Word Cards so children may check their spelling.
- Explain that you will read a spelling word, and children are to listen carefully to the word and decide if it has the letters *sh* or *wh*. They should write words with the letters *sh* under *ship* and words with the letters *wh* under *when*.
- Say the word *which*. Allow time for children to write the word. Then display the Word Card *which* so children can check their spelling. Have them make corrections as necessary. Repeat the procedure for the remaining spelling words. Save the word *fish* for last.
- When the sort is complete, have children read their lists aloud to check that they sorted the words correctly.

DAY 5 Assess

Tell children to listen carefully. Say each boldfaced word, read the sentence, and repeat the word. Have children write the word.

1. **ship**   The *ship* sails on the ocean.

2. **shop**   I like to *shop* for food.

3. **which**   *Which* hand is it in?

4. **when**   *When* will you go home?

5. **whip**   *Whip* the butter with a fork.

6. **fish**   The *fish* swim in the water.

RETEACH   **IF** children misspell two or more words, **THEN** revisit the activity on Day 3 and reassess.

OPTIONAL ASSESSMENT   As an alternate assessment, you may have children repeat the Day 1 sort.

Words with Long *a*

SPELLING LIST

1. came
2. make
3. brave
4. late
5. gave
6. shape

Review Words: bad, can, had, ran

 Reproducible Word Cards are available at **www.thinkcentral.com**.

DIFFERENTIATE INSTRUCTION

Struggling	Advanced
Words with Short Vowels	1. how
	2. now
Grade K, Lesson 30	3. cow
	4. owl
	5. ouch
	6. house
	7. found
	8. out
	9. gown
	10. town
	Grade 1, Lesson 25

 **ELL SUPPORT**

Use Minimal Pairs Some ELLs may need support pronouncing the long vowel sound /ā/. Say the following pairs of words as children listen: *cane/can, vane/van, mane/man*. Repeat the word pairs, one at a time. Ask children to raise a hand when they hear a word with /ā/. Have them say the word.

DAY 1 PHONICS **Model the Sort**

Children will sort words with you based on short *a* and long *a* vowel sounds.

- Display the Lesson 14 Word Cards, and read each one aloud. Then point to each word as you use it in a sentence.
- Remind children that they have learned the short *a* sound. Tell them that today they are going to work with another sound for *a* called the long *a* sound.
- Use the Word Cards *bad* and *late* as column headings. Suggested language: **The word *bad* has the short *a* sound, /ă/. The word *late* has the long *a* sound, /ā/. Listen for the long *a* sound: *laaaate, late*.** Have children say *late* several times, listening for the long *a* sound.
- Begin to model the sort. Suggested language: **I'm going to say a word. Listen for the vowel sound and tell me if it's the same as in *bad* or *late*. I'll do the first one.**
- Display *make* and say: ***Make*. Listen for the vowel sound. *Maaaake*. Now listen to these words together. *Make, bad. Make, late*. The vowel sound in *make* sounds like the vowel sound in *late*—the long *a* sound, /ā/. I'll put *make* under *late*.** Repeat for *ran*, placing it under *bad*. Sort the remaining words together.
- Then have children read aloud each column. Guide them to recognize the spelling patterns. Point to the short *a* column, and ask: **What is the same about these words?** (They have a consonant-vowel-consonant pattern and the short *a* sound spelled a.)
- Repeat for the other column. (The long *a* words have the a-consonant-e pattern.) Tell children that the final e does not stand for a sound; it is a clue that the vowel probably stands for its long sound.
- Give partners a set of Lesson 14 Word Cards. Have them repeat the sort.

DAY 2 **Guess My Category**

Children will guess the category names for short and long *a* words you sort.

- Remind children that this week they are learning words with the long *a* sound, /ā/, spelled a-consonant-e.
- Tell children you will sort this week's words and you want them to guess the two categories. Display and read the Word Cards *had* and *make* as headings to represent short *a* and long *a*. One by one, read the remaining Word Cards, and place them under the heading with the same vowel sound.
- When all the words have been sorted, have children read each word list. Ask: **How are the words in the first column alike?** (They all have the short *a* sound.) **How are the words in the second column alike?** (They all have the long *a* sound.) **What spelling pattern do you see in the words in the second column?** (a-consonant-e)
- Have children repeat the sort with a partner. Tell each child to write the sort in his or her Word Study Notebook.

had	make
can	came
bad	brave
ran	late
	gave
	shape

DAY 3 Speed Sort

Children will sort words as quickly as they can.

WORD STUDY NOTEBOOK

- Repeat the Day 1 sort with children. Sort between short *a* and long *a* words.
- Tell children that now they will sort the short *a* and long *a* words on their own, as quickly as they can.
- Have children place the Word Cards *can* and *gave* as category headings. Tell them that when they read a word with the short *a* sound, they should place it under *can*. When they read a word with the long *a* sound, they should place it under *gave*.
- Signal the start of the sort. After the first sort is completed, have children read the word lists. Then have them shuffle the Word Cards and repeat the sort a few times. Encourage them to try to sort the words more quickly each time.
- When the last sort is completed, have children write their sorts in two columns in their Word Study Notebooks.

DAY 4 Blind Writing Sort

Children will sort and write words that you say aloud.

WORD STUDY NOTEBOOK

- Tell children they will listen to and write words with short *a* and long *a*.
- Say the word *ran* and have children write it as a heading in their Word Study Notebooks. Point out that *ran* has the short *a* vowel sound.
- Repeat for the word *came*, having children write it as a second heading. Point out that *came* has the long *a* vowel sound. Spell the words aloud so that children can check their spellings.
- Tell children you will say a word. They are to listen and write the word under the correct heading in their Word Study Notebooks. If a word has the short *a* sound, they should write it under *ran*. If a word has the long *a* sound, they should write it under *came*.
- Say the word *brave*. After children have written the word, hold up the Word Card in order for them to check their spelling. Continue with the remaining words.
- When all the words have been written, call on children to read the lists aloud as the group checks their work.

DAY 5 Assess

Tell children to listen carefully. Say each boldfaced word, read the sentence, and repeat the word. Have children write the word.

1. **came**   Sam *came* to my party.
2. **make**   Will you *make* me a cake?
3. **brave** He was *brave* and did not cry.
4. **late**   Don't be *late* for school.
5. **gave**   I *gave* Maria a ride on my bike.
6. **shape** The cake was in a round *shape*.

RETEACH   **IF** children misspell two or more words, **THEN** revisit the activity on Day 4 and reassess.

OPTIONAL ASSESSMENT   As an alternate assessment, you may have children repeat the Day 1 sort.

Words with Long *i*

SPELLING LIST

1. time
2. like
3. kite
4. bike
5. white
6. drive

Review Words: him, sit, rip, pin

 Reproducible Word Cards are available at **www.thinkcentral.com**.

DIFFERENTIATE INSTRUCTION

Struggling	Advanced
1. am	1. mix
2. at	2. mixed
3. sat	3. hop
4. man	4. hopped
5. dad	5. hope
6. mat	6. hoping
Grade 1, Lesson 1	7. run
	8. running
	9. use
	10. used
	Grade 1, Lesson 26

 **ELL SUPPORT**

Support Word Meaning Provide additional support for ELLs to learn the meanings of the spelling words. As appropriate, use pictures (*kite, bike,* a *white* object) and demonstration (point to a clock to tell about *time,* show children something you *like,* pantomime how to *drive*).

DAY 1 PHONICS **Model the Sort**

Children will sort words with you based on their short and long vowel sounds.

- Display the Lesson 15 Word Cards, and read each word with children. Then point to each word as you use it in a sentence.
- Remind children that they have been learning about words with long vowel sounds. Tell them that today they are going to look at more words with long vowels.
- To begin the sort, display the Word Cards *sit* and *bike* as column headings. Suggested language: **Here is the word *sit*. It has the short *i* sound. Here is the word *bike*. It has the long *i* sound. We'll listen for vowel sounds in words now.**
- Display *time*. Suggested language: *Time.* **Does *time* belong under *sit* or *bike*? The vowel sound in *time* sounds like the long *i* sound, /ī/, in *bike*. I'll put *time* under *bike*.** Repeat for *pin*, placing it under *sit*.
- Continue the process, having children help you sort the remaining words. After all the words have been sorted, shuffle the Word Cards and ask children to help you sort them again.
- Focus on the words in the long *i* column. Read the words aloud with children. Guide them to notice that the long *i* sound, /ī/, can be spelled with *i*-consonant-*e*. Point out that the final *e* does not stand for a sound, but it shows that the *i* probably stands for the long *i* sound.
- Distribute the Lesson 15 Word Cards. Have children repeat the sort independently.

DAY 2 **Guess My Category**

Children will guess the categories for long *i* words you sort.

- Remind children that this week they are learning words with the long *i* sound, /ī/, spelled *i*-consonant-*e*. Repeat the Day 1 sort with children, grouping words by short or long *i*. Then remove the short *i* words.
- Display the Word Cards *like* and *kite* as column headings. Write *Other* as a third column heading. Read the words. Then read and sort the remaining words by spelling pattern (*-ike, -ite, Other*).
- After the words are sorted, have children read down each column. Ask: **In which columns are there rhyming words?** *(the first and second columns)* **What do you notice about the rhyming words in the first column?** *(They both end with the letters* ike *and the sounds /īk/.)* **What do you notice about the rhyming words in the second column?** *(They both end with the letters* ite *and the sounds /īt/.)*
- Have children read aloud the words in the third column. Ask: **Why don't these words belong under *like* or *kite*?** *(They do not end with the letters* ike *or* ite.*)*
- Have partners repeat the sort and record it in their Word Study Notebooks.

like	kite	Other
bike	white	time
		drive

DAY 3 | Word Hunt

Children will sort long and short *i* words they find in their reading.

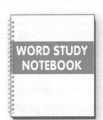

- Tell children they will go on a word hunt in a story they have read.

- Have children make two columns in their Word Study Notebooks and write *white* and *pin* as column headings. Tell them the *white* column is for long *i* words and the *pin* column is for short *i* words.

- Assign children to small groups. Have them read aloud the Decodable Reader story "Mike's Bike" together.

- Then have children look through the story again to find long *i* and short *i* words. Tell them to write the words in the appropriate column in their Word Study Notebooks.

- When children have completed their word hunt, call on group members to read aloud the words in each column.

(Possible responses: Mike's, bike, white, ride, pride, like, stripes, five, time, wide, life; is, it, his, him, its, six, this, grin)

DAY 4 | Blind Writing Sort

Children will sort and write words that you say aloud.

- Tell children that today they will listen to and write words with long and short *i*.

- Say the word *time*. Have children write it as a heading in their Word Study Notebooks. Point out the long *i* vowel sound in *time*. Repeat for the word *rip*, having children write it as a second heading. Point out the short *i* sound in *rip*.

- Display the Word Cards *rip* and *time* to allow children to check the spellings.

- Explain that you will say one word at a time. Children should write the word in the long *i* column or the short *i* column.

- Say the word *him*. Give children time to write the word before showing the Word Card *him*. Have children check the spelling and category. Continue with the remaining words.

- When the sort is complete, have children read their word lists aloud. Emphasize the spelling patterns that suggest long and short vowel sounds in the words: *i*-consonant-*e* and consonant-vowel-consonant.

DAY 5 | Assess

Tell children to listen carefully. Say each boldfaced word, read the sentence, and repeat the word. Have children write the word.

1. **time** — What *time* is it?
2. **like** — I *like* to eat oranges.
3. **kite** — The *kite* was high in the sky.
4. **bike** — My *bike* is blue.
5. **white** — Snow is *white*.
6. **drive** — Can you *drive* me to school?

RETEACH **IF** children misspell two or more words, **THEN** revisit the activity on Day 4 and reassess.

OPTIONAL ASSESSMENT As an alternate assessment, you may have children repeat the Day 1 sort.

Words with Long *o*

SPELLING LIST

1. so
2. go
3. home
4. hole
5. no
6. rope
7. joke
8. bone
9. stove
10. poke

Review Words: time, like, kite, bike, white, drive

 Reproducible Word Cards are available at **www.thinkcentral.com**.

DIFFERENTIATE INSTRUCTION

Struggling	Advanced
1. if	1. hard
2. is	2. harder
3. him	3. hardest
4. rip	4. fast
5. fit	5. faster
6. pin	6. fastest
Grade 1, Lesson 2	7. slow
	8. slower
	9. slowest
	10. sooner
	Grade 1, Lesson 27

 **ELL SUPPORT**

Use Minimal Pairs Some ELLs may need extra support hearing and saying the long *o* sound. Help children hear the correct pronunciation by having them listen to the following pairs of words: *bone/bean, lone/lean, tone/teen*. Say each pair of words again, and have children repeat them.

DAY 1 PHONICS Model the Sort

Children will sort words with you based on their long vowel sounds.

- Display the Lesson 16 Word Cards. Read each word with children. Then point to each word as you use it in a sentence.
- Remind children that they have been learning about words with long vowel sounds. Tell them that today they will look at some more words with long vowels.
- Model sorting the words by vowel sound. Display the Word Cards *kite* and *rope* as column headings. Then say: **I'm going to make one group of words with the same vowel sound as *kite* and another group with the same vowel sound as *rope*.**
- Display the Word Card *bike*. Suggested language: *Bike*. **I will listen for the vowel sound in *bike*: *biiiike*. I hear that *bike* has the same long vowel sound as *kite*. I'll put *bike* under *kite*.** Repeat the process for *go*, placing it under *rope*.
- Sort the remaining words by reading one at a time and asking children where to place it. Read the word lists with children. Then shuffle the cards and have children sort the words with you a second time.
- Read the words in each column with children. Then focus on the column of long *o* words. Guide children to notice that the long *o* sound, /ō/, can be spelled in different ways: with the letter *o* by itself and with *o*-consonant-*e*. Work with children to group the long *o* words by spelling pattern, *o* and *o*-consonant-*e*.
- Distribute the Lesson 16 Word Cards. Have children repeat the sort independently.

DAY 2 Pattern Sort

Children will sort long *o* words according to spelling patterns.

- Remind children that this week's spelling words have the long *o* sound, /ō/, spelled *o* and *o*-consonant-*e*.
- Repeat the Day 1 sort with children. Then set aside the long *i* words.
- Display the Word Cards *no* and *home* side by side to represent the *o* and *o*-consonant-*e* spellings for long *o*. Read the words. Then read the Word Card *so*, and sort it according to spelling pattern. Suggested language: **So ends with the letter *o* and the long *o* sound. The spelling pattern and vowel sound are the same as in the word *no*. I'll put *so* under *no*.**
- Continue to sort the remaining words, asking children to name the category for each word. Then read the words in each column with children. Point out that the words *no, so,* and *go* are rhyming words.
- Tell partners to repeat the sort of long *o* words. Have children write their sorts in their Word Study Notebooks.

no	home
so	hole
go	rope
	joke
	bone
	stove
	poke

DAY 3 Blind Writing Sort

Children will sort and write words that a partner says aloud.

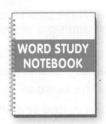

- Point out to children that they know how to write and sort words that you say. Tell them that today they will do the same kind of sort with a partner. They will take turns reading and writing words.
- Have children make two columns by folding and then unfolding a page of their Word Study Notebooks. Tell them to write the column headings *go* and *joke*.
- Explain that one partner will read the long *o* Word Cards one at a time without showing the word. The other partner is to write the word in the correct column based on the long *o* spelling pattern.
- After the writing partner writes each word, the reading partner should show the Word Card. Then the writing partner can check the spelling of the word.
- When all the long *o* words have been written, children should read down each column to check their sort.
- Then children should shuffle the Word Cards and switch roles.

DAY 4 Speed Sort

Children will sort words as quickly as they can.

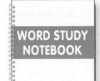

- Remind children that they have done speed sorts on their own. Tell them that today they will work on speed sorts with a partner.
- Provide partners with a set of long *o* Word Cards. Have them read the words together.
- Then have partners set out the Word Cards *so* and *hole* as headings. Tell them that they are to sort the rest of the long *o* words as quickly as they can. They will read each word aloud and place the Word Card in the correct column according to the spelling for long *o*.
- Have partners sort the words. Monitor children's work. When the first speed sort is finished, have partners repeat the sort a few more times to improve their speed.
- After the last sort, have partners write their sorts in their Word Study Notebooks.

DAY 5 Assess

Tell children to listen carefully. Say each boldfaced word, read the sentence, and repeat the word. Have children write the word.

1.	**so**	She runs *so* fast.
2.	**go**	Will you *go* to the party?
3.	**home**	My *home* is close to the school.
4.	**hole**	We dug a *hole* in the ground.
5.	**no**	There are *no* classes today.
6.	**rope**	I use a *rope* to get up the tree.
7.	**joke**	James tells a funny *joke*.
8.	**bone**	The dog chews a *bone*.
9.	**stove**	The *stove* is hot.
10.	**poke**	*Poke* him to wake him up.

RETEACH **IF** children misspell three or more words, **THEN** revisit the activity on Day 2 and reassess.

OPTIONAL ASSESSMENT As an alternate assessment, you may have children repeat the Day 1 sort.

Words with Long *e*

SPELLING LIST

1. me
2. be
3. read
4. feet
5. tree
6. keep
7. eat
8. mean
9. sea
10. these

Review Words: so, go, home, hole, rope, joke

 Reproducible Word Cards are available at **www.thinkcentral.com**.

DIFFERENTIATE INSTRUCTION

Struggling	Advanced
1. log	1. my
2. dot	2. try
3. top	3. sky
4. hot	4. fly
5. lot	5. by
6. ox	6. dry
	7. pie
Grade 1, Lesson 3	8. cried
	9. night
	10. light
	Grade 1, Lesson 28

 **ELL SUPPORT**

Linguistic Transfer The long *e* phoneme should not cause difficulties for most ELLs. However, be sure to point out that in English, long vowel sounds are often spelled with more than one letter and more than one spelling pattern.

DAY 1 PHONICS Model the Sort

Children will sort words with you based on their long vowel sounds.

- Display the Lesson 17 Word Cards. Read each word with children.
- Remind children that they have been learning about words with long vowel sounds. Tell them that today they will look at more words with long vowels.
- Display the Word Cards *so* and *be*. Suggested language: **I will put *so* at the top of one column and *be* at the top of another column. I will read a word, and you tell me if the vowel sound is the same as in *so* or *be*. I'll do the first one by myself.**
- Pick up the Word Card *home,* and read it aloud. Suggested language: *Home.* **Listen for the vowel sound. *Hoooome. Home, so. Home, be.*** The vowel sound in *home* sounds like the long *o* sound, /ō/, in *so*. **I'll put *home* under *so*.** Repeat the process for *me,* placing it under *be*.
- Continue the process with each Word Card, allowing children to name the correct column for each word. After all the words have been sorted, shuffle the Word Cards and ask children to help you sort them again.
- Then draw attention to the Word Cards in the long *e* column. Explain that the long *e* sound, /ē/, can be spelled with *e* by itself, *ea, ee,* and *e*-consonant-*e*. Have children help you group Word Cards with the same spelling for /ē/, leaving *these* in a category by itself. Point out that in *these,* the *e* at the end is silent.
- Distribute the Lesson 17 Word Cards. Have children repeat the sort independently.

DAY 2 Guess My Category

Children will recognize long *e* spelling patterns in words that you sort.

- Repeat the sort from Day 1, allowing children to help you sort the words by long vowel sound. Then set aside the words with long *o*.
- Display the Word Cards *me, sea, feet,* and *these* as column headings. Read each remaining word aloud, and place it under the word with the same spelling pattern.
- After all the long *e* Word Cards have been sorted, have children read down each column and explain how the words are similar. *(They have the same spelling for long* e.*)* After you have discussed each column by itself, point out the four different spellings that stand for the long *e* sound, /ē/.
- Highlight several rhyming words to draw attention to different spellings for the same sound. Display the Word Cards *be, tree,* and *sea*. Remind children that all the words have the long *e* sound.
- Have children read the words aloud to listen for another way in which they are alike. Suggested language: **These words rhyme even though they each have a different spelling for the long *e* sound.**
- Have children repeat the sort independently and write their sorts in their Word Study Notebooks.

me	sea	feet	these
be	read	tree	
	eat	keep	
	mean		

DAY 3 Blind Writing Sort

Children will sort and write words that a partner says aloud.

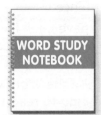

- Have children divide two facing pages in their Word Study Notebooks into two columns each for a total of four columns. Have them write these column headings: *read, tree, be, these*.
- Ask children to work with a partner. One child should read each long *e* Word Card aloud without showing the word to his or her partner.
- The other child should write the word under the correct column heading according to the long *e* spelling pattern.
- After each word has been written, the child reading the Word Card should place the card face up on the desk so the partner can confirm or correct the spelling.
- Have children read down each column after all the words have been written correctly.
- Then have partners shuffle the Word Cards and switch roles.

DAY 4 Word Hunt

Children will sort words that they find in their reading.

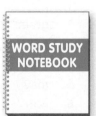

- Remind children that they have been reading and writing words with the long *e* sound. Ask them to make a three-column chart in their Word Study Notebooks and write *eat, tree,* and *these* as column headings.

- Have partners read the Decodable Reader story "At the Beach." Then tell partners to read the story again, this time hunting for words with the long *e* sound.
- Tell children to record each word they find under the heading with the same long *e* spelling.
- When complete, ask children to read their word lists aloud and check that they are correct.

(Possible responses: Pete, meet, beach, each, week, green, eat, sweet, peaches, keep, sea, feet, neat, beast, eel)

DAY 5 Assess

Tell children to listen carefully. Say each word, read the sentence, and repeat the word. Have children write the word.

1.	**me**	Bring the coat to *me*.
2.	**be**	When will you *be* home?
3.	**read**	I like to *read* books.
4.	**feet**	My *feet* help me move.
5.	**tree**	The tall *tree* had many leaves.
6.	**keep**	Can you *keep* my dog at your house?
7.	**eat**	I like to *eat* apples.
8.	**mean**	I did not *mean* to drop the glass.
9.	**sea**	I like to swim in the *sea*.
10.	**these**	I love *these* cookies.

RETEACH **IF** children misspell three or more words, **THEN** revisit the activity on Day 2 and reassess.

Words with Long *a*

1. play
2. grain
3. sail
4. mail
5. may
6. rain
7. way
8. day
9. stay
10. pain

Review Words: sea, read, mean, feet, keep, tree

 Reproducible Word Cards are available at **www.thinkcentral.com**.

DIFFERENTIATE INSTRUCTION

Struggling	Advanced
1. yet	1. sad
2. web	2. sadly
3. pen	3. slow
4. wet	4. slowly
5. leg	5. dust
6. hen	6. dusty
Grade 1, Lesson 4	7. trick
	8. tricky
	9. help
	10. helpful
	Grade 1, Lesson 29

 ELL SUPPORT

Linguistic Transfer Spanish speakers may substitute the short *e* sound for the long *a* sound, pronouncing the word *pain* as *pen*. Read the list of spelling words, emphasizing the long *a* sound in each word. Point out your mouth position as you say the long *a* sound. Then read the words again. Have children repeat the words after you.

DAY 1 PHONICS **Model the Sort**

Children will sort words with you based on their long vowel sounds.

- Display the Lesson 18 Word Cards, and read each word aloud. Then point to each word as you use it in a sentence.
- Remind children that they have been learning different spellings for long vowel sounds. Tell them that today they will learn some spellings for long *a* and review spellings for long *e*.
- Model sorting the words. Use the Word Cards *tree* and *stay* as column headings. Suggested language: **I'm going to read a word. Listen for the vowel sound and tell me if it's the same as in *tree* or *stay*. Listen as I do the first one.**
- Display the Word Card *rain*: *Rain*. **Listen for the vowel sound.** *Rain*. **Now listen to these words together.** *Rain, tree. Rain, stay.* **The vowel sound in *rain* sounds like the vowel sound in *stay*—the long *a* sound, /ā/. I'll put *rain* under *stay*.** Repeat the process for *read*, placing it under *tree*.
- Continue the process, prompting children to guide you in placing each word in the correct column. When the sort is finished, read the word lists together. Then shuffle the Word Cards and ask children to help you sort the words again.
- Focus on the long *a* column. Help children notice the different spellings for long *a*: *ay*, *ai*. Ask them to help you group the long *a* words according to the spelling patterns *ay* and *ai*.
- Give partners a set of Lesson 18 Word Cards. Have them repeat the sort together.

DAY 2 **Pattern Sort**

Children will sort long *a* words according to spelling patterns.

- Remind children that this week's words have the long *a* sound, /ā/, spelled *ay* and *ai*.
- Repeat the Day 1 sort, having children help you sort the Word Cards by long *e* or long *a*. Then remove the long *e* words.
- Display the Word Cards *way* and *mail* as column headings. Read the words. Begin a sort of *ay* and *ai* words. Read the Word Card *pain*. Ask: **Does the long *a* sound in *pain* come in the middle or at the end of the word?** After children respond, place the Word Card under *mail*. Repeat for each long *a* word until they have all been sorted.
- Read aloud the first column of words with children. Remind them that these words all have the long *a* sound at the end. Ask: **How is the long *a* sound spelled when it comes at the end of a word?** *(ay)* Repeat for the second column of words, eliciting that the long *a* sound in the middle of these words is spelled with *ai*.
- Tell children to repeat the sort independently and write it in their Word Study Notebooks.

way	mail
play	pain
may	grain
day	sail
stay	rain

DAY 3   Word Hunt

Children will sort long *a* words they find in their reading.

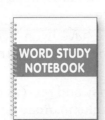

WORD STUDY NOTEBOOK

- Remind children that they have been reading and writing words with long *a*. Tell them that today they will hunt for long *a* words in a story they have read.

- Have children write the words *day* and *sail* as column headings in their Word Study Notebooks. Tell them they will write *ay* words they find under *day*. They will write *ai* words under *sail*.

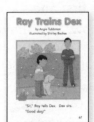

- Have partners read the Decodable Reader story "Ray Trains Dex." Then have them page through the story again to find words with the long *a* sound. Tell children to write each long *a* word in the correct column in their Word Study Notebooks.

- When children have finished their word hunt, tell partners to take turns reading their word lists aloud. Have them check that each long *a* word is in the correct column.

(Possible responses: Ray, trains, stay, waits, tail, stray, Kay)

DAY 4   Speed Sort

Children will sort words as quickly as they can.

WORD STUDY NOTEBOOK

- Sort the long *a* Word Cards with children, grouping the words according to spelling patterns: *ai* or *ay*.

- Tell children that now they will work with a partner to sort the long *a* words as quickly as they can.

- Direct partners to place the Word Cards *may* and *pain* as column headings. Explain that they are to read aloud each of the long *a* words and put the Word Card in the correct column according to the spelling pattern.

- Have partners complete one speed sort. Ask children to read down the columns and check their work. Then have partners shuffle the Word Cards and repeat the sort a few times, each time working to improve their speed.

- After the last sort, have children write their sorts in their Word Study Notebooks.

DAY 5   Assess

Tell children to listen carefully. Say each boldfaced word, read the sentence, and repeat the word. Have children write the word.

1. **play**   Lisa likes to *play*.
2. **grain**   Wheat is a *grain*.
3. **sail**   We saw the boat *sail* away.
4. **mail**   I like getting *mail*.
5. **may**   *May* I have an apple?
6. **rain**   The sky grew dark and *rain* fell.
7. **way**   Mike knows the *way* home.
8. **day**   What *day* are you leaving?
9. **stay**   Will you *stay* at my house?
10. **pain**   I felt a *pain* in my arm.

RETEACH   **IF** children misspell three or more words, **THEN** revisit the activity on Day 2 and reassess.

OPTIONAL ASSESSMENT   As an alternate assessment, you may have children repeat the Day 1 sort.

Words with Long *o*

SPELLING LIST

1. show
2. row
3. grow
4. low
5. blow
6. snow
7. boat
8. coat
9. road
10. toad

Review Words: play, may, day, grain, mail, rain

 Reproducible Word Cards are available at **www.thinkcentral.com**.

DIFFERENTIATE INSTRUCTION

Struggling	Advanced
1. up	1. even
2. bug	2. open
3. mud	3. begin
4. nut	4. baby
5. hug	5. tiger
6. tub	6. music
Grade 1, Lesson 5	7. paper
	8. zero
	9. table
	10. below
	Grade 1, Lesson 30

 ELL SUPPORT

Use Minimal Pairs Hmong speakers may pronounce the long vowel sound /ō/ as /ô/ (as in *thought*). Say the word pairs *boat/bought* and *coat/caught* to help children hear the distinction in vowel sounds. Then have children repeat the pairs of words after you.

DAY 1 PHONICS Model the Sort

Children will sort words with you based on long vowel sounds.

- Display the Lesson 19 Word Cards. Read the words aloud. Then point to each word as you use it in a sentence.
- Remind children that they have been learning about spellings for long vowel sounds. Explain that today they will learn about more spellings for long *o* and review spellings for long *a*.
- Display the Word Cards *day* and *road* as column headings. Suggested language: ***Day* is at the top of the first column. *Road* is at the top of the second column. I'm going to read a word. You will tell me if the word has the same vowel sound as *day* or *road*. I'm going to do the first one.**
- Display the Word Card *snow*. Say: *Snow.* **Listen for the vowel sound.** *Snow. Snow, day. Snow, road. Snow* **has the same vowel sound as** *road*, **the long *o* sound, /ō/. So I'll put *snow* under *road*.** Use the same procedure for *mail*, placing it under *day*.
- Sort the remaining words, prompting children to help you. Read the word lists with children. Then shuffle the cards. Ask children to help you sort the words again.
- Call attention to the words in the long *o* column. Guide children to recognize that the long *o* sound, /ō/, can be spelled with the letter pairs *ow* and *oa*. Have children help you group the long *o* words by spelling patterns, *ow* and *oa*.
- Give each child a set of Lesson 19 Word Cards. Have children repeat the sort independently.

DAY 2 Pattern Sort

Children will sort long *o* words according to spelling patterns.

- Remind children that this week's words have the long *o* sound, /ō/, spelled *ow* and *oa*.
- Repeat the sort from Day 1, allowing children to help you sort the words by long *a* and long *o*. Then set aside the words with long *a*.
- Place the Word Cards *grow* and *toad* as column headings, and read the words. Then sort the remaining words by whether the long *o* sound is in the middle or at the end of the word. Begin by reading aloud the Word Card *show*. Ask: **Does the long *o* sound in *show* come in the middle or at the end of the word?**
- After children respond, place the Word Card under *grow*. Point out that in both words, the long *o* sound is at the end. Repeat the process for the remaining words.
- Read aloud the first column of words with children. Remind them that these words all have the long *o* sound at the end. Ask: **How is the long *o* sound spelled when it comes at the end of these words?** *(ow)* Repeat for the second column of words, eliciting that the long *o* sound in the middle of these words is spelled with *oa*.
- Have children repeat the sort independently and record their sorts in their Word Study Notebooks.

grow	toad
show	boat
row	coat
low	road
blow	
snow	

DAY 3 Blind Writing Sort

Children will sort and write words that a partner says.

WORD STUDY NOTEBOOK

- Tell children that today they will work with a partner to listen to and write long *o* words.
- Have children write the column headings *low* and *coat* in their Word Study Notebooks. Spell the words aloud as children check how they spelled the words.
- Have partners work together. One partner reads aloud each long *o* Word Card without showing the word. The other partner writes the word under the correct column heading, *low* or *coat*, according to how the long *o* sound is spelled in the word.
- After each word is written, the child reading the Word Cards should display the card so the partner can confirm or correct the spelling. Then the partner should read his or her list aloud to confirm that the words are in the appropriate column.
- Then ask partners to switch roles and repeat the steps.

DAY 4 Meaning Sort

Children will sort words according to meaning.

WORD STUDY NOTEBOOK

- Read and review the long *o* words with children. Name a few of the words for volunteers to act out, such as *show*, *coat*, and *low*.
- Tell children that they will help you sort the long *o* words according to their meanings. Write these words on blank cards as column headings: *Name, Action, Describe*. Explain that some of the spelling words are naming words, some are action words, and some are describing words.
- Display the Word Card *boat* and have children read it aloud. Suggested language: **The word *boat* names something that carries people on water. I'll put *boat* under the heading *Name*.** Continue in a similar way with the other words.
- Have partners work together to repeat the sort and then record it in their Word Study Notebooks. When children finish, ask them to read their lists and underline the letters that stand for the long *o* sound in each word.

DAY 5 Assess

Tell children to listen carefully. Say each boldfaced word, read the sentence, and repeat the word. Have children write the word.

1.	**show**	Can you *show* me how to ride a bike?
2.	**row**	The books are all in a *row*.
3.	**grow**	We *grow* plants in our house.
4.	**low**	The sun is *low* in the sky.
5.	**blow**	See the wind *blow*.
6.	**snow**	I want to play in the *snow*.
7.	**boat**	The *boat* sails on water.
8.	**coat**	Wear your *coat* when it is cold.
9.	**road**	Cars move fast on the *road*.
10.	**toad**	The *toad* hopped out of the mud.

RETEACH **IF** children misspell three or more words, **THEN** revisit the activity on Day 2 and reassess.

OPTIONAL ASSESSMENT As an alternate assessment, you may have children repeat the Day 1 sort.

Compound Words

SPELLING LIST

1. bedtime
2. sunset
3. bathtub
4. sailboat
5. flagpole
6. backpack
7. playpen
8. raincoat
9. inside
10. himself

 Reproducible Word Cards are available at **www.thinkcentral.com**.

DIFFERENTIATE INSTRUCTION

Struggling	Advanced
1. an	1. spin
2. bad	2. clap
3. can	3. grade
4. had	4. swim
5. cat	5. place
6. ran	6. last
Grade 1, Lesson 6	7. test
	8. skin
	9. drag
	10. glide
	11. just
	12. stage
	Grade 2, Lesson 5

ELL SUPPORT

Support Word Meaning Use pictures to help ELLs understand the meanings of the compound words. For example, show a picture of a flagpole. Point to and name the flag and the pole. Explain that knowing the meaning of each small word can help children understand the meaning of the compound word. Tell them that a *flagpole* is a *pole* for a *flag*.

DAY 1 PHONICS Model the Sort

Children will name compound words by combining base words.

- Display the Lesson 20 Word Cards, and read the words aloud. Then point to each word as you use it in a sentence. Make a duplicate set of Word Cards and cut each card to create Word Cards for the smaller words that make up each compound word.
- Tell children that today they will help you build one word from two smaller words. Model the procedure. Show the Word Cards *sun* and *set*. Suggested language: **I put the word *sun* in the first column. I put the word *set* in the second column.**
- Place the Word Card *sunset* in a third column. Say: **When I put the words *sun* and *set* together, I spell a new word, *sunset*. This kind of word is called a *compound* word.**
- Continue in the same way, placing the two smaller words in the first two columns. Read the two words. Then ask children to name the compound word before placing the corresponding Word Card in the third column.
- Read the words in the first two columns with children. Help children notice that these smaller words can have different vowel sounds and different spelling patterns.
- Then read the compound words with children. Emphasize that compound words are formed and spelled by putting two smaller words together.
- Distribute two sets of Lesson 20 Word Cards to partners. Help them use one set of cards to cut apart the base words. Then have them repeat the sort together.

DAY 2 Guess My Category

Children will guess the categories for base words and compound words.

- Briefly review the concept of compound words. Remind children that compound words are spelled by putting two smaller words together.
- Place the Word Cards *bed, time,* and *bedtime* in a row to represent the first smaller word, the second smaller word, and the compound word formed by combining the two smaller words. Then read the Word Cards *flag, pole,* and *flagpole,* and place them in columns below the first set of words.
- Continue in the same way with the remaining smaller words and compound words.
- When all the words have been sorted, have children read down the third column. Ask: **What kind of words are these?** (compound words)
- Then have children read down the first column of words. Guide them to recognize that these are the first words that make up the compound words. Do the same for the words in the second column.
- Have partners work together to repeat the sort.

bed	time	bedtime
flag	pole	flagpole
sail	boat	sailboat
in	side	inside
back	pack	backpack

Meaning Sort

Children will sort compound words according to meaning.

- Remind children that they have been learning about compound words. Tell them that today they will sort the week's words by meaning.
- Display the Word Card *flagpole*, and read the word. Explain that a flagpole is a thing, so you will start a group of words that name things. Read and place *playpen* in the same group. Then read *bedtime*, and begin a new group for words that name times.
- Continue to sort the words with children, adding the categories *Place* and *Person*.
- When all the words have been sorted, read the groups of words with children.
- Have children repeat the sort with a partner. Tell them to write their sorts in their Word Study Notebooks.

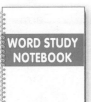 Word Hunt

Children will write compound words they find in their reading.

- Tell children that today they will look for compound words in a story they have read.
- Have partners reread the Decodable Reader story "Bedtime for Ray."
- Tell children to go through the story a second time to look for compound words. They should use their Word Study Notebooks and write each compound word, along with the two smaller words that make up the compound word.
- When complete, ask children to read their word lists aloud and check that they have correctly written the compound words and the smaller words.

(Possible responses: bedtime, weekday, bathtub, bedside)

Assess

Tell children to listen carefully. Say each boldfaced word, read the sentence, and repeat the word. Have children write the word.

1. **bedtime**   When is your *bedtime?*
2. **sunset**   The *sunset* is at the end of the day.
3. **bathtub**   I play in my *bathtub*.
4. **sailboat** A *sailboat* moves fast in the wind.
5. **flagpole** Each day the flag goes up the *flagpole*.
6. **backpack** I carry my books in a *backpack*.
7. **playpen**   The baby has a *playpen*.
8. **raincoat** I have a red *raincoat*.
9. **inside**   Look *inside* the box.
10. **himself** He made it *himself*.

RETEACH   **IF** children misspell two or more words, **THEN** revisit the activity on Day 2 and reassess.

OPTIONAL ASSESSMENT   As an alternate assessment, you may have children repeat the Day 1 sort.

Words with *ar*

SPELLING LIST

1. far
2. arm
3. yard
4. art
5. jar
6. bar
7. barn
8. bark
9. card
10. yarn

Review Words: am, at, bad, can, ran, dad

 Reproducible Word Cards are available at **www.thinkcentral.com**.

DIFFERENTIATE INSTRUCTION

Struggling	Advanced
1. in	1. next
2. will	2. end
3. did	3. camp
4. sit	4. sank
5. six	5. sing
6. big	6. drink
	7. hunt
	8. stand
	9. long
	10. stamp
	11. pond
	12. bring

Grade 1, Lesson 7

Grade 2, Lesson 6

ELL SUPPORT

Use Minimal Pairs ELLs may need additional support hearing and saying the /är/ sound. Help children hear the correct pronunciation by asking them to listen to the following pairs of words: *cat/cart, mat/mart, at/art*. Have them watch your mouth position as you say each word. Then say each pair of words again. Have children repeat them.

DAY 1 PHONICS **Model the Sort**

Children will sort words with you based on their vowel sounds.

- Display the Lesson 21 Word Cards, and read each word aloud. Then point to each word as you use it in a sentence.
- Remind children that they have learned about words with short vowel sounds. Tell them that today they are going to look at words with the sound /är/.
- Model sorting the words by vowel sound. Use the Word Cards *can* and *jar* as column headings. Suggested language: **Can. The word *can* has the short *a* sound. *Jar*. In *jar*, the *a* along with the *r* stands for a different sound, /är/. *Jar*, /är/.**
- Read the Word Card *yard*. Suggested language: **Yard. Does *yard* have the same vowel sound as *can* or *jar*? Listen for the vowel sound in *yard*. Yard, can. Yard, jar. Yard and *jar* both have the sound /är/, so I'll put *yard* under *jar*. Repeat for *dad*,** placing it under *can*.
- Continue in the same way with the remaining Word Cards, having children help you sort the words. After all the words have been sorted, shuffle the Word Cards and ask children to help you sort them again. Then read the word lists together.
- Read the words in the column under *jar* with children. Guide them to notice that the sound /är/ is spelled with the letters *ar*.
- Give each child a set of Lesson 21 Word Cards. Have them repeat the sort independently.

DAY 2 **Pattern Sort**

Children will sort *ar* words according to spelling patterns.

- Remind children that this week's spelling words have the sound /är/ spelled *ar*.
- Repeat the Day 1 sort of short *a* words and *ar* words with children. Then set aside the short *a* words.
- Display the Word Cards *card*, *bar*, and *yarn* as column headings. Write *Other* as a fourth column heading. Read the words. Then show the Word Card *barn*, and read the word. Suggested language: **Barn has the /är/ sound. It has the letters *ar* in the middle and ends with *n*. I'll put *barn* under *yarn* because they both end with *arn*.**
- Continue to sort the remaining words, asking children to tell you where to place them. Then read the words in each column with children.
- Point out the rhyming words in each of the first three columns.
- Have children repeat the sort independently and write their sorts in their Word Study Notebooks.

card	bar	yarn	Other
yard	far	barn	arm
	jar		art
			bark

DAY 3 Blind Writing Sort

Children will sort and write words that a partner says aloud.

WORD STUDY NOTEBOOK

- Tell children that today they will listen to and write words with the sound /är/.
- Have children divide two facing pages of their Word Study Notebooks into two columns each. Tell them to write these four column headings: *yard, far, barn, Other*. Spell the words aloud as children check how they spelled the words.
- Have children work in pairs. One partner will read aloud each Word Card without showing the word. The other child will write the word under the heading with the same sounds and spelling at the end of the word.
- After each word is written, the child reading the Word Cards should display the card. Then the partner can confirm or correct the spelling.
- Once all the words have been written correctly, have children read each word list.
- Then have partners switch roles and repeat the sort.

DAY 4 Open Sort

Children will sort words according to categories of their choice.

WORD STUDY NOTEBOOK

- Have partners work together to choose their own categories for sorting the week's *ar* spelling words.
- Read the words with children. Make a few suggestions for categories such as these: *words that rhyme, words that begin with the same letter, three-letter words, four-letter words.*
- Have partners discuss the words and choose their categories. Help them write the column headings in their Word Study Notebooks.
- Then tell partners to sort the Word Cards into their correct categories. Have each child write the completed sort in his or her Word Study Notebook.
- When all the children have finished, ask partners to explain how they sorted the words. Have them read the words in each column.
- Guide children to understand and correct any errors.

DAY 5 Assess

Tell children to listen carefully. Say each boldfaced word, read the sentence, and repeat the word. Have children write the word.

1. **far**   How *far* is it to school from your house?
2. **arm**   I throw with my left *arm*.
3. **yard**   I like to run in my *yard*.
4. **art**   My mother hangs my *art* on the wall.
5. **jar**   Jam comes in a *jar*.
6. **bar**   My shirt hangs on a *bar*.
7. **barn**   Cows live in a *barn*.
8. **bark**   Trees have *bark*.
9. **card**   I got a *card* for my pal.
10. **yarn**   The cat plays with *yarn*.

RETEACH   **IF** children misspell three or more words, **THEN** revisit the activity on Day 2 and reassess.

OPTIONAL ASSESSMENT   As an alternate assessment, you may have children repeat the Day 1 sort.

Words with *er, ir, ur*

SPELLING LIST

1. her
2. fern
3. girl
4. sir
5. stir
6. bird
7. fur
8. hurt
9. turn
10. third

Review Words: far, yard, art, barn, card, bark

 Reproducible Word Cards are available at **www.thinkcentral.com**.

DIFFERENTIATE INSTRUCTION

Struggling	Advanced
1. on	1. rock
2. got	2. black
3. fox	3. trick
4. pop	4. kick
5. not	5. full
6. hop	6. dress
Grade 1, Lesson 8	7. neck
	8. add
	9. spell
	10. stuck
	11. class
	12. doll
	Grade 2, Lesson 7

 **ELL SUPPORT**

Use Minimal Pairs The /ûr/ sound may be challenging for ELLs to hear and to pronounce. Help children hear the correct pronunciation by having them listen to the following pairs of words: *fin/fern, bin/burn, tin/turn.* Say each pair of words again, and have children repeat them.

DAY 1 PHONICS Model the Sort

Children will sort words with you based on their vowel sounds.

- Display the Lesson 22 Word Cards, and read them aloud. Then point to each word as you use it in a sentence.
- Remind children that they have learned about words with the /är/ sound. Tell them that today they are going to look at words with the /ûr/ sound.
- Display the Word Card *bark* as one column heading and the Word Card *turn* as another column heading. Read each word. Suggested language: **I will say a word. You will tell me if the word has the /är/ sound as in *bark* or the /ûr/ sound as in *turn*. I'll do the first one.**
- Display the Word Card *girl*. Suggested language: ***Girl*. *Girl* has the /ûr/ sound, just like *turn*. I'll put *girl* under *turn*.** Repeat for *card*, placing it under *bark*.
- Sort the remaining Word Cards by reading one at a time and asking children where to place it. Shuffle the cards and have children sort the words with you a second time. Then read the word lists with children.
- Focus on the words under *turn*. Read the words aloud with children. Guide them to recognize that the /ûr/ sound can be spelled in different ways.
- Explain that the /ûr/ sound can be spelled with the letters *er, ir,* or *ur*. Have children help you group the Word Cards according to these spelling patterns.
- Distribute the Lesson 22 Word Cards. Have children repeat the sort independently.

DAY 2 Pattern Sort

Children will sort *er, ir,* and *ur* words according to spelling patterns.

- Remind children that this week's words have the sound /ûr/ spelled *er, ir,* and *ur*.
- Work with children to repeat the sort from Day 1, grouping the words by the sounds /är/ and /ûr/. Then remove the words with *ar*.
- Display the Word Cards *fern, sir,* and *hurt* as column headings. Read each word and point out the sound /ûr/ and its spelling: *er, ir,* or *ur*. Model the sort by displaying and reading the Word Card *bird*. Suggested language: **The sound /ûr/ in *bird* is spelled with the letters *ir*. So I'll put *bird* under *sir*.**
- Have partners work with a set of *er, ir,* and *ur* Word Cards. Tell them to set up the same words that you used as column headings. *(fern, sir, hurt)* Then have partners sort the remaining words by spelling pattern.
- When all pairs have finished sorting, ask children to read the words in the first column. Ask: **How are these words alike?** *(They both have the /ûr/ sound spelled with the letters* er.*)* Repeat for the second and third columns. *(They all have the /ûr/ sound spelled* ir. *They all have the /ûr/ sound spelled* ur.*)*
- Have children repeat the sort and write their sorts in their Word Study Notebooks.

fern	sir	hurt
her	bird	fur
	girl	turn
	stir	
	third	

DAY 3 Word Hunt

Children will sort words that they find in their reading.

- Remind children that they have been learning about words with the /ûr/ sound. Tell them that today they will hunt for words with the /ûr/ sound in a story they have read.

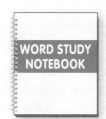

- Have children write these headings in their Word Study Notebooks: *her, girl, fur.* Tell them that when they find a word with the /ûr/ sound, they will write it under the word with the same spelling for /ûr/.

- Organize children into groups of three. Have them read aloud the Decodable Reader story "A Bath for Mert."

- Assign each group member one of the /ûr/ spellings: *er, ir, ur.* Then have children go through the story a second time, looking for words with the spelling they have been assigned. Have all group members write each word in their Word Study Notebooks under the correct heading.

- When children have finished, ask volunteers to read aloud each word list.

(Possible responses: Mert, her; dirt, first; curled, Burt)

DAY 4 Blind Writing Sort

Children will sort and write words that a partner says aloud.

- Tell children that today they will take turns reading and writing /ûr/ words with a partner.

- Have children divide a page of their Word Study Notebooks into three columns with the headings *er, ir,* and *ur.* Write the headings on the board for children to copy.

- Provide one set of the /ûr/ Word Cards. Explain that one partner reads aloud one Word Card at a time without showing the word. The other partner writes the word in the correct column based on how the /ûr/ sound is spelled: *er, ir, ur.*

- After a word is written, the reader shows the Word Card so that the writer can check or correct the spelling.

- When all the words are written, have children read the words in each column to check that they are correctly placed.

- Then have partners shuffle the Word Cards and switch roles.

DAY 5 Assess

Tell children to listen carefully. Say each boldfaced word, read the sentence, and repeat the word. Have children write the word.

1. **her**	*Her* coat was on my desk.	
2. **fern**	A green *fern* grew in my yard.	
3. **girl**	The *girl* ate a snack after school.	
4. **sir**	Please *sir,* which way is the bus?	
5. **stir**	Please *stir* the cake mix.	

6. **bird**	The *bird* sat in a tree.
7. **fur**	The cat licks its *fur.*
8. **hurt**	Kim got *hurt* on the playground.
9. **turn**	Do we *turn* right or left onto Oak Lane?
10. **third**	My brother is in *third* grade.

RETEACH   IF children misspell three or more words, **THEN** revisit the activity on Day 2 and reassess.

OPTIONAL ASSESSMENT   As an alternate assessment, you may have children repeat the Day 1 sort.

Words with *oo* (/o͝o/)

SPELLING LIST

1. look
2. book
3. good
4. hook
5. brook
6. took
7. foot
8. shook
9. wood
10. hood

Review Words: low, show, boat, coat, road, toad

 Reproducible Word Cards are available at **www.thinkcentral.com**.

DIFFERENTIATE INSTRUCTION

Struggling	Advanced
1. yes	1. dish
2. let	2. than
3. red	3. chest
4. ten	4. such
5. bed	5. thin
6. get	6. push
	7. shine
Grade 1, Lesson 9	8. chase
	9. white
	10. while
	11. these
	12. flash
	Grade 2, Lesson 8

 **ELL SUPPORT**

Use Minimal Pairs Some ELLs may need support pronouncing the vowel sound /o͝o/. Say the following pairs of words as children listen: *back/book, tack/took, shack/shook*. Repeat each word pair. Ask children to raise a hand when they hear a word with the sound /o͝o/. Have them say the word.

DAY 1 · PHONICS · Model the Sort

Children will sort words with you based on their vowel sounds.

- Display the Lesson 23 Word Cards, and read each word aloud. Then point to each word as you use it in a sentence.
- Remind children that they have learned about many different vowel sounds. Tell them that today they are going to look at words with the vowel sound /o͝o/.
- Explain that you will sort words by their vowel sound. Display the Word Cards *show* and *took* as column headings. Read each word. Suggested language: *Show* **is at the top of the first column.** *Took* **is at the top of the second column. I'm going to read a word. You will tell me if the word has the same vowel sound as** *show* **or** *took*. **I'll do the first one.**
- Say *coat* as you hold up the Word Card. Suggested language: *Coat.* **Listen for the vowel sound.** *Coat.* **Now I will compare the words.** *Coat, show. Coat, took.* **The vowel sound in** *coat* **sounds like the vowel sound in** *show*—**the long o sound, /ō/. So I'll put** *coat* **under** *show*. **Use the same procedure for** *foot*, **placing it under** *took*.
- Continue the process, allowing children to guide you in placing each Word Card in the correct column. When the sort is finished, read the word lists together. Then shuffle the Word Cards and ask children to help you sort them again.
- Read the words in the column under *took* with children. Ask them to identify the letters that stand for the vowel sound /o͝o/ in the middle of these words. *(oo)*
- Distribute the Lesson 23 Word Cards. Have children repeat the sort independently.

DAY 2 · Guess My Category

Children will guess the categories for words you sort.

- Remind children that this week's words have the vowel sound /o͝o/ spelled *oo*.
- Repeat the sort from Day 1, allowing children to help you group words by vowel sound. Then remove the long o words.
- Tell children you will sort the *oo* words and you want them to guess the categories. Read the Word Cards *book* and *hood*. Display them as column headings.
- Display and read the Word Card *good*. Place it under *hood*. Continue to read and sort *look, hook, brook, took, shook,* and *wood* into categories of rhyming words.
- Read the first column of words with children. Ask them to tell how the words are alike. *(They end with the letters* ook *and the sounds /o͝ok/.)* Repeat for the second column. *(They end with the letters* ood *and the sounds /o͝od/.)* Elicit that the words in each column rhyme.
- Then display the Word Card *foot*. Guide children to recognize that even though the word *foot* has the /o͝o/ sound, it does not rhyme with the other words. Add a third column with the heading *Other*. Place *foot* in the new category.
- Have children repeat the sort independently and write their sorts in their Word Study Notebooks.

book	hood	Other
look	good	foot
hook	wood	
brook		
took		
shook		

MAJOR UNDERSTANDING: The vowel sound /o͝o/ heard in the middle of the word *book* is spelled with the letters *oo*.

DAY 3 Blind Writing Sort

Children will sort and write words that a partner says aloud.

WORD STUDY NOTEBOOK

- Tell children that they will work with a partner to read and write words with the vowel sound /o͝o/.
- Have children set up three columns in their Word Study Notebooks. They should write *good, shook,* and *Other* as the column headings. Spell *good* and *shook* aloud as children check how they spelled the words. Write *Other* on a blank word card or on the board for children to copy.
- Explain that one partner will read aloud each Word Card without showing the word. The other child will write the word under the correct column heading according to the spelling pattern.
- After a word is written, the reader should show the Word Card so the writer can confirm or correct the spelling.
- Once all the words are written correctly, ask partners to read each list to verify that the words are in the correct column.
- Then have partners switch roles and repeat the sort.

DAY 4 Speed Sort

Children will sort words as quickly as they can.

WORD STUDY NOTEBOOK

- Sort the *oo* Word Cards with children, grouping the words according to the spelling patterns *-ook, -ood,* and *-oot.*
- Tell children that they will work with a partner to sort the *oo* words as quickly as they can. Write these headings on the board: *-ook, -ood, -oot.* Have partners take turns writing the headings on blank word cards or strips of paper.
- Tell children to set out the headings and then sort the Word Cards as quickly as possible.
- When they have finished the first sort, ask children to read the words in each category. Then have partners shuffle the Word Cards and repeat the sort a few times, trying to sort more and more quickly each time without making any errors.
- After the last sort, have children write their sorts in their Word Study Notebooks.

DAY 5 Assess

Tell children to listen carefully. Say each boldfaced word, read the sentence, and repeat the word. Have children write the word.

1. **look** — *Look* at the boat.
2. **book** — I left my *book* at home.
3. **good** — The pie was *good* to eat.
4. **hook** — Hang your coat on the *hook*.
5. **brook** — The *brook* was full of water.
6. **took** — John *took* his lunch to school.
7. **foot** — I put my shoe on my *foot*.
8. **shook** — The dog *shook* the water off.
9. **wood** — We use *wood* to make a fire.
10. **hood** — My coat has a *hood* for my head.

RETEACH **IF** children misspell three or more words, **THEN** revisit the activity on Day 2 and reassess.

OPTIONAL ASSESSMENT As an alternate assessment, you may have children repeat the Day 1 sort.

Words with *oo, ou, ew*

SPELLING LIST

1. soon
2. new
3. noon
4. zoo
5. boot
6. too
7. moon
8. blew
9. soup
10. you

Review Words: book, foot, brook, wood, good, look

 Reproducible Word Cards are available at **www.thinkcentral.com**.

DIFFERENTIATE INSTRUCTION

Struggling	Advanced
1. us	1. liked
2. sun	2. using
3. but	3. riding
4. fun	4. chased
5. bus	5. spilled
6. run	6. making
Grade 1, Lesson 10	7. closed
	8. hoping
	9. baked
	10. hiding
	11. standing
	12. asked
	Grade 2, Lesson 9

 **ELL SUPPORT**

Linguistic Transfer The vowel sound /o͞o/ should not present difficulty for most ELLs. Make sure to point out that in English this vowel sound is spelled with more than one letter and more than one spelling pattern: *oo, ou,* and *ew.*

DAY 1 PHONICS **Model the Sort**

Children will sort words with you based on their vowel sounds.

- Display the Lesson 24 Word Cards, and read each word aloud. Then point to each word as you use it in a sentence.
- Remind children that they have learned about words with the vowel sound /o͝o/. Tell them that today they are going to look at words with the vowel sound /o͞o/.
- Model sorting the words by vowel sound. Display the Word Cards *wood* and *moon* as column headings. Suggested language: **I'm going to make one group of words with the same vowel sound as *wood* and another group with the same vowel sound as *moon*.**
- Begin with the Word Card *book*. Suggested language: ***Book*. Listen for the vowel sound in *book*. *Book*. I hear that *book* has the same vowel sound as *wood*. I'll put *book* under *wood*.** Repeat the process for *too*, placing it under *moon*.
- Sort the remaining Word Cards by reading one at a time and asking children where to place it. Read the word lists with children to check the sort. Then shuffle the cards and ask children to help you sort the words again.
- Call attention to the words under *moon*. Ask: **Which letters in each of these words stand for the vowel sound /o͞o/?** *(oo, ou, ew)* Work with children to group these Word Cards by the three spelling patterns.
- Distribute the Lesson 24 Word Cards, and ask children to repeat the sound sort independently.

DAY 2 **Pattern Sort**

Children will sort words according to spelling patterns.

- Remind children that this week's words have the vowel sound /o͞o/ spelled *oo, ou,* and *ew.*
- Work with children to repeat the Day 1 sort based on the vowel sounds /o͝o/ and /o͞o/. Then remove the /o͝o/ words.
- Display the Word Cards *noon, you,* and *new* side by side to represent the *oo, ou,* and *ew* spellings. Read the words. Then display the Word Card *boot*, and sort it according to its spelling pattern. Suggested language: ***Boot* has the /o͞o/ sound spelled *oo*. So does *noon*. I'll put *boot* under *noon*.**
- Sort the remaining words, asking children to name the category for each word.
- Have children read the words in each column. Then ask them to name three words in the first column that rhyme. *(noon, soon, moon)* Point out that the words *too, zoo, you, new,* and *blew* rhyme. Circle the words as you say them. Explain that they all end with the same sound, /o͞o/, even though that sound is spelled differently.
- Tell partners to repeat the sort and then write it in their Word Study Notebooks.

noon	you	new
boot	soup	blew
soon		
zoo		
too		
moon		

DAY 3 Word Hunt

Children will sort words that they find in their reading.

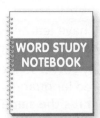

- Remind children that they have been learning about words with the vowel sound /o͞o/. Tell them that today they will hunt for words with this vowel sound in a story they have read.

- Have children make two columns in their Word Study Notebooks. Have them write the words *zoo* and *blew* as column headings.

- Explain that children are to write *oo* words they find under *zoo* and *ew* words under *blew*.

- Have partners read the Decodable Reader story "Moose's Tooth." Then have them page through the story, looking for words with the vowel sound /o͞o/. Tell children to write each word with the /o͞o/ sound in the correct column in their Word Study Notebooks.

- When children have completed their word hunt, call on individuals to read aloud their word lists to the group. *(Possible responses: Moose, loose, tooth, chew, new, brew)*

DAY 4 Blind Writing Sort

Children will sort and write words that a partner says aloud.

- Tell children that today they will work with a partner to listen to and write words with the vowel sound /o͞o/.

- Have children write these column headings in their Word Study Notebooks: *soon, soup, new*. Display the corresponding Word Cards to allow children to check the spellings.

- Explain that one partner is to read aloud each Word Card without showing the word. The other partner is to write the word under the heading with the /o͞o/ sound spelled in the same way.

- After each word has been written, the child reading the Word Card should show it to his or her partner for a spelling check.

- Have children read down each column once all the words have been written correctly.

- Then have partners switch roles and sort the words again.

DAY 5 Assess

Tell children to listen carefully. Say each boldfaced word, read the sentence, and repeat the word. Have children write the word.

1. **soon**   How *soon* can you be home?
2. **new**   James got a *new* bike.
3. **noon**   I eat lunch at *noon*.
4. **zoo**   I like to see the bears at the *zoo*.
5. **boot**   Where is my other *boot*?
6. **too**   May I go, *too*?
7. **moon**   The *moon* is round.
8. **blew**   The wind *blew* past me.
9. **soup**   The *soup* was hot.
10. **you**   Do *you* like to skate?

RETEACH IF children misspell three or more words, **THEN** revisit the activity on Day 2 and reassess.

OPTIONAL ASSESSMENT As an alternate assessment, you may have children repeat the Day 1 sort.

Words with *ou*, *ow*

SPELLING LIST

1. how
2. now
3. cow
4. owl
5. ouch
6. house
7. found
8. out
9. gown
10. town

Review Words: zoo, too, moon, boot, new, blew

 Reproducible Word Cards are available at **www.thinkcentral.com**.

DIFFERENTIATE INSTRUCTION

Struggling	Advanced
1. that	1. I'm
2. then	2. don't
3. this	3. isn't
4. them	4. can't
5. with	5. we'll
6. bath	6. it's
Grade 1, Lesson 11	7. I've
	8. didn't
	9. you're
	10. that's
	11. wasn't
	12. you've
	Grade 2, Lesson 10

 ELL SUPPORT

Linguistic Transfer Spanish speakers may need additional practice pronouncing the vowel sound /ou/. Read the list of spelling words, emphasizing the /ou/ sound in each word. Point out your mouth position as you say the /ou/ sound. Then read the words again. Have children repeat the words after you.

DAY 1 PHONICS **Model the Sort**

Children will sort words with you based on their vowel sounds.

- Display the Lesson 25 Word Cards. Read each word aloud. Then point to each word as you use it in a sentence.
- Remind children that they have learned about words with the vowel sound /o͞o/. Tell them that today they are going to look at words with the vowel sound /ou/.
- Model sorting the words by vowel sound. Use the Word Cards *moon* and *house* as column headings. Suggested language: **I'm going to read a word. Listen for the vowel sound and tell me if it's the same as in *moon* or *house*. I'll do the first one.**
- Read aloud the Word Card *cow*. Suggested language: *Cow.* **Listen for the vowel sound.** *Cow.* **Now listen to these words together.** *Cow, moon. Cow, house.* **The vowel sound in *cow* sounds like the vowel sound in *house*—the vowel sound /ou/. I'll put *cow* under *house*.** Repeat the process for *too*, placing it under *moon*.
- Continue to sort the remaining words, asking children to guide you in placing each Word Card in the correct column. When all the words have been sorted, shuffle the Word Cards and sort the words with children again.
- Read the words in both columns with children. Then reread the words under *house*. Elicit that these words all have the /ou/ sound, but it is spelled in different ways—*ou* and *ow*. Have children help you group the words by the spelling patterns *ou* and *ow*.
- Give partners a set of Lesson 25 Word Cards. Have children work together to repeat the sort.

DAY 2 **Guess My Category**

Children will guess the categories for words you sort.

- Remind children that this week's spelling words have the vowel sound /ou/ spelled with the letters *ou* and *ow*.
- Repeat the Day 1 sort with children, grouping the words by vowel sound. Then remove the words with the vowel sound /o͞o/.
- Display the Word Cards *ouch* and *how* as column headings. Read each word. Then sort the remaining words by the spelling patterns *ou* and *ow*. Read *gown* and place the Word Card under *how*. Read *found* and place the Word Card under *ouch*. Continue in the same way with the other Word Cards.
- Once all the words are sorted, guide children to identify the categories. Have them read aloud the words in the first column. Ask them to tell how the words are alike. *(They all have the sound /ou/ spelled* ou.*)* Have children read aloud the words in the second column and tell how they are alike. *(They all have the sound /ou/ spelled* ow.*)*
- Have children repeat the sort. Tell them to write their sorts in their Word Study Notebooks.

ouch	how
found	gown
house	now
out	cow
	owl
	town

DAY 3 Speed Sort

Children will sort words as quickly as they can.

WORD STUDY NOTEBOOK

- Work with children to sort the /ou/ Word Cards by their spelling pattern, *ou* or *ow*.
- Tell children that next they will work with a partner to sort these words as quickly as they can.
- Have partners set out the Word Cards *out* and *now* as column headings. Children should read each remaining Word Card and place it in the correct column according to the spelling pattern for /ou/.
- Have partners sort the words. Then ask them to read down the columns and make sure each word is in the correct place. Have partners repeat the sort a few more times to improve their speed.
- When the last sort is finished, have children write their sorts in their Word Study Notebooks.

DAY 4 Blind Writing Sort

Children will sort and write words that a partner says aloud.

WORD STUDY NOTEBOOK

- Tell children that today they will read and write words with the vowel sound /ou/.
- Have children divide a page in their Word Study Notebooks into two columns and then write the headings *found* and *town*.
- Display the corresponding Word Cards to allow children to check the spellings.
- Ask children to work with a partner. Explain that one partner will read aloud each Word Card without showing the word. The other partner is to write the word under the heading with the same spelling for the vowel sound /ou/.
- After each word is written, the first partner should show the Word Card. Then the second partner can check the spelling of the word.
- When all the words have been written, children should read the words in each column to check that they are sorted correctly.
- Then have partners shuffle the Word Cards, switch roles, and repeat the steps.

DAY 5 Assess

Tell children to listen carefully. Say each boldfaced word, read the sentence, and repeat the word. Have children write the word.

1. **how**   *How* are you feeling?
2. **now**   Would you like to eat *now*?
3. **cow**   The *cow* eats hay.
4. **owl**   The *owl* is in the tree.
5. **ouch**   I hurt my foot and said, *"Ouch!"*
6. **house**   Maria lives in a *house* by me.
7. **found**   I *found* the pen.
8. **out**   Take it *out* of the bag.
9. **gown**   My mom wore a *gown*.
10. **town**   I like my *town*.

RETEACH IF children misspell three or more words, **THEN** revisit the activity on Day 2 and reassess.

OPTIONAL ASSESSMENT As an alternate assessment, you may have children repeat the Day 1 sort.

Base Words with -ed, -ing

Model the Sort

Children will sort words with you according to base words and endings.

- Display the Lesson 26 Word Cards. Read each word aloud. Then point to each word as you use it in a sentence. Tell children that today they will be looking at base words and the endings -ed and -ing.

- Display the Word Cards *mix*, *used*, and *hoping* as column headings. Read aloud the words and point out the endings. Suggested language: **Mix is a base word. Used is a word with the ending -ed. Hoping is a word with the ending -ing.**

- Model sorting the Word Cards by base words and base words with endings. Suggested language: **Now I'll read another word. You'll tell me if it is a base word or a base word with the ending -ed or -ing. I'll do the first one.**

- Display and read the Word Card *running*. Suggested language: **Running. Running has the ending -ing, just like *hoping*. I'll put *running* under *hoping*.** Repeat for *hop*, placing it under *mix*, and for *mixed*, placing it under *used*.

- Continue the process with each Word Card, asking children to guide you in placing each word in the correct column. When all the words have been sorted, shuffle the Word Cards and sort the words with children again.

- Read aloud the words in each column. Help children understand that when endings are added to some base words, it can affect the spelling of the new words. Point out *hope/hoping* and *use/used*. Explain that the final e in the base words is dropped before the ending is added. Then point out *run/running* and *hop/hopped*. Explain that the final consonant in the base words is doubled before the ending is added.

- Distribute a set of Lesson 26 Word Cards to partners. Have children repeat the sort.

Pattern Sort

Children will sort base words and words with endings.

- Remind children that they have been learning about base words and the endings -ed and -ing.

- To repeat the Day 1 sort with children, place the Word Cards *run*, *mixed*, and *running* in a row. Display and read the Word Card *hopped*. Ask: **Is *hopped* a base word? Is it a word with the ending -ed? Is it a word with the ending -ing?**

- Once children respond, place the Word Card *hopped* under *mixed*. Point out that the final consonant p in *hop* was doubled before the ending -ed was added.

- Sort the remaining Word Cards with children using the same procedure. Point out that the final e in *use* was dropped before the ending -ed was added. When all the words have been sorted, ask children to read each word list.

- Tell partners to repeat the sort. Have children write their sorts in their Word Study Notebooks.

run	mixed	running
mix	hopped	hoping
hop	used	
hope		
use		

SPELLING WORDS

1. mix
2. mixed
3. hop
4. hopped
5. hope
6. hoping
7. run
8. running
9. use
10. used

 Go Digital Reproducible Word Cards are available at **www.thinkcentral.com**.

DIFFERENTIATE INSTRUCTION

Struggling	Advanced
1. chin	1. hens
2. chop	2. eggs
3. much	3. ducks
4. chip	4. bikes
5. rich	5. boxes
6. chick	6. wishes
Grade 1, Lesson 12	7. dresses
	8. names
	9. bells
	10. stamps
	11. dishes
	12. grapes
	Grade 2, Lesson 11

ELL SUPPORT

Linguistic Transfer In many languages, verb forms are constructed differently from those in English. Read aloud the spelling list to familiarize children with verbs formed by adding -ed and -ing. Tell them to listen to the correct pronunciation of these endings. Have children practice saying the words with you a few times.

DAY 3 Blind Writing Sort

Children will sort and write words that a partner says aloud.

- Tell children that today they will listen to and write base words and words with endings.
- Have children divide a page of their Word Study Notebooks into three columns and write these headings: *use, hopped, hoping.* Explain that the first column is for base words, the second column is for words ending with *-ed*, and the third column is for words ending with *-ing*.
- Have children work in pairs. One partner will read aloud each Word Card without showing the word. The other child will write the word under the correct column heading.
- After each word is written, the child reading the Word Cards should display the card. Then the partner can confirm or correct the spelling.
- Once all the words have been written correctly, have children read each word list.
- Then have partners switch roles and repeat the sort.

DAY 4 Meaning Sort

Children will sort words according to meaning.

- Remind children that they have been learning about base words and the endings *-ed* and *-ing*. Tell them that today they will sort the spelling words by meaning.
- Read aloud the words. Explain that all the words are verbs, or action words.
- Display and read the Word Card *hope*. Explain that *hope* tells about something happening now. Begin a group for present-tense verbs. Repeat with the Word Card *used* to begin a group for past-tense verbs.
- Then sort the words *mix, hop, use, run, hopped,* and *mixed* according to present and past tense.
- Place the words *running* and *hoping* in a third group. Explain that sometimes these words tell about now (*is running*) and sometimes they tell about the past (*was running*).
- Shuffle the Word Cards and sort them with children again. Have children copy the sort into their Word Study Notebooks.

DAY 5 Assess

Tell children to listen carefully. Say each boldfaced word, read the sentence, and repeat the word. Have children write the word.

1. **mix**   Can you *mix* the paint?
2. **mixed**   I *mixed* the fruit together.
3. **hop**   A frog can *hop*.
4. **hopped**   The bunny *hopped* across the yard.
5. **hope**   I *hope* you can come to my party!
6. **hoping**   Everyone is *hoping* for snow.
7. **run**   How fast can you *run*?
8. **running** He is *running* to the store.
9. **use**   Can you *use* another hat?
10. **used**   I *used* paint for my poster.

RETEACH **IF** children misspell three or more words, **THEN** revisit the activity on Day 2 and reassess.

OPTIONAL ASSESSMENT As an alternate assessment, you may have children repeat the Day 1 sort.

Base Words with -er, -est

SPELLING LIST

1. hard
2. harder
3. hardest
4. fast
5. faster
6. fastest
7. slow
8. slower
9. slowest
10. sooner

 Reproducible Word Cards are available at **www.thinkcentral.com**.

DIFFERENTIATE INSTRUCTION

Struggling	Advanced
1. ship	1. pay
2. shop	2. wait
3. which	3. paint
4. when	4. train
5. whip	5. pail
6. fish	6. clay
Grade 1, Lesson 13	7. tray
	8. plain
	9. stain
	10. hay
	11. gray
	12. away
	Grade 2, Lesson 12

 **ELL SUPPORT**

Linguistic Transfer Note that speakers of Hmong, Khmer, Korean, and Spanish may be unfamiliar with the endings -er and -est in comparison words. Khmer speakers may omit the endings, while other ELLs may insert the words *more* and *most* (such as *more slow* and *most slow*). Model the correct use of -er and -est words by saying the spelling words in simple oral sentences for children to repeat.

DAY 1 PHONICS **Model the Sort**

Children will sort words with you according to base words and endings.

- Display the Lesson 27 Word Cards. Read each word aloud. Then point to each word as you use it in a sentence. Use sentences that emphasize comparisons.
- Remind children that they have been learning about base words and endings. Tell them that today they will look at more base words and endings.
- Display the Word Cards *slow, slower,* and *slowest* as column headings. Read the words. Suggested language: **Slow is a base word. Slower is a word with the base word *slow* and the ending -er. Slowest is a word with the base word *slow* and the ending -est.**
- Model sorting the base words and base words with endings. Suggested language: **I'm going to read a word. Listen and tell me if it's a base word or a base word with the ending -er or the ending -est. Listen as I do the first one.**
- Say *fastest* as you hold up the Word Card. Suggested language: **Fastest. I hear and see that *fastest* has the ending -est. It's the same ending as in *slowest*. I'll put the word *fastest* under *slowest*.** Repeat for *sooner,* placing it under *slower,* and for *hard,* placing it under *slow.*
- Sort the remaining Word Cards by reading one at a time and asking children where to place it. Shuffle the cards and have children sort the words with you a second time. Then read down each column with children.
- Call attention to the words under *slower* and *slowest.* Guide children to understand that the endings -er and -est can be added to a base word to form a new word.
- Give each child a set of Lesson 27 Word Cards. Have them repeat the sort independently.

DAY 2 **Pattern Sort**

Children will sort base words and words with endings.

- Remind children that they have been learning about base words and the endings -er and -est.
- Work with children to repeat the Day 1 sort by placing the Word Cards *fast, faster,* and *fastest* as column headings. Display and read the Word Card *sooner.* Ask: **Is *sooner* a base word? Is it a word with the ending -er? Is it a word with the ending -est?** Once children respond, place the Word Card *sooner* under *faster.*
- Continue to sort the remaining Word Cards with children in the same way. When all the words have been sorted, ask children to read each word list aloud.
- Have partners repeat the sort and record it in their Word Study Notebooks.

fast	faster	fastest
hard	sooner	hardest
slow	harder	slowest
	slower	

DAY 3 | Word Hunt

Children will sort words that they find in their reading.

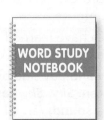

- Have partners read the Decodable Reader story "Seed Sisters."

- Tell them to page through the story a second time and find words with the *-er* and *-est* endings. Ask children to write the words they find in their Word Study Notebooks.

- When children finish, ask volunteers to read aloud their word lists to the group.

  (Possible responses: smaller, bigger, rounder, longer, flatter, faster, slower, quicker, higher, shorter, nicest)

- Ask children to write each word again, changing the *-er* ending to *-est* and the *-est* ending to *-er* to form a new word. Provide an example. Suggested language: **Here's the word *smaller*. The base word is *small*. I'll change the ending *-er* to *-est* and write the new word: *smallest*.**

DAY 4 | Speed Sort

Children will sort words as quickly as they can.

- Sort the Word Cards with children, grouping the words into three categories: base words, words with *-er*, and words with *-est*.

- Have partners work together. Ask them to place the Word Cards *hard, harder,* and *hardest* to represent the sorting categories. Explain that they should place base words under *hard*, words with *-er* under *harder*, and words with *-est* under *hardest*.

- Tell partners to sort the Word Cards as quickly as possible and then read aloud their word lists.

- Then have partners shuffle the Word Cards and repeat the sort several times, trying to sort more and more quickly each time.

- After the last sort, have children write their sorts in their Word Study Notebooks.

DAY 5 | Assess

Tell children to listen carefully. Say each boldfaced word, read the sentence, and repeat the word. Have children write the word.

1. **hard** — I will try *hard* to pass my test.
2. **harder** — I need to try *harder* to get an A.
3. **hardest** — I tried my *hardest* in class.
4. **fast** — She is a *fast* runner.
5. **faster** — He can run *faster* than I can.
6. **fastest** — She is the *fastest* in our class.
7. **slow** — The bus was *slow*.
8. **slower** — A bike is *slower* than a bus.
9. **slowest** — Walking is the *slowest* way to get home.
10. **sooner** — The *sooner* I do my work, the *sooner* I can play.

RETEACH **IF** children misspell three or more words, **THEN** revisit the activity on Day 2 and reassess.

OPTIONAL ASSESSMENT As an alternate assessment, you may have children repeat the Day 1 sort.

Words with Long *i*

DAY 1 PHONICS Model the Sort

Children will sort words with you based on their long vowel sounds.

- Display the Lesson 28 Word Cards, and read each word aloud. Then point to each word as you use it in a sentence.
- Remind children that they have learned about words with long vowel sounds. Tell them that today they are going to look at more words with long vowel sounds.
- Place the Word Cards *sky* and *day* side by side. Point to and read each word aloud. Suggested language: **Listen: *Sky*. *Sky* has the long *i* sound, /ī/. *Day* has a different vowel sound—the long *a* sound, /ā/. I'll start one group for words with the same vowel sound as *sky*. I'll start another group for words with other long vowel sounds.**
- Hold up the Word Card *cried*. Suggested language: ***Cried*. Listen for the vowel sound. The vowel sound in *cried* sounds like the vowel sound in *sky*—the long *i* sound. So I'll put *cried* under *sky*.** Then sort the word *no* under *day* to continue the category of other long vowels.
- Use the same process for each Word Card, asking children to tell where each word belongs. Read the word lists with children. Then shuffle the Word Cards, and work with children to sort the words again.
- Focus on the column of words under *sky*. Guide children to notice that the long *i* sound, /ī/, can be spelled with different letters: *y, ie,* and *igh*.
- Distribute the Lesson 28 Word Cards. Ask children to repeat the sort independently.

DAY 2 Pattern Sort

Children will sort long *i* words according to spelling patterns.

- Remind children that this week's spelling words have the long *i* sound, /ī/, spelled with the letters *y, ie,* and *igh*.
- Repeat the sort from Day 1, working with children to sort the words by long vowel sounds. Then remove the long *a, e,* and *o* words.
- Display the Word Cards *by, pie,* and *night* to represent the spelling patterns for long *i*. Read the words. Then read the Word Card *light*, and sort it according to its spelling pattern for long *i*. Suggested language: ***Light* has the vowel sound /ī/ spelled *igh*. So does *night*. I'll put *light* under *night*.** Continue to sort the remaining Word Cards, asking children to name the category for each word. Then read the words in each column with children.
- Point out that the words in the first column are rhyming words. Ask children to find one more spelling word that rhymes with these words. *(pie)* Help them notice that *pie* and *by* rhyme even though they each have different spellings for the long *i* sound.
- Have partners repeat the sort. Have children write their sorts in their Word Study Notebooks.

by	pie	night
my	cried	light
try		
sky		
fly		
dry		

MAJOR UNDERSTANDING: One sound can be spelled with different letters. The long *i* sound /ī/ can be spelled *igh, y,* and *ie.*

DAY 3 Word Hunt

Children will sort words that they find in their reading.

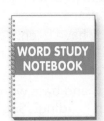

- Tell children they will hunt for words with long *i* in a story they have read.
- Have children write the words *dry, pie,* and *light* as column headings in their Word Study Notebooks.
- Then have small groups read aloud the Decodable Reader story "Sally Jane and Beth Ann."

- Ask the groups to page through the story a second time to hunt for long *i* words. Tell them to write words with long *i* spelled *y* under *dry,* words with long *i* spelled *ie* under *pie,* and words with long *i* spelled *igh* under *light.*
- When children have finished, call on group members to read aloud the words in each column. Have children check that each long *i* word is in the correct column. *(Possible responses: by, fly, sky, try, my; cried; night, bright, tight, flight, high, sighed)*

DAY 4 Blind Writing Sort

Children will sort and write words that a partner says aloud.

- Tell children that today they will work with a partner and take turns reading and writing long *i* words.
- Have children divide a page of their Word Study Notebooks into three columns with the headings *my, cried,* and *night.* Spell the words aloud as children check how they spelled the words.
- Explain that one partner will read aloud the Word Cards one at a time without showing the word. The other partner is to write the word in the correct column based on the spelling of the long *i* sound: *y, ie,* or *igh.*
- After a word is written, the first partner should show the Word Card. Then the second partner can check the spelling of the word.
- When all the words have been written, children should read the words in each column to check that they are sorted correctly. Then partners should shuffle the Word Cards and switch roles.

DAY 5 Assess

Tell children to listen carefully. Say each boldfaced word, read the sentence, and repeat the word. Have children write the word.

1. **my**   *My* hat is in my bag.
2. **try**   Will you *try* to sing?
3. **sky**   The *sky* was full of clouds.
4. **fly**   Watch the bird *fly.*
5. **by**   The glass is *by* the sink.
6. **dry**   My painting is *dry.*
7. **pie**   Dad baked a yummy *pie.*
8. **cried**   Toad *cried* when he lost the kite.
9. **night**   I go to bed at *night.*
10. **light** Where is the *light* switch?

RETEACH IF children misspell three or more words, **THEN** revisit the activity on Day 2 and reassess.

OPTIONAL ASSESSMENT As an alternate assessment, you may have children repeat the Day 1 sort.

Words with Suffixes *-ly, -y, -ful*

SPELLING LIST

1. sad
2. sadly
3. slow
4. slowly
5. dust
6. dusty
7. trick
8. tricky
9. help
10. helpful

 Reproducible Word Cards are available at **www.thinkcentral.com**.

DIFFERENTIATE INSTRUCTION

Struggling	Advanced
1. time	1. own
2. like	2. most
3. kite	3. soap
4. bike	4. float
5. white	5. both
6. drive	6. know
Grade 1, Lesson 15	7. loan
	8. goat
	9. flow
	10. loaf
	11. throw
	12. coach
	Grade 2, Lesson 14

ELL SUPPORT

Access Prior Knowledge Help Spanish speakers realize that for some word parts they know in Spanish there are equivalent word parts in English. Tell ELLs that the English word part *-ly* is used in words as much as *-mente* is used in Spanish. Point out the Spanish words *tristemente (sadly)* and *lentamente (slowly)* as examples.

DAY 1 PHONICS Model the Sort

Children will sort words with you according to base words and suffixes.

- Display the Lesson 29 Word Cards. Read each word aloud. Then point to each word as you use it in a sentence.
- Remind children that they have been learning about base words and endings. Tell them that today they will look at more base words and endings. Explain that the endings are called *suffixes*.
- Model sorting base words and base words with suffixes. Display the Word Cards *trick* and *tricky* as column headings. Suggested language: **We are going to sort some words into two groups—one group of base words and another group of base words with suffixes. I'll do some examples.**
- Hold up the Word Card *sadly*. Suggested language: **The first word is *sadly*. Is *sadly* a base word or is it a base word with a suffix? I see the suffix *-ly* at the end of *sadly*. I'll put *sadly* under *tricky*.** Repeat for the base word *help*, placing it under the heading *trick*.
- Use a similar procedure with the remaining words, having children name the correct column for each word. Read the lists together to confirm that the words are sorted correctly. Then shuffle the cards and have children help you sort the words again.
- Read aloud the words in the suffix column with children. Have them help you group the words: words with *-ly*, words with *-y*, and words with *-ful*. Tell children that the suffixes *-ly, -y,* and *-ful* can be added to base words to form new words.
- Distribute the Lesson 29 Word Cards, and have children repeat the sort independently.

DAY 2 Pattern Sort

Children will sort base words and base words with suffixes.

- Remind children that they have been learning about base words and the suffixes *-ly, -y,* and *-ful*.
- Work with children to repeat the sort from Day 1, sorting by base words and base words with suffixes.
- Then have partners display the Word Cards *slow* and *slowly* as column headings. Explain that they are to read each Word Card and decide if the word is a base word or a base word with a suffix. Tell them to place base words under *slow* and base words with suffixes under *slowly*.
- When children have finished sorting all the words, have pairs read their word lists to one another. Ask them to explain why they sorted the words as they did. Then ask them to copy their sorts into their Word Study Notebooks.

slow	slowly
sad	sadly
dust	dusty
trick	tricky
help	helpful

 DAY 3 Blind Writing Sort

Children will sort and write words that a partner says.

 WORD STUDY NOTEBOOK

- Tell children that today they will work with a partner to sort and write base words and base words with suffixes.

- Have children divide two facing pages of their Word Study Notebooks into two columns each. Write these column headings on the board for children to copy: *no suffix*, *-ly*, *-y*, *-ful*.

- Explain that one partner is to read aloud each Word Card without showing the word. The other is to write the word under the correct heading according to the type of word it is: a base word with no suffix or a word with the suffix *-ly*, *-y*, or *-ful*.

- After each word has been written, the child reading the Word Card should show it to his or her partner for a spelling check.

- After checking spelling, the child should read down each column to make sure that the words have been sorted correctly.

- Then have partners switch roles and repeat the activity.

DAY 4 Speed Sort

Children will sort words as quickly as they can.

WORD STUDY NOTEBOOK

- Write these headings on the board: *no suffix*, *-ly*, *-y*, *-ful*. Then have partners copy the headings on blank word cards.

- Have partners place the headings in a row to create categories for a speed sort.

- Ask children to take out their Word Cards. Tell them to work together to read the Word Cards as quickly as they can and to place each one in the correct column.

- When all the words have been sorted, partners should take turns reading the words in each column to make sure they have sorted them correctly.

- Then have partners shuffle the Word Cards and repeat the sort a few times, trying to sort the words more quickly each time without making any errors.

- After the last sort, ask children to write their sorts in their Word Study Notebooks. Suggest that they draw and label pictures to illustrate word meanings.

DAY 5 Assess

Tell children to listen carefully. Say each boldfaced word, read the sentence, and repeat the word. Have children write the word.

1. **sad**   He was *sad*.
2. **sadly**   He *sadly* watched the dog run away.
3. **slow**   Horses are not *slow*.
4. **slowly**   Can you talk *slowly* so I can hear?
5. **dust**   The *dust* was on the chair.
6. **dusty**   The chair was *dusty*.
7. **trick**   Do a card *trick*.
8. **tricky**   Cleaning up was *tricky*.
9. **help**   Can you *help* me clean?
10. **helpful** My neighbor is very *helpful*.

RETEACH   **IF** children misspell three or more words, **THEN** revisit the activity on Day 2 and reassess.

OPTIONAL ASSESSMENT   As an alternate assessment, you may have children repeat the Day 1 sort.

SPELLING LIST

1. even
2. open
3. begin
4. baby
5. tiger
6. music
7. paper
8. zero
9. table
10. below

 Reproducible Word Cards are available at **www.thinkcentral.com**.

DIFFERENTIATE INSTRUCTION

Struggling	Advanced
1. so	1. cannot
2. go	2. pancake
3. home	3. maybe
4. hole	4. baseball
5. no	5. playground
6. rope	6. someone
7. joke	7. myself
8. bone	8. classroom
9. stove	9. sunshine
10. poke	10. outside
Grade 1, Lesson 16	11. upon
	12. nothing
	Grade 2, Lesson 15

 **ELL SUPPORT**

Support Word Meaning Provide additional support for ELLs to learn the meanings of the spelling words. As appropriate, use props *(paper, table)*, pictures *(baby, tiger)*, and demonstrations (set up two *even* rows of chairs, place an object *below* a table, *open* a door).

DAY 1 PHONICS **Model the Sort**

Children will sort two-syllable words with you based on vowel sounds.

- Display the Lesson 30 Word Cards, and read them aloud. Then point to each word as you use it in a sentence.
- Tell children that this week's spelling words all have two syllables. Remind them that each syllable has a vowel sound.
- Model sorting the words by first-syllable vowel sounds. Hold up and read the Word Card *baby*. Suggested language: *Baby.* **Listen for the vowel sound in the first syllable of *baby*. Ba-by. I hear the long a sound, /ā/. I'll start a group for words with long a in the first syllable.** Repeat with the word *even*, beginning a new group for words with long e in the first syllable.
- Continue to sort the remaining words with children. Place each of the words *tiger, open,* and *music* in a category of its own to represent long *i, o,* and *u* in the first syllable. Read the word lists with children. Then shuffle the Word Cards, and work with children to sort the words again.
- Read the words in each column with children. Guide them to notice that the vowel sounds in the syllables can help them spell long words.
- Provide partners with a set of Lesson 30 Word Cards. Have them work together to repeat the sort.

DAY 2 **Guess My Category**

Children will guess the categories for two-syllable words you sort.

- Remind children that this week's spelling words have two syllables.
- Display the Word Card *tiger*. Read the word with children and clap the syllables together. Do the same with the remaining words.
- Then begin a sort of words by first-syllable vowel sound. Display the Word Cards *paper, zero, tiger, open,* and *music* in a row. Point to and read each word. Read each remaining Word Card aloud, and place it under the word with the same first-syllable vowel sound. There is just one word each for long *i*, long *o*, and long *u*.
- After all the words have been sorted, ask children to read the words in each column. Guide them to identify each category. Ask: **How are the words in the first column the same?** *(They each have the letter a and the long a sound in the first syllable.)* Repeat the question for the second column. *(They each have the letter e and the long e sound in the first syllable.)*
- Ask children to name the letter and vowel sound in the first syllable of *tiger, open,* and *music*. *(i, long i; o, long o; u, long u)*
- Have partners repeat the sort. Ask them to write their sorts in their Word Study Notebooks.

paper	zero	tiger	open	music
baby	even			
table	begin			
	below			

MAJOR UNDERSTANDING: When spelling two-syllable words, it is helpful to think about the vowel sound in each syllable. The vowel sound can be a clue to the spelling pattern.

DAY 3 · Speed Sort

Children will sort words as quickly as they can.

WORD STUDY NOTEBOOK

- Repeat the Day 1 sort with children, grouping words by the vowel sound in the first syllable.
- Explain that children will work with a partner to sort these words as quickly as they can.
- Have partners display the Word Cards *table, below, tiger, open,* and *music* as column headings.
- Tell children they will read each remaining word and place the Word Card in the column with the same vowel sound in the first syllable of the word.
- Allow time for partners to sort the words. Have them read the word lists when they are finished. Then have them shuffle the Word Cards and repeat the sort a few times, with the goal of improving their speed.
- When the last sort is completed, have partners take turns reading and writing the words in their Word Study Notebooks.

DAY 4 · Blind Writing Sort

Children will sort and write words that a partner says aloud.

WORD STUDY NOTEBOOK

- Tell children that today they will listen to and write two-syllable words. Remind them to listen for the vowel sound in each syllable to help them spell the whole word.
- Have children set up five columns across two facing pages of their Word Study Notebooks. They should write these five column headings: *baby, begin, tiger, open, music.*
- Display the corresponding Word Cards to allow children to check the spellings.
- Ask children to work with a partner. Explain that one partner will read aloud each Word Card without showing the word. The other partner is to write the word under the heading with the same long vowel sound in the first syllable of the word.
- After each word is written, the first partner should show the Word Card for a spelling check.
- When all the words have been written, children should read the words in each column to check that they are sorted correctly. Then have partners shuffle the Word Cards and switch roles.

DAY 5 · Assess

Tell children to listen carefully. Say each boldfaced word, read the sentence, and repeat the word. Have children write the word.

1. **even** We made two *even* rows.
2. **open** Please *open* the door.
3. **begin** Let's *begin* the movie.
4. **baby** My aunt has a new *baby*.
5. **tiger** We saw a *tiger* at the zoo.
6. **music** Ann loves *music*.
7. **paper** Do you have any *paper*?
8. **zero** *Zero* comes before one.
9. **table** Dinner is on the *table*.
10. **below** Kitty is *below* the chair.

RETEACH IF children misspell three or more words, **THEN** revisit the activity on Day 2 and reassess.

OPTIONAL ASSESSMENT As an alternate assessment, you may have children repeat the Day 1 sort.

Oral Vocabulary Development

ORAL VOCABULARY

1. **beautiful** Something that is *beautiful* is very nice to look at or to hear.

2. **excellent** Something that is *excellent* is very, very good.

3. **invitation** If someone sends you an *invitation*, that person asks you to come somewhere or do something.

4. **miss** If you *miss* catching a ball, you do not catch it.

5. **ruin** If you *ruin* something, you damage or wreck it.

6. **suddenly** When something happens *suddenly*, it happens very quickly.

Read Aloud Passages

The Oral Vocabulary words appear in the Read Aloud Passage, "The Lion and the Mouse." See page 348 of this Guide.

▶ Discuss Oral Vocabulary

Children will answer questions about the Oral Vocabulary words from the Read Aloud "The Lion and the Mouse" to deepen their understanding of the words.

- Write each Oral Vocabulary word on a strip of paper.

- Review with children the meaning of each Oral Vocabulary word, displaying each word as you share its meaning, shown to the left.

- Ask questions about the words, such as the ones below. Encourage children to use the Oral Vocabulary words in their responses.

  1. **Name some things you think are beautiful.**
  2. **Would you rather eat an excellent dinner or a dinner that is just okay? Why?**
  3. **What kinds of things have you received an invitation for?**
  4. **If you kick a soccer ball at the goal and you miss, how would you feel? Why?**
  5. **How would you feel if you made a painting and saw someone ruin it? Why?**
  6. **If you were outside and it started raining suddenly, what would you do?**

- As children answer the questions, encourage them to explain their responses and to share their ideas about the words.

▶ Paired Yes/No Questions

Children will answer paired questions about Oral Vocabulary words to show understanding of how to use the words correctly.

- Prepare two cards for each child, one card with a smile and one card with a frown. You may also have children make their own cards.

- Tell children that today they will be answering questions about the Oral Vocabulary words with a smile card for *yes* and a frown card for *no*.

- Review the meanings of the Oral Vocabulary words, displaying each word as you share its meaning.

- Read a set of paired questions. Say: *Beautiful.* **Would I feel happy if I heard beautiful music?** *(yes/smile)* **Would I feel angry if I heard beautiful music?** *(no/frown)* Encourage children to explain their answers. Continue in the same way with the remaining paired questions.

  1. **Would you want to see an excellent movie?** *(yes/smile)* **Would you want to see a movie that is not excellent at all?** *(no/frown)*
  2. **Would you send an invitation to a person you did not want to come to your party?** *(no/frown)* **Would you send an invitation to a person you wanted to come to your party?** *(yes/smile)*
  3. **If you shoot a basketball into the hoop, do you miss?** *(no/frown)* **If you shoot a basketball outside the hoop, do you miss?** *(yes/smile)*
  4. **If you ruin your shoes walking in mud, would you feel upset?** *(yes/smile)* **If you ruin your shoes walking in mud, would you feel happy?** *(no/frown)*
  5. **If a cat suddenly left the room, would it have left slowly?** *(no/frown)* **If a cat suddenly left the room, would it have left quickly?** *(yes/smile)*

▶ Word Sort

Children will sort the Oral Vocabulary words to learn more about how the words are used.

- Use the word strips from Discuss Oral Vocabulary. On the board or on chart paper, draw a chart like the one shown below. Tell children they will help you sort the Oral Vocabulary words.

- Review the meanings of the Oral Vocabulary words, displaying each word as you share its meaning.

- Then explain the chart headings. Tell children they will sort the Oral Vocabulary words into three groups: words about feeling happy, words about feeling sad, and words about feeling surprised.

- Choose one of the word strips, and read the word aloud. For example, say: **Ruin. If you build a sand castle at the beach and waves wash up and ruin it, how would you feel? Where should I put *ruin*?** Place the word strip in the *Sad* column of the chart.

- Continue with the other words. Encourage children to tell why they think a word belongs in the category they have named.

Happy	Sad	Surprised
beautiful	ruin	invitation
excellent	miss	suddenly

· ·

▶ Dictate, Draw, and Write

Children will dictate sentences and draw pictures to illustrate some of this week's Oral Vocabulary words.

- Review the meanings of the Oral Vocabulary words with children. Hold up the word strip from Discuss Oral Vocabulary as you review each word. Display the word strips along the chalk ledge.

- Have children think of a sentence using one of the Oral Vocabulary words. As a child says a sentence, record it on the board or on chart paper. Call on another child to say a different sentence using the word, and record that child's sentence as well.

- Continue until there is at least one sentence for each Oral Vocabulary word.

- Then have children choose three words to draw and write about in their Word Study Notebooks to show what they have learned about the words *beautiful, excellent, invitation, miss, ruin,* or *suddenly*.

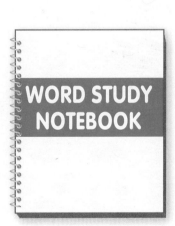

WORD STUDY NOTEBOOK

Oral Vocabulary Development

ORAL VOCABULARY

1. **bandits** *Bandits* are robbers or people who steal things.

2. **brave** Someone who is *brave* faces danger even if she or he is afraid.

3. **chattered** Someone who *chattered* talked very fast.

4. **ears** *Ears* are the body parts that hear.

5. **steady** When you are *steady*, you are calm.

6. **still** When you are *still*, you are not moving.

Read Aloud Passages

The Oral Vocabulary words appear in the Read Aloud Passage, "Susie and the Bandits." See page 348 of this Guide.

▶ Discuss Oral Vocabulary

Children will answer questions about the Oral Vocabulary words from the Read Aloud "Susie and the Bandits" to deepen their understanding of the words.

- Write each Oral Vocabulary word on a strip of paper.

- Review with children the meaning of each Oral Vocabulary word, displaying each word as you share its meaning, shown to the left.

- Ask questions about the words, such as the ones below. Encourage children to use the Oral Vocabulary words in their responses.

  1. **How would you feel if you saw bandits?**
  2. **Who do you know that is brave? Why do you think that person is brave?**
  3. **What is something you have chattered about with a friend?**
  4. **What can you hear with your ears?**
  5. **Name some times when it is important to be steady.**
  6. **Name some times when it is important to be still.**

- As children answer the questions, encourage them to explain their responses and to share their ideas about the words.

▶ Guess the Word

Children will listen to clues and identify the Oral Vocabulary words.

- Review the Oral Vocabulary words and meanings with children.

- Tell children you will be saying some clues. They are to listen carefully and then name the Oral Vocabulary word that matches each clue.

- Read aloud the first clue. Say: **The clue is "to be calm." I know that when you are calm, you are steady. So the word that matches this clue is *steady*.**

- Read aloud the remaining clues, and ask children to name the Oral Vocabulary word for each clue. If children have difficulty answering, provide two answer choices for each clue.

  1. **To be calm** *(steady)*
  2. **What you hear with** *(ears)*
  3. **When you are sleeping you are this** *(still)*
  4. **People who took things without asking** *(bandits)*
  5. **Two friends talked very fast about their day** *(chattered)*
  6. **A firefighter who faces danger every day** *(brave)*

- After children have guessed the correct word, ask volunteers to give examples of how they might use the word when talking to a friend or an adult.

▶ "Because" Sentences

Children will use the Oral Vocabulary words to complete sentences.

- Review the meanings of the Oral Vocabulary words with children.

- Tell children you will be saying part of a sentence that ends with the word *because*. Explain that they will finish the sentence by telling more about the meaning of the Oral Vocabulary word.

- Then say each of the following sentences, allowing children to finish the sentences to show understanding of the Oral Vocabulary words. Model the process by completing the first sentence for them.

- Ask two or more children to complete each sentence to demonstrate a variety of possible responses.

    1. **It's important to be steady in an emergency because…** *(Possible response: you want to stay safe.)*

    2. **Bandits should not steal because…** *(Possible response: it's not nice to take things that belong to others.)*

    3. **It can be hard to be brave at night because…** *(Possible response: sometimes you hear strange sounds.)*

    4. **Gina was asked to be quiet when she chattered in the library because…** *(Possible response: other people were trying to work quietly.)*

    5. **Our teacher asks us to "open our ears" because…** *(Possible response: she wants us to hear what she has to say.)*

    6. **You should stay still when you are watching birds because…** *(Possible response: if you move the birds might fly away.)*

▶ Dictate, Draw, and Write

Children will dictate sentences and draw pictures to illustrate some of this week's Oral Vocabulary words.

- Review the meanings of the Oral Vocabulary words with children. Hold up the word strip from Discuss Oral Vocabulary as you review each word. Display the word strips along the chalk ledge.

- Have children think of a sentence using one of the Oral Vocabulary words. As a child says a sentence, record it on the board or on chart paper. Call on another child to say a different sentence using the word, and record that child's sentence as well.

- Continue until there is at least one sentence for each Oral Vocabulary word.

- Then have children choose three words to draw and write about in their Word Study Notebooks to show what they have learned about the words *bandits, brave, chattered, ears, steady,* or *still.*

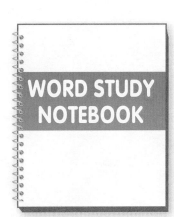

WORD STUDY NOTEBOOK

Oral Vocabulary Development

ORAL VOCABULARY

1. **apart** If you stay *apart* from other people, you stay away from them.

2. **crept** If you *crept*, you moved slowly and quietly so no one would notice.

3. **proud** If you are *proud*, you feel happy to have done something well.

4. **sneaked** If someone *sneaked* around, he or she moved in a way so that no one else would see.

5. **snout** A *snout* is a nose.

6. **worried** When you are *worried*, you think something bad may happen.

Read Aloud Passages

The Oral Vocabulary words appear in the Read Aloud Passage, "Stone Stew." See page 349 of this Guide.

▶ Discuss Oral Vocabulary

Children will answer questions about the Oral Vocabulary words from the Read Aloud "Stone Stew" to deepen their understanding of the words.

- Write each Oral Vocabulary word on a strip of paper.

- Review with children the meaning of each Oral Vocabulary word, displaying each word as you share its meaning, shown to the left.

- Ask questions about the words, such as the ones below. Encourage children to use the Oral Vocabulary words in their responses.

  1. **How do you feel when you are apart from your friends? Why?**
  2. **If you crept around, would you be loud or quiet? Why?**
  3. **Name a time you felt proud. Why did you feel that way?**
  4. **If a squirrel sneaked up a tree trunk, did it want to be seen or be hidden? Why do you think so?**
  5. **How can a dog use its snout?**
  6. **If you are worried, do you feel bad or good? Why?**

- As children answer the questions, encourage them to explain their responses and to share their ideas about the words.

▶ Paired Yes/No Questions

Children will answer paired questions about Oral Vocabulary words to show understanding of how to use the words correctly.

- Prepare two cards for each child, one card with a smile and one card with a frown. You may also have children make their own cards.

- Tell children that today they will be answering questions about the Oral Vocabulary words with a smile card for *yes* and a frown card for *no*.

- Review the meanings of the Oral Vocabulary words, displaying each word as you share its meaning.

- Read a set of paired questions. Say: *Crept.* **Would I have crept in a parade?** *(no/frown)* **Would I have crept in a room where my baby brother was sleeping?** *(yes/smile)* Encourage children to explain their answers. Continue in the same way with the remaining paired questions.

  1. **Would you feel proud if you gave up in a race?** *(no/frown)* **Would you feel proud if you won a race?** *(yes/smile)*
  2. **Would you stay apart from others if you were sick?** *(yes/smile)* **Would you stay apart from others if you wanted to play?** *(no/frown)*
  3. **Would you feel worried if your pet was at home?** *(no/frown)* **Would you feel worried if your pet was missing?** *(yes/smile)*
  4. **If someone sneaked into a room, would he or she make a lot of noise?** *(no/frown)* **If someone sneaked into a room, would he or she move very quietly?** *(yes/smile)*
  5. **Does a pig smell with its snout?** *(yes/smile)* **Does a pig hear with its snout?** *(no/frown)*

▶ Describe It or Act It Out

Children will describe or act out Oral Vocabulary words to demonstrate understanding.

- Review the meanings of the Oral Vocabulary words with children.

- Tell children that you are going to give some directions and ask some questions using the Oral Vocabulary words. Explain that they will respond by acting out the meanings or by describing the meanings.

- Read the following items. Allow a few children to provide descriptions and to act out the word meanings.

  1. **What does a pig's snout look like?** *(Possible response: short, pink)*

  2. **Stand apart from your classmates.** *(Possible response: The child stands away from the group.)*

  3. **What might you do if you feel proud?** *(Possible response: smile, clap)*

  4. **Show how a very young child might have sneaked a cookie from a cookie jar.** *(Possible response: The child moves quietly on tiptoe, looking behind to see if anyone is watching.)*

  5. **Show how you look if you are worried.** *(Possible response: The child frowns.)*

  6. **Show how a mouse might have crept away from a cat.** *(Possible response: The child creeps low to the ground.)*

▶ Dictate, Draw, and Write

Children will dictate sentences and draw pictures to illustrate some of this week's Oral Vocabulary words.

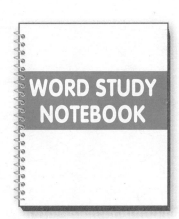

- Review the meanings of the Oral Vocabulary words with children. Hold up the word strip from Discuss Oral Vocabulary as you review each word. Display the word strips along the chalk ledge.

- Tell children that together they will write a little story about a fox sneaking into a henhouse, using as many of the Oral Vocabulary words as possible. Ask volunteers to think of sentences using the words to tell the story. As each child says a sentence, record it on the board or on chart paper.

- Continue until there is at least one sentence for each Oral Vocabulary word.

- Then have children draw and write in their Word Study Notebooks to tell about the class story. Have them try to use the words *apart, crept, proud, sneaked, snout,* or *worried* to tell about their drawings.

Oral Vocabulary Development

ORAL VOCABULARY

1. **canvas** A *canvas* is a kind of strong cloth that an artist uses to paint on.

2. **combinations** *Combinations* are mixes of two or more things.

3. **ease** If you do something with *ease*, you do it without trouble.

4. **important** Something that is *important* matters a lot.

5. **rhythm** *Rhythm* is a pattern of beats in poetry or music.

6. **row** Things in a *row* are lined up one after the other.

Read Aloud Passages

The Oral Vocabulary words appear in the Read Aloud Passage, "Painting Word Pictures." See page 349 of this Guide.

▶ Discuss Oral Vocabulary

Children will answer questions about the Oral Vocabulary words from the Read Aloud "Painting Word Pictures" to deepen their understanding of the words.

- Write each Oral Vocabulary word on a strip of paper.

- Review with children the meaning of each Oral Vocabulary word, displaying each word as you share its meaning, shown to the left.

- Ask questions about the words, such as the ones below. Encourage children to use the Oral Vocabulary words in their responses.

  1. **What would you paint on a blank canvas?**
  2. **Which are combinations of foods—peanut butter and jelly sandwiches or bananas?**
  3. **Name some things you can do with ease.**
  4. **What are some things that are important to you? Why are they important?**
  5. **Do you hear rhythm when you listen to ducks quacking or to music? Why do you think so?**
  6. **Look around the classroom. What things do you see in a row?**

- As children answer the questions, encourage them to explain their responses and to share their ideas about the words.

▶ Word Associations

Children will answer questions about the Oral Vocabulary words.

- Tell children that today you will ask some questions and they will answer with the Oral Vocabulary words.

- Review the meanings of the Oral Vocabulary words, displaying each word as you share its meaning.

- Read aloud the first question, and model how to figure out the answer.

- Then read aloud the remaining questions. Remind children to answer each question with an Oral Vocabulary word. If children have difficulty answering, provide two answer choices for each question.

  1. **Which word means something that matters a lot?** *(important)*
  2. **Which word describes things lined up side by side?** *(row)*
  3. **Which word means being able to do something without much trouble?** *(ease)*
  4. **Which word describes what you make when you mix together paint colors to make new colors?** *(combinations)*
  5. **Which word tells what you hear from a drummer in a band?** *(rhythm)*
  6. **Which word names a place for a painter to make a painting?** *(canvas)*

▶ True or Not True

Children will determine whether statements using the Oral Vocabulary words are true or not true.

- Review the meanings of the Oral Vocabulary words with children.

- Tell children you are going to say some sentences about the Oral Vocabulary words. They are to listen carefully and decide whether the sentence is true or not true. If the sentence is true, children should show thumbs up. If the sentence is not true, children should show thumbs down.

- Read aloud each sentence. If children disagree whether a statement is true or not true, guide them to understand the correct response.

  1. **Chairs that are set in a circle are in a row.** *(not true)*
  2. **An important day is usually marked on the calendar.** *(true)*
  3. **An artist might use a canvas to paint on.** *(true)*
  4. **Combinations have only one thing.** *(not true)*
  5. **Music has a rhythm that you can clap to.** *(true)*
  6. **To read with ease means it is very hard to do.** *(not true)*

- Revisit the items that are not true. Encourage children to reword the sentences to make them true.

▶ Dictate, Draw, and Write

Children will dictate sentences and draw pictures to illustrate some of this week's Oral Vocabulary words.

- Review the meanings of the Oral Vocabulary words with children. Hold up the word strip from Discuss Oral Vocabulary as you review each word. Display the word strips along the chalk ledge.

- Have children think of a sentence using one of the Oral Vocabulary words. As a child says a sentence, record it on the board or on chart paper. Call on another child to say a different sentence using the word, and record that child's sentence as well.

- Continue until there is at least one sentence for each Oral Vocabulary word.

- Then have children choose three words to draw and write about in their Word Study Notebooks to show what they have learned about the words *canvas, combinations, ease, important, rhythm,* or *row.*

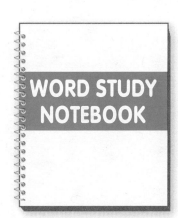

WORD STUDY NOTEBOOK

Oral Vocabulary Development

ORAL VOCABULARY

1. **alleys** *Alleys* are narrow streets, usually between or behind buildings.

2. **dash** When you *dash*, you move quickly.

3. **ferry** To *ferry* people or things means to carry them from one place to another, usually by boat or by some other means.

4. **space** *Space* is an open area.

5. **subways** *Subways* are underground trains.

6. **sealed** If something is *sealed*, it is closed up.

Read Aloud Passages

The Oral Vocabulary words appear in the Read Aloud Passage, "Training Around the Town." See page 350 of this Guide.

▶ Discuss Oral Vocabulary

Children will answer questions about the Oral Vocabulary words from the Read Aloud "Training Around the Town" to deepen their understanding of the words.

• Write each Oral Vocabulary word on a strip of paper.

• Review with children the meaning of each Oral Vocabulary word, displaying each word as you share its meaning, shown to the left.

• Ask questions about the words, such as the ones below. Encourage children to use the Oral Vocabulary words in their responses.

   1. Where would you see alleys—behind buildings or inside closets?

   2. If you dash, are you moving slowly or quickly? Why would someone dash?

   3. Which things could be used to ferry a group of people from one place to another—a bus? a chair? a boat? a train? a bike? Explain why.

   4. Do you need a lot of space to play hide and seek? Why?

   5. If you were riding on subways, would you be under the ground or above the ground? Why?

   6. Which can be sealed—a table or an envelope? How can it be sealed?

• As children answer the questions, encourage them to explain their responses and to share their ideas about the words.

▶ Guess the Word

Children will listen to clues and identify the Oral Vocabulary words.

• Review the Oral Vocabulary words and meanings with children.

• Tell children you will be saying some clues. They are to listen carefully and then name the Oral Vocabulary word that matches each clue.

• Model the process with the first clue. Then read aloud the remaining clues, and ask children to name the Oral Vocabulary word for each one. If children have difficulty answering, provide two answer choices for each clue.

   1. Closed up an envelope *(sealed)*

   2. To move things from one place to another *(ferry)*

   3. The empty area around you *(space)*

   4. What you might ride underground in a big city *(subways)*

   5. Run across the finish line in a race *(dash)*

   6. Narrow spaces between buildings *(alleys)*

• After children have guessed the correct word, ask volunteers to give examples of how they might use the word when talking to a friend or an adult.

▶ This or That

Children will sort Oral Vocabulary words into groups of words that name places and words that do not name places.

- Use the word strips from Discuss Oral Vocabulary. On the board or on chart paper, draw a chart like the one below. Tell children they will help you sort the Oral Vocabulary words.

- Review the meanings of the Oral Vocabulary words, displaying each word as you share its meaning. Then explain the chart headings. Tell children that they will sort the Oral Vocabulary words into two groups: one for words that name places where people can go and one for words that do not name places.

- Display and read each word aloud. For example, say: **Help me sort these words. Think about which words name places and which words do not. This word is** *dash*. **Does** *dash* **name a place? No, so we'll put it under the X.** Place the word strip under the X.

- Continue in the same way until all the words have been sorted. Then read aloud the words in each column with children to confirm that they have been sorted correctly.

√ Name Places	X Do Not Name Places
alleys	dash
space	sealed
ferry	
subways	

▶ Dictate, Draw, and Write

Children will dictate sentences and draw pictures to illustrate some of this week's Oral Vocabulary words.

- Review the meanings of the Oral Vocabulary words with children. Hold up the word strip from Discuss Oral Vocabulary as you review each word. Display the word strips along the chalk ledge.

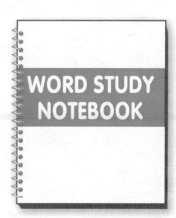

WORD STUDY NOTEBOOK

- Have children think of a sentence using one of the Oral Vocabulary words. As a child says a sentence, record it on the board or on chart paper. Call on another child to say a different sentence using the word, and record that child's sentence as well.

- Continue until there is at least one sentence for each Oral Vocabulary word.

- Then have children draw and write in their Word Study Notebooks to tell about a city scene. Encourage them to use the words *alleys, dash, ferry, space, subways,* or *sealed* to tell about their drawings.

Oral Vocabulary Development

ORAL VOCABULARY

1. clang A *clang* is a loud sound caused by banging metal.

2. fault If it is someone's *fault* that something goes wrong, that person caused the mistake.

3. figure If you *figure* something will happen, you think it will happen.

4. jumbled When things are *jumbled*, they are mixed together without any order.

5. plenty When you have *plenty*, you have more than enough.

6. tossed If you *tossed* something, you threw it gently or easily.

Read Aloud Passages

The Oral Vocabulary words appear in the Read Aloud Passage, "Night of the Wolf." See page 350 of this Guide.

▶ Discuss Oral Vocabulary

Children will answer questions about the Oral Vocabulary words from the Read Aloud "Night of the Wolf" to deepen their understanding of the words.

- Write each Oral Vocabulary word on a strip of paper.

- Review with children the meaning of each Oral Vocabulary word, displaying each word as you share its meaning, shown to the left.

- Ask questions about the words, such as the ones below. Encourage children to use the Oral Vocabulary words in their responses.

  1. Would you hear a clang from a notebook or from a bell? Why?

  2. If it was your fault that you missed the school bus, what might you say?

  3. What do you figure will happen after school?

  4. If you jumbled all the classroom books in a box, would it be hard to find one special book? Why?

  5. If you had plenty of fruit, would you need to buy more? Why?

  6. Which of these could be tossed—a ball or a brick? Why?

- As children answer the questions, encourage them to explain their responses and to share their ideas about the words.

▶ Riddles

Children will answer riddles by naming Oral Vocabulary words.

- Review the Oral Vocabulary words and meanings with children.

- Tell children you will say some riddles. They should listen carefully and then name the Oral Vocabulary word that answers each riddle.

- Model the process by showing how to figure out the first riddle. Then read aloud the remaining riddles. Ask children to name the Oral Vocabulary word that answers each riddle. Provide two answer choices if children need extra support.

  1. I am what you have when you have more than enough. What am I? *(plenty)*

  2. If you mixed things up, you did this. *(jumbled)*

  3. I am the reason for something going wrong. What am I? *(fault)*

  4. If you threw a beanbag gently to a friend, you did this. *(tossed)*

  5. I am the sound a bell might make. What am I? *(clang)*

  6. When you think about what might happen, you do this. *(figure)*

▶ Complete Sentences

Children will use Oral Vocabulary words to complete sentences.

- Review the meanings of the Oral Vocabulary words with children.

- Tell children you will be saying sentences with a word missing. Tell them to listen carefully so they can choose the Oral Vocabulary word that completes a sentence.

- Say each of the following sentences, pausing or indicating the missing word by saying *blank*. Repeat the sentence, and have children supply the missing Oral Vocabulary word. You may repeat the Oral Vocabulary words as often as children need to hear them. Model the process by completing the first sentence.

  1. **There are _____ of flowers in the garden, so you may pick as many as you like.** *(plenty)*

  2. **I _____ we'll have recess indoors because it is raining.** *(figure)*

  3. **I heard a loud _____ when the metal hammer hit the floor.** *(clang)*

  4. **The girl _____ the ball to her friend.** *(tossed)*

  5. **It is Ken's _____ that he is late for school because he forgot to set his alarm clock.** *(fault)*

  6. **Dad _____ all the clothes in the laundry basket.** *(jumbled)*

- Call on volunteers to say sentences using the Oral Vocabulary words.

▶ Dictate, Draw, and Write

Children will dictate sentences and draw pictures to illustrate some of this week's Oral Vocabulary words.

- Review the meanings of the Oral Vocabulary words with children. Hold up the word strip from Discuss Oral Vocabulary as you review each word. Display the word strips along the chalk ledge.

- Have children think of a sentence using one of the Oral Vocabulary words. As a child says a sentence, record it on the board or on chart paper. Call on another child to say a different sentence using the word, and record that child's sentence as well.

- Continue until there is at least one sentence for each Oral Vocabulary word.

- Then have children choose three words to draw and write about in their Word Study Notebooks to show what they have learned about the words *clang*, *fault*, *figure*, *jumbled*, *plenty*, or *tossed*.

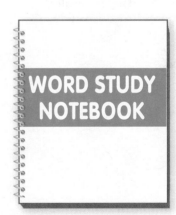

WORD STUDY NOTEBOOK

Oral Vocabulary Development

ORAL VOCABULARY

1. **agreement** If people are in *agreement*, they have the same feeling or opinion about something.

2. **bills** *Bills* are ideas for laws that are put before the government.

3. **creek** A *creek* is a small stream of water.

4. **crowd** A *crowd* is a large group of people or animals.

5. **discussed** If you *discussed* something, you talked about it with one or more people.

6. **warn** To *warn* means to tell others about danger.

Read Aloud
Passages

The Oral Vocabulary words appear in the Read Aloud Passage, "Prairie Dogs." See page 351 of this Guide.

▶ Discuss Oral Vocabulary

Children will answer questions about the Oral Vocabulary words from the Read Aloud "Prairie Dogs" to deepen their understanding of the words.

- Write each Oral Vocabulary word on a strip of paper.

- Review with children the meaning of each Oral Vocabulary word. Display and read each word as you share its meaning, shown to the left.

- Ask questions about the words, such as the ones below. Encourage children to use the Oral Vocabulary words in their responses.

  1. **What are some things you are in agreement about with your friends?**
  2. **What bills would you like to see the government pass? Why?**
  3. **What would be fun to do in a creek?**
  4. **Name some places where you might see a crowd.**
  5. **What are some things you have discussed with your friends?**
  6. **Would you warn someone about a thunderstorm or about a sunny day? Why?**

- As children answer the questions, encourage them to explain their responses and to share their ideas about the words.

▶ Secret Word Game

Children will ask yes/no questions to guess a secret Oral Vocabulary word.

- Review the meanings of the Oral Vocabulary words. Then tell children that they will play a game called the Secret Word Game.

- Explain that you will choose a word, and they have to ask questions to figure out the word. The questions must be answered *yes* or *no*.

- For the first few words, practice by assigning a "secret word" to children. Then ask yes/no questions for children to answer about the word.

- Ask questions such as these: **Does the word name an action? Does the word describe a group of people? Does the word rhyme with *torn*? Is the secret word *warn*?**

- Then choose your secret word, and have children ask yes/no questions until they identify the word. Help them with clues as necessary.

▶ Sentence Clue Game

Children will use sentence clues to explain the meanings of Oral Vocabulary words.

- Review the meanings of the Oral Vocabulary words with children. Then tell them that they will play a game called the Sentence Clue Game.

- Tell children that you will ask what a word means. Then you will say sentences that give clues about the word's meaning. In the first sentence clue, provide general information. Add details in subsequent sentences until children can define the word.

- Begin with the word *agreement*. Ask: **What is an *agreement*?** Pause after each sentence clue to allow children to identify the word: **My friend and I have an *agreement*. We talked things over and came to an *agreement*. Our *agreement* is that we can share toys.** (*Possible response: An* agreement *is a plan that everyone likes.*)

- Repeat with *discussed*. Ask: **What does *discussed* mean? Tim and Louise *discussed* something. They *discussed* a story they read. They *discussed* what happened in the story.** (*Possible response:* Discussed *means that you talked about something.*)

- Repeat the steps with the other Oral Vocabulary words as time allows.

- -

▶ Dictate, Draw, and Write

Children will dictate sentences and draw pictures to illustrate some of this week's Oral Vocabulary words.

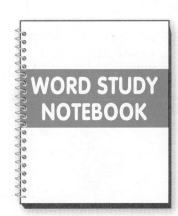

- Review the meanings of the Oral Vocabulary words with children. Hold up the word strip from Discuss Oral Vocabulary as you review each word. Display the word strips along the chalk ledge.

- Have children think of a sentence using one of the Oral Vocabulary words. As a child says a sentence, record it on the board or on chart paper. Call on another child to say a different sentence using the word, and record that child's sentence as well.

- Continue until there is at least one sentence for each Oral Vocabulary word.

- Then have children choose three words to draw and write about in their Word Study Notebooks to show what they have learned about the words *agreement*, *bills*, *creek*, *crowd*, *discussed*, or *warn*.

Oral Vocabulary Development

ORAL VOCABULARY

1. **crisp** When the word *crisp* is used to describe air, it means cool and fresh.

2. **edges** *Edges* are the outside parts of things.

3. **faraway** When something is *faraway*, it is a long way from where you are.

4. **peeked** If someone *peeked* at something, he or she looked at it quickly and secretly.

5. **smudge** If you *smudge* something, you make it blurry by rubbing it.

6. **village** A *village* is a small town, usually in the country.

Read Aloud Passages

The Oral Vocabulary words appear in the Read Aloud Passage, "The Neighbors." See page 352 of this Guide.

▶ Discuss Oral Vocabulary

Children will answer questions about the Oral Vocabulary words from the Read Aloud "The Neighbors" to deepen their understanding of the words.

- Write each Oral Vocabulary word on a strip of paper.

- Review with children the meaning of each Oral Vocabulary word, displaying each word as you share its meaning, shown to the left.

- Ask questions about the words, such as the ones below. Encourage children to use the Oral Vocabulary words in their responses.

  1. Where might you feel a crisp breeze—in a closet or at the beach? Why?
  2. Would you expect to see a fence or a castle at the edges of your schoolyard? Why?
  3. How could you travel to faraway places?
  4. How would you feel if your friend peeked at a surprise you had made for him or her? Why?
  5. What can you do if you smudge a picture you just made?
  6. Which is bigger—a village or a city? Why?

- As children answer the questions, encourage them to explain their responses and to share their ideas about the words.

▶ True or Not True

Children will determine whether statements using the Oral Vocabulary words are true or not true.

- Review the meanings of the Oral Vocabulary words, displaying each word as you share its meaning.

- Tell children you are going to say some sentences about the Oral Vocabulary words. They are to listen carefully and decide if the sentence is true or not true. If the sentence is true, children should show thumbs up. If the sentence is not true, children should show thumbs down.

- Read aloud each sentence. If children disagree whether a statement is true or not true, guide them to understand the correct response.

  1. You will need to wear a sweater if the air feels crisp at night. *(true)*
  2. If players stand at the edges of a soccer field, they are in the middle of the field. *(not true)*
  3. The moon is a faraway place. *(true)*
  4. When the owl peeked out of its nest, it did not want to be seen. *(true)*
  5. If you smudge your name after you write it, it is clear for everyone to read. *(not true)*
  6. There are skyscrapers in a village. *(not true)*

- Revisit the items that are not true. Encourage children to reword the sentences to make them true.

▶ "Because" Sentences

Children will use the Oral Vocabulary words to complete sentences.

- Review the meanings of the Oral Vocabulary words with children.

- Tell children you will say the beginning of a sentence that ends with the word *because*. Explain that they will finish the sentence by telling more about the meaning of the Oral Vocabulary word.

- Then say each of the following sentences, having children finish the sentences to show understanding of the Oral Vocabulary words. Model the process by completing the first sentence for them.

- Allow two or more children to complete each sentence to demonstrate a variety of possible responses.
    1. **This village does not have traffic lights because…** *(Possible response: there are not many cars.)*
    2. **A barnyard has a fence around the edges because…** *(Possible response: the animals must be kept in the yard.)*
    3. **It's not a good idea to smudge your homework because…** *(Possible response: then your teacher can't read it.)*
    4. **The air felt crisp because…** *(Possible response: it was the first day of fall.)*
    5. **You might not visit a faraway place because…** *(Possible response: it takes too long to get there.)*
    6. **Carol peeked at her friend's book because…** *(Possible response: she wanted to see what her friend was reading.)*

- -

▶ Dictate, Draw, and Write

Children will dictate sentences and draw pictures to illustrate some of this week's Oral Vocabulary words.

- Review the meanings of the Oral Vocabulary words with children. Hold up the word strip from Discuss Oral Vocabulary as you review each word. Display the word strips along the chalk ledge.

- Have children think of a sentence using one of the Oral Vocabulary words. As a child says a sentence, record it on the board or on chart paper. Call on another child to say a different sentence using the word, and record that child's sentence as well.

- Continue until there is at least one sentence for each Oral Vocabulary word.

- Then have children work with a partner. Have them discuss how they could illustrate the words *crisp, edges, faraway, peeked, smudge,* or *village* to show what they have learned. Tell children to choose three of the words to draw and write about in their Word Study Notebooks.

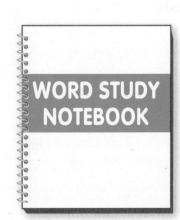

WORD STUDY NOTEBOOK

Oral Vocabulary Development

ORAL VOCABULARY

1. awake When you are *awake*, you are not asleep.

2. trip When you take a *trip*, you go to a place and then return.

3. try When you *try* to do something, you work to make it happen.

4. twice Something that is done *twice* is done two times.

5. wonder If you *wonder* about something, you want to know about it.

6. yanking If someone is *yanking* something, he or she is pulling it with a jerk.

Read Aloud Passages

The Oral Vocabulary words appear in the Read Aloud Passage, "The Little Red Hen." See page 352 of this Guide.

▶ Discuss Oral Vocabulary

Children will answer questions about the Oral Vocabulary words from the Read Aloud "The Little Red Hen" to deepen their understanding of the words.

- Write each Oral Vocabulary word on a strip of paper.

- Review with children the meaning of each Oral Vocabulary word, displaying each word as you share its meaning, shown to the left.

- Ask questions about the words, such as the ones below. Encourage children to use the Oral Vocabulary words in their responses.

  1. What things keep you awake at night?

  2. Where would you like to take a trip? Why?

  3. What is something you try to do at school?

  4. What is something you do twice in the same day?

  5. What are some things you wonder about?

  6. If someone was yanking your book out of your hand, how would you feel? Why?

- As children answer the questions, encourage them to explain their responses and to share their ideas about the words.

▶ Riddles

Children will answer riddles by naming Oral Vocabulary words.

- Review the meanings of the Oral Vocabulary words with children.

- Tell children you will say some riddles. They should listen carefully and then name the Oral Vocabulary word that answers each riddle. Model the process by showing how to figure out the first riddle.

- Then read aloud the remaining riddles. Provide two answer choices if children need extra support.

  1. I am one more time than once. What am I? *(twice)*

  2. If I travel to another country, I take this. What am I? *(trip)*

  3. If I work to play the piano, I do this. *(try)*

  4. If I am not sleeping, I am this. What am I? *(awake)*

  5. I do this if I am interested in knowing about something. What am I? *(wonder)*

  6. You might have done this if you were pulling your clothes out of the closet. What am I? *(yanking)*

▶ Describe It or Act It Out

Children will describe or act out Oral Vocabulary words to demonstrate understanding.

- Review the meanings of the Oral Vocabulary words with children.

- Tell children that you are going to ask some questions and give some directions using the Oral Vocabulary words. Explain that they will answer the questions by giving a description. They will follow the directions by acting out the meaning of the word.

- Read the following items. Encourage several children to provide descriptions or act out the word meanings.

  1. **Show how you would try to ice skate for the first time.** (*Possible response: The child makes slow, careful gliding movements.*)

  2. **What kind of trip have you taken?** (*Possible response: I took a trip on a train to visit my grandfather.*)

  3. **What things does a dog do when it is awake?** (*Possible response: It eats, plays, and goes for walks.*)

  4. **Show how to turn around twice.** (*Possible response: The child turns around two times.*)

  5. **What do you wonder about dinosaurs?** (*Possible response: I wonder why some dinosaurs could fly.*)

  6. **Show how a farmer might be yanking carrots out of the ground.** (*Possible response: The child pantomimes pulling carrots from the ground.*)

▶ Dictate, Draw, and Write

Children will dictate sentences and draw pictures to illustrate some of this week's Oral Vocabulary words.

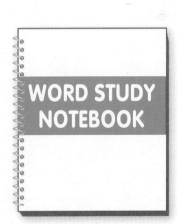

- Review the meanings of the Oral Vocabulary words with children. Hold up the word strip from Discuss Oral Vocabulary as you review each word. Display the word strips along the chalk ledge.

- Have children think of a sentence using one of the Oral Vocabulary words. As a child says a sentence, record it on the board or on chart paper. Call on another child to say a different sentence using the word, and record that child's sentence as well.

- Continue until there is at least one sentence for each Oral Vocabulary word.

- Then have children choose three words to draw and write about in their Word Study Notebooks to show what they have learned about the words *awake*, *trip*, *try*, *twice*, *wonder*, or *yanking*.

Oral Vocabulary Development

ORAL VOCABULARY

1. **enemies** *Enemies* are people or animals that can bring harm to others.

2. **forest** A *forest* is a place with a lot of trees.

3. **hibernate** When animals *hibernate*, they find or make a safe place to sleep for the winter.

4. **must** If you *must* do something, you have to do it.

5. **pouches** *Pouches* are pockets for holding or carrying things.

6. **predators** *Predators* are animals that hunt other animals for food.

Read Aloud Passages

The Oral Vocabulary words appear in the Read Aloud Passage, "Chipper Chips In." See page 353 of this Guide.

▶ Discuss Oral Vocabulary

Children will answer questions about the Oral Vocabulary words from the Read Aloud "Chipper Chips In" to deepen their understanding of the words.

- Write each Oral Vocabulary word on a strip of paper.

- Review with children the meaning of each Oral Vocabulary word, displaying each word as you share its meaning, shown to the left.

- Ask questions about the words, such as the ones below. Encourage children to use the Oral Vocabulary words in their responses.

  1. **Do animals like to be with their enemies? Why?**
  2. **What might you see in a forest?**
  3. **When animals hibernate, would you see them hunting for food? Why?**
  4. **Name something you must do every day.**
  5. **Do chipmunks store pizzas or nuts in their pouches?**
  6. **Would animals want to meet their predators? Why?**

- As children answer the questions, encourage them to explain their responses and to share their ideas about the words.

▶ Paired Yes/No Questions

Children will answer paired questions about Oral Vocabulary words to show understanding of how to use the words correctly.

- Tell children that today they will be answering yes/no questions about the Oral Vocabulary words.

- Review the meanings of the Oral Vocabulary words, displaying each word as you share its meaning.

- Read a set of paired questions. Say: *Pouches.* **Do tigers have pouches?** *(no)* **Do chipmunks have pouches?** *(yes)* Encourage children to explain their answers. Continue in the same way with the remaining paired questions.

  1. **Does a forest have many trees?** *(yes)* **Does a forest have only sand and rocks?** *(no)*
  2. **Are hens and foxes enemies?** *(yes)* **Are hens and roosters enemies?** *(no)*
  3. **Is wearing a purple shirt something you must do?** *(no)* **Is brushing your teeth something you must do?** *(yes)*
  4. **Would a bear hibernate in a cave?** *(yes)* **Would a bear hibernate in a school?** *(no)*
  5. **Are predators helpful to other animals?** *(no)* **Are predators a danger to other animals?** *(yes)*

▶ Word Sort

Children will sort the Oral Vocabulary words to learn more about how the words are used.

- Use the word strips from Discuss Oral Vocabulary. On the board or on chart paper, draw a chart like the one shown below. Tell children they will help you sort the Oral Vocabulary words.

- Review the meanings of the Oral Vocabulary words, displaying each word as you share its meaning.

- Then explain the chart headings. Tell children they will sort the Oral Vocabulary words into three groups: words about things that make animals feel scared, words about things that make animals feel safe, and other words.

- Choose one of the word strips, and read the word aloud. For example, say: *Hibernate.* **When animals hibernate, do they feel scared or safe? Who can tell me what** *hibernate* **means? Where should I put** *hibernate*? Place the word strip in the *Safe* column of the chart.

- Continue with the remaining words. Ask children to tell why they think a word belongs in the category they have named.

Scared	Safe	Other Words
enemies	hibernate	forest
predators	pouches	must

- -

▶ Dictate, Draw, and Write

Children will dictate sentences and draw pictures to illustrate some of this week's Oral Vocabulary words.

- Review the meanings of the Oral Vocabulary words with children. Hold up the word strip from Discuss Oral Vocabulary as you review each word. Display the word strips along the chalk ledge.

- Tell children that together you will write a short story about animals in the forest, using as many of the Oral Vocabulary words as possible. Ask volunteers to think of sentences using the words to tell the story. As a child says a sentence, record it on the board or on chart paper.

- Continue until there is at least one sentence for each Oral Vocabulary word.

- Then have children draw and write in their Word Study Notebooks to tell about the class story. Help them use the words *enemies, forest, hibernate, must, pouches,* or *predators* to tell about or label their drawings.

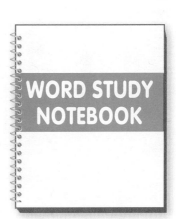

WORD STUDY NOTEBOOK

Oral Vocabulary Development

ORAL VOCABULARY

1. **companions** *Companions* are people who spend time together.

2. **exchange** If you *exchange* something, you give one thing for another.

3. **gracefully** If you do something *gracefully,* you do it smoothly and with skill.

4. **portions** *Portions* are parts of things.

5. **practice** When you *practice,* you do something over and over to get better at it.

6. **strict** Someone who is *strict* has firm rules.

Read Aloud Passages

The Oral Vocabulary words appear in the Read Aloud Passage, "The Piano Lessons." See page 353 of this Guide.

▶ Discuss Oral Vocabulary

Children will answer questions about the Oral Vocabulary words from the Read Aloud "The Piano Lessons" to deepen their understanding of the words.

- Write each Oral Vocabulary word on a strip of paper.

- Review with children the meaning of each Oral Vocabulary word, displaying each word as you share its meaning, shown to the left.

- Ask questions about the words, such as the ones below. Encourage children to use the Oral Vocabulary words in their responses.

  1. **Who are your companions at school?**

  2. **Would it be fair to exchange a penny for your friend's favorite toy? Why?**

  3. **If you dance gracefully, are you tripping and falling or are you moving smoothly? Why?**

  4. **Are portions of a pie parts of the pie or the whole pie? Why do you think so?**

  5. **What is something you practice doing? Why do you practice?**

  6. **Would a teacher who is strict ask you to follow the rules or let you do as you like? Why?**

- As children answer the questions, encourage them to explain their responses and to share their ideas about the words.

▶ Paired Yes/No Questions

Children will answer paired questions about Oral Vocabulary words to show understanding of how to use the words correctly.

- Prepare two cards for each child, one card with a smile and one card with a frown. You may also have children make their own cards.

- Tell children that today they will be answering questions about the Oral Vocabulary words with a smile card for *yes* and a frown card for *no.*

- Review the meanings of the Oral Vocabulary words, displaying each word as you share its meaning.

- Read a set of paired questions to children. Say: *Strict.* **Are Carl's parents strict if they tell him to do his chores before he can play?** *(yes/smile)* **Are Carl's parents strict if they let him play whenever he likes?** *(no/frown)* Have children explain their answers.

- Continue in the same way with the remaining paired questions.

  1. **Are you moving gracefully if you trip on the stairs?** *(no/frown)* **Are you moving gracefully if you glide on ice skates?** *(yes/smile)*

  2. **Can you divide a cake into portions?** *(yes/smile)* **Can you divide a shirt into portions?** *(no/frown)*

  3. **If you exchange books with a friend, do you trade books?** *(yes/smile)* **If you exchange books with a friend, do you each keep your own book?** *(no/frown)*

  4. **Would you practice eating a sandwich?** *(no/frown)* **Would you practice singing a song?** *(yes/smile)*

  5. **Would you want to run away from your companions?** *(no/frown)* **Would you want to play a game with your companions?** *(yes/smile)*

▶ Synonyms

Children will name synonyms for Oral Vocabulary words.

- Tell students that synonyms are words that have the same or almost the same meaning. Provide a few examples, such as *big* and *large*, *fast* and *quick*, and *talk* and *speak*.

- On the board or on chart paper, draw a chart like the one shown below. Tell children they will help you name synonyms for the Oral Vocabulary words.

- Review the meanings of the Oral Vocabulary words, displaying each word as you share its meaning.

- Write the word *gracefully* in the first column. Guide children to describe or name words that mean the same thing. List their ideas in the second column. If children need help naming synonyms, use a picture dictionary or other resource for support.

- Continue with the remaining Oral Vocabulary words. Then read the words and synonyms with children.

Word	Synonyms
gracefully	skillfully
strict	firm, stern
companions	pals, friends, buddies
exchange	trade, swap
portions	parts, pieces, sections
practice	rehearse

▶ Dictate, Draw, and Write

Children will dictate sentences and draw pictures to illustrate some of this week's Oral Vocabulary words.

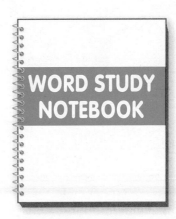

- Review the meanings of the Oral Vocabulary words with children. Hold up the word strip from Discuss Oral Vocabulary as you review each word. Display the word strips along the chalk ledge.

- Have children think of a sentence using one of the Oral Vocabulary words. As a child says a sentence, record it on the board or on chart paper. Call on another child to say a different sentence using the word, and record that child's sentence as well.

- Continue until there is at least one sentence for each Oral Vocabulary word.

- Then have children choose three words to draw and write about in their Word Study Notebooks to show what they have learned about the words *companions*, *exchange*, *gracefully*, *portions*, *practice*, or *strict*.

Oral Vocabulary Development

ORAL VOCABULARY

1. **adventure** An *adventure* is an exciting or dangerous activity.

2. **frisky** Someone who is *frisky* is playful and full of energy.

3. **shivered** If someone *shivered,* he or she shook with cold or fear.

4. **spied** If you *spied* something, you saw it.

5. **tumbled** If you *tumbled,* you fell suddenly.

6. **view** The *view* is what you can see from a certain place.

Read Aloud Passages

The Oral Vocabulary words appear in the Read Aloud Passage, "Turtle, Frog, and Rat." See page 354 of this Guide.

▶ Discuss Oral Vocabulary

Children will answer questions about the Oral Vocabulary words from the Read Aloud "Turtle, Frog, and Rat" to deepen their understanding of the words.

- Write each Oral Vocabulary word on a strip of paper.

- Review with children the meaning of each Oral Vocabulary word, displaying each word as you share its meaning, shown to the left.

- Ask questions about the words, such as the ones below. Encourage children to use the Oral Vocabulary words in their responses.

  1. **Which do you think is an adventure—going to the grocery store or going on a field trip to the zoo? Why?**

  2. **Would you take a nap if you felt frisky? Why?**

  3. **If you shivered, did you feel afraid or unafraid? Why?**

  4. **If you spied a beautiful sunset, did you use your eyes or your ears? What would you see?**

  5. **Would you be surprised if you tumbled off your chair? Why?**

  6. **Would you have a better view from the top of a mountain or from the back of a cave? Why?**

- As children answer the questions, encourage them to explain their ideas. Explore responses that seem to indicate misunderstanding.

▶ Word Sort

Children will sort the Oral Vocabulary words to learn more about how the words are used.

- Use the word strips from Discuss Oral Vocabulary. Display each word, read it, and review its meaning.

- On the board or on chart paper, draw a chart like the one shown below. Tell children they will help you sort the words into three groups: words about actions, words about things, and words about feelings.

- Display one of the word strips, and read the word. For example, say: *Spied.* **Is** *spied* **an action, a thing, or a feeling? Who can tell me what** *spied* **means? Where should I put** *spied*? Place the word strip in the *Actions* column of the chart.

- Continue in the same way, asking children to tell why they think a word belongs in a particular category. If a child thinks the word *view* is an action, explain that some words, such as *view,* can name an action or a thing. Provide context sentences to illustrate the two meanings of *view.* Then add the word to both categories.

Actions	Things	Feelings
spied	adventure	frisky
shivered	view	
tumbled		
view		

▶ "Because" Sentences

Children will use the Oral Vocabulary words to complete sentences.

- Review the meanings of the Oral Vocabulary words with children.

- Tell children you will be saying part of a sentence that ends with the word *because*. Explain that they will finish the sentence by telling more about the meaning of the Oral Vocabulary word.

- Then say each of the following sentences, allowing children to finish the sentences to show understanding of the Oral Vocabulary words. Model the process by completing the first sentence for them.

- Allow two or more children to complete each sentence to demonstrate a variety of possible responses.

  1. **I like the view from our classroom window because…** *(Possible response: I can see tall buildings.)*
  2. **Hannah spied a bird in a faraway tree because…** *(Possible response: she was looking through binoculars.)*
  3. **Going to the beach is an adventure because…** *(Possible response: you might see lots of interesting animals.)*
  4. **Dad tumbled in the yard because…** *(Possible response: he tripped over a rock.)*
  5. **I know Martin's kitten is frisky because…** *(Possible response: it likes to play with a toy mouse.)*
  6. **Pablo shivered because…** *(Possible response: he heard thunder outside.)*

▶ Dictate, Draw, and Write

Children will dictate sentences and draw pictures to illustrate some of this week's Oral Vocabulary words.

- Review the meanings of the Oral Vocabulary words with children. Hold up the word strip from Discuss Oral Vocabulary as you review each word. Display the word strips along the chalk ledge.

- Have children think of a sentence using one of the Oral Vocabulary words. As a child says a sentence, record it on the board or on chart paper. Call on another child to say a different sentence using the word, and record that child's sentence as well.

- Continue until there is at least one sentence for each Oral Vocabulary word.

- Then have partners draw and write in their Word Study Notebooks to tell about some frisky animals that have an adventure. Tell them to try to use the words *adventure*, *frisky*, *shivered*, *spied*, *tumbled*, or *view* to tell about their drawings.

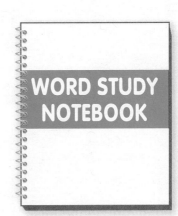

WORD STUDY NOTEBOOK

Oral Vocabulary Development

ORAL VOCABULARY

1. **bouquet** A *bouquet* is a bunch of flowers.

2. **burst** A *burst* is a short, sudden action.

3. **glows** When something *glows*, it shines brightly.

4. **plow** A *plow* is a tool that pushes things over or to the side.

5. **shrivel** When things *shrivel*, they shrink and become wrinkled.

6. **vines** *Vines* are the long, twisting stems on a plant.

Read Aloud
Passages

The Oral Vocabulary words appear in the Read Aloud Passage, "The Prickly Pride of Texas." See page 355 of this Guide.

▶ Discuss Oral Vocabulary

Children will answer questions about the Oral Vocabulary words from the Read Aloud "The Prickly Pride of Texas" to deepen their understanding of the words.

• Write each Oral Vocabulary word on a strip of paper.

• Review with children the meaning of each Oral Vocabulary word, displaying each word as you share its meaning, shown to the left.

• Ask questions about the words, such as the ones below. Encourage children to use the Oral Vocabulary words in their responses.

1. **Would you find roses or peanuts in a bouquet? Why?**
2. **If you saw a burst of fireworks in the sky, would they explode slowly or quickly? Why?**
3. **Which glows in the sun—a red brick or water in a swimming pool? Why?**
4. **Would you need a mirror or a plow to move dirt? Why?**
5. **When grapes shrivel in the sun, do they stay round and smooth? What happens to the grapes?**
6. **Would you see vines in a garden or on an airplane? Why?**

• As children answer the questions, encourage them to explain their responses and to share their ideas about the words. Use a picture dictionary or other resource to support their understanding of concepts that may be unfamiliar, such as a *plow*.

▶ True or Not True

Children will determine whether statements using the Oral Vocabulary words are true or not true.

• Review the meanings of the Oral Vocabulary words, displaying each word as you share its meaning.

• Tell children you are going to say some sentences about the Oral Vocabulary words. They are to listen carefully and decide if the sentence is true or not true. If the sentence is true, children should raise a hand. If the sentence is not true, children should not raise a hand.

• Read aloud each sentence. If children disagree whether a statement is true or not true, guide them to understand the correct response.

1. **When flowers shrivel, they become wrinkled.** *(true)*
2. **A plow can be used to cook dinner.** *(not true)*
3. **You can hear a burst of laughter.** *(true)*
4. **A pile of mud glows.** *(not true)*
5. **There may be vines in a vegetable garden.** *(true)*
6. **A bouquet is made up of fish.** *(not true)*

• Revisit the items that are not true. Encourage children to reword the sentences to make them true.

▶ Word Associations

Children will answer questions about the Oral Vocabulary words.

- Tell children that today you will ask some questions and they will answer with the Oral Vocabulary words.

- Review the meanings of the Oral Vocabulary words, displaying each word as you share its meaning.

- Read aloud the first question and model how to figure out the answer.

- Then read aloud the remaining questions. Remind children to answer each question with an Oral Vocabulary word. If children have difficulty answering, provide two answer choices for each question. For example, ask: **Are the long, twisting stems on a plant called vines or a plow?**

  1. Which word means a short, sudden action? *(burst)*

  2. Which word tells what the moon does on a clear night? *(glows)*

  3. Which word names the long and twisting parts of plants? *(vines)*

  4. Which word describes something you can buy at a flower shop? *(bouquet)*

  5. Which word names a tool that a farmer might use? *(plow)*

  6. Which word describes when something gets smaller and wrinkled? *(shrivel)*

▶ Dictate, Draw, and Write

Children will dictate sentences and draw pictures to illustrate some of this week's Oral Vocabulary words.

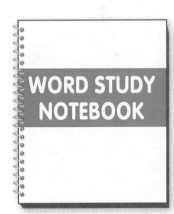

- Review the meanings of the Oral Vocabulary words with children. Hold up the word strip from Discuss Oral Vocabulary as you review each word. Display the word strips along the chalk ledge.

- Have children think of a sentence using one of the Oral Vocabulary words. As a child says a sentence, record it on the board or on chart paper. Call on another child to say a different sentence using the word, and record that child's sentence as well.

- Continue until there is at least one sentence for each Oral Vocabulary word.

- Then have children choose three words to draw and write about in their Word Study Notebooks to show what they have learned about the words *bouquet, burst, glows, plow, shrivel,* or *vines*.

Oral Vocabulary Development

ORAL VOCABULARY

1. **cactus** A *cactus* is a plant with sharp spikes that grows in hot, dry places.

2. **habitat** A *habitat* is the place in nature where an animal or plant lives.

3. **howl** A *howl* is a loud cry.

4. **mainly** *Mainly* means for the most part.

5. **search** When you *search* for something, you look for it.

6. **stems** *Stems* are the long parts of plants that leaves and flowers grow on.

Read Aloud Passages

The Oral Vocabulary words appear in the Read Aloud Passage, "The Tortoise and the Hare." See page 355 of this Guide.

▶ Discuss Oral Vocabulary

Children will answer questions about the Oral Vocabulary words from the Read Aloud "The Tortoise and the Hare" to deepen their understanding of the words.

- Write each Oral Vocabulary word on a strip of paper.

- Review with children the meaning of each Oral Vocabulary word, displaying each word as you share its meaning, shown to the left.

- Ask questions about the words, such as the ones below. Encourage children to use the Oral Vocabulary words in their responses.

  1. Would it be a good idea to touch a cactus? Why?
  2. Is a habitat a place to live or something to eat?
  3. Would you expect a howl to come from a wolf or a fish? Why?
  4. Is it mainly cold or hot in the summer?
  5. Would you search for a snack in the refrigerator or in a washing machine? Why?
  6. Where would you find stems, on stars or on flowers? Why?

- As children answer the questions, encourage them to explain their responses and to share their ideas about the words.

▶ Describe It

Children will respond to prompts about the Oral Vocabulary words to demonstrate understanding.

- Review the meanings of the Oral Vocabulary words by displaying each word and sharing its meaning.

- Tell children that you are going to ask them to describe and tell about things to show that they understand the Oral Vocabulary words.

- Model the process by completing the first item below.

- Then read aloud the remaining prompts and have children respond. Allow several children to provide descriptions for each prompt.

  1. **Describe how you could search for a lost library book.** *(Possible response: I could look in my book bag and in my room.)*
  2. **Tell how a cactus looks and feels.** *(Possible response: It has spikes all over it that are sharp.)*
  3. **Describe the habitat of a turtle.** *(Possible response: Turtles live in lakes and ponds.)*
  4. **Tell how stems are an important part of plants.** *(Possible response: They hold up the plants; they are a place where leaves and flowers can grow.)*
  5. **Tell what you mainly do during your day in school.** *(Possible response: I learn new things.)*
  6. **Describe the howl of a coyote.** *(Possible response: It is a loud crying noise.)*

▶ Complete Sentences

Children will use Oral Vocabulary words to complete sentences.

- Review the meanings of the Oral Vocabulary words with children.

- Tell children you will be saying sentences with a word missing. Tell them to listen carefully so they can choose the Oral Vocabulary word that completes each sentence.

- Then say each of the following sentences, pausing or indicating the missing word by saying *blank*. Repeat the sentence, and have children supply the missing Oral Vocabulary word. You may repeat the Oral Vocabulary words as often as children need to hear them. Model the process by completing the first sentence.

  1. **Sometimes dogs _____ at night.** *(howl)*
  2. **The mall is a place you go _____ for shopping.** *(mainly)*
  3. **I will cut the long _____ on these flowers so they will fit in the vase.** *(stems)*
  4. **Rattlesnakes live in a desert _____.** *(habitat)*
  5. **Inez can _____ for shells at the beach.** *(search)*
  6. **A _____ is a plant that grows in the desert.** *(cactus)*

- Call on volunteers to say sentences using the Oral Vocabulary words.

▶ Dictate, Draw, and Write

Children will dictate sentences and draw pictures to illustrate some of this week's Oral Vocabulary words.

- Review the meanings of the Oral Vocabulary words with children. Hold up the word strip from Discuss Oral Vocabulary as you review each word. Display the word strips along the chalk ledge.

- Have children think of a sentence using one of the Oral Vocabulary words. As a child says a sentence, record it on the board or on chart paper. Call on another child to say a different sentence using the word, and record that child's sentence as well.

- Continue until there is at least one sentence for each Oral Vocabulary word.

- Then have children work with a partner. Have them discuss how they could draw pictures for the words *cactus, habitat, howl, search,* or *stems* to show what they have learned. Tell each child to choose three of the words to draw and write about in his or her Word Study Notebook.

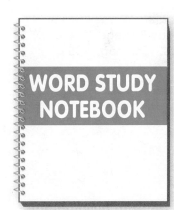

WORD STUDY NOTEBOOK

Oral Vocabulary Development

ORAL VOCABULARY

1. alert When you are *alert*, you pay attention to what is happening and are ready to act.

2. directions *Directions* are instructions for how to do something.

3. scale A *scale* is a tool that measures weight.

4. sensitive Someone who is *sensitive* pays attention to changes or details.

5. swivel If you *swivel*, you turn or spin on one spot.

6. threatened If someone *threatened* others, he or she meant to do harm.

Read Aloud Passages

The Oral Vocabulary words appear in the Read Aloud Passage, "The Dancing Wolves." See page 355 of this Guide.

▶ Discuss Oral Vocabulary

Children will answer questions about the Oral Vocabulary words from the Read Aloud "The Dancing Wolves" to deepen their understanding of the words.

- Write each Oral Vocabulary word on a strip of paper.
- Review with children the meaning of each Oral Vocabulary word, displaying each word as you share its meaning, shown to the left.
- Ask questions about the words, such as the ones below. Encourage children to use the Oral Vocabulary words in their responses.

  1. When would you be more alert, riding a bike or eating a sandwich? Why?

  2. Would you need directions to take a bath or to learn a new dance? Why?

  3. Would you be more likely to use a scale during a science lesson or during a spelling lesson? Why?

  4. If you are sensitive to changes in the weather, what might you do on a very cold day? Why?

  5. Can you swivel if you are sitting on the floor? How would you do it?

  6. When the wolf threatened to eat the three little pigs, how do you think they felt? Why?

- As children answer the questions, encourage them to explain their responses and to share their ideas about the words.

▶ True or Not True

Children will determine whether statements using the Oral Vocabulary words are true or not true.

- Review the meanings of the Oral Vocabulary words, displaying each word as you share its meaning.
- Tell children you are going to say some sentences about the Oral Vocabulary words. They are to listen carefully and decide if the sentence is true or not true.
- Read aloud each sentence, one at a time. If children disagree whether a statement is true or not true, guide them to understand the correct response.

  1. A doctor uses a scale to measure people's weight. *(true)*

  2. If you are sensitive to what is happening around you, you notice what the people around you are doing. *(true)*

  3. You are very alert when you are sleeping. *(not true)*

  4. Someone who threatened animals is a kind person. *(not true)*

  5. A globe can swivel on its stand. *(true)*

  6. You can find directions for making soup in a cookbook. *(true)*

- Revisit the items that are not true. Encourage children to reword the sentences to make them true.

▶ Sentence Clue Game

Children will use sentence clues to explain the meanings of Oral Vocabulary words.

- After reviewing the Oral Vocabulary words, tell children that they will play the Sentence Clue Game.

- Tell children that you will ask what a word means. Then you will give sentence clues, and they will use the clues to tell the word's meaning.

- Provide general information in the first sentence clue. Add details in subsequent sentences until children can explain the word's meaning.

- Begin with the word *swivel*. Ask: **What does it mean to** *swivel***?** Then give these sentence clues, pausing after each to allow children to make guesses: **The ballerina can** *swivel***. She can stand on her toes and** *swivel* **three times. She can** *swivel* **by turning her body in a circle without taking a step.** *(Possible response: To* swivel *means to turn in place without taking a step.)*

- Repeat with *alert*. Ask: **What does** *alert* **mean? The rabbit was** *alert***. The rabbit was** *alert* **when it saw a fox. The** *alert* **rabbit quickly hopped away from the fox.** *(Possible response:* Alert *means knowing what is going on around you and being prepared.)*

- Continue in the same way with the other words.

▶ Dictate, Draw, and Write

Children will dictate sentences and draw pictures to illustrate some of this week's Oral Vocabulary words.

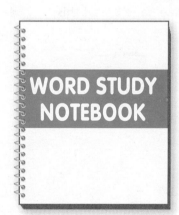

- Review the meanings of the Oral Vocabulary words with children. Hold up the word strip from Discuss Oral Vocabulary as you review each word. Display the word strips along the chalk ledge.

- Tell children that together you will write a group story about staying alert when a big storm threatened to come, using as many of the Oral Vocabulary words as possible. Ask volunteers to think of sentences using the words to tell the story. As a child says a sentence, record it on the board or on chart paper.

- Continue until there is at least one sentence for each Oral Vocabulary word.

- Then have children draw and write in their Word Study Notebooks to tell about the class story. Have them try to use the words *alert, directions, scale, sensitive, swivel,* or *threatened* to tell about their drawings.

Oral Vocabulary Development

ORAL VOCABULARY

1. atmosphere The *atmosphere* is the air and other gases around Earth.

2. decision A *decision* is what happens when a person makes up his or her mind about something.

3. landscape A *landscape* is a view of a large area of land.

4. miniature Something that is *miniature* is very, very small.

5. surface The *surface* of an object is the outside part.

6. vast Something that is *vast* is very large.

Read Aloud Passages

The Oral Vocabulary words appear in the Read Aloud Passage, "One Giant Leap." See page 356 of this Guide.

▶ Discuss Oral Vocabulary

Children will answer questions about the Oral Vocabulary words from the Read Aloud "One Giant Leap" to deepen their understanding of the words.

- Write each Oral Vocabulary word on a strip of paper.

- Review with children the meaning of each Oral Vocabulary word, displaying each word as you share its meaning, shown to the left.

- Ask questions about the words, such as the ones below. Encourage children to use the Oral Vocabulary words in their responses.

  1. Where is Earth's atmosphere, under the ground or around Earth?

  2. What is a good decision you have made at school?

  3. Which is a landscape, a view of a desert or a bedroom? Why?

  4. Could you ride in a miniature car? Why?

  5. Is the surface of a marble rough or smooth? How do you know?

  6. Which would you describe as vast, a puddle or the ocean? Why?

- As children answer the questions, encourage them to explain their responses and to share their ideas about the words.

▶ Complete Sentences

Children will use Oral Vocabulary words to complete sentences.

- Review the meanings of the Oral Vocabulary words with children.

- Tell children you will be saying sentences with a word missing. Tell them to listen carefully so they can choose the Oral Vocabulary word that completes each sentence.

- Then say each of the following sentences, pausing or indicating the missing word by saying *blank*. Repeat the sentence, and have children supply the missing Oral Vocabulary word.

- You may repeat the Oral Vocabulary words as often as children need to hear them. Model the process by completing the first sentence.

  1. It took many days to cross the _____ desert. *(vast)*

  2. The _____ horse was the smallest animal in the barn. *(miniature)*

  3. A rocket can travel through Earth's _____. *(atmosphere)*

  4. The _____ of the box is blue. *(surface)*

  5. A country _____ is quite different from the way a city looks. *(landscape)*

  6. When you go to a restaurant, you must make a _____ about what to eat. *(decision)*

- Call on volunteers to say sentences using the Oral Vocabulary words.

▶ This or That

Children will sort Oral Vocabulary words into groups of words that are about the world outside and words that are not.

- Use the word strips from Discuss Oral Vocabulary. On the board or on chart paper, draw a chart like the one shown below.

- Review the meanings of the Oral Vocabulary words, displaying each word as you share its meaning. Tell children they will help you sort the Oral Vocabulary words.

- Then explain the chart headings. Tell children that they will sort the Oral Vocabulary words into two groups: one for words about the world outside and one for words that are not about the world outside.

- Choose one of the word strips, and read the word aloud. For example, say: **Help me sort these words. Think about which words are about the world outside and which words are not. This word is** *landscape*. **Is** *landscape* **a word about the world outside? Yes, so we'll put it in the first column.**

- Continue in the same way until all the words have been sorted. Then read aloud the words in each column with children to confirm that they are sorted correctly.

✓ About the World Outside	✗ Not About the World Outside
landscape atmosphere surface vast	decision miniature

▶ Dictate, Draw, and Write

Children will dictate sentences and draw pictures to illustrate some of this week's Oral Vocabulary words.

- Review the meanings of the Oral Vocabulary words with children. Hold up the word strip from Discuss Oral Vocabulary as you review each word. Display the word strips along the chalk ledge.

- Have children think of a sentence using one of the Oral Vocabulary words. As a child says a sentence, record it on the board or on chart paper. Call on another child to say a different sentence using the word, and record that child's sentence as well.

- Continue until there is at least one sentence for each Oral Vocabulary word.

- Then have children choose three words to draw and write about in their Word Study Notebooks to show what they have learned about the words *atmosphere*, *decision*, *landscape*, *miniature*, *surface*, or *vast*.

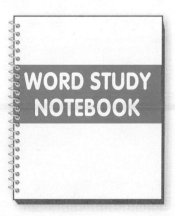

WORD STUDY NOTEBOOK

Oral Vocabulary Development

ORAL VOCABULARY

1. **shelter** A *shelter* is a place that covers or protects you.

2. **delighted** You are *delighted* when something pleases you or makes you happy.

3. **complain** If you *complain*, you tell about something you do not like.

4. **pleaded** When someone has *pleaded* with you, they have begged or asked for something they really want.

5. **lonely** If you feel *lonely*, you feel sad from being alone.

6. **horizon** The *horizon* is the line in the far distance where the sky meets the ground.

Read Aloud Passages

The Oral Vocabulary words appear in the Read Aloud Passage, "The Rainy Trip." See page 357 of this Guide.

▶ Discuss Oral Vocabulary

Children will answer questions about the Oral Vocabulary words from the Read Aloud "The Rainy Trip" to deepen their understanding of the words.

- Write each Oral Vocabulary word on a strip of paper.

- Review with children the meaning of each Oral Vocabulary word, displaying each word as you share its meaning, shown to the left.

- Ask questions about the words, such as the ones below. Encourage children to use the Oral Vocabulary words in their responses.

  1. **Would you need a shelter more if it were raining or sunny outside? Why?**
  2. **What kinds of things would make you feel delighted?**
  3. **Would you complain if someone were nice to you? Why or why not?**
  4. **If you pleaded for something, what would you say?**
  5. **When would you feel lonely? Why?**
  6. **If you want to see the horizon, would you look inside or outside? Why?**

- As children answer the questions, encourage them to explain their responses and to share their ideas about the words.

▶ Word Sort

Children will sort the Oral Vocabulary words to deepen their understanding of word meanings.

- Use the word strips from Discuss Oral Vocabulary. On the board or on chart paper, draw a chart like the one shown below, and tell children they will help you sort the Oral Vocabulary words.

- Review the meanings of the Oral Vocabulary words, displaying each word as you share its meaning.

- Then explain the chart headings. Tell children they will sort the Oral Vocabulary words into three groups: words about places, words about feelings, and words about things you do.

- Choose one of the word strips, and read the word aloud. For example, say: *Shelter.* **Is a shelter a place, a feeling, or something you can do? Who can tell me what a shelter is? Where should I put *shelter*?** Place the word strip in the *Places* column of the chart.

- Continue with the other words, and encourage children to tell why they think a word belongs in the category they have named.

Places	Feelings	Things You Do
shelter	delighted	complain
horizon	lonely	pleaded

▶ "Because" Sentences

Children will use the Oral Vocabulary words to complete sentences.

- Review the meanings of the Oral Vocabulary words with children.

- Tell children you will be saying part of a sentence that ends with the word *because*. Explain that they will finish the sentence by telling more about the meaning of the Oral Vocabulary word.

- Then say each of the following sentences, allowing children to finish the sentences to show understanding of the Oral Vocabulary words. Model the process by completing the first sentence for them.

- Allow two or more children to complete each sentence to demonstrate a variety of possible responses.

  1. Ben looked for a shelter because... *(Possible response: it started to snow.)*

  2. I was delighted because... *(Possible response: I got a new bike.)*

  3. Jess wanted to complain because... *(Possible response: she didn't get the main part in the class play.)*

  4. I pleaded with my mom because... *(Possible response: I wanted to go to my friend's birthday party.)*

  5. Mr. Ham was lonely because... *(Possible response: he lived all alone.)*

  6. He looked in the far distance to find the horizon because... *(Possible response: he wanted to see the sun going down.)*

▶ Dictate, Draw, and Write

Children will dictate sentences and draw pictures to illustrate some of this week's Oral Vocabulary words.

- Review the meanings of the Oral Vocabulary words with children. Hold up the word strip from Discuss Oral Vocabulary as you review each word. Display the word strips along the chalk ledge.

- Have children think of a sentence using one of the Oral Vocabulary words. As a child says a sentence, record it on the board or on chart paper. Call on another child to say a different sentence using the word, and record that child's sentence as well.

- Continue until there is at least one sentence for each Oral Vocabulary word.

- Then have children choose three words to draw and write about in their Word Study Notebooks to show what they have learned about the words *shelter, delighted, complain, pleaded, lonely,* or *horizon.*

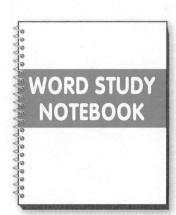

WORD STUDY NOTEBOOK

Oral Vocabulary Development

ORAL VOCABULARY

1. **disappointed** When you feel *disappointed,* you feel let down.

2. **eagerly** If you do something *eagerly,* you do it with excitement.

3. **fancy** Something that is *fancy* is very special.

4. **scampered** If someone *scampered,* he or she ran or moved quickly.

5. **slippery** Something that is *slippery* is smooth and hard to grab onto.

6. **spotted** If you *spotted* something, you saw it.

Read Aloud Passages

The Oral Vocabulary words appear in the Read Aloud Passage, "The Three Wishes." See page 357 of this Guide.

▶ Discuss Oral Vocabulary

Children will answer questions about the Oral Vocabulary words from the Read Aloud "The Three Wishes" to deepen their understanding of the words.

- Write each Oral Vocabulary word on a strip of paper.

- Review with children the meaning of each Oral Vocabulary word, displaying each word as you share its meaning, shown to the left.

- Ask questions about the words, such as the ones below. Encourage children to use the Oral Vocabulary words in their responses.

  1. **Would you feel disappointed if your best friend couldn't play with you after school? Why?**
  2. **If you are eagerly playing a game, is it exciting or boring? Why?**
  3. **Would you wear fancy clothes to do work in a garden or to go to a party? Why?**
  4. **If a mouse scampered through the grass, did it move slowly or quickly? Why?**
  5. **Which is slippery, an ice cube or a pretzel? Why?**
  6. **If you spotted something you had lost, how would you feel? Why?**

- As children answer the questions, encourage them to explain their responses and to share their ideas about the words.

▶ Describe It or Act It Out

Children will describe or act out Oral Vocabulary words to demonstrate understanding.

- Review the meanings of the Oral Vocabulary words with children.

- Tell children that you are going to ask some questions and give some directions using the Oral Vocabulary words. Explain that they will answer the questions by giving a description. They will follow the directions by acting out the meaning of the word.

- Read the following items. Allow a few children to provide descriptions and to act out the word meanings.

  1. **Show how you would look if you spotted a whale in the ocean.** *(Possible response: The child shows a look of amazement or happiness.)*
  2. **Show how a cat might have scampered in a circle.** *(Possible response: The child runs quickly in a circle.)*
  3. **What might a fancy cake look like?** *(Possible response: It might have three layers and flowers made of different colored frosting.)*
  4. **What do slippery noodles feel like?** *(Possible response: smooth, wet)*
  5. **Show how you look when you feel disappointed.** *(Possible response: The child shows a sad face.)*
  6. **What feelings do you have if you are eagerly waiting to go on vacation?** *(Possible response: excitement, impatience)*

▶ Multiple-Meaning Words

Children will explore the concept of multiple-meaning words.

- Tell children that some words have more than one meaning. Explain that today they will be learning about some of these words.

- Display the Oral Vocabulary word *spotted* and review its meaning. *(saw)* Explain that *spotted* has another meaning; it can mean "covered with a pattern of small marks." To help children understand the two meanings of *spotted,* say these sentences: **I spotted my friend at the playground. This dog has spotted fur.**

- Discuss each sentence with students. Then have volunteers think of a sentence for each meaning.

- Next, say the word *last.* Ask children to tell what they think the word means. They might indicate that *last* means "coming after all the others." Give another meaning for the word *last,* such as "to continue for a time." Say these sentences and ask children to explain the meaning of *last* in each: **The concert will *last* for two hours. I am *last* in line.**

- Use the same procedure for the following multiple-meaning words: *fair, play, shop, bat.* After you have discussed the different meanings of each word with children, ask volunteers to say sentences to show the different meanings.

▶ Dictate, Draw, and Write

Children will dictate sentences and draw pictures to illustrate some of this week's Oral Vocabulary words.

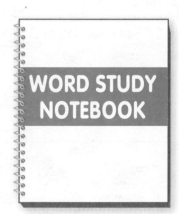

- Review the meanings of the Oral Vocabulary words with children. Hold up the word strip from Discuss Oral Vocabulary as you review each word. Display the word strips along the chalk ledge.

- Have children think of a sentence using one of the Oral Vocabulary words. As a child says a sentence, record it on the board or on chart paper. Call on another child to say a different sentence using the word, and record that child's sentence as well.

- Continue until there is at least one sentence for each Oral Vocabulary word.

- Then have children work with a partner. Have them discuss how they could illustrate the words *disappointed, eagerly, fancy, scampered, slippery,* or *spotted* to show what they have learned. Tell each child to choose three of the words to draw and write about in his or her Word Study Notebook.

Oral Vocabulary Development

ORAL VOCABULARY

1. **author** An *author* is a person who writes stories or poems.

2. **exactly** Something that is *exactly* right means that it is perfect.

3. **incomplete** Something that is *incomplete* is not finished.

4. **permission** When someone gives you *permission,* that person tells you it is okay to do something.

5. **signature** A *signature* is the name of a person written in his or her own handwriting.

6. **welcomed** If you *welcomed* the chance to do something, you were glad to do it.

Read Aloud Passages

The Oral Vocabulary words appear in the Read Aloud Passage, "Christina's Work." See page 358 of this Guide.

▶ Discuss Oral Vocabulary

Children will answer questions about the Oral Vocabulary words from the Read Aloud "Christina's Work" to deepen their understanding of the words.

- Write each Oral Vocabulary word on a strip of paper.

- Review with children the meaning of each Oral Vocabulary word, displaying each word as you share its meaning, shown to the left.

- Ask questions about the words, such as the ones below. Encourage children to use the Oral Vocabulary words in their responses.

  1. **What might an author do while he or she is working?**
  2. **If you answered every question on a test exactly right, did you do well?**
  3. **What might happen if your school work is incomplete? Why?**
  4. **What are some things you need permission to do? Why?**
  5. **Would you expect to see someone's signature on a street sign or at the end of a letter? Why?**
  6. **If you were outside in very hot weather, would you have welcomed the chance to swim in a pool or to take a long hike in the sun? Why?**

- As children answer the questions, encourage them to explain their responses and to share their ideas about the words.

▶ Paired Yes/No Questions

Children will answer paired questions about Oral Vocabulary words to show understanding of how to use the words correctly.

- Tell children that today they will be answering yes/no questions about the Oral Vocabulary words.

- Review the meanings of the Oral Vocabulary words, displaying each word as you share its meaning.

- Read a set of paired questions. Say: *Exactly.* **If you want to paint a picture of an elephant exactly how it looks, should you use yellow paint?** *(no)* **If you want to paint a picture of an elephant exactly how it looks, should you use gray or brown paint?** *(yes)* Encourage children to explain their answers. Continue in the same way with the remaining paired questions.

  1. **Do you write your signature?** *(yes)* **Do you clap your signature?** *(no)*
  2. **If you welcomed the chance to take a trip, did you want to stay home?** *(no)* **If you welcomed the chance to take a trip, did you want to go away?** *(yes)*
  3. **Does an author make the paper in a book?** *(no)* **Does an author write the words in a book?** *(yes)*
  4. **Is a puzzle with all the pieces in place incomplete?** *(no)* **Is a puzzle with some pieces missing incomplete?** *(yes)*
  5. **Do you need permission to borrow a book from the library?** *(yes)* **Do you need permission to laugh at a joke?** *(no)*

▶ "Because" Sentences

Children will use the Oral Vocabulary words to complete sentences.

- Review the meanings of the Oral Vocabulary words with children.

- Tell children you will be saying part of a sentence that ends with the word *because*. Explain that they will finish the sentence by telling more about the meaning of the Oral Vocabulary word.

- Then say each of the following sentences, allowing children to finish the sentences to show understanding of the Oral Vocabulary words. Model the process by completing the first sentence.

- Allow two or more children to complete each sentence to demonstrate a variety of possible responses.

  1. **Lian welcomed the chance to go to the fair because…** *(Possible response: she had never gone before.)*

  2. **The story was incomplete because…** *(Possible response: it had no ending.)*

  3. **The teacher asked for everyone's signature on the wall painting because…** *(Possible response: all the children had painted it.)*

  4. **This author likes to write books about animals because…** *(Possible response: she knows a lot about them.)*

  5. **Jed looked for a pizza recipe that was exactly right because…** *(Possible response: he wanted the pizza to taste good.)*

  6. **I wanted permission to sleep over at my friend's house because…** *(Possible response: we have fun together.)*

▶ Dictate, Draw, and Write

Children will dictate sentences and draw pictures to illustrate some of this week's Oral Vocabulary words.

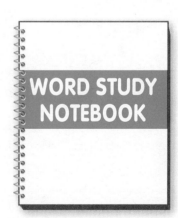

- Review the meanings of the Oral Vocabulary words with children. Hold up the word strip from Discuss Oral Vocabulary as you review each word. Display the word strips along the chalk ledge.

- Have children think of a sentence using one of the Oral Vocabulary words. As a child says a sentence, record it on the board or on chart paper. Call on another child to say a different sentence using the word, and record that child's sentence as well.

- Continue until there is at least one sentence for each Oral Vocabulary word.

- Then have children draw and write in their Word Study Notebooks to tell about an author they would like to have visit the classroom. Tell them to try to use the Oral Vocabulary words *author, exactly, incomplete, permission, signature,* or *welcomed* to tell about their drawings.

Oral Vocabulary Development

ORAL VOCABULARY

1. **calf** A *calf* is a young cow or bull.

2. **flooded** When something is *flooded*, it is covered with water.

3. **meadow** A *meadow* is a field.

4. **rippled** If something *rippled* the water in a pond or small lake, it made very small waves.

5. **swarm** A *swarm* is a very large group, usually of insects.

6. **wade** When you *wade*, you walk slowly through water that is not deep.

Read Aloud Passages

The Oral Vocabulary words appear in the Read Aloud Passage, "Chicken Little." See page 358 of this Guide.

▶ Discuss Oral Vocabulary

Children will answer questions about the Oral Vocabulary words from the Read Aloud "Chicken Little" to deepen their understanding of the words.

- Write each Oral Vocabulary word on a strip of paper.

- Review with children the meaning of each Oral Vocabulary word, displaying each word as you share its meaning, shown to the left.

- Ask questions about the words, such as the ones below. Encourage children to use the Oral Vocabulary words in their responses.

  1. **Would you see a calf in the city or on a farm? Why?**

  2. **If the schoolyard was flooded, what would you see?**

  3. **Which animal would live in a meadow, a rabbit or a whale? Why?**

  4. **Would a big boat or a small stone have rippled the water in a lake? Why?**

  5. **If you saw a swarm of bees, were there many bees or just two bees?**

  6. **Would you wade in a tree or in a pond? Why?**

- As children answer the questions, encourage them to explain their responses and to share their ideas about the words.

▶ Word Sort

Children will sort the Oral Vocabulary words to learn more about how the words are used.

- Use the word strips from Discuss Oral Vocabulary. On the board or on chart paper, draw a chart like the one shown below. Tell children they will help you sort the Oral Vocabulary words.

- Review the meanings of the Oral Vocabulary words, displaying each word as you share its meaning.

- Then explain the chart headings. Tell children they will sort the Oral Vocabulary words into three groups: words about water, words about animals, and words about places.

- Choose one of the word strips, and read the word aloud. For example, say: *Calf.* **Is *calf* a word about water, animals, or places? Who can tell me the meaning of *calf*? Where should I put *calf*?** Place the word strip in the *Animals* column of the chart.

- Continue with the other words. Encourage children to tell why they think a word belongs in the category they have named.

Water	Animals	Places
flooded	calf	meadow
rippled	swarm	
wade		

▶ Word Associations

Children will answer questions about the Oral Vocabulary words.

- Tell children that today you will ask some questions and they will answer with the Oral Vocabulary words.

- Review the meanings of the Oral Vocabulary words, displaying each word as you share its meaning.

- Read aloud the first question and model how to figure out the answer.

- Then read aloud the remaining questions. Remind children to answer each question with an Oral Vocabulary word. If children have difficulty answering, provide two answer choices for each question. For example, ask: **If an acorn fell into a pond, was the water flooded or rippled?**

  1. **Which word is the name for a big group of mosquitoes?** *(swarm)*
  2. **Which word tells what the water in a pond might have done if an acorn fell into it?** *(rippled)*
  3. **Which word means almost the same as *field*?** *(meadow)*
  4. **Which word means a young cow or bull?** *(calf)*
  5. **Which word tells how you might walk in a pond that is not deep?** *(wade)*
  6. **Which word means that water has covered something that should not be covered?** *(flooded)*

▶ Dictate, Draw, and Write

Children will dictate sentences and draw pictures to illustrate some of this week's Oral Vocabulary words.

- Review the meanings of the Oral Vocabulary words with children. Hold up the word strip from Discuss Oral Vocabulary as you review each word. Display the word strips along the chalk ledge.

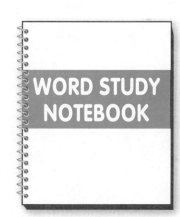

- Tell children that together you will write a group story about a calf in a flooded meadow, using as many of the Oral Vocabulary words as possible. Ask volunteers to think of sentences using the words to tell the story. As a child says a sentence, record it on the board or on chart paper.

- Continue until there is at least one sentence for each Oral Vocabulary word.

- Then have children draw and write in their Word Study Notebooks to tell about the class story. Have them try to use the words *calf, flooded, meadow, rippled, swarm,* or *wade* to tell about their drawings.

Oral Vocabulary Development

ORAL VOCABULARY

1. **clever** Someone who is *clever* is smart.

2. **clues** *Clues* are bits of information that help solve a problem or a mystery.

3. **detectives** *Detectives* are people who use clues to solve problems or mysteries.

4. **poked** If you *poked* your head out the window, you moved your head quickly to look out.

5. **sneaky** Someone who is *sneaky* acts in a way that is secret or tricky.

6. **whispered** If someone *whispered*, he or she spoke in a soft voice.

Read Aloud Passages

The Oral Vocabulary words appear in the Read Aloud Passage, "Grandpa's Tree." See page 359 of this Guide.

▶ Discuss Oral Vocabulary

Children will answer questions about the Oral Vocabulary words from the Read Aloud "Grandpa's Tree" to deepen their understanding of the words.

- Write each Oral Vocabulary word on a strip of paper.

- Review with children the meaning of each Oral Vocabulary word, displaying each word as you share its meaning, shown to the left.

- Ask questions about the words, such as the ones below. Encourage children to use the Oral Vocabulary words in their responses.

  1. Would a clever person probably be able to solve a puzzle? Why?
  2. Whose job is it to look for clues—a police officer or a pet shop owner? Why?
  3. What job do detectives do?
  4. If a visitor poked her head into your classroom, what did she do?
  5. Would you have to be sneaky to keep a family member from finding a secret birthday present? Why?
  6. If you whispered to your friend, would just your friend hear you or would the whole class hear you? Why?

- As children answer the questions, encourage them to explain their responses and to share their ideas about the words.

▶ Word Associations

Children will answer questions about the Oral Vocabulary words.

- Tell children that today you will ask some questions and they will answer with the Oral Vocabulary words.

- Review the Oral Vocabulary words, displaying each word as you share its meaning.

- Read aloud the first question, and model how to figure out the answer.

- Then read aloud the remaining questions. Remind children to answer each question with an Oral Vocabulary word. If children have difficulty answering, provide two answer choices for each question.

  1. Which word names people who use clues to solve mysteries? *(detectives)*
  2. Which word describes someone who plans a surprise birthday party for a friend without her knowing? *(sneaky)*
  3. Which word describes someone who is smart? *(clever)*
  4. Which word tells what a dog did with its head when it peeked around the corner? *(poked)*
  5. Which word means pieces of information that can be used to solve a mystery? *(clues)*
  6. Which word tells how you talked when you told someone a secret? *(whispered)*

▶ Complete Sentences

Children will use Oral Vocabulary words to complete sentences.

- Review the meanings of the Oral Vocabulary words with children.

- Tell children you will say a sentence with a word missing. Tell them to listen carefully so they can choose the Oral Vocabulary word that best completes the sentence.

- Say each of the following sentences, pausing or indicating the missing word by saying *blank*.

- Repeat the sentence, and have children supply the missing Oral Vocabulary word. You may repeat the Oral Vocabulary words as often as children need to hear them. Model the process by completing the first sentence.

  1. The _____ fox hid in the shadows until the farmer had passed by. *(sneaky)*
  2. Mr. Rizzo hired _____ to find out where his missing money was. *(detectives)*
  3. The _____ dog knows how to do many tricks. *(clever)*
  4. Rebecca _____ a secret to her sister. *(whispered)*
  5. The police looked for _____ to help them solve the mystery. *(clues)*
  6. The bear _____ its nose into a pot of honey. *(poked)*

- Call on volunteers to say sentences using the Oral Vocabulary words.

▶ Dictate, Draw, and Write

Children will dictate sentences and draw pictures to illustrate some of this week's Oral Vocabulary words.

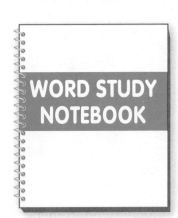

- Review the meanings of the Oral Vocabulary words with children. Hold up the word strip from Discuss Oral Vocabulary as you review each word. Display the word strips along the chalk ledge.

- Have children think of a sentence using one of the Oral Vocabulary words. As a child says a sentence, record it on the board or on chart paper. Call on another child to say a different sentence using the word, and record that child's sentence as well.

- Continue until there is at least one sentence for each Oral Vocabulary word.

- Then have partners draw and write in their Word Study Notebooks to tell about some clever detectives. Help them use the words *clever, clues, detectives, poked, sneaky,* or *whispered* to tell about or label their drawings.

Oral Vocabulary Development

ORAL VOCABULARY

1. **misty** Something *misty* is covered in mist or fog.

2. **promised** If you *promised* to do something, you said you would do it.

3. **receive** When you *receive* something, you get it or catch it.

4. **roamed** If someone *roamed*, he or she walked around from place to place.

5. **slender** Something *slender* is thin.

6. **sparkling** Something that is *sparkling* is shining.

Read Aloud Passages

The Oral Vocabulary words appear in the Read Aloud Passage, "How Bat Learned to Fly." See page 359 of this Guide.

▶ Discuss Oral Vocabulary

Children will answer questions about the Oral Vocabulary words from the Read Aloud "How Bat Learned to Fly" to deepen their understanding of the words.

- Write each Oral Vocabulary word on a strip of paper.

- Review with children the meaning of each Oral Vocabulary word, displaying each word as you share its meaning, shown to the left.

- Ask questions about the words, such as the ones below. Encourage children to use the Oral Vocabulary words in their responses.

  1. Would it be easy to see things far away on a misty day? Explain why.
  2. If you promised to make your bed each morning, do you need to do it? Why?
  3. If you receive a gift, do you give the gift away or get the gift from someone else?
  4. If a person roamed in the woods, was he sitting or walking? Why?
  5. Would it be hard to fit a slender wallet in your pocket? Why?
  6. If the sun shines brightly on the water, would the water be sparkling? Why?

- As children answer the questions, encourage them to explain their responses and to share their ideas about the words.

▶ Paired Yes/No Questions

Children will answer paired questions about Oral Vocabulary words to show understanding of how to use the words correctly.

- Tell children that today they will be answering yes/no questions about the Oral Vocabulary words.

- Review the meanings of the Oral Vocabulary words, displaying each word as you share its meaning.

- Read a set of paired questions. Say: *Roamed.* **If you roamed at the park, did you stay in one place?** *(no)* **If you roamed at the park, did you move around?** *(yes)* Encourage children to explain their answers. Continue in the same way with the remaining paired questions.

  1. Is a diamond ring sparkling? *(yes)* Is a potato sparkling? *(no)*
  2. Is the sky clear if it is misty? *(no)* Is the sky foggy if it is misty? *(yes)*
  3. If you promised to help your friend with his homework, should you do something else? *(no)* If you promised to help your friend with his homework, should you do it? *(yes)*
  4. Do spiders have slender legs? *(yes)* Do elephants have slender legs? *(no)*
  5. If you receive a gift, do you get angry? *(no)* If you receive a gift, do you say "thank you"? *(yes)*

▶ Word Sort

Children will sort the Oral Vocabulary words to learn more about how the words can be used.

- Use the word strips from Discuss Oral Vocabulary. On the board or on chart paper, draw a chart like the one shown below. Tell children they will help you sort the Oral Vocabulary words.

- Review the meanings of the Oral Vocabulary words, displaying each word as you share its meaning.

- Then explain the chart headings. Tell children they will sort the Oral Vocabulary words into two groups: action words and describing words.

- Choose one of the word strips, and read the word aloud. For example, say: **Slender. Is *slender* an action word or a describing word? Who can tell me the meaning of *slender*? Where should I put *slender*?** Place the word strip in the *Describing Words* column of the chart.

- Continue with the other words. Encourage children to tell why they think a word belongs in the category they have named.

- If a child responds that *sparkling* is an action word, point out that many words have several meanings. Use these sentences as examples for *sparkling*: The *sparkling* lights are beautiful. The stars are *sparkling* in the sky. Make another word strip for *sparkling* and add it to the Action Words column.

Action Words	Describing Words
promised	slender
receive	misty
roamed	sparkling

. . . .

▶ Dictate, Draw, and Write

Children will dictate sentences and draw pictures to illustrate some of this week's Oral Vocabulary words.

- Review the meanings of the Oral Vocabulary words with children. Hold up the word strip from Discuss Oral Vocabulary as you review each word. Display the word strips along the chalk ledge.

- Have children think of a sentence using one of the Oral Vocabulary words. As a child says a sentence, record it on the board or on chart paper. Call on another child to say a different sentence using the word, and record that child's sentence as well.

- Continue until there is at least one sentence for each Oral Vocabulary word.

- Then have children choose three words to draw and write about in their Word Study Notebooks to show what they have learned about the words *misty*, *promised*, *receive*, *roamed*, *slender*, or *sparkling*.

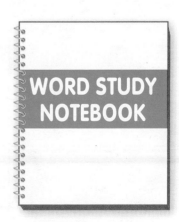

WORD STUDY NOTEBOOK

Oral Vocabulary Development

ORAL VOCABULARY

1. accent If you say a word with an *accent*, you say it the way a certain group of people say it.

2. behave When you *behave*, you follow the rules.

3. gooey Something that is *gooey* is sticky.

4. siesta A *siesta* is an afternoon nap.

5. sizzling Something that is *sizzling* is very, very hot.

6. translated If someone *translated*, that person put words into another language.

Read Aloud Passages

The Oral Vocabulary words appear in the Read Aloud Passage, "Around the World in a Day." See page 360 of this Guide.

▶ Discuss Oral Vocabulary

Children will answer questions about the Oral Vocabulary words from the Read Aloud "Around the World in a Day" to deepen their understanding of the words.

• Write each Oral Vocabulary word on a strip of paper.

• Review with children the meaning of each Oral Vocabulary word, displaying each word as you share its meaning, shown to the left.

• Ask questions about the words, such as the ones below. Encourage children to use the Oral Vocabulary words in their responses.

   1. Would you hear an accent when someone is humming or when someone is speaking? Why?

   2. Is it important to behave at school? Explain why.

   3. Which is gooey, honey or water? Why?

   4. Would you take a siesta if you felt tired? Why?

   5. Should you wait before eating sizzling meat? Why?

   6. If someone translated a sentence, would that person say the sentence in the same language or in a different language? Why?

• As children answer the questions, encourage them to explain their responses and to share their ideas about the words.

▶ True or Not True

Children will determine whether statements using the Oral Vocabulary words are true or not true.

• Review the meanings of the Oral Vocabulary words, displaying each word as you share its meaning.

• Tell children you are going to say some sentences about the Oral Vocabulary words. They are to listen carefully and decide whether the sentence is true or not true.

• Read aloud each sentence. If children disagree whether a statement is true or not true, guide them to understand the correct response.

   1. A sizzling pan is cool to the touch. *(not true)*

   2. You behave if you follow the rules. *(true)*

   3. Nuts are gooey. *(not true)*

   4. An accent is a way of saying a word. *(true)*

   5. A story in English that is translated is told in another language. *(true)*

   6. You keep your eyes open when you take a siesta. *(not true)*

• Revisit the items that are not true. Encourage children to reword the sentences to make them true.

▶ Word Associations

Children will answer questions about the Oral Vocabulary words.

- Tell children that today you will ask some questions and they will answer with the Oral Vocabulary words.

- Review the Oral Vocabulary words, displaying each word as you share its meaning.

- Read aloud the first question and model how to figure out the answer.

- Then read aloud the remaining questions. Remind children to answer each question with an Oral Vocabulary word. If children have difficulty answering, provide two answer choices for each question.

  1. **Which word means a nap in the afternoon?** *(siesta)*
  2. **Which word describes how someone whose first language is French might speak another language?** *(accent)*
  3. **Which word means that someone put words from one language into another language?** *(translated)*
  4. **Which word describes an egg in a very hot pan?** *(sizzling)*
  5. **Which word describes the sticky syrup that you pour on pancakes?** *(gooey)*
  6. **Which word describes what you do if you follow the classroom rules?** *(behave)*

. . . .

▶ Dictate, Draw, and Write

Children will dictate sentences and draw pictures to illustrate some of this week's Oral Vocabulary words.

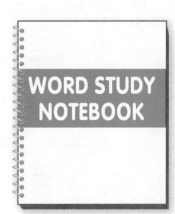

- Review the meanings of the Oral Vocabulary words with children. Hold up the word strip from Discuss Oral Vocabulary as you review each word. Display the word strips along the chalk ledge.

- Have children think of a sentence using one of the Oral Vocabulary words. As a child says a sentence, record it on the board or on chart paper. Call on another child to say a different sentence using the word, and record that child's sentence as well.

- Continue until there is at least one sentence for each Oral Vocabulary word.

- Then have children work with a partner. Have them discuss how they could illustrate the words *accent*, *behave*, *gooey*, *siesta*, *sizzling*, or *translated* to show what they have learned. Tell children to choose three of the words to draw and write about in their Word Study Notebooks.

ORAL VOCABULARY

1. **completely** *Completely* means totally or fully.

2. **gentle** Someone or something *gentle* is kind and will not cause any harm.

3. **lonely** Someone who is *lonely* feels sad about being alone.

4. **recognize** When you *recognize* something, you know what it is.

5. **reflection** A *reflection* is an image of something on a shiny surface such as a mirror.

6. **settle** When things *settle*, they come to rest.

Read Aloud Passages

The Oral Vocabulary words appear in the Read Aloud Passage, "Visiting Butterflies." See page 361 of this Guide.

▶ Discuss Oral Vocabulary

Children will answer questions about the Oral Vocabulary words from the Read Aloud "Visiting Butterflies" to deepen their understanding of the words.

- Write each Oral Vocabulary word on a strip of paper.

- Review with children the meaning of each Oral Vocabulary word, displaying each word as you share its meaning, shown to the left.

- Ask questions about the words, such as the ones below. Encourage children to use the Oral Vocabulary words in their responses.

  1. **If you are completely full after eating lunch, do you want more food? Why?**

  2. **Which animal is gentle, a lion or a lamb? Why?**

  3. **Would you feel lonely with a group of friends or by yourself? Why?**

  4. **Which person would you recognize, your teacher or a new student at school? Why?**

  5. **Would you see your reflection in a blanket or in a mirror? Why?**

  6. **If birds settle in a tree, are they sitting still or hopping around? Why?**

- As children answer the questions, encourage them to explain their responses and to share their ideas about the words.

▶ Paired Yes/No Questions

Children will answer paired questions about Oral Vocabulary words to show understanding of how to use the words correctly.

- Tell children that today they will be answering yes/no questions about the Oral Vocabulary words.

- Review the meanings of the Oral Vocabulary words, displaying each word as you share its meaning.

- Read a set of paired questions. Say: *Recognize*. **Do you recognize a person you know?** *(yes)* **Do you recognize a stranger?** *(no)* Encourage children to explain their answers. Continue in the same way with the remaining paired questions.

  1. **Would you call a kitten gentle?** *(yes)* **Would you call a tiger gentle?** *(no)*

  2. **Is a ball completely round?** *(yes)* **Is an apple completely round?** *(no)*

  3. **If you see a cat settle on a bed, is the cat moving?** *(no)* **If you see a cat settle on a bed, is the cat still?** *(yes)*

  4. **Can you see your reflection in a rug?** *(no)* **Can you see your reflection in a mirror?** *(yes)*

  5. **Would you feel lonely if you ate lunch by yourself?** *(yes)* **Would you feel lonely if you ate lunch with your friends?** *(no)*

▶ Describe It or Act It Out

Children will describe or act out Oral Vocabulary words to demonstrate understanding.

- Review the meanings of the Oral Vocabulary words with children.

- Tell children that you are going to ask some questions and give some directions using the Oral Vocabulary words. Explain that they will answer the questions by giving a description. They will follow the directions by acting out the meaning of the word.

- Read each of the following items. Allow a few children to provide descriptions or to act out the word meanings, as appropriate.

  1. **How do you feel when you are lonely?** *(Possible response: sad, upset)*

  2. **Show how you look when you recognize a favorite person at a party.** *(Possible response: The child shows a look of happiness or excitement.)*

  3. **Show how you can close your eyes completely.** *(Possible response: The child shuts his or her eyes tight.)*

  4. **How does a gentle person act?** *(Possible response: A gentle person is kind, nice, and calm.)*

  5. **What do you see when you look at your reflection in the mirror?** *(Possible response: I see my smiling face with brown eyes and my long, brown hair.)*

  6. **Show how you settle in your chair.** *(Possible response: The child moves around to get comfortable and then sits still in his or her chair.)*

▶ Dictate, Draw, and Write

Children will dictate sentences and draw pictures to illustrate some of this week's Oral Vocabulary words.

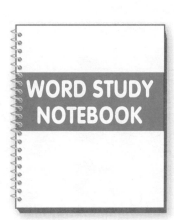

- Review the meanings of the Oral Vocabulary words with children. Hold up the word strip from Discuss Oral Vocabulary as you review each word. Display the word strips along the chalk ledge.

- Have children think of a sentence using one of the Oral Vocabulary words. As a child says a sentence, record it on the board or on chart paper. Call on another child to say a different sentence using the word, and record that child's sentence as well.

- Continue until there is at least one sentence for each Oral Vocabulary word.

- Then have children choose three words to draw and write about in their Word Study Notebooks to show what they have learned about the words *completely*, *gentle*, *lonely*, *recognize*, *reflection*, or *settle*.

ORAL VOCABULARY

1. **blossoms** *Blossoms* are flowers.

2. **cavern** A *cavern* is a large cave.

3. **ledge** A *ledge* is a flat space like a shelf sticking out on the side of a mountain.

4. **lugging** If you are *lugging* something, you are carrying a heavy load.

5. **shady** A *shady* place is an area out of the sun.

6. **shallow** Something that is *shallow* is not deep.

Read Aloud
Passages

The Oral Vocabulary words appear in the Read Aloud Passage, "Señor Coyote, the Judge." See page 361 of this Guide.

▶ Discuss Oral Vocabulary

Children will answer questions about the Oral Vocabulary words from the Read Aloud "Señor Coyote, the Judge" to deepen their understanding of the words.

- Write each Oral Vocabulary word on a strip of paper.

- Review with children the meaning of each Oral Vocabulary word, displaying each word as you share its meaning, shown to the left.

- Ask questions about the words, such as the ones below. Encourage children to use the Oral Vocabulary words in their responses.

  1. Where would you see blossoms growing?

  2. Would someone use a flashlight or a bike to explore a cavern? Why?

  3. Would you see a ledge if you were hiking in the mountains or walking in a field? Why?

  4. Would it be easy or hard to be lugging a big suitcase? Explain why.

  5. Do you feel the sun if you are standing in a shady spot? Why?

  6. Could an elephant hide in shallow water? Why?

- As children answer the questions, encourage them to explain their responses and to share their ideas about the words.

▶ This or That

Children will sort Oral Vocabulary words into two groups: words that tell about the outdoors and words that do not.

- Use the word strips from Discuss Oral Vocabulary. On the board or on chart paper, draw a chart like the one shown below. Tell children they will help you sort the Oral Vocabulary words.

- Review the meanings of the Oral Vocabulary words with children. Then explain the chart headings. Tell children that they will sort the Oral Vocabulary words into two groups: one for words that tell about the outdoors and one for words that do not tell about the outdoors.

- Display and read each word aloud. For example, say: *Cavern.* **Is *cavern* a word that tells about something you would see outdoors or not? Yes, so we'll put it in the first column under the checkmark.**

- Continue in the same way until all the words have been sorted.

✓ About the Outdoors	✗ Not About the Outdoors
cavern	lugging
blossoms	shallow
ledge	
shady	

▶ Antonyms

Children will name antonyms for some of the Oral Vocabulary words.

- Tell students that antonyms are words that have opposite meanings. Provide a few examples, such as *start* and *finish*, *easy* and *hard*, and *lost* and *found*.

- On the board or on chart paper, draw a chart like the one below. Write the examples discussed above into the chart as you reinforce the opposite meanings. Tell children that now they will help you name antonyms for some of the Oral Vocabulary words.

- Write the Oral Vocabulary word *shady* in the first column. Guide children to describe or name words that mean the opposite. List their ideas in the second column. If children need help with word meanings, encourage them to use a picture dictionary.

- Repeat with the Oral Vocabulary word *shallow*. Then read the words and antonyms with children.

Word	Antonyms
start	finish
easy	hard
lost	found
shady	sunny, bright
shallow	deep

▶ Dictate, Draw, and Write

Children will dictate sentences and draw pictures to illustrate some of this week's Oral Vocabulary words.

- Review the meanings of the Oral Vocabulary words with children. Hold up the word strip from Discuss Oral Vocabulary as you review each word. Display the word strips along the chalk ledge.

- Tell children that together you will write a class story about a bear that lives in a cavern, using as many of the Oral Vocabulary words as possible. Ask volunteers to think of sentences using the words to tell the story. As a child says a sentence, record it on the board or on chart paper.

- Continue until there is at least one sentence for each Oral Vocabulary word.

- Then have children draw and write in their Word Study Notebooks to tell about the class story. Help them use the words *blossoms*, *cavern*, *ledge*, *lugging*, *shady*, or *shallow* to tell about or label their drawings.

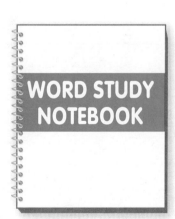

WORD STUDY NOTEBOOK

Oral Vocabulary Development

ORAL VOCABULARY

1. **field** A *field* is an area of open land.

2. **magical** Something *magical* is special in a way that seems unlike everyday life.

3. **shrubbery** *Shrubbery* is a group of bushes.

4. **softly** If you speak *softly*, you speak quietly.

5. **universe** The *universe* is all of the things in space.

6. **wondrous** Something *wondrous* gives you a feeling of amazement.

Read Aloud Passages

The Oral Vocabulary words appear in the Read Aloud Passage, "The Art Contest." See page 362 of this Guide.

▶ Discuss Oral Vocabulary

Children will answer questions about the Oral Vocabulary words from the Read Aloud "The Art Contest" to deepen their understanding of the words.

- Write each Oral Vocabulary word on a strip of paper.

- Review with children the meaning of each Oral Vocabulary word, displaying each word as you share its meaning, shown to the left.

- Ask questions about the words, such as the ones below. Encourage children to use the Oral Vocabulary words in their responses.
    1. **Do you think a field might be a good place to fly a kite? Why?**
    2. **Which would be magical, a hen that lays white eggs or a hen that lays golden eggs? Why?**
    3. **Where would you find shrubbery? Why?**
    4. **If you played the piano softly, would the music be quiet or loud? Why?**
    5. **Is Earth part of the universe? Why do you think so?**
    6. **Would seeing a shooting star be a wondrous event? Why?**

- As children answer the questions, encourage them to explain their responses and to share their ideas about the words.

▶ True or Not True

Children will determine whether statements using the Oral Vocabulary words are true or not true.

- Review the meanings of the Oral Vocabulary words, displaying each word as you share its meaning.

- Tell children you are going to say some sentences about the Oral Vocabulary words. They are to listen carefully and decide whether the sentence is true or not true.

- Read aloud each sentence. If children disagree whether a statement is true or not true, guide them to understand the correct response.
    1. **When you shout, you talk softly.** *(not true)*
    2. **The moon and sun are part of the universe.** *(true)*
    3. **Shrubbery is a kind of animal.** *(not true)*
    4. **A field is full of buildings and roads.** *(not true)*
    5. **A beautiful rainbow with many colors is wondrous.** *(true)*
    6. **A magical creature such as a unicorn does not really exist.** *(true)*

- Revisit the items that are not true. Encourage children to reword the sentences to make them true.

▶ Complete Sentences

Children will use Oral Vocabulary words to complete sentences.

- Review the meanings of the Oral Vocabulary words with children.

- Tell children you will be saying sentences with a word missing. Tell them to listen carefully so they can choose the Oral Vocabulary word that completes a sentence.

- Say each of the following sentences, pausing or indicating the missing word by saying *blank*. Repeat the sentence, and have children supply the missing Oral Vocabulary word. You may repeat the Oral Vocabulary words as often as children need to hear them. Model the process by completing the first sentence.

  1. There were talking trees in the _____ forest. *(magical)*

  2. There are many stars in the _____. *(universe)*

  3. The _____ adds plenty of green color to our backyard. *(shrubbery)*

  4. The farmer grows corn in the _____. *(field)*

  5. Neal saw a _____ sight when the full moon rose at night. *(wondrous)*

  6. The kitten meowed so _____ that I could hardly hear it. *(softly)*

- Call on volunteers to say sentences using the Oral Vocabulary words.

- -

▶ Dictate, Draw, and Write

Children will dictate sentences and draw pictures to illustrate some of this week's Oral Vocabulary words.

- Review the meanings of the Oral Vocabulary words with children. Hold up the word strip from Discuss Oral Vocabulary as you review each word. Display the word strips along the chalk ledge.

- Have children think of a sentence using one of the Oral Vocabulary words. As a child says a sentence, record it on the board or on chart paper. Call on another child to say a different sentence using the word, and record that child's sentence as well.

- Continue until there is at least one sentence for each Oral Vocabulary word.

- Then have children draw and write in their Word Study Notebooks to tell about something wondrous and magical. Have them try to use the words *field, magical, shrubbery, softly, universe,* or *wondrous* to tell about their drawings.

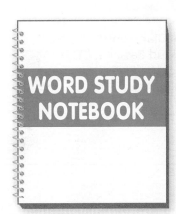

WORD STUDY NOTEBOOK

Oral Vocabulary Development

ORAL VOCABULARY

1. **cobweb** Spiders make a kind of silky thread and spin it into a design called a *cobweb*.

2. **demanded** If someone *demanded* something, he or she asked strongly for it.

3. **dreadful** Something *dreadful* is awful and causes unhappiness.

4. **grumbled** If you *grumbled*, you complained in a low, unhappy voice.

5. **panted** If someone *panted*, he or she breathed with short, quick breaths.

6. **terrified** To be *terrified* means to be very scared.

Read Aloud Passages

The Oral Vocabulary words appear in the Read Aloud Passage, "The Shoemaker and the Elves." See page 362 of this Guide.

▶ Discuss Oral Vocabulary

Children will answer questions about the Oral Vocabulary words from the Read Aloud "The Shoemaker and the Elves" to deepen their understanding of the words.

- Write each Oral Vocabulary word on a strip of paper.

- Review with children the meaning of each Oral Vocabulary word, displaying each word as you share its meaning, shown to the left.

- Ask questions about the words, such as the ones below. Encourage children to use the Oral Vocabulary words in their responses.

  1. **Would a spider or a monkey leave a cobweb behind? Why?**
  2. **If a teacher demanded quiet in the classroom, what did she do?**
  3. **Which is dreadful, winning a game or losing a favorite toy? Why?**
  4. **What kinds of things have you grumbled about?**
  5. **Would someone have panted if she just ran a long race? Why?**
  6. **Would you feel terrified if your friend said hello? Why?**

- As children answer the questions, encourage them to explain their responses and to share their ideas about the words.

▶ Guess the Word

Children will listen to clues and identify the Oral Vocabulary words.

- Review the Oral Vocabulary words and meanings with children.

- Tell children you will be saying some clues. They are to listen carefully and then name the Oral Vocabulary word for each clue.

- Model the process with the first clue. Then read aloud the remaining clues and ask children to name the Oral Vocabulary word for each one. If children have difficulty answering, provide two answer choices for each clue.

  1. **Complained about the rainy weather** *(grumbled)*
  2. **Very afraid during a loud thunderstorm** *(terrified)*
  3. **Had to have a snack right away** *(demanded)*
  4. **Breathed heavily after jumping rope** *(panted)*
  5. **What a spider spins** *(cobweb)*
  6. **An awful day** *(dreadful)*

- After children have guessed the correct word, ask volunteers to give examples of how they might use the word when talking to a friend or an adult.

▶ Describe It or Act It Out

Children will describe or act out Oral Vocabulary words to demonstrate understanding.

- Review the meanings of the Oral Vocabulary words with children.

- Tell children that you are going to ask some questions and give some directions using the Oral Vocabulary words. Explain that they will answer the questions by giving a description. They will follow the directions by acting out the meaning of the word.

- Read each of the following items. Encourage several children to provide descriptions or to act out the word meanings.

  1. **Show how you would have panted after running around the playground.** *(Possible response: The child takes short, quick breaths.)*

  2. **What does a cobweb look like?** *(Possible response: silky, white, round with crisscrossed threads)*

  3. **Show how you would look if you were terrified of a bug.** *(Possible response: The child looks scared or anxious.)*

  4. **What kind of voice would you use if you demanded something?** *(Possible response: loud, strong)*

  5. **What kind of voice would you use if you grumbled about something?** *(Possible response: low, unhappy, whiny)*

  6. **Show how you would look if you wanted to go out to play, but the weather was dreadful.** *(Possible response: The child looks unhappy or grumpy.)*

▶ Dictate, Draw, and Write

Children will dictate sentences and draw pictures to illustrate some of this week's Oral Vocabulary words.

- Review the meanings of the Oral Vocabulary words with children. Hold up the word strip from Discuss Oral Vocabulary as you review each word. Display the word strips along the chalk ledge.

- Have children think of a sentence using one of the Oral Vocabulary words. As a child says a sentence, record it on the board or on chart paper. Call on another child to say a different sentence using the word, and record that child's sentence as well.

- Continue until there is at least one sentence for each Oral Vocabulary word.

- Then have children choose three words to draw and write about in their Word Study Notebooks to show what they have learned about the words *cobweb, demanded, dreadful, grumbled, panted,* or *terrified.*

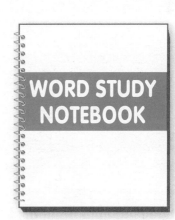

WORD STUDY NOTEBOOK

Oral Vocabulary Development

ORAL VOCABULARY

1. **assures** If someone *assures* you, he or she promises you.

2. **audience** An *audience* is a group of people watching or listening to a performance.

3. **chorus** A *chorus* is a group of singers.

4. **determined** Someone who is *determined* sticks to his or her goal.

5. **enthusiasm** *Enthusiasm* is what you feel when you like something a lot.

6. **stomped** If you *stomped*, you hit one or both feet loudly on the floor.

Read Aloud Passages

The Oral Vocabulary words appear in the Read Aloud Passage, "A Hopeful Song." See page 363 of this Guide.

▶ Discuss Oral Vocabulary

Children will answer questions about the Oral Vocabulary words from the Read Aloud "A Hopeful Song" to deepen their understanding of the words.

- Write each Oral Vocabulary word on a strip of paper.

- Review with children the meaning of each Oral Vocabulary word, displaying each word as you share its meaning, shown to the left.

- Ask questions about the words, such as the ones below. Encourage children to use the Oral Vocabulary words in their responses.

  1. **How would you feel if someone assures you that you can go on a class field trip? Why?**

  2. **Would you find an audience at a concert or at a cookout? Why?**

  3. **Would you expect a chorus to play baseball or to sing? Why?**

  4. **If you are determined to be a good student, what will you do?**

  5. **What is something that you have enthusiasm for? Why do you like it so much?**

  6. **Who is more likely to have stomped on the floor, a dancer or a painter? Why?**

- As children answer the questions, encourage them to explain their responses and to share their ideas about the words.

▶ Paired Yes/No Questions

Children will answer paired questions about Oral Vocabulary words to show understanding of how to use the words correctly.

- Tell children that today they will be answering yes/no questions about the Oral Vocabulary words.

- Review the meanings of the Oral Vocabulary words, displaying each word as you share its meaning.

- Read a set of paired questions. Say: *Assures.* **If your friend assures you he will share his crayons, will he keep the crayons to himself?** *(no)* **If your friend assures you he will share his crayons, will he let you use the crayons?** *(yes)* Encourage children to explain their answers. Continue in the same way with the remaining paired questions.

  1. **If you were determined to learn about dinosaurs, would you look at library books?** *(yes)* **If you were determined to learn about dinosaurs, would you go to a zoo?** *(no)*

  2. **Would you see an audience at a grocery store?** *(no)* **Would you see an audience at a movie theater?** *(yes)*

  3. **If someone stomped on a wooden floor, would you hear it?** *(yes)* **If someone stomped on a thick rug, would you hear it?** *(no)*

  4. **Does a chorus rake leaves?** *(no)* **Does a chorus sing songs?** *(yes)*

  5. **Is clapping your hands a way to show enthusiasm?** *(yes)* **Is going to sleep a way to show enthusiasm?** *(no)*

▶ Word Sort

Children will sort the Oral Vocabulary words to learn more about how the words are used.

- Use the word strips from Discuss Oral Vocabulary. On the board or on chart paper, draw a chart like the one shown below. Tell children they will help you sort the Oral Vocabulary words.

- Review the meanings of the Oral Vocabulary words, displaying each word as you share its meaning.

- Then explain the chart headings. Tell children they will sort the Oral Vocabulary words into two groups: words about a good show and other words.

- Choose one of the word strips, and read the word aloud. For example, say: *Audience.* **Is *audience* a word about a good show? Who can tell me the meaning of *audience*? Where should I put *audience*?** Place the word strip in the *Words About a Good Show* column of the chart.

- Continue with the other words. Encourage children to tell why they think a word belongs in the category they have named. Make adjustments if a child presents a good argument for moving a word or creating a third category. For example, the word *determined* could describe how a performer feels.

Words About a Good Show	Other Words
audience	determined
chorus	assures
enthusiasm	
stomped	

- -

▶ Dictate, Draw, and Write

Children will dictate sentences and draw pictures to illustrate some of this week's Oral Vocabulary words.

- Review the meanings of the Oral Vocabulary words with children. Hold up the word strip from Discuss Oral Vocabulary as you review each word. Display the word strips along the chalk ledge.

- Have children think of a sentence using one of the Oral Vocabulary words. As a child says a sentence, record it on the board or on chart paper. Call on another child to say a different sentence using the word, and record that child's sentence as well.

- Continue until there is at least one sentence for each Oral Vocabulary word.

- Then have children choose three words to draw and write about in their Word Study Notebooks to show what they have learned about the words *assures, audience, chorus, determined, enthusiasm,* or *stomped.*

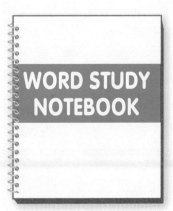

WORD STUDY NOTEBOOK

Oral Vocabulary Development

ORAL VOCABULARY

1. corner A *corner* is a place where two sides come together.

2. disguised Someone who is *disguised* is dressed in a way that hides who the person is.

3. mystery A *mystery* is something puzzling that has to be figured out.

4. seriously *Seriously* means in a way that is thoughtful and not joking.

5. signs *Signs* are things that give clues about something that happened or something that might happen later.

6. solve If you *solve* something, you figure it out.

Read Aloud Passages

The Oral Vocabulary words appear in the Read Aloud Passage, "A Stone Goes to Court." See page 364 of this Guide.

▶ Discuss Oral Vocabulary

Children will answer questions about the Oral Vocabulary words from the Read Aloud "A Stone Goes to Court" to deepen their understanding of the words.

- Write each Oral Vocabulary word on a strip of paper.

- Review with children the meaning of each Oral Vocabulary word, displaying each word as you share its meaning, shown to the left.

- Ask questions about the words, such as the ones below. Encourage children to use the Oral Vocabulary words in their responses.

  1. Look in one corner of the classroom. What do you see there?

  2. Have you ever been disguised? What did you wear?

  3. Would it be a mystery if you sharpened your pencil or if your pencil disappeared from your desk? Why?

  4. What is something that people must do seriously? Explain why.

  5. What signs tell you that it might rain—a dark and cloudy sky or a sky filled with bright sunshine? Why?

  6. Do you solve a math problem or a telephone call? Why?

- As children answer the questions, encourage them to explain their responses and to share their ideas about the words.

▶ "Because" Sentences

Children will use the Oral Vocabulary words to complete sentences.

- Review the meanings of the Oral Vocabulary words with children.

- Tell children you will say the beginning of a sentence that ends with the word *because*. Explain that they will finish the sentence by telling more about the meaning of the Oral Vocabulary word.

- Then say each of the following sentences, having children finish the sentences to show understanding of the Oral Vocabulary words. Model the process by completing the first sentence for them.

- Ask two or more children to complete each sentence to demonstrate a variety of possible responses.

  1. It is a mystery where the raccoon lives because... *(Possible response: no one has seen its home.)*

  2. Joseph sat in the corner because... *(Possible response: there was a comfortable chair there.)*

  3. The principal speaks seriously because... *(Possible response: she is announcing there will be a fire drill.)*

  4. He can solve the word puzzle because... *(Possible response: he uses a dictionary.)*

  5. Elena was disguised as a tiger because... *(Possible response: she was going to a costume party.)*

  6. I know that the sun going down and streetlights coming on are signs of nighttime because... *(Possible response: I have seen this happen many times.)*

Word Associations

Children will answer questions about the Oral Vocabulary words.

- Tell children that today you will ask some questions and they will answer with the Oral Vocabulary words.
- Review the meanings of the Oral Vocabulary words, displaying each word as you share its meaning.
- Read aloud the first question and model how to figure out the answer.
- Then read aloud the remaining questions. Remind children to answer each question with an Oral Vocabulary word. If children have difficulty answering, provide two answer choices for each question.

  1. **Which word describes clues that show something happened?** *(signs)*
  2. **Which word means something that people have to try to figure out?** *(mystery)*
  3. **Which word names a place in a room where two walls meet?** *(corner)*
  4. **Which word describes something a detective might do?** *(solve)*
  5. **Which word tells how you might talk about the weather if a dangerous storm were coming?** *(seriously)*
  6. **Which word describes the way you would be if you wore a costume?** *(disguised)*

Dictate, Draw, and Write

Children will dictate sentences and draw pictures to illustrate some of this week's Oral Vocabulary words.

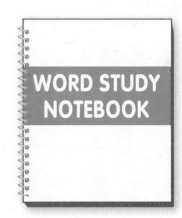

- Review the meanings of the Oral Vocabulary words with children. Hold up the word strip from Discuss Oral Vocabulary as you review each word. Display the word strips along the chalk ledge.
- Have children think of a sentence using one of the Oral Vocabulary words. As a child says a sentence, record it on the board or on chart paper. Call on another child to say a different sentence using the word, and record that child's sentence as well.
- Continue until there is at least one sentence for each Oral Vocabulary word.
- Then have partners draw and write in their Word Study Notebooks to tell about or make up a classroom mystery they would like to solve. Have them try to use the words *corner, disguised, mystery, seriously, signs,* or *solve* to tell about their drawings.

Oral Vocabulary Development

ORAL VOCABULARY

1. careful To be *careful* means to think about what you are doing.

2. mightiest Something that is the *mightiest* is the strongest.

3. show-off A *show-off* is someone who does things so that others will notice.

4. waste If something is useless, it is a *waste*.

5. wild Something *wild* is noisy and out of control.

6. wobble If you *wobble*, you move or shake from side to side.

Read Aloud Passages

The Oral Vocabulary words appear in the Read Aloud Passage, "The Parts of the House Have a Fight." See page 364 of this Guide.

▶ Discuss Oral Vocabulary

Children will answer questions about the Oral Vocabulary words from the Read Aloud "The Parts of the House Have a Fight" to deepen their understanding of the words.

- Write each Oral Vocabulary word on a strip of paper.

- Review with children the meaning of each Oral Vocabulary word, displaying each word as you share its meaning, shown to the left.

- Ask questions about the words, such as the ones below. Encourage children to use the Oral Vocabulary words in their responses.

   1. Why should you be careful when you cross the street?

   2. Do you think a lion is the mightiest animal in the jungle? Why?

   3. Does a show-off want to hide from everyone or be noticed by everyone? Why?

   4. Which is a waste of time—talking to a tree or talking to a friend? Why?

   5. What might a teacher say if two classmates had a wild argument?

   6. Would a person who is just learning to ride a bike wobble? Why?

- As children answer the questions, encourage them to explain their responses and to share their ideas about the words.

▶ Secret Word Game

Children will ask yes/no questions to guess a secret Oral Vocabulary word.

- Review the Oral Vocabulary words with children. Then tell them that they will play the Secret Word Game.

- Remind children that you will choose a word, and they have to ask questions to figure out the word. The questions must be able to be answered *yes* or *no*.

- Model how to ask yes/no questions by assigning a secret word to children. Ask questions such as these: **Does the word name an action? Does the word describe a person? Is the word made up of two words? Does the word describe how you might move? Does the word rhyme with *paste*?**

- Then choose your secret word, and have children ask yes/no questions to identify the word. Help them with additional clues as necessary.

- Repeat with the other Oral Vocabulary words, as time allows.

▶ Describe It or Act It Out

Children will describe or act out Oral Vocabulary words to demonstrate understanding.

- Review the meanings of the Oral Vocabulary words with children.

- Tell children that you are going to ask some questions and give some directions using the Oral Vocabulary words. Explain that they will answer the questions by giving a description. They will follow the directions by acting out the meaning of the word.

- Read each of the following items. Encourage several children to provide descriptions or to act out the word meanings.

  1. **Show how you might wobble if you were walking on a tightrope.** *(Possible response: The child pantomimes walking on a tightrope, wobbling from side to side to keep his or her balance.)*

  2. **If a wild person came into the library, how would the people around him or her feel?** *(Possible response: They would probably be mad and ask the person to be quiet or leave.)*

  3. **How does a show-off act in gym class?** *(Possible response: The child might run fast or jump high.)*

  4. **Tell about something that is a waste of time.** *(Possible response: Trying to teach a pet hamster to fly is a waste of time.)*

  5. **Show how you would be careful to carry a full glass of water across the room.** *(Possible response: The child pantomimes holding a glass and walks carefully across the room.)*

  6. **Tell what the mightiest person in the world might do.** *(Possible response: She might lift a large animal or a car.)*

▶ Dictate, Draw, and Write

Children will dictate sentences and draw pictures to illustrate some of this week's Oral Vocabulary words.

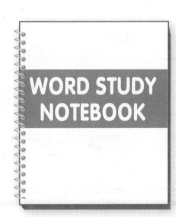

- Review the meanings of the Oral Vocabulary words with children. Hold up the word strip from Discuss Oral Vocabulary as you review each word. Display the word strips along the chalk ledge.

- Have children think of a sentence using one of the Oral Vocabulary words. As a child says a sentence, record it on the board or on chart paper. Call on another child to say a different sentence using the word, and record that child's sentence as well.

- Continue until there is at least one sentence for each Oral Vocabulary word.

- Then have children work with a partner. Have them discuss how they could illustrate the words *careful, mightiest, show-off, waste, wild,* or *wobble* to show what they have learned. Tell children to choose three of the words to draw and write about in their Word Study Notebooks.

Teacher's Notes

Meet Irene Fountas

Journeys Leveled Readers offer a variety of engaging, interesting fiction and nonfiction text— very carefully leveled, so you can count on the supports and challenges in each text to be appropriate for children in their development.

Irene Fountas
Consulting Author

The **Journeys** Reader's Workshop approach supports an emphasis on children reading and writing complex literature and informational text.

Weekly Plans for Whole Group and Small Group instruction enable teachers to:

- increase children's ability to read, think, and write critically about text.

- meet children at their instructional level and move them forward.

- allow for lesson flexibility to fit the strengths and needs of children.

Irene Fountas is a Professor in the School of Education of Lesley University in Cambridge, Massachusetts. Irene's research has focused on leveled texts, reader's and writer's workshop, assessment, classroom management, and professional development.

Reading Minilessons

Table of Contents

Whole-Group Lessons

- Interactive Read-Aloud/Shared Reading
- Reading Minilessons

Introduction

What Are Effective Instructional Practices in Literacy?

Your goal in literacy teaching is to bring each child from where he is to as far as you can take him in a school year, with the clear goal of helping each child develop the competencies of proficiency at the level. Proficient readers and writers not only think deeply and critically about texts but also develop a love of reading. The roots of lifelong literacy begin with a rich foundation in the elementary school.

The lessons in this section provide a structure for organizing your literacy teaching, linking understandings across the language and literacy framework, and building a strong foundation of reading strategies and skills. On the pages that follow, you will find an overview of how to use this section along with your *Journeys* materials in three different instructional contexts: Whole-Group Teaching, Small-Group Teaching, and Independent Literacy Work.

WHOLE GROUP
Interactive Read-Aloud/Shared Reading
(heterogeneous)

WHOLE GROUP
Reading Minilesson
(heterogeneous)

SMALL GROUP
Guided Reading
(temporary homogeneous)

SMALL GROUP
Literature Discussion
(heterogeneous)

INDEPENDENT
Independent Reading,
Literacy Work

Whole-Group Teaching

Whole-Group Lessons are related lesson sequences you may want to use across a week. At the core of each lesson is a Journeys literature selection, chosen to highlight a certain aspect of reading that is important for children to learn and apply in various contexts.

Interactive Read-Aloud/Shared Reading sets the stage for the day's focus and provides a common foundation of experience for children at various levels of reading proficiency (Fountas and Pinnell, 2006).

As you read aloud to children, use the questions and prompts at planned stopping points in the text to encourage discussion of the reading through classroom collaboration.

Reading aloud to children in this context

- helps children appreciate literature.

- gives children a model of how to think about ideas in the text and from the thinking of their peers.

- models fluent, expressive, phrased reading.

- has children think actively about what they read.

- allows children to hear and share a variety of perspectives and interpretations through classroom collaboration.

- is the common text used in the Reading Minilesson.

The **Reading Minilesson** is focused instruction about a specific topic or skill, called the Minilesson Principle (Fountas and Pinnell, 2001). Using this principle, you help your children think like effective, independent readers. The literature selection from the Interactive Read-Aloud/Shared Reading context is used as the example to demonstrate the principle.

The **Group Share** has children apply the minilesson principle to the text. As children think deeply about the text, they are able to make the connection to the minilesson principle, deepening their comprehension.

Whole-Group Lessons

What Is a Pal?
Student Book, Lesson 1

The Lion and the Mouse
See page 348 of this Guide.

Friends Forever
Student Book, Lesson 1

▶ What Is a Pal?

INTERACTIVE READ-ALOUD/SHARED READING

Read the book aloud to children. Stop periodically for very brief discussion of the book. Use the following suggested stopping points and prompts for quick group response, or give a specific prompt and have partners or threes turn and talk.

- After children read that Sam and Nat can help Dan, ask: "How are these pals helping? How do you know that?"
- After children read about who can be a pal, ask: "Who can be a pal? Who are some of your pals? Turn and talk about your ideas with a partner."
- After children read that a pal is fun to be with, ask: "What do you do with your pals?" Follow-up: "Why are your pals fun to be with?"
- At the end, ask: "How are you a pal?"

MINILESSON Main Idea

TEACH Display the minilesson principle on chart paper, and read it aloud to children. Tell children they are going to learn how to notice that authors tell mostly about one thing in information books.

1. Discuss the principle with children, using *What Is a Pal?* as an example. Suggested language: "There are different kinds of books. Some books tell stories. Other books give information or tell about real things. What kind of book is *What Is a Pal?*" *(an information book)* Follow-up: "How do you know?" *(It gives information about pals.)*

2. Focus on one part of the book, such as what pals can do with you. Suggested language: "This book tells about some things a pal can do with you. What are two things a pal can do with you?" *(A pal can help you and play with you.)*

3. Use children's responses to explain that authors tell mostly about one thing in information books. Suggested language: "The author tells mostly about pals. Pals are the one thing that this information book is mostly about."

4. Elicit from children additional details that support the idea that pals are the one thing this book is mostly about. Record children's ideas in a Web like the one shown here.

> **MINILESSON PRINCIPLE**
> Notice that authors tell mostly about one thing in information books.

Pals

SUMMARIZE AND APPLY Restate the minilesson principle. Then tell children to apply it to their independent reading. Suggested language: "When you read an information book, think about the one thing that the author tells mostly about. Think about how you know what that one thing is."

GROUP SHARE Ask children to share what they learned from reading an information book. Tell children to identify the one thing that the author tells mostly about and how they identified it.

186 • Lesson 1

TEACHER'S ROLE

- Engage children in thinking deeply about texts.
- Provide a learning environment in which children feel comfortable sharing their thinking with each other.
- Prepare explicit lessons that are tailored to children's needs.
- Provide a model of phrased, fluent reading in interactive read-aloud.

- Prompt children with comments and questions at planned stopping points to promote active thinking in interactive read-aloud/shared reading.
- Provide explicit teaching of critical literacy concepts in reading minilessons.
- Expose children to a wide variety of genres, authors, and topics.
- Monitor children's understanding to plan for future lessons.

CHILD'S ROLE

- Listen actively.
- Share ideas and opinions with others.
- Make connections to other readings and to own experiences.
- Ask genuine questions and build on the ideas of others.
- Demonstrate understanding of critical literacy concepts.

Genre instruction is a powerful tool for helping children develop the competencies of effective readers and writers. The questions and teaching points in this section can be used over and over across the year as children encounter different genres and increasingly difficult texts within a particular genre.

Discussion Starters are provided to spark discussion about genre characteristics.

Prompts for **Comparing Texts** guide children to compare the various texts they have read in a particular genre.

Informational Text

SUPPORT THINKING

DISCUSSION STARTERS During whole-group and small-group discussion, use questions to spark conversation about genre characteristics.

- What is this book about?
- What different kinds of type do you see?
- What kinds of pictures does the author use?
- What can you learn from the pictures?
- What does the author do to make the book interesting?
- How does the author organize the book to help you understand what you are reading?
- How do you know that the information in the book is true?
- How do you think the author feels about the topic? How do you know?

COMPARING TEXTS After children have read and listened to several informational selections, prompt them to compare selections and to recognize common characteristics. Use questions such as these:

- How are the animals in [title] and [title] the same?
- Think about [title] and [title]. How are they the same? How are they different?
- How do the pictures in [title] and [title] help you understand the author's ideas?

Genre Characteristics

Informational text gives facts about a topic.

Through repeated exposure to informational text, children should learn to notice common genre characteristics, though at Grade 1 they will not be expected to use the technical labels. Use friendly language to help them understand the following concepts.

- **Author's Purpose:** to inform
- **Graphic Features:** pictures that help the reader understand information or show more about the topic
  - **Diagrams:** pictures with labels
  - **Maps:** pictures that show where something is or how to get from one place to another
  - **Graphs/Charts:** pictures that help readers compare information
- **Text Features:** ways the author makes words stand out
  - **Headings:** type—usually larger, darker, or both—at the beginning of a new section
  - **Captions:** words or sentences that explain a picture
  - **Sizes/Colors:** authors use different sizes and colors to help readers see what is most important
- **Main Idea:** what the book is mostly about
- **Details:** pieces of information that tell more about the main idea or topic
- **Text Structure:** how the book is organized
- **Fact:** a piece of information that is true and can be proved
- **Opinion:** a statement of what the author thinks or believes

JOURNEYS Literature

Lucia's Neighborhood, Student Book, Lesson 4

At Home in the Ocean, Student Book, Lesson 11

STUDENT BOOK
Amazing Animals
Animal Groups
At Home in the Ocean
Be a Team Player
City Zoo
Drums
Four Seasons for Animals
Garden Good Guys
Grow, Apples, Grow!
How Animals Communicate
Insect Messages
Let's Go to the Moon!
Lewis and Clark's Big Trip
Life Then and Now
Lucia's Neighborhood
Measuring Weather
The Rain Forest
Rules and Laws

School Long Ago
Seasons
Storms!
Symbols of Our Country
A Tree Is a Plant
Water
What Can You Do?
What Is a Pal?
Where Does Food Come From?
Winners Never Quit!

TEACHER'S EDITION READ-ALOUD
A Hopeful Song
One Giant Leap
Prairie Dogs
The Prickly Pride of Texas

Training Around the Town
Visiting Butterflies

LEVELED READERS
All About Bats **J**
Always Learning **K**
The Amazing Octopus **L**
An Acorn Grows **H**
Animal Homes **E**
Animal Talk **C**
Animals **E**
Animals at Night **D**
Apples **D**
At the Park **A**
Baby Birds **E**
Baby Kangaroos **I**
Bald Eagles **L**
The Baseball Game **I**

254 • Teaching Genre: Informational Text

Small-Group Teaching

Small-group lessons are the individualized sessions in which you help children develop as readers based on their needs, challenges, and sometimes their preferences.

In **GUIDED READING** lessons, you use *Journeys* Leveled Readers to work with small groups of children who will benefit from teaching at a particular instructional level. You select the text and guide the readers by supporting their ability to use a variety of reading strategies (Fountas and Pinnell, 1996, 2001). Guided reading groups are flexible and should change as a result of your observations of your children's growth.

In this section, whole-group lessons provide the foundation for small-group instruction. Skills introduced in whole group can be developed and expanded according to children's needs in a smaller group with the appropriate level text. On the planning pages, Leveled Readers that connect to the whole-group experience are suggested, though you may need to select from the complete Leveled Readers Database (pp. 388–397) to match your children's instructional levels.

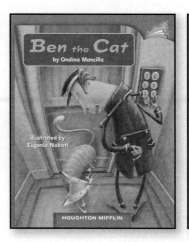 

▲ JOURNEYS Leveled Readers

Select Leveled Readers according to the instructional levels of your children.

Guided Reading Level

Every Reader has been carefully analyzed and leveled by Irene Fountas, and the titles are presented in ascending order.

Reading Recovery Level

Each Reader has been assessed with a quantitative readability score, indicating its Lexile level..

Genre

The Leveled Readers have been written in a wide variety of genres, directly corresponding to those of the Anchor Texts with which they appear. Instruction for and additional information about each genre can be found in the Teaching Genre section of this Guide.

Leveled Readers Database

Guided Reading Level	Title	Grade Pack	DRA Level	Lexile Level	Reading Recovery Level	Genre	Word Count
A	At the Park	1 ●	A	BR	A, B	Informational Text	36
A	Granny	1 ●	A	180	A, B	Realistic Fiction	36
A	Helping	1 ●	1	BR	1	Informational Text	36
A	Sledding	1 ●	A	290	A, B	Fantasy	58
B	Curious About School	1 VR	2	20	2	Informational Text	50
B	Curious George Finds Out About School	1 ●	4	60	4	Fantasy	51
B	Dogs	1 ●	2	BR	2	Informational Text	79
B	Drawing	1 ●	2	BR	2	Informational Text	48
B	Dress Up	1 ●	2	BR	2	Realistic Fiction	49
B	Favorite Things	1 VR	2	BR	2	Informational Text	47
B	Grandpa	1 VR	2	50	2	Informational Text	50
B	Pigs, The	1 ●	2	BR	2	Fable	83
B	Trip to the Rock	1 ●	2	130	2	Fantasy	90
B	Winter	1 ●	2	20	2	Informational Text	79
C	Animal Talk	1 VR	3	240	3	Informational Text	55
C	Curious George Visits School	1 ●	4	140	4	Fantasy	88
C	Curious George's Day at School	1 ▲	4	140	4	Fantasy	87
C	Firehouse	1 VR	3	BR	3	Informational Text	58
C	Friends Who Share	1 ◆	4	180	4	Informational Text	118
C	Grandpa and Me	1 ▲	3	420	3	Realistic Fiction	86
C	Happy Birthday!	1 VR	4	BR	4	Informational Text	78
C	Music	1 VR	3	BR	3	Informational Text	58
C	Our Town	1 ▲	3	240	3	Informational Text	103
C	Places in Our Town, The	1 ◆	6	200	6	Informational Text	108
C	Reading Together	1 VR	4	BR	4	Informational Text	62
C	Sharing	1 ▲	4	100	4	Informational Text	107
C	Trains	1 VR	3	150	3	Informational Text	65
C	When Grandpa Was a Boy	1 ●	4	450	4	Realistic Fiction	93
D	Animals at Night	1 ▲	6	220	6	Informational Text	161
D	Apples	1 ●	6	240	5	Informational Text	100

388 • Leveled Readers Database

👤 TEACHER'S ROLE

GUIDED READING

- Form groups based on children's instructional levels.
- Establish routines and meeting times.
- Select and introduce the book.
- Monitor children's reading through the use of running records and specific questioning.
- Record observations.

LITERATURE DISCUSSION

- Form groups based on children's reading preferences.
- Demonstrate routines for effective discussion.
- Facilitate discussions, and redirect student talk as needed.
- Summarize children's ideas and engage them in self-evaluation of their contributions.

👥 CHILD'S ROLE

GUIDED READING

- Apply skills learned during whole-group instruction.
- Share ideas.
- Make connections to other readings and to own experiences.
- Ask questions.
- Support thinking with evidence from the text.

LITERATURE DISCUSSION

- Choose a book.
- Prepare by reading and thinking about the text.
- Listen politely and respectfully to others.
- Share opinions and raise questions.

▼  Leveled Readers Teacher's Guides

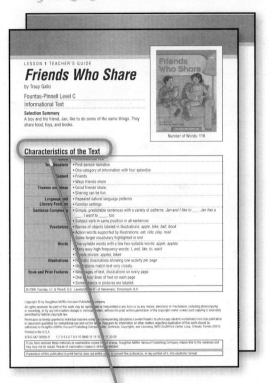

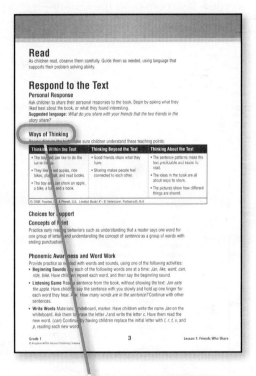

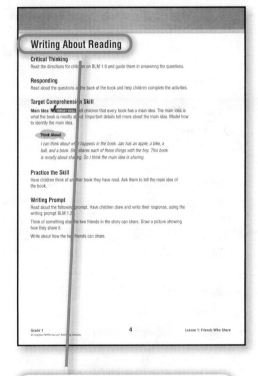

Characteristics of the Text

The qualitative features of each Reader include genre, text structure, content, book and print features, themes and ideas, language and literary features, and sentence complexity.

Ways of Thinking

The Leveled Readers Teacher's Guides outline how to lead children to read closely as they are prompted to think within, beyond, and about the text.

Writing About Reading

Children have multiple opportunities to demonstrate through writing their thinking within, beyond, and about the text they have just read.

In **LITERATURE DISCUSSION,** a small group of children of varying abilities and a common interest—a topic, a genre, or an author—selects one book to read. Each child comes prepared to discuss it.

In this collaborative group, you facilitate discussion of the book and encourage children to share their thinking and to build upon each other's ideas as they gain a deeper understanding of the text (Fountas and Pinnell, 2001).

Literature discussion groups will change as children select different books to read. Guide children to select books by encouraging them to page through a book or read a short segment in order to determine whether it is too easy or too difficult before they make a final selection.

The suggested trade book titles on pp. 398–402 are appropriate for Grade 1 children to engage in literature discussions and represent a wide variety of genres, authors, and topics.

Independent Literacy Work

Independent literacy work includes meaningful and productive activities for your children to do while you work with small groups.

INDEPENDENT READING The best way to develop reading skills is to read more. Independent reading is a time for children to explore their interests, select books that are "just right" for them, and read continuous text for an established period of time.

Support your children as they make book choices because too-hard books will only frustrate them. Teach them how to choose books that they can read with understanding and that don't present too many challenges. Having a large, accessible collection of books—whether in your classroom or in the library—is the best way to support readers.

Suggested Trade Book Titles
Select books from a variety of genres, topics, and themes for children to read independently or in Literature Discussion Groups.

TEACHER'S ROLE

- Establish classroom routines for independent work time.
- Set expectations for what children should accomplish.
- Confer with individual children to discuss books or sample oral reading.

CHILD'S ROLE

- Follow established classroom routines.
- Engage thoughtfully in reading and writing tasks.
- Take responsibility for assignments, and demonstrate progress.

Literature Discussion

For small-group literature discussion, use the suggested trade book titles on the pages that follow, or select age-appropriate texts from your library or classroom collection.

Engage children in discussions to build understanding of the text, deepen comprehension, and foster children's confidence in talking about what they read. Encourage children to share their ideas about the text and also to build upon one another's ideas.

 Classic

 Science

 Social Studies

 Music

 Math

Art

Suggested Trade Book Titles

BIOGRAPHY

Carson, Cheryl. *Charles M. Schultz.* Cartoonist Charles M. Schultz is profiled here. Capstone Press, 2005 (24p).

Jaffe, Elizabeth D. *Ellen Ochoa.* This basic biography profiles the United States' first Latina astronaut. Children's Press, 2005 (32p).

Knox, Barbara. *George Washington.* This easy-to-read introduction to the life of George Washington includes a timeline. Capstone, 2004 (24p).

Krensky, Stephen. *A Man for All Seasons: The Life of George Washington Carver.* This biography profiles the man whose discoveries put the peanut on the map. Amistad, 2008 (32p).

Marzolla, Jean, and Jerry Pinkney. *Happy Birthday, Martin Luther King.* This brief narrative of Dr. King's life is presented in an easy-to-read format. Scholastic, 1993 (32p).

FABLE

Herman, Gail. *The Lion and the Mouse.* This fable is an easy-to-read retelling of Aesop's classic tale. Random House, 1998 (32p).

Poole, Amy Lowry. *The Ant and the Grasshopper.* Grasshopper plays the summer days away while Ant works hard to prepare for winter. Holiday House, 2000 (32p).

FAIRY TALE

Andersen, Hans Christian, and Jerry Pinkney. *The Ugly Duckling.* Hans Christian Andersen's classic tale is illustrated with Caldecott Honor–winning illustrations. Harper, 1999 (40p).

Gorbachev, Valeri. *Goldilocks and the Three Bears.* Three bears return home to discover an unexpected visitor in their home in this appealing retelling of the classic tale. North-South/Night Sky, 2001 (40p).

FANTASY

Andersen, Peggy Perry. *Chuck's Band.* Chuck and his barnyard friends form a band in this toe-tapping story. Houghton Mifflin, 2008 (32p).

Bang-Campbell, Monika. *Little Rat Makes Music.* With the help of Kitty and lots of practice, Little Rat learns to play the violin. Harcourt, 2007 (48p).

Banks, Kate. *Fox.* A baby fox observes the changing seasons while his parents teach him to care for himself. Farrar, Straus and Giroux, 2007 (40p).

Brett, Jan. *Honey. . . Honey. . . Lion!* When greedy Badger will not share honey with his friend, his friend has a surprise for him. Putnam, 2005 (32p).

Campoy, F. Isabel. *Get Up, Rick!* Brief text and supportive illustrations describe what happens on a farm when the rooster oversleeps. Green Light Readers, 2007 (24p).

Carle, Eric. *The Very Hungry Caterpillar.* A caterpillar eats its way through the week and turns into a beautiful butterfly. Philomel, 1969 (32p).

Cazet, Denys. *Minnie and Moo and the Case of the Missing Jelly Donut.* The brave bovine buddies are on the case when Minnie discovers that her jelly donut has gone missing. HarperTrophy, 2006 (48p).

Chaconas, Dori. *Cork and Fuzz: Good Sports.* Two friends learn a lesson about sportsmanship when they compete against one another. Viking, 2007 (32p).

Cronin, Doreen. *Dooby Dooby Moo.* Determined Duck and the rest of Farmer Brown's animals set their sights on first prize at the county fair's talent show, unbeknownst to Farmer Brown. **Available in Spanish as** *Dubi Dubi Muu/Dooby Dooby Moo.* Atheneum, 2006 (40p).

Cyrus, Kurt. *Tadpole Rex.* In a swamp frequented by dinosaurs, a tiny tadpole looks forward to growing as big as his mighty neighbors. Harcourt, 2008 (40p).

DiCamillo, Kate. *Mercy Watson to the Rescue.* When Mr. and Mrs. Watson find

Teacher's Notes

Whole-Group Lessons

What Is a Pal?
Student Book, Lesson 1

The Lion and the Mouse
See page 348 of this Guide.

Friends Forever
Student Book, Lesson 1

▶ **What Is a Pal?**

INTERACTIVE READ-ALOUD/SHARED READING

Read the book aloud to children. Stop periodically for very brief discussion of the book. Use the following suggested stopping points and prompts for quick group response, or give a specific prompt and have partners or threes turn and talk.

- After children read that Sam and Nat can help Dan, ask: "How are these pals helping? How do you know that?"
- After children read about who can be a pal, ask: "Who can be a pal? Who are some of your pals? Turn and talk about your ideas with a partner."
- After children read that a pal is fun to be with, ask: "What do you do with your pals?" Follow-up: "Why are your pals fun to be with?"
- At the end, ask: "How are you a pal?"

MINILESSON Main Idea

TEACH Display the minilesson principle on chart paper, and read it aloud to children. Tell children they are going to learn how to notice that authors tell mostly about one thing in information books.

1. Discuss the principle with children, using *What Is a Pal?* as an example. Suggested language: "There are different kinds of books. Some books tell stories. Other books give information or tell about real things. What kind of book is *What Is a Pal?*" *(an information book)* Follow-up: "How do you know?" *(It gives information about pals.)*

2. Focus on one part of the book, such as what pals can do with you. Suggested language: "This book tells about some things a pal can do with you. What are two things a pal can do with you?" *(A pal can help you and play with you.)*

3. Use children's responses to explain that authors tell mostly about one thing in information books. Suggested language: "The author tells mostly about pals. Pals are the one thing that this information book is mostly about."

4. Elicit from children additional details that support the idea that pals are the one thing this book is mostly about. Record children's ideas in a Web like the one shown here.

> **MINILESSON PRINCIPLE**
>
> Notice that authors tell mostly about one thing in information books.

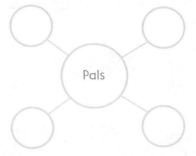

SUMMARIZE AND APPLY Restate the minilesson principle. Then tell children to apply it to their independent reading. Suggested language: "When you read an information book, think about the one thing that the author tells mostly about. Think about how you know what that one thing is."

GROUP SHARE Ask children to share what they learned from reading an information book. Tell children to identify the one thing that the author tells mostly about and how they identified it.

▶ The Lion and the Mouse

INTERACTIVE READ-ALOUD/SHARED READING

Read aloud the story to children. Stop periodically for brief discussion of the story. Use the following suggested stopping points and prompts:

- After the lion releases the mouse, ask: "Why does the lion let the mouse go?"
- After the mouse runs to find the lion, ask: "Why do you think the mouse comes back to help the lion?"
- At the end of the story, say: "How did the lion feel at the end of the story? Turn and talk about your ideas with a partner."

MINILESSON Genre: Fable

TEACH Display the minilesson principle on chart paper, and read it aloud to children. Explain that *The Lion and the Mouse* is a fable and that a fable is a story that has a lesson. Tell children they are going to think about how the lion in this fable learns a lesson.

1. Discuss with children the character of the lion. Suggested language: "What was the lion like at the beginning of the story?" *(He thought he was better than anyone else because he was the King of the Beasts.)*

> **MINILESSON PRINCIPLE**
> Think about how the people or animals in a story learn a lesson.

2. Talk with children about how the lion changed by the end of the story. Suggested language: "What was the lion like at the end of the story? What lesson did he learn?" *(He found out that he wasn't as powerful as he had thought. He learned that as powerful as he was, he needed help from a small, unimportant mouse.)*

3. Discuss with children the lessons that people or animals have learned in other stories they have read before. Write their ideas in a T-Map labeled *People or Animals* and *Lesson Learned*.

SUMMARIZE AND APPLY Restate the minilesson principle. Tell children to apply it to their independent reading. Suggested language: "When you read, think about how the people or animals in a story learn a lesson."

GROUP SHARE Ask children to share an example from independent reading of how the people or animals in a story learn a lesson.

▶ Friends Forever

INTERACTIVE READ-ALOUD/SHARED READING

Read aloud the introduction and the poems to children. Stop periodically for brief discussion. Use the following suggested stopping points and prompts:

- After reading "Damon & Blue," ask: "What is this poem about?" Follow-up: "What does the poet mean when she says *Can't beat us when we're side by side*?"
- After reading "Wait for Me," ask: "What is this poem about?" Follow-up: "How is this poem like 'Damon & Blue'? Turn and talk about your ideas with a partner."

MINILESSON Genre: Poetry

TEACH Remind children that they have read three poems: "Damon & Blue," "Wait for Me," and "Jambo." Explain to children that some poems have words that rhyme, which can make them fun to read.

1. Model how to notice rhyming words in poems. Read aloud the first three lines of "Damon & Blue," emphasizing the word at the end of each line. Have children follow along. Then say the three rhyming words in isolation: *Blue, two, avenue*. Point out that these words rhyme because they have the same ending sound.

> **MINILESSON PRINCIPLE**
> Notice that some poems have words that rhyme.

2. Help children notice the rhyming words in poems. Read aloud the remaining lines of "Damon & Blue," and help children identify the rhyming words *glide, stride*, and *side*. Repeat with "Wait for Me" and "Jambo."

3. Ask children to share what they noticed about the poems they read, prompting them to recognize that some poems have words that rhyme. Then write the minilesson principle on chart paper, and read it aloud. Explain to children that noticing rhyming words in a poem will help them enjoy it more.

SUMMARIZE AND APPLY Restate the minilesson principle. Tell children to apply it to their independent reading. Suggested language: "When you read poems, notice that some of them have words that rhyme."

GROUP SHARE Ask children to tell about poems with rhyming words that they read for independent reading. Have them explain how the rhyming words made the poems fun to read.

Whole-Group Lessons

The Storm
Student Book, Lesson 2

Read Aloud Passages

Susie and the Bandits
See page 348 of this Guide.

Storms!
Student Book, Lesson 2

▶ **The Storm**

INTERACTIVE READ-ALOUD/SHARED READING

Read aloud the story to children. Stop periodically for very brief discussion of the story. Use the following suggested stopping points and prompts for quick group response, or give a specific prompt and have partners or threes turn and talk.

- After Tim and Rip run to Pop, ask: "Who are the people and animals in this story? Where does the story take place?"
- After Pop tells Tim to go to bed, ask: "Why is Pop at Tim's house? How do you know? Turn and talk about your ideas with a partner."
- After Rip hides, ask: "Why do Tim and Rip hide?" Follow-up: "What do you think will happen next?"
- At the end of the story, ask: "What does Pop do for Tim? How does this help Tim?"

MINILESSON Understanding Characters

TEACH Display the minilesson principle on chart paper, and read it aloud to children. Tell children they are going to learn how to think about the people and animals in a story to understand how they feel.

1. Discuss the principle with children, using examples of characters from *The Storm*. Suggested language: "In the story *The Storm,* we got to know a few people and animals as we read. Who were these people and animals?" *(Pop, Tim, and Rip)*

2. Focus on Tim and Rip in the story. Suggested language: "What did Tim and Rip see out the window when they went to bed?" *(Tim and Rip saw a lightning storm.)* Follow-up: "What did they do?" *(They hid.)*

3. Use children's responses to explain that what people and animals do in a story are clues that help readers understand how the people and animals feel. Suggested language: "The author uses what Tim and Rip did (hid) to show readers that Tim and Rip were afraid of the lightning storm."

4. Elicit from children additional examples from the story. Record children's ideas in a T-Map like the one shown here.

> **MINILESSON PRINCIPLE**
>
> Notice what the people and animals do to help you understand how they feel.

What the Person or Animal Did	How the Person or Animal Felt

SUMMARIZE AND APPLY Restate the minilesson principle. Then tell children to apply it to their independent reading. Suggested language: "When you read, think about what the people and animals do in stories. Find out about how they feel by noticing what they do."

GROUP SHARE Ask children to share what they learned about one person or animal in their story. Tell them to explain what the person or animal did that helped them learn about how the person or animal felt.

▶ Susie and the Bandits

INTERACTIVE READ-ALOUD/SHARED READING

Read aloud the story to children. Stop periodically for brief discussion of it. Use the following suggested stopping points and prompts:

- After Paulie Opossum speaks, ask: "What is the problem in this story?"
- After the raccoons run to the creek for a bath, ask: "How did Susie Skunk get the bandits to stop? What do you think will happen next?"
- At the end of the story, say: "Susie Skunk tells the raccoons that finding their own food takes a lot more bravery. What do you think she meant? Turn and talk about your ideas with a partner."

MINILESSON Understanding Characters

TEACH Display the minilesson principle on chart paper, and read it aloud to children. Tell children they are going to learn to think about what characters, the people and animals in a story, do to understand what they are like.

1. Using the character Susie from *Susie and the Bandits,* discuss with children that the way characters act gives clues about what they are like. Suggested language: "In the story *Susie and the Bandits,* Susie made a deal with the other animals. What was the deal she made?" (*Susie promised to get the raccoons to stop raiding the garbage if the animals would stop calling her Stinky.*)

> **MINILESSON PRINCIPLE**
> Think about what characters do to understand what they are like.

2. Talk with children about Susie's reason for making that deal. Suggested language: "Susie wanted the animals to stop calling her Stinky. Why did Susie want that?" (*Being called Stinky hurt her feelings.*) Follow-up: "What did her plan show about her?" (*She was smart because she thought of a way to make everyone happy.*)

3. Discuss with children the raccoons' actions in the story and how those actions show what the characters are like. Write their ideas in a T-Map labeled *What the Character Does* and *What the Character Is Like.*

SUMMARIZE AND APPLY Restate the minilesson principle. Tell children to apply it to their independent reading. Suggested language: "When you read, think about what characters do to help you understand what the characters are like."

GROUP SHARE Ask children to share an example from independent reading of something a character does and how it shows what the character is like.

▶ Storms!

INTERACTIVE READ-ALOUD/SHARED READING

Read aloud the book to children. Stop periodically for brief discussion. Use the following suggested stopping points and prompts:

- After the section about kinds of storms, ask: "What is this book mostly about?" Follow-up: "What are some kinds of storms?"
- At the end of the book, ask: "What are some tools for measuring storms?" Follow-up: "Why is it important for scientists to measure storms? Turn and talk about your ideas with a partner."

MINILESSON Genre: Informational Text

TEACH Tell children they are going to think about the information the author tells in *Storms!*

1. Discuss the principle with children, using *Storms!* as an example. Suggested language: "There are different kinds of books. Some books tell stories. Other books give information or tell about facts. What kind of book is *Storms!*?" (*an information book*) Follow-up: "How do you know?" (*It gives information and facts about storms.*)

> **MINILESSON PRINCIPLE**
> Think about the information the author tells.

2. Ask children to share the information from *Storms!* Suggested language: "What information do you remember from *Storms!*?" (*Answers will vary.*) Follow-up: "What information did you think was most interesting? Why?" (*Answers will vary.*) Then guide children to retell facts from *Storms!* as you write the minilesson principle on chart paper. Explain to children that thinking about the information the author tells will help them understand what they read in an information book.

SUMMARIZE AND APPLY Restate the minilesson principle. Tell children to apply it to their independent reading. Suggested language: "When you read an information book, think about the information the author tells."

GROUP SHARE Ask children to share some information from an information book that they read for independent reading.

Whole-Group Lessons

Curious George at School
Student Book, Lesson 3

Read Aloud Passages

Stone Stew
See page 349 of this Guide.

School Long Ago
Student Book, Lesson 3

▶ Curious George at School

INTERACTIVE READ-ALOUD/SHARED READING

Read aloud the story to children. Stop periodically for very brief discussion of the story. Use the following suggested stopping points and prompts for quick group response, or give a specific prompt and have partners or threes turn and talk.

- After George can see the paints, ask: "Who is the most important character in this story? Where is he?"
- After George spills the paints, ask: "What problem does George have? How do you think he will solve his problem? Turn and talk about your ideas with a partner."
- After George gets a mop, ask: "How is George going to try to solve his problem? How do you know?" Follow up: "What do you think will happen next?"
- At the end of the story, ask: "What happened when George tried to clean up the mess by himself? How did the mess get cleaned up?"

MINILESSON Sequence of Events

TEACH Display the minilesson principle on chart paper, and read it aloud to children. Tell children they are going to think about what happens first, next, and last in a story. Explain that thinking about the story events in order will help them better understand the story.

> **MINILESSON PRINCIPLE**
>
> Think about what happens first, next, and last in the story.

1. Use *Curious George at School* to discuss the principle with children. Suggested language: "What happened in the beginning of the story *Curious George at School*?" (*A monkey named Curious George went to school.*) Follow-up: "What problem did George have first?" (*He made a mess with the paints.*)

2. Tell children to think about how George tried to solve his problem after he made a mess. Suggested language: "First George made a mess with the paints. What happened next?" (*He tried to clean up the paints and made an even bigger mess.*)

3. Ask children to think about how the story ended. Suggested language: "First George made a mess with the paints. Next he tried to clean up the paints and made an even bigger mess. What happened last, at the end of the story?" (*The children helped George clean up the mess.*)

4. Work with children to use their answers to the previous questions to tell what happened first, next, and last in the story. Point out that using the words *first, next,* and *last* will help them remember the order of what happened. Record children's ideas in a Flow Chart like the one shown here.

SUMMARIZE AND APPLY Restate the minilesson principle. Explain to children that they can apply it to their independent reading. Suggested language: "When you read a story, think about what happens first, next, and last."

GROUP SHARE Have children share stories they read by telling what happened first, next, and last. Remind them to use the words *first, next,* and *last* to help tell the correct order of what happened.

▶ Stone Stew

INTERACTIVE READ-ALOUD/SHARED READING

Read aloud the story to children. Stop periodically for brief discussion of the story. Use the following suggested stopping points and prompts:

- After the sailor asks for a bite to eat, ask: "What did the townspeople do when the sailor came into town? Why?"
- After the boy gives the sailor some okra, ask: "Why does the boy have to sneak out to give the sailor okra?"
- At the end of the story, say: "Think about the townspeople. What kind of people are they?" Follow-up: "Think about the sailor. What kind of person is he? Turn and talk about your ideas with a partner."

MINILESSON Sequence of Events

TEACH Display the minilesson principle on chart paper, and read it aloud to children. Remind children that thinking about what happens first, next, and last in a story will help them better understand what the story is about.

1. Help children identify the sequence of events in *Stone Stew.* Suggested language: "In *Stone Stew,* what happened first when the sailor comes to town?" *(He asked for food, but the townspeople wouldn't give him any.)*

> **MINILESSON PRINCIPLE**
> Think about what happens first, next, and last in the story.

2. Tell children to think about what the sailor did next to solve this problem. Suggested language: "First the sailor asked for food, but the townspeople wouldn't give him any. So what did the sailor do next?" *(He took out a stone and began to make stone stew.)*
3. Ask children to think about how the problem was solved at the end of the story. Suggested language: "First the sailor asked for food, but the townspeople wouldn't give him any. So, next, he took out a stone and began to make stone stew. What happened last?" *(One at a time the townspeople added foods to the stew, and they all ate the stew with the sailor.)*
4. Work with children to use their answers to the previous questions to tell what happened first, next, and last in the story. Write their ideas in a Flow Chart labeled *First, Next,* and *Last.*

SUMMARIZE AND APPLY Restate the minilesson principle. Explain to children that they should apply it to their independent reading. Suggested language: "When you read a story, think about what happens first, next, and last. This will help you understand what the story is about."

GROUP SHARE Have children tell what happened first, next, and last in a story they read.

▶ School Long Ago

INTERACTIVE READ-ALOUD/SHARED READING

Read aloud the book to children. Stop periodically for brief discussion. Use the following suggested stopping points and prompts:

- After the first paragraph, ask: "What will this book be mostly about? How do you know?"
- At the end, ask: "What are some of the ways school was different long ago? Turn and talk about your ideas with a partner."

MINILESSON Genre: Informational Text

TEACH Explain to children that *School Long Ago* is different from the other two stories they read this week. Point out that the book gives information about real people, places, and things that happened. Display the minilesson principle on chart paper, and read it aloud to children. Explain that an information book may include charts that give information.

1. Help children understand the information in the chart. Suggested language: "What are the words at the top of the columns?" *(Then, Now)* "Why is the slate in the *Then* column and the notebook in the *Now* column?" *(They show what children wrote on in school long ago and what they use today.)* Follow-up: "Why are the slate and the notebook next to each other in this chart?" *(They are both writing tools. The chart shows them next to each other to tell about how tools have changed.)*

> **MINILESSON PRINCIPLE**
> Notice how the charts in a book give information.

2. Discuss how charts give information. Suggested language: "This chart uses words and pictures to give information. What information does this chart help you understand?" *(how school has changed from long ago)* Help children understand that authors use charts to show information in a way that is easy to understand. Explain that reading charts for information will help them better understand what they read.

SUMMARIZE AND APPLY Restate the minilesson principle. Tell children to apply it to their independent reading. Suggested language: "When you read, look for charts and read them to understand the information they give."

GROUP SHARE Ask children to share examples of charts in the books they chose for independent reading and tell about the information the charts give.

Whole-Group Lessons

Lucia's Neighborhood
Student Book, Lesson 4

Read Aloud Passages

Painting Word Pictures
See page 349 of this Guide.

City Mouse and Country Mouse
Student Book, Lesson 4

▶ Lucia's Neighborhood

INTERACTIVE READ-ALOUD/SHARED READING

Read aloud the book to children. Stop periodically for very brief discussion of it. Use the following suggested stopping points and prompts for quick group response, or give a specific prompt and have partners or threes turn and talk.

- After Lucia visits the pet shop, ask: "Is there a pattern in this book? What is it?"
- After Lucia and her mother stop in the street, ask: "How is Lucia's neighborhood like your neighborhood? How is it different?"
- After Lucia visits the library, ask: "Which place in Lucia's neighborhood would you most like to visit? Why? Turn and talk about your ideas with a partner."
- At the end of the story, ask: "Why do you think Lucia says that it's fun to be home?" Follow-up: "How do you feel when you get home after a busy day?"

MINILESSON Text and Graphic Features

TEACH Display the minilesson principle on chart paper, and read it aloud to children.

1. Guide children through the process of using pictures to understand the words in *Lucia's Neighborhood*. Display the page that shows the bakery. Cover the text and ask: "What do you see in this picture?" *(Lucia is eating a pastry. One woman has a tray of pastries. Another woman wears a white apron. Behind the people are display cases with rolls and muffins.)*

> **MINILESSON PRINCIPLE**
>
> You can look at the pictures to understand the words.

2. Tell children to think about all the clues in the picture. Then point to the word at the top of the page and ask: "How could you use the picture clues to figure out the word at the top of the picture?" *(You could tell from the picture that they are at a bakery. The word at the top of the page begins with b, so I can guess that is says bakery.)*

3. Ask children to reread the sentences at the bottom of this page. Then talk about how the clues from the picture help them better understand the words. Suggested language: "What is Lucia talking about when she says *Look what we get here*?" *(They get pastries to eat.)* Follow-up: "How do you know?" *(You can tell by looking at the picture.)*

4. Work with children to explain how to use clues in other pictures to better understand the words in this book. Record children's ideas in a T-Map like the one shown here.

What the Pictures Show	What the Words Say

SUMMARIZE AND APPLY Restate the minilesson principle. Explain to children that they can apply it to their independent reading. Suggested language: "When you read a book, look at the pictures to help you read words you don't know and to understand what is happening."

GROUP SHARE Have children share books they read and explain how they used pictures to figure out a word or understand what they read.

▶ Painting Word Pictures

INTERACTIVE READ-ALOUD/SHARED READING

Read aloud the introduction and the poems to children. Stop periodically for brief discussion. Use the following suggested stopping points and prompts:

- After the introduction, ask: "How are poets like painters?"
- After "The Wind," ask: "Which words rhyme in this poem?" Follow-up: "How do they make the poem more fun to read?"
- After "Autumn Leaves," ask: "How is this poem like a song? Turn and talk about your ideas with a partner."

MINILESSON Genre: Poetry

TEACH Display the minilesson principle on chart paper, and read it aloud to children. Tell children they are going to think about how poems make pictures in their minds.

1. Ask children to close their eyes and listen as you reread the first two lines of "The Wind." Then have them describe the word picture it created. Suggested language: "What did you see in your mind when I read these lines?" *(the wind blowing kites and birds around the sky)*

> **MINILESSON PRINCIPLE**
>
> Think about how words in poems make pictures in your mind.

2. Ask children to close their eyes and listen as you reread the last stanza of "Autumn Leaves." Next ask volunteers to pretend they are autumn leaves and act out what they do when they are tired, as others watch. Then ask children to think about the picture they made in their own minds when they heard these words. Suggested language: "How was the picture in your mind like what the children acted out? How was it different?"

3. Discuss with children other word pictures in "The Wind" and "Autumn Leaves." Write their ideas in a T-Map labeled *Words in the Poem* and *Pictures in My Mind.*

SUMMARIZE AND APPLY Restate the minilesson principle. Explain to children that they should apply it to their independent reading. Suggested language: "When you read a poem, think about how the words make pictures in your mind. This will help you understand and enjoy the poem."

GROUP SHARE After reading a poem, have children describe or draw the picture the poem made in their mind.

▶ City Mouse and Country Mouse

INTERACTIVE READ-ALOUD/SHARED READING

Before reading, discuss the format of this play with children. Then read it aloud using different voices for the characters, or ask three volunteers to take the parts and read them aloud. Stop periodically for brief discussion of the play. Use the following suggested stopping points and prompts:

- After the second page, ask: "Why didn't City Mouse want to go to the country? How do you know?"
- At the end of the story, ask: "How is the city different from the country? Turn and talk about your ideas with a partner."

MINILESSON Genre: Fable

TEACH Display the minilesson principle on chart paper, and read it aloud to children. Explain that *City Mouse and Country Mouse* is a fable and that a fable is a story that has a lesson. Tell children they are going to think about how a character in this fable learned a lesson.

1. Discuss the character Country Mouse and why he went to the city. Suggested language: "Why did Country Mouse go to the city?" *(City Mouse wouldn't visit him in the country and said the food was better in the city.)*

> **MINILESSON PRINCIPLE**
>
> Think about the lesson that a character learns in a story.

2. Talk about what Country Mouse thought about the city at first and why this changed. Suggested language: "What did Country Mouse think about the city at first?" *(He liked it.)* "How do you know?" *(He said,* Look at all this yummy food!*)* Follow-up: "What made Country Mouse change his mind?" *(A cat tried to eat him and City Mouse.)*

3. Discuss the lesson in this story. Suggested language: "Why did Country Mouse go back to the country?" *(He wanted to be safe.)* Follow-up: "What lesson did he learn?" *(It is better to live in a safe place than in one that has nicer things but is very dangerous.)*

4. Discuss with children the lessons that characters have learned in other stories they have read before. Write their ideas in a T-Map labeled *Character* and *Lesson Learned.*

SUMMARIZE AND APPLY Restate the minilesson principle. Tell children to apply it to their independent reading. Suggested language: "When you read, think about the lesson a character learns."

GROUP SHARE Ask children to share an example from independent reading of a lesson that a character has learned.

Whole-Group Lessons

Gus Takes the Train
Student Book, Lesson 5

Read Aloud
Passages

Training Around the Town
See page 350 of this Guide.

City Zoo
Student Book, Lesson 5

▶ **Gus Takes the Train**

INTERACTIVE READ-ALOUD/SHARED READING

Read aloud the story to children. Stop periodically for very brief discussion of the story. Use the following suggested stopping points and prompts for quick group response, or give a specific prompt and have partners or threes turn and talk.

- After the train conductor looks at his watch, ask: "Who is the most important character in this story? What is his problem?"
- After Gus sits, ask: "How does the train conductor help Gus?"
- After Peg and Gus have a sip, ask: "How do you think Gus feels about meeting a friend? How can you tell? Talk about your ideas with a partner."
- At the end of the story, ask: "What do you think Gus will do now that he is off the train?" Follow-up: "Why do you think so?"

MINILESSON Story Structure

TEACH Display the minilesson principle on chart paper, and read it aloud to children. Tell children that they are going to think about how a story begins and how it ends.

1. Discuss the principle with children, using *Gus Takes the Train*. Suggested language: "What happened in the beginning of the story *Gus Takes the Train*?" (*Gus ran to catch a train with a bag that was big and heavy.*) "How do you think he felt?" (*He probably felt worried that he would miss the train.*)

> **MINILESSON PRINCIPLE**
> Think about how a story begins and how it ends.

2. Tell children to think about what happened to Gus on the train and how the story ends. Suggested language: "What happened at the end of the story?" (*Gus and Peg got off the train at the zoo.*) "How did Gus feel then?" (*happy*) "Why was he happy?"(*He had fun on the train with Peg and may go to the zoo with her.*)

3. Work with children to use their answers to the previous questions to tell what happened in the beginning, middle, and end of the story. Record children's ideas in a Flow Chart like the one shown here.

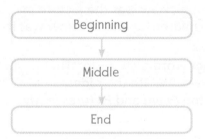

SUMMARIZE AND APPLY Restate the minilesson principle. Explain to children that they can apply it to their independent reading. Suggested language: "When you read a story, think about how it begins and how it ends."

GROUP SHARE Have children each share a story they have read by telling how the story begins and how it ends. Suggest that they use the words *In the beginning* and *at the end of the story.*

▶ Training Around the Town

INTERACTIVE READ-ALOUD/SHARED READING

Read aloud the passage to children. Stop periodically for brief discussion. Use the following suggested stopping points and prompts:

- After reading the first paragraph, ask: "What problem do cities have?" Follow-up: "What is one way some cities solve this problem?"
- After reading about the closing of the Fort Worth subway, ask: "How was the Fort Worth subway special?"
- At the end of the passage, ask: "How are subways and streetcars the same? How are they different? Turn and talk about your ideas with a partner."

MINILESSON Genre: Informational Text

TEACH Display the minilesson principle on chart paper, and read it aloud to children. Tell children they are going to think about ideas that go together when they read.

1. Point out that *Training Around the Town* tells about two different kinds of city trains. Suggested language: "What two kinds of trains did you learn about?" *(subway and streetcar)*

2. Help children recall that the author first explained what a subway is and then told more about subways by describing a subway in Fort Worth. Explain that both of these ideas go together to help readers learn about subways.

3. Help children see the same pattern in the section about streetcars. Suggested language: "First the author explained what a streetcar is. What did the author describe next?" *(the Dallas streetcar system)* Follow-up: "Why did the author do that?" *(to help readers understand more about streetcars)*

4. Work with children to use their answers to the previous questions to complete an Idea-Support Map for the topic of streetcars.

> **MINILESSON PRINCIPLE**
> Think about ideas that go together when you read.

SUMMARIZE AND APPLY Restate the minilesson principle. Explain to children that they should apply it to their independent reading. Suggested language: "When you read an information book, think about the ideas that go together. This will help you better understand what the book is about."

GROUP SHARE Have children tell about an information book that they read for independent reading by telling what it was about and the ideas that went together.

▶ City Zoo

INTERACTIVE READ-ALOUD/SHARED READING

Read aloud the book to children. Stop periodically for brief discussion. Use the following suggested stopping points and prompts:

- After reading the first page, ask: "What animals might you see at this zoo?" Follow-up: "Why do you think the author says the animals are interesting?"
- At the end of the book, ask: "Why does the author give these tips?" Follow-up: "How could they help if you went to a zoo? Turn and talk about your ideas with a partner."

MINILESSON Genre: Informational Text

TEACH Display the minilesson principle on chart paper, and read it aloud to children. Point out that *City Zoo* has a map and that maps use pictures and words to show where things are.

1. Help children understand the information in the map. Suggested language: "A map is a picture of a place. A key shows what the pictures on a map mean."

2. Have children use the key to find and name different zoo animals on the map. Ask volunteers to demonstrate how they match the words on the key to the animal pictures on the map. Tell children that using these words and pictures together helps them learn where the animals are at the zoo. Explain that noticing how pictures and words go together will help them better understand books that have picture tools such as maps.

> **MINILESSON PRINCIPLE**
> Notice how pictures and words go together in books.

SUMMARIZE AND APPLY Restate the minilesson principle. Tell children to apply it to their independent reading. Suggested language: "When you read today, notice how pictures and words go together."

GROUP SHARE Ask children to share examples of maps and picture tools in the books they chose for independent reading. Have them tell about how the pictures and words go together.

Whole-Group Lessons

Jack and the Wolf
Student Book, Lesson 6

Read Aloud Passages

Night of the Wolf
See page 350 of this Guide.

The Three Little Pigs
Student Book, Lesson 6

▶ Jack and the Wolf

INTERACTIVE READ-ALOUD/SHARED READING

Read aloud the story to children. Stop periodically for very brief discussion of the story. Use the following suggested stopping points and prompts for quick group response, or give a specific prompt and have partners or threes turn and talk.

- After children read about Jack's job, ask: "Would you like to have Jack's job? Why or why not?"
- After Jack yells *Wolf!* the second time, ask: "What would you say to Jack if you were one of his friends? Tell why."
- After Jack says *You did not come,* ask: "Why didn't Jack's friends come when he called? Turn and talk about your ideas with a partner."
- At the end of the story, ask: "What lesson did Jack learn in this story?" Follow-up: "Is this a good lesson for other people to learn, too? Why?"

MINILESSON Understanding Characters

TEACH Display the minilesson principle on chart paper, and read it aloud to children. Tell children they are going to learn how to think about characters as they read. Point out that this will help them understand ways that characters change.

1. Discuss the principle with children, using examples of characters from *Jack and the Wolf.* Suggested language: "In the story *Jack and the Wolf,* you got to know a few different characters as you read. Who were they?" *(Jack, Jack's friends, Wolf, Nell)*

> **MINILESSON PRINCIPLE**
>
> Think about how the characters change.

2. Focus on Jack and have children tell what he was like at the beginning of the story. Suggested language: "What did you learn about Jack at the beginning of the story?" *(Jack was a little boy. He sat with the sheep on a hill. He called* Wolf *over and over because he was bored.)*

3. Have children tell what Jack was like at the end of the story. Suggested language: "How did Jack feel when he promised Nell not to play tricks anymore? Do you think he will yell *Wolf* again just for fun?" *(Possible answer: Jack felt sorry that he had played a mean trick, so I don't think he will do it again.)*

4. Use children's responses to the above questions to fill in a T-Map labeled *Beginning* and *End* like the one shown here.

Beginning	End

SUMMARIZE AND APPLY Restate the minilesson principle. Then tell children to apply it to their independent reading. Suggested language: "When you read, think about how the characters change in a story."

GROUP SHARE Ask children to share a description of a character they read about in a story. Tell them to explain how the character changed by the end of the story.

▶ Night of the Wolf

INTERACTIVE READ-ALOUD/SHARED READING

Read aloud the story to children. Stop periodically for brief discussion of the story. Use the following suggested stopping points and prompts:

- After the wind tosses a snow shovel across the yard, ask: "Where and when does this story take place?"
- After the girls hear the wolf howl a second time, ask: "What do you think will happen next? Turn and talk about your ideas with a partner."
- At the end of the story, say: "What happened right before Meg and Ellie saw the wolves run away? What happened after?"

MINILESSON Understanding Characters

TEACH Display the minilesson principle on chart paper, and read it aloud to children. Tell children they are going to learn to use what characters say and do to notice when characters are like real people.

1. Discuss with children how some story characters are like real people and others are not. Suggested language: "Think of a story character you know who could not be a real person." Discuss the characteristics that children used to figure it out. Ask: "What makes you think that character could not be real?"

> **MINILESSON PRINCIPLE**
>
> Notice when the characters in stories are like real people.

2. Guide children to think about Meg and Ellie in *Night of the Wolf*. Suggested language: "Think about what Meg and Ellie said and did. Were they like real people? What makes you think so?" *(Yes, they talked like real people and had feelings like real people. They wished they could have a snow day and were scared of the wolf's howl. These are both things real children might do.)*

SUMMARIZE AND APPLY Restate the minilesson principle. Tell children to apply it to their independent reading. Suggested language: "When you read, think about whether the characters are like real people and how you know."

GROUP SHARE Have children choose a character from a story they read and tell how they knew that the character was or was not like a real person.

▶ The Three Little Pigs

INTERACTIVE READ-ALOUD/SHARED READING

Read aloud the story to children. Stop periodically for brief discussion of the story. Use the following suggested stopping points and prompts:

- After the Wolf blows over the first house, ask: "Who are the important characters in the story so far? What are they like?"
- At the end of the story, ask: "What happened first in this story? What happened next? What happened last?"

MINILESSON Genre: Fairy Tale

TEACH Display the minilesson principle on chart paper, and read it aloud to children. Explain that *The Three Little Pigs* is different from the other two stories they read this week. Tell children that *The Three Little Pigs* is a special type of story called a fairy tale. Explain that they will think about whether the things that happen in a fairy tale could happen in real life.

1. Focus on *The Three Little Pigs* to introduce the idea that fairy tales tell about things that could not happen in real life. Suggested language: "The story *The Three Little Pigs* tells about things that could not happen in real life. In real life, a pig could not a build a house out of straw, sticks, or bricks."

> **MINILESSON PRINCIPLE**
>
> Think about what happens in a story and if it could really happen.

2. Ask children to name other things that happen in *The Three Little Pigs* that could not happen in real life. Guide children to explain how they know which events could happen in real life and which could not. Explain to children that they will better understand what they read if they pay attention to whether things that happen in a story could happen in real life.

SUMMARIZE AND APPLY Restate the minilesson principle. Tell children to apply it to their independent reading. Suggested language: "When you read, ask yourself whether what is happening in a story could happen in real life."

GROUP SHARE Ask children to tell something that happened in the story they read for independent reading and whether it could happen in real life.

Whole-Group Lessons

How Animals Communicate
Student Book, Lesson 7

Read Aloud Passages

Prairie Dogs
See page 351 of this Guide.

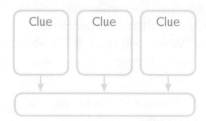

Insect Messages
Student Book, Lesson 7

▶ How Animals Communicate

INTERACTIVE READ-ALOUD/SHARED READING

Read aloud the book to children. Stop periodically for very brief discussion. Use the following suggested stopping points and prompts for quick group response, or give a specific prompt and have partners or threes turn and talk.

- After children read the section about how animals touch, ask: "What was this part about? What did you learn about animals?"
- Before children reach the page that shows a snake, pause to point out the heading. Read it aloud and ask: "What do you think this page will be about?"
- After children read the page that shows a skunk, ask: "How do the words and picture tell you that the skunk smells bad?"
- At the end of the book, ask: "How did the author break this book into parts? Turn and talk about it with a partner."

MINILESSON Details

TEACH Display the minilesson principle on chart paper and read it aloud to children. Tell children they are going to learn to look for word and picture clues about how things look, feel, sound, and smell. Point out that this will help them understand what they read.

1. Discuss the principle with children, using examples from *How Animals Communicate*. Suggested language: "In the information book *How Animals Communicate,* we got clues about how animals look, feel, sound, and smell. Look at the elephants. What do you think their skin feels like? What clues tell you so?" *(It feels bumpy and rough. I think so because in the picture, the elephants have wrinkly skin.)*

> **MINILESSON PRINCIPLE**
>
> Notice the information that tells how things look, feel, sound, and smell.

2. Continue, using the bird as an example. Suggested language: "How do you think the bird sounds when it sings? What makes you think so?" *(I think the bird makes a soft, nice sound. I think so because the bird is small, so maybe it is not very loud. Also, the words say that the bird sings, so it must sound nice.)*

3. Use children's responses to the above question about the bird to fill in an Inference Map like the one shown here. Record what they think the bird might sound like in the big box at the bottom. Record the clues they used in boxes above.

Clue	Clue	Clue

SUMMARIZE AND APPLY Restate the minilesson principle. Then tell children to apply it to their independent reading. Suggested language: "When you read, look for information that tells how things look, feel, sound, and smell. Find clues in the words and pictures."

GROUP SHARE Ask children to share examples of information from another book they have read that tells how something looks, feels, sounds, or smells.

▶ Prairie Dogs

INTERACTIVE READ-ALOUD/SHARED READING

Read aloud the passage to children. Stop periodically for brief discussion. Use the following suggested stopping points and prompts:

- After you read the first paragraph, ask: "What do you think this will be about? What makes you think so?"
- After you read the section about how prairie dogs watch out for each other, ask: "What might cause prairie dogs to run for safety in their holes?"
- At the end, ask: "Do you think people should help to protect prairie dogs? Talk with a partner about your ideas."

MINILESSON Details

TEACH Display the minilesson principle on chart paper, and read it aloud to children. Tell children they are going to learn to use the author's words to figure out how things look.

1. Discuss with children what prairie dogs look like. Suggested language: "How big are prairie dogs?" *(They are the size of rabbits.)* Follow-up: "What other animals do you think they look like? What else do you know about how they look?" *(Answers will vary.)*

> **MINILESSON PRINCIPLE**
>
> Think about how the author uses describing words to tell how things look.

2. Reread the paragraph that begins *Prairie dogs live on prairies.* Tell children to listen for describing words as you read. Then ask: "Which words helped you get a picture of how prairie dogs look?" *(Possible answers include: brown/black fur; stubby tails; short, strong legs; sharp claws)*

3. Use the words children identified to fill in a Web with *Prairie Dogs* in the middle and words that tell what they look like in outside circles.

SUMMARIZE AND APPLY Restate the minilesson principle. Tell children to apply it to their independent reading. Suggested language: "When you read, pay attention to words that tell how things look."

GROUP SHARE Have children tell about describing words they found in their independent reading.

▶ Insect Messages

INTERACTIVE READ-ALOUD/SHARED READING

Read aloud the book to children. Stop periodically for brief discussion. Use the following suggested stopping points and prompts:

- After you read the first page, ask: "Do you think this book tells facts, or is it a made-up story? How do you know?"
- At the end of the book, ask: "What do the pictures show? Why do you think the author chose those pictures? Talk with a partner about your ideas."

MINILESSON Genre: Informational Text

TEACH Explain that *Insect Messages* is similar to the other two books they read this week because it contains facts and information.

1. Focus on *Insect Messages* to introduce the idea that the pictures and labels that go with informational texts contain important information. Suggested language: "*Insect Messages* has four pictures. What does each one show?" *(an insect that can send messages)*

> **MINILESSON PRINCIPLE**
>
> Look for important information in the pictures and the labels on the pictures.

2. Point out the label that goes with each picture and read it aloud. Ask: "How are the labels alike? What do they tell about the pictures?" *(They are each one word. They each give the name of the insect shown in the picture.)*

3. Write the minilesson principle on chart paper. Guide children to explain the important information they got from the words and pictures in *Insect Messages.* Explain that they will better understand what they read if they use the pictures and their labels to find important information.

SUMMARIZE AND APPLY Restate the minilesson principle. Tell children to apply it to their independent reading. Suggested language: "When you read, look for important information in pictures and labels."

GROUP SHARE Ask children to tell about pictures and labels in books they have read independently.

Whole-Group Lessons

A Musical Day
Student Book, Lesson 8

Read Aloud Passages

The Neighbors
See page 352 of this Guide.

Drums
Student Book, Lesson 8

▶ A Musical Day

INTERACTIVE READ-ALOUD/SHARED READING

Read aloud the story to children. Stop periodically for very brief discussion. Use the following suggested stopping points and prompts for quick group response, or give a specific prompt and have partners or threes turn and talk.

- After the children hug Aunt Viv, ask: "What is happening in the story?"
- After the children in the story yell *Yes!* with excitement, ask: "How do the children feel? Why do they feel that way?"
- After the two girls make guitars to pluck, ask: "What do the girls use to make their guitars? Find clues in the picture. Turn and talk about it with a partner."
- At the end of the story, ask: "What is the last thing that happened in this story?"

MINILESSON Sequence of Events

TEACH Display the minilesson principle on chart paper, and read it aloud to children. Tell children they are going to learn to think about what happens first and next in a story. Point out that this will help them understand the story better.

1. Discuss the principle with children, using examples from *A Musical Day.* Suggested language: "In the story *A Musical Day,* the first thing that happened was that Mom and Dad got ready for their trip. What happened next?" *(Aunt Viv arrived.)*

2. Have children name other story events in order. Suggested language: "What happened after the kids got a big hug from Aunt Viv?" *(They clapped, hopped, and sang.)*

3. Focus children's attention on the sequence of events in the story as a whole. Suggested language: "Now let's tell what happened in the whole story."

4. Ask children to tell about the whole story by explaining what happened first, next, and last. Record their ideas in a Flow Chart such as the one below.

> **MINILESSON PRINCIPLE**
>
> Think about what happens first and next in a story.

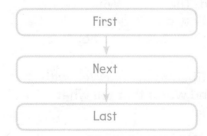

```
┌─────────────┐
│    First    │
└─────────────┘
       ↓
┌─────────────┐
│    Next     │
└─────────────┘
       ↓
┌─────────────┐
│    Last     │
└─────────────┘
```

SUMMARIZE AND APPLY Restate the minilesson principle. Then tell children to apply it to their independent reading. Suggested language: "When you read, think about what happens first and next in a story."

GROUP SHARE Ask children to share what happened first and next in other stories they have read recently.

▶ The Neighbors

INTERACTIVE READ-ALOUD/SHARED READING

Read aloud the story to children. Stop periodically for brief discussion of the story. Use the following suggested stopping points and prompts:

- After you read the first paragraph, ask: "Where does this story happen? How do you know?"
- After Chen is interrupted by laughter from Li's house, ask: "How do you think Chen and Li are alike? How are they different?"
- At the end of the story, ask: "What important things happened in this story?"

MINILESSON Sequence of Events

TEACH Display the minilesson principle on chart paper, and read it aloud to children. Tell children they are going to use the order of what happened in a story to understand the story better.

1. Discuss with children the first important thing that happened in *The Neighbors*. Suggested language: "What happened first in the story?" *(Chen wanted to get rid of Li. He gave Li a box of gold coins.)*

> **MINILESSON PRINCIPLE**
>
> Think about the order of what happens in a story.

2. Have children discuss what happened next, or in the middle of the story. Suggested language: "What happened next?" *(Li spent all his time worrying about the money. Both he and his family were unhappy.)* Then work with children to tell what happened last, or at the end of the story. Ask: "What happened last?" *(Li gave back the money and learned a lesson.)*

3. Use children's responses to the above questions to fill in a Flow Chart for *The Neighbors*. Point out that a Flow Chart may not include every small thing that happened in the story, but the most important events should be shown in the order of first, next, and last.

SUMMARIZE AND APPLY Restate the minilesson principle. Tell children to apply it to their independent reading. Suggested language: "When you read, think about the order of what happens in a story."

GROUP SHARE Have children tell about the order of events in stories they read for independent reading.

▶ Drums

INTERACTIVE READ-ALOUD/SHARED READING

Read aloud the book to children. Stop periodically for brief discussion. Use the following suggested stopping points and prompts:

- After you read the first page, ask: "How do you think Yolanda Martinez feels about drums? How can you tell?"
- After you read the second page, ask: "What are some things all drums have?"
- After you read the last page, ask: "What are the steps to making a drum?"

MINILESSON Diagram

TEACH Explain to children that *Drums* has special parts that help readers because it includes photographs with labels. Tell them that the labeled pictures of drum parts help readers understand information that is not in the rest of the book.

1. Focus on the diagram in *Drums* to help children understand how pictures and labels can help them understand information. Suggested language: "What do the pictures show? How do the labels help tell about the pictures?" *(The picture shows three parts of a drum and each part's name.)*

> **MINILESSON PRINCIPLE**
>
> Think about how pictures and labels help you understand the information.

2. Write the minilesson principle on chart paper. Guide children to explain how the pictures and their labels helped them understand the different parts of a drum. Explain to children that pictures and their labels sometimes give information that is not found in other parts of a book.

SUMMARIZE AND APPLY Restate the minilesson principle. Tell children to apply it to their independent reading. Suggested language: "When you read, look at pictures and labels to help you understand important information."

GROUP SHARE Ask children to tell about pictures and labels in books they read for independent reading.

Whole-Group Lessons

Dr. Seuss
Student Book, Lesson 9

The Little Red Hen
See page 352 of this Guide.

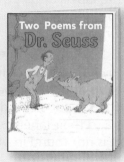

Two Poems from Dr. Seuss
Student Book, Lesson 9

▶ Dr. Seuss

INTERACTIVE READ-ALOUD/SHARED READING

Read aloud the book to children. Stop periodically for very brief discussion of the book. Use the following suggested stopping points and prompts for quick group response, or give a specific prompt and have partners or threes turn and talk.

- After children read the page that says Ted was a funny man, ask: "How does the picture show that Ted was funny?"
- On the page that shows Dr. Seuss writing, ask: "Who is this story mostly about? How do you know?"
- On the page that shows Dr. Seuss reading to kids, ask: "Have you ever read or heard a Dr. Seuss story? What was it like?"
- At the end of the story, ask: "Why is Dr. Seuss famous today? Turn and talk about it with two partners."

MINILESSON Genre: Biography

TEACH Display the minilesson principle on chart paper, and read it aloud to children. Tell children that *Dr. Seuss* is a biography, or a story about a special person's life. In a biography, the author gives information to explain what makes that person special.

> **MINILESSON PRINCIPLE**
>
> Notice how the author tells what is special about the person she is writing about.

1. Discuss the principle with children, using examples from *Dr. Seuss*. Suggested language: "In the story *Dr. Seuss,* we learned that Ted wrote many books for children. How did this show that Ted was special?" *(Writing books is probably hard. Also, Ted drew pictures for his books. These things show that he was special.)*

2. Focus on other details from the story that show how Ted was special. Suggested language: "What was special about Ted's book *The Cat in the Hat?*" *(The main character is famous. Many people loved the book.)* Follow-up: "How did people feel about Ted's other books?" *(Many people loved his other books, too.)*

3. Create a Web such as the one shown below. In the center circle, write *Ways Ted Was Special*. Then use children's responses to the above questions to fill in the outer circles. If any circles are left blank, ask children to suggest other special things they learned about Ted from the story.

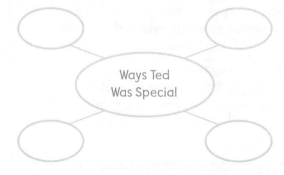

Ways Ted Was Special

SUMMARIZE AND APPLY Restate the minilesson principle. Then tell children to apply it to their independent reading. Suggested language: "When you read, think about what makes the people you read about special."

GROUP SHARE Ask children to share something special about a person they have read about recently.

▶ The Little Red Hen

INTERACTIVE READ-ALOUD/SHARED READING

Read aloud the story to children. Stop periodically for brief discussion of the story. Use the following suggested stopping points and prompts:

- After you read the first paragraph of the story, ask: "Who are the important characters in the story so far?"
- After the duck, pig, and cat refuse to help take the wheat to the miller, ask: "Would you like to have the duck, pig, and cat as friends? Why or why not?"
- At the end of the story, ask: "How do you think the duck, pig, and cat feel at the end of the story? How do you think the Little Red Hen feels?"

MINILESSON Genre: Fairy Tale

TEACH Display the minilesson principle on chart paper, and read it aloud. Tell children that *The Little Red Hen* is a kind of story called a fairy tale. A fairy tale is a story about characters and things that could not happen in real life.

1. Discuss with children how the same thing happened over and over in the story. Suggested language: "How did the duck, pig, and cat answer every time the Little Red Hen asked for help?" *(Not I!)*

> **MINILESSON PRINCIPLE**
> Notice when the same thing happens over and over to think about what might happen next.

2. Review how the Little Red Hen asked for help planting the wheat, cutting the wheat, and taking it to the miller. Have children tell what they expected to happen when the Little Red Hen asked for help with the dough. Suggested language: "Did you think the other animals would help the Little Red Hen make her dough?" *(no)*

3. Help children understand that they should use clues, such as things that happen over and over, whenever they think about what might happen next in a story. Suggested language: "What made you think the duck, pig, and cat would not want to help the hen make her dough?" *(They said* no *to everything else she asked them to help with.)*

SUMMARIZE AND APPLY Restate the minilesson principle. Tell children to apply it to their independent reading. Suggested language: "When something happens over and over in a story, use this information to think about what might happen next."

GROUP SHARE Have children tell clues they used to guess what might happen next in stories from their independent reading.

▶ Two Poems from Dr. Seuss

INTERACTIVE READ-ALOUD/SHARED READING

Read aloud the introduction and poems to children. Stop periodically for brief discussion. Use the following suggested stopping points and prompts:

- After you read the first poem, say: "What was 'Pete Pats Pigs' about?"
- After you read the second poem, ask: "What was 'Quack Quack!' about?"
- Have children compare the two poems. "How were the poems the same? How were they different?"

MINILESSON Genre: Poetry

TEACH Remind children of ways that poems are different from other things they might read. Many poems rhyme, for example. Poems also include words that help readers make pictures in their minds. Then write the minilesson principle on chart paper, and read it aloud for children.

1. Have children close their eyes so they cannot see the pictures. Then reread "Pete Pats Pigs" for children, telling them to listen for words that help them picture Pete and his pigs. Suggested language: "Which words help you picture Pete? Which words help you picture the pigs and their playpen?" *(pink, big)*

> **MINILESSON PRINCIPLE**
> Think about how words in a poem make pictures in your mind.

2. Repeat the first step using the other poem, "Quack Quack!" Have children name words that help them picture each duck.

SUMMARIZE AND APPLY Restate the minilesson principle. Tell children to apply it to their independent reading. Suggested language: "When you read, think about how the author's words help you make pictures in your mind."

GROUP SHARE Ask children to tell about how they used words from their independent reading to make pictures in their minds.

Whole-Group Lessons

A Cupcake Party
Student Book, Lesson 10

Read Aloud Passages

Chipper Chips In
See page 353 of this Guide.

Happy Times
Student Book, Lesson 10

▶ A Cupcake Party

INTERACTIVE READ-ALOUD/SHARED READING

Read aloud the story to children. Stop periodically for very brief discussion of the story. Use the following suggested stopping points and prompts for quick group response, or give a specific prompt and have partners or threes turn and talk.

- After Fritz says that he misses his friends, ask: "What do you think Fritz will do next?"
- On the page that shows Fritz putting cupcakes into the oven, ask: "What does Fritz do after he invites all his friends over for a party?"
- On the page that shows Fritz's friends giving him an acorn, ask: "Why do you think Fritz's friends brought him a snack?"
- At the end of the story, ask: "Do you think it would be fun to go to a party like Fritz's? Turn and talk about your ideas with a partner."

MINILESSON Story Structure

TEACH Display the minilesson principle on chart paper, and read it aloud to children. Explain that in most stories an important character has a problem. Tell children that they are going to learn to notice what problem a character has in a story and how he or she tries to solve it.

1. Discuss the principle with children, using examples from *A Cupcake Party.* Suggested language: "In the story *A Cupcake Party,* we learned that Fritz missed his friends. This was a problem. What was the first thing he did to try to solve this problem?" *(He decided to have a party.)*

2. Focus on the steps Fritz took to solve his problem. Suggested language: "What did Fritz do next to solve his problem?" *(He invited his friends to his party. Then he baked special cupcakes for his friends so the party would be fun.)*

3. Create a Flow Chart such as the one below to show Fritz's problem and what he did to solve it. In the top box, record Fritz's problem. Then use Fritz's ways of solving his problem to fill in the chart. Discuss how the chart shows both Fritz's problem and how he solved it.

> **MINILESSON PRINCIPLE**
> Notice how the characters in a story solve a problem.

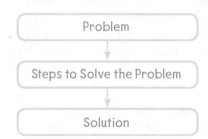

SUMMARIZE AND APPLY Restate the minilesson principle. Then tell children to apply it to their independent reading. Suggested language: "When you read, think about the problems that characters have and how they try to solve their problems."

GROUP SHARE Ask children to share a problem that a character faced in a story they read. Have them tell how the character solved his or her problem.

▶ Chipper Chips In

INTERACTIVE READ-ALOUD/SHARED READING

Read aloud the story to children. Stop periodically for brief discussion of the story. Use the following suggested stopping points and prompts:

- After Chipper's brothers tell her that she is too small to collect seeds, ask: "Who are the important characters in this story so far?"
- After the chipmunks are told that the first frost is coming soon, ask: "How do you think Chipper feels here? Why do you think so?"
- At the end of the story, ask: "What lesson do you think Chipper's brothers learned in the story? Turn and talk about your ideas with a partner."

MINILESSON Story Structure

TEACH Display the minilesson principle on chart paper and read it aloud to children. Tell children they are going to learn to notice the problems that different characters have in stories.

1. Discuss with children the problem that Chipper had at the beginning of *Chipper Chips In*. Suggested language: "What did Chipper's brothers tell her at the beginning of the story? How do you think that made her feel?" *(They told her that she was too small to help collect seeds for winter. That probably made her feel mad and left out.)*

> **MINILESSON PRINCIPLE**
>
> Notice that the characters in stories have problems to solve.

2. Help children understand that Chipper's problem was that her brothers did not want her to help. Suggested language: "What was Chipper's big problem?"

3. Explain to children that in some stories, more than one character has a problem. Use the example of the chipmunks needing to gather seeds quickly to help children understand. Suggested language: "In the middle of the story, all the chipmunks had a problem. What was it?" *(They needed to gather seeds very quickly.)*

SUMMARIZE AND APPLY Restate the minilesson principle. Tell children to apply it to their independent reading. Suggested language: "When you read, think about the problems that characters try to solve."

GROUP SHARE Ask children to share more examples from their independent reading of problems characters can have.

▶ Happy Times

INTERACTIVE READ-ALOUD/SHARED READING

Read aloud the poems to children. Stop periodically for brief discussion of the text. Use the following suggested stopping points and prompts:

- After reading "Singing Time," ask: "Which words in this poem rhyme?" Follow-up: "How do the rhyming words make the poem more fun to read?"
- After reading "I'm Glad," ask: "What makes the poet glad?" Follow-up: "What does the poet mean by saying that fresh air is *sandwiched in between*?"
- After reading "Laughing Boy," ask: "What is this poem about?" Follow-up: "How is this poem like 'I'm Glad'? How is it different? Turn and talk about your ideas with a partner."

MINILESSON Genre: Poetry

TEACH Display the minilesson principle on chart paper, and read it aloud to children. Explain that rhythm is a pattern of sound like the beat in music. Tell children that they are going to learn to identify the rhythm of a poem.

1. Focus on "Singing Time" to lead children in identifying the rhythm of a poem. Have them listen as you read "Singing Time" aloud and clap along to the rhythm. Ask: "Which words did I clap for to show the rhythm?" *(wake, morning, early, always, very, thing, poke, head, sit, bed, sing, sing, sing)*

> **MINILESSON PRINCIPLE**
>
> Notice the rhythm of a poem.

2. Reread "I'm Glad" aloud and have children listen for the beat. Then repeat each line, clapping to the rhythm. Repeat for "Laughing Boy." Ask: "Which poem's rhythm was easier to hear?" *("I'm Glad")*

SUMMARIZE AND APPLY Restate the minilesson principle. Tell children they can apply it to their independent reading. Suggested language: "When you read a poem, pay attention to the rhythm."

GROUP SHARE Ask children to share an example of a poem they read. Have them identify the rhythm by clapping to the beat of the poem as they read.

Whole-Group Lessons

At Home in the Ocean
Student Book, Lesson 11

Read Aloud Passages

The Piano Lessons
See page 353 of this Guide.

Water
Student Book, Lesson 11

▶ At Home in the Ocean

INTERACTIVE READ-ALOUD/SHARED READING

Read aloud the book to children. Stop periodically for very brief discussion of the text. Use the suggested stopping points and prompts below for quick group response, or give a specific prompt and have partners or threes turn and talk.

- After reading about the blue whale, ask: "What does the word in blue under each photo tell you?"
- After reading about manatees, ask: "Do you think a manatee could live where penguins live? Why or why not?"
- After reading about sea otters, ask: "What kind of plants do sea otters eat?"
- At the end of the selection, ask: "How are animals that live in the ocean alike? How are they different? Turn and talk about your ideas with a partner."

MINILESSON Author's Purpose

TEACH Display the minilesson principle on chart paper, and read it aloud to children. Explain that authors have different reasons for writing their books. Tell them that they are going to think about how authors sometimes write to give information.

1. Discuss the principle with children using *At Home in the Ocean* as an example. Focus on the first two pages. Suggested language: "In *At Home in the Ocean*, the author writes about how big the ocean is. What else does the author tell you about the ocean?" *(It is home to many plants and animals.)*

> **MINILESSON PRINCIPLE**
> Think about how authors sometimes write to give information.

2. Focus on the pages that tell about penguins, manatees, and turtles. Suggested language: "These pages tell about different animals that live in the ocean and what they do. Think about two of the animals and what they do. What information does the author give?" *(Penguins swim fast. Manatees swim slow, eat a lot, and rest.)*

3. Elicit from children additional facts from the text. Record children's ideas in an Inference Map like the one shown here.

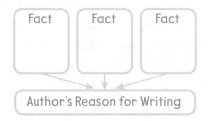

4. Use children's responses to identify the author's purpose. Suggested language: "You can see that each page gives facts about an animal or plant that lives in the ocean. This helps you figure out that the author wrote this book to give information."

SUMMARIZE AND APPLY Restate the minilesson principle. Tell children to apply it to their independent reading. Suggested language: "When you read a book, think about why the author wrote it. Does the book give information or was it written for a different reason?"

GROUP SHARE Have children share why they think the author wrote the book they are reading. Ask them to share details from the book that support their ideas.

▶ The Piano Lessons

INTERACTIVE READ-ALOUD/SHARED READING

Read aloud the story to children. Stop periodically for brief discussion of it. Use the following suggested stopping points and prompts:

- After you read how Kim practices at home, ask: "How would you describe Mrs. Johnson? What does she say and do to help you figure out what she is like?"
- After Mrs. Johnson suggests that the girls practice together, ask: "Did Mrs. Johnson surprise you here? Why or why not?"
- At the end of the story, say: "How has Kim changed from the beginning of the story to the end? Turn and talk with a partner about how and why she changed."

MINILESSON Author's Purpose

TEACH Display the minilesson principle on chart paper, and read it aloud to children. Tell children they are going to think about how authors can write stories for readers to enjoy.

1. Discuss the principle with children, using *The Piano Lessons* as an example. Focus on one part of the story, such as when Kim is practicing in the beginning. Suggested language: "The author helps you create a picture in your mind as you listen to the story. You heard the words *plink, plunk, thud*. These helped you understand how terrible Kim was at practicing and might have made you laugh. What did Kim say about practicing that sounded like a real girl talking?" *(This is soooo boring.)*

> **MINILESSON PRINCIPLE**
>
> Think about how authors sometimes write to help readers enjoy their stories.

2. Use children's responses to explain that authors have different reasons for writing. Suggested language: "You can tell that the author of *The Piano Lessons* wants you to laugh at this part. This helps you figure out that the author wrote the story for readers to enjoy."

3. Help children identify other parts of the story that help them understand the author's purpose. Write their ideas in an Inference Map.

SUMMARIZE AND APPLY Restate the minilesson principle. Tell children to apply it to their independent reading. Suggested language: "When you read, think about what the author does to help you enjoy the story."

GROUP SHARE Have children share why they think the author wrote the story that they read independently. Ask them to share details from the story that show how the author helped them enjoy it.

▶ Water

INTERACTIVE READ-ALOUD/SHARED READING

Read aloud the book to children. Stop periodically for brief discussion of it. Use the following suggested stopping points and prompts:

- After the first page, ask: "What is a liquid? How does the picture help you understand the words?"
- At the end, ask: "How is liquid water different from frozen water? Turn and talk about your ideas with a partner."

MINILESSON Genre: Informational Text

TEACH Explain to children that two of the books they read this week, *At Home in the Ocean* and *Water,* were written to give information.

1. Focus on the first two pages to introduce how authors can make information interesting. Suggested language: "In *Water*, the author used different kinds of sentences. The first part has questions and answers. This can make information more interesting to read."

> **MINILESSON PRINCIPLE**
>
> Notice how authors make information interesting.

2. Explain that the author of *Water* also used pictures to give information. Tell children that pictures are often used to make information more interesting.

3. Ask children to share parts of *Water* that they found interesting. Write the minilesson principle on chart paper. Guide children to identify features, such as diagrams and pictures, that make information interesting.

SUMMARIZE AND APPLY Restate the minilesson principle. Tell children to apply it to their independent reading. Suggested language: "When you read, think about how the author keeps you interested in the information you are reading."

GROUP SHARE Ask children to share a part of a book they chose for independent reading. Have them tell how the author made it interesting.

Whole-Group Lessons

How Leopard Got His Spots
Student Book, Lesson 12

Read Aloud Passages

Turtle, Frog, and Rat
See page 354 of this Guide.

The Rain Forest
Student Book, Lesson 12

▶ How Leopard Got His Spots

INTERACTIVE READ-ALOUD/SHARED READING

Read aloud the story to children. Stop periodically for very brief discussion of it. Use the following suggested stopping points and prompts for quick group response, or give a specific prompt and have partners or threes turn and talk.

- After Fred gets stuck, ask: "Why do you think Fred felt very sad? How do you think he feels about Hal?"
- After Fred paints Zel and Jill, ask: "How do you think Leopard will get his spots?"
- After Hal says *Paint me, too,* ask: "What do you think Fred will do? Turn and talk with your partner about what you think will happen next."
- At the end of the story, ask: "What lesson can you learn from this story?" Follow-up: "Has anyone ever played a trick on you? How did it make you feel?"

MINILESSON Sequence of Events

TEACH Display the minilesson principle on chart paper, and read it aloud to children. Tell children they are going to learn how to think about order as they read. Explain that most stories happen in a certain order. They tell what happens first, next, and last.

1. Discuss the principle with children, using events from the first part of *How Leopard Got His Spots.* Suggested language: "In the story *How Leopard Got His Spots,* things happen in order. Let's look at the first five pages of the story. What happened first?" *(Hal and Fred were playing catch, and Hal tricked Fred.)*

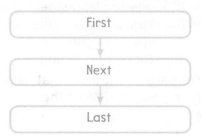

> **MINILESSON PRINCIPLE**
> Think about what happens first, next, and last in a story.

2. Focus on what happened directly after Hal tricked Fred. Suggested language: "What happened to Fred after he got tricked?" *(He got stuck in the plant and yelled for help.)* "What happened last?" *(Len cut the plants and let Fred out.)*

3. Use children's responses to explain how authors put events in an order that makes sense. Suggested language: "The author told what happened first, next, and last. When you think about the order in which things happen, it helps you understand the story."

4. Work with children to sequence the most important events from the whole story. Record children's ideas in a flow chart like the one shown here.

```
┌─────────────────┐
│      First      │
└─────────────────┘
         ↓
┌─────────────────┐
│      Next       │
└─────────────────┘
         ↓
┌─────────────────┐
│      Last       │
└─────────────────┘
```

SUMMARIZE AND APPLY Restate the minilesson principle. Explain to children that they can apply it to their independent reading. Suggested language: "When you read a story, think about what happens first, next, and last."

GROUP SHARE Have children share the sequence of events from a story they read for independent reading. Ask them to tell what happened first, next, and last.

▶ Turtle, Frog, and Rat

INTERACTIVE READ-ALOUD/SHARED READING

Read aloud the story to children. Stop periodically for brief discussion of it. Use the following suggested stopping points and prompts:

- After the animals compliment each other, ask: "Do you think Rat, Turtle, and Frog are good friends to each other? Why or why not?"
- After Rat finds his friends, ask: "How do you think Rat feels when he finds his friends?" Follow-up: "How do you think Turtle and Frog feel when they see Rat?"
- At the end of the story, say: "What lesson can you learn from Rat's wife? Turn and talk with a partner about whether you think it is a good lesson."

MINILESSON Genre: Folktale

TEACH Display the minilesson principle on chart paper, and read it aloud to children. Tell children they are going to learn to think about how a folktale can explain something in nature.

1. Focus on *Turtle, Frog, and Rat* to introduce the idea that some folktales explain why things in nature came to be. Suggested language: "In the story *Turtle, Rat, and Frog*, the animals changed. What did each animal look like at the beginning of the story?" (*Frog had flat eyes. Turtle had a smooth shell. Rat had a furry tail.*)

> **MINILESSON PRINCIPLE**
>
> Notice that a folktale explains why something is the way it is.

2. Use children's responses to point out how this folktale explains why something is the way it is. Suggested language: "You know that today these animals look different. Frogs have bulging eyes, turtles have rough shells, and rats have skinny, furless tails. How did the story explain why this is?" (*The animals had an accident when they were trying to meet Rat's wife.*)

3. As children share the events that led to each animal's appearance, write the minilesson principle on chart paper. Explain to children that some folktales have funny ways of explaining things in nature.

SUMMARIZE AND APPLY Restate the minilesson principle. Tell children to apply it to their independent reading. Suggested language: "When you read a folktale, look for ways it explains why something is the way it is."

GROUP SHARE Ask children to summarize folktales they have read that tell why something is the way it is.

▶ The Rain Forest

INTERACTIVE READ-ALOUD/SHARED READING

Read aloud the book to children. Stop periodically for brief discussion of it. Use the following suggested stopping points and prompts:

- After the Understory paragraph, ask: "Why is the understory layer shady?"
- After the Forest Floor paragraph, ask: "Which part of the rainforest do you think has the largest animals? Why?"
- At the end of the selection, ask: "How do the pictures, labels, and map help you better understand the information? Turn and talk about your ideas with a partner."

MINILESSON Genre: Informational Text

TEACH Explain to children that *The Rain Forest* is different from the other two stories they read this week. Point out that it gives information about a real place.

1. Focus on the headings to introduce how authors call attention to information. Suggested language: "In *The Rain Forest*, the author included some words in red type. These words are also darker than the words around them."

> **MINILESSON PRINCIPLE**
>
> Think about why the author made the letters different colors and sizes.

2. Page through the text with children to identify the three headings in red, bold type. Point out how each heading tells what the paragraph is going to be about. Suggested language: "Look at the words *Canopy Layer*. They are a different color and bigger than the words around them. If you read the sentences that follow it, you can see that they all tell about the canopy layer. If you want to find information about a part of the rain forest, you can easily find it by looking for the words in red that name the part."

3. Write the minilesson principle on chart paper. Guide children to see how the headings stand out from the other words. Explain to children that authors put words in different colors or sizes to draw a reader's attention to them or to help them find information.

SUMMARIZE AND APPLY Restate the minilesson principle. Explain to children that they can apply it to their independent reading. Suggested language: "When you read, look for words that are shown in different colors or sizes from the rest of the words in the book."

GROUP SHARE Ask children to share examples of words shown in special colors or sizes in a book they read.

Whole-Group Lessons

Seasons
Student Book, Lesson 13

Read Aloud Passages

The Prickly Pride of Texas
See page 355 of this Guide.

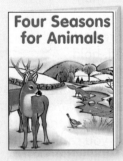

Four Seasons for Animals
Student Book, Lesson 13

▶ Seasons

INTERACTIVE READ-ALOUD/SHARED READING

Read aloud the book to children. Stop periodically for very brief discussion of it. Use the following suggested stopping points and prompts for quick group response, or give a specific prompt and have partners or threes turn and talk.

- After the last page of the Spring section, ask: "How do the words on this page help you make a picture in your mind of what spring is like?"
- After the last page of the Fall section, ask: "Why do you think animals pack away nuts in the fall?"
- At the end, ask: "Why do you think the author chose to write this information like a poem? Turn and talk to a partner about whether or not this was a good way to learn about the seasons."

MINILESSON Cause and Effect

TEACH Display the minilesson principle on chart paper, and read it aloud to children. Tell children they are going to learn how to notice how one thing can make another thing happen. Explain that understanding why things happen will help them better understand a whole story.

1. Discuss the principle with children, using examples from *Seasons*. Suggested language: "In the Spring section of *Seasons*, you read that the grass made a squish sound. What happened to make the grass squish?" *(It rained, and the grass got wet.)*

2. Use children's responses to explain how to notice when one thing causes another. Suggested language: "The rain made the grass squish. The rain was one thing that made another thing happen. As you read, it is important to look for the reasons why things happen."

3. Work with children to find events that made other things happen. Record children's ideas in a T-Map like the one shown here.

> **MINILESSON PRINCIPLE**
>
> Notice when one thing makes another thing happen.

What Happened?	Why?

SUMMARIZE AND APPLY Restate the minilesson principle. Explain to children that they can apply it to their independent reading. Suggested language: "When you read a story, notice how one thing can make another thing happen."

GROUP SHARE Have children share an example of one thing that made another thing happen from their independent reading.

▶ The Prickly Pride of Texas

INTERACTIVE READ-ALOUD/SHARED READING

Read aloud the selection to children. Stop periodically for brief discussion of it. Use the following suggested stopping points and prompts:

- After the retelling of the legend, ask: "Why do you think the author began this with a story?"
- After the paragraph that describes how parts of the plant can be used for food, say: "Turn and talk with a partner about how different parts of prickly pear cactus might taste." Follow-up: "Do you think you would like to eat any parts of the prickly pear cactus? If you have before, what was it like?"
- At the end, ask: "How does the author feel about the prickly pear cactus? How can you tell?"

MINILESSON Genre: Informational Text

TEACH Display the minilesson principle on chart paper, and read it aloud to children. Tell children they are going to think about words the author used to tell what the prickly pear cactus is like.

1. Tell children that authors often use words that help readers picture what something is like. Suggested language: "In *The Prickly Pride of Texas,* the author used words that help you understand what the plant is like. These words told about how the cactus looks, feels, and tastes. Do you remember what the author said the leaves looked like?" *(flat, green paddles shaped like tears)*

> **MINILESSON PRINCIPLE**
>
> Notice when an author tells what something is like.

2. Work with children to find other descriptive details from the story. Write their ideas in a Web with *Prickly Pear Cactus* in the center circle. Have children suggest details that tell about the cactus in the outer circles.

SUMMARIZE AND APPLY Restate the minilesson principle. Explain to children that they should apply it to their independent reading. Suggested language: "When you read, pay attention to words that tell what something is like."

GROUP SHARE Have children choose a description they have read in a book. Ask them to share words the author used to tell what something is like. You may wish to have the group tell which words helped them best picture the thing being described.

▶ Four Seasons for Animals

INTERACTIVE READ-ALOUD/SHARED READING

Read aloud the book to children. Stop periodically for brief discussion of the text. Use the following suggested stopping points and prompts:

- After reading the section Spring, ask: "How does the picture of the flower buds help you understand what happens to them in the spring?"
- After reading the section Fall, ask: "How does life for the animals change from summer to fall?"
- At the end, ask: "Why do you think the author wrote this? Turn and talk about your ideas with a partner."

MINILESSON Genre: Informational Text

TEACH Explain to children that *Four Seasons for Animals* is an informational text. It gives information about what animals do during the four seasons of the year.

1. Focus on the headings to introduce how authors call attention to and organize information. Suggested language: "In *Four Seasons for Animals,* the author included some words in colored type. These words are larger than the words that follow them."

> **MINILESSON PRINCIPLE**
>
> Notice the headings authors use to tell about sections of a text.

2. Page through the text with children to identify the headings. Point out how each heading tells what the text that follows will be about. Suggested language: "Look at the word *Spring.* It is a different color and larger than the words that follow it. If you read the section, you will see that the sentences all tell about what happens in the spring."

3. Display the minilesson principle on chart paper, and read it aloud to children. Guide children to notice how the headings stand out from the other words. Explain that authors use headings to help readers understand what each section is about.

SUMMARIZE AND APPLY Restate the minilesson principle. Tell children they can apply it to their independent reading. Suggested language: "When you read, look for headings that tell what each section is about."

GROUP SHARE Ask children to share examples of headings in a book they read. Have them tell how the headings helped them understand the information in each section.

Whole-Group Lessons

The Big Race
Student Book, Lesson 14

Read Aloud Passages

The Tortoise and the Hare
See page 355 of this Guide.

Rules and Laws
Student Book, Lesson 14

▶ The Big Race

INTERACTIVE READ-ALOUD/SHARED READING

Read aloud the story to children. Stop periodically for very brief discussion of it. Use the following suggested stopping points and prompts for quick group response, or give a specific prompt and have partners or threes turn and talk.

- After Red Lizard gets to the race, ask: "What is special about the race? Why does Red Lizard want to run in it?"
- After all the animals arrive at the starting line, ask: "Who is running in this race? Who do you think will win? Why do you think this?"
- After Roadrunner trips over the rake, ask: "Who do you think will win the race now? Turn and talk with your partner about who you think will win."
- At the end of the story, ask: "What lesson can you learn from this story?" Follow-up: "When have you shared something with your friends?"

MINILESSON Conclusions

TEACH Display the minilesson principle on chart paper, and read it aloud to children. Tell children they are going to learn how to notice clues about characters as they read. Explain that the clues will help them figure out what a character is like.

1. Discuss the principle with children, using examples of characters from *The Big Race*. Suggested language: "In *The Big Race*, five characters ran in the race. Which character finished the race?" (*Red Lizard*) "What happened to the other characters?" (*They either fell or stopped paying attention.*)

> **MINILESSON PRINCIPLE**
>
> Notice clues about characters to help you understand what they are like.

2. Focus on the character Red Lizard. Suggested language: "Red Lizard won the race and the cake. Do you remember what he did with his prize?" (*At first, he was going to eat the cake all by himself. Then he saw that his pals looked sad. He decided to share the cake with his pals.*)

3. Use children's responses to explain how authors give clues about what characters are like. Suggested language: "What Red Lizard did at the end shows you that he was kind and generous. The author did not tell you that Red Lizard was kind, but you can figure it out because of what he did."

4. Work with children to draw conclusions about other characters in the story. Record children's ideas in an Inference Map like the one shown here.

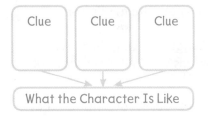

SUMMARIZE AND APPLY Restate the minilesson principle. Explain to children that they can apply it to their independent reading. Suggested language: "When you read a story, think about what the characters are like. Look for clues that the author gives you about them."

GROUP SHARE Have children share a description of one character in a story they read for independent reading. Ask them to tell what the character is like. Then have them give clues from the story that helped them figure out what the character is like.

▶ The Tortoise and the Hare

INTERACTIVE READ-ALOUD/SHARED READING

Read aloud the story to children. Stop periodically for brief discussion of it. Use the following suggested stopping points and prompts:

- After the tortoise challenges the hare to a race, ask: "Why do you think the tortoise wants to race the hare?"
- After the hare sits down, ask: "Why does the hare decide to take a rest?" Follow-up: "Do you think this is a good idea? Why or why not?"
- At the end of the story, say: "Think about what the coyote says. Do you think it is a good lesson? Turn and talk about your ideas with a partner."

MINILESSON Conclusions

TEACH Display the minilesson principle on chart paper, and read it aloud to children. Tell children they are going to learn to use what characters say and do to figure out what they are like.

1. Remind children how authors give clues about what characters are like. Explain that clues can be what a character says and does. Suggested language: "In the story *The Tortoise and the Hare,* what did the hare do when the tortoise asked him to race?" (*The hare laughed. He said there was no one faster.*)

> **MINILESSON PRINCIPLE**
>
> Think about what characters say and what they do to help you know what they are like.

2. Point out to children that what characters say and what they do help you know what they are like. Suggested language: "The author used what the hare said—when he bragged to the tortoise—and what he did—laughed—to show you what the hare was like. You can figure out that the hare was sure of himself and thought he could not lose."

3. Work with children to draw additional conclusions about the tortoise from the story. Write their ideas in an Inference Map.

SUMMARIZE AND APPLY Restate the minilesson principle. Explain to children that they should apply it to their independent reading. Suggested language: "When you read, think about what characters say and what they do to figure out what they are like."

GROUP SHARE Have children choose a character from a story and tell what the character said and did. Then have them tell what the character was like.

▶ Rules and Laws

INTERACTIVE READ-ALOUD/SHARED READING

Read aloud the book to children. Stop periodically for brief discussion of the text. Use the following suggested stopping points and prompts:

- After reading the section Rules, ask: "What game rule is shown in the photo?" Follow-up: "Why are game rules important?"
- After reading the section Laws, ask: "How do laws help us to be good citizens?"
- At the end ask: "Why are rules and laws important for people to follow? Turn and talk about your ideas with a partner."

MINILESSON Genre: Informational Text

TEACH Display the minilesson principle on chart paper, and read it aloud to children. Explain to children that thinking about the information in labels will help them better understand what they read.

1. Tell children they are going to think about how labels give them information in *Rules and Laws*. Suggested language: "Look at the photo of the girl at school. What is she doing?" (*raising her hand*) Follow-up: "Read the words below the photo. What information do you get from reading these words?" (*that raising a hand is a school rule*)

> **MINILESSON PRINCIPLE**
>
> Think about how labels give you information.

2. Ask children to look at the other photos and labels on the page. Suggested language: "Why do you think the author included these labels?" (*to help you understand what the photos show*)

3. Page through the selection, discussing the photos and having children read the labels. Help children to summarize what they learned by filling in a T-Map with the following headings: *Label* and *Information It Gives*.

SUMMARIZE AND APPLY Restate the minilesson principle. Tell children they can apply it to their independent reading. Suggested language: "When you read, look at the pictures and read the labels to get more information."

GROUP SHARE Ask children to share some information from a label in a book they read. Have them tell how the label helped them better understand the information in the book.

Whole-Group Lessons

Animal Groups
Student Book, Lesson 15

Read Aloud Passages

The Dancing Wolves
See page 355 of this Guide.

Animal Picnic
Student Book, Lesson 15

▶ Animal Groups

INTERACTIVE READ-ALOUD/SHARED READING

Read aloud the book to children. Stop periodically for very brief discussion of it. Use the following suggested stopping points and prompts for quick group response, or give a specific prompt and have partners or threes turn and talk.

- After the section about fish, ask: "Why do fish have gills?" Follow-up: "What is different about the way you breathe?"
- After the section about reptiles, ask: "What are some of the different ways that reptiles move around?"
- After the bird section, ask: "What are some animals that hatch from eggs?"
- At the end of the book, ask: "What is the same about all mammals? Turn and talk about your ideas with a partner."

MINILESSON Compare and Contrast

TEACH Display the minilesson principle on chart paper, and read it aloud to children. Tell children they are going to learn how to think about the ways in which things can be the same and different.

1. Discuss the principle with children, using *Animal Groups* as an example. Suggested language: "In *Animal Groups*, you learned about five different animal groups. The animals in each group are the same in some ways. What is the same about all amphibians?" (*They have wet skin. They live on land and water. They hatch from eggs.*)

> **MINILESSON PRINCIPLE**
>
> Think about how things are the same and how they are different.

2. Then choose another animal group for children to compare to amphibians. Suggested language: "Can you remember what is the same about all birds?" (*They have feathers and wings. They hatch from eggs.*)

3. Use children's responses to explain how to compare and contrast. Suggested language: "Think about the two animal groups Amphibians and Birds. How are they the same? How are they different?" (*They are the same because they both hatch from eggs. They are different because amphibians have wet skin, but birds have feathers and wings.*)

4. Work with children to tell how two of the animal groups are the same and different. Record children's ideas in a Venn Diagram like the one shown here.

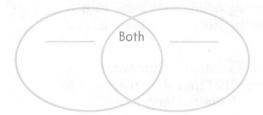

Both

SUMMARIZE AND APPLY Restate the minilesson principle. Explain to children that they can apply it to their independent reading. Suggested language: "When you read a book, think about how things are the same and different."

GROUP SHARE Have children tell about how two different books they read were the same and different.

▶ The Dancing Wolves

INTERACTIVE READ-ALOUD/SHARED READING

Read aloud the story to children. Stop periodically for brief discussion of it. Use the following suggested stopping points and prompts:

- After the rabbit suggests a dance contest, ask: "What is rabbit like?" Follow-up: "Do you really think he is giving himself up as a prize? What do you think will happen next?"

- At the end of the story, ask: "Why do you think the author wrote this story? How do you know? Turn and talk about your ideas with a partner."

MINILESSON   Story Structure

TEACH Display the minilesson principle on chart paper, and read it aloud to children. Tell children they are going to think about characters and what has happened in a story to figure out what might happen next.

1. Explain to children that authors sometimes give clues about what might happen next in a story. Use *The Dancing Wolves* as an example. Suggested language: "In *The Dancing Wolves*, what did the rabbit do after the wolves finished the first dance?" (*He moved farther away and gave the wolves a harder dance to do.*) Follow-up: "What did the rabbit do after the wolves finished the second dance?" (*He moved even father away and gave the wolves an even harder dance.*)

> **MINILESSON PRINCIPLE**
>
> Think about the characters and what happened to think what might happen next.

2. Remind children that they can make guesses about what might happen next using what they know about the characters and events in a story. Suggested language: "As you listened, you heard that the rabbit moved farther away with each dance. This is a good clue that rabbit will get away in the end. Because the author gave the story a pattern, it helped you make a good guess about what would happen next."

SUMMARIZE AND APPLY Restate the minilesson principle. Explain to children that they should apply it to their independent reading. Suggested language: "When you read, think about what characters say and do and what happens to figure out what might happen next."

GROUP SHARE Have children tell about the events in a story they are reading. If they have not finished, have them tell what they think might happen next and explain why. If they have finished, have them tell what they thought would happen while reading and whether or not it was correct.

▶ Animal Picnic

INTERACTIVE READ-ALOUD/SHARED READING

Read aloud the play to children. Stop periodically for brief discussion of it. Use the following suggested stopping points and prompts:

- After Bird says *I had to fly,* ask: "How did each animal get to the picnic. How do you know?"

- At the end of the play, ask: "Do you think the animals will try eating each other's food? Turn and talk about your ideas with a partner."

MINILESSON   Compare and Contrast

TEACH Remind children that it is important to think about how things are the same and different as they read. Point out that they can think about how characters are the same and different to help them better understand a story.

1. Discuss the principle with children, using Fox and Cow as an example. Suggested language: "In *Animal Picnic*, the animals Fox, Cow, and Bird all meet for a picnic. What is the same about Cow and Fox?" (*They both brought food to the picnic. They both have teeth.*)

> **MINILESSON PRINCIPLE**
>
> Think about how the characters in a story are the same and how they are different.

2. Use children's responses to explain how to contrast. Suggested language: "Think about Fox and Cow's food and teeth. How are Fox and Cow different?" (*Cow brought grass and has flat teeth. Fox brought meat and has sharp teeth.*)

3. Work with children to compare and contrast Bird to either Fox or Cow. Record children's ideas in a Venn Diagram.

SUMMARIZE AND APPLY Restate the minilesson principle. Explain to children that they can apply it to their independent reading. Suggested language: "When you read, think about how characters are the same and different."

GROUP SHARE Ask children to share how characters in a story they read were the same and different.

Whole-Group Lessons

Let's Go to the Moon!
Student Book, Lesson 16

Read Aloud Passages

One Giant Leap
See page 356 of this Guide.

Mae Jemison
Student Book, Lesson 16

▶ Let's Go to the Moon!

INTERACTIVE READ-ALOUD/SHARED READING

Read aloud the book to children. Stop periodically for very brief discussion of the text. Use the following suggested stopping points and prompts for quick group response, or give a specific prompt and have partners or threes turn and talk.

- After reading the section called Blast Off!, ask: "Where is the spaceship going? How do you know?"
- After reading the page titled Moon Rocks, ask: "How do the words *Moon Rocks* look different from other words in the book? What information do they help you find?"
- After reading about Taking Pictures, ask: "Who is telling about the Moon and the events that happened there? How do you know?"
- At the end of the book, ask: "Would like to visit the Moon? Why or why not? Turn and talk about your ideas with a partner."

MINILESSON Main Idea and Details

TEACH Display the minilesson principle on chart paper, and read it aloud to children. Tell children they are going to learn how to think about the most important idea in a book as they read.

1. Discuss the principle with children, using the main idea from *Let's Go to the Moon!* Suggested language: "*Let's Go to the Moon!* is mostly about one idea. What is the book mostly about?" *(The book is mostly about astronauts visiting the Moon.)*

2. Focus on one detail that supports the main idea, such as the details in the Moon Walk section. Suggested language: "In the section called Moon Walk, the author told about astronauts walking on the Moon. What did you learn about walking on the Moon?" *(People and things are light on the Moon because there is less gravity.)*

3. Use children's responses to explain how details tell more information about the main idea of the book. Suggested language: "The information about moon walks told us more about what it is like when astronauts visit the Moon."

4. Elicit additional details from the book. Record children's ideas in a Web like the one shown here.

> **MINILESSON PRINCIPLE**
>
> Notice that an author tells mostly about one idea and tells information about the idea.

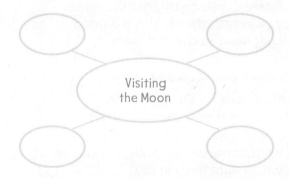

Visiting the Moon

SUMMARIZE AND APPLY Restate the minilesson principle. Then tell children to apply it to their independent reading. Suggested language: "When you read, think about what the book is mostly about. Think about how the other information tells about that idea."

GROUP SHARE Ask children to talk about a book from their independent reading by telling what it is mostly about. Have them explain how information in the book tells about that idea.

▶ One Giant Leap

INTERACTIVE READ-ALOUD/SHARED READING

Read aloud the book to children. Stop periodically for brief discussion of the text. Use the following suggested stopping points and prompts:

- After the first paragraph, ask: "Who were the first two people to land on the Moon?"
- After the second paragraph, ask: "What was the purpose of the *Apollo 11* project?"
- At the end of the book, ask: "How were Armstrong's and Aldrin's visit to the Moon the same as Collins's? How were they different?"

MINILESSON Main Idea and Details

TEACH Display the minilesson principle on chart paper, and read it aloud to children. Tell children that they are going to learn to think about what a book is mostly about.

1. Using the events from *One Giant Leap,* discuss with children that a book is mostly about one thing. Suggested language: "In *One Giant Leap,* you read about the *Apollo 11* astronauts. What special thing did they do?" *(They went to the Moon. Two of them were the first people to land on the Moon.)*

> **MINILESSON PRINCIPLE**
>
> Notice what the book is mostly about.

2. Talk with children about the events that took the astronauts to the Moon. Suggested language: "The astronauts' adventure began on July 16, 1969. What happened on that date?" *(The spaceship blasted off.)* Follow-up: "What were the important things that happened over the next four days?" *(The astronauts traveled to the Moon. Armstrong and Aldrin landed a small craft on the Moon.)*

3. Tell children that all the ideas in a book will help them notice what a book is mostly about. In an Idea-Support Map, write some of the details that children have mentioned. Then guide them to tell what all the details are mostly about, and write the main idea in the top box.

SUMMARIZE AND APPLY Restate the minilesson principle. Tell children to apply it to their independent reading. Suggested language: "When you read, think about what the book is mostly about to help you understand it."

GROUP SHARE Ask children to tell what a book they are reading is mostly about.

▶ Mae Jemison

INTERACTIVE READ-ALOUD/SHARED READING

Read aloud the book to children. Stop periodically for brief discussion of the text. Use the following suggested stopping points and prompts:

- After the first page, ask: "Who is this book about? Why is she special?"
- At the end of the book, have children look at the timeline: "In what year did Mae become an astronaut?" Follow-up: "Did Mae become an astronaut before or after she started her company? How does the timeline help you know?"

MINILESSON Genre: Biography

TEACH Remind children that they have read three books this week: *Let's Go to the Moon!, One Giant Step,* and *Mae Jemison.* Explain that the books have something in common—they are information books that tell about astronauts and the events in their lives.

1. Focus on *Mae Jemison* to introduce the idea that a biography tells about the events in a person's life. Suggested language: "The book *Mae Jemison* is a biography that tells about a real person, Mae Jemison. It tells where she was born and what she wanted to be. As you read biographies, think about the important things that happened in the real person's life."

> **MINILESSON PRINCIPLE**
>
> Think about the important things that happen in a person's life.

2. Ask children to share some of the important things that Mae Jemison did in her life. Suggested language: "What are some important things that happened in Mae Jemison's life?" *(She became a doctor and an astronaut; she started a company.)*

3. Guide children to summarize the events as you write the minilesson principle on chart paper.

SUMMARIZE AND APPLY Restate the minilesson principle. Tell children to apply it to their independent reading. Suggested language: "When you read a biography, look for the important events that happen in a person's life."

GROUP SHARE Ask children to retell the important things that happen in a person's life from the book they read for independent reading.

Whole-Group Lessons

The Big Trip
Student Book, Lesson 17

Read Aloud
Passages

The Rainy Trip
See page 357 of this Guide.

Lewis and Clark's Big Trip
Student Book, Lesson 17

▶ The Big Trip

INTERACTIVE READ-ALOUD/SHARED READING

Read aloud the story to children. Stop periodically for very brief discussion of the text. Use the following suggested stopping points and prompts for quick group response, or give a specific prompt and have partners or threes turn and talk.

* After Pig and Goat discuss taking a trip by bike, ask: "Who are the characters in the story?" Before continuing the story, say: "Listen to see if Goat changes during this story."

* After Pig suggests taking a trip by donkey, ask: "Why does Pig think taking a donkey cart is a good idea? Why does Goat think it is a bad idea?"

* At the end of the story, ask: "How has Goat changed during this story? What makes you think so?" Follow-up: "Do you like to take trips? How do you like to get where you are going? Why?"

MINILESSON Compare and Contrast

TEACH Display the minilesson principle on chart paper, and read it aloud to children. Tell children they are going to learn how to think about how things in a story are the same and different. Explain that they will use story clues to help them.

1. Discuss the principle with children, using examples from *The Big Trip*. Suggested language: "In the story *The Big Trip*, Pig had the idea to take his trip by plane and hot air balloon. How are these two ways of taking a trip the same?" *(They travel in the air.)* "How are they different?" *(A plane is a metal frame lifted by an engine. A hot air balloon is a basket lifted by a balloon.)*

2. Focus on the hot air balloon. Suggested language: "How did Pig feel about taking a trip in a hot air balloon?" *(Pig thought it was a good idea because it would get him where he wanted to go.)* "How did Goat feel about it?" *(Goat worried that the balloon would get a hole.)*

3. Use children's responses to explain how authors show that things in a story, such as characters, places, or things, are the same and different. Suggested language: "Pig and Goat had different ideas about hot air balloon travel. Pig thought it was a good idea. Goat, though, did not think it was safe."

4. Work with children to list other parts of the story that are the same and that are different. Record children's ideas in a T-Map like the one shown here.

> **MINILESSON PRINCIPLE**
>
> Think about how the things in a story are the same and how they are different.

Same	Different

SUMMARIZE AND APPLY Restate the minilesson principle. Then tell children to apply it to their independent reading. Suggested language: "When you read, think about how things in the story are the same and how they are different. Look for clues that the author gives you to see how two things are the same or how they are different."

GROUP SHARE Have children name two characters or places from a story they read independently. Ask them to tell one way those things were the same. Then have them tell one way they were different.

▶ The Rainy Trip

INTERACTIVE READ-ALOUD/SHARED READING

Read aloud the story to children. Stop periodically for brief discussion of the story. Use the following suggested stopping points and prompts:

- After Kyra's dad takes everyone to the museum and dinner, ask: "What was the group supposed to be doing on the trip? Why can't they follow their plan?"
- After Ellie and Kyra learn the new game, ask: "What is the problem between Kyra and Ellie?" Follow-up: "How is their problem solved?"
- At the end of the story, say: "The writer was trying to teach you a lesson with this story. What is the lesson? Turn and talk about your ideas with a partner."

MINILESSON Compare and Contrast

TEACH Display the minilesson principle on chart paper, and read it aloud to children. Tell children they are going to learn to notice what is the same and different from the beginning of a story to the end.

1. Remind children that a story has a beginning, a middle, and an end. Explain that a story can be exciting because of the way things change from the beginning to the end. Suggested language: "In the story *The Rainy Trip,* what happened at the beginning?" *(Kyra's family and her friend were on a camping trip. The trip was not fun because it kept raining.)*

> **MINILESSON PRINCIPLE**
> Think about what is the same and what is different from the beginning of a story to the end.

2. Point out to children that looking at how the beginning and end of a story are the same and different helps them better understand the important parts of the story. Suggested language: "At the beginning and end of the story, some things were the same and some things were different. One thing that was the same was that the group was still on the camping trip. One thing that was different was that Ellie and Kyra learned how to have fun."

3. Work with children to identify other things that are the same and different from the beginning to the end of the story. Write their ideas in a T-Map with the labels *Same* and *Different*.

SUMMARIZE AND APPLY Restate the minilesson principle. Tell children to apply it to their independent reading. Suggested language: "When you read, think about what is the same and different from the beginning of the story to the end."

GROUP SHARE Have children explain one way a story they read was the same at the beginning and the end. Then have them explain one way the story was different.

▶ Lewis and Clark's Big Trip

INTERACTIVE READ-ALOUD/SHARED READING

Read aloud the book to children. Stop periodically for brief discussion. Use the following suggested stopping points and prompts:

- After the first page, ask: "Who were Lewis and Clark? What did they do?"
- At the end, say: "Suppose that you took the same trip today that Lewis and Clark took long ago. How would your trip be like theirs? How would it be different? Turn and talk about your ideas with a partner."

MINILESSON Genre: Informational Text

TEACH Explain to children that *Lewis and Clark's Big Trip* is different from the other two stories they read this week because it gives facts and the other stories are made-up. Information books tell about real people, places, and events.

1. Focus on the map to introduce how maps show information. Suggested language: "The book *Lewis and Clark's Big Trip* includes a map. A map is a picture that shows where things are and what is near and far away. The title at the top tells that the map shows Lewis and Clark's path across the United States. The key in the bottom left corner explains all of the shapes and colors on the map."

> **MINILESSON PRINCIPLE**
> Think about how maps show information.

2. Write the minilesson principle on chart paper. Work with children to use the features on the map in *Lewis and Clark's Big Trip.* Guide children to find its features, such as rivers and cities. Help them use the key to see what the different shapes and colors on the map stand for. Explain to children that paying attention to maps will help them understand what they read.

SUMMARIZE AND APPLY Restate the minilesson principle. Tell children to apply it to their independent reading. Suggested language: "When you read, look for and use maps to better understand the information you read."

GROUP SHARE Ask children to share examples of maps they have seen in their independent reading. Have them explain the information shown on the map.

Whole-Group Lessons

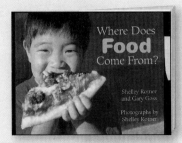

Where Does Food Come From?
Student Book, Lesson 18

Read Aloud Passages

The Three Wishes
See page 357 of this Guide.

Jack and the Beanstalk
Student Book, Lesson 18

▶ Where Does Food Come From?

INTERACTIVE READ-ALOUD/SHARED READING

Read aloud the book to children. Stop periodically for very brief discussion of it. Use the following suggested stopping points and prompts for quick group response, or give a specific prompt and have partners or threes turn and talk.

- After reading about potatoes, ask: "What kind of food are potatoes? Where do they grow?"
- After reading about wheat, ask: "What is wheat? How is it used to make bread?"
- After reading about eggs, ask: "How are milk and eggs the same? How are they different? Turn and talk about your ideas with a partner."
- At the end of the book, ask: "What did you learn about where foods come from?" Follow-up: "What is your favorite food? Where does it come from? How could you find out?"

MINILESSON Author's Purpose

TEACH Display the minilesson principle on chart paper, and read it aloud to children. Tell children they are going to think about why the author wrote the book. Explain that text clues will help them figure that out.

> **MINILESSON PRINCIPLE**
> Think about why the author wrote the book and what you might learn.

1. Discuss the principle with children, using examples from *Where Does Food Come From?* Suggested language: "In *Where Does Food Come From?*, what did the author write about?" (*The author wrote about where food comes from.*) "How did the author organize the information?" (*The information is organized by the kind of food.*)

2. Focus on milk. Suggested language: "What did the author tell about milk?" (*The author told where milk comes from and how it is used to make other foods.*) "Why do you think the author told that information?" (*Possible answer: The author wanted to teach that milk comes from cows and that many foods come from milk.*)

3. Use children's responses to explain that authors write for a reason. Suggested language: "An author can write for different reasons. Sometimes it is to teach about a topic. Sometimes it is to tell an entertaining story. In this book, the author gives a lot of information. This gives you a clue that the author wrote to teach you about a topic."

4. Work with children to identify other clues that support the idea that the author wrote the book to teach about a topic. Record children's ideas in an Inference Map like the one shown here.

The author wrote to teach.

SUMMARIZE AND APPLY Restate the minilesson principle. Then tell children to apply it to their independent reading. Suggested language: "When you read, think about why the author wrote the book."

GROUP SHARE Have children identify the reason the author wrote a book they have read. Then have them tell the clues they used to identify that reason.

▶ The Three Wishes

INTERACTIVE READ-ALOUD/SHARED READING

Read aloud the story to children. Stop periodically for brief discussion. Use the following suggested stopping points and prompts:

- After the tree speaks for the first time, ask: "Why does the tree ask the woodcutter not to cut it down? How does the tree reward the woodcutter for saving it?"
- After the sausage falls on the plate, ask: "Do you think that the woodcutter uses his wish well? Why or why not?"
- At the end of the story, ask: "What lessons do you think the woodcutter learns? Do you think he will act differently in the future? Turn and talk about your ideas with a partner."

MINILESSON Genre: Fairy Tale

TEACH Display the minilesson principle on chart paper, and read it aloud to children. Tell children they are going to learn to notice that characters in fairy tales can do amazing things. They will also learn to recognize how those things can help or hurt the characters.

1. Remind children that a fairy tale is a made-up story with imaginary or unbelievable events. The characters can often do things that real people cannot. Suggested language: "In the fairy tale *The Three Wishes*, the characters did amazing things. What did the tree do that real trees cannot?" (*The tree could talk and grant wishes.*)

> **MINILESSON PRINCIPLE**
>
> Notice that fairy tale characters can do amazing things that help or hurt them.

2. Point out to children that figuring out the amazing things that happen in a fairy tale can help them understand the story. Suggested language: "One amazing thing that happened in this fairy tale was that the tree could talk. Talking saved the tree from being cut down."

3. Work with children to identify other amazing things that happened in the story and discuss how those things helped or hurt the characters. Write their ideas in a T-Map with the labels *Amazing Thing That Happened* and *How It Hurt or Helped*.

SUMMARIZE AND APPLY Restate the minilesson principle. Tell children to apply it to their independent reading. Suggested language: "When you read, think about the amazing things that a character can do. Think about how those amazing things help or hurt the character."

GROUP SHARE Have children identify an amazing thing from independent reading. Then have them identify how that amazing thing helped or hurt the characters.

▶ Jack and the Beanstalk

INTERACTIVE READ-ALOUD/SHARED READING

Read aloud the story to children. Stop periodically for brief discussion. Use the following suggested stopping points and prompts:

- After the first page, ask: "What did Jack get when he traded the cow? What does that trade tell you about Jack?"
- After the beanstalk grows, ask: "What amazing things happen in the fairy tale? How does each of those amazing things change the rest of the story? Turn and talk about your ideas with a partner."

MINILESSON Genre: Fairy Tale

TEACH Explain to children that *Jack and the Beanstalk* is like *The Three Wishes* because both stories are fairy tales. Point out that both made-up stories tell about amazing things that happen.

1. Introduce the idea that fairy tales have characters that can be nice or mean. Suggested language: "A character is a person or animal in a story. In a fairy tale, a character might also be a talking object or made-up creature like a tree or a giant. In *Jack and the Beanstalk*, there were many characters. They were Jack, his mother, the man who trades the beans, the goose, the cow, and the giant."

> **MINILESSON PRINCIPLE**
>
> Notice that fairy tales have nice characters and mean characters.

2. Write the minilesson principle on chart paper. Explain that nice characters do kind and helpful things and that mean characters are cruel or unkind. Ask children to decide whether the characters Jack, his mother, the man with the beans, and the giant were nice or mean. Have them use story clues and the pictures to explain their ideas. Explain to children that understanding characters will help them understand what they read.

SUMMARIZE AND APPLY Restate the minilesson principle. Tell children to apply it to their independent reading. Suggested language: "When you read, think about each character. Decide if the character is nice or mean."

GROUP SHARE Ask children to share an example of a character from a story they chose for independent reading. Have them tell whether that character is nice or mean.

Whole-Group Lessons

Tomás Rivera
Student Book, Lesson 19

Christina's Work
See page 358 of this Guide.

Life Then and Now
Student Book, Lesson 19

▶ Tomás Rivera

INTERACTIVE READ-ALOUD/SHARED READING

Read aloud the book to children. Stop periodically for very brief discussion of it. Use the following suggested stopping points and prompts for quick group response, or give a specific prompt and have partners or threes turn and talk.

- After Grandpa takes Tomás to the library, ask: "What do Grandpa and Tomás do together? Why is Grandpa important to Tomás?"
- After Tomás goes to the library, ask: "What do you think will happen to Tomás after he goes to the library? How might the visit to the library change his life?"
- At the end of the book, ask: "How did this book make you feel?" Follow-up: "When have you gone somewhere that changed your life? Turn and talk with a partner about your ideas."

MINILESSON Sequence of Events

TEACH Display the minilesson principle on chart paper, and read it aloud to children. Tell children that they are going to think about what happens first, next, and last in a book. Explain that understanding what happens first, next, and last will help them understand a book better.

1. Discuss the principle with children, using events from *Tomás Rivera*. Suggested language: "The first part of the book tells about Tomás as a boy. What did Tomás's family do?" *(They moved from place to place picking crops.)* Follow-up: "What did Tomás like to do after picking crops all day?" *(He liked to listen to his grandfather's stories.)*

> **MINILESSON PRINCIPLE**
>
> Think about what happens first, next, and last in a book.

2. Guide children to think about what happened next. Suggested language: "Tomás wanted to tell stories too. What happened next?" *(Tomás's grandfather took him to a library.)*

3. Guide children to think about what happened last. Suggested language: "After reading lots of books, Tomás began to write his own stories. What happened last in the book?" *(Tomás became a teacher, and he still wrote stories.)*

4. Use children's responses to record what happened first, next, and last in a Flow Chart like the one shown here.

First
↓
Next
↓
Last

SUMMARIZE AND APPLY Restate the minilesson principle. Tell children to apply it to their independent reading. Suggested language: "When you read a book, think about what happens first, next, and last."

GROUP SHARE Have children share the sequence of events from a book they read for independent reading. Ask them to tell what happened first, next, and last.

▶ Christina's Work

INTERACTIVE READ-ALOUD/SHARED READING

Read aloud the book to children. Stop periodically for brief discussion. Use the following suggested stopping points and prompts:

- After reading the introduction about Christina, ask: "What words would you use to tell about Christina? What clues in the book tell what she was like?"
- After reading "What Is Pink?," say: "'What Is Pink?' is a poem. How is it the same as other poems you have read? How is it different?"
- At the end of the book, ask: "How are you and Christina the same? How are you different? Turn and talk with a partner about these ideas."

MINILESSON Conclusions

TEACH Display the minilesson principle on chart paper, and read it aloud to children. Tell children they are going to learn to use what characters say and do to figure out what they are like.

1. Remind children how authors give clues about what characters are like. Explain that clues can be what a person does, says, thinks, and writes. Suggested language: "In *Christina's Work,* the author said that Christina was often sick but kept writing anyway. What does that tell you about Christina?" (*Christina loved to write. Nothing would stop Christina from doing what she loved.*)

> **MINILESSON PRINCIPLE**
>
> Think about how information in a book helps you know what someone is like.

2. Point out to children that information about what people think and do are clues to what they are like. Suggested language: "The author used what Christina thought (she had strong beliefs) and what she did (wrote poems about those beliefs) to show you what Christina was like. You can figure out that Christina was brave and stood up for what she believed in."

3. Work with children to draw additional conclusions from *Christina's Work.* Write their ideas in an Inference Map.

SUMMARIZE AND APPLY Restate the minilesson principle. Explain to children that they should apply it to their independent reading. Suggested language: "When you read, think about what people say, think, and do to figure out what they are like."

GROUP SHARE Have children choose a person they have read about and tell what he or she thought, said, and did. Then have them tell what the person is like.

▶ Life Then and Now

INTERACTIVE READ-ALOUD/SHARED READING

Read aloud the book to children. Stop periodically for brief discussion. Use the following suggested stopping points and prompts:

- After reading the first paragraph, ask: "What does *life then* mean? What words helped you figure it out?"
- At the end of the book, ask: "What might your life have been like if you lived 100 years ago? Turn and talk about your ideas with a partner."

MINILESSON Compare and Contrast

TEACH Explain to children that *Life Then and Now* is both the same as and different from the other two books they read this week. All three books are the same because they are information books. *Life Then and Now,* though, is not a biography. It does not tell about a real person.

1. Focus on types of communication to introduce how authors tell how things are the same and how they are different. Suggested language: "In *Life Then and Now,* the author shows that people used phones in the past and today. The pictures show that phones have changed. They look different today."

> **MINILESSON PRINCIPLE**
>
> Notice how authors tell how things are the same and how they are different.

2. Page through the book with children to identify a way that things are the same today and in the past. Find a way things are different. Suggested language: "What are some things that families did for fun in the past? How is this different from what families do for fun today?" (*In the past, families listened to the radio. Now they watch TV.*)

3. Then write the minilesson principle on chart paper. Guide children to see how the author can use words and pictures to tell how things are the same and how they are different. Explain to children that paying attention to these clues will help them understand what they read.

SUMMARIZE AND APPLY Restate the minilesson principle. Explain to children that they can apply it to their independent reading. Suggested language: "When you read, look for how things are the same and how they are different."

GROUP SHARE Ask children to share an example from their independent reading of things that are the same. Then have them tell about things that are different.

Whole-Group Lessons

Little Rabbit's Tale
Student Book, Lesson 20

Read Aloud Passages

Chicken Little
See page 358 of this Guide.

Silly Poems
Student Book, Lesson 20

▶ Little Rabbit's Tale

INTERACTIVE READ-ALOUD/SHARED READING

Read aloud the story to children. Stop periodically for very brief discussion of it. Use the following suggested stopping points and prompts for quick group response, or give a specific prompt and have partners or threes turn and talk.

- After Little Rabbit hops off to find Goose, ask: "Why does Little Rabbit think the sky is falling?"
- After Little Rabbit and his friends start off to see Little Rabbit's mother, ask: "Which friends does Little Rabbit tell that the sky is falling? What do they think when he tells them the news?"
- After Little Rabbit asks if his friends can stay for a meal, ask: "How did Little Rabbit's friends feel when they found out that the sky was not falling?"
- At the end of the story, ask: "What lesson can you learn from this story?" Follow-up: "When have you made a mistake? What did you learn from it? Turn and talk with a partner about what happened."

MINILESSON Cause and Effect

TEACH Display the minilesson principle on chart paper, and read it aloud to children. Tell children that they are going to learn to notice how one thing happens in a story and then makes other things happen. Explain that word clues and pictures in a story will help them figure out how one thing makes other things happen.

1. Discuss the principle with children, using examples from *Little Rabbit's Tale.* Suggested language: "In the story *Little Rabbit's Tale,* things happen that make other things happen. What happened with the wind while Little Rabbit was sleeping under the tree?" *(The wind blew.)* "What happened because the wind blew?" *(An apple fell from the tree and hit Little Rabbit.)*

> **MINILESSON PRINCIPLE**
>
> Think about how one thing happens and makes other things happen.

2. Focus on what happened after the apple hit Little Rabbit. Suggested language: "One thing that happened was that the apple hit Little Rabbit. That made other things happen. What happened after the apple hit Little Rabbit?" *(Little Rabbit thought the sky was falling and ran off to tell his friends.)*

3. Use children's responses to explain how authors give clues about how one thing in a story makes other things happen. Suggested language: "Right after the apple hit Little Rabbit, he said *The sky is falling. I've got to try to tell everyone.* The picture shows Little Rabbit hopping off to tell his friends. These clues show that the falling apple made Little Rabbit want to find his friends."

4. Work with children to name one thing in the story that made other things happen. Record children's ideas in a T-Map like the one shown here.

What Happened	Why It Happened
An apple fell and hit Little Rabbit.	The wind blew.

SUMMARIZE AND APPLY Restate the minilesson principle. Explain to children that they can apply it to their independent reading. Suggested language: "When you read a story, think about how one thing that happens makes other things happen."

GROUP SHARE Have children share one thing that happened in a story they read. Ask them to tell how that thing made other things happen.

▶ Chicken Little

INTERACTIVE READ-ALOUD/SHARED READING

Read aloud the story to children. Stop periodically for brief discussion. Use the following suggested stopping points and prompts:

- After the acorn falls on Chicken Little's head, ask: "Why did Chicken Little think the sky was falling?"
- After Chicken Little and the other friends meet Foxy Loxy, ask: "What plan did Foxy Loxy have for Chicken Little and the other friends? Why did Foxy Loxy have that plan?"
- At the end of the story, ask: "What lesson did Chicken Little learn? Turn and talk with a partner about whether you think it is a good lesson."

MINILESSON Genre: Folktale

TEACH Display the minilesson principle on chart paper, and read it aloud to children. Tell children they are going to learn how to think about how different characters can tell the same story.

1. Remind children that many parts of the stories *Little Rabbit's Tale* and *Chicken Little* are the same. Suggested language: "How are the stories *Little Rabbit's Tale* and *Chicken Little* the same?" (*Something fell on the main character's head. The character in each story thought the sky was falling and went off to tell others.*)

> **MINILESSON PRINCIPLE**
> Think about how different characters can tell the same story.

2. Point out that the stories are not exactly the same. Suggested language: "The story *Little Rabbit's Tale* is not exactly the same as *Chicken Little*. The characters are different. Some details are different, too. Little Rabbit went off to tell his friends that the sky was falling. Chicken Little went to tell the king."

3. Work with children to review the setting, characters, and events from *Little Rabbit's Tale* and *Chicken Little*. Write their ideas in separate Story Maps. Use the Story Maps to help children think about how characters can tell the same story. Point out that the stories are usually a little bit different.

SUMMARIZE AND APPLY Restate the minilesson principle. Explain to children that they should apply it to their independent reading. Suggested language: "When you read, think about how different characters can tell the same story. Think about how the stories are the same and how they are different."

GROUP SHARE Have children choose an example of characters that tell the same story. Then have them tell about how the different characters tell the same story.

▶ Silly Poems

INTERACTIVE READ-ALOUD/SHARED READING

Read aloud the introduction and poems to children. Stop periodically for brief discussion of the text. Use the following suggested stopping points and prompts:

- After reading the first page, point out the photo. Suggested language: "Reader 2 says he would like to fly like a bird when he grows up. How do you think the readers feel about birds? How can you tell?"
- After reading "Wouldn't You?" ask: "Does this poem make you want to fly like a bird? Why or why not? Turn and talk about your ideas with a partner."

MINILESSON Genre: Poetry

TEACH Explain to children that poetry is a special kind of writing. Tell them that poems may have lines that are the same length and that they often have words that rhyme.

1. Focus on the Langston Hughes poem about the elephant and the mouse to introduce how poems can have silly ideas. Suggested language: "In the poem about the elephant and the mouse, the poet writes that the elephant is afraid of a mouse. This idea sounds silly because an elephant is so big and a mouse is so small."

> **MINILESSON PRINCIPLE**
> Notice the silly words and ideas in poems.

2. Page through the poems with children to identify silly words and ideas. Then write the minilesson principle on chart paper. Guide children to see how the author can use silly words and ideas to make the poem more fun to read. Explain to children that paying attention to silly words and ideas will help them understand and enjoy the poems they read.

SUMMARIZE AND APPLY Restate the minilesson principle. Explain to children that they can apply it to their independent reading. Suggested language: "When you read poems, look for silly words and ideas."

GROUP SHARE Ask children to share an example of a poem they read. Then have them identify some of the silly words and ideas in the poem.

Whole-Group Lessons

The Garden
Student Book, Lesson 21

Read Aloud Passages

Grandpa's Tree
See page 359 of this Guide.

Garden Good Guys
Student Book, Lesson 21

▶ The Garden

INTERACTIVE READ-ALOUD/SHARED READING

Read aloud the story to children. Stop periodically for very brief discussion of the text. Use the suggested stopping points and prompts below for quick group response, or give a specific prompt and have partners or threes turn and talk.

- After reading the first page, ask: "What does Toad want to do?" Follow-up: "How soon do you think the seeds will start to grow?"
- After Frog comes to help Toad, ask: "How does Frog help Toad?"
- After Toad falls asleep, ask: "What else does Toad do to help the seeds grow?" Follow-up: "Do you think doing those things will help them grow? Why or why not?"
- At the end of the story, ask: "What advice would you give Toad about growing a garden? Turn and talk about your ideas with a partner."

MINILESSON Story Structure

TEACH Display the minilesson principle on chart paper, and read it aloud to children. Tell children that they are going to learn how to think about the problem in a story and how the characters try to solve it.

1. Discuss the principle with children, using examples from *The Garden*. Suggested language: "In the story *The Garden*, Toad wanted to grow a garden. What problem did Toad have?" *(The seeds wouldn't grow.)*

> **MINILESSON PRINCIPLE**
>
> Notice the problem in the story and how the characters solve it.

2. Focus on Toad's first attempt at solving his problem. Suggested language: "Toad shouted at the seeds to start growing, but they didn't grow. Why didn't shouting at the seeds solve the problem?" *(because seeds need water, sunshine, and time to grow)*

3. Point out that Toad tried several other things to try and solve his problem. Suggested language: "When shouting didn't work, what did Toad think the problem was?" *(He thought the seeds were afraid of the dark.)* Follow-up: "What did he do?" *(He lit candles and read to the seeds.)*

4. Help children tell about other things Toad did to try to solve his problem. Record their ideas in a Story Map like the one shown here. List attempts at solving the problem under *Middle*, and how the problem was solved under *End*.

Setting	Characters
Plot	
Beginning	
Middle	
End	

SUMMARIZE AND APPLY Restate the minilesson principle. Then tell children to apply it to their independent reading. Suggested language: "When you read a story, think about the problem the character has. Look for different things the character does to try to solve the problem and how the problem is solved."

GROUP SHARE Have children share the problem in a story they chose for independent reading. Ask them to tell what the character did to try to solve the problem. Then have them tell how the problem was solved.

▶ Grandpa's Tree

INTERACTIVE READ-ALOUD/SHARED READING

Read aloud the story to children. Stop periodically for brief discussion. Use the following suggested stopping points and prompts:

- After the first paragraph, ask: "Why is Grandpa's tree special?"
- After Tara suggests that they make a bird feeder, ask: "Why does Grandpa frown when Tara says they should make a bird feeder for the robin?"
- At the end of the story, say: "How did making a bird feeder help Grandpa? Turn and talk about your ideas with a partner."

MINILESSON Story Structure

TEACH Display the minilesson principle on chart paper, and read it aloud to children. Tell children they are going to learn how to look for ways characters work together to solve a problem in a story.

1. Remind children that most stories have a problem that the characters try to solve. Explain that a problem can affect many characters. Suggested language: "In the story *Grandpa's Tree*, Grandpa was grumpy because he broke his leg. How was this also a problem for Tara and Justin?" *(They were sad because they missed doing things with Grandpa.)*

> **MINILESSON PRINCIPLE**
> Notice how characters work together to solve a problem.

2. Point out to children that characters often have to work together to solve a problem. Suggested language: "Why did Tara and Justin think a project would solve Grandpa's problem?" *(Grandpa would have something to do.)* Follow-up: "How did finding a project for Grandpa also help Tara and Justin?" *(They were happy because they were doing a project with Grandpa.)*

3. Guide children to complete a Story Map for *Grandpa's Tree*. Help children tell how Tara, Justin, and Dad work together to solve the problem.

SUMMARIZE AND APPLY Restate the minilesson principle. Tell children to apply it to their independent reading. Suggested language: "When you read, think about the problem and how the characters work together to solve it."

GROUP SHARE Have children share the problem in a story they read independently. Then have them tell how the characters in the story work together to solve the problem.

▶ Garden Good Guys

INTERACTIVE READ-ALOUD/SHARED READING

Read aloud the book to children. Stop periodically for brief discussion of the text. Use the following suggested stopping points and prompts:

- After reading the introduction, ask: "Why is it important to know about different kinds of bugs?"
- After reading about the praying mantis, ask: "How do a ladybug and a praying mantis help a garden?"
- At the end, ask: "Why does the author say that dragonflies are good for people, too?"

MINILESSON Genre: Informational Text

TEACH Display the minilesson principle on chart paper, and read it aloud to children. Explain to children that thinking about the information in labels will help them better understand what they read.

1. Tell children they are going to think about how labels give them information in *Garden Good Guys*. Suggested language: "Look at the photos on the second page. Read the label below each one. What information do you get from reading these labels?" *(the name of each bug)*

> **MINILESSON PRINCIPLE**
> Think about how labels give you information.

2. Ask children to look at the photo of the dragonfly, and read the labels. Ask: "What information do these labels give?" *(One label tells the name of the bug, and one label names a part of the bug.)*

3. Page through the selection and have children read each label. Help them to summarize what they learned by filling in a T-Map with the headings *Label* and *Information It Gives*.

SUMMARIZE AND APPLY Restate the minilesson principle. Tell children they can apply it to their independent reading. Suggested language: "When you read, look at the pictures and read the labels to get more information."

GROUP SHARE Ask children to share some information from a label in a book they read. Have them tell how the label helped them better understand the information in the book.

Whole-Group Lessons

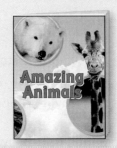

Amazing Animals
Student Book, Lesson 22

Read Aloud Passages

How Bat Learned to Fly
See page 359 of this Guide.

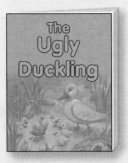

The Ugly Duckling
Student Book, Lesson 22

▶ **Amazing Animals**

INTERACTIVE READ-ALOUD/SHARED READING

Read aloud the book to children. Stop periodically for very brief discussion of it. Use the following suggested stopping points and prompts for quick group response, or give a specific prompt and have partners or threes turn and talk.

- After reading about the polar bear, ask: "Where is the young polar bear hiding? What clues helped you figure this out?"
- After reading about the camel, ask: "What do the words and pictures tell you about where a camel lives?"
- After reading about the porcupine, ask: "How would you describe a porcupine's quills? How do you think other animals learn to stay away from a porcupine's quills?"
- At the end, ask: "Which animal do you think is the most amazing? Why do you think that? Turn and talk about your ideas with a partner."

MINILESSON Conclusions

TEACH Display the minilesson principle on chart paper, and read it aloud to children. Tell children they are going to learn how to use what they already know to figure out things that the author does not tell them.

1. Discuss the principle with children, using examples from *Amazing Animals*. Suggested language: "A polar bear has thick fur that looks white in the sun. How does what you know about snow and snowy places explain why thick, white fur is important to a polar bear?" *(Snowy places are cold, so thick fur helps keep the polar bear warm. Snow is white, so white fur makes it hard for a polar bear to be seen.)*

> **MINILESSON PRINCIPLE**
>
> Think about what you already know when you read.

2. Focus on what children know about a desert. Suggested language: "What do you know about deserts?" *(A desert is a hot, dry place with sandy soil and few plants.)* "How does this help you understand why the hump on a camel is an important body part?" *(A camel's hump stores fat for food. There is little food in the desert.)*

3. Explain that children can use what they already know to figure things out in a selection. Suggested language: "You learned that ducks use their beaks to eat plants and bugs. What do you think a duck does when it cleans another duck with its beak?" *(It looks for any bugs hiding in the duck's feathers. It eats the bugs it finds.)*

4. Work with children to complete an Inference Map about other animals in the book. Help them understand that they can use the words and pictures along with what they already know to figure out things as they read.

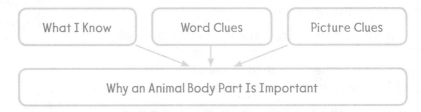

SUMMARIZE AND APPLY Restate the minilesson principle. Then tell children to apply it to their independent reading. Suggested language: "When you read a book, think about what you already know as you read the words and look at the pictures. Use what you already know to help you better understand the book."

GROUP SHARE Have children share an example of something they figured out while reading. Ask them to tell how they used what they already knew along with the words and pictures to figure something out.

▶ How Bat Learned to Fly

Read aloud the story to children. Stop periodically for brief discussion. Use the following suggested stopping points and prompts:

- After learning that Mouse always drops the ball, ask: "What is Mouse's problem?"
- After Mouse sits under the tree sniffling, ask: "Why does Mouse decide to quit playing ball?"
- After Mother Earth shares her idea, ask: "Will Mother Earth's idea work? Why or why not?"
- At the end of the story, ask: "What does this story explain? Is it like any other stories you have heard or read? Turn and talk about your ideas with a partner."

MINILESSON Conclusions

TEACH Display the minilesson principle on chart paper, and read it aloud to children. Tell children they are going to learn to use what characters do and say to figure out how they feel.

1. Have children recall how at the beginning of *How Bat Learned to Fly*, Mouse was always dropping the ball. Suggested language: "What did Coyote say when Mouse kept dropping the ball?" (*Coyote scolded Mouse. He said, Why do you always drop the ball when you run?*)

> **MINILESSON PRINCIPLE**
>
> Think about how the characters feel and the clues that help you know.

2. Point out to children that what characters say and do are clues to how they feel. Suggested language: "The way that Coyote spoke is a clue to how he felt. He scolded Mouse. I know that when someone scolds, they are complaining about something. I can figure out that Coyote was upset and annoyed with Mouse."

3. Help children draw additional conclusions about the way the characters in the story feel. Write their ideas in an Inference Map.

SUMMARIZE AND APPLY Restate the minilesson principle. Tell children to apply it to their independent reading. Suggested language: "When you read, think about how the characters feel and the clues that help you know."

GROUP SHARE Have children choose a character from a story they read and tell what the character said and did. Then have them tell how these clues helped them figure out how the character felt.

▶ The Ugly Duckling

Read aloud the story to children. Stop periodically for brief discussion. Use the following suggested stopping points and prompts:

- After the first paragraph, ask: "How is the gray duck different from the other ducks?"
- After the gray duck leaves the other ducks, ask: "Why do you think the gray duck leaves the other ducks?"
- At the end, ask: "How are ducks and swans alike? How are they different? Turn and talk about your ideas with a partner."

MINILESSON Genre: Folktale

TEACH Explain to children that *The Ugly Duckling* is a folktale. Tell them that a folktale is an old story that is passed down through the years. Folktales often tell about the world or have a lesson to learn. Sometimes they begin with the words *Once upon a time* and end with the words *happily ever after.*

1. Focus on the first two paragraphs of the story. Suggested language: "In the story *The Ugly Duckling,* you learned that one duckling was different from the others. How was the ugly duckling different?" (*He was the last duckling to hatch. He was big and gray. The other ducks did not want to play with him.*)

> **MINILESSON PRINCIPLE**
>
> Notice how characters change in a story.

2. Point out details in the sentences and pictures that tell how the ugly duckling grew and changed. Then write the minilesson principle on chart paper. Guide children to note that even though the ugly duckling was the last to hatch, the pictures show that he grew faster than the other ducklings. Help them realize that the last picture shows the ugly duckling grown up. Ask children to tell how the ugly duckling's feelings changed. Suggested language: "How did the ugly duckling's feelings change once he learned he was a swan?" (*He felt proud and beautiful.*)

SUMMARIZE AND APPLY Restate the minilesson principle. Tell children to apply it to their independent reading. Suggested language: "When you read a story, look for clues that tell how the characters change from the beginning of the story to the end."

GROUP SHARE Ask children to share how another character from a story changed. Have them tell what the character was like at the beginning of the story and what the character was like at the end of the story.

Whole-Group Lessons

Whistle for Willie
Student Book, Lesson 23

Read Aloud Passages

Around the World in a Day
See page 360 of this Guide.

Pet Poems
Student Book, Lesson 23

▶ Whistle for Willie

INTERACTIVE READ-ALOUD/SHARED READING

Read aloud the story to children. Stop periodically for very brief discussion of the story. Use the following suggested stopping points and prompts for quick group response, or give a specific prompt and have partners or threes turn and talk.

- After Peter tries to whistle for the second time, ask: "What problem does Peter have? What do you think Peter should do to learn how to whistle?"
- After Peter puts on his father's hat, ask: "Why do you think Peter thought feeling grown-up would help him whistle?"
- At the end of the story, say: "How does being able to whistle make Peter feel? Why do you think he keeps whistling? Turn and talk about your ideas with a partner."

MINILESSON Cause and Effect

TEACH Display the minilesson principle on chart paper, and read it aloud to children. Tell children they are going to learn to think about how one thing in a story makes another thing happen.

1. Discuss the principle with children, using examples from *Whistle for Willie*. Suggested language: "In the story *Whistle for Willie*, one thing that Peter did was spin around and around. What happened when Peter stopping spinning?" *(Everything turned down and up and up and down.)* "Why did everything seem to keep moving?" *(Peter was dizzy from spinning. That's the way things look when you are dizzy.)*

> **MINILESSON PRINCIPLE**
>
> Notice when one thing in a story makes another thing happen.

2. Focus on the event to help children see how the first event causes the second event to happen. Suggested language: "What happens when you spin around and then stop spinning?" *(Things seem to keep moving. It's hard to stand up straight.)*

3. Tell children that when they read, they should think about what happens in a story and why. Suggested language: "What happened when Peter hid in the carton and whistled?" *(Willie stopped and looked around.)* "What happened when Peter said, It's me, and stood up?" *(Willie raced straight to him.)*

4. Help children identify other events in the story. Record their ideas in a Flow Chart like the one shown here. List the first thing that happens in the first box and then list what it made happen in the second box.

SUMMARIZE AND APPLY Restate the minilesson principle. Then tell children to apply it to their independent reading. Suggested language: "When you read a story, think about what happens in the story. Look for things that make other things happen."

GROUP SHARE Have children choose a story event from their independent reading to share. Have them tell how this thing made another thing in the story happen.

▶ Around the World in a Day

INTERACTIVE READ-ALOUD/SHARED READING

INTERACTIVE READ-ALOUD/SHARED READING

Read aloud the story to children. Stop periodically for brief discussion. Use the following suggested stopping points and prompts:

- After Dad shares the information about the street fair, ask: "What kinds of things do you think happen at a street fair? Do you think a street fair sounds like fun?"
- After the description of the performers, ask: "Which performer would you most like to see? Why?"
- At the end of the story, say: "Do you think the family will go to the street fair next year? Why or why not? Turn and talk about your ideas with a partner."

MINILESSON Genre: Realistic Fiction

TEACH Display the minilesson principle on chart paper, and read it aloud to children. Tell children they are going to learn how thinking about where a story takes place can help them picture what happens.

> **MINILESSON PRINCIPLE**
>
> Think about where a story takes place to help you picture what happens.

1. Remind children that some stories tell about people, places, and things that happen that could be true. Suggested language: "In the story *Around the World in a Day,* where did the family go?" *(They went to an Around the World Street Fair.)*

2. Point out to children that thinking about where a story takes place can help them picture what happens in a story. Suggested language: "This street fair had food, crafts, and souvenirs from many different countries. How did this help you picture what the family did at the street fair?" *(Sample answer: I pictured the family buying food at different stands and eating their food as they walked along.)*

3. Work with children to complete a Web that describes the setting of the story. Help children tell how they pictured the family enjoying the different places in the setting.

SUMMARIZE AND APPLY Restate the minilesson principle. Tell children to apply it to their independent reading. Suggested language: "When you read, think about where a story takes place. Try to picture what happens in the story."

GROUP SHARE Have children share where a story they read takes place. Then have them tell how knowing where the story took place helped them picture one thing that happened.

▶ Pet Poems

INTERACTIVE READ-ALOUD/SHARED READING

Read aloud the introduction and poems to children. Stop periodically for brief discussion. Use the following suggested stopping points and prompts:

- After reading "Bingo," ask: "Who knows this poem as a song?" Invite children who know the song to sing it with you.
- After reading "Little White Horse," ask: "What do you like most about this poem?"
- At the end of "Pet Snake," ask: "Does this poem make you want a pet snake? Why or why not? Turn and talk about your ideas with a partner."

MINILESSON Genre: Poetry

TEACH Explain that poems use words to show things and feelings in different ways. Point out that many poems rhyme, or have words with the same ending sound. Tell children they are going to learn to notice the rhyming words in a poem.

> **MINILESSON PRINCIPLE**
>
> Notice the rhyming words in a poem.

1. Have children focus on the Spanish and English versions of "Little White Horse." Suggested language: "Listen for rhyming words as I read these poems again. What rhyming words did you hear?" *(blanco/reblanco, aquí/nací, snow/go, sea/be)*

2. Review the other two poems with children. Then write the minilesson principle on chart paper. Work with children to identify the rhyming words in "Bingo" and "Pet Snake." Explain to children that rhyming words help make poems fun to read and listen to.

SUMMARIZE AND APPLY Restate the minilesson principle. Tell children to apply it to their independent reading. Suggested language: "When you read a poem, remember to look for rhyming words. Think about how the rhyming words make the poem more interesting to read."

GROUP SHARE Ask children to share examples of rhyming words they found in poems they read for independent reading.

Whole-Group Lessons

A Tree Is a Plant
Student Book, Lesson 24

Read Aloud Passages

Visiting Butterflies
See page 361 of this Guide.

Grow, Apples, Grow!
Student Book, Lesson 24

▶ A Tree Is a Plant

INTERACTIVE READ-ALOUD/SHARED READING

Read aloud the book to children. Stop periodically for very brief discussion of the text. Use the suggested stopping points and prompts below for quick group response, or give a specific prompt and have partners or threes turn and talk.

- After reading the second page, ask: "What information do the labels in the pictures give?" Follow-up: "What other kinds of trees do you know?"
- After reading about young apple tree plants, ask: "What does an apple tree need to grow?"
- After reading about the tree's leaves, ask: "How does an apple tree get its food?"
- At the end, ask: "How are apple trees like other plants? How are they different? Turn and talk about your ideas with a partner."

MINILESSON Sequence of Events

TEACH Display the minilesson principle on chart paper, and read it aloud to children. Tell children that they are going to learn how to use the information an author gives to figure out how things grow and change.

1. Discuss the principle with children, using examples from *A Tree Is a Plant*. Suggested language: "In *A Tree Is a Plant*, the author tells how an apple tree can grow from a seed that falls to the ground. How does a seed that falls to the ground get planted?" *(Wind blows leaves and soil over the seed. Then it is pushed into the ground by ice and snow.)*

2. Explain to children that they can think about the order in which things happen to understand how an apple tree grows and changes. Suggested language: "What happens to the apple seed in the first spring?" *(It grows into a small tree.)* Follow-up: "What happens next?" *(The tree takes seven years to grow. Then it blossoms.)*

3. Point out to children that words such as *first, next, then,* and *last* help tell the order of when things happen. Suggested language: "How can you use these words to tell what happens to apples in the spring, summer, and fall?"

4. Work with children to tell how an apple tree changes throughout the year. Record their ideas in a Flow Chart like the one shown here.

> **MINILESSON PRINCIPLE**
> Notice how the author gives information to show how things grow and change.

In the spring trees blossom. → In the summer apples grow. → In the fall → In the winter

SUMMARIZE AND APPLY Restate the minilesson principle. Then tell children to apply it to their independent reading. Suggested language: "When you read a book, look for information that tells how things grow and change. Put the things that happen in order to help you better understand when the changes happen."

GROUP SHARE Have children share a few events from a book they have read. Ask them to tell how the information helped them understand how things grew or changed. Encourage children to use the words *first, next, then,* and *last* to describe the order of events.

▶ Visiting Butterflies

INTERACTIVE READ-ALOUD/SHARED READING

Read aloud the book to children. Stop periodically for brief discussion. Use the following suggested stopping points and prompts:

- After reading about leaving the butterfly house at the Bronx Zoo, say: "Think about seeing animals at a zoo. How is seeing butterflies at a zoo different from seeing other animals at a zoo?"
- At the end of the story, say: "How is visiting butterflies at the Bronx Zoo like visiting butterflies at the Houston Museum of Natural Science? How is it different? Turn and talk about your ideas with a partner."

MINILESSON Sequence of Events

TEACH Display the minilesson principle on chart paper, and read it aloud to children. Tell children they are going to learn to tell what happens first, next, and last in a selection.

1. Remind children that things often happen in a certain order. Suggested language: "In *Visiting Butterflies*, what did you learn you do before you go into the butterfly house?" (*You walk around an outside garden to learn about butterflies and how they grow.*)

> **MINILESSON PRINCIPLE**
> Notice what happens first, next, and last when you read.

2. Point out to children that clue words can help tell the order in which things happen. Suggested language: "What do you do after you enjoy the outdoor garden?" (*You walk through one door of the butterfly house into a small space.*)

3. Work with children to use a Flow Chart to sequence the events for visiting butterflies at the Bronx Zoo. Help them tell what happens first, next, and last. Repeat the activity for visiting butterflies at the Houston Museum of Natural Science.

SUMMARIZE AND APPLY Restate the minilesson principle. Tell children to apply it to their independent reading. Suggested language: "When you read, think about the order in which things happen. Think about what happens first, next, and last."

GROUP SHARE Have children tell what happened first, next, and last in a book they have read.

▶ Grow, Apples, Grow!

INTERACTIVE READ-ALOUD/SHARED READING

Read aloud the book to children. Stop periodically for brief discussion of the text. Use the following suggested stopping points and prompts:

- After reading the first page, ask: "What kind of food is an apple?" Follow-up: "Where do apples grow?"
- At the end, ask: "How do you think the author feels about apples? Turn and talk about your ideas with a partner."

MINILESSON Genre: Informational Text

TEACH Display the minilesson principle on chart paper, and read it aloud to children. Remind children that informational texts give facts about a topic. Explain that captions give information that can help you understand the topic better.

1. Discuss the principle with children, using examples from *Grow, Apples, Grow!* Suggested language: "Look at the photos on the second page. Read the captions below each one. What information do you get from reading these captions?" (*what happens to apple trees from spring to fall*)

> **MINILESSON PRINCIPLE**
> Think about how captions give you information.

2. Ask children to look at the photos on the last page and read the caption. Ask: "What information does this caption give?" (*It tells what people like to do with apples.*)

3. Point out the importance of the captions in this selection. Suggested language: "This selection would have been very different without the captions. Why would the selection have been difficult to understand without the captions?" (*The captions give important facts that are not stated in the text.*)

SUMMARIZE AND APPLY Restate the minilesson principle. Tell children they can apply it to their independent reading. Suggested language: "When you read, look for captions to help you understand a topic."

GROUP SHARE Ask children to share some information from a caption in a book they read. Have them tell how the caption helped them better understand the information in the book.

Whole-Group Lessons

The New Friend
Student Book, Lesson 25

Read Aloud Passages

Señor Coyote, the Judge
See page 361 of this Guide.

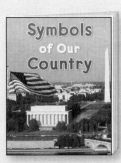

Symbols of Our Country
Student Book, Lesson 25

▶ The New Friend

INTERACTIVE READ-ALOUD/SHARED READING

Read aloud the story to children. Stop periodically for very brief discussion of it. Use the following suggested stopping points and prompts for quick group response, or give a specific prompt and have partners or threes turn and talk.

- After the men begin unloading the moving truck, ask: "Why do you think the boys are so interested in what is happening at the house?"
- After Makoto's parents go to buy food, ask: "How do you think the boys feel about Makoto moving into the house? How might their feelings be different if Makoto was younger or older?"
- At the end of the story, say: "What do you think will happen on Makoto's first day at his new school? Turn and talk about your ideas with a partner."

MINILESSON Understanding Characters

TEACH Display the minilesson principle on chart paper, and read it aloud to children. Remind children that some stories tell about people, places, and things that could be true. Tell children they are going to learn to use the words and pictures in a story to see if the characters act like real people.

1. Discuss the principle with children, using examples from *The New Friend*. Suggested language: "In the story *The New Friend*, a work crew came to wash and paint the empty house. What did the workers bring with them?" *(pails and paintbrushes)* "Is this what real workers would bring if they were painting a house?"

2. Draw attention to the picture of the work crew. Suggested language: "Look at the people painting the house. What kind of clothes did they wear to paint the house?" *(overalls, T-shirts, caps)* "Are these clothes a real painter might wear?"

3. Tell children that when they read, they should think about what the characters look like and what they do to decide if they act like real people. Suggested language: "Think about the words and the pictures in the story. What did the boys look like? What were some things that the boys did that were like what real boys their age do? Did they do anything that a real boy could not do?"

4. Help children record their ideas on a T-Map. Guide them to list what the characters look like and what they do that are like what real people do.

> **MINILESSON PRINCIPLE**
>
> Notice that characters in some stories look and act like real people.

What the Boys Looked Like	What the Boys Did

SUMMARIZE AND APPLY Restate the minilesson principle. Then tell children to apply it to their independent reading. Suggested language: "When you read a story, think about what the characters look like and what the characters do. Decide if the characters act like real people or if they are make-believe."

GROUP SHARE Have children choose a character from a story to share. Have them describe the character. Then ask children to tell if their character acted like a real person.

▶ Señor Coyote, the Judge

INTERACTIVE READ-ALOUD/SHARED READING

Read aloud the story to children. Stop periodically for brief discussion. Use the following suggested stopping points and prompts:

- After Señor Rattlesnake tells Señor Rabbit to get the stone off him, ask: "Does this story tell about make-believe characters or real characters? How do you know?"
- After the snake says that a good deed deserves a reward, ask: "Why do you think Señor Rabbit helped the snake? Should people expect a reward for helping others?"
- At the end of the story, say: "Do you think Señor Rattlesnake will learn his lesson? Why or why not? Turn and talk about your ideas with a partner."

MINILESSON Understanding Characters

TEACH Display the minilesson principle on chart paper, and read it aloud to children. Tell children they are going to learn to think about what characters do to better understand the characters.

> **MINILESSON PRINCIPLE**
>
> Think about what characters do.

1. Recall the character Señor Rattlesnake with children. Explain that the way a character behaves can help them better understand the character. Suggested language: "In the story Señor Coyote, the Judge, how did Señor Rattlesnake act after Señor Rabbit helped him?" (*He said he wanted to reward Señor Rabbit, but he really planned to eat him.*)

2. Point out to children that thinking about what a character does helps them figure out what the character is like. Suggested language: "The way that Señor Rattlesnake behaved tells me that he is not a nice character and cannot be trusted."

3. Work with children to complete an Inference Map for each character. Record what the character does in the top three boxes. Then record what the character is like in the bottom box.

SUMMARIZE AND APPLY Restate the minilesson principle. Tell children to apply it to their independent reading. Suggested language: "When you read, think about what the story characters do. Use the things that the characters do to decide what the characters are like."

GROUP SHARE Have children share a character from a story they have read and tell what the character did. Then ask children to tell what the character is like based on what he or she did.

▶ Symbols of Our Country

INTERACTIVE READ-ALOUD/SHARED READING

Read aloud the book to children. Stop periodically for brief discussion of the text. Use the following suggested stopping points and prompts:

- After reading about the Lincoln memorial, say: "The author tells about important symbols in our country. Why are the Washington Monument and Lincoln Memorial important?"
- After reading about the Supreme Court, say: "Buildings can be symbols, too. What is special about these buildings?"
- At the end, say: "Symbols are everywhere. What symbols do you see in our community? What do they mean? Turn and talk about your ideas with a partner."

MINILESSON Genre: Informational Text

TEACH Explain to children that Symbols of Our Country is an informational text. It gives information about important symbols of our country.

> **MINILESSON PRINCIPLE**
>
> Notice headings to think about what each section is about.

1. Focus on the headings to introduce how authors call attention to and organize information. Suggested language: "In Symbols of Our Country, the author includes some words in colored type. These words are larger than the words that follow them."

2. Page through the text with children to identify the headings. Point out how each heading tells what the text that follows will be about. Suggested language: "Look at the words American Flag. They are a different color and size than the words that follow them. If you read the section, you will see that the sentences all tell about the American flag."

3. Display the minilesson principle on chart paper, and read it aloud to children. Guide children to notice how the headings stand out from the other words. Explain that authors use headings to help readers understand what each section is about.

SUMMARIZE AND APPLY Restate the minilesson principle. Tell children they can apply it to their independent reading. Suggested language: "When you read, look for headings that tell what each section is about."

GROUP SHARE Ask children to share examples of headings in a book they read. Have them tell how the headings helped them understand the information in each section.

Whole-Group Lessons

The Dot
Student Book, Lesson 26

Read Aloud Passages

The Art Contest
See page 362 of this Guide.

Artists Create Art!
Student Book, Lesson 26

▶ The Dot

INTERACTIVE READ-ALOUD/SHARED READING

Read aloud the story to children. Stop periodically for very brief discussion of it. Use the following suggested stopping points and prompts for quick group response, or give a specific prompt and have partners or threes turn and talk.

- After Vashti grabs a marker and jabs the paper, ask: "How does Vashti feel about drawing? How do you know that? Turn and talk about your ideas with a partner."
- After the teacher asks Vashti to sign her paper, ask: "Why does Vashti's teacher ask her to sign the paper?"
- After Vashti sees her dot framed above the teacher's desk, ask: "Why do you think Vashti's teacher framed and hung up her dot?" Follow-up: "What do you think will happen next?"
- At the end of the story, ask: "How do you think the boy felt when Vashti asked him to sign his paper?"

MINILESSON Compare and Contrast

TEACH Display the minilesson principle on chart paper, and read it aloud to children. Tell children they are going to learn how to think about characters as they read.

1. Discuss the principle with children, using an example from *The Dot*. Suggested language: "At the beginning of the story *The Dot,* the main character Vashti said that she couldn't draw. How did her feelings toward drawing change by the end of the story?" *(Vashti liked drawing and she even encouraged the boy to draw.)*

2. Focus on when Vashti's teacher asked her to sign the paper. Suggested language: "After Vashti drew her first dot, her teacher said, *Now sign it.* How is this like something that happened later in the story? Do you remember what happened?" *(After the boy said that he couldn't draw a straight line, Vashti asked him to show her. Then she asked him to sign the paper, just like her teacher did.)*

3. Elicit from children additional examples from the story. Prompt them to talk about how Vashti's feelings about trying something new may have changed or how Vashti's teacher's feelings may have changed. Record children's ideas in a T-Map like the one shown here.

> **MINILESSON PRINCIPLE**
>
> Notice how characters' feelings are different at the beginning and at the end of a story.

Beginning of the Story	End of the Story

SUMMARIZE AND APPLY Restate the minilesson principle. Then tell children to apply it to their independent reading. Suggested language: "When you read, pay attention to the character's feelings. Think about how the character feels differently at the beginning of the story from how he or she feels at the end."

GROUP SHARE Ask children to share what they learned about one character in a story they have read. Have them tell how the character changed from the beginning of the story to the end.

▶ The Art Contest

INTERACTIVE READ-ALOUD/SHARED READING

Read aloud the story to children. Stop periodically for brief discussion. Use the following suggested stopping points and prompts:

- After John exclaims that he can't think of anything to do, ask: "What is the problem in this story?"
- After the line *his mom saved the day*, ask: "How do you think his mom will save the day?"
- At the end of the story, say: "Think about John's new understanding that art doesn't have to be perfect. What do you think the author is trying to tell you? Turn and talk about your ideas with a partner."

MINILESSON Compare and Contrast

TEACH Display the minilesson principle on chart paper, and read it aloud to children. Tell children they are going to learn to think about how characters in different stories are similar.

1. Using the character John from *The Art Contest,* ask children to think about the ways that his feelings changed throughout the story. Suggested language: "In the story *The Art Contest,* we read about John, who didn't like his fire truck painting the year before. By the end of the story, he realized that art doesn't have to be perfect. How do you think he felt about his sunset painting at the end of the story?" *(He was probably proud of his painting. He thought it was beautiful and hoped it would win the art contest.)*

> **MINILESSON PRINCIPLE**
>
> Think about the ways characters in stories are the same.

2. Talk with children about how Mr. Murphy encourages John to like art. Suggested language: "Mr. Murphy encouraged John to try creating art. How did Mr. Murphy try to encourage John?" *(He told him to close his eyes. He told him that art doesn't have to be perfect.)*

3. Remind children of their discussion about Vashti from *The Dot.* Talk about the ways in which Vashti and John are the same. Point out that the characters' feelings changed in similar ways as well. Write children's ideas in a Venn Diagram.

SUMMARIZE AND APPLY Restate the minilesson principle. Tell children to apply it to their independent reading. Suggested language: "When you read, think about the ways the characters are the same as characters in another story."

GROUP SHARE Ask children to share an example from independent reading of how a character from that story is the same as John or Vashti.

▶ Artists Create Art!

INTERACTIVE READ-ALOUD/SHARED READING

Read aloud the book to children. Stop periodically for brief discussion. Use the following suggested stopping points and prompts:

- After the paragraph about Georges Seurat, say: "The author tells you that you will see many brushstrokes if you look closely at one of Georges Seurat's paintings. How is this different from David Wynne's grizzly bear sculpture?"
- At the end of the story, ask: "How are the three people in this story the same and different? Turn and talk about your ideas with a partner."

MINILESSON Genre: Biography

TEACH Explain to children that *Artists Create Art!* is a biography. Tell them that they are going to learn to notice how the author of a biography tells what is special about the person she is writing about.

1. Introduce the idea that an author writing a biography tells what is special about the person. Suggested language: "In *Artists Create Art!,* the author wrote about three artists. They each created a different kind of art. Their art makes them special."

> **MINILESSON PRINCIPLE**
>
> Notice how the author tells what is special about the person she is writing about.

2. Ask children to share what else is special about the artists in *Artists Create Art!* Suggested language: "What is special about Grandma Prisbrey?" *(She learned to make art by herself.)* Continue by asking the same question about the other artists.

3. Then guide children to summarize the common features of a biography as you write the minilesson principle on chart paper. Explain to children that knowing what to expect when they read a biography will help them understand what they read.

SUMMARIZE AND APPLY Restate the minilesson principle. Tell children to apply it to their independent reading. Suggested language: "When you read, think about what is special about the person you are reading about."

GROUP SHARE Ask children to explain the things that made a person they read about for independent reading special.

Whole-Group Lessons

What Can You Do?
Student Book, Lesson 27

Read Aloud Passages

The Shoemaker and the Elves
See page 362 of this Guide.

The Wind and the Sun
Student Book, Lesson 27

▶ **What Can You Do?**

INTERACTIVE READ-ALOUD/SHARED READING

Read aloud the book to children. Stop periodically for very brief discussion of it. Use the following suggested stopping points and prompts for quick group response, or give a specific prompt and have partners or threes turn and talk.

- After the quote about learning to swim, ask: "Did this girl always know how to swim? How did she become good at it?"
- After the sentence, *We're happy when we do something well*, ask: "How do you feel when you do something well?" Follow-up: "How do you feel when you're learning something new?"
- After the sentences about Marie, Jill, and Gene, ask: "How do you think Marie, Jill, and Gene became good at spelling, printing, and working with computers? Turn and talk about your ideas with a partner."
- At the end, repeat the final question and ask: "What can you do? What would you like to learn how to do?"

MINILESSON Author's Purpose

TEACH Display the minilesson principle on chart paper, and read it aloud to children. Tell children that they are going to learn how the details in a book can help you understand an author's reason for writing.

1. Discuss the principle with children using *What Can You Do?* as an example. Focus on the first page. Suggested language: "In *What Can You Do?* the author writes that everyone is good at something. What details does the author give about a boy and girl she knows?" *(The boy can draw well. The girl can climb high.)*

2. Focus on the girl and boy on the next two pages. Ask: "What are these children good at?" *(The girl is good at swimming. The boy is good at skiing.)*

3. Elicit from children additional details from the text. Record children's ideas in an Inference Map like the one shown here.

> **MINILESSON PRINCIPLE**
>
> Think about how writers sometimes write to help you learn things.

4. Use children's responses to identify the author's purpose. Suggested language: "You can see that this book tells about many different things that children are good at. What is the author's reason for writing this book?" *(to help you learn that everyone is good at something)*

SUMMARIZE AND APPLY Restate the minilesson principle. Then tell children to apply it to their independent reading. Suggested language: "When you read a book, think about details that can help you figure out why the author wrote the book."

GROUP SHARE Have children share why they think the author wrote the book they are reading. Ask them to share details from the book that support their ideas.

▶ The Shoemaker and the Elves

INTERACTIVE READ-ALOUD/SHARED READING

Read aloud the story to children. Stop periodically for brief discussion. Use the following suggested stopping points and prompts:

- After the first paragraph, ask: "When and where does this story take place?"
- After the shoemaker's wife suggests that they stay up to find out what is going on, ask: "Why does the shoemaker's wife want to stay up? What do you think will happen next?"
- At the end of the story, say: "Think about how the story ends. What lesson can you learn from this story? Turn and talk about your ideas with a partner."

MINILESSON Genre: Fairy Tale

TEACH Display the minilesson principle on chart paper, and read it aloud to children. Tell children they are going to learn to think about what happens to characters in a story.

> **MINILESSON PRINCIPLE**
>
> Think about what happens to characters in a story.

1. Using the shoemaker from *The Shoemaker and the Elves,* discuss with children what happened to characters in the story. Suggested language: "In the story *The Shoemaker and the Elves,* the shoemaker had trouble running his shoe store. Something amazing happened that helped the shoemaker. What happened to him?" *(The elves came and made a beautiful pair of shoes for him.)*

2. Talk with children about what happened to the elves. Suggested language: "We learned in the story that the shoemaker wanted to thank the elves for their help. What did the shoemaker do to thank the elves?" *(He and his wife made special shoes for the elves.)*

3. Discuss with children what happens to characters in the story. Remind them to think about the amazing things that happen in order. Fill out a Flow Chart with what happens to the characters in *The Shoemaker and the Elves.*

SUMMARIZE AND APPLY Restate the minilesson principle. Tell children to apply it to their independent reading. Suggested language: "When you read a fairy tale, think about what happens to characters in the story."

GROUP SHARE Ask children to share an example from independent reading of something amazing that happens to a character.

▶ The Wind and the Sun

INTERACTIVE READ-ALOUD/SHARED READING

Read aloud the story to children. Stop periodically for brief discussion. Use the following suggested stopping points and prompts:

- After Wind suggests having a contest, ask: "Why do Sun and Wind decide to have a contest?" Follow-up: "Who do you think will win?"
- After the traveler wraps his jacket tighter, ask: "Did Wind's idea turn out the way he thought it would?" Follow-up: "Why or why not?"
- At the end of the story, ask: "What other stories have we read that are like this one? Turn and talk about your ideas with a partner."

MINILESSON Genre: Fable

TEACH Explain to children that *The Wind and the Sun* is different from the other two stories children read this week. Point out that it is a fable, and that a fable is a story that teaches a lesson.

> **MINILESSON PRINCIPLE**
>
> Think about what the characters do and how the author is teaching you a lesson.

1. Focus on what the characters do in *The Wind and the Sun* to introduce the idea that fables teach lessons. Suggested language: "In the story *The Wind and the Sun,* Wind and Sun did different things. Wind tried to use force to get Traveler to take off his coat. Sun used warmth, and that worked better. The lesson is that it is better to use kindness instead of force."

2. Write the minilesson principle on chart paper. Help children to understand that what the characters do can teach a lesson. Have children retell Wind's and Sun's actions in their own words and connect that to the story's lesson. Explain to children that figuring out what the characters in a story do will help them understand the lesson.

SUMMARIZE AND APPLY Restate the minilesson principle. Tell children to apply it to their independent reading. Suggested language: "When you read, look for a lesson that the author is teaching."

GROUP SHARE Ask children to retell a lesson from a story they read for independent reading. Have them explain how what the characters did helped teach the lesson.

Whole-Group Lessons

The Kite
Student Book, Lesson 28

A Hopeful Song
See page 363 of this Guide.

Measuring Weather
Student Book, Lesson 28

▶ The Kite

INTERACTIVE READ-ALOUD/SHARED READING

Read aloud the story to children. Stop periodically for very brief discussion of it. Use the following suggested stopping points and prompts for quick group response, or give a specific prompt and have partners or threes turn and talk.

- After the robins tell Frog and Toad to give up, ask: "Why did the robins laugh?" Follow-up: "Do you think Frog and Toad will give up? Why or why not?"
- After the kite falls down with a thud, ask: "Which word helps you best picture what happened to the kite? Why?"
- After Toad suggests going home, ask: "How do you think Toad feels? Turn and talk about your ideas with a partner."
- At the end of the story, ask: "What can you learn from this story?"

MINILESSON Story Structure

TEACH Display the minilesson principle on chart paper, and read it aloud to children. Tell children they are going to learn to think about how characters in a story solve a problem.

1. Discuss how characters solve a problem using examples from *The Kite*. Focus on Frog and how he solved the problem of getting the kite to fly. Suggested language: "In order to know how a character solved a problem, we need to know what that problem was. What was the problem in *The Kite*?" *(The kite wouldn't fly.)*

MINILESSON PRINCIPLE

Think about how the characters in a story solve a problem.

2. Use children's responses to talk about how Frog solved the problem. Suggested language: "Frog didn't quit when the kite wouldn't fly. He kept trying different things, like telling Toad to run, jump, wave, and shout."

3. Work with children to complete a Story Map that shows the setting, characters, and plot. Make sure that children recognize the problem and how it is solved.

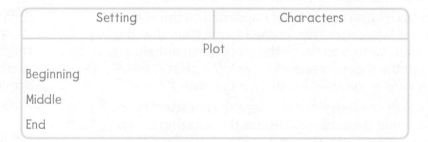

Setting	Characters
Plot	
Beginning	
Middle	
End	

SUMMARIZE AND APPLY Restate the minilesson principle. Then tell children to apply it to their independent reading. Suggested language: "When you read, think about how the characters in a story solve a problem."

GROUP SHARE Ask children to share what the characters did to solve the problem in a story they have read.

▶ A Hopeful Song

INTERACTIVE READ-ALOUD/SHARED READING

Read aloud the book to children. Stop periodically for brief discussion. Use the following suggested stopping points and prompts:

- After the first paragraph, ask: "How does the opening paragraph make you feel?"
- After the third paragraph, ask: "Why did Ray Barnett go to Africa?"
- At the end of the story, say: "Why is the title of this book *A Hopeful Song*? Turn and talk about your ideas with a partner."

MINILESSON Genre: Informational Text

TEACH Display the minilesson principle on chart paper, and read it aloud to children. Tell children they are going to learn to think about how the author of an informational text feels about what he is writing about.

1. Using the book *A Hopeful Song,* discuss with children that authors show how they feel about a topic through what they write. Suggested language: "Authors write for specific reasons. Often, the reason an author writes a book gives us a clue about how he or she feels. Why do you think the author of *A Hopeful Song* wrote this book?" *(to inform people about a choir that he likes very much)*

> **MINILESSON PRINCIPLE**
> Think about how the author of informational text feels about what he is writing about.

2. Explain to children that an author will include clues to show his or her feelings and reasons for writing. Suggested language: "What words in the book give you clues about how the author feels about the African Children's Choir?" *(The word "successful" makes me think that the author thinks that the African Children's Choir is doing well.)*

3. Discuss with children other clues that tell how an author feels about what he is writing about. Write their ideas in an Inference Map.

SUMMARIZE AND APPLY Restate the minilesson principle. Tell children to apply it to their independent reading. Suggested language: "When you read, look for clues that tell you how the author feels."

GROUP SHARE Ask children to explain how the author of their independent reading book feels. Have them support this idea with clues they have found in the book.

▶ Measuring Weather

INTERACTIVE READ-ALOUD/SHARED READING

Read aloud the book to children. Stop periodically for brief discussion. Use the following suggested stopping points and prompts:

- After the paragraph about the thermometer, ask: "How are a thermometer and a rain gauge the same?" Follow-up: "How are they different?"
- At the end of the story, ask: "How is it helpful to know what the temperature is going to be each day? Turn and talk about your ideas with a partner."

MINILESSON Genre: Informational Text

TEACH Write the minilesson principle on chart paper, and read it aloud. Explain to children that *Measuring Weather* is an information book that gives information about a topic. It includes a graph to give more information about the topic.

> **MINILESSON PRINCIPLE**
> Think about the information in graphs.

1. Focus on the graph to introduce how graphs give information. Suggested language: "In *Measuring Weather,* the author included a graph that showed the daily temperature for a week. This type of graph is called a *bar graph.*"

2. Ask children to share what they remember about the graph in *Measuring Weather.* Guide children to understand how the information found in a graph is often easier to understand because it uses pictures and words together. Help them recognize the parts of a bar graph that help them understand information, such as headings and bars.

SUMMARIZE AND APPLY Restate the minilesson principle. Tell children to apply it to their independent reading. Suggested language: "When you read a book with graphs, think about the information in graphs."

GROUP SHARE Ask children to explain the information they learned from a graph found in their independent reading.

Whole-Group Lessons

Hi! Fly Guy
Student Book, Lesson 29

Read Aloud Passages

A Stone Goes to Court
See page 364 of this Guide.

Busy Bugs
Student Book, Lesson 29

▶ Hi! Fly Guy

INTERACTIVE READ-ALOUD/SHARED READING

Read aloud the story to children. Stop periodically for very brief discussion of the text. Use the suggested stopping points and prompts below for quick group response, or give a specific prompt and have partners or threes turn and talk.

- After Buzz captures Fly Guy, ask: "How does Fly Guy feel when he first meets Buzz? Why?"
- After Buzz tries to let Fly Guy go, ask: "How do Fly Guy's feelings change about Buzz?" Follow-up: "What makes his feelings change?"
- After the judges let Fly Guy in the show, ask: "Why do the judges change their minds about having Fly Guy in the show?"
- At the end of the story, ask: "Do you think a fly would make a good pet? Why or why not? Turn and talk about your ideas with a partner."

MINILESSON Understanding Characters

TEACH Display the minilesson principle on chart paper, and read it aloud to children. Tell children that they are going to think about what the people and animals in a story do to help readers understand what they are like.

1. Discuss the principle with children, using examples of characters from *Hi! Fly Guy*. Suggested language: "In the first chapter of *Hi! Fly Guy*, we met two characters. Who are these characters?" *(a fly and a boy)*

> **MINILESSON PRINCIPLE**
>
> Think about what characters do to understand what they are like.

2. Focus on what Fly Guy did to understand what he is like. Suggested language: "When Buzz took Fly Guy to the pet show, the judges laughed. What did Fly Guy do?" *(He did tricks, said "Buzz," and flew into the jar.)* Follow-up: "Why did he do those things?" *(He wanted to help Buzz by showing the judges he is a pet.)*

3. Use children's responses to explain how what characters do are clues to what they are like. Suggested language: "The author used what Fly Guy did to show readers that Fly Guy is clever and a good friend."

4. Work with children to think about what Buzz is like. Record children's responses in a T-Map like the one shown here.

What the Character Does	Why the Character Does It

SUMMARIZE AND APPLY Restate the minilesson principle. Then tell children to apply it to their independent reading. Suggested language: "When you read a story, think about what the characters do to help you understand what they are like."

GROUP SHARE Have children share what they learned about a character they read about. Have them explain what the character did that helped them understand what the character is like.

▶ A Stone Goes to Court

INTERACTIVE READ-ALOUD/SHARED READING

Read aloud the story to children. Stop periodically for brief discussion. Use the following suggested stopping points and prompts:

- After reading the sentence containing the word *disguised,* ask: "What clues in this sentence would help you understand the word *disguised?*"
- After Robert points to the stone, say: "Think about the title of the story. What do you think will happen next?"
- At the end of the story, say: "Think about the main problem in this story. How was the problem solved? Turn and talk about your ideas with a partner."

MINILESSON Cause and Effect

TEACH Display the minilesson principle on chart paper, and read it aloud to children. Tell children they are going to learn to think about what characters do and why.

1. Using the character of the Mayor from *A Stone Goes to Court,* discuss with children that characters do certain things for a reason. Suggested language: "In the story *A Stone Goes to Court,* we read about a boy named Robert whose money was stolen. The Mayor arrested a stone for the crime. How did the Mayor get the money back?" *(When the townspeople laughed about the stone being charged with a crime, the Mayor fined them for being disrespectful and gave the money to Robert.)*

> **MINILESSON PRINCIPLE**
>
> Think about what characters do and why.

2. Talk with children about the Mayor's reason for doing this. Suggested language: "The Mayor must have had a reason for arresting a stone. Why do you think he did this?" *(He knew he would never find the man in green clothing, so he came up with a plan to get Robert's money back.)*

3. Discuss with children the cause of other characters' actions. Write their ideas in a T-Map labeled *What the Character Does* and *Why.*

SUMMARIZE AND APPLY Restate the minilesson principle. Tell children to apply it to their independent reading. Suggested language: "When you read, think about what characters do and why."

GROUP SHARE Ask children to share an example from independent reading of something a character did and why the character did it.

▶ Busy Bugs

INTERACTIVE READ-ALOUD/SHARED READING

Read aloud the introduction and poems to children. Stop periodically for brief discussion. Use the following suggested stopping points and prompts:

- After the snail poems, say: "The first poem is written in Spanish. The second poem is the English version of the first poem. What do you think the Spanish word for *snail* is?"
- After reading "Song of the Bugs," ask: "What line is repeated in this poem?" Follow-up: "Why did the author repeat the same line twice? Turn and talk about your ideas with a partner."

MINILESSON Genre: Poetry

TEACH Point out that *Busy Bugs* is a collection of poems. Tell children that poets include specific words in their poems to make readers feel a certain way.

1. Focus on "Worm" to introduce the way a poem can make you feel. Suggested language: "In 'Worm,' the poet used many words that rhymed. When you read this poem out loud, the words are fun to say. This can make you feel happy, or it can make you feel nervous if you don't like worms."

> **MINILESSON PRINCIPLE**
>
> Think about how a poem makes you feel.

2. Write the minilesson principle on chart paper. Guide children to think about how the different poems in *Busy Bugs* made them feel. Encourage them to choose specific lines or words that made them feel a certain way. Have children explain the words they chose.

SUMMARIZE AND APPLY Restate the minilesson principle. Tell children to apply it to their independent reading. Suggested language: "When you read, think about how a poem makes you feel."

GROUP SHARE Ask children to explain the feeling they got from a poem they read for independent reading.

Whole-Group Lessons

Winners Never Quit!
Student Book, Lesson 30

Read Aloud Passages

The Parts of the House Have a Fight
See page 364 of this Guide.

Be a Team Player
Student Book, Lesson 30

▶ Winners Never Quit!

INTERACTIVE READ-ALOUD/SHARED READING

Read aloud the book to children. Stop periodically for very brief discussion of it. Use the following suggested stopping points and prompts for quick group response, or give a specific prompt and have partners or threes turn and talk.

- After Garrett tells Mia, *Better luck next time!*, ask: "How do you think Mia feels when she can't score a goal and no one cheers?" Follow-up: "How is this feeling different from how she feels when she scores a goal and her teammates cheer?"

- After Mia stomps to the house, ask: "Why did the author use the word *stomped*? Turn and talk with your partner about how words can help you make a picture in your mind."

- After Mia stands by the side and watches, ask: "How do you think Mia feels watching everyone else play soccer?" Follow-up: "How do you think she feels now about quitting?"

- At the end of the story, ask: "What lesson did Mia learn?"

MINILESSON Main Idea and Details

TEACH Display the minilesson principle on chart paper, and read it aloud to children. Explain that the main idea of a book is what the book is mostly about. Tell children that they are going to think about how details give information about the main idea.

1. Discuss the principle with children, using *Winners Never Quit!* Suggested language: "In *Winners Never Quit!* you learned about a girl named Mia Hamm who loved to play soccer. What is this book mostly about?" *(Being a team player is more important than winning or losing.)*

> **MINILESSON PRINCIPLE**
>
> Think about how details give information about the main idea.

2. Talk with children about the details that give information about the main idea. Suggested language: "The author tells how Mia Hamm loved to play soccer but hated to lose. She quit the game when she didn't score a goal. What happened after she quit?" *(Her brothers and sisters didn't let her play the next day.)* Follow-up: "How did not being able to play change Mia?" *(She realized that not playing was worse than losing.)*

3. Help children identify other details in the book that give information about the main idea. Record their ideas in a Web like the one shown here.

Playing is more important than winning or losing.

SUMMARIZE AND APPLY Restate the minilesson principle. Then tell children to apply it to their independent reading. Suggested language: "When you read, think about how the details give information about the main idea."

GROUP SHARE Have children share the main idea from a book they read for independent reading. Have them give a few examples of details that give more information about the main idea.

▶ The Parts of the House Have a Fight

INTERACTIVE READ-ALOUD/SHARED READING

Read aloud the story to children. Stop periodically for brief discussion. Use the following suggested stopping points and prompts:

- After the tree house hears the family fighting, ask: "Do you think this story really happened? Why or why not?"
- At the end of the story, say: "Think about the whole story. How are the family members and the parts of the house the same? Turn and talk about your ideas with a partner."

MINILESSON Genre: Folktale

TEACH Explain to children that *The Parts of the House Have a Fight* is a folktale from the Philippines. Tell children that folktales are stories that were made up many years ago. Folktales are often not real, but they may teach a lesson.

1. Using the story *The Parts of the House Have a Fight*, discuss with children that a folktale includes things which could not actually happen. Suggested language: "In the folktale *The Parts of the House Have a Fight*, you read about a family fighting about who is the most important member. What happened because of their fighting?" *(Their fighting caused the parts of the house to begin arguing over which part was the most important.)*

> **MINILESSON PRINCIPLE**
>
> Think about what a story really means.

2. Talk with children about why the author might have included a similar fight among the family members and among the parts of the house. Suggested language: "The family members have the same argument that the parts of the house have. Why do you think the author made the parts of the house fight, too?" *(to show that the family members are like parts of a house, all different, but all important)*

3. Write the minilesson principle on chart paper. Guide children to understand that an author might not come out and say what a story really means. Help them recognize that they can use clues from the story and what they already know to help them understand what a story really means.

SUMMARIZE AND APPLY Restate the minilesson principle. Tell children to apply it to their independent reading. Suggested language: "When you read, think about what a story really means."

GROUP SHARE Ask children to share an example from independent reading of what they think a story really means.

▶ Be a Team Player

INTERACTIVE READ-ALOUD/SHARED READING

Read aloud the book to children. Stop periodically for brief discussion. Use the following suggested stopping points and prompts:

- After the fourth paragraph, ask: "Why is it important to be a team player?"
- After the checklist, say: "One of the things on this checklist is to follow the rules. Why do you think it is important to follow all, and not just some, of the rules on this checklist? Turn and talk about your ideas with a partner."

MINILESSON Genre: Informational Text

TEACH Explain to children that *Be a Team Player* is different from the other two stories they read this week. Point out that it is an information book. It tells how to do something.

1. Focus on the checklist at the end of the book. Suggested language: "In *Be a Team Player*, the author included a checklist that gives rules about how to be a team player."

> **MINILESSON PRINCIPLE**
>
> Think about the most important information.

2. Write the minilesson principle on chart paper. Then guide children to read back through *Be a Team Player* and to name important information in the book. Suggested language: "Which is more important: *People may play on a field or on a court* or *No matter what kind of team it is, it's important to be a good team player*? Why?" *(The second sentence; it tells about a big idea that is important no matter what you do.)*

SUMMARIZE AND APPLY Restate the minilesson principle. Tell children to apply it to their independent reading. Suggested language: "When you read, think about the most important information."

GROUP SHARE Ask children to explain what the most important information is in a book they read for independent reading and why that is the most important information.

Teacher's Notes

Teaching Genre

Table of Contents

Genre instruction and repeated exposure to a variety of genres are essential components of any high-quality literacy program. Access to the tools children need to understand information in different genres will make them better readers. When children understand the characteristics of a variety of genres, they will be able to:

• gain an appreciation for a wide range of texts
• develop a common vocabulary for talking about texts
• begin reading texts with a set of expectations related to genre
• make evidence-based predictions
• develop preferences as readers
• understand purposes for reading and writing
• recognize the choices an author makes when writing
• compare and contrast texts
• think deeply about what they read

The pages in this section provide a framework for discussing genre with your children in an age-appropriate way. You can use the lists on the following pages to organize for genre discussion.

• **Genre Characteristics:** teach and review the salient features
• **Discussion Starters:** begin and maintain productive discussions
• **Comparing Texts:** encourage children to make connections across texts
• **Literature:** select *Journeys* literature for discussion

Fantasy

SUPPORT THINKING

DISCUSSION STARTERS During whole-group and small-group discussion, use questions to spark conversation about genre characteristics.

- Who is this story about?
- What is [character name] like? What can he/she do that is special?
- What is happening in this story?
- What problem does [character name] have?
- Where is this story happening? Is it a place that you would like to visit? Explain.
- Which parts of this story could not happen in real life?
- Which people could not live in the real world? How do you know?
- Would you like to read more stories that are like [title]? Why or why not?

COMPARING TEXTS After children have read and listened to several fantasy stories, prompt them to compare selections and to recognize common characteristics. Use questions such as these:

- How are the people in [title] and [title] alike? How are they different?
- How is [title] the same as other stories you have read? How is it different?
- How is the ending of [title] different from the ending of [title]?

 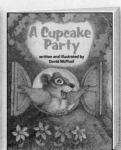

Gus Takes the Train,
Student Book,
Lesson 5

A Cupcake Party,
Student Book,
Lesson 10

Genre Characteristics

A fantasy story is a made-up story that could not happen in real life.

Through repeated exposure to fantasy stories, children should learn to notice common genre characteristics, though at Grade 1 they will not be expected to use the technical labels (except for *characters* and *setting*). Use friendly language to help them understand the following concepts:

- **Author's Purpose:** to entertain
- **Characters:** the people or animals in a story; characters in fantasy stories often have special abilities
- **Characters' Actions/Qualities:** may have both real and make-believe qualities
  - animals and objects may talk and act like people
  - people may have feelings like those of real people but can do amazing things
- **Setting:** where and when the story takes place
  - may be a real place or a make-believe place
  - the story may be set in a different time
- **Plot:** what happens in the story
  - includes a problem at the beginning, things that happen as characters try to solve the problem, and an ending
  - the problem may be similar to problems in real life
  - characters may have realistic or make-believe solutions to problems
- **Dialogue:** the words that characters say to each other
- **Theme/Message:** what the author is trying to say to readers

JOURNEYS Literature

STUDENT BOOK

The Big Race

The Big Trip

A Cupcake Party

Curious George at School

The Garden

Gus Takes the Train

Hi! Fly Guy

The Kite

TEACHER'S EDITION READ-ALOUD

Chipper Chips In

The Dancing Wolves

Susie and the Bandits

LEVELED READERS

Bear Swims E

Ben the Cat D

The Boat Race J

Bobcat Tells a Tale J

Cam the Camel K

A Cat Named Ben D

Chipmunk's New Home I

A Chunk of Cheese F

Curious George at the Library I

Curious George Finds Out About School B

Curious George Visits School C

Curious George's Day at School C

Flying H

Flying in an Airplane H

Forest Stew H

Happy Birthday, Toad E

Izzy's Move D

A Job for Jojo J

Lena's Garden J

The Map and the Treasure I

The Mountain J

Polar Bear Pete H

Polly's Pet Polar Bear G

Putting Frosting on the Cake D

The Sailboat Race J

The Sand Castle K

A Seed for Sid E

Skunk Cooks Soup G

Toad's Birthday E

The Treasure Map I

Trip to the Rock B

SUPPORT THINKING

DISCUSSION STARTERS During whole-group and small-group discussion, use questions to spark conversation about genre characteristics.

- Who is this story about?
- What happens in this story?
- What problem does [character name] have?
- How do things turn out for people who are good? For people who are bad?
- Where is this story happening?
- Which characters get along? Which characters do not get along?
- Which parts of this story could not happen in real life?
- Which people could not live in the real world? How do you know?
- Which words are clues that this story is a fairy tale?
- Do you like the way the story ended? Why or why not?

COMPARING TEXTS After children have read and listened to several fairy tales, prompt them to compare stories and to recognize common characteristics. Use questions such as these:

- How is [title] the same as other stories you have read?
- How is [character name] like characters in other stories you have read?
- Have you read about any other characters that can do the same things as [character name]?
- Which fairy tale do you like better—[title] or [title]?

The Three Little Pigs,
Student Book,
Lesson 6

Jack and the Beanstalk,
Student Book,
Lesson 18

Genre Characteristics

A fairy tale is a made-up story in which characters can do amazing things. It has been told over and over for many years.

Through repeated exposure to fairy tales, children should learn to notice common genre characteristics, though at Grade 1 they will not be expected to use the technical labels (except for *characters* and *setting*). Use friendly language to help them understand the following concepts:

- **Author's Purpose:** to entertain
- **Characters:** the people or animals in a story; characters in fairy tales often have special powers or can do amazing things; some characters are good and some are bad
- **Setting:** where and when the story takes place; usually set long ago in a faraway place
- **Plot:** what happens in the story; includes a problem at the beginning, things that happen as characters try to solve the problem, and an ending
- **Dialogue:** the words that characters say to each other
- **Storybook Language:** memorable beginning and ending language such as *Once upon a time* and *happily ever after*
- **Transformations:** a change in form of a person or an object
- **Theme/Message:** what the author is trying to say to readers

JOURNEYS Literature

STUDENT BOOK	TEACHER'S EDITION READ-ALOUD
Jack and the Beanstalk The Three Little Pigs	The Little Red Hen The Shoemaker and the Elves The Three Wishes

Folktale

Genre Characteristics

A folktale is a made-up story that was first told aloud to explain something or to teach a lesson. It has been told over and over for many years.

Through repeated exposure to folktales, children should learn to notice common genre characteristics, though at Grade 1 they will not be expected to use the technical labels (except for *characters* and *setting*). Use friendly language to help them understand the following concepts:

- **Author's Purpose:** to entertain; to teach a lesson
- **Characters:** the people or animals in a story; animals may talk and act like people
- **Setting:** where and when the story takes place; usually set long ago in a specific place (often where the story originated)
- **Plot:** what happens in the story; includes a problem that characters face, things that happen as characters try to solve the problem, and an ending
- **Dialogue:** the words that characters say to each other
- **Theme/Message:** what the author is trying to say to readers
  - often tells what a group of people believes
  - may tell a group's explanation for why things are the way they are

JOURNEYS Literature

STUDENT BOOK
How Leopard Got His Spots
Little Rabbit's Tale
The Ugly Duckling

TEACHER'S EDITION READ-ALOUD
Chicken Little

How Bat Learned to Fly
The Neighbors
The Parts of the House Have a Fight
Señor Coyote, the Judge
A Stone Goes to Court
Stone Stew
Turtle, Frog, and Rat

LEVELED READERS
Bear's Long, Brown Tail **H**
Bear's Tail **H**
Giraffe's Neck **E**
Peacock's Tail **L**

SUPPORT THINKING

DISCUSSION STARTERS During whole-group and small-group discussion, use questions to spark conversation about genre characteristics.

- Who is this story about?
- What is [character name] like?
- What is happening in this story?
- What problem does [character name] have? How does [character name] work out the problem?
- Where is this story happening? What is the place like?
- What can you tell about [character name] by what he/she says?
- Which parts of this story could not happen in real life? Explain how you know.
- What lesson can you learn by reading this story?

COMPARING TEXTS After children have read and listened to several folktales, prompt them to compare stories and to recognize common characteristics. Use questions such as these:

- How are the characters in [title] and [title] the same?
- How is [title] the same as other stories you have read? How is it different?
- Think about the ending of [title]. How is this ending similar to the ending of [title]?

How Leopard Got His Spots, Student Book, Lesson 12

Little Rabbit's Tale, Student Book, Lesson 20

Fable

SUPPORT THINKING

DISCUSSION STARTERS During whole-group and small-group discussion, use questions to spark conversation about genre characteristics.

- Who is this story about?
- What is [character name] like?
- What is happening in this story?
- What problem does [character name] have?
- What does [character name] learn?
- Where is this story happening?
- What can you tell about [character name] by what he/she says? What can you tell about [character name] from the pictures?
- What is the lesson of the story?

COMPARING TEXTS After children have read and listened to several fables, prompt them to compare stories and to recognize common characteristics. Use questions such as these:

- How are the characters in [title] and [title] the same?
- How is [title] the same as other stories you have read?
- How are the lessons the characters learn in [title] and [title] the same?
- How is [title] different from another fable you have read?

City Mouse and Country Mouse, Student Book, Lesson 4

Jack and the Wolf, Student Book, Lesson 6

Genre Characteristics

A fable is a short, made-up story that teaches a lesson.

Through repeated exposure to fables, children should learn to notice common genre characteristics, though at Grade 1 they will not be expected to use the technical labels (except for *characters, setting,* and *lesson*). Use friendly language to help them understand the following concepts:

- **Author's Purpose:** to entertain; to teach a lesson
- **Characters:** the people or animals in a story; characters in fables are often animals or objects that talk and act like people
- **Setting:** where and when the story takes place
- **Plot:** what happens in the story; includes a problem that characters face, what happens as characters try to solve the problem, and an ending
- **Dialogue:** the words that characters say to each other
- **Message/Moral:** the lesson characters learn from what happens in the story

JOURNEYS Literature

STUDENT BOOK	TEACHER'S EDITION READ-ALOUD	LEVELED READERS
City Mouse and Country Mouse	The Lion and the Mouse	Fox and Crow **I**
Jack and the Wolf	The Tortoise and the Hare	Go Turtle! Go Hare! **D**
The Wind and the Sun		The Pigs **B**
		Turtle and Hare **D**

Realistic Fiction

Genre Characteristics

Realistic fiction is a made-up story that could happen in real life.

Through repeated exposure to realistic fiction, children should learn to notice common genre characteristics, though at Grade 1 they will not be expected to use the technical labels (except for *characters* and *setting*). Use friendly language to help them understand the following concepts:

- **Author's Purpose:** to entertain
- **Characters:** the people or animals in a story; characters in realistic fiction might remind children of people they know
- **Setting:** where and when the story happens; could be a real place
- **Plot:** what happens in the story; includes a problem that characters face, things that happen as characters try to solve the problem, and an ending
- **Dialogue:** the words that characters say to each other; characters talk like real people

JOURNEYS Literature

STUDENT BOOK
The Dot
A Musical Day
The New Friend
The Storm
Whistle for Willie

TEACHER'S EDITION READ-ALOUD
Around the World in a Day
The Art Contest
Grandpa's Tree
Night of the Wolf
The Piano Lessons
The Rainy Trip

LEVELED READERS
Amy's Airplane **E**
The Beach **J**
The Bumpy Snowman **H**
Dress Up **B**
First Day of Second Grade **H**
Grandpa and Me **C**
Granny **A**
The Lemonade Stand **L**
Len's Tomato Plant **I**
Len's Tomatoes **I**
A Mexican Festival **J**
Molly's New Team **F**
Nana's House **D**
Our Bakery **H**

Our Day at Nana's House **D**
Our Day at the Bakery **H**
Our School **F**
Paco's Snowman **I**
Ready for Second Grade **I**
A Surprise for Ms. Green **J**
Tag-Along Tim **J**
What I Want to Be **J**
When Grandpa Was a Boy **C**
Working in the Park **E**

SUPPORT THINKING

DISCUSSION STARTERS During whole-group and small-group discussion, use questions to spark conversation about genre characteristics.

- Who is this story about?
- What is [character name] like?
- What is happening in this story?
- What problem does [character name] have?
- How do things turn out for [character name]?
- Where is this story happening?
- When is this story happening?
- What parts of the story could really happen?
- Which person in [title] makes you think about someone you know?

COMPARING TEXTS After children have read and listened to several realistic fiction stories, prompt them to compare stories and to recognize common characteristics. Use questions such as these:

- How are the people in [title] and [title] alike?
- How is [title] the same as other stories you have read? How is it different?
- Which story seems more real—[title] or [title]? Explain.

The Storm, Student Book, Lesson 2

A Musical Day, Student Book, Lesson 8

Informational Text

Genre Characteristics

Informational text gives facts about a topic.

Through repeated exposure to informational text, children should learn to notice common genre characteristics, though at Grade 1 they will not be expected to use the technical labels. Use friendly language to help them understand the following concepts:

- **Author's Purpose:** to inform
- **Graphic Features:** pictures that help the reader understand information or show more about the topic
  - **Diagrams:** pictures with labels
  - **Maps:** pictures that show where something is or how to get from one place to another
  - **Graphs/Charts:** pictures that help readers compare information
- **Text Features:** ways the author makes words stand out
  - **Headings:** type—usually larger, darker, or both—at the beginning of a new section
  - **Captions:** words or sentences that explain a picture
  - **Sizes/Colors:** authors use different sizes and colors to help readers see what is most important
- **Main Idea:** what the book is mostly about
- **Details:** pieces of information that tell more about the main idea or topic
- **Text Structure:** how the book is organized
- **Fact:** a piece of information that is true and can be proved
- **Opinion:** a statement of what the author thinks or believes

JOURNEYS Literature

SUPPORT THINKING

DISCUSSION STARTERS During whole-group and small-group discussion, use questions to spark conversation about genre characteristics.

- What is this book about?
- What different kinds of type do you see?
- What kinds of pictures does the author use?
- What can you learn from the pictures?
- What does the author do to make the book interesting?
- How does the author organize the book to help you understand what you are reading?
- How do you know that the information in the book is true?
- How do you think the author feels about the topic? How do you know?

COMPARING TEXTS After children have read and listened to several informational selections, prompt them to compare selections and to recognize common characteristics. Use questions such as these:

- How are the animals in [title] and [title] the same?
- Think about [title] and [title]. How are they the same? How are they different?
- How do the pictures in [title] and [title] help you understand the author's ideas?

Lucia's Neighborhood, Student Book, Lesson 4

At Home in the Ocean, Student Book, Lesson 11

JOURNEYS Literature

LEVELED READERS *CONT.*

Busy Animals at Night **D**
Butterflies **H**
Coral Reefs **H**
Curious About School **B**
Desert Animals **E**
Dogs **B**
Dog Talk **J**
Drawing **B**
Ducks **D**
Fall Changes **I**
Favorite Things **B**
Firehouse **C**
Food for You **H**
Friends **I**
Friends Who Share **C**
From Pit to Plum **J**
A Fun Baseball Game **H**
Going to School **E**
Grandpa **B**
Happy Birthday! **C**
Helping **A**
Helping at Home **E**

How Animals Move **J**
How We Get Food **G**
In the Fall **H**
In the Sea **D**
In the Sky **D**
Jim Henson, the Puppet Man **E**
Kamala's Art **H**
Kite Flying **F**
Lance Armstrong **L**
Life in the Coral Reefs **G**
Living and Working in Space **J**
Making a Home **D**
The Man Who Made Puppets **E**
Many Kinds of Bats **J**
Margret and Hans Rey **J**
Michelle Wie **F**
Moving **G**
Music **C**
My Favorite Foods **D**
Neighbors **I**
Our Class **E**
Our Town **C**
People in the Town **D**

The Places in Our Town **C**
A Plum Grows **J**
Reading **D**
Reading Together **C**
Seasons **I**
Seasons Around the World **K**
The Seasons of the Year **I**
Sharing **C**
Shark **D**
Soccer **G**
So Many Sounds **F**
Spots **D**
The Story of a Rose **M**
The Sun **D**
Tiny Baby Kangaroos **I**
Trains **C**
Trees **G**
Two Sisters Play Tennis **J**
The Weather **E**
The Williams Sisters **J**
Winter **B**
A World of Food **K**
Worms **J**

Biography

SUPPORT THINKING

DISCUSSION STARTERS During whole-group and small-group discussion, use questions to spark conversation about genre characteristics.

- Who is this book about?
- What is/was [subject name] like?
- What important things happened to [subject name]?
- Where did [subject name] live?
- What did other people think about [subject name]?
- What is the author trying to tell readers about [subject name]?
- Why is it important to know about [subject name]'s life?
- What can you learn from [subject name]'s life?

COMPARING TEXTS After children have read and listened to several biographies, prompt them to compare selections and to recognize common characteristics. Use questions such as these:

- How are [subject name] and [subject name] the same?
- How is [title] the same as other biographies you have read? How is it different?
- Which person would you like to read more about? Explain.
- Of all the biographies you've read, which tells about the most interesting person? Explain.

Dr. Seuss,
Student Book,
Lesson 9

Mae Jemison,
Student Book,
Lesson 16

Genre Characteristics

A biography is the true story of a real person's life.

Through repeated exposure to biographies, children should learn to notice common genre characteristics, though at Grade 1 they will not be expected to use the technical labels. Use friendly language to help them understand the following concepts:

- **Author's Purpose:** to inform; to show why this person's life is important
- **Important Events:** told in the order they happened
- **Facts and Opinions:** help readers understand how the author feels and why the person's life is important
- **Narrative Structure:** events told in order as a story; may tell about all or just part of the person's life

JOURNEYS Literature

STUDENT BOOK

Artists Create Art!

Dr. Seuss

Mae Jemison

Tomás Rivera

TEACHER'S EDITION READ-ALOUD

Christina's Work

LEVELED READERS

Jim Henson, The Puppet Man **E**

Lance Armstrong **L**

The Man Who Made Puppets **E**

Margret and Hans Rey **J**

Mia Hamm, Soccer Star **J**

Michelle Wie **F**

Two Sisters Play Tennis **J**

The Williams Sisters **J**

Poetry

Genre Characteristics

Poetry is a piece of writing in which words are used to show feelings and ideas.

Through repeated exposure to poetry, children should learn to notice common genre characteristics, though at Grade 1 they will not be expected to use the technical labels (except for *rhyme*). Use friendly language to help them understand the following concepts:

- **Author's Purpose:** to entertain; to express
- **Forms:** include traditional rhymes, songs, chants, free verse, and list poems
- **Rhyme:** to have the same ending sound; rhyming words can make a poem fun to read
- **Rhythm:** the beat of how the words are read
- **Sensory Words:** words that describe how things look, feel, taste, smell, and sound
- **Repeated Readings:** can often help readers enjoy and understand a poem more

JOURNEYS Literature

STUDENT BOOK
Busy Bugs
Friends Forever
Happy Times

Pet Poems
Silly Poems
Two Poems from Dr. Seuss

TEACHER'S EDITION READ-ALOUD
Painting Word Pictures

SUPPORT THINKING

DISCUSSION STARTERS During whole-group and small-group discussion, use questions to spark conversation about genre characteristics.

- What does this poem tell about?
- Which words in the poem rhyme?
- Which words in the poem help you picture something?
- Which words in the poem describe sounds? Which words describe smells? Which words describe tastes?
- Is the poem silly or serious? How do you know?

COMPARING TEXTS After children have read and listened to several poems, prompt them to compare poems and to recognize common characteristics. Use questions such as these:

- How are [title] and [title] the same?
- How are the poems in [title] the same as other poems you have read?
- How are the poems in *Two Poems from Dr. Seuss* like other things that Dr. Seuss has written?
- Which poem in *The Four Seasons* best helps you picture the season? Explain.

Friends Forever, Student Book, Lesson 1

Silly Poems, Student Book, Lesson 20

Teacher's Notes

Writing Handbook Minilessons

Writing Handbook Minilessons

Writing Handbook Minilessons

How to Use This Book

The *Writing Handbook* was designed to complement the writing instruction in your reading program as well as meet academic standards for writing. It consists of two components: a handbook for children that they can use as a resource as well as practice writing in throughout the year, and a Teacher's Guide that supports instruction by providing minilessons for every handbook topic.

Components

Two easy-to-use components make up the Grade 1 *Writing Handbook* program:

- A 96-page partially consumable student handbook with 30 writing topics that correlate to your reading program's key writing lessons, followed by a resource section on writing strategies, such as the writing process and writing traits.

  The first section of the handbook includes writing models along with interactive practice to scaffold or reinforce children's understanding of opinion, informational/explanatory, and narrative writing. As children practice writing, they build additional examples of the forms to refer to throughout the year as well as develop a deeper understanding of each form's structure.

  The second section of the handbook is a resource tool that children can refer to whenever they write. Topics range from writing strategies to how to use checklists and rubrics.

- A Teacher's Guide with 60 minilessons (two minilessons for each topic

in the first section of the handbook) plus one minilesson, as needed, for use with each remaining page in the handbook.

Minilessons

Minilessons are short, focused lessons on specific topics. In this Teacher's Guide, minilessons are provided for each topic in the Student Handbook. In the first section are two minilessons for each student handbook topic. Each of these minilessons consists of the following parts:

- Topic title
- Tab with section name
- Minilesson number and title
- Objective and guiding question
- Easy-to-follow instruction in an *I Do*, *We Do*, and *You Do* format
- Modeled, collaborative, and independent writing
- Conference and evaluation information
- Technology references

6 • Writing Handbook

How to Use This Book

This handbook will help you write. It will give you ideas. It will also help you share your ideas.

First, you will read about how to write. Then you will practice writing. Have fun using this book!

6 • Grade 1

How to Use This Book • 7

- Reduced facsimiles of student handbook pages
- Tips for corrective feedback
- A feature that further explores the lesson's writing trait

Each writing minilesson has been correlated to your reading program's writing lessons so that all minilessons and corresponding writing handbook pages within this section are used at least once during the school year. Additional minilessons are provided in the Teacher's Guide that correlate to each remaining page in the handbook. Use these minilessons, as needed, to clarify concepts for children and provide additional support.

Student-Page Walk-Through

Guide children to turn to pages 6 and 7 in their books. Read aloud the information. Explain to them that their handbook is a tool that they can use to help them whenever they write. It can help them answer any writing question they have, and they can use it during writing. Guide children to turn to and look at each of these parts in their handbooks:

- Table of contents
- Introductory pages, including overviews of the writing process and the writing traits
- Writing form pages, each with a section tab, title, definition, and helpful bulleted points, followed by a clear example of the writing model as well as a write-in activity page
- Additional pages on topics ranging from writing strategies to revising to using technology, which they may need or want to refer to during the year for projects and other assignments

Grade 1 • 7

Purposes for Writing

The *Writing Handbook* spirals writing instruction up the grade levels to coincide with writing standards that spiral. Beginning in Grade 1, children will explore and practice writing, and their sophistication in writing for different purposes and audiences will grow. Students across all grades will learn about and practice opinion/argument, informative/explanatory, and narrative writing.

Purpose and Form

Writers choose specific writing forms to communicate their intended meaning. To choose effectively, they target their purpose and audience before and while they write. Children will be introduced to and practice writing in different genres to build up a repertoire of writing forms from which to choose. This increasing practice as well as access to information about writing will help children feel more comfortable about writing and help them enjoy doing it.

In this handbook, the writing forms and models presented coincide primarily with the purposes expressed through academic standards. These are to inform, to explain, to narrate, and to persuade. There are other purposes for writing as well, but these four are emphasized to best prepare students at all grade levels for college and career readiness.

TO INFORM The purpose for writing to inform is to share facts and other information. Informational texts make statements that are supported by facts and truthful evidence.

TO EXPLAIN The purpose for writing to explain is to tell *what, how,* and *why* about a topic. An example is to explain in writing how to do or make something.

TO NARRATE The purpose of writing to narrate is to tell a story. The story can be made up or truthful. Most forms of narrative writing have a beginning, middle, and end. Examples

are fictional stories and personal narratives.

TO PERSUADE Writing that has a purpose to persuade states an opinion or goal and supports it with reasons and supporting details in order to get the audience to agree, take action, or both.

Success in School and Life

Older students and adults are often judged by how well they can communicate. Students at all grade levels are thus encouraged to learn to write well to be successful in their studies. In particular, by the upper grades, students will need to master the basic essay format that includes

- An introductory paragraph that identifies the topic or statement of purpose.

- Supporting paragraphs that provide related details and examples.

- A closing paragraph that sums up and concludes.

Students will use this essay form to produce reports, literary analyses, theses, and critiques throughout their academic career. They will also be tested on their ability to write effective essays in standardized tests. In later life, as adults, they will need to be able to communicate clearly in writing to coworkers, bosses, and clients. This requires extensive and ongoing exposure to exemplary writing models and explicit instruction in a variety of areas, as well as opportunities to practice different forms of writing.

8 • Writing Handbook

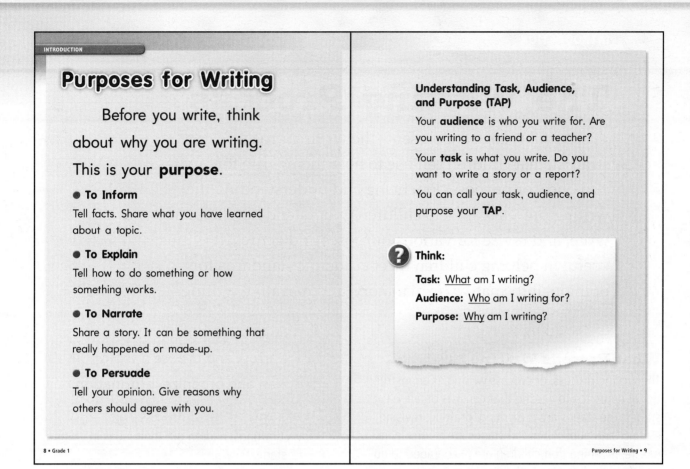

Purposes for Writing

Before you write, think about why you are writing. This is your **purpose**.

● **To Inform**

Tell facts. Share what you have learned about a topic.

● **To Explain**

Tell how to do something or how something works.

● **To Narrate**

Share a story. It can be something that really happened or made-up.

● **To Persuade**

Tell your opinion. Give reasons why others should agree with you.

Understanding Task, Audience, and Purpose (TAP)

Your **audience** is who you write for. Are you writing to a friend or a teacher?

Your **task** is what you write. Do you want to write a story or a report?

You can call your task, audience, and purpose your **TAP**.

? Think:

Task: <u>What</u> am I writing?

Audience: <u>Who</u> am I writing for?

Purpose: <u>Why</u> am I writing?

opportunities to practice different forms of writing. In all cases, their purpose for writing must always be clear. Evidence suggests that the more time student writers spend on writing, developing their writing skills, and deepening their writing experience, the better writers they become.

At Grade 1, children begin to solidify their understanding of basic sentence construction, first through modeled and interactive writing and then through independent practice. This approach enables children to progress to building solid paragraphs. Children will learn that a paragraph has at least a topic sentence that reflects their purpose, supporting sentences, and a closing sentence. As they progress up the grades, knowledge of basic sentence and paragraph construction will enable children to write longer pieces such as essays, which contain multiple paragraphs connected by transitional words and phrases.

The Reading-Writing Connection

The ability to communicate their thinking about texts for a variety of purposes and audiences will serve children well in several ways. When children write about what they read, reflecting on content, craft, or another aspect of a text, they provide evidence of their thinking. This helps teachers know how well children have understood a text. Additionally, the more children write in response to texts, the more they increase their ability to reflect and improve their critical writing ability. Also, children will learn how to cite evidence from texts to support their claims or main ideas.

Introduce the Purposes

Have children turn to page 8, and read aloud the text to them. Explain that these are the key purposes for writing that will be explored in their handbooks. Give or elicit an example of writing that might be used for each purpose. Examples might include a report about an animal *to inform*, a recipe or directions about how to make a sandwich *to explain*, a story about what happened at school yesterday *to narrate*, and a poster about the need to recycle *to persuade*. Then read the next page to children. Discuss how children should always consider their TAP—or task, audience, and purpose—to help them better target the message of their writing.

Grade 1 • 9

The Writing Process

The *Writing Handbook* presents the writing process as a strategy that children can use to help them write for any task, audience, or purpose. Practicing and understanding the writing process can help children understand how to plan, write, and revise for various purposes and genres. It is thus useful in helping children meet academic standards for opinion, informative/explanatory, and narrative writing.

What Process Writing Is

The writing process, or process writing, is an instructional approach to writing that consists of five basic stages. The stages are prewriting, drafting, revising, editing, and publishing. The stages are recursive in nature, meaning that children are encouraged to go back and forth between the stages as needed.

The *Writing Handbook* is set up so that you will have the opportunity to demonstrate the writing process stages through interactive writing exercises before you ask children to try it themselves. See pages 74–77 of this teacher's guide for the minilessons you might choose to use in teaching the writing process to your children. Use these minilessons, as needed, to scaffold the writing instruction presented in your main reading program. Also, encourage children to refer to writing process pages in their handbooks whenever they need additional help in writing.

The characteristics of the stages of the writing process are as follows:

Prewriting

This is the stage where children begin to plan their writing. Children:

- Define a task and purpose.
- Identify an audience.
- Brainstorm ideas.

- Narrow and choose a topic.
- Plan and organize information.

Drafting

During drafting, children put their ideas in writing. In this stage, they

- Write a first draft.
- Do not yet worry about perfecting their writing.
- Know that they can revise, edit, and proofread later.
- Use their plan and checklists to help them write or to return to prewriting, as needed.

Revising

A draft is reread and decisions are made to rework and improve it. In this stage, children might:

- Read aloud their work to others to determine how it sounds and how it might be improved.
- Conference with other children or their teacher.
- Add information.
- Delete unnecessary information.
- Rearrange sentences.
- Combine sentences.

10 • Writing Handbook

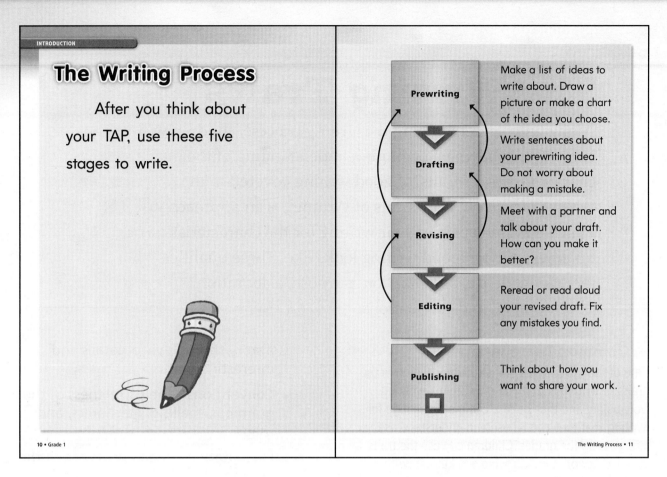

The Writing Process

After you think about your TAP, use these five stages to write.

Prewriting	Make a list of ideas to write about. Draw a picture or make a chart of the idea you choose.
Drafting	Write sentences about your prewriting idea. Do not worry about making a mistake.
Revising	Meet with a partner and talk about your draft. How can you make it better?
Editing	Reread or read aloud your revised draft. Fix any mistakes you find.
Publishing	Think about how you want to share your work.

Editing

During editing, the draft is polished. In this stage, children reread and correct their writing for the following:

- Grammar
- Spelling
- Mechanics
- Usage

Publishing

Children share their writing with others. In this stage, children typically:

- Make a final, clean copy.
- Use their best handwriting, if writing by hand. If they are sharing their work electronically, they typically choose typefaces and other elements to make their writing readable and attractive.
- Combine their writing with art or graphics.
- Make multiple copies, read their writing aloud, post it electronically, or share and display it in some other way.

Introduce the Process

Read aloud Student Handbook pages 10–11. Explain to children that the writing process is a strategy that they can use to help them write about any topic. Point out how the graphic on p. 11 starts with prewriting at the top and then moves down to the last stage at the bottom, which is publishing. For children who have no previous orientation to the writing process, simplify your introduction by emphasizing at first only the three key stages of planning, drafting, and revising. Explain how most tasks of any nature require planning, doing or making something, and then thinking about what might be done better and making those improvements. Compare how these same basic stages can be used to help children write well.

The Writing Traits

Along with understanding the writing process, children will benefit from having a beginning understanding of the characteristics, or traits, of good writing covered in the *Writing Handbook*. The "Traits of Writing" is an approach in which children analyze their writing for the characteristics, or qualities, of what good writing looks like. These qualities include evidence, organization, purpose, elaboration, development, and conventions.

A Common Language

One of the advantages of instructing children in the traits of writing is that you give them a working vocabulary and thus build a common language for writing that they can all use and understand as they progress up the grades. Children can use the traits as a framework for improving any kind of writing they are doing. To this end, a systematic, explicitly taught focus on the traits of writing has proved to be an effective tool for discussing writing, enabling children to analyze and improve their own writing, and providing teachers with a way to assess children's compositions and developing skills in a fair, even-handed manner.

Writers typically focus on six traits, with presentation—or the appearance of writing—sometimes considered an additional trait.

- **Evidence**—the details and examples that explain ideas and support opinions.
- **Organization**—the structure of the writing.
- **Purpose**—the reason for writing, which supports the type of writing and the audience.
- **Elaboration**—the words and phrases the writer uses to convey the message and add interest.
- **Development**—the advancement of

a story through vivid details and interesting plot.

- **Conventions**—the correctness of the grammar, spelling, mechanics, and usage.
- **Presentation**—the appearance of the writing.

The Writing Workshop

Since writing is an involved process that children accomplish at varying speeds, it is usually a good idea to set aside a block of time for them to work on their writing. One time-tested model that has worked well in classrooms is the Writing Workshop. In this model, during a set period of time, children work individually and collaboratively (with classmates and/or with the teacher) on different writing activities. Two of these activities are for children to comment on interactive writing produced during class time or to collaborate in reviewing each other's manuscripts. One effective technique used in many workshops as a way for children to comment on aspects of each other's writing is to use the language of the traits when they comment.

Some tasks are started and finished during a workshop, while others are ongoing. A writing workshop can serve many writing-related functions:

- Children can work on a class writing assignment (ongoing or quickly accomplished).

12 • Writing Handbook

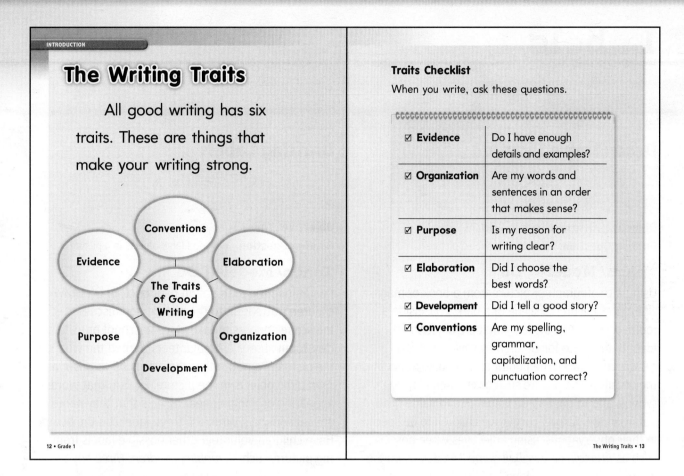

The Writing Traits

All good writing has six traits. These are things that make your writing strong.

- Conventions
- Evidence
- Elaboration
- The Traits of Good Writing
- Purpose
- Organization
- Development

Traits Checklist

When you write, ask these questions.

☑ Evidence	Do I have enough details and examples?
☑ Organization	Are my words and sentences in an order that makes sense?
☑ Purpose	Is my reason for writing clear?
☑ Elaboration	Did I choose the best words?
☑ Development	Did I tell a good story?
☑ Conventions	Are my spelling, grammar, capitalization, and punctuation correct?

12 • Grade 1

The Writing Traits • 13

- Children can engage in independent writing, jotting down or consulting ideas in their writing log or journal, starting or working on pieces of their own devising.

- As previously mentioned, children can engage in peer-conferencing, giving one another advice about a piece of writing or sharing writing ideas.

- Children can select pieces for inclusion in their writing portfolio, where they keep their best work.

- Teachers can conference with individual children, reviewing student writing and discussing a given student's strengths and weaknesses as well as instructional progress.

- Teachers can engage in small-group instruction with children who need extra help with practice in specific areas of writing.

Writing Workshops are often most effective when they adhere to a dependable schedule and follow a set of clearly posted guidelines (for example, keep voices down, point out the good things about someone's writing as well as comment on parts that might be revised, listen politely, put away materials when the workshop is over). In addition, children should know what areas of the classroom they can use during the workshop and should have free access to writing materials, including their handbooks.

Introduce the Traits

Share the Writing Traits overview pages with children. Discuss each trait briefly and explain to children that their handbooks contain more information on the traits, which they can use to help them as they plan, draft, revise, edit, and publish their writing.

When you use the minilessons to instruct children on different topics in writing, use the language of the traits with them. Encourage them to use it, too, any time they interact with text.

Grade 1 • 13

Writing Handbook Minilessons

Labels

Minilesson 1

Describing a Picture

Objective: Describe objects in a picture.

Guiding Question: How do I describe a picture?

Teach/Model—I Do

Using a photograph or picture from a book or magazine, show children a scene of a park, zoo, inside a room, or any place that has multiple objects in it. Identify the place for children by saying *this is a picture of [a park]*. Then point to and name a few of the details in the picture such as children playing, swings, and so on. Call on volunteers to name other details in the picture. Encourage children to be specific in their observations, using adjectives when possible, such as *little girl* or *baseball game*. List details on the board as they are mentioned. Make sure children understand that they are describing a picture.

Guided Practice—We Do

Display a different photograph or picture of a scene. Guide children to describe various details in it. Help children to be specific in their descriptions by encouraging them to tell exactly what they see such as *two adults and a child* instead of *people* and a *big dog* or *a white dog* instead of *a dog*. Record details on the board as children mention them. Then work together to determine the main idea of the scene such as a beach or a skating rink.

Practice/Apply—You Do

COLLABORATIVE Distribute another scene to each small group. Have children discuss details in the scene and name what the whole scene is about.

INDEPENDENT Instruct children to draw or write another detail that could be added to the picture they just worked on in their groups.

Conference/Evaluate

Circulate and help children come up with another detail to add to the scene. Encourage them to both write and draw the detail.

14 • Writing

Minilesson 2

Drafting Labels

Objective: Write labels.

Guiding Question: How do I label objects in a picture?

Teach/Model—I Do

Read aloud the material on handbook p. 14. Draw children's attention to the picture and discuss that the scene appears to take place in school or a classroom library. Ask volunteers to read the words in the picture. Point out that the words *book, shelf*, and *mat* name objects in the picture. Explain that words appearing or hanging near objects that they name are called *labels*. Write the three labels on the board. Have children volunteer other possible labels from the picture, such as *mobile, children, three boys, three girls, male librarian* or *teacher*. Record their labels on the board, as well. Review that a one or two word name that describes something or someone in a picture is called a label.

Guided Practice—We Do

 Have children turn to Activity 1 on p. 15. Work with them to identify the picture as a park scene and to name objects that they see such as *trees, bench, plants, path, duck*. Point out the three separate pictures below the scene and guide children to write a label for each one: *tree, pond, duck*.

Practice/Apply—You Do

 INDEPENDENT Read directions aloud with children. Tell them to draw a picture of a familiar scene with several objects in it. Direct children to label three or more of the objects in the picture.

Conference/Evaluate

Circulate and offer encouragement and help as children draw their scenes and write labels. Evaluate using the rubric on p. 96.

Labels

A **label** names an object. It tells what something is or what it looks like.

✎ Parts of a Label

- A label can be one word such as <u>chair</u> or <u>book</u>.
- A label can be more than one word such as <u>red chair</u> or <u>big book</u>.

14 • Grade 1

Name _____

Follow your teacher's directions.

 Draw a picture.
Label three objects in it.

Labels • 15

✔ Corrective Feedback

IF . . . children are having trouble finding objects in their picture to label,

THEN . . . have them draw more objects or else run a finger along the picture and stop whenever they recognize an object they can name. Encourage children to be specific when labeling each object, such as *striped cat* or *snow boots* instead of *cat* or *shoes*.

✐ Focus Trait: Evidence

Explain to children that labels can name the big idea of a picture or the smaller ideas. Tell children that the smaller ideas are called details. On the board, draw a simple stick picture of a farm with a barn and a few animals, such as a horse and a cat. Have volunteers label the details in the picture.

Then have another volunteer label the whole picture *Farm*. Explain that both kinds of labels are fine. The first kind labels the small ideas in the picture. The second kind labels the whole picture. If you wish, repeat with another picture, such as one of a school lunchroom.

Grade 1 • **15**

Captions

WRITING FORMS

Minilesson 3

Talking About a Picture

Objective: Name details that give information about a picture.

Guiding Question: What places and things do pictures show?

Teach/Model—I Do

Read aloud the definition, parts, and model on handbook p. 16. Explain that the words *the park* in the caption give a detail about the picture. These words name the place. The words *a bench* give another detail about the picture. Tell children that good captions often name the places and things in pictures. Point out that, without a caption, children might be unsure about the details of the picture.

Guided Practice—We Do

Have children study the picture in the model on handbook p. 16. Discuss other things they see in the picture that could be part of a caption. Help children list the words on chart paper: *sun, tree, flowers, grass, path.*

Practice/Apply—You Do

COLLABORATIVE Make available pictures of different locations, such as a classroom, a schoolyard, a playground, a garden, a farm, and a city. Have small groups choose one picture and talk about what they see. Ask them to name the place and the different things they see in the picture.

INDEPENDENT Have children choose a different picture. Instruct them to write the place name and one thing shown in the picture.

Conference/Evaluate

Circulate and help children name details about the pictures. Ask *What place is this? What things do you see?* Encourage children to write their captions as complete sentences, including a capital letter at the beginning and a period at the end.

16 • Writing

Minilesson 4

Drafting Captions

Objective: Write captions.

Guiding Question: How do I write about a picture?

Teach/Model—I Do

Review handbook p. 16 with children. On chart paper, draw a simple sketch of a library room, including books, shelves, a table, chairs, a computer, and a clock. Tell children *The library is one place a family might visit. We can write a few captions about the picture.* Discuss things children see, explaining that these are details that might be included in a caption. Below the picture, write this sentence frame: *Here _____ at the _____.* Call on volunteers to complete the caption and have them write any words they know in the blanks.

Guided Practice—We Do

 Have children turn to the frame on handbook p. 17. Discuss the details in the picture. Elicit suggestions for captions from children, encouraging complete sentences. Together, choose one caption for the picture. Have children write in their books as you write on the board.

Practice/Apply—You Do

 INDEPENDENT Have children read the directions. Tell them to use their prewriting plan from Lesson 2 or to brainstorm new ideas, using Graphic Organizer 5 to list details.

Conference/Evaluate

During the writing process, circulate and give corrective feedback as needed while children work independently. Evaluate using the rubric on p. 96.

Captions

A **caption** tells about a picture.

 Parts of a Caption

- A few words or a sentence about a picture
- Details about what a picture shows

Here is a bench at the park.

16 • Grade 1

Name _____

Follow your teacher's directions.

1 The family _____

_____

_____

2 Use your plan. Write a caption. You can write about a place to visit with your family.

Captions • 17

✓ Corrective Feedback

IF . . . children's captions do not explain what is happening in the picture,

THEN . . . point to concrete details in the picture and have children name them. Work together to decide on one detail children can include in their caption. Then have them revise their writing accordingly.

Focus Trait: Evidence

Remind children that sometimes a caption gives the big idea of a picture; at other times it tells about one or more picture details. Mention that whatever the caption is about, it is usually written as a full sentence.

Display some pictures from a book or magazine for children. Have volunteers state captions about the big idea as well as captions about picture details. Make sure children are using full sentences.

Grade 1 • **17**

Writing Handbook Minilessons

Sentences

Minilesson 5

Writing a Complete Thought

Objective: Write a complete thought in sentence form.

Guiding Question: How do I write a complete thought?

Teach/Model—I Do

Read aloud the definition and the list on handbook p. 18. Point to the picture in the model and say *children*. Shake your head and tell the class that the picture shows children, but that the word *children* is not a complete idea because it just tells who is in the picture. Explain that a complete idea would tell who is in the picture *and* what they are doing. Point to the picture again and say *playing*. Shake your head again and explain that this is still not a complete thought; you need to tell who and what. Read the first model sentence aloud. Explain that this is a complete idea because it tells *who* is doing something and *what* they are doing. Repeat with the other sentences.

Guided Practice—We Do

Show children a simple picture in a picture book. Ask them to tell what is happening in the picture. Remind them that they need to tell *who* is in the picture and *what* they are doing. Compliment children on telling complete thoughts; if they do not, help rephrase their ideas to include both the who and the what. Write their sentences on the board and point out how they begin with capital letters and end with periods.

Practice/Apply—You Do

COLLABORATIVE Have small groups choose a picture book. Ask them to describe a picture in the book by using a complete sentence.

INDEPENDENT Ask children to sketch a picture. Then have them write a complete sentence that tells what is happening in the picture.

Conference/Evaluate

Move through the room, guiding children to remember to put periods at the ends of their sentences.

18 • Writing

Minilesson 6

Drafting Sentences

Objective: Write sentences about pictures.

Guiding Question: How do I write a full sentence about a picture?

Teach/Model—I Do

Have children turn to handbook p. 18. Review the definition, the Parts of a Sentence and the model. Point out that each of the sentences begins with a capital letter and ends with a period. Emphasize that the sentences all tell about the picture. On the board, draw a sketch of a bird sitting in a tree. Below it, write *I see a bird. It is in a tree.* Read the sentences aloud. Repeat this activity by drawing a cloud and a sun, and writing the sentences *There is a cloud. The cloud is near the sun.* Point out the capital letters and final periods.

Guided Practice—We Do

 Have children turn to the frame on handbook p. 19. Direct their attention to the picture and discuss its contents. Then work together to complete the frame with sentences that are about the picture. Remind children to end their sentences with punctuation. Have children write in their books as you write on the board.

Practice/Apply—You Do

 INDEPENDENT Read the directions with children. Tell them to use their prewriting plan from Lesson 3 or brainstorm new ideas to write one or more sentences.

Conference/Evaluate

Walk around the room, checking that children are on task. Offer help as necessary. Make sure that children use initial capital letters and final periods appropriately. Evaluate using the rubric on p. 96.

Sentences

A **sentence** gives information. It is a group of words that tells who or what does something.

Parts of a Sentence

- A sentence starts with a capital letter.
- A sentence ends with an end mark.

We play outside.

Jay and Anne run fast.

Pat rides a bike.

Name _____

Follow your teacher's directions.

1 The girl _____

_____

_____

 2 The boy _____

_____

_____

 3 Use your plan. Write a sentence. Tell what you do at school.

Corrective Feedback

IF . . . children are not using initial capital letters or final periods,

THEN . . . read the sentences aloud with children, having them listen for how your voice goes up and down. Explain that when your voice goes down, it usually marks the end of the sentence, so adding a period is necessary. Explain that when one sentence ends, a new one begins and requires an initial capital letter.

Focus Trait: Elaboration

On the board, write the sentence *My friend draws things.* Read it aloud. Then explain that the word *things* in the sentence is not very exact. Tell children that when you get a picture in your head of what is happening in the sentence, you aren't sure what kinds of things your friend is drawing.

Erase the word *things* and replace it with *fish.* Read the sentence aloud. Explain that using the word *fish* makes it easier to picture what your friend is doing.

Then replace *fish* with *cars.* Read the new sentence with children. Stress that this more exact word helps you know what the sentence is telling about.

Close by asking children to think of other good choices for words to take the place of *things.* Write the words and discuss why they are better choices than the word *things.*

Grade 1 • **19**

Writing Handbook Minilessons

Class Story

Minilesson 7	Minilesson 8

Thinking of Events

Objective: Brainstorm events that happened at school.

Guiding Question: How do I make a list of events?

Teach/Model—I Do

Read aloud the definition, the list, and the model on handbook p. 20. Explain that the class story in the model describes a real hike. Remind children that they have done lots of interesting things in their lives. Add that these things are often called *events* or *activities* and that these can make a great story. Tell the class that your life has included some events that might make a good story. Make a list of 3–4 of these events on the board, using phrases rather than full sentences; examples might include *when I went to Mexico; getting a new cat;* or *the big argument with Sam.* Read the completed list with children.

Guided Practice—We Do

Guide children to name several activities they have done as a class. Have them think about field trips, special events, performances, and the like. Jot the events they mention in note form on a large sheet of paper. After 5–6 suggestions, read the list aloud. Compliment children on their excellent memories.

Practice/Apply—You Do

COLLABORATIVE Give small groups a sheet of paper. Ask them to continue listing events that have happened to date during the school year. Children can record their ideas in words, pictures, or both.

INDEPENDENT Have children make their own list of events that happened to them, either at school or elsewhere. Tell them that they can record their events by using words, pictures, or a combination. Ask them to share their work with a classmate.

Conference/Evaluate

Circulate, and ask children about their lists. Note which children are writing words and which are not.

Drafting a Class Story

Objective: Write a story as a class.

Guiding Question: How can we turn some events that happened to us into a class story?

Teach/Model—I Do

Have children turn to handbook p. 20. Review the definition, list, and model. Then review the list of activities you compiled with children during the *We Do* section of the previous minilesson. Choose one event from the list. On the board, write an opening sentence, such as *One day we played soccer outside.* Then ask children to remember some of the things that happened that day. Write 3–4 of their ideas on the board, using initial capitals and final periods. Read the completed story aloud with children. Congratulate them on writing a class story about real events.

Guided Practice—We Do

 Have children turn to the frame on handbook p. 21. Tell them to imagine that they took a class trip to a market. Guide them to think about what they know about markets and what might happen there. Then work with children to write sentences about the trip. Have children write in their books as you write on the board.

Practice/Apply—You Do

 INDEPENDENT Read the directions with children. Ask them to add one or more sentences to the story about visiting the market. Have children share their work.

Conference/Evaluate

Move through the room, checking to see if children are using initial capital letters and final periods. Make sure their sentences tell about the market. Evaluate using the rubric on p. 96.

Class Story

A **class story** is a story we write as a class. It can tell about something that really happened. It can describe people and things.

Parts of a Class Story

- Events that are told in complete sentences
- Sentences that include interesting details

The Hike

Our class went for a hike. We climbed up a tall hill. We could see a big lake. The hike made us tired. But we had fun anyway.

Name _____

Follow your teacher's directions.

 Our class went to the market.

_____
_____

We _____
_____
_____
_____

_____
We also _____
_____
_____
_____

_____
We _____
_____
_____
_____

 Think of a detail you could add to the class story. Write a sentence about it.

✓ Corrective Feedback

IF . . . children are writing about events that are unrelated to the story topic,

THEN . . . ask them to use this sentence frame to describe important events: *When we were at the market/playing soccer/eating lunch outside, _____.* For instance, children might say *When we were playing soccer, Jamie scored a goal* or *When we were eating lunch outside, Tavon saw some ants.*

Focus Trait: Elaboration

On the board, write the sentence *We saw some _____ grapes at the market.* Read it aloud with children. Tell them that a sentence like this one helps the reader understand what happened at the market, but add that children can include more detail to make the sentence even better. Ask children to close their eyes and picture grapes that could be in a market. Then invite children to suggest adjectives that could be written in the blank. Guide them to think of color words, size words, and other words that could tell about grapes; examples might include *purple, tiny,* and *squishy.* Write each word in turn in the blank and read the resulting sentence with children. Talk with the class about how the choice of words can make the original sentence clearer and more interesting.

Grade 1 • **21**

Class Story

WRITING FORMS

Minilesson 9

Revising a Class Story

Objective: Revise a class story.

Guiding Question: How can I make a story better?

Teach/Model—I Do

Read aloud the definition, list, and model on handbook p. 22. Remind children that people work together when they write a class story. Then explain that even a good story can be made better by revising it, or making changes that will make it clearer and more interesting. Write the following on the board: *We played a game. It was fun.* Tell children it is the beginning of a class story. Read it aloud and shake your head. Explain that the story doesn't tell the reader very much. Make changes so the story now reads *We played a fun game last week. It was a lot like basketball.* Read this aloud and point out that it is clearer and more informative than the original.

Guided Practice—We Do

On the board, write a simple and not very informative description of something that the class did recently, such as *We heard a concert. We liked it.* Read this brief story aloud. Guide children to make changes to make the story clearer, such as by saying who performed the concert or what part was most interesting. Read the new story aloud and help children compare it to the original.

Practice/Apply—You Do

COLLABORATIVE Ask partners to work together to find another way to revise the class story you began in the *We Do* section of the lesson.

INDEPENDENT Read aloud the revision you made to the class story from the *I Do* section. Ask children to find a different way to revise the story.

Conference/Evaluate

Circulate, offering help with spelling as needed. Ask children to tell you why they made the revisions they did. Encourage children to share their ideas.

22 • Writing

Minilesson 10

Publishing a Class Story

Objective: Make a clean copy of a class story.

Guiding Question: What does it mean to publish a story?

Teach/Model—I Do

Have children turn to handbook p. 22. Review the definition and the list. Go over the model with children. Point out that there are no editing or revising marks on the text. Explain that this is called a clean copy or a published version of the class story; all the changes have already been made and the story has been recopied. Tell children that authors often start with a "messy copy" in which they are only interested in getting their ideas on paper; after that, they revise and edit their work and close by publishing their work as a clean copy.

Guided Practice—We Do

 Have children turn to the frame on handbook p. 23. Read aloud the opening sentence of the story and explain that this story tells about a time when a class went to the zoo. Invite children to use their own experiences with zoos to tell what might happen on that trip. Then have them settle on three events and determine their order. Guide children to describe what might have happened first when the class went to the zoo, such as *we saw a zebra* or *we watched the seals diving*; then write the sentence on the board and have children copy it. Repeat with second and third events.

Practice/Apply—You Do

 INDEPENDENT Read the directions with children. Have them add another sentence to the zoo story on a separate sheet of paper.

Conference/Evaluate

Remind children to write as neatly as possible, leaving spaces between words and using lower case letters. Evaluate using the rubric on p. 96.

Class Story

A **class story** is written together by the class and the teacher.

Parts of a Class Story

- Sentences that tell events in time order
- Words that describe
- An ending to the story

> Our class went to visit a farm. **First**, we saw five cows. **Next**, we got to feed the red hens. **Last**, we all went for a ride in a big wagon. We had a fun day at the farm.

Name _____

Follow your teacher's directions.

 1 Our class went to the zoo.

_____

First, _____

_____

_____ .

_____

Then _____

_____

_____

Later, _____

_____

_____ .

 2 Think of another event you could add to the class story. Write a sentence about it.

✔ Corrective Feedback

IF . . . children do not understand why revision is sometimes necessary,

THEN . . . ask guiding questions to help establish why revising writing can make it better. As an example, use the story *We played a game. It was fun.* Ask questions such as *Does the story tell you what kind of a game it was?*, *Does the story tell you if the game was an indoor game or an outdoor game?*, and *Does the story tell when we played the game?* Draw out that information like this is not included in the story and would be interesting to readers.

Focus Trait: Development

Brainstorming is an excellent way for children to come up with writing topics of all kinds, and it makes good sense for children to use this procedure in determining a topic for a class story. Brainstorming is not always easy for children, however. Children need to feel that they will be able to make any suggestion without worrying that someone else will dismiss the idea as "stupid" or "silly." Before brainstorming with the class in this lesson, be sure children understand that the process is simply about getting ideas, not evaluating them. In particular, when a child makes a suggestion, no one else should comment on it. Enforcing this rule will help make children feel comfortable offering their ideas in group settings.

Writing Handbook Minilessons

Sentences That Describe

Minilesson 11	Minilesson 12

Using Sensory Words

Drafting Sentences That Describe

Objective: List and use words that describe how things look, sound, feel, taste, and smell.

Guiding Question: What words tell what things are like?

Objective: Write sentences that describe an object or a place.

Guiding Question: How can I write a sentence that describes?

Teach/Model—I Do

Read aloud the definition and the list on handbook p. 24. Then read the model aloud. As you read, emphasize the describing words. Explain that words like *soft* and *green* are called sensory words; they let readers use their senses to know what objects look like, feel like, sound like, and so on. Then display a tennis ball or other common object. Explain that you are going to make a list of sensory words that describe the ball. Write words such as *round, fuzzy, bouncy*, and *yellow* on the board, saying the words as you write them. Repeat with another object.

Teach/Model—I Do

Have children turn to handbook p. 24. Review the definition, list, and model. Reread the model, asking children to raise their hands when they hear a word that describes. Then tell children that you went to a restaurant recently. Explain that you can use sensory words to describe the restaurant and what it looked like, smelled like, or sounded like. Write a few brief sentences on the board about a restaurant, such as *They had blue napkins, The soup was spicy and warm*, and *There was loud music.* Read the sentences and ask children to use their senses to imagine what the restaurant was like.

Guided Practice—We Do

Display another classroom object such as a marble or a bell. Have children look at the object closely. Then guide them to suggest sensory words that tell how the object looks. Repeat for how the object feels and sounds, or smells. Write the words on butcher paper and read the list with children.

Guided Practice—We Do

 Have children turn to the frame on handbook p. 25. Guide them to think about a big city. If you think most children have not visited a large city, show pictures of one. Then work together with children to complete the sentences with sensory words that describe a city. You may want to review the describing words you wrote with children in the previous minilesson. Have children write in their books as you write on the board.

Practice/Apply—You Do

COLLABORATIVE Give small groups 4-5 classroom objects. Have children play a guessing game. One child thinks of one of the objects and then uses the sentence frame *My object is _____* to describe it with an appropriate sensory word (such as *red, rough*, or *big*). Other children guess the object. Continue until everyone has had a turn.

INDEPENDENT Have children choose an object and make a list of 3–4 sensory words that describe it.

Practice/Apply—You Do

 INDEPENDENT Read the directions aloud. Have children use sensory words to write their own description of a place they like to visit.

Conference/Evaluate

Move through the room, checking that children are on task. Ask children if their words tell what the object feels, looks, or sounds like, or something else.

Conference/Evaluate

Remind children to use final periods and initial capitals in their sentences. Compliment children on their use of sensory words: *The word* tall *helps me know what buildings in the city look like!* Evaluate using the rubric on p. 96.

24 • Writing

Sentences That Describe

Sentences that describe work together to tell how something looks, sounds, smells, tastes, or feels. Describing words are called adjectives.

Parts of Sentences That Describe

- Details that tell how something looks, sounds, smells, tastes, or feels
- Sentences that tell about just one thing

The Woods

The leaves are soft and green.

The trees feel very bumpy.

I hear loud buzzing.

The air smells fresh.

24 • Grade 1

Name _____

Follow your teacher's directions.

 The buildings _____

The streets _____

The people _____

 Use your plan. Write sentences that describe. You can tell about a place you like to visit.

Sentences That Describe • 25

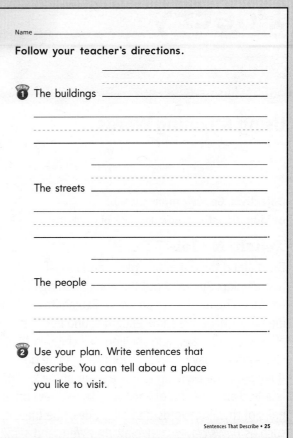

Corrective Feedback

IF . . . children have difficulty thinking of any descriptive words,

THEN . . . ask them to close their eyes and think about what the place they are describing looks like. Guide them to find words that tell about color, size, and so forth. Repeat with what the place sounds like. You can also provide children with sentence frames to help them find words. For example, if children are struggling to describe the streets of a city, tell them that the streets are not *quiet*, but _____, and guide them to supply *noisy* or *loud*.

Focus Trait: Evidence

Tell children that good ideas for writing can come from almost anywhere. Point out that when people go to different places, they often write about what the saw. Emphasize that much of the writing in this lesson is based on visits to different places. Add, however, that writers can get good ideas for writing about things they see even if they stay close to home. Ask children to generate a list of objects, people, or animals they can describe that are in or near their own homes. Start the list yourself if necessary with examples such as *the cereal I ate for breakfast*, *the store down the street*, or *the toy cars in my room*. Write suggestions on the board and read them with children; sum up by reminding them that ideas for writing can come from many different places and activities.

Grade 1 • **25**

Writing Handbook Minilessons | **283**

Writing Handbook Minilessons

Poetry

Minilesson 13	Minilesson 14

Using Rhyming Words

Objective: Generate rhyming words.

Guiding Question: How do I think of words that rhyme?

Teach/Model—I Do

Read aloud the definition, parts, and model on handbook p. 26. Point out the underlined rhyming words in the model, *fur* and *purr*. Explain that rhyming words have the same ending sound but not always the same ending spelling. Tell children that some poems have rhyming words and some don't. In this poem, the rhyming words appear at the end of line two and the end of line four. Name a few other pairs of rhyming words that might describe the cat, such as *paws/claws*, *gray/play*, *mew/few*, and *silky/milky*. Mention that the topic of the poem is a cat.

Guided Practice—We Do

With children, choose an animal topic such as a horse. Elicit and record words that could have something to do with a horse, such as *white* or *neigh*. Then work together to name rhyming words for some of the words on the board. For example, *white (right, quite, light)* and *neigh (hay, stay, weigh)*.

Practice/Apply—You Do

INDEPENDENT Have children choose another animal and write words that have something to do with the animal. Then have them rhyme some of the words.

Conference/Evaluate

Circulate and help children generate rhyming words. Remind them that rhyming words can have endings that are spelled differently, such as *might* and *bite* or *her* and *fur*.

Drafting Poetry

Objective: Write a poem.

Guiding Question: How do I write a poem?

Teach/Model—I Do

Review handbook p. 26 with children. Point out that the poem tells how the cat looks and sounds. Tell children that together you will write a poem about a turtle. Brainstorm words that describe a turtle: *small, four feet, claws, green, brown, hard shell, pointy tail.* On the board, write these lines of the poem: *The turtle has four short feet, And a shell that's very ____(hard). There's a small brown turtle, Creeping through the ____(yard).* Read the poem together and have children think of rhyming words to complete the lines. Invite volunteers to write the rhyming words on the board.

Guided Practice—We Do

 Have children turn to the frame on handbook p. 27. Tell them that, together, you are all going to write a poem about an animal. Help children choose the animal for the topic and then come up with interesting words about the animal as well as some rhyming word pairs. Then, together, write the lines of the poem. Have children write in their books as you write on the board. (Example: *I would like to see a rabbit, with its fuzzy little tail, I would like to feed that bunny, with carrots from a pail.*)

Practice/Apply—You Do

 INDEPENDENT Have children read the directions. Tell them to use their prewriting plan from Lesson 7 or to brainstorm new ideas, using Graphic Organizer 5.

Conference/Evaluate

During the writing process, circulate and give corrective feedback as needed while children work independently. Evaluate using the rubric on p. 96.

26 • Writing

Poetry

A **poem** is a group of words put together in a special way. A poem can be about a thing or a feeling.

Parts of a Poem
- Interesting words about the topic
- Some words that may rhyme

The Cat

I would like to see a cat
with black stripes in its <u>fur</u>.

I would like to pet the cat
to hear its low, soft <u>purr</u>.

Name _____

Follow your teacher's directions.

 1 I would like to see _____
_____
_____
_____
_____
_____
_____

I would like to _____
_____
_____
_____
_____
_____

 2 Use your plan. Write a poem. You can write about a favorite animal.

✓ Corrective Feedback

IF . . . children are having difficulty finding words about their animal,

THEN . . . guide their thinking with questions, such as *What size is the animal? What color is it? What noise does it make? How does its skin or fur feel?* If children started a graphic organizer, they can add descriptive words that answer these questions.

Focus Trait: Elaboration

Write these sentences on the board:

A whale is a big animal.

A mouse is a small animal.

Point out that the words *big* and *small* tell about the size of the animals, but they are not very interesting words. To make the sentences better, you can replace *big* and *small* with more interesting words. Work with children to make lists of words for *big* and *small*.

Examples:

<u>big</u>	<u>small</u>
huge	tiny
enormous	teeny
gigantic	miniature

Then read the sentences, replacing *big* and *small* with the words from the lists.

Grade 1 • **27**

Thank-You Note

Minilesson 15

Using Formal and Informal Language

Objective: Choose the right kind of language for a reader.

Guiding Question: What kind of language should I use for different readers?

Teach/Model—I Do

Read aloud the definition and list on handbook p. 28. On the board, write in letter form and read aloud the following: *Dear Mr. Ruiz, Thank you so much for visiting our class. We learned a lot about planning and writing books. If you have time, please come back again and tell us more. Yours truly, Ms. Ford's Class.* Explain to children that Mr. Ruiz is someone the class has met but does not know well. The tone of the note is very polite but not too friendly. Mention that the words used in a note should match the person who will be getting it.

Guided Practice—We Do

Work with children to write the body of a note thanking another class for inviting them to a class play. Guide children to understand that, this time, words such as *very cool*, *super*, and other less formal language would be fine since the children know each other better than they know someone like Mr. Ruiz.

Practice/Apply—You Do

COLLABORATIVE Instruct small groups to write the body of a note thanking their principal for throwing a pizza party. Remind them to think about whether the words they choose would be more like those used for the note to Mr. Ruiz or those used in the *We Do*.

INDEPENDENT Have children write the body of a note thanking a friend for a gift. Remind them to use words that suit the person who will receive the note.

Conference/Evaluate

Circulate and help children come up with ideas for the body of their note. Encourage them to think of suitable words and tone as they write.

28 • Writing

Minilesson 16

Drafting a Thank-You Note

Objective: Write a thank-you note.

Guiding Question: How do I tell a story about myself?

Teach/Model—I Do

Have children turn to handbook p. 28. Review the definition and list. Point out the parts of the thank-you note in the model. Mention that *Love* is a closing used for family members or close friends. Write the following on the board or on chart paper. Call on volunteers to complete the missing parts.

Dear Uncle _____,

         Thank you _____.

It is _____.

I really like _____.

         _____,

Guided Practice—We Do

 Have children turn to the frame on handbook p. 29. Guide them to choose the person who will receive the note and what the person will be thanked for. Work together to complete the note, using a suitable tone and words. Have children write in their books as you write on the board.

Practice/Apply—You Do

 INDEPENDENT Have children read the directions. Tell them to use their prewriting plan from Lesson 8 or to brainstorm new ideas, using Graphic Organizer 6.

Conference/Evaluate

During the writing process, circulate and offer encouragement and help as needed. Evaluate using the rubric on p. 96.

Thank-You Note

A **thank-you note** thanks someone for a favor or a gift.

Parts of a Thank-You Note

- A date, greeting, closing, and your name
- A sentence that tells what you are thanking someone for
- Details that tell your feelings

March 1, 2013

Dear Grandpa,

    Thank you for the ant farm. It is a great gift! I like to see the ants work. They are so busy.

          Love,

           Eli

28 • Grade 1

Name _____

Follow your teacher's directions.

 1

_____ _____

_____ _____

Dear _____,

_____

Thank you for _____

_____

I like _____

_____

_____

          Your friend,

          _____

          _____

 2 Write a thank-you note to a friend or family member.

Thank-You Note • 29

✓ Corrective Feedback

IF . . . children leave out a part of their thank-you notes,

THEN . . . have them return to the model and rename each part: date, greeting, body, closing, name. Remind children to be clear about what they are thanking someone for and to add details that tell their feelings.

✏ Writing Trait: Purpose

Explain to children that the tone of their note and the words they choose should suit their audience (the person who will be getting the note). For example, they probably wouldn't call a book author who visited the school *super cool*; nor would they sign their note *Love*.

Write the following on the board. Choose a sentence with the word choice that best fits each person.

the mayor, grandparent, good friend

I enjoyed learning about our town. (mayor)
That baseball game was way cool! (good friend)
I miss you. Please visit us soon. (grandparent)

Grade 1 • 29

Writing Handbook Minilessons

Description: Prewriting

WRITING FORMS

Minilesson 17

Listing Topics and Choosing One

Objective: Make a list of possible writing topics and choose a subject from among them.

Guiding Question: What topics can I write about?

Teach/Model—I Do

Read aloud the definition, list, and model on handbook p. 30. Explain that when people write a description, they often write about a topic they like. Tell children that you are going to choose a good writing topic by making a list of possible topics first. Say *I could write about our first day of school.* Write *first day* on the board. Then say *I'm interested in dinosaurs too,* and write *dinosaurs.* Keep going until you have a list of 5–6 topics. Read them aloud; then circle one. Tell children that this topic is most interesting to you, so this is the topic you will write about.

Guided Practice—We Do

Ask children what topics they might like to write about. Guide them to make a list of possible writing topics. Record key words and phrases on a large sheet of paper. Ask children what made them think of the topics they named; accept all responses. After 6–8 suggestions, read the list aloud with children. Congratulate children on listing great topics.

Practice/Apply—You Do

COLLABORATIVE Have children work in pairs. Ask partners to think of 4–5 animals they would like to write about and have them make a list of these animals. Tell them to circle the animal they would most like to write about. Then have pairs share their work.

INDEPENDENT Have children use words or pictures to list 2–4 good writing topics. Have them circle the one they like best and share their work.

Conference/Evaluate

Circulate, asking children what makes each topic interesting to them and why they chose the one they did.

30 • Writing

Minilesson 18

Brainstorming Sensory Words

Objective: List sensory words.

Guiding Question: What words tell about the way things look, feel, and sound?

Teach/Model—I Do

Have children turn to handbook p. 30. Reread the definition and the list. Then review the model with children. Explain that a web can help authors organize their thoughts before beginning to write. Help children identify sensory words in the model, such as *short* and *floppy.* Then point out that many words describe how things feel, smell, look, and sound. Make a brief list of words that describe how things feel; possible words include *hot, rough, soft, squishy, cold,* and *curved.* Read the list with children; if possible, provide real-life examples for each, such as an apple for *smooth.*

Guided Practice—We Do

 Have children turn to Activity 1 on handbook p. 31. Choose a common animal such as a horse. Ask children to write the word *horse* in the box marked *My Topic.* Then guide children to generate words that could describe a horse, focusing on sensory words like *big* or *fast.* Ask children to write 4 of these words in the smaller boxes around the *My Topic* box.

Practice/Apply—You Do

 INDEPENDENT Have children make a diagram like the one in the handbook p. 31. Ask them to write the name of a favorite animal in the middle. In each of the surrounding four boxes, children should write an adjective that tells about the animal.

Conference/Evaluate

Check children's ability to generate describing words. Evaluate using the rubric on p. 96.

Description: Prewriting

A **description** can tell how something looks. The writer helps the reader picture a thing in his or her mind.

✏ Parts of a Description

- The topic sentence tells what the description is about.
- Detail sentences use adjectives that tell size, shape, color, or number.

Tail:		Fur:
short		soft and black

My Topic:
Sam the rabbit

Eyes:		Ears:
brown		floppy

Name _____

Follow your teacher's directions.

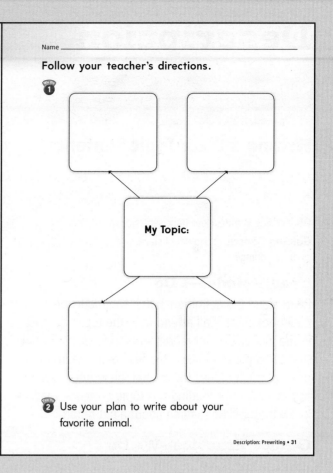

My Topic:

 Use your plan to write about your favorite animal.

✔ Corrective Feedback

IF . . . children can write just one or two descriptive words about their animals,

THEN . . . ask them to focus on describing specific features of the animal, such as *what its fur feels like* or *how big its head is.* Write key words such as *fur* or *head* in the boxes as reminders.

Focus Trait: Evidence

Tell children that books are often a good source of ideas for writing. Choose a book that gives information about different kinds of animals. Then go through the pages slowly, noting interesting details aloud. For example, you might say *I like zebras because they have stripes. I think giraffes look funny with their long necks. It might be fun to write about rabbits because they are so cute!* After 4–5 examples like this, choose an animal described in the book and explain your choice, such as by saying *I think I'll write about seals. I love the way they swim, and this picture makes me think about how soft their fur is and how shiny their noses can be!* Give children an opportunity to try this process on their own to find animals to write about.

Grade 1 • **31**

Writing Handbook Minilessons

Description

Minilesson 19

Writing a Clear Topic Sentence

Objective: Write a clear topic sentence to inform.

Guiding Question: How do I start my description with a clear beginning?

Teach/Model—I Do

Read aloud the definition, parts, and model on handbook p. 32. Call attention to the topic sentence in the model: *My pet rabbit is named Sam.* Point out that the topic sentence is the first sentence in the description. It names the animal the writer is going to describe. After reading this topic sentence, readers know they will be reading about a pet rabbit.

Guided Practice—We Do

Have children name animals they know about—pets, farm animals, and wild animals. Record children's suggestions on the board. Continue until you have a list of at least eight animals. Work together to generate topic sentences about a few of the animals on the list. Write the topic sentences on the board, such as *An owl lives in a tree by my house* or *My neighbor has a horse.*

Practice/Apply—You Do

COLLABORATIVE Have partners choose an animal from the list and work together to write a topic sentence about the animal.

INDEPENDENT Instruct children to choose a different animal from the list or to think of another animal. Then ask them to write a topic sentence that tells about the animal they chose.

Conference/Evaluate

Circulate and support children by asking them to state their topic sentence orally before writing it. Tell children to write a complete sentence. Remind them that a complete sentence has a naming part and a telling part.

32 • Writing

Minilesson 20

Drafting a Description

Objective: Write a description, using relevant details.

Guiding Question: How do I write a good description?

Teach/Model—I Do

Have children review the material on handbook p. 32. Point out that the boldfaced words name details about the pet rabbit. Then tell children *Let's write a description of a squirrel together.* On the board or on chart paper, write *I see a squirrel.* Say *This is the topic sentence.* Read the topic sentence with children. Then write a few sentences with blanks, giving children the opportunity to provide details about the squirrel. For example, *The squirrel has _____. It looks _____.* Work with children to create a closing statement. Then mention that a drawing might have helped make the description clearer.

Guided Practice—We Do

 Have children turn to the frame on handbook p. 33. Work together to choose and then write a description of a favorite animal. Have children write in their books as you write on the board. Encourage them to draw the animal.

Practice/Apply—You Do

 INDEPENDENT Have children read the directions. Tell them to use their prewriting plan from Lesson 10 or brainstorm new ideas for writing a description, using Graphic Organizer 3.

Conference/Evaluate

During the writing process, give corrective feedback as needed while children work collaboratively and independently. Evaluate using the rubric on p. 96.

Description: Drafting/Revising

A **description** is writing that tells how something looks, sounds, tastes, smells, and feels.

Parts of a Description

- A topic sentence tells what the description is about.
- Descriptive words and other details tell more about the topic.

> My pet rabbit is named Sam. Sam has **soft**, **black** fur. His eyes are **brown**. His ears are **floppy**. He has a short tail. Sam is a **nice**, **quiet** pet.

32 • Grade 1

Name _____

Follow your teacher's directions.

1 My favorite animal is

_____
- .

_____
It looks _____
_____
- .
_____
- .
_____
It is _____
_____
- .
It has _____
_____
- .
_____
- .

2 Use your plan to write a description. If you like, write about a pet you have or would like to have.

Description: Drafting/Revising • 33

✔ Corrective Feedback

IF . . . children are including details that only describe how the animal looks,

THEN . . . remind them that a description can also include details that tell how the animal sounds, feels, and smells. If children wish, they can go back to their writing and add sound words such as *noisy*, *barking*, and *roaring*; feeling words such as *soft*, *rough*, and *smooth*; and smell words such as *clean*, *sour*, and *stale*.

Focus Trait: Organization

Explain that there is more than one way to organize a paragraph, but that it is usually a good idea to put the topic sentence first. That way, readers will know the topic right away.

Write the following sentence on the board:

She has long black ears. She likes to cuddle. I have a dog named Marlee. She likes to run a lot. She is three colors: black, brown, and white.

Have children rewrite the sentences, placing the topic sentence first: *I have a dog named Marlee.*

Grade 1 • **33**

Writing Handbook Minilessons

Sentences That Inform

Minilesson 21

Using Words That Tell *How, When*, and *Where*

Objective: Use adverbs in sentences.

Guiding Question: How do I use adverbs to make my sentences interesting?

Teach/Model—I Do

Read aloud handbook p. 34. Point out words that show how things happen, such as *slowly, quietly,* and *quickly.* Explain that many words tell how, when, and where things happen and that some of these words end in *-ly.* Mention that writers use these kinds of words to make their writing more interesting. Share a brief story about an interesting animal you have seen, using words that tell how, when and where, such as *silently, yesterday, inside.*

Guided Practice—We Do

Ask children to think about things animals do, such as *play, eat, run, chew, climb, hide* and write them on the board. Guide children to come up with words that tell how, when, and where the action might be happen, such as *a lion roars loudly, the mouse scampers inside.* Together, use the phrases to complete the sentence frame: *A___.* (Example: *A bear sleeps soundly.*)

Practice/Apply—You Do

COLLABORATIVE Have small groups think of another animal and how, when, and where it might eat. Have children write three sentences to complete the frame: *A ____.* Remind them to include a word for *how, when,* or *where.* Have children share sentences with the class.

INDEPENDENT Tell children to select an animal. Then have them draw their animal doing an action and complete the sentence frame: *A___.*

Conference/Evaluate

Circulate and help children think of words to describe actions.

34 • Writing

Minilesson 22

Drafting Sentences That Inform

Objective: Write sentences that inform.

Guiding Question: How do I write sentences that tell facts?

Teach/Model—I Do

Have children turn to handbook p. 34. Review the definition, Parts of Sentences That Inform, and model. Say, *I'd like to write about sheep. You can help me write sentences that tell facts about sheep.* On the board, write *A sheep _____.* Ask *What is a sheep? Where does a sheep live?* to guide suggestions for completing the sentence. Then ask *What can a sheep do? How does a sheep do that?* Write ideas on the board or on chart paper. Then write *It can _____. It _____.* Elicit suggestions to complete the sentences, making sure children understand that this kind of writing has facts and real information, not opinions.

Guided Practice—We Do

 Have children turn to the frame on handbook p. 35. Discuss horses with children and list what they know about them on the board. Together, use the information from the list to complete sentences for the frame. Have children write in their books as you write on the board.

Practice/Apply—You Do

 INDEPENDENT Have children read the directions. Tell them to use their prewriting plan from Lesson 11 or brainstorm new ideas, using Graphic Organizer 5.

Conference/Evaluate

During the writing process, circulate and offer encouragement and help as needed. Evaluate using the rubric on p. 96.

Sentences That Inform

Sentences that inform work together to tell facts, or information that is true. Writers use sentences that inform to share what they know.

Parts of Sentences That Inform

- A topic sentence that tells what all the sentences are about
- Detail sentences that tell facts, not opinions
- Some details that describe how something happens

Cows

Cows are big animals on farms.

They walk very slowly.

Cows lie quietly in the grass.

They flick their tails quickly to push away flies.

Name _____

Follow your teacher's directions.

 1 A horse _____

_____

It can _____

_____

It _____

_____

2 Use your plan. Write sentences that inform. You can write about the animal you chose.

Corrective Feedback

IF . . . children are not using adverbs when writing,

THEN . . . have them complete a few actions in a certain way, using an adverb to guide *how*. For example, ask children to smile *widely*, dance *wildly*, stretch *slowly*, and yawn *loudly*. Write the verbs and adverbs on the board and brainstorm a list of actions animals do. Then add adverbs to describe *how* they could do each action. Instruct children to use adverbs from the list in their sentences that inform.

Focus Trait: Evidence

On the board, write and read aloud: *The man is a farmer.*

Tell children that they can make their sentences more informative and interesting to read by using specific nouns. Write and read aloud: *Mr. Todd is a farmer.*

Point to the proper noun, *Mr. Todd.* Remind children that specific names, animals, places, things, and titles are proper nouns that must be capitalized. Tell children that the titles *Mr., Mrs.,* and *Dr.* always

have a period after them. Then write the following sentences and read together:

The dog lives far away in the city.

I have a blue car.

She gave me a little toy.

Replace each underlined common noun with a proper noun to make sentences more interesting and precise.

Grade 1 • **35**

Instructions

WRITING FORMS

Minilesson 23

Writing Step-by-Step Instructions

Objective: Include steps for instructions.

Guiding Question: How do I write a list of steps?

Teach/Model—I Do

Read aloud the definition and Parts of Instructions on handbook p. 36. Explain that you are going to tell children how to make a drum. Write in list form and read aloud the following: *1. Get an empty can. 2. Lay paper over the top. 3. Put a rubber band around the can and the paper. 4. Get two sticks and play.* Discuss with children what would happen if one of the steps, such as step 2, was missing. (*There would be no top for the drum.*) Or, what if steps 2 and 1 were reversed? (*There would be no can to lay the paper over.*) Explain that unless the steps are complete and in the correct order, the instructions probably won't work.

Guided Practice—We Do

Show children a paper plate, a length of string, a hole punch, and bird seed. Guide them to make a bird feeder. Help children suggest the steps; record steps in a list on the board. For example, *1. Punch four holes in the plate. 2. Push string through opposite holes. 3. Tie the string together so the plate hangs down. 4. Put birdseed on the feeder and hang it on a branch.*

Practice/Apply—You Do

COLLABORATIVE Have small groups write steps for making an alphabet book of things found in nature. Have them list possible materials and write the steps. For example, *Construction paper, hole punch, string, crayons or collage materials. 1. Punch holes in paper. 2. Sew the pages together with string. 3. Write a title. 4. Draw and write something from nature for each letter,* such as ant *for* A *and* bug *for* B.

Conference/Evaluate

Circulate and help groups come up with reasonable steps for their books. Make sure all materials are included.

36 • Writing

Minilesson 24

Drafting Instructions

Objective: Write a complete set of instructions.

Guiding Question: How do I write a paragraph of instructions?

Teach/Model—I Do

Have children read the model on handbook p. 36. Mention that in the previous lesson, you gave them the steps for making a drum. Explain that the model shows the same information in paragraph form. Compare the steps from Minilesson 23 to the information in the model to see if the instructions are complete. Point out the boldfaced words that help tell the order of the steps without using numbers.

Guided Practice—We Do

 Have children turn to the frame on handbook p. 37. Guide them to choose a project for the instructions, such as the bird feeder from the *We Do* in Minilesson 23. Work with children to suggest all the necessary information for the instructions. Encourage children to use time-order words in their paragraphs. Have children write in their books as you write on the board.

Practice/Apply—You Do

 INDEPENDENT Have children read the directions. Tell them to use their prewriting plan from Lesson 12 or to brainstorm new ideas, using Graphic Organizer 6.

Conference/Evaluate

As children write, circulate and offer encouragement and help as needed. Evaluate using the rubric on p. 96.

Instructions

Instructions tell how to do or make something.

Parts of Instructions

- Things you need
- Steps to follow in order
- Time-order words such as <u>first</u> and <u>next</u>

Making a Drum

Here is how to make a drum. **First**, get an empty can. **Next**, lay paper over the top. **Then** put a rubber band around the can and the paper. **Last**, get two sticks and play.

36 • Grade 1

Name _____

Follow your teacher's directions.

_____

 1 Here is how to _____ .

_____

First, _____

_____

_____

_____

Next, _____

_____

_____

_____

Last, _____

_____

_____

2 Write instructions. Tell a friend how to make an art project.

Instructions • 37

Corrective Feedback

IF . . . children are not including all the important information in their instructions,

THEN . . . have them act out making the project. As they do each step, have them check whether that piece of information is included in their set of instructions.

Focus Trait: Elaboration

Explain to children that adding time-order words helps groups of sentences that give directions or instructions make sense. First, list with children some other examples of time-order words or phrases, such as earlier, a while ago, at first, and so on. Then write the following sentences on the board. Have children order them and use time-order words so they make sense.

We found paper and string in the desk drawer. (First...)

We cut the paper to a kite shape. (Next...)

Dad and I wanted to make a kite. (topic sentence)

The kite flew very high. (At last...)

We made a tail for the kite. (Then...)

We put string on it. (Later that day...)

Grade 1 • 37

Sentences That Inform

Minilesson 25

Writing a Main Idea and Details

Objective: Write a topic sentence.

Guiding Question: What is a main idea and how do I write about it?

Teach/Model—I Do

Read aloud the definition, list, and model on handbook p. 38. Read the topic sentence in the model *Trees are big plants.* Explain that the sentence is the main idea, or what the other sentences are about. Read each detail sentence in the model. Point out that each sentence tells a detail about the main idea. Together, determine another detail that could be added to the paragraph to support the main idea, such as *Trees need sun to grow* or *Some trees lose their leaves before winter.*

Guided Practice—We Do

Ask children to name some interesting animals and record them on the board. Select one or two animals. Guide children to create a topic sentence and detail sentences about each animal. For example, *Whales are mammals. They live in the ocean. They need to breathe air. They have live young. They feed their young milk.*

Practice/Apply—You Do

COLLABORATIVE Have small groups choose an animal from the list and draw a picture of it. Then have children write a topic sentence and one detail sentence about the animal.

INDEPENDENT Have children choose a different animal. Then ask them to write the topic sentence: *This is a _____.* Have them write one detail about the animal.

Conference/Evaluate

Circulate and help children think of details about their animal. Remind them to think about where the animal lives, what it eats, how it looks, and so on.

Minilesson 26

Drafting Sentences That Inform

Objective: Write sentences to inform.

Guiding Question: How do I write topic and detail sentences that are facts?

Teach/Model—I Do

Have children turn to handbook p. 38. Review the definition, Parts of Sentences, and model. Remind children that facts tell things that are true, while opinions tell what someone thinks or feels about something. Point out that the model sentences are facts, not opinions. On the board or on chart paper, write a topic sentence about dogs, such as *Dogs are pets for many people. A dog can_____. Dogs _____.* Ask children to share facts about dogs to complete the sentences. Confirm that the sentences are facts and not opinions.

Guided Practice—We Do

 Have children turn to the frame on handbook p. 39. Guide them to share facts about ducks, such as what they eat, where they live, how they act, what they look like. Record the information on the board. Together, use the information from the board to complete sentences for the frame, such as *Ducks are birds. A duck can swim and dive. Ducks have feathers.* Have children write in their books as you write on the board.

Practice/Apply—You Do

 INDEPENDENT Read the directions to children. Have them use their plans from Lesson 13 or another plan they create, using Graphic Organizer 3.

Conference/Evaluate

During the writing process, circulate and offer encouragement and help as needed. Evaluate using the rubric on p. 96.

38 • Writing

WRITING FORMS

Sentences That Inform

Sentences that inform tell facts about the world. Facts are things that are true.

Parts of Sentences That Inform

- A topic sentence tells what all of the sentences are about.
- Detail sentences tell facts, not opinions.
- All of the sentences are about one main idea.

All About Trees

Trees are big plants.

Leaves grow on trees.

There are lots of trees in the forest.

Birds build their nests in trees.

Name _____

Follow your teacher's directions.

 1 Ducks are _____
_____
_____
_____.

A duck can _____
_____
_____.

Ducks _____
_____
_____.

 2 Use your plan. Write sentences that inform. You can write about a season you like.

✓ Corrective Feedback

IF . . . children are having difficulty writing facts instead of opinions,

THEN . . . share facts and opinions aloud. Have children tell whether each statement is a fact or opinion and explain their reasoning. Point out that facts tell what everyone believes to be true and can be proven. Opinions tell what the writer thinks and believes.

Focus Trait: Evidence

Remind children that it is important to write about one idea, but the idea cannot be too big.

Write several big topics on the board, such as *trees, school, cats.* Choose one and model writing a topic sentence, such as: *People need trees.*

Work with children to create other topic sentences about trees, such as:

There are different kinds of trees.

Animals live in trees.

Suggest details for each topic sentence. Then guide children to suggest topic sentences for *school* and *cats* using sentence frames:

Cats are ___.   *School ___.*

(Cats are pets; Cats are mammals; School is a place to learn; School is for everyone)

Grade 1 • **39**

Report: Prewriting

WRITING FORMS

Minilesson 27

Selecting a Topic

Objective: Choose a research topic.

Guiding Question: What topics can I write about?

Teach/Model—I Do

Read aloud the definition, list, and model on handbook p. 40. Explain that when people write reports, they choose a subject that they want to know more about. Say *I'm interested in birds. I like the way they fly. I'd like to learn more about birds.* Write *birds* on the board. Then say *I like cars and trucks, too, and I'd love to learn more about them.* Write *cars and trucks.* Generate a list of 5–7 topics in this way. Read the list aloud and put a star next to one. Tell children that this is the topic you most want to learn about right now, so you would choose this topic for your report.

Guided Practice—We Do

Remind children that doing research means learning about real things. Ask children what subjects they might like to research. Use their suggestions to generate a list of possible research topics with children. Record key words and phrases. After 6–8 suggestions, read the list aloud with children.

Practice/Apply—You Do

COLLABORATIVE Have partners list different topics they might like to research. Have them draw a star to show the topic they would most like to write about. Then have pairs share their work with other pairs.

INDEPENDENT Ask children to use words or pictures to list 3–4 good research topics. They should put a star next to the topic they like best; then have them share their work with a classmate.

Conference/Evaluate

Move through the room, asking children why they chose the topics they did and making sure they are listing real subjects. Encourage children to write their lists, but allow them to draw pictures as well.

40 • Writing

Minilesson 28

Planning a Report

Objective: Outline and take notes to prepare to write a report.

Guiding Question: How can I get ready to write a report?

Teach/Model—I Do

Have children turn to handbook p. 40. Reread the definition and the list. Then walk through the model with children. Point out that the model begins with a question that children can answer by doing research on the topic: in this case, what ants can do. Display a few books or magazines about ants; be sure children understand that they need informational texts rather than fiction when they do research. Stress that authors can use diagrams like this to take notes and organize their thoughts before writing.

Guided Practice—We Do

 Have children turn to handbook p. 41. Tell children that they will be doing some research as a class. Have them write the question *What can cats do?* in the top of the organizer. Then read aloud a brief section of a nonfiction book about cats. Guide children to identify things they learned from the book. Then work together to complete the organizer based with a few facts about cats. Have children write in their books as you write on the board.

Practice/Apply—You Do

 INDEPENDENT Help children make an organizer like the one on handbook p. 41. Ask them to write a question about an animal they would like to learn about. Give children access to books, magazines, and websites about animals for help in gathering information. Have them write facts about their animals in the fact boxes in the organizer.

Conference/Evaluate

Help children find appropriate information. Evaluate using the rubric on p. 96.

Report: Prewriting

A **report** tells facts about a topic. When people write reports, they can find the facts they need in books.

Parts of a Report

- The topic sentence tells what the report is about.
- Detail sentences give facts about the topic.
- Writers do research to find facts about a topic.

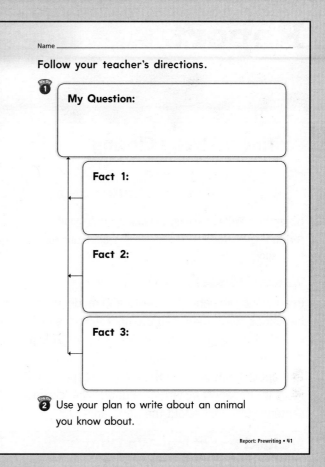

My Question: What can ants do?

Fact 1: very busy

Fact 2: build large nests

Fact 3: carry food in teams

40 • Grade 1

Name _____

Follow your teacher's directions.

 1

My Question:

Fact 1:

Fact 2:

Fact 3:

2 Use your plan to write about an animal you know about.

Report: Prewriting • 41

✓ Corrective Feedback

IF . . . children write opinions in the fact boxes (such as *I like alligators* or *Horses are fun to ride*),

THEN . . . review the difference between a fact (which everyone would agree is true) and an opinion (which not everyone would agree is true). Ask children to determine whether the following statements about ants are facts or opinions: *Ants are small; ants have six legs; ants are ugly; ants are brave.* Draw out that the first two are facts and the second two are opinions, and discuss the differences with children.

Focus Trait: Evidence

Tell children that when they write a report, they should start with an idea of what kind of topic they would like to write about, such as animals, sports, vehicles, and so on. Caution children, though, that not all topics are equally easy to write about. Explain, for example, that it is probably going to be simpler to find information about common birds such as eagles and ducks than about birds that are not as common.

Likewise, the topic *trucks* is going to be simpler than a topic about a certain model of truck. Point out that if the topic a child chooses for a report proves too hard to find information about, they should switch to something similar but easier to learn about.

Grade 1 • **41**

Writing Handbook Minilessons

Report

Minilesson 29

Writing a Strong Closing

Objective: Write a clear ending to support the topic.

Guiding Question: How do I write a good closing sentence for a report?

Teach/Model—I Do

Read aloud the definition, parts, and model on handbook p. 42. Then read the final sentence in the model: *Ants work like this all over the world!* Explain that this is a closing sentence, or the last sentence, in the report. Point out that the writer wrapped up the ideas in the report by writing a good, clear closing sentence that tells about the topic, ants.

Guided Practice—We Do

Ask children to name some animals. Write their suggestions on the board. Then choose one animal and have children tell a few facts they know about it. For example, for a giraffe, the facts might include *It has a long neck*, *It has fur with brown patches*, and *It eats leaves.* Write the facts on the board. Then talk about how to write a closing sentence for a report on a giraffe. Explain that the closing sentence should wrap up the facts about the giraffe. Write this sentence as one example: *A giraffe is interesting in many ways!* Invite children to give other closing sentences.

Practice/Apply—You Do

COLLABORATIVE Have small groups choose another animal from the list. Have them talk about facts they know about the animal. Then ask them to write a closing sentence for a report about the animal.

INDEPENDENT Instruct children to choose another animal from the list or think of a new animal. After they think of facts about the animal, have them write a closing sentence for a report about the animal.

Conference/Evaluate

Circulate and work with children as they write closing sentences. Be sure they relate to the topic.

42 • Writing

Minilesson 30

Drafting a Report

Objective: Write a report.

Guiding Question: How do I write a report with facts?

Teach/Model—I Do

Have children turn to handbook p. 42. Review the definition, Parts of a Report, and model. Point out the topic sentence and the way the detail sentences begin. Tell children *Let's write a report about a pelican together.* Before writing, display a picture of a pelican. Then on the board or on chart paper, write this topic sentence *A pelican is a big bird.* Write these sentence frames *One thing a pelican has is _____. Another thing a pelican has is _____.* Have children name facts to complete the sentences. Write their ideas, asking children to come up and write words they know. Discuss ideas for a good closing sentence, and write it on the chart paper. For example, *Pelicans are very unusual birds!*

Guided Practice—We Do

 Have children turn to the frame on handbook p. 43. Work with children to write a report in which they choose and write facts about another animal. Have children write in their books as you write on the board. Then have them draw the animal to show its qualities.

Practice/Apply—You Do

 INDEPENDENT Have children read the directions. Tell them to use their prewriting plan from Lesson 15 or brainstorm new ideas, using Graphic Organizer 3.

Conference/Evaluate

During the writing process, circulate and give corrective feedback as needed while children work independently. Evaluate using the rubric on p. 96.

Report: Drafting/Revising

A **report** gives facts about a topic. You write the facts in your own words.

Parts of a Report

- A topic sentence tells what the report is about.
- Detail sentences tell the facts.
- A closing ties ideas together.

Ants

Ants are busy little animals. One thing ants do is build large nests. Another thing they do is carry food in teams. Ants work like this all over the world!

42 • Grade 1

Name _____

Follow your teacher's directions.

 _____
_____ are animals

that _____
_____.

_____
One thing _____
_____
_____

_____
Another thing _____
_____
_____

 Use your plan. Write a report. Tell about an animal you know about.

Report: Drafting/Revising • 43

Corrective Feedback

IF . . . children do not include a topic sentence in their report,

THEN . . . remind them that a report is more than just a list of facts. Explain that a good report starts with a topic sentence so that the reader knows what the report will be about. Provide some sentence frames, such as _____ *are interesting animals* or _____ *do special things.* Then work with children to write a topic sentence for their report.

Focus Trait: Purpose

Remind children that a report gives facts and information about a topic. Personal opinions and opinion words such as *I think* or *I like* usually don't belong in report. Write the following on the board:

I think pandas are very interesting.

Pandas may look like bears, but they are not.

Pandas are the cutest animals.

They have black and white patches.

Pandas spend a lot of time in trees.

Help children identify sentences that don't belong in a report and explain why.

Grade 1 • **43**

Sentences About Yourself

Minilesson 31	Minilesson 32

Writing a Complete Idea

Objective: Write sentences about one topic that use *I* or *me*.

Guiding Question: How do write a complete idea about myself?

Teach/Model—I Do

Read aloud the definition, list, and model on handbook p. 44. Point out the words *I* and *me*. Explain that the story is about a person. It is a true story about the author. Tell children that, when they write about themselves, they are the authors, so they will use the words *I* and *me*. Point out that the sentences on p. 44 are about one main idea. Suggest some details the author might have added to support the main idea, such as *I sat in the sun until I warmed up* or *Next time, I won't be the first to jump into the lake!*

Guided Practice—We Do

Ask children to name places or events the class has attended together, such as visiting another classroom, going to a play, or exploring outdoors. Write the places on the board. Guide children to share words and phrases that describe what each place was like and what they did there, such as *exciting to see the birds.* Record the words and phrases.

Practice/Apply—You Do

COLLABORATIVE Have partners choose one place from the list. Ask them to work together to write a complete idea about one place.

INDEPENDENT Have children think of a place they have been, using the list or an idea of their own. Have them write a sentence that shows a complete idea.

Conference/Evaluate

Circulate as children work, reminding them to use *I* and *me* in their sentence.

Punctuating Sentences

Objective: Punctuate sentences correctly.

Guiding Question: How do I use punctuation to show a complete idea?

Teach/Model—I Do

Have children turn to handbook p. 44. Review the material. Discuss the punctuation in the model. Write the question on the board, *How was my swim?* Point out that a question mark ends an asking sentence. On the board or on chart paper, write several sentences about an event the class has experienced together, leaving out the punctuation, such as *I went to the nature center It was amazing to see the insects up close I want to visit there again.* Have children identify the sentences and add punctuation to them.

Guided Practice—We Do

 Have children turn to the frame on handbook p. 45. Together, choose an event the entire class has attended and discuss ideas for sentences about it. Guide children to write complete sentences about the event, making sure there are capitals at the beginning and correct punctuation at the end. Have children write in their books as you write on the board.

Practice/Apply—You Do

 INDEPENDENT Read the directions with children. Have them use their plans from Lesson 16 or another plan they created, using Graphic Organizer 3.

Conference/Evaluate

During the writing process, circulate and offer encouragement and help as needed. Evaluate using the rubric on p. 96.

44 • Writing

Sentences About Yourself

A **sentence about yourself** tells
a true story about you. It uses the words
I or me.

Parts of a Sentence About Yourself

- A topic sentence tells the main idea.
- Detail sentences tell what happened.
- Some details tell who or what.

At the Lake

I went swimming at the lake last week.

The water was freezing cold!

Mom wrapped me in a warm towel when I got out.

Name _____

Follow your teacher's directions.

_____

 1 I went _____

_____

_____

_____

_____

It was _____

_____

_____

_____

I _____

_____

_____

 2 Use your plan. Write sentences about yourself. If you like, write about nature.

✓ Corrective Feedback

IF . . . children are having trouble writing about one topic,

THEN . . . have them brainstorm a list of places they have visited, such as a zoo, museum, beach, or circus. Have them fold a piece of paper into four squares and write the sentence *I went to the ___.* in a top box. Encourage children to write a sentence in each box about three different things they saw at the place, such as *zebra, lion, penguin* for *zoo.* Then have them put the sentences together to create a story about a single topic.

✎ Focus Trait: Evidence

Remind children that the details in their writing are all ideas that should be about their topic. On the board write:

We went to the beach. There were lots of shells. My dog is brown. I built a sand castle.

Point out the detail that does not fit. Replace the sentence with one that fits the topic, *the beach.* Write:

We went to the beach. There were lots of shells. I swam in the water. I built a sand castle.

Encourage children to ask themselves these questions as they write:

Is every sentence about the main idea?

Are there any sentences that do not fit the topic?

Grade 1 • **45**

Sentences About Yourself

Minilesson 33

Drafting Sentences

Objective: Write sentences that show the order of events.

Guiding Question: How do I write sentences that tell the order things happened?

Teach/Model—I Do

Have children turn to handbook p. 46 and read it aloud. Point out the time-order words *yesterday*, *first*, and *after that* in the model. On the board or chart paper, brainstorm other words or phrases that tell order, such as *then*, *next*, *later*, *soon*, etc. Work with children to draft sentences about going fishing, using time-order words, such as: *Last week, my family went fishing. First, we put worms on the hooks. Later, I felt a tug.* Write the sentences on the board and read them together.

Guided Practice—We Do

 Have children turn to the frame on handbook p. 47. Together, brainstorm places children have gone with their families and record them on the board, such as *zoo*, *museum*, *beach*, *lake*. Have children choose one place as the topic for the frame. Guide them to write sentences about the place they chose, paying attention to the time-order clues provided. Remind children to use capitals and end punctuation. Have children write in their books as you write on the board.

Practice/Apply—You Do

 INDEPENDENT Read the directions to children. Have them use their plans from Lesson 17 or another plan they create, using Graphic Organizer 3.

Conference/Evaluate

During the writing process, circulate and offer encouragement and help as needed. Evaluate using the rubric on p. 96.

Minilesson 34

Revising Sentences

Objective: Revise sentences to tell when and where.

Guiding Question: How do I revise sentences to tell when and where things happened?

Teach/Model—I Do

Read aloud the definition, list, and model on handbook p. 46. Point out *I* and *we* in the model. Explain that good writers add details that tell where and when events happen. Point out the word *Yesterday* that tells when and the words *house* and *park* that tell where. Suggest a revision for the second sentence that tells where, such as *First, we put on a puppet show in the living room.*

Guided Practice—We Do

Write several sentences on the board about the first day of school, such as *Our First Day of School: First, we came in. We played. Then, we learned.* Guide children to revise sentences by adding details that tell when and where, such as *First, we came into the classroom and sat on the rug. After lunch, we played games in the gym. Then, we learned about classroom rules.* Write the revised sentences on the board next to the original sentences. Have children compare the two.

Practice/Apply—You Do

COLLABORATIVE Have partners choose one of the original sentences from the board and revise it differently. Ask them to collaborate and add details that tell when and where.

INDEPENDENT Have individuals write a sentence about the first day of school. Remind them to include a detail about when or where.

Conference/Evaluate

Circulate and offer support as children work. Encourage them to add details that tell times and places events happened.

Sentences About Yourself

A **sentence about yourself** tells about something real that happened to you. It has the words I, <u>me</u>, or <u>we</u>.

✏ Parts of a Sentence About Yourself

- A topic sentence tells what all the sentences will be about.
- Detail sentences tell what happened and in what order.
- Details may tell where or when things happened.

My Cousins

Yesterday **I** went to my cousin's house.

First, **we** put on a puppet show.

After that, **we** played football in the park.

46 • Grade 1

Name _____

Follow your teacher's directions.

 1 My family _____
_____
_____
_____.

_____
First, we _____
_____
_____.

_____
Later, _____
_____
_____.

 2 Use your plan. Write sentences about yourself. You can write about something you like to do.

Sentences About Yourself • 47

✓ Corrective Feedback

IF . . . children are not adding details that tell when and where,

THEN . . . list words and phrases on a chart telling when and where, such as *park, basement, zoo, class, at the game, on the field, last night, yesterday, this morning, today, earlier*, etc. Post the chart where children can see it when writing. Remind them to use the chart to add details to their sentences that tell when and where things happen.

✏ Focus Trait: Purpose

Recall with children that when writers write a true story about themselves they share information about something that happened to them. Write the following true stories on the board. Have children talk about the information each writer shared:

1) I went to a party. We played games. I lost every one. We had cake. I dropped mine on the floor.

2) I went to a party. I lost every game, but I got a great prize. It was funny when I dropped my cake. The dog ate it! I got another piece that was even bigger!

Ask children what they think the writer of each one wanted the reader to know.

Grade 1 • 47

Friendly Letter

Minilesson 35

Using Letter Format

Objective: Recognize the greeting, body, and closing of a letter.

Guiding Question: What parts need to be included in a letter?

Teach/Model—I Do
Read aloud the definition, parts, and model on handbook p. 48. Point out the date and then the boldfaced greeting in the model, *Dear Ben*. The greeting names the person to whom the letter is written. Use the model to explain that the next part of the letter is the body: it gives the message. In this case, the message tells what the writer is doing at camp. Then point out the closing, *Your pal*. Explain that a letter always ends with a closing, followed by the name of the person who wrote the letter.

Guided Practice—We Do
Write this letter on the board:

May 1, 20—

Dear Mr. Briggs,
Please visit our class. We are in Room 14.

Your friends,

Mrs. Morton's class

With children, identify each part of the letter.

Practice/Apply—You Do
COLLABORATIVE Ask partners to write a new greeting and a new closing for the letter posted on the board. Explain that children should write their own names after the closing.

INDEPENDENT Have children think of new messages for the letter posted on the board. They can write a sentence or two to give the message.

Conference/Evaluate
Circulate and help children name people to include in the greeting, such as people they know at school.

48 • Writing

Minilesson 36

Drafting a Friendly Letter

Objective: Write a letter.

Guiding Question: How do I write a letter with instructions?

Teach/Model—I Do
Have children turn to handbook p. 48. Review the definition, Parts of a Letter, and model. Say *Let's write a letter to another class.* On the board or on chart paper, write the date, greeting, and topic sentence: *Dear Mr. Dean's class, We are going to make a big rainforest mural.* Elicit one or two more sentences from children, such as *It will have many plants and animals in it. Would you like to help us make the mural?* Finish by writing the closing: *Your friends, [Ms. Jansen's] class.*

Guided Practice—We Do
 Have children turn to the frame on handbook p. 49. Guide children to write the date, a greeting, body, and closing for a friendly letter. Have them dictate correct placement and punctuation for each part. Have children write in their books as you write on the board.

Practice/Apply—You Do
 INDEPENDENT Have children read the directions. Tell them to use their prewriting plan from Lesson 18 or brainstorm new ideas for a letter about a trip they took, using Graphic Organizer 6.

Conference/Evaluate
During the writing process, circulate and give corrective feedback as needed while children work collaboratively and independently. Evaluate using the rubric on p. 96.

Friendly Letter

A **friendly letter** is written to another person.

Parts of a Letter

- The **date**
- A **greeting** to the person the letter is for
- A **body** that tells what you want to say
- A **closing** and **your name**

April 19, 2012

Dear Ben,

    I am at camp. I just made a drum. I made it from a tin can.

        Your pal,

        Jon

48 • Grade 1

Name _____

Follow your teacher's directions.

_____
_____
_____

Dear _____,

_____
_____
_____
_____
_____
_____

Your friend,

_____
_____

 Use your plan, or make a new one. Write a letter about a trip.

Friendly Letter • 49

Corrective Feedback

IF . . . children leave out any parts of the letter,

THEN . . . cut up a short sample letter into parts for children to rearrange, somewhat like a puzzle. Have children name the parts when they are done.

Focus Trait: Conventions

Tell children that whether they are writing a letter, a story, or a report, there are ways to make their sentences fit together smoothly. Explain that when sentences fit together smoothly writing is more interesting to read. One way to make writing more interesting is to combine, or put shorter sentences together to make a longer sentence. Writers combine shorter sentences with words such as *and* and *but*. Writers add a comma before *and* and *but* to separate the ideas and make the longer sentence easier to understand. Write the following sentences on the board and work with children to combine them:

1. *I want to play. I am busy.* (I want to play, but I am busy.)

2. *I will bring a drink. I will bring a snack. I will bring fruit.* (I will bring a drink, a snack, and fruit.)

3. *Jed will watch the show. I will watch the show.* (Jed and I will watch the show.)

Grade 1 • **49**

Personal Narrative: Prewriting

WRITING FORMS

Minilesson 37

Using Time Order

Objective: Use time-order words in writing.

Guiding Question: How do I use time-order words?

Teach/Model—I Do

Read aloud handbook p. 50. Emphasize that personal narratives tell the order in which things take place. Highlight the words *first*, *next*, and *last*. Write these three words on the board in list form. Then ask children to look closely at what you do. Touch your knees, then your neck, and finally your chin. On the board, write the following sentences: *First, I touched my knees. Next, I touched my neck. Last, I touched my chin.* Read the sentences aloud. Explain that the time-order words help the reader know in what order you did these actions.

Guided Practice—We Do

Ask a child to carry out three actions similar to the ones you just did. Have the class name the actions in order. Then help them write the actions as sentences, using the words *first*, *next*, and *last*. Read the sentences with children and ask them to carry out the actions in the right order. Repeat with other children carrying out a different group of three actions.

Practice/Apply—You Do

COLLABORATIVE Have children work in groups of three. Each child should think of a different action to carry out. Ask them to decide on an order for the actions and write them down using time-order words. Have groups share their work.

INDEPENDENT Ask children to write 3 actions. Have them use time-order words *first*, *next*, and *last* to order the actions. Ask them to trade papers and have each child carry out the other's list in order.

Conference/Evaluate

Check that children are using time-order words correctly. Assist with spelling as needed.

50 • Writing

Minilesson 38

Planning a Personal Narrative

Objective: Draft a personal narrative, using time-order words.

Guiding Question: How can I write a personal narrative?

Teach/Model—I Do

Have children turn to handbook p. 50. Review the definition, list, and model with children. Remind the class that the three items in the model show what happened first, next, and last in a show the author attended. Then explain that you went to the zoo once. Tell children that first, you saw the elephants; next, you saw the lions; and last, you saw the monkeys. Write phrases on the board (such as *first elephants*) to record the basic sequence of events. Read the list with children.

Guided Practice—We Do

 Have children turn to Activity 1 on handbook p. 51. Remind them about a recent event, such as a special snack, a field trip, or a P.E. class. Review what children did. Then guide children to fill the boxes with three things they did during one of the events, being sure to list them in the correct order. Work together to write short phrases and draw simple pictures. Have children write in their books as you write on the board.

Practice/Apply—You Do

 INDEPENDENT Help children make an organizer like the one on handbook p. 51. Ask them to think about a place they recently visited, such as a theater, a stadium, and so on. Have children write simple phrases to list three things they did or saw, using the time-order words *first/next/last* to sequence the events.

Conference/Evaluate

Circulate, checking that children are on task. Help children list the things they did in order. Evaluate using the rubric on p. 96.

Personal Narrative: Prewriting

A **personal narrative** tells a true story about the author. It uses the words <u>I</u> or <u>me</u>.

Parts of a Personal Narrative

- It tells events in the order they happened.
- It uses time order words like <u>first</u>, <u>next</u>, <u>soon</u>, and <u>later</u>.

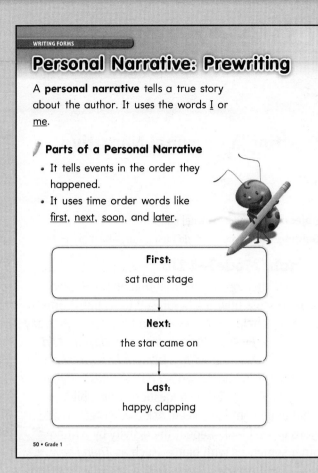

| **First:** |
| sat near stage |

↓

| **Next:** |
| the star came on |

↓

| **Last:** |
| happy, clapping |

50 • Grade 1

Name _____

Follow your teacher's directions.

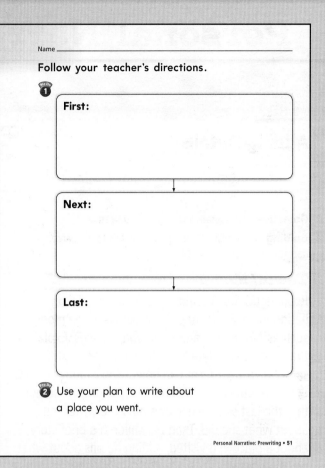

1

| **First:** |
| |

↓

| **Next:** |
| |

↓

| **Last:** |
| |

2 Use your plan to write about a place you went.

Personal Narrative: Prewriting • 51

 Corrective Feedback

IF . . . children have difficulty using time-order words,

THEN . . . relate these words to their spatial meanings. Write the word *cat* on a sheet of paper and have children touch the letters in turn. Point out that the *first* letter of *cat* is *c*, the *next* letter is *a*, and the *last* letter is *t*. Then have children say the letters in order from first to last to point out how *first/next/last* refers to the order in which children said the letters as well as to the order in which children saw the letters on the page.

 Focus Trait: Organization

Tell children that time-order is an excellent way to organize writing, partly because it helps the author put his or her ideas in sequence, but also because time order helps the reader understand what is going on. Help children generate a list of other useful time order words and phrases, such as *then*, *soon*, *later on*, *after that*, and so on. Encourage children to use these words and phrases when they seem ready to branch out beyond simply using

first, next, and *last.* Work with children to write sentences such as *Then I went on the train* or *After that it was time to go home.*

Grade 1 • **51**

Writing Handbook Minilessons

Personal Narrative

Minilesson 39	Minilesson 40

Adding Details

Objective: Add details to a personal narrative.

Guiding Question: How do I add details to my personal narrative?

Teach/Model—I Do

Read aloud the definition, parts, and model on handbook p. 52. Point out the details in the model, such as *big red hat* and *many funny songs.* Explain that writers add details to show exactly what they saw, did, or heard. For example, they sometimes add details about colors, numbers, and sounds. Also note that the last sentence shows how the writer felt about what she did. Then tell children a brief story about a place you visited, adding details about what you saw or did.

Guided Practice—We Do

Elicit several topics from children about fun places they visited with their family, such as a museum or amusement park. Record the topics on the board. Choose one of the topics and guide children to suggest some relevant details about it, such as *museum—art, paintings.*

Practice/Apply—You Do

COLLABORATIVE Tell small groups to choose another topic from the list. Instruct children to work together to brainstorm additional details to go with their topic.

INDEPENDENT Instruct children to choose a different topic from the board or to come up with a new topic. Then tell them to write an important detail about the topic.

Conference/Evaluate

Circulate and help children come up with details to add to their narratives. Encourage children to write their details in complete sentences. Completed sentences should start with a capital letter and end with a period.

52 • Writing

Drafting a Personal Narrative

Objective: Write a personal narrative.

Guiding Question: How do I tell a story about myself?

Teach/Model—I Do

Have children review the material on handbook p. 52. Discuss how the boldfaced transition words in the model help tell the events in time order. Then say *You know, I visited the zoo the other day, and I'd like you to help me write a personal narrative about my trip.* On the board write *I had the best time at the zoo. I saw _____.* Elicit suggestions from children for what you might have seen. Ask a volunteer to add a word in the blank. Repeat the activity by writing other sentences with blanks, such as *Then I saw _____. After that, I went to see _____.* Point out transition words in the sentences.

Guided Practice—We Do

 Have children turn to the frame on handbook p. 53. Together, choose a topic for a personal narrative about a family trip. Then guide children to complete the narrative, reminding them to include details in their suggested sentences. Have children write in their books as you write on the board.

Practice/Apply—You Do

 INDEPENDENT Have children read the directions. Tell them to use their prewriting plan from Lesson 20 or to brainstorm new ideas, using Graphic Organizer 6.

Conference/Evaluate

During the writing process, circulate and offer encouragement and help as needed. Evaluate using the rubric on p. 96.

Personal Narrative: Drafting/Revising

A **personal narrative** is a true story about something you did.

✎ Parts of a Personal Narrative

- Sentences tell what you did in time order.
- Sentences use words like I, me, or we.
- An ending ties ideas together.

> My family went to a play. **First**, we sat down close to the stage. **Then** the star of the show walked on stage. He wore a big red hat. He sang many funny songs. **At the end**, we felt happy. We stood and clapped.

52 • Grade 1

Name _____

Follow your teacher's directions.

1 I went on a fun trip to _____

First, _____

Then _____

At the end, _____

2 Use your plan. Write a personal narrative. If you like, write what you did with your family.

Personal Narrative: Drafting/Revising • 53

✔ Corrective Feedback

IF . . . children are not including enough details in their personal narratives,

THEN . . . remind them to think about what they saw, did, or heard. Have children look at their lists of details. Instruct them to put those details into complete sentences. Review the kinds of details they can add, including those about colors, numbers, sounds, and smells.

✎ Focus Trait: Elaboration

Tell children that, when writing, they can sometimes choose groups of words, or phrases, to help explain where something is or when it happens. For the word group *in the park*, for example, the word *in* is a preposition. The word group *in the park* is called a prepositional phrase.

Some prepositional phrases, such as *at the beach*, tell where things happen. Others, such as *before school*, tell when things happen.

Write the following sentences on the board:

> *We played baseball after school.*
> *Kayla lost her mitten at the zoo.*
> *The cat ran into the room.*

Have children identify the prepositional phrase in each sentence and say whether it tells where or when. (*after school*, when; *at the zoo*, where; *into the room*, where)

Grade 1 • 53

Story Sentences

WRITING FORMS

Minilesson 41

Using Exact Words

Objective: Use exact words characters say.

Guiding Question: How do I show how characters think and feel?

Teach/Model—I Do

Read aloud handbook p. 54. Mention that writers sometimes tell the exact words a character says to show how the character thinks or feels. Point out the dialogue in the second sentence. Instead of writing *Zoe sees the train*, the writer uses the words "I see the train!" to show what Zoe sees and how she feels. Also point out that the use of words such as *I* and *me* show that characters are talking about themselves. Assign children the roles of Zoe and Sam. Read the part of the narrator as children act out the story. Guide children to suggest other exact words Zoe and Sam could say about the train ride to show how they feel, such as: *"Oh, no! I see the train!"* or *"Do we have to go for a train ride?"*

Guided Practice—We Do

Work with children to name characters from familiar stories, such as Little Red Riding Hood and the wolf, Goldilocks and the three bears, and the hare and the tortoise. List the characters on the board and have children choose one set of characters. Then guide volunteers to create dialogue the characters might say to show their thoughts and feelings.

Practice/Apply—You Do

COLLABORATIVE Have pairs work together to choose another set of characters from the board and write dialogue for them.

INDEPENDENT Ask children to choose a third set of characters from the board and write dialogue for them.

Conference/Evaluate

Circulate as children work, offering suggestions for characters or scenarios.

54 • Writing

Minilesson 42

Drafting Story Sentences

Objective: Write story sentences with quotation marks.

Guiding Question: How do I use quotation marks when writing story sentences?

Teach/Model—I Do

Review handbook p. 54 with children. Identify the quotation marks in the model and point out that the words inside the quotation marks are the exact words the characters say. Explain that the words outside the quotation marks name the character and include words such as said, asked, or answered. Tell children that together you'll write dialogue for the nursery rhyme characters Jack and Jill. On the board write Jack said, _____. Then Jill said, _____. Elicit from children suggestions for what the characters might say. (Ex. Jack said, "I fell and broke my head. Jill said, "I tumbled all the way down the hill.") Write children's suggestions to complete the dialogue. Invite volunteers to write the quotation marks in the correct position.

Guided Practice—We Do

 COLLABORATIVE Have children turn to the frame on handbook p. 55. With children, create a story line, such as Allie and Jane were at the zoo, and then dialogue for the two girls. Guide children to choose words for *said* and to place quotation marks correctly. Have children write in their books as you write on the board.

Practice/Apply—You Do

 INDEPENDENT Read the directions to children. Have them use their plans from Lesson 21 or another plan they create, using Graphic Organizer 1.

Conference/Evaluate

During the writing process, circulate and offer encouragement and help as needed. Evaluate using the rubric on p. 96.

Story Sentences

Story sentences show us how characters think and feel. **Dialogue** can tell the exact words characters say.

Parts of Dialogue Story Sentences

- They tell the exact words that the characters say.
- The characters are make-believe.
- Quotation marks tell where the characters start and stop talking.

Here Comes the Train!

Zoe looked along the train tracks.

"I see the train!" she said.

The train slid to a stop at the station.

"We're going for a train ride!"

Zoe's brother Sam shouted.

54 • Grade 1

Name _____

Follow your teacher's directions.

1 Allie and Jane _____
_____
_____
_____.

_____

"Look at _____
_____
_____," said Allie.

_____

"It is _____," said Jane.

2 Use your plan. Write story sentences. If you like, write about the book you read.

Story Sentences • 55

 Corrective Feedback

IF . . . children are having difficulty writing sentences with exact words,

THEN . . . have children read their sentences aloud to hear the character's dialogue. Have them use double fingers on their left hand to touch their paper where the character begins speaking and double fingers on their right hand to touch where the character stops speaking. Remind children to use quotation marks at the beginning and end of each character's dialogue.

 Focus Trait: Purpose

Remind children that when writers write a story they choose words to help readers understand how they feel about a situation or character.

On the board write: *On the first day of school I felt_____because_____.*

Have children complete the sentence individually and then share what they wrote.

Discuss how children had different feelings about the first day of school and that they chose words to communicate their own feeling about the experience.

Repeat the activity with: *On the first day of vacation I was _____ because_____.*

Grade 1 • 55

Story Sentences

WRITING FORMS

Minilesson 43

Using Vivid Verbs

Objective: Use exact verbs to tell what characters do.

Guiding Question: How do I use vivid verbs to show what characters do?

Teach/Model—I Do

Read aloud the definition, list, and model on handbook p. 56. Have children tell the events in order. Point out the words *then* and *after that* that help show the order of events. Then recall with children that verbs tell about actions. Point out the verbs in the model: *swimming, spotted, swallowed, paddled, fell asleep.* Replace the verbs *spotted, swallowed,* and *paddled* with *saw, ate,* and *went.* Discuss how the common verbs make the story less interesting. Then share a short story about an animal, such as a pet, using vivid verbs. Point out the verbs that were used and how they help readers visualize the animal's actions.

Guided Practice—We Do

On the board, brainstorm a list of animals. Guide children to name specific actions for each animal, such as *horse: gallops, prances, nibbles,* etc. Record the verbs on the board. Work with children to write a sentence about one animal that includes vivid verbs, such as *A horse pranced to the fence and nibbled an apple.*

Practice/Apply—You Do

COLLABORATIVE Have partners choose another animal from the board. Ask them to write a sentence about the animal, using vivid verbs. Have partners share their sentence.

INDEPENDENT Ask children to write a sentence about another animal from the board or one of their own choosing. Remind them to use vivid verbs.

Conference/Evaluate

Circulate as children write, giving support and suggestions for vivid verbs as necessary.

56 • Writing

Minilesson 44

Publishing Story Sentences

Objective: Publish story sentences for an audience.

Guiding Question: How do I publish story sentences?

Teach/Model—I Do

Have children turn to handbook p. 56. Review the definition, sentences, and model. Explain that published sentences should be neat, error free and written for a particular audience. On the board or on chart paper, write story sentences about an animal, such as *Some kittens were playing in the barn. First, they hissed and hid. Then they peeked out from the hay.* Point out the vivid verbs *playing, hissed, hid,* and *peeked.* Have children note that the writing is ready to publish, or share with others, because it is appropriate for a first grade audience and it is neat and error free.

Guided Practice—We Do

 Have children turn to the frame on handbook p. 57. Have them suggest ideas for a story about an animal. Together, choose one story line and work with children to write the story on the board. When you have finished, mention that you will look for any mistakes you need to correct. Then model writing the story on clean chart paper so it is ready to be published. Have children write in their books as you write on chart paper. Remind children that published sentences have an intended audience and are neat and error free.

Practice/Apply—You Do

 INDEPENDENT Read the directions to children. Have them use their plans from Lesson 22 or another plan they create, using Graphic Organizer 3.

Conference/Evaluate

During the writing process, circulate and offer encouragement and help as needed. Evaluate using the rubric on p. 96.

Story Sentences

Story sentences tell what make-believe characters say and do.

Parts of Story Sentences

- The characters are make-believe.
- Details tell the events in order.
- Vivid verbs tell what the characters do.

The Geese

Two geese were swimming in the river.

Then they spotted some bread crumbs in the water.

The geese swallowed the crumbs.

After that, they paddled home and fell asleep.

---

56 • Grade 1

Name _____

Follow your teacher's directions.

_____

 1 Some _____

_____

_____

_____

First, _____

_____

_____

_____

Then _____

_____

_____

_____

2 Use your plan. Write story sentences. You can write about your favorite animal.

Story Sentences • 57

✔ Corrective Feedback

IF . . . children are not using specific verbs,

THEN . . . use a children's thesaurus to find replacements for common verbs. Create a chart showing the common verbs and their more exact replacements such as,

Instead of:	Try:
run	dash, sprint, race, bolt, jog, scamper

Post the chart in a visible spot for children to refer to when writing.

Focus Trait: Elaboration

Point out that word choice affects how readers visualize a story. Tell children to use the most specific words to show exact meaning. Write:

The dog ran.

Guide students to use the *who, what, when, where, why* strategy for adding details to sentences. For example, *Who* did something (the dog); *What* did he do (ran); *When* did he do it? (does not say); *Where* did he do it? (does not say); *Why* did he do it? (does not say).

Write a revised sentence that includes the five W's:

Yesterday, the dog ran outside because he was stealing a ham from the table.

Grade 1 • **57**

Story Summary

WRITING FORMS

Minilesson 45

Using Your Own Words

Objective: Use your own words in a summary.

Guiding Question: How do I retell a story?

Teach/Model—I Do

Read aloud handbook p. 58. Point out the boldfaced words in the model: *First, Next, At last.* These help readers understand the order of events. When children retell a story, they can use these words to help show when each event happened. Then explain that, when writing a summary of a story, a writer uses his or her own words to tell the most important events in the order in which they happened. Point out that the writer of the model summary used his own words and did not copy from the story. Briefly summarize a story the class has read. Mention that you are using your own words in your summary.

Guided Practice—We Do

Guide children to suggest stories they know; write the titles on the board. Choose one story, such as "The Grasshopper and the Ant." Guide children to retell the important story events in their own words, while you record them on the board. For example, *An ant and a grasshopper lived in a stone wall, and winter was about to come. The ant worked hard every day to store food. Meanwhile, the grasshopper sat around doing nothing and made fun of the ant for working so hard. When winter came, the ant had plenty to eat. The grasshopper went hungry, however, and had to beg the ant for food.*

Practice/Apply—You Do

INDEPENDENT Have small groups choose another story from the board and work together to retell it. Remind children to retell the story in their own words.

Conference/Evaluate

Circulate, making sure children use their own words when retelling events from the story.

58 • Writing

Minilesson 46

Drafting a Story Summary

Objective: Write a summary.

Guiding Question: How do I write a story summary?

Teach/Model—I Do

Review handbook p. 58 with children. Point out that the summary tells the three most important events from the story *Whistle for Willie.* Also note that the sentences use the writer's own words, not the exact words from the story. Say *Let's write a summary about* The Tree *together.* On the board or on chart paper, write these sentence frames: *First Poppleton _____. Then the tree _____. Finally Poppleton _____.* Elicit ideas for completing the summary. Call on volunteers to write words they know in the sentences.

Guided Practice—We Do

 Have children turn to the frame on handbook p. 59. Together, choose and write a summary for another familiar story. Guide children to use time-order words in their suggested sentences. Have children write in their books as you write on the board.

Practice/Apply—You Do

 INDEPENDENT Have children read the directions. Tell them to use their prewriting plan from Lesson 23 or to brainstorm new ideas, using Graphic Organizer 6.

Conference/Evaluate

During the writing process, circulate and give corrective feedback as needed while children work independently. Evaluate using the rubric on p. 96.

Story Summary

A **story summary** tells what happens in a story. You write the summary in your own words.

Parts of a Story Summary

- Sentences tell the parts of a story in the order they happen.
- Sentences tell only the most important parts.

Whistle for Willie

First, Peter wanted to whistle. **Next**, he tried hard, but no whistle came out. **At last**, Peter tried again and he whistled!

58 • Grade 1

Name _____

Follow your teacher's directions.

 _____

First, _____

Next, _____

At last, _____

 Use your plan, or make a new one. Write a summary about a story you like.

Story Summary • 59

✓ Corrective Feedback

IF . . . children include too many story events in their summary,

THEN . . . remind them that a summary tells only the most important parts of the story. Tell children that they can only include three events in their summary. While the beginning and end may be easy to identify, the middle usually contains a series of events. Help children state in one sentence the main part of the middle of the story. If their sentence does not focus on an important middle event, guide them to state a sentence that does.

✏ Focus Trait: Organization

Encourage children to write their story summary on the computer. This will allow them to easily insert order words, rewrite sentences that are not focused on important ideas, and cut and paste sentences that are not in the correct sequence.

Before children work on the computer, demonstrate or review any necessary skills. Be sure children understand how to enter text, insert additional words, and cut and paste words or entire sentences.

Grade 1 • **59**

Story: Prewriting

WRITING FORMS

Minilesson 47

Brainstorming Ideas

Objective: Brainstorm story ideas.

Guiding Question: How do I find ideas for stories?

Teach/Model—I Do

Read aloud the material on handbook p. 60. Tell children that when they write a story, their first job is to come up with ideas. Explain that authors can get ideas from almost anywhere, and add that it is a good idea to write ideas down to make them easier to remember. Look around the room and make comments such as the following: *I see a box of markers on the shelf; I could write a story about some children arguing because there aren't enough markers to go around,* or *Wouldn't it be funny if the door to the classroom opened up and a penguin walked inside!* Write brief phrases on the board to record these ideas, such as *penguin in the room.* List 4–5 possible topics and read the list aloud.

Guided Practice—We Do

Guide children to add to your list. Have them look around the room and tell you possible story topics related to the objects they see. Accept all story ideas. Write phrases on the board to record children's suggestions. Try to get 6–7 new ideas from the class; then read the complete list aloud.

Practice/Apply—You Do

COLLABORATIVE Have pairs make a list of 5–6 story topics related to animals. Children should record their ideas in phrases or sentences on a sheet of paper and share their lists with another set of partners.

INDEPENDENT Ask children to list 3–4 possible story topics of their own choice. Have them talk about their lists with a classmate.

Conference/Evaluate

Circulate and help children to use short phrases or sentences in their lists.

60 • Writing

Minilesson 48

Creating a Problem and Solution

Objective: Determine a problem and solution for a made-up story.

Guiding Question: How can I write a problem and a solution?

Teach/Model—I Do

Have children turn to handbook p. 60. Read through the model with children. Point out that the plot includes a problem that is solved in the end. Review with children that the problem is in the model is a lost watch. The problem is solved in the story when the watch is found in a book bag. Conclude by suggesting problems and solutions for some of the story topics you brainstormed in the previous mini-lesson; for example, a problem in the penguin story might be that the penguin distracts the children from doing their work, and the solution is to call the zoo to collect the missing penguin.

Guided Practice—We Do

 Have children turn to handbook p. 61. Choose a story you or the class brainstormed in the previous minilesson, or use a new idea. Guide children to name 2–3 characters for the story and write their names in the upper left box; do the same with a setting in the upper right box. Have children discuss possible problems and solutions that could go into the story. Fill out the boxes for the plot with children, including both a problem and a solution.

Practice/Apply—You Do

 INDEPENDENT Read the directions with children. Tell them to use their prewriting plan from Lesson 24 or to come up with new ideas to write the problem and solution of a story.

Conference/Evaluate

Circulate, offering help as necessary. Evaluate using the rubric on p. 96.

Story: Prewriting

A **story** tells something that is made-up.
It comes from the author's imagination.

Parts of a Story

- The beginning introduces the characters.
- The middle tells about a problem.
- The end tells how the characters solve the problem.

Characters 2 girls Jane and Meg	Setting school
Plot	

Beginning:
new watch
bring it to school

Middle:
watch gets lost (problem)
girls look for it

End:
found in book bag

60 • Grade 1

Name _____

Follow your teacher's directions.

Characters	Setting
Plot	

Beginning:

Middle:

End:

 Use your plan to write a new story.

Story: Prewriting • 61

✔ Corrective Feedback

IF . . . children have difficulty thinking of solutions to the problems they want to put into their stories,

THEN . . . have children use role-playing to model the problem. For example, if children want to write about a dispute over a toy, ask two children to act out the characters who are arguing. After they have pretended to argue for a short time, ask them to show how they might settle the argument. Talk with children about the way they solved the problem in the role play and how they could use those ideas in the story.

Focus Trait: Development

Tell children that asking *what if...* is often a good way to begin thinking about story ideas. Model a few what-if questions such as the following:

Think about the pencils we have in the room. What if the pencils suddenly started to move by themselves? What would happen then? or

You know that dogs have a very strong sense of smell; they can smell things that people can't smell. What if there was a person whose sense of smell was as strong as a dog's? What would that be like for this person?

Discuss possible outcomes of these made-up situations and talk about how these could be good starting points for stories. Then encourage children to come up with their own what-if scenarios like these.

Grade 1 • 61

Writing Handbook Minilessons

Story

WRITING FORMS

Minilesson 49

Drafting a Story

Objective: Write a story.

Guiding Question: How do I write a story?

Teach/Model—I Do

Read aloud the material on handbook p. 62. Discuss how the boldfaced words in the model show the order of events: *First, Then, At last.* Tell children that together you will write a story about two friends. On chart paper, write *Hector and Danny were friends.* Brainstorm with children some problems the two friends might have, such as wanting to use the computer at the same time or forgetting to bring lunch to school. With children, decide on one problem and solution and continue writing the story using these sentence frames: *First, _____, Then, _____, At last, _____.*

Guided Practice—We Do

Ask children to turn to the frame on handbook p. 63. Together, create two animal friends and discuss possible story events for them. Work together to choose one story line, and write the story using time-order words. Have children write in their books as you write on chart paper.

Practice/Apply—You Do

COLLABORATIVE Have pairs write their own stories on a topic of their choice. Ask them to use sentence frames with time-order words as in the model in the handbook.

INDEPENDENT Ask children to write their own stories, using their own characters and situations. Have them use time-order words in their writing.

Conference/Evaluate

During the writing process, circulate and give corrective feedback as needed while children work collaboratively or independently. Evaluate using the rubric on p. 96.

62 • Writing

Minilesson 50

Revising a Story

Objective: Revise a story.

Guiding Question: How can I improve my story?

Teach/Model—I Do

Have children turn to handbook p. 62 and review the material. Remind children that when they complete a draft of a story or any other piece of writing, they can revise it to make it better. Display the chart paper with the story you wrote with children in the previous minilesson. Read the story through with children. Then model making several small changes to improve the story. For example, if a sentence reads *Then Hector gave Danny some of his own lunch,* you might change *lunch* to *sandwich* because it is more descriptive. Mark the changes you make, explain why you are making them, and review them with children.

Guided Practice—We Do

 Have children turn to handbook p. 63. Have children follow along as you read aloud the story children wrote together in the previous minilesson. Then guide children to suggest revisions to make the story clearer or more interesting. Make changes on the chart paper where you originally wrote the story as children make the changes in their books.

Practice/Apply—You Do

 INDEPENDENT Have children use the stories they wrote in the *Independent* section of the previous minilesson. Ask them to read the stories again and revise them by making at least 2–3 changes. Have children mark the changes they make on their original copies.

Conference/Evaluate

Move through the room, offering help as necessary and asking children why they chose to make the revisions they did. Ask children to tell a partner how their revisions make their stories better.

Story: Drafting/Revising

A **story** tells what happens to the characters in it.

Parts of a Story

- A title
- Sentences that tell what happens at the beginning, in the middle, and at the end
- A problem that the characters solve

Jane's New Watch

    Jane got a new watch. **First**, she wore it to school. **Then** she lost the watch. Jane asked her friend Meg to help. **At last**, Jane and Meg found the watch. It was in Jane's book bag!

62 • Grade 1

Name _____

Follow your teacher's directions.

_____
_____
_____
_____

First, _____
_____
_____.

Then _____
_____
_____.

At last, _____.

2 Use your plan. Write a new story.

Story: Drafting/Revising • 63

✓ Corrective Feedback

IF . . . children have written story events out of order,

THEN . . . have them review the events they put into their story. Ask *What happens first in your story?* Have children write the number 1 beside the first event. Help children sequence the remaining events in the same way by asking them questions and having them write a number beside each event.

Focus Trait: Development

When to use a name and when to use a pronoun can be tricky for young children when they write about events in a story. Making the wrong choice can make a sentence difficult to understand; it can also make sentences seem abrupt and choppy. Help children develop an ear for when to use names and when to use pronouns by reading these sets of sentences aloud:

First, she played ball. Then, she played with cars. At last, she played with her dog.

First, Ella played ball. Then, Ella played with cars. At last, Ella played with her dog.

First, Ella played ball. Then, she played with cars. At last, she played with her dog.

Discuss the sets with children. Draw out that using *she* without a name does not tell who the sentences are about, and repeating the name *Ella* three times is unnecessary.

Grade 1 • **63**

Opinion Sentences

Minilesson 51

Thinking About Fact vs. Opinion

Objective: Understand the difference between fact and opinion.

Guiding Question: How do I write an opinion?

Teach/Model—I Do

Read aloud the definition, list, and model on handbook p. 64. To discuss the difference between fact and opinion, begin by telling children that a fact is something that can be proved, such as *There are seven days in a week*. Point out that looking at a calendar can prove this fact. Explain that an opinion is what an individual person thinks or believes, such as *My favorite day of the week is Saturday*. Ask children to share opinions about their favorite day of the week and then give a fact about that same day, such as *Monday comes right after Sunday*. Reread the model. Guide children to identify the words *my* and *favorite* that help show the topic sentence is an opinion.

Guided Practice—We Do

Work together to brainstorm topics about which children could write facts or opinions, such as *sports, animals,* or *toys*. Guide children to give specific examples for each, such as *baseball, pandas, kites*. Work with children to write one opinion and one fact for a few of the examples, such as *Flying a kite is great* and *A kite has a tail and string*.

Practice/Apply—You Do

COLLABORATIVE Have small groups choose two more examples from the board and write an opinion and a fact for each.

INDEPENDENT Have children choose another example from the board and write an opinion and a fact about it.

Conference/Evaluate

Circulate while children write, reminding them that an opinion is what they think or believe.

64 • Writing

Minilesson 52

Drafting Opinion Sentences

Objective: Write an opinion and details that support the reason for the opinion.

Guiding Question: How do I write an opinion and details that tell "why"?

Teach/Model—I Do

Have children turn to handbook p. 64. Review the definition, Parts of Opinion Sentences, and model. Review the difference between fact and opinion. Point out the topic sentence in the model and the two reasons the writer gives to support the opinion. Write an opinion sentence on the board, such as *My favorite season is summer*. Work with children to write two reasons that tell "why" such as *I like going to the beach. It is great when we can cool off in the lake.*

Guided Practice—We Do

 Have children turn to the frame on handbook p. 65. On the board, make a list of children's favorite zoo animals. Together, choose one animal to write about and guide them to write a topic sentence about the animal. Make sure the sentence is an opinion, such as *My favorite zoo animal is the penguin*. Then work with children to write two reasons to support the opinion, such as *I like to watch them dive; It is great when they slide in the snow*. Have children write in their books as you write on the board.

Practice/Apply—You Do

 INDEPENDENT Read the directions to children. Have them use their plans from Lesson 26 or another plan they create, using Graphic Organizer 3.

Conference/Evaluate

During the writing process, circulate and offer encouragement. Evaluate using the rubric on p. 96.

Opinion Sentences

Opinion sentences tell something you believe. They can show your strong feelings about a topic.

Parts of Opinion Sentences

- The topic sentence tells your opinion, or what you think.
- Detail sentences tell the reasons for your opinion.
- An exclamation shows that you feel strongly about something.

Basketball

Basketball is my favorite sport!

You have to run fast and play hard in a basketball game.

It feels great when you score some points for your team!

64 • Grade 1

Name _____

Follow your teacher's directions.

 My favorite _____

_____

_____

_____

I like _____.

_____

It is great when _____

_____

_____

 Use your plan. Write opinion sentences. You can write about your favorite thing to do.

Opinion Sentences • 65

✔ Corrective Feedback

IF . . . children are having difficulty writing an opinion,

THEN . . . encourage them to begin an opinion with words that show what they think or believe, such as "*I like…*" or "*My favorite…*" or "*The best….*" Remind children that opinions are what they believe and not everyone will have the same opinion.

Focus Trait: Purpose

Remind children that writers write for a specific reason. One reason is to explain their opinion, or how they feel about a topic. Writers use reasons and details to convince readers their opinion is correct. Write:

I like math. It is good. It can help me.

Point out that the topic sentence gives an opinion, but the sentences that follow don't support the opinion with strong reasons.

Rewrite the sentences to show how the writer feels about the topic. Example:

Math is the best subject ever! Math helps me add up the money in my account. I can figure out how much I need to buy the bike I want.

Grade 1 • **65**

Opinion Sentences

Minilesson 53

Writing to Persuade

Objective: Write sentences to persuade.

Guiding Question: How do I write sentences to convince others of my opinion?

Teach/Model—I Do

Read aloud the definition, bulleted list, and model on handbook p. 66. Then read aloud the topic sentence in the model and point out that words like *I love* signal that this is the writer's opinion, or what the writer believes. Mention that each of the other sentences gives a reason that will persuade, or convince, readers to agree with the writer's opinion. Point out the word *because* and tell children that the writer uses this word to tell why he likes to spend time in the garden.

Guided Practice—We Do

Ask children to name some hobbies they enjoy. List their ideas on the board. Continue until you have a list of at least eight hobbies. Guide children to give their opinion of a few hobbies on the list, such as *I think skateboarding is terrific* or *I think cooking is boring.* Write the opinions on the board. Then help children think of reasons they would use to persuade others to agree with their opinion, such as *You can ride on ramps on a skateboard* or *With cooking, you are stuck in the kitchen.* Write the reasons on the board.

Practice/Apply—You Do

COLLABORATIVE Instruct children to choose another hobby from the list or to think of one on their own. Have them write a topic sentence to tell their opinion, beginning with the words *I think _____*. If they wish, children can also give a reason/ detail for their opinion.

Conference/Evaluate

Circulate and help children write their topic sentence. Remind them that the sentence should tell how they feel about the hobby they have chosen to write about.

66 • Writing

Minilesson 54

Publishing Opinion Sentences

Objective: Write opinion sentences for publication.

Guiding Question: How do I publish opinion sentences for an audience?

Teach/Model—I Do

Have children turn to handbook p. 66. Review the definition, Parts of Opinion Sentences, and model. Explain that the writing in the model is neat and without mistakes. It is ready for publishing. On chart paper, write an opinion, such as *I like playing soccer.* Work with children to write a second sentence that tells "why" using the word *because*, such as *It is fun to get the ball because then I can score. I also like to pass the ball to a friend.* Practice reading the sentences together. Review the writing to correct any errors.

Guided Practice—We Do

 Have children turn to the frame on handbook p. 67. Together, create an opinion sentence about something children do together in school, such as *I like painting in art class.* Continue with the remaining sentences, which are also opinion sentences about the same topic. Have children write in their books as you write on the board. Then guide children to look over their sentences for errors and see if their work is clean and neat and ready for publishing.

Practice/Apply—You Do

 INDEPENDENT Read the directions to children. Have them use their plans from Lesson 27 or another plan they create, using Graphic Organizer 3.

Conference/Evaluate

During the writing process, circulate and offer encouragement and help as needed. Evaluate using the rubric on p. 96.

Opinion Sentences

Opinion sentences tell something you think. You can use the word <u>because</u> to explain your reasons.

Parts of Opinion Sentences

- The topic sentence gives your opinion, or what you believe.
- Detail sentences tell the reasons for your opinion.
- The word <u>because</u> tells that you are about to give a reason.

My Garden

I love spending time in my garden!

It is fun **because** I get to dig lots of holes.

It also feels good to help the plants get bigger.

66 • Grade 1

Name _____

Follow your teacher's directions.

 I like _____

_____

_____

It is fun _____

_____

_____

I also like _____

 Use your plan. Write opinion sentences. Write about something you learned how to do.

Opinion Sentences • 67

✔ Corrective Feedback

IF . . . children are having difficulty using *because* in their detail sentences,

THEN . . . tell them to state a reason that supports their opinion beginning with *because*, such as *I like to play soccer…because it is exciting to score a goal.* or *Dogs are the best pets…because they play with you.* Direct children to ask themselves when writing: *What reason tells "why" I have that opinion?*

Focus Trait: Elaboration

Explain that beginning sentences in different ways helps make the story more interesting for readers. Write:

The puppies play together. The puppies bite and growl. The puppies do not hurt each other.

Point out that all the sentences begin the same way. Rewrite to include interesting sentence beginnings:

The puppies play together. Sometimes, they bite and growl. It's all for show because their little teeth don't hurt each other.

Point out the different sentence beginnings that help the story sound interesting. Encourage children to use varied sentence beginnings when they write.

Grade 1 • **67**

Writing Handbook Minilessons

Opinion Sentences

Minilesson 55

Stating a Strong Opinion

Objective: Choose words to show exact meaning.

Guiding Question: How can I use exact words to create a strong opinion?

Teach/Model—I Do

Read aloud the definition, list, and model on handbook p. 68. Point out the word *best* and the exclamation point in the topic sentence. Explain that the word and exclamation show that the writer has strong feelings about the circus. They show a strong opinion. Point out the words *funny, a lot, tiny, blue,* and *sparkly.* Explain that using exact words like these help make ideas clear. Give a few more examples of how to state strong, clear opinions with exact words, such as *I love the fair! It has yummy treats and exciting rides. I do not like the fair! It has long lines and too many people.*

Guided Practice—We Do

Guide children to name projects the class has done together, such as *making a mural, planting seeds, or cooking food.* Write the project names on the board, listing at least five. Point to each project and guide children to choose one, suggesting words that tell how they felt about the subject, such as *cooking—exciting, fantastic, yummy.* Record the words.

Practice/Apply—You Do

COLLABORATIVE Have partners choose another project from the board. Ask them to work together to give a strong opinion about the project.

INDEPENDENT Have children think of a project about which they feel strongly, either using the list on the board or an idea of their own. Have them write a sentence that shows exact words and a strong opinion.

Conference/Evaluate

Circulate as children work, helping them think of words that tell how they feel. Remind them that a strong opinion can tell what they like or don't like about something.

68 • Writing

Minilesson 56

Revising Opinion Sentences

Objective: Revise opinion sentences.

Guiding Question: How do I revise my sentences to make my opinion strong?

Teach/Model—I Do

Have children review handbook p. 68. Explain that good writers look for words that are just right. Point out the exact words from the model that tell how things look, tell how many, or compare things. On the board, write *The fair was the most fun ever! I saw a pony. The cotton candy was good.* Work with children to add exact words to revise the sentences, such as *I saw a trick pony with gold ribbons. The pink cotton candy was delicious.*

Guided Practice—We Do

 Have children turn to the frame on handbook p. 69. Ask them to suggest opinion sentences about the zoo, such as *The zoo is fun.* Write children's suggestions on the board. Together, guide children to revise the sentences to make them clearer and more interesting, such as *The zoo is full of wonderful animals to visit; I saw three striped zebras; The lion cub was cute.* Have children write the revised opinions in their books as you write on the board

Practice/Apply—You Do

 INDEPENDENT Read the directions to children. Have them use their plans from Lesson 28 or another plan they create, using Graphic Organizer 3.

Conference/Evaluate

During the writing process, circulate and offer encouragement and help as needed. Evaluate using the rubric on p. 96.

Opinion Sentences

Opinion sentences tell what you believe. They give reasons why you have that opinion.

✎ Parts of Opinion Sentences

- The topic sentence tells your opinion, or what you think.
- Detail sentences tell the reasons for your opinion.
- Exact words make the ideas clear.

> **At the Circus**
>
> We saw the best circus ever!
>
> One funny part was when a lot of clowns hopped out of a tiny car.
>
> I loved the dancer's blue dress because it was so sparkly.

68 • Grade 1

Name _____

Follow your teacher's directions.

 1 The zoo _____

_____

_____

I saw _____

_____

_____

The _____

_____

 2 Use your plan. Write opinion sentences. If you like, you can write about the story you read.

Opinion Sentences • 69

✔ Corrective Feedback

IF . . . children cannot think of clear, exact words,

THEN . . . create a list that can be posted in the classroom for children to use when writing. Include adjectives that tell how things look, tell how many, or compare things. Invite children to add adjectives to the list when you discover them in their writing.

✎ Focus Trait: Elaboration

Remind children that good writers use a variety of words instead of using the same words over and over again. Review that adjectives are words that describe things.

Together, create a list of adjectives to describe the circus such as *huge, exciting, funny, sparkly, loud, wonderful,* etc.

Write: *I went to a fun circus where the clowns were fun.*

With children, revise the sentence with different, more exact word choices, such as:

> *I went to a huge circus where the clowns tripped over their own big shoes.*

Grade 1 • **69**

Writing Handbook Minilessons

Opinion Paragraph: Prewriting

Minilesson 57	Minilesson 58

Giving an Opinion About What You Read

Using Details to Support Your Opinion

Objective: Write an opinion about a book.

Guiding Question: What do I think about a book?

Objective: Find reasons in the text to support an opinion.

Guiding Question: How I justify my opinion about a book?

Teach/Model—I Do

Read aloud handbook p. 70. Tell children that people often write their opinions about books they read. Display a book that you have recently read aloud to the class. Do a brief picture walk to remind children of the text. Then explain to children that you will write an opinion about the book. Remind children that an opinion is something you believe, but other people may not agree. Offer 3-4 opinions about the book, such as *My favorite character is ___* or *I would/would not like to be part of the family in the book.* Write the opinions on a large sheet of paper.

Teach/Model—I Do

Have children turn to handbook p. 70. Review the definition, list, and model. Talk about the opinion, reasons, and examples in the planner. Explain that opinions are stronger when they are supported by details, such as why the writer likes something. Discuss that in this planner, the writer's main opinion is that art is the best class because mixing colors is fun and painting allows him to use his imagination. Elicit other reasons and examples from children as to why art might be the best class, such as *you can make a beautiful collages from old junk.* Tell children that this is how to support an opinion.

Guided Practice—We Do

Use the same book you used in the I Do section of the lesson, or choose a different one. Guide children express their own opinions of the book. Encourage children to say what they think about the characters, the setting, the plot, the pictures, or any other aspect of the book. Children may use words such as because to explain their thinking. Record children's opinions on a large sheet of paper.

Guided Practice—We Do

 Have children turn to the frame on handbook p. 71. Guide them to agree on an opinion about something, such as *swimming is the best sport of all* and write the opinion in the top box on the page. Then help them write detail phrases that list reasons and examples for the opinion in the other two boxes. Have children write in their books as you write on the board.

Practice/Apply—You Do

COLLABORATIVE Have partners choose a book they have both read. Ask them to agree on 2 or more opinions about the book and write them down.

INDEPENDENT Ask children to choose a book they know well. Have them write an opinion about the book and share their work with a classmate.

Practice/Apply—You Do

 INDEPENDENT Read the directions with children. Tell them to use their prewriting plan from Lesson 29 or to make a new plan that gives an opinion about something. Remind children to use details in the form of reasons and examples to support their opinion.

Conference/Evaluate

Make sure children are writing full sentences with capital letters and final periods. Check that children are writing opinions rather than factual information.

Conference/Evaluate

Move through the room, asking children what details they are using to support their opinions. Evaluate using the rubric on p. 96.

70 • Writing

Opinion Paragraph: Prewriting

An **opinion paragraph** is a group of sentences about one feeling or belief.

Parts of an Opinion Paragraph

- The topic sentence tells your opinion, or what you think.
- Detail sentences give reasons and examples.
- The closing sentence retells your opinion using different words.

My Opinion:
Best class = art class

First reason:
fun
Example:
mixing colors

Second reason:
use imagination
Example:
painting pictures

Name _____

Follow your teacher's directions.

1 My Opinion:

Reason:

Example:

Reason:

Example:

2 Use your plan to write about an opinion you have.

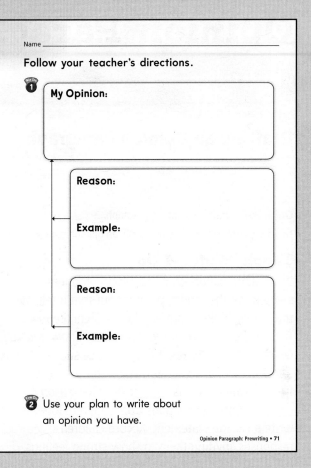

✓ Corrective Feedback

IF . . . children write facts or information instead of opinions,

THEN . . . provide a sentence frame, such as *My favorite place to visit is _____ because _____* and have children complete the sentence in a way that demonstrates what they are thinking. You can also give children a short list of adjectives such as *fun*, *scary*, and *interesting* and ask them to choose the ones that best support their opinion.

Focus Trait: Evidence

When children are asked to express their opinions about books, they need to think carefully about what they do and do not like about the story. They also need to analyze the story in simple ways, such as by determining if a particular character is kind or mean, or if the setting makes the story realistic or fantasy. Thinking about these questions leads naturally into discussions about how authors get their ideas and how they turn those ideas into stories. As children talk about their favorite parts of books, make comments such as *Savanna thinks that the book is funny; why do you think the author chose to write a funny book?* or *Tom says that his favorite character is _____; what did the author do to make this character so interesting to read about?*

Grade 1 • **71**

Opinion Paragraph

WRITING FORMS

Minilesson 59

Drafting an Opinion Paragraph

Objective: Draft an opinion paragraph.

Guiding Question: How do I write an opinion paragraph?

Teach/Model—I Do

Read aloud handbook p. 72. Discuss the topic sentence in the model, pointing out that it tells what the writer thinks about art class. Tell children *Now we'll write an opinion together about Show and Tell.* On chart paper, write a topic sentence such as *I think Show and Tell is really fun!* Write these sentence frames: *One reason is _____. Another reason is _____.* Elicit suggestions from children. Together, write a closing statement. Record children's responses, inviting them to show strong feelings.

Guided Practice—We Do

 Have children turn to handbook p. 73. Guide children to write an opinion sentence and two reasons to support the opinion, such as *I think swmming is the best sport of all. One reason is that it is good exercise. Another reason is that it keeps me cool.* Encourage them to use their prewriting plans from Minilesson 58. Have them write in their books as you write on the board.

Practice/Apply—You Do

 INDEPENDENT Have children write opinion paragraphs on their own, using the sentence frames on p. 73 as a model. Remind children to express reasons for their opinions. Children may use their prewriting plan from Minilesson 58 or brainstorm new ideas.

Conference/Evaluate

During the writing process, give corrective feedback as needed while children work in pairs or individually. Evaluate using the rubric on p. 96.

Minilesson 60

Revising an Opinion Paragraph

Objective: Revise opinion sentences.

Guiding Question: How do I improve my opinion sentences?

Teach/Model—I Do

Review handbook p. 72. Remind children that revising written work can help make it clearer and more interesting. Display the chart paper with the opinion paragraph you used in the *I Do* section of the previous minilesson. Read the paragraph with children, pointing out the words as you read. Then model making a few small changes to improve the paragraph. If your original paragraph included the sentence *One reason is that you learn about things*, for example, you might add *like rocks and pine cones* to the end of the sentence to make it more specific. Explain why you are making the changes and point out the editing symbols you use.

Guided Practice—We Do

Have children turn to handbook p. 73. Read aloud the opinion paragraph children wrote together in the *We Do* section of the previous minilesson. Then have children suggest revisions to improve the paragraph and make it easier to understand. Make changes directly on the chart paper where you wrote the initial paragraph. As you do so, have children make the changes in their books.

Practice/Apply—You Do

INDEPENDENT Have children use the opinion paragraphs they wrote in the *Independent* section of Minilesson 59. Ask them to reread their work and revise their writing by making at least 2–3 changes. Have children use editing symbols to make the changes.

Conference/Evaluate

Circulate, offering help as necessary.

72 • Writing

Opinion Paragraph: Drafting/ Revising

An **opinion paragraph** tells something that you believe.

Parts of an Opinion Paragraph

- A topic sentence gives your opinion.
- Detail sentences give reasons for your opinion.
- A closing ties ideas together.

> **I think** that art class is the best! **One reason** is that it is fun to mix colors. **Another reason** is that I can use my imagination to paint pictures. I always learn a lot in art class.

72 • Grade 1

Name _____

Follow your teacher's directions.

 I think _____
_____
_____
_____

One reason is _____
_____
_____

Another reason is _____
_____
_____

 Use your plan. Write sentences to tell your opinion.

Opinion Paragraph: Drafting/Revising • 73

✔ Corrective Feedback

IF . . . children's detail sentences do not support their opinion,

THEN . . . remind them that each detail sentence must give a reason that explains their opinion. Tell children to ask themselves, *Does this sentence tell why I like math class?* If the answer is *no,* they should delete the sentence and write a new sentence that does explain *why*.

Focus Trait: Organization

Organization can be difficult for children who are just beginning to write paragraphs. Their minds move more quickly than their ability to put words on the paper, and the result can sometimes be a hodge-podge of ideas with no particular order. Point out that in the paragraphs used in this lesson, the topic sentence always comes first and the reasons always follow. Read the following sentences to children: *I think birds are great. One reason is that they are very pretty. Another reason is that they are strong.* Point out that the first sentence tells what the writer likes; only then does it make sense to explain why. Contrast this with the following sentences: *One reason is that it tastes good. Another reason is that it's good for you. I like milk.* Point out that the first two sentences don't make much sense; the reasons should come after the topic statement.

Grade 1 • **73**

Writing Handbook Minilessons

Prewriting

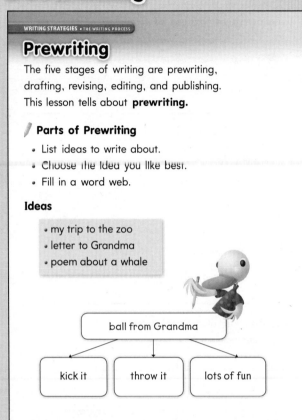

Prewriting

The five stages of writing are prewriting, drafting, revising, editing, and publishing. This lesson tells about **prewriting.**

Parts of Prewriting

- List ideas to write about.
- Choose the idea you like best.
- Fill in a word web.

Ideas

- my trip to the zoo
- letter to Grandma
- poem about a whale

ball from Grandma

| kick it | throw it | lots of fun |

74 • Grade 1

There are more organizers you can use to help fill out your ideas. Use them to plan your writing.

Flow Chart

Went to see elephants

↓

Next, to ape house

↓

Ended at petting zoo

Venn Diagram to Compare and Contrast

Whales — live in the sea

Both — mammals, weigh over a ton

Elephant — live on the land

Prewriting • 75

WRITING STRATEGY

Minilesson 61

Introducing Prewriting

Objective: Understand how to organize ideas for prewriting.

Guiding Question: How can I use these pages to help me organize my ideas?

Teach/Model

Read p. 74 with children. Explain that the list shows the writer's ideas. Discuss how the word web is organized. Explain that the word web shows an idea at the top and specific points the writer will write about below.

Practice/Apply

Read the examples on p. 75. Discuss how the writer used the flow chart to show a sequence of events and a Venn diagram to compare/contrast.

74 • Writing

Minilesson 62

Turning Ideas into Prewriting

Objective: Understand how to use graphic organizers for prewriting.

Guiding Question: How can I turn my ideas into prewriting?

Teach/Model

Explain to children that the key points the writer plans to write about are shown in each graphic organizer. The writer uses the organizer to arrange his or her ideas. Later, the writer will be able to use the prewriting ideas to write a draft.

Practice/Apply

Have children read the graphic organizers on p. 75. Discuss how each organizer fits the purpose of the writing. Work with them to brainstorm possible ideas to add to the organizers.

Drafting

WRITING STRATEGIES •THE WRITING PROCESS

Drafting

When you **draft**, you use full sentences to write what you planned.

Parts of Drafting

- Look at the ideas in your word web.
- Write about these ideas.
- Use full sentences.

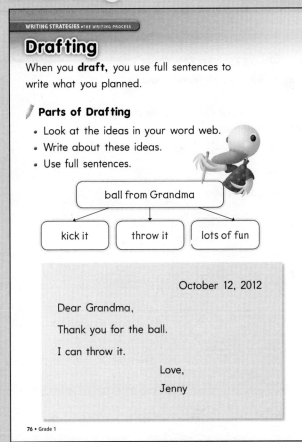

ball from Grandma

kick it   throw it   lots of fun

October 12, 2012

Dear Grandma,

Thank you for the ball.

I can throw it.

Love,

Jenny

Here is how Ben used his plan. He wrote sentences about a book from his friend Allie.

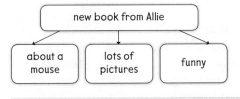

new book from Allie

about a mouse   lots of pictures   funny

Allie gave me a book.

The book is about a mouse.

It has lots of pictures.

I think it is very funny.

WRITING STRATEGY

Minilesson 63

Introducing Drafting

Objective: Understand how to use the drafting handbook pages.

Guiding Question: How can I use organizers to help me draft?

Teach/Model

Read p. 76 with children. Explain that the example shows how a writer used the prewriting graphic organizer to write a rough draft of a letter. Each detail in the organizer became a sentence in the draft.

Practice/Apply

Together, read the example on p. 77. Discuss how this organizer was used to write sentences about the topic. Work together to write an additional sentence based on the organizer.

Minilesson 64

Going from Organizer to Draft

Objective: Understand how to use a graphic organizer to draft sentences.

Guiding Question: How can I use my prewriting plan to draft sentences?

Teach/Model

Remind children that a graphic organizer is used as a guide for writing a first draft. Explain that a first draft does not have to be perfect because you will fix mistakes later.

Practice/Apply

Have children discuss how the students in both models used the key idea and details from the organizer to draft sentences.

Writing • 75

Writing Handbook Minilessons

Revising

Revising

When you **revise**, you change your writing to make it better.

Parts of Revising

- Read your writing. Share it with a partner.
- Ask it your writing is clear.
- Make your writing better.
- Use editor's marks.

Editor's Marks

∧ Insert.

⪑ Delete.

⊙ Make a period.

October 12, 2012

Dear Grandma,
                    soccer
Thank you for the ∧ball.
It is fun to throw it and kick it with my
I can throw it.⪑   friends.
∧

Love,

Jenny

Here is how Ben revised his writing.

First, he read his draft to a friend.
Next, he listened. His friend asked questions.
Last, Ben changed his writing. He changed words and sentences.

                          new
Allie gave me a ∧book.

The book is about a mouse.
              funny
It has lots of ∧pictures.
        I laughed a lot.
I think it is very funny.
                ∧

WRITING STRATEGY

Minilesson 65

Introducing Revising

Objective: Understand how to use the revising handbook pages.

Guiding Question: How can revising make my writing better?

Teach/Model

Read p. 78 and point out how the writer changed the draft. Point out that the details make the revised version sound better. One way to improve a draft is to add more details. Review the editor's marks and discuss how they help writers revise writing.

Practice/Apply

Have students read the draft on p. 78. Discuss the changes and work with students to suggest other possible changes to the draft.

76 • Writing

Minilesson 66

Revising a Draft

Objective: Understand how to revise a draft.

Guiding Question: How do I revise my writing?

Teach/Model

Explain that writers read their drafts aloud so listening partners can ask questions about the writing. The questions help a writer understand what parts of the writing are unclear or need to be changed.

Practice/Apply

Read the original student model on p. 79. Guide children to ask questions about the writing that would help Ben decide what to change such as, *Was it a new book? What were the pictures like? Was it funny?* Discuss differences between the draft and the revision.

Editing and Publishing

Editing

When you **edit**, you fix mistakes in your writing.

Parts of Editing

- Make sure your spelling is correct.
- Check that your sentences have end marks.
- Put capital letters where they belong.

March 15, 2012

Dear Arlo,

thank you for the baseball bat. I can hit very far with it.
It is a good size for me.

Your friend,

Peter

Publishing

When you **publish** your writing, you share it. You make it look as good as you can.

Parts of Publishing

- Make a clean copy.
- Maybe draw a picture or use computer art to go with it.
- Share your work.

Dear Grandma,

Thank you for the soccer ball.
It is fun to throw it and kick it with my friends.

Love,

Jenny

WRITING STRATEGY

Minilesson 67

Introducing Editing

Objective: Understand how to use the editing handbook pages.

Guiding Question: What do I need to do to edit my work?

Teach/Model

Read p. 80 with children. Explain that editing includes fixing spelling, capitalization, grammar, and punctuation mistakes.

Practice/Apply

Have children discuss the parts of editing. Discuss the purpose of editor's marks in the example. Point out that the marks are always the same for the same types of mistakes. Have children point out the types of mistakes that were fixed and how the writer fixed them.

Minilesson 68

Introducing Publishing

Objective: Understand how to publish a piece of writing.

Guiding Question: How do I publish my work?

Teach/Model

Read p. 81 with children. Point out the differences between the edited letter on the previous page and this published letter. Explain that a published piece is the best work someone can do. It should be clean and free of mistakes. It can also have pictures.

Practice/Apply

Point out that sharing can mean reading a piece of writing aloud, sending it to someone, performing, videotaping, and so on. Ask children to discuss different ways they might like to publish their own work.

Writing Handbook Minilessons

Evidence

WRITING STRATEGIES • WRITING TRAITS

Evidence

Before you write, think of **ideas**.

Ideas

- Think about what you will write.
- Draw pictures, write lists, or make webs.

Informative Writing

Think of topics for a report. Make a list of details about your topic.

Hermit Crabs

live in shells they find

ten legs

eat plants

good pets

Informative Writing

Think of how to do something. Write words about the steps in order.

Bathing a Dog

1. Fill a bathtub with water.

2. With an adult, put the dog in the tub.

3. Wet the dog's fur.

4. Wash the dog's fur with shampoo.

5. Take the dog out of the tub, and dry its fur.

Persuasive Writing

Think of an opinion. Make a list of reasons.

Eat More Vegetables!

1. vitamins

2. help you grow strong

3. taste good

WRITING STRATEGY

Minilesson 69

Introducing Ideas

Objective: Understand how to use the ideas handbook pages.

Guiding Question: How do I get ideas for writing?

Teach/Model

Read p. 82. Explain that writers write about one idea at a time. Point out that in the student example, the main topic, or idea, is at the top. Words or phrases that tell about the main idea are listed below it.

Practice/Apply

Read p. 83 with children. Review narrative, informative, and persuasive writing. Discuss how the ideas shown in the lists on this page relate to each kind of writing. Ask children what writing form they might use for each of these lists (e.g. a report).

Minilesson 70

Thinking of Ideas for Different Kinds of Writing

Objective: Understand how to develop ideas for different purposes.

Guiding Question: How do I think of ideas for my writing?

Teach/Model

Review the different kinds of writing. Explain that the kinds of ideas and details you need can be different for each kind of writing. For example, in persuasive writing, writers might think of reasons to support an opinion, while in informative writing, writers think of facts.

Practice/Apply

Look at the persuasive writing example on p. 83. Discuss how students can use these ideas to fill out a graphic organizer or draft opinion sentences.

Organization

WRITING STRATEGIES • WRITING TRAITS

Organization

Organization is when you put your ideas in order.

Organization
- Think of a good beginning.
- Make a plan.
- Put your ideas in order.

Narrative Writing

Tell about something that happened to you. Put your ideas in the order they happened.

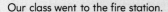

> Our class went to the fire station.
>
> We sat in the fire truck.
>
> We put on boots and helmets.

84 • Grade 1

Informative Writing

Write a topic sentence. Write facts about the topic.

> The sun is the center of the solar system.
>
> It is close to the Earth.
>
> It keeps us warm.
>
> All the planets turn around the sun.

Persuasive Writing

Tell your opinion. List your reasons. One way is to put the most important reason last.

> Baseball is the best sport.
>
> Games are very exciting.
>
> It is a fun sport to play and a fun sport to watch.
>
> My favorite part is hitting a home run.

Organization • 85

WRITING STRATEGY

Minilesson 71

Introducing Organization

Objective: Understand how to use the organization handbook pages.

Guiding Question: How do I organize my ideas for writing?

Teach/Model

Read p. 84 with children. Point out that the main idea is in the first sentence *(Our class went to fire station)*. The other sentences tell details about the main idea.

Practice/Apply

Work with students to write an additional sentence for the narrative. Then discuss the correct order for the sentences. Elicit from students that narrative writing should include events in the order they happened.

Minilesson 72

Organizing for Different Kinds of Writing

Objective: Understand how to organize ideas.

Guiding Question: How do I organize ideas for different kinds of writing?

Teach/Model

Read p. 85 with children. Review the kinds of writing. Point out that different kinds of writing are organized in different ways.

Practice/Apply

Have children discuss ways the students in the examples organized their ideas for each type of writing (examples: informative has main idea and details; persuasive has most important reason last).

Writing • 79

Writing Handbook Minilessons

Purpose and Elaboration

Purpose

Purpose is your reason for writing. You can write to tell a story, to inform, to explain, or to persuade.

Purpose
- Think about why you are writing.
- Carefully choose words.
- Grab your reader's attention at the beginning.
- End your writing in an interesting way.

> Juicy oranges are my favorite fruit.
>
> They make me think of sunshine.
>
> I love to eat oranges in the summer.
>
> The sticky juice drips all over my fingers.
>
> That's why you should like juicy oranges, too!

86 • Grade 1

Elaboration

When you **write**, think about the words you use.

Word Choice
- Use exact words.
- Use words that describe. Help make a picture in the reader's mind.

> I share a <u>warm</u> pie with my friends.
>
> We cut it into <u>six</u> pieces.
>
> The pie has a <u>tasty</u> crust.
>
> It has <u>sweet</u> apples inside.

Voice and Word Choice• 87

WRITING STRATEGY

Minilesson 73

Introducing Voice

Objective: Understand how to use the purpose handbook pages.

Guiding Question: How do I make my reason for writing clear?

Teach/Model

Read p. 86. Point out the different reasons for writing. Emphasize that writers keep their purpose for writing in mind as they choose words and plan what they are going to write about.

Practice/Apply

Discuss that the writer's purpose for writing was to give an opinion about juicy oranges. Ask children to point out words and ideas that show how the writer feels about oranges. Ask children to think about a topic they have a strong opinion about and can explain their feelings.

80 • Writing

Minilesson 74

Introducing Word Choice

Objective: Understand how to use the word choice handbook pages.

Guiding Question: How do I choose words that show exactly what I mean?

Teach/Model

Read p. 87 with children. Explain that readers make pictures in their minds while reading, so writers should choose strong describing words.

Practice/Apply

Discuss the underlined words used in the example that help readers get a picture in their minds. Ask children to think about other words that could give readers a different picture in their minds (*soft, four, crunchy, tart*).

Development

Development

When you write a story, add details that tell about the characters, setting, and the events.

Development

- Choose words that help readers picture where the story takes place.
- Add details that give information about who the story is about.
- Keep readers interested in what is happening in the story by adding intersting details.

It was a dark, stormy night. Jimmy and his mom were home alone watching a movie. Then there was a loud clap of thunder. Everything in the house shook. The lights went out. In a flash, Jimmy was in his mom's arms.

Make every sentence in your story count.

- Add time-order words.
- Make your sentences fun to read.
- Use statements and questions.

Jimmy wondered if his mom was as scared as he was. One glance at her face told him she was. What were they going to do? First his mom told Jimmy to be brave. As they went to get a flashlight, the lights came back on. It was still rainy and very windy outside. Inside Jimmy and his mom were once again cozy!

WRITING STRATEGY

Minilesson 75

Introducing Sentence Fluency

Objective: Understand how to use the sentence fluency handbook pages.

Guiding Question: What kinds of sentences will make my writing fluent?

Teach/Model

Read p. 88. Explain that writing with different kinds of sentences makes writing sound smooth. Point out the sentence length, question, and exclamation.

Practice/Apply

Discuss how the model writer used different kinds of sentences. Ask children how this piece would sound if all the sentences were the same. Elicit that varying the sentences makes the writing more interesting.

Minilesson 76

Writing Varied Sentences

Objective: Understand how to write different kinds of sentences.

Guiding Question: How can I write different kinds of sentences to make my writing sound smooth?

Teach/Model

Read p. 89 with children. Explain that reading what they wrote aloud will help them hear where details, questions, or time-order words could be added to their writing. Then they can revise their sentences to make them flow more smoothly.

Practice/Apply

Have children discuss the different sentence features in the student models that make them sound smooth and interesting.

Writing • 81

Writing Handbook Minilessons

Conventions

Conventions

After you write, check for mistakes.

Conventions

- Check for spelling.
- Check for capital letters.
- Check for correct end marks.

> Dear Megan,
>
>   ice   Have
> I went to the ise rink. have you
>
> ever been there? You can skate and do
>
> spins
>
>   Your friend,
>   Susana

90 • Grade 1

Singular and Plural Nouns

A singular noun names one. A plural noun names more than one and ends in an s.

Wrong Way	Right Way
We put everything in box.	We put everything in boxes.

Complete Sentences

A complete sentence begins with a capital letter and ends with a period.

Wrong Way	Right Way
one day he ran a race	One day he ran a race.

Correct Use of I and me

I is always in the subject of a sentence.

Wrong Way	Right Way
Erin and me went home.	Erin and I went home.

Describing Words with er and est

Some describing words tell how things are different.

Wrong Way	Right Way
A baseball is small than a basketball.	A baseball is smaller than a basketball.

Conventions • 91

WRITING STRATEGY

Minilesson 77

Introducing Conventions

Objective: Understand how to use the conventions handbook pages.

Guiding Question: What conventions should I check when writing?

Teach/Model

Read p. 90 with children. Explain that conventions are rules about spelling, capital letters, and end marks. Remind students that, when they edit, they check to make sure they applied these rules correctly.

Practice/Apply

Discuss how the writer of the model on p. 90 checked her sentences for correct conventions. Point out how the writer made changes.

Minilesson 78

Using Correct Conventions

Objective: Understand common conventions.

Guiding Question: How can I write sentences with correct conventions?

Teach/Model

Walk students through each example on p. 91, and review why the Right Way is correct. Explain that these are some common errors that writers make and that children should look out for these as they write.

Practice/Apply

Write a few examples of incorrect sentences, such as *sam and me walk to school*. Ask student to identify what is wrong with the sentences. Work together to correct them (*Sam and I walk to school*).

82 • Writing

Using the Computer

Using the Computer

Use a **computer** to find information about your topic on the Internet.

Using the Computer

- Go to a web page that has information about your topic.
- Take notes to help you remember.

File   Edit   View   Favorites   Tools   Help
Address   http://www.---.org

ALL ABOUT POLAR BEARS

HOME
CONTACT
ABOUT US
NEWS

Polar bears live in a cold place called the Arctic. They have thick white fur that keeps them warm. They are good swimmers.

Polar bears

- live in the Arctic
- have thick white fur
- good at swimming

92 • Grade 1

Here is another example.

File   Edit   View   Favorites   Tools   Help
Address   http://www.---.com

Rabbits

Rabbits are small animals. Their tails are short and their ears are long. Rabbits usually live in holes. They eat twigs and grass. Sometimes they eat vegetables from people's gardens!

Rabbits

- short tails, long ears
- live in holes
- eat twigs, grass, and vegetables

Using the Computer • 93

WRITING STRATEGY

Minilesson 79

Introducing Using the Computer

Objective: Understand how to use these handbook pages.

Guiding Question: How can I find information on the computer?

Teach/Model

Read p. 92 with children. Explain that the example shows how computers can help children find information on the Internet to use in their writing. This writer found details for a report on polar bears.

Practice/Apply

Review p. 92 and point out that the writer used the information from this website to take notes about polar bears. Discuss how a writer might use this information to write a report.

Minilesson 80

Using the Computer to Find Information

Objective: Understand how to use computer information when writing.

Guiding Question: How can I use information from the computer when I write?

Teach/Model

Read p. 93 with students. Explain to children that a lot of information is found on the Internet. This writer took notes about rabbits. Point out how the facts are written in the writer's own words, not copied from the page.

Practice/Apply

Read sentences from the examples. Have children identify the key words or ideas from each sentence.

Writing • 83

Writing Handbook Minilessons

Research

How to Do Research

When you **research** you find facts for your writing. One place to find facts is in a book.

Parts of a Book

- The cover of a book shows the title, or name of the book.
- It shows the author, or the person who wrote the book.
- It also shows the illustrator, or person who made the pictures.

Cover

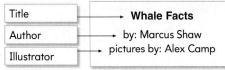

Title	→	**Whale Facts**
Author	→	by: Marcus Shaw
Illustrator	→	pictures by: Alex Camp

94 • Grade 1

Table of Contents

This page shows page numbers where you can find information in a book.

Contents

3	Kinds of Whales
16	Where Whales Live
28	What Whales Eat

Index

These pages show topics and page numbers. The topics are shown in ABC order.

Index

A		**C**	
Atlantic Ocean, 8, 19		Caribbean Sea, 17	
		Coral reef, 20, 26	
B		**D**	
Baleen, 3, 5, 8–12		Dangers, 19, 23	
Beluga whale, 4, 27		Diet, 28, 30	
Blue whale, 5, 23		Dolphins, 8, 10	

How to Do Research • 95

Minilesson 81

Introducing Research

Objective: Understand how to use the research handbook pages.

Guiding Question: Which parts of a book will help me do research?

Teach/Model

Read p. 94 with children. Explain that the example shows the important parts of a book cover. Children can use this to help with their research.

Practice/Apply

Read the examples on p. 95. Discuss how the table of contents and index can help writers quickly find information in a book. Point out that the index shows topics in ABC order. The table of contents shows topics in the order they appear in the book.

84 • Writing

Minilesson 82

Using Research for Writing

Objective: Understand how to use books to find information.

Guiding Question: How does knowing the parts of a book help me find facts for my writing?

Teach/Model

Explain that knowing how to find information in a book will help children get facts for writing. Read the topics in the table of contents and in the index. Point out that the index has more details than the table of contents.

Practice/Apply

Ask children to use the table of contents and index to find page numbers by asking questions such as *What pages would I look on to find where whales live? Which pages will have facts about blue whales?*

Checklists and Rubrics

WRITING STRATEGIES • Evaluation

Checklists and Rubrics

Use this list to check your writing. Make sure you have done everything on the list.

 **How to Use a Checklist**

- Read the checklist.
- Check your writing.
- After you check, fix your writing.
- After you fix, go back and check the list. Make sure you fixed all mistakes.

√ My writing is on topic.

√ My writing has facts or details.

√ My writing has a beginning and an ending.

√ Ideas are in order.

√ Words are spelled correctly.

√ Sentences and names start with capital letters.

√ Sentences have correct end marks.

96 • Grade 1

WRITING STRATEGY

Minilesson 83

Introducing Checklists and Rubrics

Objective: Understand how to use the evaluation handbook page.

Guiding Question: How will using a checklist help me evaluate my writing?

Teach/Model

Read p. 96 with children. Explain that the example shows a checklist for children to evaluate their writing. Explain that a rubric is like a checklist. It shows what is being evaluated.

Practice/Apply

Direct children to choose a piece of writing and evaluate it using the checklist. Discuss what children should look for as they revise.

Writing • 85

Writing Handbook Minilessons

Index

Read Aloud Passages

Table of Contents

LESSON 1

The Lion and the Mouse

an Aesop's fable

One day, a long time ago, a lion ate an **excellent** meal. As soon as he had finished, he decided to take a nap in his cool den. He stretched out, laid his head on his paws, and was asleep at once.

Soon a curious little mouse peeked around the corner into the lion's den. The mouse could hear the lion snoring, so she tiptoed in. The mouse touched the lion's paw, but he continued to snore. So the little mouse very quietly climbed right on top of the lion's nose.

This awakened the King of the Beasts, but he did not move. Slowly he opened one eye and saw the mouse. **Suddenly** his huge paw came down. He did not **miss** the tiny creature, as quick as she was. He captured her!

The little mouse was terrified. "Please sir," she begged the King of the Beasts, "Spare me, and I will never forget your kindness."

"Spare you?" roared the lion. "You had no **invitation** to be here! First you dare to awaken me. Then you ask me for a favor! Give me one good reason why I should not eat you."

"The time may come," replied the little mouse, "when I may be able to do a favor for you. You never know when you may need the help of a friend like me."

The lion began to chuckle. Then he laughed out loud! How could a tiny mouse ever help him, King of the Beasts? The lion was so amused that he let the mouse go. She scampered away and disappeared into a dark corner. The lion closed his eyes and soon forgot all about the little mouse.

Then, one day, the lion was out hunting for food. He did not know that some hunters had set a trap to catch him. All of a sudden, the King of the Beasts was stuck in a net!

The lion struggled to get free. The more he fought, however, the more he became tangled in the net. The lion began to panic. "*This will* **ruin my life**," he thought. Then he let out a giant roar. It was so terrible that it echoed through the forest.

Far away, the little mouse stopped and listened. She recognized the voice of the lion who had once spared her life.

The little mouse ran through the forest as fast as she could. She found the King of the Beasts struggling hopelessly in the tangled net.

"Hello, Your Majesty," said the mouse. "You seem to be all tied up at the moment. Perhaps I can help set you free."

The little mouse nibbled and gnawed at the ropes of the net. She worked and worked. Before long, the net began to weaken. Soon there was a hole large enough for the lion to wiggle through.

After the lion was free, he remembered the **beautiful** words that the mouse had once said to him: "*You never know when you may need the help of a friend like me.*" The lion smiled. Not only had the little mouse been right, but she had saved his life!

LESSON 2

Susie and the Bandits

Each night, after dark, **bandits** roamed the neighborhood. These were no ordinary bad guys. They were a group of raccoons who called themselves "The Brave Bandits." Their only goal was to eat as much food as possible from the neighborhood's garbage cans. These critters chomped on chicken bones, munched on rotten lettuce, and licked old tuna fish cans. By the time the sun rose, garbage was scattered all over the neighborhood.

The other animals **chattered** and complained among themselves. They were not happy about the raccoons.

"These so-called Brave Bandits have to be stopped," said Paulie Opossum. "I don't think it's very **brave** to steal things. They are making a mess in the neighborhood, and the humans are getting angry."

"That's right," said Bonnie Bunny. "Just the other day I saw a new wire fence by my bunny hole. The humans think I'm in on it!"

So Bonnie, Paulie, and a group of concerned animals paid a visit to the raccoons. They woke up the bandits and told them that they were putting all the animals in danger.

"What are the humans going to do to us?" the raccoons laughed. "Shine a light on us? Oh, so scary!"

"My sensitive **ears** overheard the humans at a meeting," said Bonnie Bunny. "They talked about fences and loud radios and sprinklers that go off in the night."

"Oh those humans think they're so clever," said Ricky Raccoon. "They've tried sheds and locks and fancy garbage can lids. But they can't stop the Brave Bandits!"

The raccoons laughed as the other animals sadly left. Just then, a skunk poked her head out of a stone wall. "I can help," she called.

"Stinky Skunk!" the animals cried and started to run.

"Hold **still**," she said. "My name is Susie, and I'm tired of those bandits, too. I will get the raccoons to stop raiding the garbage if all of you will stop calling me Stinky."

And so they agreed. That night, Susie waited on the ground by the raccoons' home in the tree. "Move out of the way, Stinky," Ricky Raccoon yelled when they came down.

"First of all, my name is Susie," she said. "Secondly, I'm here because you have to stop raiding the garbage cans."

"Too bad," said Ricky. "We need to eat."

With that, Susie sprayed her smelly spray all over the Brave Bandits. The raccoons smelled so bad that they ran to a nearby creek for a bath. Susie followed them there. As Ricky washed his face, he spotted Susie. "**Steady** now, Bandits," he said. "That skunk is back!"

"Look around you," Susie said. "There are plenty of berries, insects, and fish here. You do not need to eat the humans' garbage. Finding your own food takes a lot more bravery. I will promise not to spray you again if you promise to stay away from the garbage cans."

And so they agreed. From that night on, the neighborhood changed. The raccoons stopped eating from garbage cans, the humans left the animals alone, and Susie Skunk was never called "Stinky" again.

LESSON 3
Stone Stew

a traditional folktale

Long ago in the West Indies, a sailor wandered into a small town. He was hungry and far from port.

The townspeople feared strangers and kept themselves **apart** from others. When they saw the sailor, they **worried** that he might be dangerous. The doors and shutters throughout the town quickly slammed shut.

The sailor knocked on a door and asked for a bite to eat.

"Better keep moving on," the man said. "There is nothing to eat here."

"I'll have to make my stone stew, then," the sailor said.

Out of his bag the sailor pulled a pot. He filled it with water from the town well and built a fire under it. Then, with great care, he took a stone from a velvet bag and dropped it into the water.

The townspeople peered from behind the closed doors and shutters to keep a careful watch on the sailor.

The sailor stirred his pot, took a taste, and licked his lips. "Mmm. This is delicious," he said rather loudly, "but stone stew with okra is even better."

A boy **sneaked** out of his house and **crept** over to see what the sailor was cooking. Then he shyly approached the sailor. "Here is some okra, sir."

"Why, thank you, son," said the sailor, as he dropped the okra in the pot. "You know, I once had stone stew with okra and pork, and it was fit for a king!"

The town butcher came out of his shop with some salt pork and pig's **snout**.

"Excellent!" cried the sailor. "But, oh, if there were yams, it would be much better."

A woman soon appeared with her apron full of yams from her cupboard.

And so it went with breadfruit, coconut milk, onions, and so on. Soon there was a scrumptious meal for the whole town. They all sat down together to have some stew.

The townspeople were thrilled by the delicious stone stew and **proud** of their contributions. Never had they had such a feast!

"Imagine that," they said. "All made from a stone!"

The townspeople offered the sailor a lot of money for his special stone, but he wouldn't accept it. So the townspeople gave him directions to the port. The next day, the sailor was on his way.

To this day, the townspeople fondly remember the sailor and his wonderful stone stew.

LESSON 4
Painting Word Pictures

Poets paint pictures with words. They use paper as their **canvas**. Words are their paint. The word pictures they create are poems.

The sounds of words are **important** to poets. Rhyme and **rhythm** are the tools poets use to paint their word pictures.

Poets may use **combinations** of words that rhyme. They may also repeat words and sounds. Three or four words in a **row** may have the same sound.

The lines of poems often have a certain rhythm, or beat. The rhyme and rhythm allow a reader to read and say poems with **ease**. They also make poetry fun!

Listen to these poems. What word pictures do they make?

The Wind
by Robert Louis Stevenson

I saw you toss the kites on high
And blow the birds about the sky;
And all around I heard you pass,
Like ladies' skirts across the grass—
O wind, a-blowing all day long,
O wind, that sings so loud a song!

Read Aloud Passages

Autumn Leaves

Autumn leaves are a-falling;
Red and yellow and brown;
Autumn leaves are a-falling,
See them fluttering down.
Tra, la, la, la, la, la, la,
Tra, la, la, la, la, la,
Autumn leaves are a-falling,
See them fluttering down.

Autumn leaves from the treetops
Flutter down to the ground,
When the wind blows his trumpet,
See them whirling around.
Tra, la, la, la, la, la, la,
Tra, la, la, la, la, la,
When the wind blows his trumpet,
See them whirling around.

Autumn leaves when they're tired,
Settle down in a heap,
At the foot of the old tree,
Soon they'll all fall asleep.
Tra, la, la, la, la, la, la,
Tra, la, la, la, la, la,
At the foot of the old tree,
Soon they'll all fall asleep.

LESSON 5

Training Around the Town

Have you ever visited a big city? Perhaps you even live in a big city. Cities can be difficult to get around. Roads may be crowded with cars, buses, and bikes. Some cities solve this problem by building special trains. These trains help people get around quickly. They can be fun to ride, too!

Subways are a special kind of train. A subway is a train that runs under the ground. Because a subway is underground, it does not take up **space** on city streets and **alleys**. A subway gets people where they're going in a hurry.

For almost 40 years, Fort Worth, Texas had a very special subway. It was built by a department store. In 1963, the store built the subway line to help its customers. The main station was in the basement of the store. Other stations were located in nearby parking lots. The boxy, brightly painted subway cars would **ferry** shoppers from the parking lots to the store. That way, people did not have to walk long distances. When they finished shopping, they could **dash** from the store back to their cars in just minutes.

After many years, the department store was torn down to make way for new office towers. Then, in 2001, the office towers were sold. The company that owned the subway no longer needed it. The subway closed in 2002. Its underground tunnel was **sealed**.

Many people in Fort Worth were upset, especially people who worked and parked nearby each day. Some had been riding the subway since they were young. They were sad to see the subway go.

Today you can still ride one of the old Fort Worth subway cars. You can find it in Dallas, Texas, on a streetcar route. A streetcar is another special kind of train. Like other trains, streetcars run on rails. However, streetcar rails are built on the street next to lanes for cars and buses.

The Dallas streetcar system began more than 130 years ago. Mules pulled the early streetcars on their tracks. But soon electricity powered the streetcars. By the 1950s, people thought streetcars were old-fashioned, and cars were the future. Dallas did away with their streetcar service.

Then about 30 years ago construction work on some streets uncovered the old streetcar tracks. People's thinking about streetcars had changed. They liked the idea of bringing back some history with the streetcar. Dallas laid new streetcar tracks and started to restore historic streetcars from around the country. Now Dallas's old streetcars are a tourist attraction. More than 250,000 people ride them each year.

LESSON 6

Night of the Wolf

One night, Meg and Ellie sat by their bedroom window and stared out into the night. It was snowing and it looked like the kind of snow that would stick. The flakes were small and falling almost as fast as rain.

"I **figure** we'll have a snow day," said Ellie, "if it keeps up like this for another couple of hours."

"I don't know," said Meg. "We haven't had a snow day since we moved to Minnesota. The snow doesn't seem to bother anyone here."

"Can you imagine what people back home would say if they saw us walking to school with snow banks taller than people?" asked Ellie. "I don't think I'll ever get used to it!"

"I know," said Meg. "It's okay here, but it's so different. I wonder if we'll ever stop calling Texas 'back home'?'"

Suddenly, the wind **tossed** a snow shovel across the lawn. It hit the shed with a loud **clang**. Both girls jumped.

"Whoa!" said Meg. "Maybe we really will have a snow day. That wind is so strong!"

"We'd better get to bed just in case," said Ellie. "I don't want it to be my **fault** if you can't get up in the morning. I get blamed every time you sleep late! Mom and Dad seem to forget that you always slept late in the old house, too, and we didn't even share a room there!"

The girls climbed into their beds and snuggled under their thick, warm blankets. Ellie shut off the light.

A few moments later, Meg sat up suddenly. "Did you hear that?" she whispered. "I think I heard a howl—an animal howl."

"It's just the wind," said Ellie. "You're just trying to keep me up late again! Now go to sleep."

Then they both heard it. It was a long howl. It started low and got higher, *Ahhh—ooooo*. It did not sound like the wind. And it sounded close!

Meg and Ellie ran back to the window. They huddled together and scanned the land behind their house.

"Look!" Meg gasped. She pointed to the left. There stood a beautiful timber wolf no more than a hundred yards away. As they stared at it, it lifted its head to the sky and howled again, *Ahhh—ooooo!*

"Do you think it's lost in the snow?" asked Ellie.

"Probably not. I think they like the snow," said Meg. "My teacher said this is one of the only places where there are **plenty** of wolves. And it snows here all the time!"

The wolf stood with its ears perked up and looked around. Then four more wolves seemed to appear from nowhere. The wolves all put their heads down and **jumbled** together. They nuzzled one another and wrestled a little. Once they finished their greetings, they settled into an organized group. Then the wolves ran off into the woods.

The girls looked at each other in amazement. "Now that's definitely not something we'd see back home!" Ellie said with a laugh.

"That's true," said Meg. "It may be different here, but it sure isn't boring!"

As Meg and Ellie climbed back into bed, they both fell asleep thinking that their new home was pretty nice after all.

LESSON 7
Prairie Dogs

If you ever visit Oakley, Kansas, you can visit the world's largest prairie dog. It's about 15 feet tall and weighs 8,000 pounds! That prairie dog isn't real, of course, but a sculpture in a theme park. If you want to see real prairie dogs, though, you can go to Prairie Dog State Park. Near Prairie Dog **Creek**, you can see thousands of prairie dogs living in nature.

Prairie Dogs are not dogs, but a kind of squirrel. Like dogs, though, they bark. Their high-pitched barks **warn** each other when enemies are around. These amazing little animals can make a slightly different sound for each kind of enemy.

Prairie dogs live on prairies, or open fields and grasslands. They are about the size of a rabbit and weigh up to 4 pounds. Their fur can be almost any shade of brown to black. Their tails are stubby.

Prairie dogs have short, strong legs and sharp toenails that make them great diggers. In fact, they live in underground burrows, or holes, and tunnels that they dig themselves. You can spot a burrow by the mound of dirt on top of it. Prairie dogs sit on the dirt hills to look for enemies and to escape from floodwaters.

It's fun to watch prairie dogs eat. Like squirrels, they sit up and hold food in their paws. They eat mostly grasses, roots, and seeds, with some insects and spiders. If prairie dogs get full during a meal, they can store extra food in their chubby cheeks and save it for later.

Prairie dogs are like humans in some ways. Like people, they live together in family groups and band together in larger communities called towns. Most towns are smaller than a half square mile, but some are huge. The largest prairie dog town covered some 25,000 square miles. That town was home to millions of prairie dogs. Now that's a **crowd**!

Members of the same groups know and greet each other. Family members feed, kiss, and groom each other. The young pups are very playful, so their parents keep a careful eye on them. "Neighbors" watch out for each other, too. A call from one prairie dog will send the others running for safety in their holes. Once the danger passes, an "all-clear" call brings the animals back out.

Prairie dogs are a key part of nature's balance. The holes that they dig help keep soil healthy. They are also an important part of the food chain. Many animals hunt them for food. Their burrows are also homes for other animals.

Unfortunately, not everyone is in **agreement** about the prairie dogs. In the past 100 years, the number of prairie dogs and amount of land where they live has shrunk a lot. Much of the land where they live has turned into farms or pastures. They are not welcome there anymore. Their holes and tunnels bother many people, so they are often treated as pests. These changes have cut the number of prairie dogs down to a tiny portion of what it used to be.

As a result, towns and states have **discussed** what to do about prairie dogs. Some areas have even passed **bills** and laws that protect these important, adorable, and playful animals.

LESSON 8
The Neighbors

Long ago and **faraway** in China, there lived two neighbors, Chen and Li. Their houses were not much more than a stone's throw apart, yet they were as different as oil and water.

Chen was very rich, but unhappy. He lived in the biggest house in the **village**. The only thing that he cared about was counting his money. He counted it from morning to night.

Li, on the other hand, lived in a simple farmhouse, and was happy with his life. Each day, Li worked the land to provide for his family. Each night, Li played his flute. His family would gather around to sing and dance.

One night, Chen was counting his coins as usual. He started to write some numbers, when a burst of laughter carried through the **crisp**, night air. It made him **smudge** his work!

"That's it!" he yelled. "Every night, it's the same thing. How can I count my money with all of this noise?"

He **peeked** out his window at Li's family. He could see them dancing and laughing on the **edges** of their porch. *How can they be so happy in that little house?* he thought.

Then he had an idea. He knew a way to get rid of Li and his noisy family. *If Li was rich, he wouldn't have time for his foolish flute playing…and he might even move!*

Chen packed up some gold coins and went to Li's house. He handed a box to Li and said, "I see that you work very hard, so I am giving you this gift. You deserve to work less and move your family to a bigger house."

Li opened the box. He dropped his flute and went right up to his bedroom to count the coins. He counted them late into the night. He even fell asleep with the piles in front him.

The next morning, Li awoke with a start. "What if some of my money is missing? What if I did not count it correctly!" he exclaimed. Then he began counting it again.

Next, he started to worry that someone would steal it. He spent the rest of the day moving his money from hiding place to hiding place. Then at night, he counted it again. As he counted, he worried. He worried about where he would move and what he would buy.

He worried and worried until the sun came up.

This went on for days—the counting, the hiding, the worrying, the sleepless nights. Since Li had received the coins, he had not played his flute once. Li had not spoken to his children. Then one evening, Li's eldest daughter, Su, interrupted him.

"Father," said Su. "We miss your flute playing, and more importantly, we miss you. It is as if our house is empty, even when we are all here."

Suddenly, Li knew exactly what to do with the coins. He walked over to Chen's big, fancy house, and knocked on the door. Chen answered. He looked as tired and worn as Li.

"I'm here to give you your money back," said Li.

"But why?" asked Chen. "You could have anything. You could leave that little farm and move to a grand house!"

Li smiled and simply said, "With money, you can buy a house, but not a home."

LESSON 9
The Little Red Hen

Once upon a time, there was a little farm on a hill. On this farm lived the Little Red Hen, her three chicks, a duck, a pig, and a cat. The Little Red Hen did all the work. She cooked, washed, and swept. She mowed, raked, and gardened.

One day, while she was **yanking** the weeds out of the garden, the Little Red Hen found some grains of wheat. "Look," she clucked. "Who will help me plant this wheat?"

"Not I," quacked the duck, and he waddled away.

"Not I," oinked the pig, and he trotted away.

"Not I," meowed the cat who was barely **awake**, and she fell back asleep.

"Then I will plant it myself," said the Little Red Hen. And she did.

When the wheat was tall and golden, the Little Red Hen knew it was ready to be cut. "Who will help me cut the wheat?" she asked.

"Not I," quacked the duck.

"Not I," oinked the pig.

"Not I," meowed the cat.

"Then I will cut this wheat myself," said the Little Red Hen. And she did.

"It is time to take the wheat to the miller so he can grind it into flour," said the Little Red Hen. "Who will help me?"

"Not I," quacked the duck.

"Not I," oinked the pig.

"Not I," meowed the cat.

"Then I will make the **trip** to the miller by myself," said the Little Red Hen. And she did.

The miller ground the wheat into fine, white flour. Then he put it into a sack for the Little Red Hen. When she returned to the barnyard, the Little Red Hen asked, "Who will help me make the dough?"

"Not I," quacked the duck.

"Not I," oinked the pig.

"Not I," meowed the cat.

"Then I will make the dough myself," said the Little Red Hen. And she did.

When she finished the dough, the Little Red Hen asked, "Could any of you at least **try** to help me bake the bread?"

The duck, the pig, and the cat just groaned all together.

"I get the point. I won't ask **twice**. I will bake it myself," said the Little Red Hen. And she did.

Soon the bread was done. The Little Red Hen took it from the oven. "I **wonder** who will help me eat this bread?" she said.

"I will," quacked the duck.

"I will," oinked the pig.

"I will," purred the cat.

"Oh, no you won't," said the Little Red Hen. "You wouldn't help me plant the seeds, cut the wheat, go to the miller, or bake the bread. Now, my three chicks and I will eat this bread ourselves!"

And they did.

The duck, the cat, and the pig finally realized how selfish they had been. From then on, the friends shared the work equally.

LESSON 10
Chipper Chips In

Winter was coming. The **forest** had turned from green to gold to brown. The animals knew the snow would come soon. They could already smell it in the air.

Chipper the Chipmunk sat on a branch watching her brothers race back and forth. They have a great job, she thought. All day long, they searched for seeds and nuts. They stored them in their big cheek **pouches** and brought them back to the burrow.

Chipper wanted to look for food, too. But her brothers didn't think she was big enough. "How could a little chipmunk like you carry enough seeds to make a difference?" her oldest brother Chuck said just this morning.

"But if you could just give me a chance," Chipper said.

"Stick to what we know you're good at," Chuck replied. "There's no sense in changing our system."

Chipper was a lookout. Her job was to watch for **enemies**. If she saw any **predators**, such as a hawk or a fox, she had to warn them. Chipper knew her job was important. Still, she wanted to scurry through the leaves. And most of all, she wanted to help fill the burrow with food.

Suddenly, Chipper's thoughts were interrupted. "Chip! Chip!" a chipmunk's voice called out. "Calling all chipmunks! There is an emergency meeting at Chestnut Stump!"

All the chipmunks from the forest gathered around Chestnut Stump. They chattered about good places to find seeds and nuts. Then Chester, the head chipmunk, leapt on top of the stump. The crowd went silent.

"I have some news," he announced. "The word from Deer Hollow is that the first frost will be here within two days!"

The chipmunks were shocked. They let out squeals.

"It is time to **hibernate**, but our burrows are not full!" Chester said. "Each and every chipmunk will have to collect from sunrise to sunset. We need the extra cheeks on the job."

"But what about our lookouts?" asked Chuck.

"I have made a deal with the blue jays," Chester said. "They will be our eyes in the sky if we share food with them. So from this point on, all chipmunks **must** focus on storing!"

"Chip! Chip!" the crowd cried. And Chipper's call was the loudest of all. With a flick of her tail, she scampered off with her brothers to their favorite seed-collecting spot. Chipper started grabbing bundles of seeds with her tiny paws. Then she pushed them into her cheeks as quickly as she could.

"Whoa! Chipper, I think that's enough," said Chase. "You should go back to the burrow and drop some of those off!"

"Not yet," said Chipper. She kept stuffing and stuffing seeds until her cheeks were bigger than her head.

"I've never seen a chipmunk store so many seeds!" Chase said.

Because of Chipper's amazing cheek pouches, the burrow was filled by sunset. When the frost came, the chipmunks had enough food for the whole winter—plus plenty to share with the blue jays.

"Chipper is the seed-storing champ!" cheered Chuck. "Next year, we'll all take turns as lookouts. I'm sorry I didn't give you a chance to chip in before, baby sister!"

Chipper just smiled from cheek to chock-full cheek!

LESSON 11
The Piano Lessons

The sign above the door simply read, "Mrs. Johnson's Music School." It was small, neat, and simple, just like Mrs. Johnson.

What the sign didn't say was that Mrs. Johnson was a **strict** teacher. Everyone knew that she was the best music teacher around, but also the toughest. She had certain rules, and she made her students stick to them.

"All my students must **practice** every day," she cried at the end of each class. "One hour, or more!"

Kim and Kayla were two of Mrs. Johnson's regular students. They had been **companions** since they met in art class at age 5. Then they had ballet together at age 6, soccer camp at age 7, and now piano lessons.

Both girls liked the lessons. They were filled with loud music, laughter, and Mrs. Johnson banging her cane to keep time. But practicing at home was different. Kayla didn't mind so much, but Kim hated it.

Kim didn't like sitting alone at the big piano. *Plink, plunk, thud*, went the piano, as Kim just pounded random keys. "This is *soooo* boring," she groaned to anyone who would listen. Kim sat on the piano bench for an hour every day, but she didn't even try to learn the music.

Each week, the girls and the other students would return to Mrs. Johnson's school to show what they had learned. The students who practiced would play **gracefully**, but Kim was terrible. She would have nothing to play and Mrs. Johnson would cry, "You must practice every day! One hour, or more!"

This went on week after week. Kayla would play her piece and do pretty well. Then Kim would get up in front of the group, **exchange** a look with Kayla, and play horribly. Mrs. Johnson knew that Kim had not practiced. She would cry, "You must practice every day! One hour, or more!"

Then one day, strict Mrs. Johnson surprised Kim by bending her rules just a little. "Kim," she said in a low voice. "When I was your age, I didn't like to practice either. It was dull and lonely for me, too. I have an idea. I know that you and Kayla are friends, so the two of you will practice together. One hour or more, of course!"

After that, Kim and Kayla sat together at the piano bench every day after school. Kayla showed Kim how she made her practice fun by playing **portions** of the music really loudly. They played songs where Kayla was the left hand and Kim was the right one. They learned a lot of duets, so that they each played one part of the song.

Kim started playing really well in class. It made her even more willing to practice. Soon she found that an hour started to go by really fast. Kim didn't like to admit it at first, but sometimes she even practiced for more!

LESSON 12

Turtle, Frog, and Rat

Long ago, Turtle, Frog, and Rat were best friends. They lived together in a lovely house made of woven grasses, with a wide **view** of the ocean. When they felt **frisky**, they would dance and sing or play hide-and-seek with bugs. When they felt relaxed, they would drink tea and talk.

The friends spent many happy evenings complimenting each other.

"You have beautiful flat eyes," Turtle and Rat told Frog.

"No one has a smoother shell than you," Rat and Frog told Turtle.

"Your tail is so long and furry," Frog and Turtle told Rat.

One night, after days of rain, the friends had an unfortunate **adventure**. A flood rushed toward their house! Turtle and Frog were strong swimmers, so they were in no danger.

Rat did not swim as well as his friends, so he ran to the forest and climbed a tall tree to safety. There, he met a beautiful lady rat. She thought that his furry tail was handsome. They fell in love, married, and built a tree house together.

After the floodwaters went down and some time had passed, Rat went to check on his friends. The grass house had washed away, but Frog and Turtle were living in a fine new house with mud walls and a roof made from a giant leaf.

Rat told them, "I made a new home in the forest and now I have a wife. Will you come meet her?"

The friends agreed and went off together.

At Rat's tree, Frog and Turtle realized that it was too high for them. Rat thought for a moment and had an idea.

"You can grab my tail with your jaws," he said to Turtle, "and I will pull you up." Turtle **shivered** with fear, but he agreed and took Rat's tail in his mouth. Rat started to climb.

When they were nearly at the top, Turtle opened his mouth to say hello to Rat's wife. When he did, he lost his grip and **tumbled** down. As he fell, his sharp beak slid along Rat's tail and accidentally pulled off all the hair. When he landed, Turtle's smooth shell cracked all over. Frog **spied** the whole thing. He was so upset by what he saw that his eyes bulged out in alarm.

"I'm not hurt," said Turtle. "But my beautiful shell is ruined. Now it looks cracked!"

"It's not ruined!" said Frog. "Your shell is much more interesting now than when it was smooth. But look what happened to my eyes!"

"I like your bulging eyes," said Rat. "Now you can keep them above the water when you swim. But my tail, just look at my tail!" he wailed. "My wife won't love me without a thick, furry tail!"

"Don't be silly," his wife said. "I love you for who you are, not what you look like."

So Rat, Turtle, and Frog got used to their new looks and stayed friends forever. But to this day, turtles still have shells that look cracked, frogs have bulging eyes, and rats have hairless tails.

LESSON 13

The Prickly Pride of Texas

Have you heard the legend of the prickly pear cactus? Long ago in Mexico, a group of people called the Aztecs wanted to build a great city. They searched for the right spot for hundreds of years. Finally, a signal told them where to build. It was an eagle, with a snake in its mouth, standing on a prickly pear cactus. The signal told the Aztecs that they had found the correct location. They built the city right there and called it Tenochtitlan (teh-noch-TIT-lan) or "The Place of the Prickly Pear Cactus." Today, that city is the capital of Mexico.

It is no wonder that the Aztecs wanted to live in a place where they could find the prickly pear cactus; people have used this plant for food, medicine, hair conditioner, and more for a very long time. It grows in warm places all over the world, including the United States. The prickly pear grows so much in Texas, for example, that it is the official Texas state plant!

You can easily spot a prickly pear cactus. This plant does not have **vines**, a woody trunk, or thin leaves like other familiar plants. Instead, it has flat, green paddles. They are shaped like tears.

A prickly pear cactus can be just a few inches high or up to 7 feet tall. You would need a **plow** to knock down a large prickly pear cactus!

Whether large or small, this plant usually produces beautiful flowers. Each flower is a bright **burst** of yellow that **glows** in the sun. Don't try to gather these flowers for a **bouquet**, though, because the prickly pear cactus is covered with sharp spines that look like needles. Sometimes the flowers **shrivel** and form fruits. These reddish-pink fruits are called prickly pears because they also have prickly spines.

Many people like to eat the fruit and paddles of the prickly pear cactus. The fruits are red, sweet, and juicy inside and make delicious jams, candies, or sweet drinks. The seeds inside the fruits can even be used to make flour for bread. The paddles make tasty, healthy food too, but take a little more work. To eat them, people must first carefully pick the paddles and scrub or cut off the spines. After that, the paddles can be cooked like a vegetable or cut up and stirred like an omelet.

The prickly pear cactus has other uses besides serving as food. The red fruit can be made into dye for fabric. Other parts of the plant can be used as medicine. In some parts of the world, they are grown between houses as natural fences.

The prickly pear cactus is a beautiful, useful, and important plant. So the next time you travel across the Texas countryside, try to spot one. Don't touch it, however—it's called "prickly" for a reason!

LESSON 14

The Tortoise and the Hare

This story is about a desert tortoise and a hare. The hare is also known as a jack-rabbit because it is always running around really fast. This hare was extra fast and he knew it. "I am as fast as lightning," he said. "No animal in the desert **habitat** is as fast as I am."

The tortoise **mainly** took things more slowly. He moved at his own pace and was proud of it. One day, tired of the hare bragging about his speed, he said, "Hare, you are fast indeed, but I would like to race you anyway."

The hare laughed and laughed. "I will certainly beat you in a race," he said. "You could **search** your whole life and never find a faster opponent!"

The tortoise insisted, so the tortoise and the hare set up at the starting line. The other animals of the desert—the prairie dog, the coyote, the rattlesnake, the scorpion, and all the others—gathered to watch.

The rattlesnake called, "Get ready!" and the coyote gave a **howl** to start the race. The hare started off like a shot. He was so fast that he bent the **stems** on the plants nearby. The tortoise went off at his usual steady pace.

After two minutes, the hare stopped and looked back. He was so far ahead that he could not even see the tortoise behind him. "That silly tortoise will never catch up with me," he thought. "I will just take a rest and finish the race later."

So the hare sat down by a **cactus** and soon fell asleep by dreaming about carrot ice cream. He slept so well that he didn't notice the tortoise slowly plodding by. When the hare woke up, he quickly finished the race, but was shocked to find the tortoise already across the finish line!

All of the animals in the desert cheered when the prairie dog handed the tortoise the trophy. The coyote reminded the hare that "there are times to set a fast pace, but slow and steady wins the race."

LESSON 15

The Dancing Wolves

A rabbit walked through the woods on his way to visit his friend the woodchuck. The woodchuck lived in a deep, warm hole under an old tree stump. Excited to share the woodchuck's cookies and milk, the rabbit was not as **sensitive** to the dangers in the forest as usual. He did not notice, until it was too late, that a pack of hungry wolves surrounded him and **threatened** to eat him.

The rabbit was frightened, but stayed **alert**. He said to the wolves, "I am too small for all of you to eat. I am just a little bite for big wolves like you. One of you will get me, but which one will it be?"

The wolves looked at the rabbit and sized him up. They imagined him on a **scale** and saw that he was too small for them to share. So, of course, the wolves began to argue.

The rabbit cried, "Stop! I have an idea to solve your problem. I will teach you a new dance and the best dancer will win me as the prize."

The wolves, who loved to dance, agreed to this solution. The rabbit gave **directions**. "Line up. I will stand by this tree and sing. You dance away from me until I call 'Turn!' and then you dance back to me in a line."

The wolves did as they were told. After hearing the cry "Turn!" they danced back to the rabbit.

"Great!" said the rabbit. "You are marvelous dancers. Now for the next part, you will dance as before. But on every seventh step, you must **swivel** in place. I will sing and call to you from that tall tree *over there*."

The wolves did as they were told, having even more fun. When they came back, the rabbit said, "Terrific! You did even better than the first time. For the next part, you will dance away from me again but this time you will hop on every fourth step and clap your paws on every fifth step. I will sing from that tree *way over there*."

And so it went. The dances got harder and harder so that the wolves had to think more and more about what they were doing. The rabbit moved farther and farther away to trees that were closer and closer to the woodchuck's hole.

Finally, the rabbit yelled, "This is the last dance! It is a race. You must run away as fast as you can, do a flip every seventh step, and jump every tenth step. The first wolf that returns after I yell 'Turn!' will get to eat me."

The wolves took off. The rabbit waited until they were far away. Then he called "Turn" and darted into the woodchuck's hole. The wolves ran back, extra-hungry from all of the dancing, and expecting to eat rabbit for lunch. When they returned, though, the rabbit had disappeared.

The wolves plopped down on the ground, moaning with hunger and disappointment. Each wolf thought he could hear the distant sound of a rabbit eating cookies, but none would admit it.

LESSON 16
One Giant Leap

Would you like to travel to the Moon? Only a handful of people have ever made the trip. The first people to walk on the Moon were Buzz Aldrin and Neil Armstrong. They made their famous walk on July 20, 1969.

These men were part of a project called "Apollo 11." The United States had sent men into space before. However, no one had ever walked around on the Moon. The goal of this project was to send men to the Moon and get them home safely.

The journey began on July 16, 1969. Aldrin, Armstrong, and a pilot named Michael Collins lifted into Earth's **atmosphere** in a spaceship. The spaceship carried a special craft. This craft would come apart from the main spaceship. It would carry Aldrin and Armstrong to the Moon's **surface**.

Four days after leaving Earth, the small craft left the main spaceship. Collins stayed in the main spaceship to make sure it stayed safe. He watched the small craft below, however. The craft looked **miniature** against the Moon's **vast** surface. It finally landed.

Soon, Armstrong climbed out wearing his space suit. He looked at the strange and beautiful **landscape**. He took a few steps. Then he said these words: "That's one small step for (a) man, one giant leap for mankind." Back on Earth, millions of people heard him on the radio and on television.

Soon Aldrin climbed down to the Moon's surface. The men began to explore. They could not walk or move very quickly. Their space suits were clumsy and the ground below them was slippery. They felt light as they walked. But the two men picked up rocks and dirt to bring back home. They took photographs. They even spoke to the President of the United States on a special telephone.

Finally, after two hours, the men climbed back into their special craft. While they were moving around, however, an accident happened. One of the men broke part of an important machine. This machine was supposed to help them lift off from the Moon and return to Earth, and now it did not work! For a moment, the men feared they would be stuck. Thankfully, they worked together. They made a **decision** about how to fix the problem. They used a simple pen to fix the machine and lift off!

Back in the main spaceship, the three men spoke again to people at home. Collins thanked everyone who had built the spaceship, prepared them for their trip, and given them advice in space. He said that without them, the journey would not have been possible. Finally, on July 24, the men landed safely back on Earth. People all over the world cheered for Aldrin, Armstrong, and Collins and for their exciting, important trip.

LESSON 17
The Rainy Trip

On the second day of our camping trip, the rain started falling.

"What's going on?" my friend Kyra's dad grumbled. "The newspaper said it would be sunny all week!"

As we crouched in our tent for **shelter**, I hid my disappointment. Kyra was my best friend and her dad had been so nice to invite me on their trip. I had never been camping before. I hadn't thought about what we would do if it rained, though. I hadn't even brought a raincoat!

It kept raining, so Kyra's dad took us to visit a nearby museum. Then we ate dinner at a fast food restaurant. Kyra's little sister, Ellie, was **delighted** to eat French fries and chicken nuggets. But Kyra and I had been looking forward to eating dinner around a campfire.

"I'm sure the weather will clear up tomorrow," Kyra's dad said.

But when we woke up the next morning, the rain was falling harder than ever.

Kyra tried distracting us with her favorite camping trick: eating milk and cereal without a bowl. First, she took a miniature cereal box. She ripped off one long skinny side and one big side. Then she made another careful tear in the bag of cereal. Finally, she poured milk into the bag and ate the cereal with a spoon, just like it was in a bowl! This kept us busy for a while.

But then Ellie started to **complain**.

"When can we go swimming?" she whined. "I'm bored."

"We have to wait for the sun to come out, Squirt," Kyra said.

"When will the sun come out?" Ellie asked.

"Will you PLEASE stop asking me questions?" Kyra **pleaded**. I stuck my head in a book. I had never seen Kyra in a bad mood before. Suddenly, I felt very **lonely**.

Then I had an idea. "Do you guys want to learn a new game?" I asked.

"Sure," everyone said.

"First you take a book like this." I held up my book, called *The Big Race*. "You open to any page and read a line. You use that line to start a funny story! I'll start." I opened the book and read a line. "*Red Lizard looks at his big cake.* Now I'll add a line. Red Lizard looks at his big cake. He is very hungry. OK Ellie, now you add a line."

Ellie thought for a minute. "The cake is made of bugs."

"Eeew, Ellie!" Kyra giggled. "I guess it's my turn. Hmmmmm, let's see. Red Lizard looks at his big cake. He is very hungry. The cake is made of bugs. He tries to eat the cake, but a bug bites him on the tongue!"

Ellie squealed. "Eeew, Kyra!"

Just then an amazing thing happened. The patter of raindrops on our tent stopped! Kyra and I looked outside. On the **horizon**, we saw the sun peeking through the clouds.

"Great!" Kyra's dad cheered. "Let's go swimming while we have the chance!"

"Can we finish our game at the beach?" Kyra asked with a smile. "I want to find out what happens to Red Lizard."

LESSON 18
The Three Wishes

Long ago, in a forest far away, a woodcutter lived with his wife. Each morning, the woodcutter went into the forest to cut wood to sell for money. He did not make a lot of money this way, however, and he and his wife were very poor.

One day, the woodcutter went into the woods to chop down a large oak tree. He hurried **eagerly** through the forest to get to the tree, as it was very large and would provide a great deal of wood to sell.

Soon he reached the tree and prepared to cut it down. As he lifted his axe, however, a family of chipmunks **scampered** away from the tree in fear. Next, the woodcutter saw a **slippery** snake slither out of a hole under the tree. Then he **spotted** a beautiful bird abandoning its nest on a branch above his head. As the animals tried to escape, a deep voice rumbled from inside the tree.

"Please do not cut me down," said the voice. "I am an old tree. The forest animals need me. Without me, they will have no home!"

The woodcutter stood in front of the tree, astonished.

"Very well," he said, scratching his head.

"Thank you, kind man," said the tree. "To show how grateful I am, I will grant your next three wishes."

The woodcutter was so shocked that he wandered home without cutting any wood, forgetting what the tree had said. By the time he got home he was very hungry. He asked his wife if there was any food to eat.

"We have nothing but a little porridge, and that won't be ready for hours," she told him.

"Oh, how I wish I had a big, fine sausage to eat right now!" he said, **disappointed**. But no sooner had the woodcutter made his wish when a **fancy** sausage appeared on the table in front of him.

"My goodness!" said his wife. "Where did that come from?" Just then the woodcutter remembered the tree's promise and told his wife about the three wishes.

"You fool!" she cried. "There is no such thing as a talking tree, and now we have no wood to sell! I wish that sausage were stuck on your nose."

In the blink of an eye, the sausage stuck to the woodcutter's nose. The woodcutter's wife tried frantically to pull the sausage off her husband's nose. But it did not work.

The woodcutter realized what he must do and promptly wished for the sausage to fall off his nose. It did, and it fell right onto the big plate that sat between the woodcutter and his wife. And the two were glad, for although they had not been able to wish for lots of money, or a fine house, or a golden coach to ride in, at least they had a tasty sausage to eat for dinner.

LESSON 19
Christina's Work

Christina Rossetti was an **author**. She lived in England over one hundred years ago. Christina's father was a poet and she grew up surrounded by writers and artists. She began writing as a girl.

As a young woman, Christina published poems in a magazine. However, she would not give the magazine **permission** to print her name on the poems. She used a made-up **signature** instead.

As an adult, Christina became famous for her poetry. She often worked for a long time to choose **exactly** the right words for a poem. She also became famous for her strong beliefs.

Christina tried to write different kinds of books. She tried to write a book about the life of one of her favorite authors. The book was **incomplete**, though. Christina felt she did not have enough information to finish it.

Throughout her life, Christina always **welcomed** the chance to write poetry. She wrote poems about her beliefs and poems for children. Christina had many illnesses, but she kept writing. She became one of the most famous poets in England. People still enjoy her poetry today. Do you?

What Is Pink?
What is pink? a rose is pink
By the fountain's brink.
What is red? a poppy's red
In its barley bed.
What is blue? the sky is blue
Where the clouds float thro'.

What is white? a swan is white
Sailing in the light.
What is yellow? pears are yellow,
Rich and ripe and mellow.
What is green? the grass is green,
With small flowers between.
What is violet? clouds are violet
In the summer twilight.
What is orange? why, an orange,
Just an orange!

How Many Seconds?
How many seconds in a minute?
Sixty, and no more in it.
How many minutes in an hour?
Sixty for sun and shower.
How many hours in a day?
Twenty-four for work and play.
How many days in a week?
Seven both to hear and speak.
How many weeks in a month?
Four, as the swift moon runn'th.
How many months in a year?
Twelve the almanack makes clear.

LESSON 20
Chicken Little

One sunny afternoon, Chicken Little was strolling through the forest. All of a sudden, KERPLUNK! An acorn fell from a tree and onto Chicken Little's chicken head.

"Oh dear!" she cried. "The sky must be falling. I should be a good little chicken and tell the king." So Chicken Little set off towards the king's castle.

Chicken Little met her friend, Henny Penny, along the way. Henny Penny was looking in some soft mud for worms to eat.

"But Henny Penny," said Chicken Little, "the sky is falling! Come with me to tell the king." Henny Penny agreed, and the two friends set off towards the king's castle.

Soon the friends saw Candy Cow. She was eating grass in a beautiful green **meadow** with her little **calf**, Cory.

"But Candy Cow," said Henny Penny, "the sky is falling! Come with us to tell the king." Candy Cow agreed, and she set off with her friends and her little calf towards the king's castle.

Next the friends saw Lucky Ducky. He had just begun to **wade** into a pond for a swim. The nice, cool water **rippled** around him.

"But Lucky Ducky," called Candy Cow, "the sky is falling! Come with us to tell the king." Lucky Ducky agreed, and the whole group set off towards the king's castle.

No sooner had they started walking along their path, though, than sneaky old Foxy Loxy stopped them.

"Where are you going on this fine day?" Foxy Loxy asked the friends with his sweetest voice.

"The sky is falling!" said Lucky Ducky. "We are going to tell the king."

"Well it's a good thing I bumped into you," grinned Foxy Loxy. "The path to the king's castle has **flooded**. Fortunately, I know a shortcut. Follow me!"

Sneaky Foxy Loxy did not show the friends a shortcut, though. Instead he led them straight to his foxhole, where he planned to eat them! Chicken Little, Henny Penny, Candy Cow, and Lucky Ducky were about to step inside when they heard a loud buzzing sound. It was their friend, Betty Bee.

"Beeeee careful, my friends!" buzzed Betty Bee. "Foxy Loxy is trying to trick you!" And with that, Betty Bee chased Foxy Loxy, followed by a huge **swarm** of buzzing bee buddies. Foxy Loxy ran and ran until he was too far away to find his way back home.

After that day, Chicken Little always strolled with an umbrella over her head. The king gave it to her as a present, just in case an acorn fell from a tree as she walked by. She especially liked to stroll through the forest and visit with Henny Penny, Candy Cow, and Lucky Ducky, who were happy to discover that the sky was not falling and that they would never have to see Foxy Loxy again.

LESSON 21

Grandpa's Tree

Grandpa's favorite tree was an old maple tree that stood in the corner of his yard. Every time Tara and Justin went to visit, Grandpa would tell stories about his tree. "Have I told you how that tree was planted on the day that I was born?" he would ask. "Did you know that I carved your grandma's initials in that tree? Do you know that when your dad was your age, he fell out of that tree and broke his arm?"

Tara and Justin loved to hear these stories again and again. They also loved to visit Grandpa. He always had a new project for them to work on, and they had such fun together.

One day, Tara and Justin went to Grandpa's house expecting a usual visit, but things were different. Grandpa hardly spoke at all and didn't want to do anything. "He is just grumpy because he broke his leg and can't move around very well," Dad **whispered**. "Why don't you go out and play."

Tara and Justin went out, but they didn't play. They talked about Grandpa.

"I think Grandpa needs a project," Justin said.

"I think we all need a project," Tara said.

Just then Tara noticed a shell from a bird's egg under Grandpa's tree. "Look," she said. "A bird's egg! I wonder what kind of bird it came from."

Justin looked. "The color and size may give us **clues**. It's tiny and blue. It might be from a robin. Let's tell Grandpa!"

Justin and Tara hurried back into the house.

"Hey, Grandpa," Justin called. "Did you know that there is a bird living in your tree? We think it may be a robin."

"Humph," grunted Grandpa. "What makes you think so?"

"We found this blue eggshell under the tree," said Tara.

"So there has to be a nest in the tree," Justin chimed in.

"So you two **detectives** solved the mystery," Grandpa said. "It was very **clever** to put those clues together." Then Grandpa smiled, "Imagine that. A robin's nest in my tree."

"I have an idea," cried Tara. "Let's make a birdfeeder!"

Grandpa frowned. "Not with this leg, I can't."

Dad **poked** his head into the room. "Don't be silly," he said. "Since when do you make a birdfeeder with your legs? Justin, go get Grandpa's tools from the garage. Tara, I saw some wood in the basement. I'll clear the table."

For a moment, Grandpa almost looked happy. Then he saw the wood. "These pieces are too big," he grumbled.

"Draw a pattern," said Dad patiently. "I'll cut the wood to match."

So Grandpa started drawing the sizes for the pieces of wood. As he planned the birdfeeder, he started talking. "Have I told you how that tree was planted on the day I was born?"

Justin and Tara smiled. "Tell us about it, Grandpa."

The next few days went by quickly as they worked on the birdfeeder. Finally, it was done. Grandpa, Tara, and Justin watched from the window as Dad hung it on the tree. "That was **sneaky** of you to find a project to make me forget my leg," Grandpa said.

"It wasn't sneaky, Grandpa," said Tara. "We just know that you are happy when you do things."

"Look!" said Justin. "The bird found the feeder. It is a robin!"

Grandpa chuckled. "Imagine that. A robin in my tree."

LESSON 22

How Bat Learned to Fly

Long, long ago, when all animals were friends, there was a special group of friends who did everything together. They **roamed** through the forest gathering food. They swam and fished in a **sparkling** lake. They slept under the night sky. But most of all they loved to play games together. One **misty** morning, when it was too early to swim or fish, the animals invented a new game.

It started when Bear had an itch. As Bear rubbed his back against the tree, Raccoon noticed the green leaves that fell. He gathered the leaves and made a ball. As Raccoon made the ball, Mouse, Coyote, Bear, and Possum worked on the rules of the game. Soon they invented football.

Now the way the animals tell the story, each time Mouse had the ball and started to run, it fell out of his hands.

Coyote scolded, "Why do you drop the ball when you run?"

"It's not his fault," said Possum. "He has little hands."

"He should hold it under his arm like me," said Raccoon.

"He should hold it against his chest like me," said Bear.

Mouse knew his friends were trying to help, but he also knew that Possum was right. The other animals were bigger and had larger hands. They could hold the ball any way they wanted when they ran. But Mouse's hands were too small.

Mouse felt awful. He didn't want to ruin the game, so he went off and sat under a tree. Mouse **promised** himself that he would never play football again. He felt sorry for himself. He would miss playing with his friends.

As Mouse sat under the tree sniffling, he heard a gentle voice whisper, "Don't cry, Mouse. I know that one day you will be a good football player."

Mouse wiped his eyes and looked up. He saw a woman with hair as dark as newly turned soil and a gown sparkling like a spring rain. It was Mother Earth!

Mother Earth spoke like a summer breeze. "Next time you play," she whispered, "jump up and wrap yourself around the ball. Hold onto it with your whole body."

Mouse thought about this. "I am a good jumper," he smiled. "It might just work. Thank you, Mother Earth."

Mouse hurried back to join his friends. The next time it was his turn to **receive** the ball, he jumped high into the air to catch it. He grabbed onto the ball with his whole body and wrapped his **slender** arms and legs around it. He hung on tightly with his tiny hands and went flying through the air.

All the animals gasped. No one, not even tall Bear or fast Coyote, could catch him. Both Raccoon and Possum tried to catch the ball like Mouse, but they just fell to the ground.

Now Mouse was better at playing football than Raccoon and Possum. Soon he was better than Bear and Coyote. All the animals agreed that he was the best football player of all.

What happened next truly amazed the animals. They say that one day, Mouse jumped up to catch the ball and missed. In fact, he flew right over the ball and high into the sky.

"Look, everyone," he shouted. "I'm flying!"

"Yes," Mother Earth whispered. "You can fly because you are no longer a Mouse. You have a new name. From now on, you shall be called Bat.

And that is how Bat learned to fly.

LESSON 23
Around the World in a Day

It started just like every other Saturday morning. Jamie and I had just finished breakfast. We were sitting not so patiently across the table from Dad, watching as he read the paper. Every Saturday, Dad picks a family outing. We might go apple picking or to a museum, park, or movie. We never knew until that morning when Dad looked in the paper for ideas. Suddenly, Dad slapped the paper on the table.

"Did you find something?" Mom asked.

"Yes," Dad said, pausing for effect. "We are going around the world."

Jamie and I looked at each other and laughed. "We can't go around the world in one day!" I said.

"It's right here," Dad said, pointing to the newspaper. "*The first annual Around the World Street Fair. Crafts, Food, Entertainment.* What do you think?"

"It sounds like fun," Jamie said.

"I'll give it a try," I answered.

"Well, then," said Mom. "Let's go."

An hour later, we were in the city at the fair. It was the biggest street fair I had ever seen. The main avenue and the intersections were closed to traffic, and the street fair was many blocks long. Booths and stalls lined the avenue, each one flying the flag from its country.

"Now stay close and **behave**," Mom warned. "I don't want to lose anyone."

It was hard to stay together. There were crafts to buy and different foods to eat. Each intersection had a stage where performers entertained. We listened to bagpipes from Scotland and steel drums from Trinidad. We watched Spanish flamenco dancers and Irish step dancers.

Before we knew it, it was lunchtime. Dad and I ordered fajitas at a Mexican stand. I watched the man wrap the **sizzling** pieces of meat in the corn tortillas. He gave one to Dad and then to me and said, "Tengan cuidado! Está caliente."

"Be careful! It's hot," I **translated** for Dad. "Thank you, gracias." I said to the man.

"Ah, you speak Spanish?" the man asked.

"I'm learning in school," I said, "but my **accent** is bad."

"No. Es bueno," said the man. "Good."

Mom and Jamie got **gooey** crepes from a French vendor.

"How do you say 'thank you' in French?" Jamie asked.

"Thank you is 'merci,'" the vendor told her.

"Merci," Jamie repeated.

After we ate, we all got Italian ices for dessert. Then we took one last walk to look for souvenirs. Dad found his souvenir first. He bought a woven grass basket from Kenya. Mom decided on a set of wooden nesting dolls from Russia. Jamie bought some paper origami animals from Japan. Finally, I decided on a sombrero from Mexico.

On the ride home, we talked about how much fun we had. We also agreed that a trip around the world was very tiring. I yawned and said that I needed a **siesta**. Then I pulled my sombrero over my face to nap. Maybe I would dream about what we'd do next Saturday.

LESSON 24
Visiting Butterflies

Where can you see butterflies? Some people may see butterflies in fields and gardens. Others may see a butterfly in a park or a backyard. But did you know that many people go to zoos and museums to see hundreds of butterflies at a time?

If you live in New York, you can see these **gentle** insects at the Bronx Zoo. First, you walk around an outdoor butterfly garden where you can learn about butterflies and how they grow. Giant sculptures of butterflies and caterpillars decorate the garden. If you are tired, you can even rest on a caterpillar bench.

After you enjoy the garden, you can visit the butterfly house. First you walk through one door into a tiny space. When the door is **completely** closed, you open a second door and enter the butterfly house. Two doors help to make sure that none of the butterflies living inside get out. The butterfly house is like being in a secret garden. There is a fish pond, hundreds of plants, and more than a thousand butterflies. It is easy to see some butterflies as they fly from flower to flower. You have to look carefully, however, to see other butterflies. They might be resting on a flower or plant. If you stand still, they might even **settle** on you!

When you leave the butterfly house, you pass a big mirror. Make sure you check out your **reflection** carefully— a butterfly may be sitting on your head or shoulder.

In Texas, you can visit the Houston Museum of Natural Science to see butterflies. Inside this museum is the Cockrell Butterfly Center. This butterfly home is a three-story glass building. Inside there is a 50-foot waterfall and hundreds of rainforest plants and flowers. The butterflies here are never **lonely**. There are hundreds and hundreds of butterflies flying around. As you look at the butterflies, check your guidebook. How many different butterflies can you **recognize**?

The butterflies at the Cockrell Butterfly Center come from all around the world. Every week, shipments of chrysalises arrive at the Center. A chrysalis is a developing butterfly inside a hard shell called a cocoon. The Center takes care of the chrysalises until they grow into butterflies and come out of their cocoons. When a butterfly does comes out, it is allowed to fly free. If you watch carefully, you can see butterflies fly from flower to flower, stop to sip nectar, or land on a surprised visitor.

After visiting the Cockrell Butterfly Center, you can visit a section of the museum called "Insects and Us." Here you can learn about all kinds of insects. You can also learn about butterfly gardening. That's where you learn about the kinds of plants you can grow in your own yard to attract butterflies.

LESSON 25
Señor Coyote, the Judge

Once upon a time, on a day when the sun blazed in the sky, Señor Rattlesnake slid out of his cool hole in the ground. He slithered around the cactus **blossoms** and stretched out to nap on the hot desert sand. He was almost asleep when a large stone rolled down the mountainside and landed right on him. Señor Rattlesnake didn't know what to do. He wiggled and squiggled. But it was no use. Señor Rattlesnake was hopelessly, helplessly trapped.

Nearby, Señor Rabbit was napping in a cool mountain **cavern**. He woke up to the sounds of Señor Rattlesnake's hissing and rattling. Señor Rabbit hopped out of the **shady** cavern and into the bright sunlight. He blinked his eyes, carefully crept out onto the rocky **ledge**, and looked over the side. He saw Señor Rattlesnake, wiggling in the sun.

Señor Rabbit hurried down the mountain and up to the snake. "Señor Rattlesnake, why are you **lugging** that heavy stone on your back?" he asked. "Where are you taking it?"

"I am not *lugging* it anywhere," groaned the snake. "I am trapped and need help. Now get this stone off of me!"

Señor Rabbit was a kind creature. He sat and placed his big feet against the stone. He pushed and pressed. Then he pushed some more. Finally, the heavy stone rolled away.

"Thank you, Señor Rabbit," hissed the snake. "S-s-such a good deed deserves a reward.

"I was glad to help," said the rabbit. "I don't need a reward."

"Yes-s-s you do," hissed Señor Rattlesnake, rattling his tail.

"What?" cried Señor Rabbit. "I just saved your life!"

"Yes-s-s you did. And for your reward, I will eat you for my s-s-supper!"

Poor Señor Rabbit was too frightened to run. He just sat there as Señor Rattlesnake prepared to strike.

Just then Señor Coyote strolled by. "What is going on here?" he asked.

The rabbit and the snake both began to speak at once.

"Wait!" shouted Señor Coyote. "Speak one at a time. Señor Rabbit, you speak first."

"Señor Rattlesnake was trapped under the stone," said the rabbit. "He asked for my help. Then, after I pushed away the stone, he said he would reward me by eating me!"

"Not true," hissed the snake. "I crawled into a **shallow** space under the stone. I wanted to trick Señor Rabbit to catch him for my s-s-supper."

Señor Coyote scratched his head. "Let me think for a minute," he said. "Since you both agree that Señor Rattlesnake was under this stone, it is only fair that he crawl under it so I can see how things were," said Señor Coyote.

"Ah, but the stone has been moved," hissed Señor Rattlesnake, "I can't crawl under it. You will have to roll it onto me."

So Señor Coyote rolled the heavy stone onto the snake and asked, "Is this how you were?"

"Yes-s-s," hissed Señor Rattlesnake. "Now take it off!"

"I have a better plan," said Señor Coyote. "You stay under that stone. It is your reward for trying to trick someone who helped you. Good day, Señor Rattlesnake."

LESSON 26
The Art Contest

Every year, Honeywell School had an art contest. Each student made a project in art class, and the projects were displayed in the gym. Mr. Murphy, the art teacher, picked a first, second, and third place for each grade. He announced the winners at a big show with the parents. It was a big deal.

John was sitting in art class. He whispered **softly** to his friend Mike, "I don't know what to make for this year's contest."

"What did you do last year?" asked Mike.

"Ugh, don't remind me," John said. "I painted a fire truck that came out like a red blob. It was the worst painting in the **universe**."

"I remember it now," said Mike. "It wasn't that bad."

"Excuse me, boys," Mr. Murphy interrupted. "You should be working, not talking."

"But I can't think of anything to do!" exclaimed John.

"Start by closing your eyes," said Mr. Murphy.

John closed his eyes and said, "I see black." Mike and the rest of the class laughed.

"Okay, I'm serious," said Mr. Murphy. "We can all try this. Close your eyes and think of something beautiful or interesting or even ordinary. It could be a butterfly you saw. It could be something **magical** that you dreamed."

One by one, the other kids in the class had ideas. John tried and tried, but he still couldn't think of anything. Soon the bell rang and it was time to go home.

That night, John sat quietly at dinner. He kept thinking about the art contest, but he couldn't think of an idea. Then his mom saved the day.

"What a pretty sunset," she said and pointed out the window at the **field** behind their house.

"That's it!" John said. "I'll paint a sunset!"

At the next art class, John used a pencil to sketch what he had seen. He kept erasing and starting over because he couldn't get it just right. Mr. Murphy came over to look.

"Why are you erasing so much, John?" he asked. "One of the best things about art is that it doesn't have to be perfect. It doesn't have to be anything other than what it is and what you make it."

John took a new sheet of paper and sketched the sunset again. *That's not bad*, he thought.

At the next class, it was time to finish the project. John opened some paints and took a deep breath. The painting started out fine, but then the colors started to run into one another. "Oh no!" John cried. "The paint isn't staying inside my marks! My project is ruined! Not again!"

Then John remembered what Mr. Murphy had said about how art doesn't have to be perfect and he relaxed. He finished the painting and showed it to Mr. Murphy.

"That is a **wondrous** sunset," said Mr. Murphy. "I love the way the colors mix and how the setting sun is reflected in the trees and **shrubbery**."

John agreed. The painting wasn't perfect, but it was beautiful. Maybe it would even win a prize!

LESSON 27
The Shoemaker and the Elves

Once upon a time, a shoemaker and his wife worked hard running a small shoe store. They loved to make shoes, but there was never enough money to run the store well. One night, they had only a single scrap of leather left. It was just enough to make one last pair of shoes.

"This is a **dreadful** situation," the shoemaker **grumbled**. "How will we keep our shop open?"

"Let's go to bed," said the shoemaker's wife. "In the morning, we will figure out what to do."

"Let me cut the leather first," the shoemaker said. So he cut the leather, laid everything on the table, and went to bed.

The shoemaker woke early the next morning and went down to stitch the shoes. To his surprise, he found a beautiful pair of shoes on the table! He was wondering if his wife had finished the sewing, when a customer came into the shop. She tried on the shoes. They fit perfectly. She loved them so much that she paid twice as much as the shoemaker asked.

The shoemaker used the money to buy more leather. That night, he cut it, put the pieces on the table, and went to bed. The next morning, he and his wife came downstairs to stitch the shoes. They were doubly thrilled to see two new pairs.

While they were examining the beautiful stitching, three customers entered. They argued over the two pairs of shoes. Finally, one customer **demanded** to buy them both for triple the price!

Day after day, the shoemaker and his wife bought leather, cut the pieces, and put them on the table before bed. Each morning, they found magnificent shoes. They had many happy customers.

One night the shoemaker's wife said, "We must find out who stitches our shoes and give thanks. Let's stay up tonight and find out what is going on."

That night, they hid in the closet. As the clock struck midnight, the window blew open and a **cobweb** swung in the breeze. In came a group of tiny elves. They were not more than a few inches tall and had pointy little ears.

At first, the shoemaker and his wife were **terrified**. "What is happening?" the shoemaker **panted**.

The shoemaker and his wife watched the elves joyfully dance around the shop. They stitched the leather, cut trim, made soles and heels, and laced laces. Before daybreak, the elves lined up the new pairs of beautiful shoes on the table.

The shoemaker asked, "How can we repay the elves?"

"I have an idea," his wife said. "Did you notice that they were dressed in rags? They make such fine shoes for us, but have none for themselves."

The shoemaker and his wife made special shoes for the elves. When they finished, they put the shoes on the table.

As the clock struck midnight, the elves came. They found the gifts and put them on happily. All night long, they danced. Just before dawn, they ran out the window.

The shoemaker and his wife never saw the elves again, but they now had enough money to live a very happy life making shoes without worry.

LESSON 28
A Hopeful Song

Excited and nervous, the children filed into the brightly-lit room. They took their places in front of an **audience** of important leaders, including the President of the United States. For a minute, the whole room was silent. Then, with smiles on their faces, the children began to perform. Music filled the air as the children **stomped**, danced, and sang. Soon the President had a smile on his face, too.

These singers were part of a **chorus** called the African Children's Choir. The chorus is made up of children aged 7 to 12 years old. They all come from Africa, a large group of countries far from the United States. The children sing many different songs.

The choir was started by a man named Ray Barnett. Ray was not born in Africa. He was born in Ireland. Many years ago, however, he heard about a terrible war happening in Africa. He heard that many children were hurt by the war. They could not go to school. Some of them were sick, but had no money to see a doctor. Some children were separated from their families. Ray decided to visit the place he had heard about. When he got there, he saw that what he had heard was true.

Ray was **determined** to do something. He wanted people to know that many African children needed help. However, he also wanted to show the world how talented and special these children were. He formed a chorus of African children. This chorus would sing and perform for money. Ray would use the money to help needy children.

Ray's project was a huge success. Today, the African Children's Choir travels all over the world to dance and sing. The children wear traditional African costumes. The costumes are made from colorful cloth and beads. People pay to see the choir perform and to buy its CDs.

Even though the choir is successful, it changes from one year to the next. The children may sing new songs or wear new costumes. Also, a new group of children is chosen to perform each year. These children are sometimes nervous to leave their homes to travel with the choir. Ray promises the children and their families that they will be safe. He also **assures** them that they can attend school when they return home at the end of the year. Many of them would not be able to go to school otherwise.

The African Children's Choir has become famous for the energy and **enthusiasm** it brings to concerts. It has performed for world leaders and even appeared on television. More importantly, it continues to help African children grow up healthy and attend school. It also gives the rest of the world a chance to hear young African singers' bright, hopeful songs.

LESSON 29
A Stone Goes to Court

Late one afternoon, a boy named Robert was walking through a forest on his way to visit his grandmother.

As the forest grew dark, Robert stopped to rest in an out-of-the-way **corner** near a small town. A patch of soft ferns looked so inviting that Robert decided to sleep there and complete his trip in the morning. He looked around for **signs** of passing robbers. Even though he saw none, he worried that someone might take his pennies from his pocket while he slept. So Robert hid the coins under a large stone, curled up on the ferns, and fell asleep.

Robert was not alone. Nearby a man, **disguised** in the forest by his green clothing, watched Robert hide his money.

The next morning Robert woke up and reached for his money. The coins had vanished! Robert looked under every rock, but could not find his money. What would he do? It was all the money he had. Robert began to cry.

Robert cried and cried. Soon the Mayor, the Police Chief, and many townspeople came to see what was the matter.

Robert told his story.

"Hmm," said the Police Chief. "We must **solve** this **mystery**! We'll get our best detectives!"

"Yes, yes . . ." said the Mayor to the Chief. Turning to Robert, the Mayor asked, "Did you see or hear anyone last night or this morning?"

"No," Robert said glumly.

"Where is the stone where you hid the coins?" asked the Mayor. Robert pointed to the stone.

The Mayor thought a minute. "Arrest this stone at once!" the Mayor commanded the Chief. "We will put the stone on trial for robbery."

The townspeople looked at each other and did not move.

"Well, get on with it" said the Mayor. "Chief, take this stone to the courtroom."

Soon Robert, the Mayor, the Chief, and the townspeople crowded into the courtroom. The stone and the boy stood in front of the Mayor.

"Stone, did you steal the boy's money?" the Mayor asked **seriously**.

The stone did not answer. The Mayor told the court reporter to record that the stone refused to answer. A man in the front row covered his mouth to hide his laughter. A woman giggled. The Mayor glared at them both.

"Stone, have you ever seen this boy before?" the Mayor continued.

Again the stone did not reply. The Mayor told the reporter to record that the stone was uncooperative and would be punished. The crowd burst out laughing.

The Mayor yelled over to the court reporter, "Record that the crowd showed disrespect to the court." Then the Mayor fined every person in the crowd one penny. The Police Chief collected the coins and brought them to the Mayor.

The Mayor gave all the coins to Robert who grinned from ear to ear. Robert bought himself a delicious breakfast and was soon back on the road to his grandmother's house.

To this day, people in that town still talk about the stone that went to court.

LESSON 30
The Parts of the House Have a Fight
a folktale from the Philippines

A family once lived together in a tree house high in a large palm tree. One hot morning, every member of this large family was sitting around the table. One person bragged that he was the most important member of the family, and, before you could say "Wait," the family burst into a **wild** argument.

"I am the most important member of the family because I was born first," said the oldest daughter.

"No, I am the most important because I am the most handsome," said one son.

"Ha!" said the younger daughter. "You're just a big **show-off** with your fancy clothes. I am most important because I am the smartest."

The tree house heard all of the arguing, and soon the parts of the house were fighting, too.

The poles that supported the house started grumbling. One boasted, "I am the most important because I am the **mightiest**! I was the very first pole driven into the earth."

The other poles replied, "Nonsense! Without us, you could not do your job of keeping the house off the wet ground. We are every bit as strong and important as you are."

As the poles fought about their strength and importance, the floor supports sneered, "You poles would be useless if we were not here to connect you!"

This caused the beams that connected the floor supports to cry out to them, "Without us, you would **wobble** and sag!"

The floor snapped at the beams and the floor supports, "For goodness sake! You wouldn't even have a reason to exist if it weren't for me!"

The woven bamboo walls lashed out at the floor, "What kind of house would this be without walls to make the rooms?"

The roof beams answered back, "You walls need our support just to stand up. If you're not **careful**, we'll stop supporting you. Then you'll see what happens!"

Insulted, the bamboo ceiling reminded the beams, "I hold all the walls together!"

The palm-leaf roof yelled to the other parts of the house, "You'd all rot in a month if I didn't keep the rain off all of you!"

As they fought, they realized that there could be no winner in this argument because they were all of equal use to the house. Together, they agreed, "It is a waste of time to argue. None of us is important without the others."

At that very moment, each member of the family came to the same conclusion. The squabbling between the members of the family stopped. Wiser and more peaceful, the family lived well from that day forward.

Teacher's Notes

Resources

Table of Contents

Linguistic Transfer Support

In the charts that follow, the mark • identifies areas in which primary language speakers may have some difficulty pronouncing and perceiving spoken English. The sound may not exist in the primary language, may exist but be pronounced somewhat differently, or may be confused with another sound. Sound production and perception issues affect phonics instruction.

CONSONANTS

Sound	Spanish	Vietnamese	Hmong	Cantonese	Haitian Creole	Korean	Khmer
/b/ as in bat			•	•		•	
/k/ as in cat and kite			•				
/d/ as in dog				•		•	
/f/ as in fan						•	
/g/ as in goat			•	•		•	•
/h/ as in hen					•		
/j/ as in jacket	•	•	•	•		•	
/l/ as in lemon						•	
/m/ as in money							
/n/ as in nail							
/p/ as in pig			•				
/r/ as in rabbit	•		•	•	•	•	
/s/ as in sun			•				
/t/ as in teen		•	•				
/v/ as in video	•			•		•	•
/w/ as in wagon	•		•				•
/y/ as in yo-yo							
/z/ as in zebra	•		•	•		•	•
/kw/ as in queen			•				
/ks/ as in X-ray			•	•			

SHORT VOWELS

Sound	Spanish	Vietnamese	Hmong	Cantonese	Haitian Creole	Korean	Khmer
short a as in hat	•	•		•		•	
short e as in set	•		•	•	•	•	
short i as in sit	•	•	•	•	•	•	
short o as in hot	•		•			•	
short u as in cup	•		•	•	•	•	

LONG VOWELS

Sound	Spanish	Vietnamese	Hmong	Cantonese	Haitian Creole	Korean	Khmer
long *a* as in d<u>a</u>te			•	•			
long *e* as in b<u>e</u>				•		•	
long *i* as in <u>i</u>ce				•			
long *o* as in r<u>oa</u>d			•	•			
long *u* as in tr<u>ue</u>				•		•	

VOWEL PATTERNS

Sound	Spanish	Vietnamese	Hmong	Cantonese	Haitian Creole	Korean	Khmer
oo as in b<u>oo</u>k	•	•	•		•	•	•
aw as in s<u>aw</u>	•					•	

DIPHTHONGS

Sound	Spanish	Vietnamese	Hmong	Cantonese	Haitian Creole	Korean	Khmer
oy as in b<u>oy</u>			•				
ow as in h<u>ow</u>	•						

R-CONTROLLED VOWELS

Sound	Spanish	Vietnamese	Hmong	Cantonese	Haitian Creole	Korean	Khmer
ir as in b<u>ir</u>d	•	•	•	•	•	•	•
ar as in h<u>ar</u>d	•	•	•	•	•	•	•
or as in f<u>or</u>m	•	•	•	•	•	•	•
air as in h<u>air</u>	•	•	•	•	•	•	•
ear as in h<u>ear</u>	•	•	•	•	•	•	•

CONSONANT DIGRAPHS

Sound	Spanish	Vietnamese	Hmong	Cantonese	Haitian Creole	Korean	Khmer
sh as in <u>sh</u>oe	•*	•		•			•
ch as in <u>ch</u>ain		•	•				
th as in <u>th</u>ink	•	•	•	•	•	•	•
ng as in si<u>ng</u>	•		•		•		

CONSONANT BLENDS

Sound	Spanish	Vietnamese	Hmong	Cantonese	Haitian Creole	Korean	Khmer
bl, tr, dr, etc. (start of words) as in <u>bl</u>ack, <u>tr</u>ee, <u>dr</u>ess		•	•	•		•	
ld, nt, rt, etc. (end of words) as in co<u>ld</u>, te<u>nt</u>, sta<u>rt</u>		•	•	•	•	•	•

* Spanish speakers from Mexico or Central America who also speak Nahuatl or a Mayan language will be familiar with this sound, written as an *x* in words like *mixteca* (pronounced *mishteca*).

Sound–Symbol Transfer Support

The following charts identify sound–symbol transfer issues for four languages that use the Roman alphabet. (The remaining three do not.) The mark • identifies symbols which do not represent the corresponding sound in the writing system of the primary language.

CONSONANTS

Sound	Spanish	Vietnamese	Hmong	Haitian Creole
b as in bat			•	
c as in cat		•	•	•
as in cent		•	•	
d as in dog				
f as in fish				
g as in goat			•	
as in giant	•		•	
h as in hen	•			
j as in jacket	•	•	•	
k as in kite			•	
l as in lemon				
m as in moon				
n as in nice				
p as in pig				
qu as in queen	•		•	•
r as in rabbit	•		•	
s as in sun			•	
t as in teen			•	
v as in video	•			
w as in wagon		•	•	
x as in X-ray		•	•	•
y as in yo-yo	•			
z as in zebra	•	•	•	

CONSONANT DIGRAPHS

Sound	Spanish	Vietnamese	Hmong	Haitian Creole
sh as in shoe	•			
ch as in chair				•
th as in think / as in that	•			•

VOWELS AND VOWEL PATTERNS

Sound	Spanish	Vietnamese	Hmong	Haitian Creole
a as in b<u>a</u>t	•		•	
aCe as in d<u>a</u>te	•	•		
ai as in r<u>ai</u>n	•	•	•	•
ay as in d<u>ay</u>	•		•	•
au as in <u>au</u>thor	•	•	•	•
aw as in s<u>aw</u>	•	•	•	•
e as in b<u>e</u>t	•		•	•
ee as in s<u>ee</u>d	•	•	•	•
ea as in t<u>ea</u>	•	•	•	•
ew as in f<u>ew</u>	•	•	•	•
i as in s<u>i</u>t	•		•	•
iCe as in p<u>i</u>pe	•	•	•	•
o as in h<u>o</u>t	•		•	•
o as in r<u>o</u>de	•	•	•	•
oo as in m<u>oo</u>n	•	•	•	•
oo as in b<u>oo</u>k	•		•	•
oa as in b<u>oa</u>t	•	•	•	•
ow as in r<u>ow</u>	•	•	•	•
ow as in h<u>ow</u>	•	•	•	
ou as in s<u>ou</u>nd	•	•	•	•
oi as in b<u>oi</u>l			•	•
oy as in b<u>oy</u>		•	•	•
u as in c<u>u</u>p	•	•	•	•
uCe as in J<u>u</u>ne	•	•		
ui as in s<u>ui</u>t	•	•	•	•
ue as in bl<u>ue</u>	•	•	•	•
y as in tr<u>y</u>	•	•	•	•
ar as in st<u>ar</u>			•	•
er as in f<u>er</u>n	•		•	•
ir as in b<u>ir</u>d	•		•	•
or as in t<u>or</u>n	•		•	
ur as in b<u>ur</u>n	•		•	

English–Spanish Vocabulary Transfer Support

English and Spanish share some basic linguistic characteristics. Both languages use word parts like prefixes and suffixes, and both have verbs that change in form. The example words below are not intended to be cognates, but words that illustrate the similar meanings of the word parts. Note that Haitian Creole, Cantonese, Hmong, and Vietnamese do not use word parts to construct new words in the same way that English does.

PREFIXES

English Word Part or Parts	English Example Words	Spanish Word Part or Parts	Spanish Example Words	Word Part Purpose
un-, non-, in-, dis-	unhappy nonstop incorrect dislike	*in-, des-/dis-* *no* plus the verb *sin* plus the noun or verb	infeliz, incorrecto desconocido disparejo no gustar sin parar	Means "not"
re-	redo	*re-*	rehacer	Means "again"
pre-	preteen	*pre-*	preescolar	Means "before"

SUFFIXES

English Word Part or Parts	English Example Words	Spanish Word Part or Parts	Spanish Example Words	Word Part Purpose
-ful	powerful	*-oso/a*	poderoso/a	Means "with"; turns a noun into an adjective
-able	readable likeable	*-ible* *-able*	legible agradable	Turns a verb into an adjective
-less	fearless careless	*sin* plus the noun prefix *des-*	sin miedo descuidado	Means "without"; turns a noun into an adjective
-ness	happiness	*-idad*	felicidad	Turns an adjective into a noun
-ion/-tion, -ment	reaction payment amazement	*-ción/-sión* verb stem + *-o*	reacción conclusión pago asombro	Turns a verb into a noun
-ly	quickly	*-mente*	rápidamente	Turns an adjective into an adverb

Qualitative Spelling Inventory (QSI)

You may use this inventory and the **Qualitative Spelling Inventory Checklist** (pages 374–375) to gather information about where students fall within a specific developmental level. In this QSI, the words are presented in increasing difficulty. As the spelling assessment proceeds, you will see what features students are learning by the quality of their spelling and the number of words and features they spell correctly. With the words in ascending difficulty, consider stopping the assessment when students make enough errors to determine a phase of spelling. To avoid frustration level testing, small groups can continue this or another list the next day.

The inventory and the checklist will help you identify what students have learned, what they are still "using but confusing" and thus need to learn, and what is beyond their present level. The inventory can be given at the beginning and end of the year and one or two times in between to monitor progress.

Students who score between 40% and 90% on the **Qualitative Spelling Inventory** can begin instruction on grade level. Consider alternate lists for students who score below 40% and above 90%.

Grade 1	Grade 2	Grade 3	Grade 4	Grade 5	Grade 6
1. net	1. class	1. paint	1. shown	1. scowl	1. pledge
2. pig	2. went	2. find	2. thirst	2. beneath	2. advantage
3. job	3. chop	3. comb	3. lodge	3. pounce	3. changeable
4. bell	4. when	4. knife	4. curve	4. brighten	4. inspire
5. trap	5. milk	5. scratch	5. suit	5. disgrace	5. conference
6. chin	6. shell	6. crawl	6. bounce	6. poison	6. relying
7. with	7. sock	7. throat	7. middle	7. destroy	7. amusement
8. drum	8. such	8. voice	8. clue	8. weary	8. conclusion
9. track	9. sleep	9. nurse	9. traced	9. sailors	9. carriage
10. bump	10. boat	10. weigh	10. hurry	10. whistle	10. advertisement
11. smoke	11. size	11. waving	11. noisier	11. chatting	11. description
12. pool	12. plain	12. letter	12. striped	12. legal	12. appearance
13. slide	13. tight	13. useful	13. collar	13. human	13. cooperation
14. shade	14. knife	14. tripping	14. medal	14. abilities	14. democratic
15. brave	15. start	15. early	15. skipping	15. decided	15. responsible
16. white	16. fought	16. dollar	16. palace	16. settlement	16. invisible
17. pink	17. story	17. mouthful	17. civil	17. surround	17. official
18. father	18. clapped	18. starry	18. wrinkle	18. treasure	18. commission
19. batted	19. saving	19. slammed	19. fossil	19. service	19. civilize
20. hugging	20. funny	20. thousand	20. disappear	20. confession	20. inherited
	21. patches	21. circle	21. damage	21. frequency	21. accidental
	22. pinned	22. laughter	22. capture	22. commotion	22. spacious
	23. village	23. carried	23. parading	23. evidence	23. sensibility
	24. pleasure	24. happiest	24. trouble	24. predict	24. composition
	25. question		25. imagine	25. community	25. accomplish
			26. favorite	26. president	26. opposition
				27. responsible	
				28. sensibility	
				29. symphonies	
				30. permission	

Qualitative Spelling Inventory Checklist

This checklist can assist you in identifying a phase of spelling development for each student and whether the student is in the early, middle, or late part of that phase.

When a feature is regularly spelled correctly, check "Yes." If the feature is spelled incorrectly or is omitted, check "No." The last feature that you check as "Often" corresponds to the student's phase of development.

Student's Name_____

Letter Name–Alphabetic Phase

EARLY

- Are beginning and ending consonants included?   Yes _____   No _____   Often _____
- Is there a vowel in each word?   Yes _____   No _____   Often _____

MIDDLE

- Are consonant digraphs and blends correct? (**sh**ade/**tr**ack)   Yes _____   No _____   Often _____

LATE

- Are short vowels spelled correctly? (h**i**d, ch**o**p, s**u**ch)   Yes _____   No _____   Often _____
- Are *m* and *n* included in front of other consonants? (bu**m**p, pi**n**k)   Yes _____   No _____   Often _____

Within Word Pattern Phase

EARLY

- Are long vowel spellings in single-syllable words "used but confused"? (SLIED for *slide*, MAIK for *make*)   Yes _____   No _____   Often _____
- Is there a vowel in each word?   Yes _____   No _____   Often _____

MIDDLE

- Are most long vowels in single-syllable words spelled correctly but some long vowel spellings still "used but confused"? (MANE for *main*)   Yes _____   No _____   Often _____

LATE

- Are *r*- and *l*-controlled vowels in single-syllable words spelled correctly? (sta**r**t/mi**l**k)   Yes _____   No _____   Often _____

Syllables and Affixes Phase

EARLY

- Are inflectional endings added correctly to base words with short vowel patterns? (hug**ging**, pin**ned**)   Yes _____ No _____ Often _____

MIDDLE

- Are inflectional endings added correctly to base words with long vowel patterns? (wa**ving**, stri**ped**)   Yes _____ No _____ Often _____

LATE

- Are unaccented final syllables spelled correctly? (cat**tle**, accur**ate**)   Yes _____ No _____ Often _____

- Are less frequent prefixes and suffixes spelled correctly? (**con**fession, **pro**duction, cap**ture**, coll**ar**)   Yes _____ No _____ Often _____

Derivational Relations Phase

EARLY

- Are multisyllabic words spelled correctly? (expansion, community)   Yes _____ No _____ Often _____

MIDDLE

- Are unaccented vowels in derived words spelled correctly? (prohibition, opp**o**sition)   Yes _____ No _____ Often _____

LATE

- Are words from derived forms spelled correctly? (compe**t**ition, confi**d**ent)   Yes _____ No _____ Often _____

- Are absorbed prefixes spelled correctly? (**ir**relevant, **ac**complish)   Yes _____ No _____ Often _____

Adapted from Words Their Way *by Donald Bear, Marcia Invernizzi, Shane Templeton, & Francine Johnston (Englewood Cliff, NJ: Prentice-Hall 2004).*

▶ Comprehensive List of Spelling/Phonics Lessons and Words, Grades K–6

The effectiveness of word study instruction begins with its word list. The lessons and words on pages 376–386 are organized by the phases of spelling development to guide your selection of lessons for students, based on assessment results. Lessons that are not in your grade-level version of this Guide can be accessed online at **www.thinkcentral.com**.

Emergent Phase

LATE

Letters Aa–Jj
Grade K, Lesson 1

The Letters in Your Name
Grade K, Lesson 2

Letters Aa–Tt
Grade K, Lesson 3

The Alphabet
Grade K, Lesson 4

Beginning Sounds in Words
Grade K, Lesson 5

Beginning Sounds in Words
Grade K, Lesson 6

Beginning Sounds /m/m, /s/s
Grade K, Lesson 7

Beginning Sounds /m/m, /s/s, /t/t
Grade K, Lesson 8

Beginning Sounds /t/t, /k/c, /p/p
Grade K, Lesson 9

Beginning Sounds /n/n, /m/m
Grade K, Lesson 14

Beginning Sounds /p/p, /f/f
Grade K, Lesson 16

Beginning Sounds /d/d, /r/r, /g/g
Grade K, Lesson 21

Letter Name–Alphabetic Phase

EARLY

Ending Sounds in Words
Grade K, Lesson 10

Ending Sounds /s/s, /p/p, /t/t
Grade K, Lesson 11

Ending Sounds /g/g, /b/b
Grade K, Lesson 18

Short a /ă/
Grade K, Lesson 12

Words with -an, -ap, -at
Grade K, Lesson 13

Short a Words and High-Frequency Words
Grade K, Lesson 15

Short i /ĭ/
Grade K, Lesson 17

Words with Short a and Short i
Grade K, Lesson 19

Words with -ig, -in, -it
Grade K, Lesson 20

Short o /ŏ/
Grade K, Lesson 22

MIDDLE

Words for One and More than One (-s)
Grade K, Lesson 23

Words with -at, -it, -ot
Grade K, Lesson 24

Words with Short o and Short e
Grade K, Lesson 25

Words with -et and -en
Grade K, Lesson 26

Short u /ŭ/
Grade K, Lesson 27

Words with Short e and Short u
Grade K, Lesson 28

Words with -ap, -up, -op
Grade K, Lesson 29

Words with Short Vowels
Grade K, Lesson 30

Words with Short a
Grade 1, Lesson 1
1. am
2. at
3. sat
4. man
5. dad
6. mat

Words with Short i
Grade 1, Lesson 2
1. if
2. is
3. him
4. rip
5. fit
6. pin

Words with Short o
Grade 1, Lesson 3
1. log
2. dot
3. top
4. hot
5. lot
6. ox

Words with Short e
Grade 1, Lesson 4
1. yet
2. web
3. pen
4. wet
5. leg
6. hen

Words with Short u
Grade 1, Lesson 5
1. up
2. bug
3. mud
4. nut
5. hug
6. tub

Words with Short a
Grade 1, Lesson 6
1. an
2. bad
3. can
4. had
5. cat
6. ran

Words with Short i
Grade 1, Lesson 7
1. in
2. will
3. did
4. sit
5. six
6. big

Words with Short o
Grade 1, Lesson 8
1. on
2. got
3. fox
4. pop
5. not
6. hop

Words with Short e
Grade 1, Lesson 9
1. yes
2. let
3. red
4. ten
5. bed
6. get

Words with Short u
Grade 1, Lesson 10
1. us
2. sun
3. but
4. fun
5. bus
6. run

Words with th
Grade 1, Lesson 11
1. that
2. then
3. this
4. them
5. with
6. bath

Words with ch
Grade 1, Lesson 12
1. chin
2. chop
3. much
4. chip
5. rich
6. chick

Words with sh, wh
Grade 1, Lesson 13
1. ship
2. shop
3. which
4. when
5. whip
6. fish

Short Vowels a, i
Grade 2, Lesson 1
1. sad
2. dig
3. jam
4. glad
5. list
6. win
7. flat
8. if
9. fix
10. rip
11. kit
12. mask

Short Vowels o, u, e
Grade 2, Lesson 2
1. wet
2. job
3. hug
4. rest
5. spot
6. mud
7. left
8. help
9. plum

10. nut
11. net
12. hot

LATE

Consonant Blends with *r, l, s*
Grade 2, Lesson 5
1. spin
2. clap
3. grade
4. swim
5. place
6. last
7. test
8. skin
9. drag
10. glide
11. just
12. stage

Common Final Blends *nd, ng, nk, nt, xt, mp*
Grade 2, Lesson 6
1. next
2. end
3. camp
4. sank
5. sing
6. drink
7. hunt
8. stand
9. long
10. stamp
11. pond
12. bring

Words with *ar*
Grade 1, Lesson 21
1. far
2. arm
3. yard
4. art
5. jar
6. bar
7. barn
8. bark
9. card
10. yarn

Double Consonants and *ck*
Grade 2, Lesson 7
1. rock
2. black
3. trick
4. kick
5. full
6. dress
7. neck
8. add
9. spell
10. stuck
11. class
12. doll

Words with *th, sh, wh, ch*
Grade 2, Lesson 8
1. dish
2. than
3. chest
4. such
5. thin
6. push
7. shine
8. chase
9. white
10. while
11. these
12. flash

Short Vowels
Grade 3, Lesson 1
1. crop
2. plan
3. thing
4. smell
5. shut
6. sticky
7. spent
8. lunch
9. pumpkin
10. clock
11. gift
12. class
13. skip
14. swing

Within Word Pattern Phase

EARLY

Words with Long *a*
Grade 1, Lesson 14
1. came
2. make
3. brave
4. late
5. gave
6. shape

Words with Long *i*
Grade 1, Lesson 15
1. time
2. like
3. kite
4. bike
5. white
6. drive

Long Vowels *a, i*
Grade 2, Lesson 3
1. cake
2. mine
3. plate
4. size
5. ate
6. grape
7. prize
8. wipe
9. race

10. line
11. pile
12. rake

Words with Long *o*
Grade 1, Lesson 16
1. so
2. go
3. home
4. hole
5. no
6. rope
7. joke
8. bone
9. stove
10. poke

Words with Long *e*
Grade 1, Lesson 17
1. me
2. be
3. read
4. feet
5. tree
6. keep
7. eat
8. mean
9. sea
10. these

Words with Long *a*
Grade 1, Lesson 18
1. play
2. grain
3. sail
4. mail
5. may
6. rain
7. way
8. day
9. stay
10. pain

Words with Long *o*
Grade 1, Lesson 19
1. show
2. row
3. grow
4. low
5. blow
6. snow
7. boat
8. coat
9. road
10. toad

Words with *er, ir, ur*
Grade 1, Lesson 22
1. her
2. fern
3. girl
4. sir
5. stir
6. bird
7. fur
8. hurt
9. turn
10. third

Words with *oo* (/o͞o/)
Grade 1, Lesson 23
1. look
2. book
3. good
4. hook
5. brook
6. took
7. foot
8. shook
9. wood
10. hood

Words with *oo, ou, ew*
Grade 1, Lesson 24
1. soon
2. new
3. noon
4. zoo
5. boot
6. too
7. moon
8. blew
9. soup
10. you

Words with Long *i*
Grade 1, Lesson 28
1. my
2. try
3. sky
4. fly
5. by
6. dry
7. pie
8. cried
9. night
10. light

Long Vowels *o, u*
Grade 2, Lesson 4
1. doze
2. nose
3. use
4. rose
5. pole
6. close
7. cute
8. woke
9. mule
10. rode
11. role
12. tune

Contractions
Grade 2, Lesson 10
1. I'm
2. don't
3. isn't
4. can't
5. we'll
6. it's
7. I've
8. didn't
9. you're
10. that's
11. wasn't
12. you've

Words with *ai, ay*
Grade 2, Lesson 12
1. pay
2. wait
3. paint
4. train
5. pail
6. clay
7. tray
8. plain
9. stain
10. hay
11. gray
12. away

Words with *ee, ea*
Grade 2, Lesson 13
1. free
2. teach
3. teeth
4. please
5. beach
6. wheel
7. team
8. speak
9. sneeze
10. sheep
11. meaning
12. weave

Long *o (o, oa, ow)*
Grade 2, Lesson 14
1. own
2. most
3. soap
4. float
5. both
6. know
7. loan
8. goat
9. flow
10. loaf
11. throw
12. coach

Long *i (i, igh, y)*
Grade 2, Lesson 17
1. night
2. kind
3. spy
4. child
5. light
6. find
7. right
8. high
9. wild
10. July
11. fry
12. sigh

MIDDLE

Words with *ar*
Grade 2, Lesson 19
1. car
2. dark
3. arm
4. star
5. park
6. yard

7. party
8. hard
9. farm
10. start
11. part
12. spark

Words with or, ore
Grade 2, Lesson 20
1. horn
2. story
3. fork
4. score
5. store
6. corn
7. morning
8. shore
9. short
10. born
11. tore
12. forget

Words with er
Grade 2, Lesson 21
1. father
2. over
3. under
4. herd
5. water
6. verb
7. paper
8. cracker
9. offer
10. cover
11. germ
12. master

Homophones
Grade 2, Lesson 22
1. meet
2. meat
3. week
4. weak
5. mane
6. main
7. tail
8. tale
9. be
10. bee
11. too
12. two

Words with oo (ew, oo, ou)
Grade 2, Lesson 26
1. root
2. crew
3. spoon
4. few
5. bloom
6. grew
7. room
8. you
9. stew
10. boost
11. scoop
12. flew

Words with oo (book)
Grade 2, Lesson 27
1. took
2. books
3. foot
4. hoof
5. cook
6. nook
7. hood
8. wood
9. stood
10. shook
11. crook
12. cookbook

Words with ai, ay, igh, y
Grade 2, Lesson 29
1. aim
2. snail
3. bay
4. braid
5. ray
6. always
7. gain
8. sly
9. chain
10. shy
11. bright
12. fright

Words with oa, ow, ee, ea
Grade 2, Lesson 30
1. seated
2. keeps
3. speed
4. seen
5. means
6. clean
7. groan
8. roast
9. bowls
10. crow
11. owe
12. grown

V-C-e Spellings
Grade 3, Lesson 2
1. spoke
2. mile
3. save
4. excuse
5. cone
6. invite
7. cube
8. price
9. erase
10. ripe
11. broke
12. flame
13. life
14. rule

More Long a and Long e Spellings
Grade 3, Lesson 3
1. lay
2. real

3. trail
4. sweet
5. today
6. dream
7. seem
8. tea
9. treat
10. afraid
11. leave
12. bait
13. screen
14. speed

More Long o Spellings
Grade 3, Lesson 4
1. load
2. open
3. told
4. yellow
5. soak
6. shadow
7. foam
8. follow
9. glow
10. sold
11. window
12. coach
13. almost
14. throat

Spelling Long i
Grade 3, Lesson 5
1. slight
2. mild
3. sight
4. pie
5. mind
6. tie
7. pilot
8. might
9. lie
10. tight
11. blind
12. fight
13. die
14. midnight

Vowel + /r/ Sounds in air and fear
Grade 3, Lesson 16
1. air
2. wear
3. chair
4. stairs
5. bare
6. bear
7. hair
8. care
9. pear
10. pair
11. share
12. near
13. ear
14. beard

Words with aw, al, o
Grade 2, Lesson 25
1. tall
2. saw
3. dog
4. draw
5. call
6. fall
7. soft
8. paw
9. ball
10. yawn
11. log
12. small

More Short and Long Vowels
Grade 3, Lesson 6
1. math
2. toast
3. easy
4. socks
5. Friday
6. stuff
7. paid
8. cheese
9. June
10. elbow
11. program
12. shiny
13. piles
14. sticky

Words with ou, ow
Grade 1, Lesson 25
1. how
2. now
3. cow
4. owl
5. ouch
6. house
7. found
8. out
9. gown
10. town

Words with ow, ou
Grade 2, Lesson 28
1. cow
2. house
3. town
4. shout
5. down
6. mouse
7. found
8. loud
9. brown
10. ground
11. pound
12. flower

LATE

Three-Letter Clusters
Grade 3, Lesson 7
1. three
2. scrap
3. street

4. spring
5. thrill
6. scream
7. strange
8. throw
9. string
10. scrape
11. spray
12. threw
13. strong
14. scratch

Unexpected Consonant Spellings
Grade 3, Lesson 8
1. itch
2. wreck
3. knee
4. patch
5. wrap
6. knot
7. watch
8. knife
9. stretch
10. write
11. knew
12. knock
13. match
14. wrong

Vowel Sound in town
Grade 3, Lesson 9
1. clown
2. round
3. bow
4. cloud
5. power
6. crown
7. thousand
8. crowd
9. sound
10. count
11. powder
12. blouse
13. frown
14. pound

Vowel Sound in talk
Grade 3, Lesson 10
1. talk
2. cross
3. awful
4. law
5. cloth
6. cost
7. crawl
8. chalk
9. also
10. raw
11. salt
12. wall
13. lawn
14. always

Vowel Sound in joy
Grade 3, Lesson 11
1. joy
2. point

3. voice
4. join
5. oil
6. coin
7. noise
8. spoil
9. toy
10. joint
11. boy
12. soil
13. choice
14. boil

Homophones
Grade 3, Lesson 12
1. hole
2. whole
3. its
4. it's
5. hear
6. here
7. won
8. one
9. our
10. hour
11. their
12. there
13. fur
14. fir

Contractions
Grade 3, Lesson 13
1. I'd
2. he's
3. haven't
4. doesn't
5. let's
6. there's
7. wouldn't
8. what's
9. she's
10. aren't
11. hasn't
12. couldn't
13. he'd
14. they're

Vowel + /r/ Sounds
Grade 3, Lesson 14
1. horse
2. mark
3. storm
4. market
5. acorn
6. artist
7. March
8. north
9. barking
10. stork
11. thorn
12. forest
13. chore
14. restore

Vowel + /r/ Sound in nurse
Grade 3, Lesson 15
1. nurse
2. work
3. shirt

4. hurt
5. first
6. word
7. serve
8. curly
9. dirt
10. third
11. worry
12. turn
13. stir
14. firm

Words with /j/ and /s/
Grade 3, Lesson 17
1. age
2. space
3. change
4. jawbone
5. jacket
6. giant
7. pencil
8. circle
9. once
10. large
11. dance
12. jeans
13. bounce
14. huge

Spelling the /k/ and /kw/ Sounds
Grade 3, Lesson 18
1. shark
2. check
3. queen
4. circus
5. flake
6. crack
7. second
8. squeeze
9. quart
10. squeak
11. quick
12. coldest
13. Africa
14. Mexico

Vowel Sounds in *spoon* and *wood*
Grade 3, Lesson 19
1. mood
2. wooden
3. drew
4. smooth
5. blue
6. balloon
7. true
8. crooked
9. chew
10. tooth
11. hooves
12. cool
13. food
14. pooch

ough* and *augh
Grade 3, Lesson 28
1. taught
2. thought

3. rough
4. laugh
5. bought
6. cough
7. ought
8. caught
9. fought
10. daughter
11. tough
12. through
13. enough
14. brought

Short *o* and Long *o*
Grade 4, Lesson 4
1. block
2. shown
3. oatmeal
4. wrote
5. fellow
6. scold
7. coast
8. odd
9. locate
10. slope
11. throat
12. host
13. online
14. shock
15. solve
16. known
17. remote
18. stock
19. boast
20. globe

Homophones
Grade 4, Lesson 5
1. wait
2. weight
3. heard
4. herd
5. days
6. daze
7. heel
8. heal
9. peak
10. peek
11. sent
12. cent
13. scent
14. feet
15. feat
16. vain
17. vane
18. vein
19. miner
20. minor

Short *a* and Long *a*
Grade 4, Lesson 1
1. blade
2. gray
3. past
4. afraid
5. magic
6. delay
7. amaze
8. drain
9. maybe

10. break
11. sale
12. hang
13. stain
14. glass
15. raft
16. jail
17. crayon
18. fact
19. stale
20. steak

Short *e* and Long *e*
Grade 4, Lesson 2
1. west
2. steep
3. member
4. gleam
5. fresh
6. freedom
7. speed
8. steam
9. beast
10. believe
11. speck
12. kept
13. cheap
14. pretend
15. greed
16. shelf
17. least
18. eager
19. reason
20. chief

Short *i* and Long *i*
Grade 4, Lesson 3
1. skill
2. crime
3. grind
4. tonight
5. brick
6. flight
7. live
8. chill
9. delight
10. build
11. ditch
12. decide
13. witness
14. wind
15. district
16. inch
17. sigh
18. fright
19. remind
20. split

Vowel Sounds /ŭ/, /yo͞o/, and /o͞o/
Grade 4, Lesson 6
1. bunch
2. fruit
3. argue
4. crumb
5. crew
6. tune
7. juice
8. refuse
9. truth

10. young
11. clue
12. trunk
13. amuse
14. suit
15. rude
16. trust
17. dew
18. stuck
19. rescue
20. brush

Vowel Sounds /o͞o/ and /o͝o/
Grade 4, Lesson 7
1. bloom
2. cookbook
3. tool
4. shampoo
5. put
6. wool
7. stool
8. proof
9. prove
10. group
11. brook
12. foolish
13. bush
14. crooked
15. booth
16. raccoon
17. hook
18. groom
19. roof
20. soup

Vowel Sounds /ou/ and /ô/
Grade 4, Lesson 8
1. aloud
2. bald
3. hawk
4. south
5. faucet
6. proud
7. claw
8. tower
9. stalk
10. couple
11. howl
12. false
13. dawn
14. allow
15. drown
16. pause
17. fault
18. cause
19. amount
20. cloudier

Vowel + /r/ Sounds
Grade 4, Lesson 9
1. spark
2. prepare
3. cheer
4. tear
5. scarf
6. scare
7. repair
8. earring

9. scarce
10. weird
11. sharp
12. rear
13. spare
14. gear
15. hairy
16. compare
17. alarm
18. harsh
19. upstairs
20. square

More Vowel + /r/ Sounds
Grade 4, Lesson 10
1. learn
2. dirty
3. worn
4. sore
5. thirst
6. burn
7. record
8. cure
9. board
10. course
11. worth
12. early
13. return
14. pure
15. world
16. search
17. worse
18. thirteen
19. sport
20. current

Syllables and Affixes Phase

EARLY

Compound Words
Grade 1, Lesson 20
1. bedtime
2. sunset
3. bathtub
4. sailboat
5. flagpole
6. backpack
7. playpen
8. raincoat
9. inside
10. himself

Base Words with -ed, -ing
Grade 1, Lesson 26
1. mix
2. mixed
3. hop
4. hopped
5. hope
6. hoping
7. run
8. running
9. use
10. used

Base Words with -er, -est
Grade 1, Lesson 27
1. hard
2. harder
3. hardest
4. fast
5. faster
6. fastest
7. slow
8. slower
9. slowest
10. sooner

Words with Suffixes -ly, -y, -ful
Grade 1, Lesson 29
1. sad
2. sadly
3. slow
4. slowly
5. dust
6. dusty
7. trick
8. tricky
9. help
10. helpful

Compound Words
Grade 2, Lesson 15
1. cannot
2. pancake
3. maybe
4. baseball
5. playground
6. someone
7. myself
8. classroom
9. sunshine
10. outside
11. upon
12. nothing

Base Words with Endings -ed, -ing
Grade 2, Lesson 9
1. liked
2. using
3. riding
4. chased
5. spilled
6. making
7. closed
8. hoping
9. baked
10. hiding
11. standing
12. asked

Base Words with Endings -ed, -ing
Grade 2, Lesson 16
1. running
2. clapped
3. stopped
4. hopping
5. batted
6. selling
7. pinned
8. cutting

9. sitting
10. rubbed
11. missed
12. grabbed

Base Words with Endings -s, -es
Grade 2, Lesson 11
1. hens
2. eggs
3. ducks
4. bikes
5. boxes
6. wishes
7. dresses
8. names
9. bells
10. stamps
11. dishes
12. grapes

Suffixes -ly, -ful
Grade 2, Lesson 23
1. helpful
2. sadly
3. hopeful
4. thankful
5. slowly
6. wishful
7. kindly
8. useful
9. safely
10. painful
11. mouthful
12. weakly

Long e Spelled y
Grade 2, Lesson 18
1. happy
2. pretty
3. baby
4. very
5. puppy
6. funny
7. carry
8. lucky
9. only
10. sunny
11. penny
12. city

Prefixes re-, un-
Grade 2, Lesson 24
1. unhappy
2. retell
3. untangle
4. unkind
5. repaint
6. refill
7. unlike
8. remake
9. unpack
10. reread
11. unlock
12. replay

Compound Words
Grade 3, Lesson 20
1. birthday
2. anyone

3. sometimes
4. everything
5. homework
6. afternoon
7. airplane
8. grandmother
9. something
10. without
11. himself
12. faraway
13. sunburned
14. daylight

Words with -ed and -ing
Grade 3, Lesson 21
1. coming
2. swimming
3. dropping
4. tapping
5. taping
6. invited
7. saving
8. stared
9. planned
10. changing
11. joking
12. loved
13. gripped
14. tasted

Changing Final y to i
Grade 3, Lesson 22
1. cities
2. cried
3. puppies
4. hurried
5. stories
6. flies
7. parties
8. tried
9. pennies
10. fried
11. carried
12. babies
13. spied
14. ponies

The Suffixes -ful, -ly, and -er
Grade 3, Lesson 23
1. singer
2. loudly
3. joyful
4. teacher
5. fighter
6. closely
7. powerful
8. farmer
9. quickly
10. careful
11. friendly
12. speaker
13. wonderful
14. truly

The Prefixes re- and un-
Grade 3, Lesson 24
1. unfold
2. rejoin
3. untie
4. reheat
5. unfair
6. unclear
7. repaid
8. rewrite
9. unhurt
10. recheck
11. unlucky
12. unwrap
13. reuse
14. unsure

The Suffixes -less and -ness
Grade 3, Lesson 25
1. painless
2. sickness
3. sadness
4. helpless
5. thankless
6. kindness
7. hopeless
8. darkness
9. fearless
10. thickness
11. careless
12. goodness
13. spotless
14. softness

Compound Words
Grade 4, Lesson 11
1. somebody
2. fireplace
3. nearby
4. toothbrush
5. homesick
6. make-believe
7. anything
8. all right
9. goodbye
10. forehead
11. classmate
12. flashlight
13. haircut
14. twenty-two
15. driveway
16. alarm clock
17. baby-sit
18. airport
19. forever
20. mailbox

Words with -ed or -ing
Grade 4, Lesson 12
1. rising
2. traced
3. stripped
4. slammed
5. dancing
6. striped
7. winning

8. snapping
9. bragging
10. handled
11. dripped
12. begged
13. dared
14. skipped
15. hitting
16. spotted
17. raced
18. dimmed
19. spinning
20. escaped

More Words with -ed or -ing
Grade 4, Lesson 13
1. wiped
2. covered
3. mapped
4. pleasing
5. slipped
6. putting
7. traveled
8. seeking
9. visiting
10. mixed
11. shipped
12. phoning
13. offered
14. smelling
15. hiking
16. checking
17. fainted
18. landed
19. becoming
20. wandering

Final Long e
Grade 4, Lesson 14
1. turkey
2. lonely
3. colony
4. steady
5. hungry
6. valley
7. hockey
8. starry
9. melody
10. movie
11. duty
12. drowsy
13. chimney
14. plenty
15. daily
16. alley
17. fifty
18. empty
19. injury
20. prairie

Changing Final y to i
Grade 4, Lesson 15
1. tiniest
2. hobbies
3. copied
4. countries
5. pitied
6. easier

7. laziest
8. families
9. spied
10. happiest
11. ladies
12. friendlier
13. studied
14. busier
15. breezier
16. prettiest
17. noisier
18. healthier
19. butterflies
20. funniest

Words with /k/, /ng/, and /kw/
Grade 4, Lesson 16
1. risky
2. track
3. topic
4. blank
5. question
6. pocket
7. monkey
8. junk
9. equal
10. ache
11. public
12. attack
13. struck
14. earthquake
15. picnic
16. banker
17. electric
18. blanket
19. mistake
20. stomach

Prefixes re-, un-, dis-
Grade 4, Lesson 18
1. unused
2. refresh
3. dislike
4. replace
5. unpaid
6. redo
7. disorder
8. unplanned
9. distrust
10. rewind
11. untrue
12. unload
13. recall
14. displease
15. uneven
16. rebuild
17. restart
18. uncover
19. untidy
20. discolor

Suffixes -ful, -less, -ness, -ment
Grade 4, Lesson 19
1. colorful
2. weakness
3. movement
4. endless

5. truthful
6. illness
7. cheerful
8. useless
9. beautiful
10. restless
11. clumsiness
12. pavement
13. peaceful
14. fondness
15. neatness
16. speechless
17. statement
18. wasteful
19. penniless
20. treatment

Words with -ed or -ing
Grade 5, Lesson 16
1. scrubbed
2. listening
3. stunned
4. knitting
5. carpeting
6. wandered
7. gathering
8. beginning
9. skimmed
10. chatting
11. shrugged
12. bothering
13. whipped
14. quizzed
15. suffering
16. scanned
17. ordered
18. totaled
19. answered
20. upsetting

More Words with -ed or -ing
Grade 5, Lesson 17
1. tiring
2. borrowed
3. freezing
4. delivered
5. whispered
6. losing
7. decided
8. amazing
9. performing
10. resulting
11. related
12. attending
13. damaged
14. remarked
15. practicing
16. supported
17. united
18. expected
19. amusing
20. repeated

Changing Final y to i
Grade 5, Lesson 18
1. duties
2. earlier

3. loveliest
4. denied
5. ferries
6. sunnier
7. terrified
8. abilities
9. dirtier
10. scariest
11. trophies
12. cozier
13. enemies
14. iciest
15. greediest
16. drowsier
17. victories
18. horrified
19. memories
20. strategies

Suffixes: -ful, -ly, -ness, -less, -ment
Grade 5, Lesson 19
1. lately
2. settlement
3. watchful
4. countless
5. steadily
6. closeness
7. calmly
8. government
9. agreement
10. cloudiness
11. delightful
12. noisily
13. tardiness
14. forgetful
15. forgiveness
16. harmless
17. enjoyment
18. appointment
19. effortless
20. plentiful

Prefixes: in-, un-, dis-, mis-
Grade 5, Lesson 24
1. mislead
2. dismiss
3. insincere
4. unable
5. indirect
6. mistreat
7. disaster
8. dishonest
9. insecure
10. unknown
11. incomplete
12. unequal
13. unstable
14. misspell
15. disagree
16. informal
17. discover
18. unwise
19. mislaid
20. disgrace

Words with Syllable Pattern CV
Grade 1, Lesson 30
1. even
2. open
3. begin
4. baby
5. tiger
6. music
7. paper
8. zero
9. table
10. below

VCCV Syllabication
Grade 3, Lesson 26
1. person
2. helmet
3. until
4. carpet
5. Monday
6. enjoy
7. forget
8. problem
9. Sunday
10. garden
11. order
12. mistake
13. umpire
14. herself

Words with Double Consonants
Grade 3, Lesson 27
1. jelly
2. bottom
3. pillow
4. happen
5. butter
6. lesson
7. cherry
8. sudden
9. arrow
10. dollar
11. hello
12. rabbit
13. letter
14. button

Words Ending with -er or -le
Grade 3, Lesson 29
1. apple
2. river
3. little
4. October
5. ladder
6. summer
7. purple
8. later
9. November
10. giggle
11. uncle
12. winter
13. center
14. double

Words that Begin with a- or be-
Grade 3, Lesson 30
1. below
2. about
3. belong
4. around
5. again
6. alone
7. because
8. above
9. between
10. alive
11. behind
12. begin
13. along
14. before

Words with VCV Pattern
Grade 4, Lesson 21
1. event
2. humor
3. rapid
4. music
5. relief
6. planet
7. detail
8. unite
9. frozen
10. figure
11. siren
12. polite
13. hotel
14. protest
15. punish
16. defend
17. relay
18. habit
19. student
20. moment

VCCV and VCV Patterns
Grade 4, Lesson 22
1. dentist
2. final
3. finish
4. narrow
5. shelter
6. ahead
7. corner
8. hollow
9. divide
10. famous
11. recent
12. silver
13. capture
14. cabin
15. dinner
16. minus
17. minute
18. value
19. reward
20. broken

Words with VCCV Pattern
Grade 4, Lesson 23
1. poster
2. secret
3. whether
4. author
5. rocket
6. bushel
7. agree
8. bucket
9. ticket
10. declare
11. chicken
12. clothing
13. apron
14. whiskers
15. degree
16. gather
17. achieve
18. rather
19. bracket
20. machine

Words with VCCCV Pattern
Grade 4, Lesson 24
1. hundred
2. supply
3. single
4. middle
5. explain
6. surprise
7. pilgrim
8. sandwich
9. instead
10. complete
11. monster
12. settle
13. address
14. farther
15. sample
16. although
17. turtle
18. athlete
19. orchard
20. kingdom

Words with VV Pattern
Grade 4, Lesson 25
1. idea
2. lion
3. usual
4. radio
5. liar
6. poem
7. India
8. piano
9. January
10. quiet
11. poet
12. science
13. diary
14. violin
15. period
16. February
17. cereal
18. video
19. meteor
20. rodeo

Final Schwa + /r/ Sound
Grade 4, Lesson 26
1. enter
2. banner
3. sugar
4. shower
5. motor
6. collar
7. labor
8. finger
9. mirror
10. beggar
11. favor
12. bother
13. fever
14. doctor
15. temper
16. actor
17. polar
18. sweater
19. traitor
20. whenever

Final Schwa + /l/ Sound
Grade 4, Lesson 27
1. title
2. towel
3. battle
4. pedal
5. metal
6. simple
7. eagle
8. special
9. total
10. trouble
11. nickel
12. gentle
13. barrel
14. model
15. tangle
16. ankle
17. marvel
18. juggle
19. squirrel
20. riddle

More Vowel + /r/ Sounds
Grade 5, Lesson 7
1. earth
2. peer
3. twirl
4. burnt
5. smear
6. further
7. appear
8. worthwhile
9. nerve
10. pier
11. squirm
12. weary
13. alert
14. murmur
15. thirsty

16. reverse
17. worship
18. career
19. research
20. volunteer

Short Vowels
Grade 6, Lesson 1
1. batch
2. reject
3. vanish
4. sloppy
5. rhythm
6. blunder
7. strict
8. meadow
9. recover
10. cleanse
11. text
12. mystery
13. expand
14. bluff
15. promptly
16. initials
17. statue
18. polish
19. somehow
20. dreadful

Short Vowels
Grade 5, Lesson 1
1. breath
2. wobble
3. blister
4. crush
5. direct
6. promise
7. grasp
8. numb
9. hymn
10. shovel
11. gravity
12. frantic
13. swift
14. feather
15. comic
16. bundle
17. solid
18. weather
19. energy
20. stingy

Long a and Long e
Grade 5, Lesson 2
1. awake
2. feast
3. stray
4. greet
5. praise
6. disease
7. repeat
8. display
9. braces
10. thief
11. ashamed
12. sleeve
13. waist
14. beneath
15. sheepish

16. release
17. remain
18. sway
19. training
20. niece

Long i and Long o
Grade 5, Lesson 3
1. sign
2. groan
3. reply
4. thrown
5. strike
6. mighty
7. stroll
8. compose
9. dough
10. height
11. excite
12. apply
13. slight
14. define
15. odor
16. spider
17. control
18. silent
19. brighten
20. approach

Vowel Sounds: /o͞o/, /yo͞o/
Grade 5, Lesson 4
1. glue
2. flute
3. youth
4. accuse
5. bruise
6. stew
7. choose
8. loose
9. lose
10. view
11. confuse
12. cruise
13. jewel
14. execute
15. route
16. cartoon
17. avenue
18. include
19. assume
20. souvenir

VCCV Pattern
Grade 5, Lesson 11
1. bargain
2. journey
3. pattern
4. arrive
5. object
6. suppose
7. shoulder
8. permit
9. sorrow
10. tunnel
11. subject
12. custom
13. suggest
14. perhaps

Comprehensive Word List

15. lawyer
16. timber
17. common
18. publish
19. burden
20. scissors

VCV Pattern
Grade 5, Lesson 12

1. human
2. exact
3. award
4. behave
5. credit
6. basic
7. vivid
8. evil
9. modern
10. nation
11. robot
12. panic
13. select
14. cousin
15. item
16. police
17. prefer
18. menu
19. novel
20. deserve

VCCCV Pattern
Grade 5, Lesson 13

1. conflict
2. orphan
3. instant
4. complex
5. simply
6. burglar
7. laundry
8. laughter
9. employ
10. anchor
11. merchant
12. improve
13. arctic
14. mischief
15. childhood
16. purchase
17. dolphin
18. partner
19. complain
20. tremble

VV Pattern
Grade 5, Lesson 14

1. actual
2. cruel
3. patriot
4. diet
5. museum
6. casual
7. ruin
8. pioneer
9. trial
10. visual
11. realize
12. create
13. riot
14. genuine

15. area
16. annual
17. audio
18. dial
19. theater
20. influence

Vowel Sounds: /ou/, /ô/, /oi/
Grade 5, Lesson 5

1. ounce
2. sprawl
3. launch
4. loyal
5. avoid
6. basketball
7. moist
8. haunt
9. scowl
10. naughty
11. destroy
12. saucer
13. pounce
14. poison
15. August
16. auction
17. royal
18. coward
19. awkward
20. encounter

Vowel + /r/ Sounds
Grade 5, Lesson 6

1. glory
2. aware
3. carton
4. adore
5. aboard
6. dairy
7. ordeal
8. pardon
9. warn
10. vary
11. barely
12. torch
13. barge
14. soar
15. beware
16. absorb
17. armor
18. stairway
19. perform
20. former

Words with VCCV Pattern
Grade 4, Lesson 20

1. million
2. collect
3. lumber
4. pepper
5. plastic
6. borrow
7. support
8. thirty
9. perfect
10. attend
11. canyon
12. traffic

13. fortune
14. danger
15. soccer
16. engine
17. picture
18. survive
19. seldom
20. effort

LATE

Words with Final /j/ and /s/
Grade 4, Lesson 17

1. glance
2. judge
3. damage
4. package
5. twice
6. stage
7. carriage
8. since
9. practice
10. marriage
11. baggage
12. office
13. message
14. bridge
15. chance
16. notice
17. ridge
18. manage
19. palace
20. bandage

Words with Silent Consonants
Grade 4, Lesson 29

1. half
2. comb
3. mortgage
4. honor
5. fasten
6. kneel
7. wreath
8. calm
9. answer
10. handsome
11. wrinkle
12. listen
13. fetch
14. yolk
15. climb
16. honest
17. knuckle
18. plumber
19. limb
20. folktale

Unusual Spellings
Grade 4, Lesson 30

1. meant
2. routine
3. style
4. flood
5. month
6. pleasant
7. guess
8. women

9. either
10. against
11. disguise
12. sweat
13. magazine
14. guard
15. receive
16. wonder
17. league
18. type
19. ceiling
20. money

Three-Syllable Words
Grade 4, Lesson 28

1. library
2. another
3. hospital
4. example
5. deliver
6. history
7. however
8. several
9. vacation
10. important
11. victory
12. imagine
13. camera
14. potato
15. remember
16. together
17. memory
18. favorite
19. continue
20. president

Homophones
Grade 5, Lesson 8

1. steel
2. steal
3. aloud
4. allowed
5. ring
6. wring
7. lesson
8. lessen
9. who's
10. whose
11. manor
12. manner
13. pedal
14. peddle
15. berry
16. bury
17. hanger
18. hangar
19. overdo
20. overdue

Compound Words
Grade 5, Lesson 9

1. wildlife
2. uproar
3. home run
4. headache
5. top-secret
6. teammate
7. wheelchair

8. light bulb
9. well-known
10. throughout
11. life preserver
12. barefoot
13. part-time
14. warehouse
15. overboard
16. post office
17. outspoken
18. up-to-date
19. awestruck
20. newscast

Final Schwa + /r/ Sound
Grade 5, Lesson 10

1. cellar
2. flavor
3. cougar
4. chapter
5. mayor
6. anger
7. senator
8. passenger
9. major
10. popular
11. tractor
12. thunder
13. pillar
14. border
15. calendar
16. quarter
17. lunar
18. proper
19. elevator
20. bitter

Final Schwa + /l/ Sound
Grade 5, Lesson 15

1. formal
2. whistle
3. label
4. puzzle
5. legal
6. angle
7. normal
8. needle
9. angel
10. pupil
11. struggle
12. level
13. local
14. bicycle
15. channel
16. global
17. stumble
18. quarrel
19. article
20. fossil

Final /n/ or /ən/, /chər/, /zhər/
Grade 5, Lesson 21

1. nature
2. certain
3. future
4. villain

5. mountain
6. mixture
7. pleasure
8. captain
9. departure
10. surgeon
11. texture
12. curtain
13. creature
14. treasure
15. gesture
16. fountain
17. furniture
18. measure
19. feature
20. adventure

Unstressed Syllables
Grade 5, Lesson 23
1. entry
2. limit
3. talent
4. disturb
5. entire
6. wisdom
7. dozen
8. impress
9. respond
10. fortress
11. neglect
12. patrol
13. kitchen
14. forbid
15. pirate
16. spinach
17. adopt
18. frighten
19. surround
20. challenge

Words from Other Languages
Grade 5, Lesson 20
1. salsa
2. mattress
3. tycoon
4. burrito
5. bandana
6. tomato
7. poncho
8. dungarees
9. lasso
10. patio
11. siesta
12. cargo
13. vanilla
14. tsunami
15. iguana
16. plaza
17. caravan
18. hammock
19. pajamas
20. gallant

Plurals
Grade 6, Lesson 19
1. echoes
2. halves
3. solos

4. leaves
5. heroes
6. cliffs
7. scarves
8. potatoes
9. pianos
10. volcanoes
11. sheriffs
12. calves
13. tomatoes
14. cellos
15. wolves
16. ratios
17. stereos
18. yourselves
19. studios
20. bookshelves

Long Vowels
Grade 6, Lesson 2
1. scene
2. bracelet
3. mute
4. strive
5. faithful
6. devote
7. rhyme
8. succeed
9. coax
10. rely
11. conceal
12. forgave
13. lonesome
14. delete
15. confine
16. exceed
17. terrain
18. reproach
19. abuse
20. defeat

Vowel Sounds: /ou/, /o͞o/, /ô/, /oi/
Grade 6, Lesson 3
1. mound
2. gloomy
3. caution
4. annoy
5. dawdle
6. counter
7. haughty
8. rejoice
9. devour
10. thoughtful
11. flawless
12. maroon
13. droop
14. doubt
15. bamboo
16. hoist
17. oyster
18. exhausted
19. scoundrel
20. boundary

Vowel + /r/ Sounds
Grade 6, Lesson 4
1. source
2. flirt
3. hurdle

4. parka
5. frontier
6. forward
7. radar
8. earnest
9. afford
10. urban
11. discard
12. smirk
13. rehearse
14. mourn
15. surface
16. parcel
17. yearn
18. fierce
19. starch
20. formula

Words with /e or e/
Grade 6, Lesson 6
1. brief
2. field
3. reign
4. review
5. fiery
6. receipt
7. relieve
8. conceited
9. neither
10. foreign
11. grief
12. veil
13. freight
14. belief
15. deceive
16. yield
17. beige
18. perceive
19. seize
20. leisure

Derivational Relations Phase

EARLY

Final /ĭj/, /ĭv/, /ĭs/
Grade 5, Lesson 22
1. storage
2. olive
3. service
4. relative
5. cabbage
6. courage
7. native
8. passage
9. voyage
10. knowledge
11. image
12. creative
13. average
14. justice
15. detective
16. postage
17. cowardice
18. adjective

Suffix: -ion
Grade 5, Lesson 25
1. elect
2. election
3. tense
4. tension
5. react
6. reaction
7. confess
8. confession
9. decorate
10. decoration
11. contribute
12. contribution
13. express
14. expression
15. imitate
16. imitation
17. connect
18. connection
19. admire
20. admiration

Word Parts: com-, con-, pre-, pro-
Grade 5, Lesson 26
1. produce
2. company
3. protect
4. preview
5. contain
6. combat
7. prejudge
8. commotion
9. contest
10. prefix
11. progress
12. computer
13. confide
14. convince
15. prospect
16. confirm
17. preflight
18. provide
19. propose
20. promotion

Homophones
Grade 6, Lesson 5
1. waist
2. waste
3. patience
4. patients
5. rite
6. right
7. write
8. muscle
9. mussel
10. principal
11. principle
12. summary
13. summery
14. sight
15. cite
16. site
17. stationary
18. stationery

Final /ər/
Grade 6, Lesson 7
1. fiber
2. similar
3. regular
4. barrier
5. superior
6. grammar
7. rumor
8. character
9. director
10. acre
11. consider
12. junior
13. senior
14. solar
15. scholar
16. razor
17. surrender
18. particular
19. familiar
20. laser

Final /ən/, /əl/, and /ər/
Grade 6, Lesson 8
1. triangle
2. mental
3. error
4. panel
5. litter
6. pollen
7. gallon
8. cancel
9. abandon
10. rival
11. soldier
12. recycle
13. salmon
14. counsel
15. rural
16. vehicle
17. citizen
18. monitor
19. physical
20. oxygen

Words with -ed or -ing
Grade 6, Lesson 9
1. happening
2. limited
3. forgetting
4. equaled
5. fitting
6. reasoning
7. labored
8. permitting
9. scrapped
10. tutoring
11. admitted
12. honored
13. skidding
14. pardoned
15. modeling
16. preferred
17. scarred

18. favored
19. glistening
20. shuddered

Endings and Suffixes
Grade 6, Lesson 10
1. reserved
2. unlikely
3. purposeful
4. adorable
5. amazement
6. gentleness
7. sparkling
8. homeless
9. excitement
10. mileage
11. graceful
12. sincerely
13. advanced
14. usable
15. amusement
16. entirely
17. wireless
18. excluding
19. scarcely
20. changeable

Final /ĭz/, /ĭv/, and /ĭj/
Grade 6, Lesson 15
1. revise
2. advantage
3. memorize
4. active
5. organize
6. criticize
7. shortage
8. advertise
9. attractive
10. college
11. explosive
12. exercise
13. encourage
14. summarize
15. wreckage
16. recognize
17. positive
18. percentage
19. sensitive
20. heritage

Suffixes: -ion or -ation
Grade 6, Lesson 11
1. correct
2. correction
3. explore
4. exploration
5. admire
6. admiration
7. subtract
8. subtraction
9. examine
10. examination
11. separate
12. separation
13. alter
14. alteration
15. preserve

16. preservation
17. reflect
18. reflection
19. substitute
20. substitution

Spelling /sh/
Grade 6, Lesson 18
1. section
2. shallow
3. direction
4. musician
5. rash
6. position
7. astonish
8. pressure
9. attention
10. crucial
11. impression
12. official
13. emotion
14. bashful
15. delicious
16. establish
17. ancient
18. situation
19. suspicion
20. permission

Prefixes: dis-, ex-, inter-
Grade 6, Lesson 20
1. disobey
2. explosion
3. dislike
4. interview
5. disapprove
6. interoffice
7. Internet
8. disallow
9. disappear
10. international
11. disrespect
12. exchange
13. exclaim
14. dissolve
15. disconnect
16. interact
17. distaste
18. export
19. disappoint
20. interstate

Prefixes: pre-, pro-
Grade 6, Lesson 21
1. prediction
2. project
3. prevent
4. prepaid
5. prevail
6. proclaim
7. prehistoric
8. prejudge
9. preapprove
10. pregame
11. precaution
12. preorder
13. prescreen
14. preshow
15. pretreat

16. prolong
17. process
18. protrude
19. provision
20. production

More Words with -ion
Grade 6, Lesson 13
1. circulate
2. circulation
3. conclude
4. conclusion
5. instruct
6. instruction
7. possess
8. possession
9. introduce
10. introduction
11. except
12. exception
13. discuss
14. discussion
15. collide
16. collision
17. oppose
18. opposition
19. estimate
20. estimation

Suffixes: -ent, -ant, -able, -ible, -ism, -ist
Grade 5, Lesson 27
1. vacant
2. insistent
3. reversible
4. patriotism
5. finalist
6. honorable
7. contestant
8. observant
9. urgent
10. pessimist
11. comfortable
12. absorbent
13. optimism
14. journalism
15. novelist
16. terrible
17. frequent
18. laughable
19. radiant
20. collectible

Greek Word Parts
Grade 5, Lesson 28
1. telephone
2. autograph
3. microscope
4. photograph
5. televise
6. biology
7. microphone
8. paragraph
9. symphony
10. telegraph
11. megaphone
12. microwave
13. photocopy
14. biography

15. saxophone
16. telescope
17. calligraphy
18. xylophone
19. homophone
20. homograph

Latin Word Roots
Grade 5, Lesson 29
1. inspect
2. export
3. erupt
4. predict
5. respect
6. bankrupt
7. dictate
8. porter
9. report
10. spectacle
11. deport
12. interrupt
13. dictator
14. import
15. disrupt
16. portable
17. transport
18. spectator
19. verdict
20. dictionary

More Words from Other Languages
Grade 5, Lesson 30
1. ballet
2. echo
3. bouquet
4. cassette
5. coupon
6. safari
7. portrait
8. barrette
9. depot
10. courtesy
11. petite
12. denim
13. brunette
14. buffet
15. garage
16. khaki
17. crochet
18. chorus
19. essay
20. alphabet

MIDDLE

Prefixes: in-, im-, ir-, il-
Grade 6, Lesson 12
1. illegal
2. indent
3. imperfect
4. irregular
5. insecure
6. illogical
7. inappropriate
8. impatient
9. individual
10. inability
11. impolite

12. illegible
13. irresistible
14. immobile
15. impartial
16. inaudible
17. improper
18. ineffective
19. immovable
20. irrational

Word Parts: com-, con-
Grade 6, Lesson 14
1. contrast
2. contact
3. compound
4. concentrate
5. combine
6. comment
7. conference
8. compete
9. community
10. convert
11. conversation
12. commute
13. constitution
14. conduct
15. consumer
16. continent
17. composition
18. communicate
19. compliment
20. condition

Suffixes: -ent, -ant
Grade 6, Lesson 16
1. confident
2. confidence
3. fragrant
4. fragrance
5. excellent
6. excellence
7. decent
8. decency
9. truant
10. truancy
11. brilliant
12. brilliance
13. resident
14. residence
15. evident
16. evidence
17. occupant
18. occupancy
19. reluctant
20. reluctance

Suffixes: -able/-ible, -ate
Grade 6, Lesson 17
1. visible
2. enjoyable
3. celebrate
4. incredible
5. horrible
6. desperate
7. cooperate
8. valuable
9. appreciate
10. considerate

11. audible
12. delicate
13. washable
14. graduate
15. capable
16. miserable
17. sensible
18. fortunate
19. noticeable
20. responsible

Words with Silent Letters
Grade 6, Lesson 22

1. aisle
2. align
3. island
4. crumbs
5. gnaw
6. design
7. knotty
8. bustle
9. shepherd
10. soften
11. sword
12. thistle
13. knock
14. wrestle
15. column
16. autumn
17. knowledge
18. debt
19. numb
20. raspberry

Suffixes: -ic, -ure, -ous
Grade 6, Lesson 23

1. fantastic
2. culture
3. curious
4. nervous
5. posture
6. jealous
7. scientific
8. generous
9. signature
10. dangerous
11. tragic
12. gigantic
13. sculpture
14. precious
15. lecture
16. serious
17. specific
18. fracture
19. romantic
20. ambitious

Prefixes: de-, trans-
Grade 6, Lesson 24

1. transform
2. deject
3. destruct
4. detour
5. transmit
6. default
7. describe
8. defend
9. transplant
10. descend
11. derail
12. defrost
13. transcript
14. deploy
15. dethrone
16. deodorize
17. transatlantic
18. decompose
19. decrease
20. transaction

Word Parts
Grade 6, Lesson 25

1. existence
2. refreshment
3. convention
4. intermission
5. uneventful
6. perfectly
7. completion
8. improvement
9. information
10. attendance
11. reversible
12. invention
13. development
14. respectful
15. unhappiness
16. preparation
17. irrigate
18. disagreement
19. unbelievable
20. concentration

Words from Other Languages
Grade 6, Lesson 26

1. opera
2. vague
3. antique
4. drama
5. tornado
6. debut
7. stampede
8. gourmet
9. unique
10. academy
11. sonnet
12. brochure
13. cocoon
14. fatigue
15. mosquito
16. diploma
17. fiesta
18. debris
19. cafeteria
20. quartet

Greek Word Parts
Grade 6, Lesson 27

1. geography
2. democracy
3. microbiology
4. technology
5. thermos
6. automatic
7. mythology
8. democratic
9. thermometer
10. chronology
11. automobile
12. aristocrat
13. thermal
14. geology
15. aristocracy
16. geometry
17. anthology
18. apology
19. thermostat
20. psychology

Latin Word Roots
Grade 6, Lesson 28

1. prescribe
2. contract
3. manufacture
4. progression
5. vocal
6. manual
7. audience
8. eject
9. impose
10. management
11. Congress
12. expose
13. inject
14. audition
15. manuscript
16. vocabulary
17. objection
18. manicure
19. proposal
20. extract

Greek and Latin Word Parts
Grade 6, Lesson 29

1. pedal
2. peddler
3. pedestrian
4. pedestal
5. centipede
6. dental
7. dentist
8. dentures
9. vocalize
10. vocalist
11. vocation
12. memoir
13. memorial
14. tripod
15. podium
16. memorable
17. manager
18. manifest
19. mortal
20. mortified

Words Often Confused
Grade 6, Lesson 30

1. desert
2. dessert
3. hardy
4. hearty
5. moral
6. morale
7. laying
8. lying
9. personal
10. personnel
11. formally
12. formerly
13. healthy
14. healthful
15. precede
16. proceed
17. conscious
18. conscience
19. immigrate
20. emigrate

Teacher's Notes

Leveled Readers Database

Guided Reading Level	Title	Grade Pack	DRA Level	Lexile Level	Reading Recovery Level	Genre	Word Count
A	At the Park	1 ●	A	BR	A, B	Informational Text	36
A	Granny	1 ●	A	180	A, B	Realistic Fiction	36
A	Helping	1 ●	1	BR	1	Informational Text	36
A	Sledding	1 ●	A	290	A, B	Fantasy	58
B	Curious About School	1VR	2	20	2	Informational Text	50
B	Curious George Finds Out About School	1 ●	4	60	4	Fantasy	51
B	Dogs	1 ●	2	BR	2	Informational Text	79
B	Drawing	1 ●	2	BR	2	Informational Text	48
B	Dress Up	1 ●	2	BR	2	Realistic Fiction	49
B	Favorite Things	1VR	2	BR	2	Informational Text	47
B	Grandpa	1VR	2	50	2	Informational Text	50
B	Pigs, The	1 ●	2	BR	2	Fable	83
B	Trip to the Rock	1 ●	2	130	2	Fantasy	90
B	Winter	1 ●	2	20	2	Informational Text	79
C	Animal Talk	1VR	3	240	3	Informational Text	55
C	Curious George Visits School	1 ◆	4	140	4	Fantasy	88
C	Curious George's Day at School	1 ▲	4	140	4	Fantasy	87
C	Firehouse	1VR	3	BR	3	Informational Text	58
C	Friends Who Share	1 ◆	4	180	4	Informational Text	118
C	Grandpa and Me	1 ▲	3	420	3	Realistic Fiction	86
C	Happy Birthday!	1VR	4	BR	4	Informational Text	78
C	Music	1VR	3	BR	3	Informational Text	58
C	Our Town	1 ▲	3	240	3	Informational Text	103
C	Places in Our Town, The	1 ◆	6	200	6	Informational Text	108
C	Reading Together	1VR	4	BR	4	Informational Text	62
C	Sharing	1 ▲	4	100	4	Informational Text	107
C	Trains	1VR	3	150	3	Informational Text	65
C	When Grandpa Was a Boy	1 ◆	4	450	4	Realistic Fiction	93
D	Animals at Night	1 ▲	6	220	6	Informational Text	161
D	Apples	1 ●	6	240	5	Informational Text	100

- Go to www.thinkcentral.com for the complete *Journeys* Online Leveled Readers Database.
- Search by grade, genre, title, or level.

Author's Purpose	Cause and Effect	Compare and Contrast	Conclusions	Fact and Opinion	Main Idea and Details	Sequence of Events	Story Structure	Text and Graphic Features	Theme	Understanding Characters
				•	•			•		
			•			•				•
•	•				•					
	•					•	•			•
•					•					
	•					•			•	•
		•		•	•			•		
	•		•		•	•		•		
	•		•		•	•				•
•		•		•	•					
•		•			•					
						•				•
			•			•	•			
•	•		•		•	•				
•			•		•					
	•					•			•	•
	•					•			•	•
•					•					
•					•					
•		•	•			•			•	•
•					•					
•			•		•			•		
•	•				•			•		
•					•			•		
•					•					
•					•					
•					•					
		•							•	•
					•			•		
•					•					

Leveled Readers Database

Guided Reading Level	Title	Grade Pack	DRA Level	Lexile Level	Reading Recovery Level	Genre	Word Count
D	Ben the Cat	1 ▲	6	90	6	Fantasy	124
D	Busy Animals at Night	1 ◆	6	270	5	Informational Text	183
D	Cat Named Ben, A	1 ◆	6	70	5	Fantasy	131
D	Ducks	1VR	6	30	5	Informational Text	65
D	Go Turtle! Go Hare!	1 ◆	6	80	5	Fable	100
D	In the Sea	1 ●	6	360	5	Informational Text	87
D	In the Sky	1VR	6	120	6	Informational Text	101
D	Izzy's Move	1 ●	6	290	6	Fantasy	129
D	Making a Home	1 ●	6	220	6	Informational Text	102
D	My Favorite Foods	1VR	6	130	6	Informational Text	95
D	Nana's House	1 ▲	6	320	6	Realistic Fiction	133
D	Our Day at Nana's House	1 ◆	6	330	5	Realistic Fiction	137
D	People in the Town	1VR	6	140	5	Informational Text	107
D	Putting Frosting on the Cake	1 ●	6	360	6	Fantasy	120
D	Reading	1VR	6	80	6	Informational Text	76
D	Shark	1VR	6	20	6	Informational Text	85
D	Spots	1VR	6	90	6	Informational Text	83
D	Sun, The	1 ●	6	BR	5	Informational Text	119
D	Turtle and Hare	1 ▲	6	40	6	Fable	94
E	Amy's Airplane	1 ●	8	270	8	Realistic Fiction	147
E	Animal Homes	1 ●	8	170	8	Informational Text	170
E	Animals	1VR	8	190	7	Informational Text	115
E	Baby Birds	1VR	8	270	8	Informational Text	180
E	Bear Swims	1 ●	8	240	7	Fantasy	151
E	Desert Animals	1VR	8	330	8	Informational Text	171
E	Going to School	1VR	8	270	7	Informational Text	114
E	Giraffe's Neck	1 ●	8	310	8	Folktale	109
E	Happy Birthday, Toad	1 ◆	8	270	7	Fantasy	144
E	Helping at Home	1VR	8	380	7	Informational Text	158
E	Jim Henson, the Puppet Man	1 ▲	8	200	7	Informational Text	93

ONLINE LEVELED READERS DATABASE

- Go to www.thinkcentral.com for the complete *Journeys* Online Leveled Readers Database.
- Search by grade, genre, title, or level.

Author's Purpose	Cause and Effect	Compare and Contrast	Conclusions	Fact and Opinion	Main Idea and Details	Sequence of Events	Story Structure	Text and Graphic Features	Theme	Understanding Characters
			●			●	●			●
					●			●		
			●			●	●			●
●			●		●					
●	●	●	●			●	●		●	●
●					●	●				
●		●			●					
	●	●	●			●	●		●	
●		●		●	●			●		
●		●	●		●					
	●		●			●				●
	●		●			●				●
●		●	●		●					
	●		●			●	●			●
●		●		●	●					
●					●			●		
●					●					
●					●			●		
●	●	●	●			●	●		●	●
	●		●			●	●			●
●			●		●					
●		●			●					
●					●					
		●					●			●
●		●	●		●					
●			●		●					
●	●					●	●			
						●	●			
●			●		●					
●				●	●			●		

Leveled Readers Database

Guided Reading Level	Title	Grade Pack	DRA Level	Lexile Level	Reading Recovery Level	Genre	Word Count
E	Man Who Made Puppets, The	1 ◆	8	350	8	Informational Text	106
E	Our Class	1 ●	8	190	7	Informational Text	200
E	Seed for Sid, A	1 ●	8	260	8	Fantasy	180
E	Toad's Birthday	1 ▲	8	230	8	Fantasy	135
E	Weather, The	1VR	8	290	8	Informational Text	81
E	Working in the Park	1 ●	8	380	8	Realistic Fiction	118
F	Chunk of Cheese, A	1 ●	10	370	10	Fantasy	215
F	Kite Flying	1VR	10	440	9	Informational Text	192
F	Let's Play Ball	1 ●	10	190	9	Realistic Fiction	215
F	Michelle Wie	1 ●	10	120	10	Narrative Nonfiction	153
F	Molly's New Team	1 ●	10	180	10	Realistic Fiction	161
F	Our School	1 ●	10	350	9	Realistic Fiction	182
F	So Many Sounds	1VR	10	400	10	Informational Text	166
G	How We Get Food	1 ◆	12	320	12	Informational Text	291
G	Life in the Coral Reefs	1 ◆	12	430	12	Informational Text	198
G	Moving	1VR	12	170	12	Informational Text	170
G	Polly's Pet Polar Bear	1 ◆	12	300	12	Fantasy	279
G	Soccer	1VR	12	510	12	Informational Text	201
G	Trees	1VR	12	310	12	Informational Text	161
H	An Acorn Grows	1 ●	14	470	12	Informational Text	171
H	Bear's Long, Brown Tail	1 ◆	14	250	14	Folktale	332
H	Bear's Tail	1 ▲	14	480	14	Folktale	292
H	Bumpy Snowman, The	1 ◆	14	370	14	Realistic Fiction	334
H	Butterflies	1VR	14	410	9	Informational Text	132
H	Coral Reefs	1 ▲	14	570	13	Informational Text	203
H	First Day of Second Grade	1 ◆	14	360	14	Realistic Fiction	263
H	Flying	1 ▲	14	390	13	Fantasy	226
H	Flying in an Airplane	1 ◆	14	200	14	Fantasy	272
H	Food for You	1 ▲	14	440	14	Informational Text	232
H	Forest Stew	1 ▲	14	390	14	Fantasy	242

- Go to www.thinkcentral.com for the complete *Journeys* Online Leveled Readers Database.
- Search by grade, genre, title, or level.

Author's Purpose	Cause and Effect	Compare and Contrast	Conclusions	Fact and Opinion	Main Idea and Details	Sequence of Events	Story Structure	Text and Graphic Features	Theme	Understanding Characters
•				•	•			•		
					•			•		
			•			•	•			
						•	•			
•					•					
			•			•				
	•		•			•	•		•	
•					•					
			•			•	•			•
•					•					•
						•	•		•	•
		•	•							•
•			•		•					
•	•				•					
•				•	•			•		
•					•					
	•						•			•
•					•					
•		•			•					
•	•		•		•	•				
•	•	•	•		•	•	•		•	•
•	•	•	•		•	•	•		•	•
•	•	•	•		•	•	•		•	•
•			•		•					
•				•	•			•		
			•			•	•			•
		•				•	•		•	•
		•				•	•		•	•
•	•				•					
•	•					•	•		•	

Leveled Readers Database

Guided Reading Level	Title	Grade Pack	DRA Level	Lexile Level	Reading Recovery Level	Genre	Word Count
H	Fun Baseball Game, A	1 ◆	14	480	13	Informational Text	376
H	In the Fall	1 ◆	14	300	14	Informational Text	286
H	Kamala's Art	1VR	14	430	13	Informational Text	184
H	Our Bakery	1 ▲	14	380	14	Realistic Fiction	230
H	Our Day at the Bakery	1 ◆	14	210	14	Realistic Fiction	274
H	Polar Bear Pete	1 ▲	14	480	14	Fantasy	273
H	Skunk Cooks Soup	1 ◆	14	330	14	Fantasy	202
I	Baby Kangaroos	1 ▲	16	540	15	Informational Text	256
I	Baseball Game, The	1 ▲	16	540	16	Informational Text	358
I	Birds	1 ◆	16	260	15	Realistic Fiction	370
I	Chipmunk's New Home	1 ■	16	400	16	Fantasy	300
I	Curious George at the Library	1 ■	16	280	16	Fantasy	281
I	Fall Changes	1 ▲	16	460	16	Informational Text	320
I	Fox and Crow	1 ■	16	380	15	Fable	333
I	Friends	1 ■	16	400	15	Informational Text	302
I	Len's Tomato Plant	1 ◆	16	380	15	Realistic Fiction	294
I	Len's Tomatoes	1 ▲	16	430	15	Realistic Fiction	289
I	Map and the Treasure, The	1 ◆	16	300	15	Fantasy	292
I	More Than One Bird	1 ▲	16	350	16	Realistic Fiction	326
I	Neighbors	1 ■	16	330	15	Informational Text	244
I	Paco's Snowman	1 ▲	16	380	16	Realistic Fiction	330
I	Ready for Second Grade	1 ▲	16	360	15	Realistic Fiction	295
I	Seasons	1 ▲	16	400	15	Informational Text	253
I	Seasons of the Year, The	1 ◆	16	430	16	Informational Text	332
I	Tiny Baby Kangaroos	1 ◆	16	620	15	Informational Text	296
I	Treasure Map, The	1 ▲	16	320	15	Fantasy	306
J	All About Bats	1 ▲	18	520	18	Informational Text	296
J	Beach, The	1 ■	18	320	18	Realistic Fiction	292
J	Boat Race, The	1 ◆	18	380	18	Fantasy	366
J	Bobcat Tells a Tale	1 ■	18	310	18	Fantasy	255

- Go to www.thinkcentral.com for the complete *Journeys* Online Leveled Readers Database.
- Search by grade, genre, title, or level.

Author's Purpose	Cause and Effect	Compare and Contrast	Conclusions	Fact and Opinion	Main Idea and Details	Sequence of Events	Story Structure	Text and Graphic Features	Theme	Understanding Characters
				•	•	•		•		
	•	•			•	•				
•					•					
•	•		•		•	•				
•	•		•		•	•				
	•						•			•
					•	•	•			•
•			•		•	•				
				•	•	•		•		
			•			•	•			•
	•					•	•			
	•					•	•			•
	•	•			•	•				
•	•					•	•		•	•
•	•	•			•					
•	•					•				
•	•					•				
•	•		•			•	•		•	
					•	•	•			•
								•		
•	•	•	•			•	•		•	•
					•	•	•			•
•			•		•			•		
•			•		•			•		
•			•		•					
•	•		•			•	•		•	
•		•			•			•		
•			•			•				
•	•		•			•			•	•
	•		•			•	•			

Leveled Readers Database

Guided Reading Level	Title	Grade Pack	DRA Level	Lexile Level	Reading Recovery Level	Genre	Word Count
J	Dog Talk	1 ■	18	310	18	Informational Text	324
J	From Pit to Plum	1 ▲	18	520	18	Informational Text	259
J	How Animals Move	1 ■	18	650	18	Informational Text	401
J	Job for Jojo, A	1 ■	10	210	10	Fantasy	326
J	Lena's Garden	1 ■	18	520	18	Fantasy	296
J	Living and Working in Space	1 ■	18	650	18	Informational Text	383
J	Many Kinds of Bats	1 ◆	18	530	18	Informational Text	292
J	Margret and Hans Rey	1 ■	18	520	18	Informational Text	237
J	Mexican Festival, A	1 ■	18	340	18	Realistic Fiction	267
J	Mountain, The	1 ■	18	320	18	Fantasy	348
J	Plum Grows, A	1 ◆	18	350	18	Informational Text	258
J	Sailboat Race, The	1 ▲	18	330	18	Fantasy	330
J	Surprise for Ms. Green, A	1 ■	18	300	18	Realistic Fiction	393
J	Tag-Along Tim	1 ■	18	410	18	Realistic Fiction	358
J	Two Sisters Play Tennis	1 ◆	18	480	18	Narrative Nonfiction	327
J	What I Want to Be	1 ■	18	320	18	Realistic Fiction	377
J	Williams Sisters, The	1 ▲	18	450	18	Narrative Nonfiction	318
J	Worms	1VR	18	460	18	Informational Text	178
K	Always Learning	1 ■	20	480	18	Informational Text	392
K	Cam the Camel	1 ■	20	440	18	Fantasy	334
K	Cat Trick, A	1 ■	20	490	18	Realistic Fiction	372
K	Sand Castle, The	1 ■	20	370	18	Fantasy	388
K	Seasons Around the World	1 ■	20	600	18	Informational Text	353
K	World of Food, A	1 ■	20	580	18	Informational Text	340
L	Amazing Octopus, The	1 ■	24	520	20	Informational Text	346
L	Bald Eagles	1 ■	24	640	20	Informational Text	420
L	Lance Armstrong	1 ■	24	540	20	Narrative Nonfiction	444
L	Lemonade Stand, The	1 ■	24	560	20	Realistic Fiction	386
L	Peacock's Tail	1 ■	24	530	20	Folktale	344
M	Story of a Rose, The	1 ■	28	590	20	Informational Text	375

ONLINE LEVELED READERS DATABASE

• Go to www.thinkcentral.com for the complete *Journeys* Online Leveled Readers Database.
• Search by grade, genre, title, or level.

Author's Purpose	Cause and Effect	Compare and Contrast	Conclusions	Fact and Opinion	Main Idea and Details	Sequence of Events	Story Structure	Text and Graphic Features	Theme	Understanding Characters
●					●					
●	●			●	●	●		●		
●			●		●			●		
			●			●	●			●
	●		●				●	●		●
●	●				●			●		
●		●			●			●		
●					●			●		
						●				●
		●				●	●			
●	●		●	●	●	●		●		
●	●		●			●	●		●	●
		●	●				●		●	●
●			●			●	●		●	●
●					●					●
	●	●	●							
●					●					●
●			●	●	●					
●				●	●	●	●			
			●			●	●		●	●
			●			●	●			●
	●					●	●		●	●
●	●	●			●					
●					●				●	
●	●			●	●					
●		●		●	●					
●				●	●	●				●
	●					●	●			
●	●	●	●			●	●		●	●
●	●	●		●	●	●		●		

Literature Discussion

For small-group literature discussion, use the suggested trade book titles on the pages that follow, or select age-appropriate texts from your library or classroom collection.

Engage children in discussions to build understanding of the text, deepen comprehension, and foster children's confidence in talking about what they read. Encourage children to share their ideas about the text and also to build upon one another's ideas.

 Classic

 Science

 Social Studies

 Music

 Math

 Art

Suggested Trade Book Titles

BIOGRAPHY

Carson, Cheryl. *Charles M. Schultz.* Cartoonist Charles M. Schultz is profiled here. Capstone Press, 2005 (24p).

Jaffe, Elizabeth D. *Ellen Ochoa.* This basic biography profiles the United States' first Latina astronaut. Children's Press, 2005 (32p).

Knox, Barbara. *George Washington.* This easy-to-read introduction to the life of George Washington includes a timeline. Capstone, 2004 (24p).

Krensky, Stephen. *A Man for All Seasons: The Life of George Washington Carver.* This biography profiles the man whose discoveries put the peanut on the map. Amistad, 2008 (32p).

Marzolla, Jean, and Jerry Pinkney. *Happy Birthday, Martin Luther King.* This brief narrative of Dr. King's life is presented in an easy-to-read format. Scholastic, 1993 (32p).

FABLE

Herman, Gail. *The Lion and the Mouse.* This fable is an easy-to-read retelling of Aesop's classic tale. Random House, 1998 (32p).

Poole, Amy Lowry. *The Ant and the Grasshopper.* Grasshopper plays the summer days away while Ant works hard to prepare for winter. Holiday House, 2000 (32p).

FAIRY TALE

Andersen, Hans Christian, and Jerry Pinkney. *The Ugly Duckling.* Hans Christian Andersen's classic tale is illustrated with Caldecott Honor–winning illustrations. Harper, 1999 (40p).

Gorbachev, Valeri. *Goldilocks and the Three Bears.* Three bears return home to discover an unexpected visitor in their home in this appealing retelling of the classic tale. North-South/Night Sky, 2001 (40p).

FANTASY

Andersen, Peggy Perry. *Chuck's Band.* Chuck and his barnyard friends form a band in this toe-tapping story. Houghton Mifflin, 2008 (32p).

Bang-Campbell, Monika. *Little Rat Makes Music.* With the help of Kitty and lots of practice, Little Rat learns to play the violin. Harcourt, 2007 (48p).

Banks, Kate. *Fox.* A baby fox observes the changing seasons while his parents teach him to care for himself. Farrar, Straus and Giroux, 2007 (40p).

Brett, Jan. *Honey. . . Honey. . . Lion!* When greedy Badger will not share honey with his friend, his friend has a surprise for him. Putnam, 2005 (32p).

Campoy, F. Isabel. *Get Up, Rick!* Brief text and supportive illustrations describe what happens on a farm when the rooster oversleeps. Green Light Readers, 2007 (24p).

Carle, Eric. *The Very Hungry Caterpillar.* A caterpillar eats its way through the week and turns into a beautiful butterfly. Philomel, 1969 (32p).

Cazet, Denys. *Minnie and Moo and the Case of the Missing Jelly Donut.* The brave bovine buddies are on the case when Minnie discovers that her jelly donut has gone missing. HarperTrophy, 2006 (48p).

Chaconas, Dori. *Cork and Fuzz: Good Sports.* Two friends learn a lesson about sportsmanship when they compete against one another. Viking, 2007 (32p).

Cronin, Doreen. *Dooby Dooby Moo.* Determined Duck and the rest of Farmer Brown's animals set their sights on first prize at the county fair's talent show, unbeknownst to Farmer Brown. **Available in Spanish as *Dubi Dubi Muu/Dooby Dooby Moo.*** Atheneum, 2006 (40p).

Cyrus, Kurt. *Tadpole Rex.* In a swamp frequented by dinosaurs, a tiny tadpole looks forward to growing as big as his mighty neighbors. Harcourt, 2008 (40p).

DiCamillo, Kate. *Mercy Watson to the Rescue.* When Mr. and Mrs. Watson find themselves in trouble, their pig, Mercy, saves the day. Candlewick, 2005 (80p).

Henkes, Kevin. *A Good Day.* Four animals triumph when they find they can turn a potentially bad day into a good day. Greenwillow, 2007 (32p).

Henkes, Kevin. *Lilly's Big Day.* High-spirited Lilly is disappointed when she is not asked to be the flower girl in her teacher's wedding, but she still finds a way to shine. Greenwillow, 2006 (40p).

Hill, Susan. *Ruby Paints a Picture.* Ruby captures the best part of each of her animal friends in her artwork. HarperCollins, 2005 (32p).

Howe, James. *Houndsley and Catina.* In this early chapter book, a cat and a dog explore ways of sharing themselves and realize that doing what they love is most important. Candlewick, 2006 (40p).

Inkpen, Mick. *Kipper's A to Z: An Alphabet Adventure.* In this innovative alphabet book, Kipper and his little friend Arnold search for things that begin with each letter of the alphabet. Red Wagon, 2001 (56p).

Johnson, Crockett. *Harold and the Purple Crayon.* Harold and his purple crayon go on a whimsical journey in this classic tribute to the imagination. **Available in Spanish as** *Harold y el lápiz color morado.* HarperCollins, 1955 (64p).

Kreloff, Elliot. *Tic and Tac Clean Up.* Once their house is clean, Tic and Tac try to come up with activities that won't make a mess. Sterling, 2007 (32p).

Kvasnosky, Laura McGee. *Zelda and Ivy and the Boy Next Door.* A new neighbor gives fox sisters Zelda and Ivy an opportunity to embark on new capers in this early chapter book. Candlewick, 2008 (48p).

Lies, Brian. *Bats at the Beach.* A typical day at the beach is turned on its head when a family of bats sets out for the sand and sea—at night! Houghton Mifflin, 2006 (32p).

Lionni, Leo. *Swimmy.* Swimmy teaches a school of little fish to swim together to avoid danger in this Caldecott Honor book. **Available in Spanish as** *Nadarín.* Knopf, 1963 (32p).

Lobel, Anita. *Nini Here and There.* Nini the cat fears her family is going away without her but soon learns they would never dream of leaving her behind. Greenwillow, 2007 (32p).

Lobel, Arnold. *Frog and Toad All Year.* The beloved friends enjoy adventures and happy times together during every season of the year. **Available in Spanish as** *Sapo y sepo, un año entero.* HarperCollins, 1976 (64p).

Lucas, Sally. *Dancing Dinos Go to School.* It's an exciting day at school when two irrepressible dinosaurs dance into the classroom in this rhyming story. Random House, 2006 (32p).

McCloskey, Robert. *Make Way for Ducklings.* Follow the Mallard family on their journey through Boston in this children's classic. Viking, 1941 (68p).

McMillan, Bruce. *How the Ladies Stopped the Wind.* A group of resourceful ladies from Iceland use their problem-solving skills to stop the wind. Houghton Mifflin, 2007 (32p).

McMullan, Kate. *I'm Dirty.* With sound words and great enthusiasm, a hard-working backhoe describes how he helps keep his neighborhood clean. Joanna Cotler, 2006 (40p).

Noble, Trinka Hakes. *The Day Jimmy's Boa Ate the Wash.* A school field trip to a farm is full of hilarious surprises when Jimmy brings his pet boa along. Dial, 1980 (32p).

Numeroff, Laura. *If You Give a Pig a Party.* A pig's request to throw a party sets off a chain of funny and unexpected consequences. **Available in Spanish as** *Si le haces una fiesta a una cerdita.* HarperCollins, 2005 (32p).

Pinkwater, Daniel. *Bear's Picture.* Bear stands up for himself when two fine gentlemen criticize his picture. Houghton Mifflin, 2008 (32p).

Rankin, Laura. *Fluffy and Baron.* A duckling and a German shepherd form an unlikely friendship in this gentle story about growing up. Dial, 2006 (32p).

Seuss, Dr. *The Cat in the Hat.* Chaos ensues when the Cat in the Hat pays a visit to Sally and her brother. **Available in Spanish as** *El gato en el sombrero/The Cat in the Hat.* Random House, 1957 (60p).

Seuss, Dr. *Oh, the Thinks You Can Think!* This Seuss classic describes all the imaginative things you can think, if only you try. Random House, 1975 (48p).

Shannon, George. *Rabbit's Gift.* Rabbit shares his winter store of food with friends and starts a wave of generosity that spreads among all the forest animals. Harcourt, 2007 (32p).

Shaw, Nancy. *Sheep Blast Off!* When a spacecraft lands in a nearby field, the lovable, blundering sheep go on board and embark on the ride of their lives. Houghton Mifflin, 2008 (32p).

Sherry, Kevin. *I'm the Biggest Thing in the Ocean.* In this lighthearted tale, a giant squid repeatedly announces that it's the biggest thing in the ocean . . . until it meets an even bigger whale. Dial, 2007 (32p).

Thomas, Jan. *What Will FAT CAT Sit On?* Familiar animals, repetitive text, and humor make this book ideal for new readers. Harcourt, 2007 (40p).

Walsh, Ellen Stoll. *Dot & Jabber and the Big Bug Mystery.* Dot and Jabber investigate a field where all the bugs seem to have disappeared and discover that they have all been camouflaged. Harcourt, 2003 (40p).

Willems, Mo. *There Is a Bird on Your Head!* Gerald is surprised to discover that a bird has made itself at home on his head. Hyperion, 2007 (64p).

Literature Discussion

FOLKTALE

Barton, Byron. *The Little Red Hen.* The little red hen finds that none of her lazy friends want to help her with chores, but all are happy to help her share the rewards. HarperFestival, 1997 (32p).

Bruchac, Joseph. *The Great Ball Game: A Muskogee Story.* When birds and animals challenge each other to a ball game to prove who is better, Bat shows that he has special qualities from both groups. Dial, 1994 (32p).

Demi. *The Empty Pot.* Honesty makes a Chinese boy the winner of the Emperor's flower-growing contest when he admits that he couldn't get his seed to grow. Holt, 1996 (32p).

Tolstoy, Alexei. *The Enormous Turnip.* One by one, family members help pull the enormous turnip out of the ground. Harcourt, 2003 (24p).

Tuchman, Gail. *How the Sky Got Its Stars: A Hopi Legend.* A Hopi legend tells how all animals, except for Coyote, create things on Earth until Coyote plays with the stars and makes something, too. Harcourt, 1997 (16p).

INFORMATIONAL TEXT

Ada, Alma Flor. *I Love Saturdays y domingos.* Weekends are special for a girl who spends time with both her English-speaking grandparents and her Spanish-speaking ones. **Available in Spanish as *Me encantan los Saturdays y Domingos*.** Atheneum, 2002 (32p).

Ajmera, Maya and John D. Ivanko. *Be My Neighbor.* This photo essay shows kids all over the world in the communities they call home. Charlesbridge, 2005 (32p).

Arnold, Katya. *Elephants Can Paint Too!* This profile describes an unusual conservation project, in which an art teacher teaches a group of elephants in Thailand to paint. Atheneum/Anne Schwartz, 2005 (40p).

Arnosky, Jim. *Babies in the Bayou.* This is a clearly illustrated introduction to the littlest inhabitants of the Southern marshland habitat. Penguin, 2007 (32p).

Bauer, Marion Dane. *Clouds.* Clear text presents basic facts about cirrus, stratus, and cumulus clouds for young readers. Tandem, 2004 (32p).

Clements, Andrew. *Tara and Tiree, Fearless Friends: A True Story.* This true story tells how two loyal dogs rescued their owner from a frozen lake. Aladdin, 2003 (32p).

DeGezelle, Terri. *Snowplows.* Easy-to-read text and color photographs introduce children to what snowplows can do. **Avaiable in Spanish as *Barredoras de nieve/Snowplows*.** Capstone, 2006 (24p).

Endres, Hollie J. *Fair Share.* Readers are introduced to the concept of division in this book about sharing. Capstone Press, 2005 (16p).

Gray, Susan Heinrichs. *Dinosaur Dig!* Readers find out what it is like to go on a dinosaur dig. Children's Press, 2007 (24p).

Helbrough, Emma. *How Flowers Grow.* Photographs and diagrams are featured in this description of how flowers grow. Usborne, 2007 (32p).

Jenkins, Martin. *The Emperor's Egg.* This colorful book chronicles how the male emperor penguin keeps his egg warm for two months in subzero temperatures while he waits for his mate's return. Candlewick, 2008 (32p).

Jones, Melanie Davis. *BIG Machines.* Simple text introduces different machines at work in a community. Children's Press, 2003 (24p).

Kalman, Bobbie. *Animals Grow and Change.* Color photographs and informative text introduce the growth cycles of animals. Crabtree, 2007 (24p).

Kalman, Bobbie. *A Forest Habitat.* Photos of baby animals in their natural surroundings help to inform children about forest habitats. **Available in Spanish as *Un habitat de bosque*.** Crabtree, 2006 (32p).

Kenah, Katharine. *Big Beasts.* Photographs and "extreme facts" will keep readers turning the pages in this book about the biggest animals on earth. School Specialty, 2007 (32p).

Lock, David. *Animals at Home.* Readers are introduced to different kinds of homes that animals make for themselves. DK Children, 2007 (32p).

Lock, Deborah. *Let's Make Music.* Informative text supported by photographs describes ways people make music. DK Children, 2005 (32p).

Milbourne, Anna, and Benji Davies. *On the Moon.* Readers take a trip with an astronaut in this friendly intro–duction to the moon. Usborne, 2004 (24p).

Murphy, Patricia J. *Let's Play Soccer.* Erik has fun at his first day of soccer practice. DK Children, 2008 (32p).

Nelson, Robin. *Communication Then and Now.* Readers compare current methods of communication with those of years ago. Lerner, 2003 (24p).

Peterson, Cris. *Fantastic Farm Machines.* A farming family describes machines that help them grow and harvest crops. Boyds Mills, 2006 (32p).

Rau, Dana Meachen. *Buzz, Bee, Buzz!* Bright, colorful photographs and a word list are features of this simple introduction to the bee. **Available in Spanish as *Zumba, abeja, zumba*.** Marshall Cavendish, 2007 (24p).

Rau, Dana Meachen. *Firefighter.* Simple text and rebuses provide an easy-to-read introduction to the job of a firefighter. **Available in Spanish as *Un bombero*.** Marshall Cavendish, 2007 (24p).

Ring, Susan. *From Here to There.* Photographs and informative text explore the different ways people travel. **Available in Spanish as *De aquí a allá*.** Yellow Umbrella, 2004 (16p).

Rotner, Shelley. *Senses at the Seashore.* This photo essay with minimal text evokes the sights, sounds, and smells of the seashore. Millbrook, 2005 (32p).

Ryder, Joanne. *A Pair of Polar Bears.* Twin polar bear cubs play, learn, and grow at the San Diego Zoo. Simon & Schuster, 2006 (32p).

Stone, Lynn M. *How Do Animals Use Their Voices and Sound?* Simple text and color photographs depict what various animals have to say. **Available in Spanish as *¿Cómo usan los animales su vos y sus sonidos?*** Rourke, 2007 (24p).

Time for Kids with Brenda Iasevoli. *Time for Kids: Plants!* Photos and informative text give facts about plants. HarperCollins, 2006 (32p).

Time for Kids with Leslie Dickstein. *Time for Kids: Storms!* Vivid photos complement the informative text about severe weather. HarperCollins, 2006 (32p).

Udry, Janet May. *A Tree Is Nice.* Poetic text reveals the reasons trees are so nice. **Available in Spanish as *Un árbol es hermoso.*** Harper, 1956 (32p).

VanVoorst, Jennifer. *Can You Guess?* Colorful photographs and informative text introduce the concept of estimation. Yellow Umbrella, 2004 (16p).

Wallace, Karen. *Rockets and Spaceships.* Photographs and informative text provide an exciting look at the technology that makes space exploration possible. Dorling Kindersley, 2001 (32p).

POETRY

Brown, Richard. *Street Music.* Rhythmic text and lively illustrations introduce readers to the music of the city. Sterling, 2006 (24p).

Crews, Nina. *The Neighborhood Mother Goose.* Traditional Mother Goose rhymes are paired with colorful photographs of children in this award-winning collection. Amistad, 2003 (64p).

Ehlert, Lois. *Oodles of Animals.* Playful rhymes and bold illustrations capture the spirit of 64 different animals. Harcourt, 2008 (56p).

Falwell, Cathryn. *Scoot!* Collage artwork and spirited action words introduce the inhabitants of a lively pond habitat. Greenwillow, 2008 (32p).

Lansky, Bruce. *I Hope I Don't Strike Out.* A collection of silly poems that focuses on the funny side of sports. Meadowbrook, 2008 (32p).

Lillegard, Dee. *Go! Poetry in Motion.* A lively collection of poetry featuring rhyme and sound words that celebrates the ways we get from here to there. Knopf, 2006 (32p).

Lumley, Jemima. *The Journey Home from Grandpa's.* A family enjoys the sights as they travel from the country to the city in this rhythmic story. Barefoot Books, 2006 (24p).

Mora, Pat. *Yum! Mmmm! Qué Rico!: America's Sproutings.* This poetry collection is a delicious introduction to fourteen types of food that grow. **Available in Spanish as *Yum! ¡MmMm! ¡Qué rico! Brotes de las Américas.*** Lee & Low, 2007 (32p).

Prelutsky, Jack. *My Dog May Be a Genius.* This collection of silly poems is sure to make readers giggle. Greenwillow, 2008 (160p).

Roemer, Heidi. *Come to My Party and Other Shape Poems.* Playful poems featuring sound words and repetition describe seasonal activities. Henry Holt and Co., 2004 (32p).

REALISTIC FICTION

Adler, David A. *Young Cam Jansen and the Lions' Lunch Mystery.* Young Cam Jansen uses her sleuthing skills to find a lost lunch bag on a school trip to the zoo. Viking, 2007 (32p).

dePaola, Tomie. *The Art Lesson.* Tommy loves drawing and can't wait to attend art lessons in school. Putnam, 1997 (32p).

Diakite, Penda. *I Lost My Tooth in Africa.* This story recounts a child's trip to Mali, where she loses her tooth. Scholastic, 2006 (32p).

Figley, Marty Rhodes. *The Schoolchildren's Blizzard.* During the blizzard of 1888, a brave teacher leads her students to safety in this story based on a true event. Carolrhoda Books, 2004 (48p).

Guest, Elissa Haden. *Iris and Walter and the Field Trip.* In this early chapter book, Iris and Walter take a field trip to the aquarium. Harcourt, 2007 (48p).

Harrison, David L. *Johnny Appleseed: My Story.* In this fictionalized biography, Johnny Appleseed tells his own story to the children of a pioneer family. Random House, 2001 (48p).

Himmelman, John. *Pipaluk and the Whales.* In a story based on an actual event, a girl named Pipaluk and the people of her Arctic village help rescue beluga whales trapped in the ice. National Geographic, 2002 (32p).

Hoff, Syd. *The Littlest Leaguer.* Harold is not the biggest player on his team, but he doesn't let his size hold him back when his chance comes to show what he can do on the baseball field. HarperTrophy, 2008 (48p).

Holub, Joan. *The Pizza That We Made.* Rhyming text tells the story of three friends working together to make a pizza. Puffin, 2001 (32p).

Hulme, Joy N. *Mary Clare Likes to Share: A Math Reader.* Mary Clare uses math to share with her friends and family. Random House, 2006 (32p).

Hutchins, Pat. *The Doorbell Rang.* Sam and Victoria have to figure out how to divide a dozen cookies equally to share them with their friends. **Available in Spanish as *Llaman a la puerta.*** Harper, 1989 (32p).

Literature Discussion

Jones, Christianne C. *Room to Share.* Readers find out what happens when neat Anne and messy Gina share a room. Picture Window, 2005 (24p).

Keats, Ezra Jack. *Peter's Chair.* When Peter sees that his baby furniture is being painted pink for his new baby sister, he rescues his chair, only to discover that he has outgrown it. **Available in Spanish as** *La silla de Pedro.* Viking,1998 (40p).

Klein, Andria F. *Max Goes to the Farm.* Max and his friend Don visit Max's grandparents' farm. Picture Window, 2008 (24p).

Lin, Grace. *Lissy's Friends.* When Lissy feels lonely at school she makes an origami bird and soon has more friends than she can count. Viking, 2007 (40p).

McKissack, Robert. *Try Your Best.* On Sports Day, Ann learns the importance of trying her best. Harcourt, 2004 (24p).

McNamara, Margaret. *Dad Goes to School.* During Parents Week, the students in Ms. Connor's classroom find out what one another's parents do for a living. Aladdin, 2007 (32p).

McNamara, Margaret. *Fall Leaf Project.* The students in Mrs. Connor's class collect colorful fall leaves and send them to a class in the Southwest where leaves don't change color in the fall. Aladdin, 2006 (32p).

McNamara, Margaret. *Happy Graduation!* The first-graders at Robin Hill School celebrate their graduation with an unexpected guest. Aladdin, 2006 (32p).

Millman, Isaac. *Moses Sees a Play.* A group of hearing children visit Moses' school to see a play performed by the Little Theater of the Deaf. Insets demonstrating American Sign Language are included. Farrar, 2004 (32p).

Mora, Pat. *A Birthday Basket for Tía.* Cecilia prepares a special birthday gift for her great aunt. **Available in Spanish as** *Una canasta de cumpleaños para Tía.* Aladdin, 1997 (32p).

Nevius, Carol. *Baseball Hour.* Boys and girls find out how teamwork makes them better baseball players. Marshall Cavendish, 2008 (32p).

Osofsky, Audrey. *My Buddy.* This heartwarming picture book describes the friendship between a young boy with muscular dystrophy and his service dog. Henry Holt, 1994 (32p).

Recorvits, Helen. *My Name Is Yoon.* A Korean child adjusts to life in her new American classroom in this heartwarming narrative. Farrar, 2003 (32p).

Ries, Lori. *Aggie and Ben: Three Stories.* Ben brings home a puppy after his father surprises him with a trip to the pet store in this early chapter book. Charlesbridge, 2006 (48p).

Robbins, Jacqui. *The New Girl . . . and Me.* A friendship is born when Shakeeta joins Mia's class. Atheneum, 2006 (32p).

Rylant, Cynthia. *Mr. Putter and Tabby Run the Race.* Mr. Putter signs up for a marathon in the hopes of winning a train set. Harcourt, 2008 (44p).

Sullivan, Paula. *Todd's Box.* Todd makes a special gift for his mother. Green Light, 2004 (24p).

Tompert, Ann. *Harry's Hats.* Each time Harry puts on a new hat, he finds a new way of expressing himself. Children's Press, 2004 (32p).

Torres, Leyla. *The Kite Festival.* All of the members of Fernando's family work together to create a kite for the festival. Farrar, Straus and Giroux, 2004 (32p).

Uegaki, Chieri. *Suki's Kimono.* Suki wears a kimono to the first day of school and bravely demonstrates a traditional Japanese dance in front of her class. Kids Can, 2005 (32p).

Yaccarino, Dan. *Every Friday.* Follow a father and son on their weekly ritual of spending the day together in their urban neighborhood. Henry Holt, 2007 (32p).

Yee, Wong Herbert. *Who Likes Rain?* A girl muses about an early spring rain and the animals and things that are affected by it. Holt, 2007 (32p).

Abbott, M. (2001). Effects of traditional versus extended word-study spelling instruction on students' orthographic knowledge. *Reading Online, 5*(3).

Barrentine, Shelley. "Engaging with reading through interactive read-alouds." *The Reading Teacher, 50(1):* 36–43.

Baumann, J. F., Edwards, E. C., Font, G., Tereshinski, C. A., Kame'enui, E. J., & Olejnik, S. (2003). Teaching morphemic and contextual analysis to fifth-grade students. *Reading Research Quarterly, 37*(2), 150–176.

Bear, D. R., Invernizzi, M., Templeton, S., & Johnston, F. (2012). *Words their way: Word study for phonics, vocabulary, and spelling instruction* (5th Ed.). Upper Saddle River, NJ: Pearson/Prentice-Hall.

Beck, I., McKeown, M. G., & Kucan, L. (2008). *Creating robust vocabulary.* New York: Guilford.

Berninger, V. W., Abbott, R. D., Nagy, W., & Carlisle, J. (2009). Growth in phonological, orthographic, and morphological awareness in grades 1 to 6. *Journal of Psycholinguistic Research. 39*(2), 141–163.

Berninger, V. W., Vaughan, K., & Abbott, R. D. (2000). Language-based spelling instruction: Teaching children to make multiple connections between spoken and written words. *Learning Disability Quarterly,* 23, 117–135.

Biemiller, A. (2005). Size and sequence in vocabulary development: Implications for choosing words for primary grade vocabulary instruction. In E. H. Hiebert & M. L. Kamil (Eds.), *Teaching and learning vocabulary: Bringing research to practice* (pp. 223–242). Mahwah, NJ: Lawrence Erlbaum Associates.

Bowers, P. N., & Kirby, J. R. (2010). Effects of morphological instruction on vocabulary acquisition. *Reading and Writing: An Interdisciplinary Journal.* 23(5), 515–537.

Brooks, A., Begay, K., Curtin, G., Byrd, K., & Graham, S. (2000). Language-based spelling instruction: Teaching children to make multiple connections between spoken and written words. *Learning Disability Quarterly,* 2, 117–135.

Carlisle, J. F. (2010). Effects of instruction in morphological awareness on literacy achievement: An integrative review. *Reading Research Quarterly, 45*(4), 464–487.

Clay, Marie M. *Becoming Literate: The Construction of Inner Control.* Heinemann, 1991.

Clay, Marie M. *Change Over Time in Children's Literacy Development.* Heinemann, 2001.

Conrad, N. J. (2008). From reading to spelling and spelling to reading: Transfer goes both ways. *Journal of Educational Psychology, 100*(4), 869–878.

Dale, E., & O'Rourke, J. (1981). *Living word vocabulary.* Chicago: World Book/Childcraft International.

Ehri, L. C. (2005). Learning to read words: Theory, findings, and issues. *Scientific Studies of Reading, 9*(2), 167–188.

Fountas, Irene. C. and G. S. Pinnell. *Guided Reading: Good First Teaching for All Children.* Heinemann, 1996.

Fountas, Irene C. and G. S. Pinnell. *Guiding Readers and Writers: Teaching Comprehension, Genre, and Content Literacy.* Heinemann, 2001.

Fountas, Irene C. and G. S. Pinnell. *Leveled Books, K–8: Matching Texts to Readers for Effective Teaching.* Heinemann, 2005.

Fountas, Irene C. and G. S. Pinnell. *Teaching for Comprehending and Fluency: Thinking, Talking, and Writing About Reading, K–8.* Heinemann, 2006.

Henderson, E. H., & Templeton, S. (1986). The development of spelling abilities through alphabet, pattern, and meaning. *Elementary School Journal, 86,* 305–316.

Hiebert, E. H. (2005). In pursuit of an effective, efficient vocabulary curriculum for elementary students. In E. H. Hiebert & M. L. Kamil (Eds.), *Teaching and learning vocabulary: Bringing research to practice* (pp. 243–263). Mahwah, NJ: Lawrence Erlbaum Associates.

Holdaway, Don. *The Foundations of Literacy.* Ashton Scholastic, 1979 (also Heinemann).

Invernizzi, M., & Hayes, L. (2004). Developmental-spelling research: A systematic imperative. *Reading Research Quarterly, 39,* 2–15.

Juel, C, & Minden-Cupp, C. (2000). Learning to read words: linguistic units and instructional strategies. *Reading Research Quarterly, 35,* 458–492.

Kieffer, M. J., & Lesaux, N. K. (2007). Breaking down words to build meaning: Morphology, vocabulary, and reading comprehension in the urban classroom. *Reading Teacher, 61*(2), 134–144.

Morris, D., Bloodgood, J. W., Lomax, R. G., & Perney, J. (2003). Developmental steps in learning to read: A longitudinal study in kindergarten and first grade. *Reading Research Quarterly, 38,* 302–328.

Morris, D., Nelson, L., & Perney, J. (1986). Exploring the concept of "spelling instructional level" through the analysis of error-types. *Elementary School Journal, 87,* 181–200.

Nunes, T., & Bryant, P. (2006). *Improving literacy by teaching morphemes.* London: Routledge.

Ouellette, G. P., & Sénéchal, M. (2008). A window into early literacy: Exploring the cognitive and linguistic underpinnings of invented spelling. *Scientific studies of reading, 12*(2), 195–219.

Pikulski, J., & Templeton, S. (2010). *Comprehensive vocabulary instruction for reading and school success* (Professional Paper). Boston: Houghton Mifflin Harcourt.

Pinnell, Gay Su and Irene C. Fountas. *The Continuum of Literacy Learning, Grades K–8: Behaviors and Understandings to Notice, Teach, and Support.* Heinemann, 2007.

Santoro, L. E., Chard, D. J., Howard, L., & Baker, S. K. (2008). Making the most of classroom read-alouds to promote comprehension and vocabulary. *The Reading Teacher, 61,* 396–408.

Templeton, S. (2003). Teaching of spelling. In J. Guthrie (Senior Ed.), *Encyclopedia of Education* (2nd Ed.) (pp. 2302–2305). New York: Macmillan.

Templeton, S. (2011). Teaching spelling in the English/language arts classroom. In D. Lapp & D. Fisher (Eds.), *The handbook of research on teaching the English language arts* (3rd ed.) (pp. 247–251). IRA/NCTE: Erlbaum/Taylor Francis.

Templeton, S. (2012). The vocabulary-spelling connection and generative instruction: Orthographic development and morphological knowledge at the intermediate grades and beyond. In J. F. Baumann & E. J. Kame'enui (Eds.), *Vocabulary instruction: Research to Practice* (2nd ed.) New York: Guilford Press.

Templeton, S., & Bear, D. R. (Eds.). (1992). *Development of orthographic knowledge and the foundations of literacy: A memorial festschrift for Edmund H. Henderson.* Hillsdale, NJ: Lawrence Erlbaum Associates.

Templeton, S., & Bear, D. R. (2006). *Spelling and Vocabulary.* Boston: Houghton Mifflin.

Templeton, S., & Bear, D. R. (2011). Phonemic awareness, word recognition, and spelling. In T. Rasinski (Ed.), *Developing reading instruction that works.* Bloomington, IN: Solution Tree Press.

Templeton, S., Bear, D. R., Invernizzi, M., & Johnston, F. (2010). *Vocabulary their way: Word study with middle and secondary students.* Boston: Allyn & Bacon.

Templeton, S., Bear, D. R., & Madura, S. (2007). Assessing students' spelling knowledge: Relationships to reading and writing. In J. R. Paratore & R. L. McCormack (Eds.), *Classroom literacy assessment: Making sense of what students know and do.* New York: Guilford Press.

Templeton, S., & Gehsmann, K. (in press). *Teaching reading and writing, K-8: The developmental approach.* Boston: Pearson/ Allyn & Bacon.

Templeton, S., & Morris, D. (1999). Questions teachers ask about spelling. *Reading Research Quarterly, 34,* 102–112.

Templeton, S., & Morris, D. (2000). Spelling. In M. Kamil, P. Mosenthal, P. D. Pearson, & R. Barr (Eds.), *Handbook of reading research: Vol. 3* (pp. 525–543). Mahwah, NJ: Lawrence Erlbaum Associates.

White, T. G. (2005). Effects of systematic and strategic analogy-based phonics on Grade 2 students' word reading and reading comprehension. *Reading Research Quarterly, 40*(2), 234–255.

Zeno, S. M., Ivens, S. H., Millard, R. T., & Duvvuri, R. (1996). *The educator's word frequency guide.* New York: Touchstone Applied Science Associates